Penguin Education

Self-Manag
Economic Liberation of
Man

Edited by Jaroslav Vanek

Penguin Modern Economics Readings

General Editor

B. J. McCormick

Advisory Board

K. J. W. Alexander
R. W. Clower
G. R. Fisher
P. Robson
J. Spraos
H. Townsend

Self-Management:
Economic Liberation of Man

Selected Readings

Jaroslav Vanek

Penguin Education

Penguin Education
A Division of Penguin Books Ltd,
Harmondsworth, Middlesex, England
Penguin Books Inc, 7110 Ambassador Road,
Baltimore, Maryland 21207, USA
Penguin Books Australia Ltd,
Ringwood, Victoria, Australia
Penguin Books Canada Ltd,
41 Steelcase Road West,
Markham, Ontario, Canada
Penguin Books (N.Z.) Ltd,
182-190 Wairau Road, Auckland 10, New Zealand

First published 1975

Printed in the United States of America
Set in Monotype Times

To the memory of my brother Jan

Acknowledgements

I should like to acknowledge the invaluable
help which was given to me in preparing
this volume by Tom Bayard, Connell Fanning,
Florence Finch, Patricia Haines, Derek Jones,
Andy and Liz Pienkos.

J. Vanek

Contents

Part Three
Performance

Part Four
Economic Theory

Introduction

1 General considerations

The participation of man in running the affairs and activities which directly concern him has been the object of an upsurge of interest in recent years. Two major directions can be distinguished: on the one hand, in political life in the immediate political environment and activities; and on the other, the participation of the working man in his place of work. The first subject approaches and actually merges with the problem of political democracy and as such is very well known, and has been extensively discussed; the second subject is far less developed and is more obscure. In a sense it can be said that the process of economic democratization or economic participation trails considerably behind the process of political democratization and political self-determination. This is also reflected in the state of our knowledge. Nonetheless, enough of significance has been written on the subject of economic participation under the various headings of self-management, labour management, workers' management, workers' control, industrial democracy or producer cooperation, to make it possible to put together a volume of readings on the subject. What follows is the result of such an attempt.

The subject of labour management and industrial democracy is extremely diverse. It ranges from a significant historical dimension to the present, and in fact to the future; from a mathematically exact theory to discussion of a wide variety of concrete cases of application, and to sociological studies of workers' attitudes towards labour management. This diversity makes it impossible to cover the whole field in any degree of completeness within a single volume and I am consequently forced to be selective with respect to the areas treated. The most important criterion of selection was that by and large the volume should be primarily one in economics.

Another way in which we were able to restrict the scope considerably was to give a narrow definition to what we actually mean by labour management and industrial democracy. Our definition implies the *direct* involvement of workers and employees in the process of control, management and exploitation of their enterprises, but we exclude participation through union countervailing power, collective bargaining and other indirect ways of influencing the policy of an enterprise through the action of labour unions.

The third and last consideration which permits us to limit the scope of our subject is that we have produced a volume primarily concerned with the present, and in some sense the future. This does not imply that we should entirely neglect anything that is historical, but that only such historical writings may be included as would have relevance for the state of labour management and economic participation today. This orientation to the present not only permits us to stay within manageable dimensions, but also reflects the present state of concern of most of those interested in the subject. Economic participation and labour management are not academic subjects of primarily historical interest, but rather very lively issues of today, when individuals, groups of people and whole nations are becoming acutely aware of the difficulties arising from capital domination and control, and are seeking alternatives. Among these, labour management and industrial democracy appear by far the most significant, if not the only solution.

Besides acquainting the reader with the subject of labour management, the purpose of this volume is also to offer answers to some fundamental questions regarding the feasibility, desirability and implementation of labour management in the real world. Certain misconceptions and erroneous judgements have, in my opinion, become part of the accepted thinking about labour management, and in many cases transmitted from teachers to students, resulting in a complete discarding of the possibility of letting the working man become master in his own working place. There is a widespread view that labour management is syndicalism and that syndicalism does not work. The equally problematic position of Hugh Clegg on the subject of industrial democracy, that would forever doom the working man to subservience, is disputed below by Paul Blumberg in the section on doctrine (Reading 6).

In order to avoid such misconceptions and to let the reader penetrate the maze of different forms that the participation of labour and employees can assume, we need a comprehensive definitional survey. Such a survey does not at present exist and we have had to produce it ourselves. Only by using more precise definitions will it be possible to speak meaningfully about the efficiency and social desirability of labour-managed and co-operative forms of productive organizations. To these definitions we will devote the second half of this section.

Let us now turn to the major areas which remain after the three restricting criteria are applied. There appear to be four such areas, and this volume has therefore been organized into four distinct parts. We will outline these headings here and devote a separate, more detailed discussion to each in the subsequent four sections. In the last section of this introductory chapter we summarize the necessary characteristics of a viable and fully efficient labour-managed system, as they emerge from the various contributions, both factual and theoretical, included in this volume.

We will let doctrine precede reality and analysis, and devote the first part of the volume to the doctrine of self-management. In the subsequent section of this introduction we make an attempt to introduce the various readings in their historical context. In Part Two we present the reader with selected cases of labour management and industrial democracy as they exist in various parts of the world today. In Part Three we gather the various pieces of evidence which have been produced to date – which are neither numerous nor complete – on the efficiency of the participatory organization of production. In other words, in Part Three we attempt to show the reader how economically effective labour management actually is. The emphasis here is on economic performance rather than on broad social or psychological desirability, which is only rarely disputed. Finally, in Part Four we turn to the formal economic theory of self-management. We have placed that part last in the volume expecting that because of its comparative technicality its audience will be more restricted than that for the other three parts. But, in order to keep the entire content of the volume easily accessible to comprehension, in section five of this introduction we outline in nontechnical terms the content of the theoretical papers.

Let us now consider the definitions. Specifically, what exactly do we mean when we say that a firm is labour-managed, self-managed, worker-managed or that it is a participatory firm? To answer these questions and to give a more precise definition, it will be convenient to develop a general categorization of economic systems and forms of productive organizations. In this way we will be able not only to draw the lines among various forms of economic participation but also to distinguish between the participatory systems on the one hand and nonparticipatory systems on the other.

As is indicated in Table 1, we use two significant criteria of classification. The first criterion leading to what we call the first-order distinction refers to the position of the working man in the enterprise and differentiates between enterprises and systems where the working man is 'master in his own house' and systems where he is controlled by those who own the capital assets with which he works. It is useful to define the first category as *self-managed* or based on economic self-determination, and the second category as *capital-controlled* or *dehumanized* systems, the term dehumanized referring to the fact that those within a working collective are dominated by and serving the objectives of those who own capital, most often external to the collective. The second criterion, leading to what we refer to as the second-order distinction, is of a more conventional and customary type. It refers to the actual owner of the productive resources used in production. The whole spectrum of alternatives – in our case, eight in number – ranges from state, social or socialist ownership, to private ownership. Several intermediate categories between the two extremes are introduced precisely to permit us to speak about various forms of production cooperatives or labour-managed enterprises or systems. Moreover, a large number of combinations under the second-order distinction is conceivable with, for example, combined ownership by private individuals and by the state, or by those employed in the enterprise and those external to the enterprise.

Table 1 Categorization, economic systems and the types of productive organization (arrows means 'corresponds to')

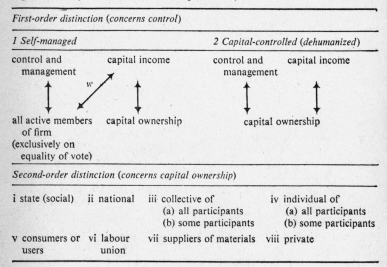

First-order distinction (concerns control)

1 Self-managed | *2 Capital-controlled (dehumanized)*

control and management — capital income | control and management — capital income

all active members of firm (exclusively on equality of vote) — capital ownership | capital ownership

Second-order distinction (concerns capital ownership)

i state (social) ii national iii collective of iv individual of
                            (a) all participants   (a) all participants
                            (b) some participants (b) some participants

v consumers or users vi labour union vii suppliers of materials viii private

In section three, where we discuss the different cases of participatory or labour-managed firms as they arise in different parts of the world, we will be able to use our table in identifying each specific case. Here it will suffice to give a few examples and to use our categorization in defining certain basic forms of participation.

Let us look more closely at the self-managed category. Its essential characteristic, as indicated in Table 1, is the *exclusive* control and management of productive organizations by their *full* active membership on a basis of equality of vote.[1] It is only firms fulfilling this definition that can be referred to as self-managed. Whenever others are given the right to control and manage, even if it is together with the active members, whenever some of the active members are left out of the process of self-management and whenever men are not equal in voting strength, we can no longer speak of

1 Of course, as in the political sphere, this management will normally be carried out through an efficient system of delegation of authority.

self-management and are facing a situation dehumanized in one way or another. Of course, depending on specific conditions, the degree of dehumanization can vary from case to case, the extreme form being found in the capitalist firms or systems, whether of the Western (private) or the Soviet (state) variety.

We can now propose several definitions to disentangle this definitional maze. What we mean by self-managed enterprises or systems has just been made clear. It is a strict definition but this is necessary for it reflects both the need for organizational purity and a philosophical and moral resistance to adulteration. However, it is necessary to recognize that there are many forms besides self-management in which members partake in the management and exploitation of an enterprise. All such cases should be referred to as *participatory*. The self-managed systems are defined in the Table by 1 and i to viii.

The broader category of participatory systems or firms corresponds, in addition to the self-managed, to 2 in the Table, combined with either iii or iv, or a combination of either of these two with the remaining six headings of the second-order distinction. Thus, for example, a participatory firm would be one controlled and managed by those who own the capital, the latter being in part regular stock holders and in part an industrial community holding collectively a block of shares of the company in the name of the working collective. In terms of symbols, such a participatory firm could be written as 2–iii(a), viii. As participatory we should also describe systems where workers take part to some degree in management and/or control without sharing in ownership. Such situations, most often referred to as 'codetermination' (*Mitbestimmung*), could be denoted as 2(1)–viii.

Next it appears useful to propose a new distinction between worker-managed firms and labour-managed firms. The first should be used for describing firms, as in Yugoslavia, where all the conditions of exclusive control and management by all active members on the basis of equality are fulfilled. However, the income of any capital is basically assigned to the active participants and not to capital ownership which in Yugoslavia is taken to be social ownership. Thus as we have indicated by the arrow marked with 'w' in Table 1 we can think of the *worker-managed* system as an alternative self-managed system, that is 1w–i.

By contrast, let us refer to self-managed systems which pay an economic, or scarcity-reflecting remuneration for the use of capital to its owners, whoever they may be, as *labour-managed* systems or firms. Within the category of labour-managed firms or systems, the one identified with 1–ii, that is, the self-managed with national ownership, occupies a special position, to which we will return in sections five and six of this introduction. Let it only be noted that in all other situations under the second-order distinction, that is, i to viii with the exclusion of ii, either conflicts of interest or the possibility of domination by capital can occur. What we have defined here as national ownership is precisely designed in order to avoid such complications.

Next to the worker-managed and labour-managed categories, we can also distinguish the more traditional category of the producer cooperative. Producer cooperatives are productive organizations, all having in common, under the second-order distinction, ownership of the types iii and iv (a) or (b). But they can fall under 1 or 2 on the first-order distinction depending on the specific nature of their organization.

Finally, we have what is a very frequent occurrence today all over the world, which we may refer to as a *cooperative, for the purpose of production or service* (as distinguished from producer cooperative) wherein consumers, users or suppliers (such as suppliers of milk in agriculture) cooperate in funding and control, and produce products or services linked to their respective needs. In some instances these cooperatives will also admit as members the workers and employees of the enterprise. We can define the cooperative for purposes of production as 2–v and/or vii, with the possible combination of these two headings with iii or iv under the second-order distinction.

Because syndicalism sometimes meant no more than a strategy of taking over economic power, and because in most instances syndicalist attempts did not succeed (or at least did not crystallize into a well-defined organizational form of production), it is hard to say what syndicalism is exactly in terms of our definitional scheme. Perhaps closest to the true form of syndicalism is that found in Israel today within the Histadut movement, where the labour union (as distinct from the working community) assumes the ownership, control and management of the firm. If we refer to that as syndicalism, then it would be defined using our schema as 2–vi. It remains a question as to whether that form should be referred to as participatory at all.

2 Historical development of the idea of workers' participation

The modern idea of workers' participation or self-management emerged in the critical reaction to the industrial revolution which began in the eighteenth century. In England and continental Europe by the mid-nineteenth century, the intellectual reaction to industrialism had assumed a whole spectrum of different forms.

The most important figures among those whom we think of as the utopian socialists were Saint-Simon and Charles Fourier in France, and Robert Owen in England. Saint-Simon advocated the redirecting of the industrial age under greater state control, while Fourier and Owen placed their hopes in autonomous communities organized for the good of all who worked in them. In the utopian communities, the producers were subordinate to the general management of the community. Although they were concerned with the organization of industry, and of agriculture, none of these men had a clear vision of workers' self-management, but each led a movement and had a school of followers, out of which sprang other movements aiming more directly at economic democracy.

The earliest true precursor of workers' participation lived in France in the nineteenth century and began his intellectual career as a Saint-Simoniar. His name was Philippe-Joseph-Baptiste Buchez; his conception was that of the 'workingman's association'. Buchez was a man of many talents: medical doctor, philosopher, historian, journalist. He moved through the intellectual world of Paris between the revolutions of 1830 and 1848, evolving, like the earlier utopians, his plans for a society better than the one around him. His ideal world was to be characterized by putting Christianity into practice, which he felt had never yet happened. In his egalitarian view, this implied democracy in the everyday life of a man's work as well as in his form of government.

Through a series of newspaper articles, a preface to one volume of his lengthy *Parliamentary History of the French Revolution* and model statutes for such a group, Buchez provides the philosophy, the theory and a clear outline for the functioning of 'workmen's associations' which truly embodied workers' self-management. His aim, as one of his followers put it, was to institute 'the republic in the workshop'. He confronted squarely the problem of the controlling power attached to whoever supplied capital for an undertaking. Buchez's solution, which in retrospect had its shortcomings, was unique: the association would be based on the accumulation of a stock of 'social, inalienable capital' contributed by the members, which became the permanent property of the association and a guarantee of its perpetuity.

Clearly, this was a highly altruistic demand, and Buchez's model statutes of 1831 contained others as well. Nonetheless, a number of associations on Buchez's pattern were founded up to the time of the revolution of 1848. How they fared is among the matters discussed in our selection on Buchez. Also of interest is his relationship to Louis Blanc, whose 'national workshops' had something in common with the workmen's associations. However, given the extent of state intervention in their structure and control, the national workshops did not represent a type of worker-managed unit, and hence Blanc is not represented by a reading here.

During the decade of the 1840s there developed in England the first really successful alternative to capitalist industrialism. We refer, of course, to the Pioneers of Rochdale, who, partly under the influence of Owen, founded in 1844 what became the first lasting cooperative of consumers.

Emulation of their success expanded the cooperatives into a worldwide movement, which is important today in many countries. A further stage of the Rochdale programme for a complete cooperative society called for cooperation in production, but this never became reality to any significant degree. The cooperative movement serves its members' wants as consumers, and in related areas such as credit and marketing; but it has had relatively little to do with workers' participation, and there has been little development of producers' cooperatives within the movement in the hundred years following Rochdale. Only in the most recent years, in some developing countries, does this general pattern appear to be changing.

The English Christian Socialist movement of the 1840s and 1850s, begun by John Malcolm Ludlow, transferred to Britain the ideas and goals of Buchez and his school. But the Christian Socialists' strivings for workingmen's associations and producers' cooperatives did not endure long, and in the end their main impact was to bolster the mainstream of the cooperative movement.

We cannot leave the 1840s without naming two other figures of capital importance: Pierre-Joseph Proudhon, and Karl Marx. Proudhon, who in 1840 startled France with his seemingly radical doctrine on property (*What is Property?*) more precisely opposing its abuses, was a man of many apparent contradictions. He moved in socialist circles, but he was inclined to favour the petty-bourgeois class. His style was that of a revolutionary, but he became an opponent of Marx; he opposed excessive property rights, but also opposed nationalization of property. Proudhon's conception of workers' associations was clearest towards the role of the *artisanat* or small craftsmen, in line with his class origins and sympathies. Later he also evolved a framework for large industrial associations and placed his hopes in an alliance of the proletariat with the petty-bourgeois. He took exception, however, to the types of associations that Fourier and Louis Blanc had brought into being, and the only project he guided to reality was a 'People's Bank', based on his advocacy of mutual free credit for producers, which failed roundly. Yet this solitary thinker who claimed he never wanted a following became one of the most influential men of his generation. Outside socialism, his idea of mutual credit was adopted by mutual aid or 'friendly' societies in Europe and America. Within the socialist movement his influence filtered in several directions. He was a hero to those who opposed the authoritarianism of Marx; to very many of the leaders of the Paris Commune; and to those who developed the anarchist and syndicalist movements. Insofar as all these groups favoured workers' association or, later, 'workers' control', Proudhon is a seminal figure, even though he did not provide any clear new direction.

It is unnecessary to assess the role of Marx as a giant of social criticism.

His leadership in the reform of society is more ambiguous, as the whole subsequent, complex history of socialism will testify. Thus the position of Marx on workers' associations and his role in promoting self-management are problematical. Radoslav Selucky (see Reading 2) makes us realize how little Marx said which was consistent and unequivocal. He distinguishes two major streams of thought – inferred from Marx, Engels and even Lenin – the centralist and the participatory. Examining the logical consistency of each, he tries to suggest which is more valid.

A further historical problem is the interpretation of that signal event of March to May 1871, the Paris Commune. Its leadership was influenced by the ideas of Proudhon. After the Commune was brutally crushed, Marx became its belated champion, maximizing for his own ends the symbolic political significance of what was no longer an actuality. Did the Commune have workers' self-determination? Its decrees announced free associations of producers, but its few brief weeks of life provided no opportunity to test their success or failure.

This very brief sketch is by no means exhaustive, and we are in effect passing over some who have a rightful place in the development of the ideas for workers' self-management. These include Ferdinand Lassalle and his influence for associations within the socialist movement in Germany in the 1860s; the Russian Prince Peter Kropotkin, who, within the anarchist movement, gave the greatest attention to associations of mutual aid; and La Tour du Pin, who, in the milieu of French Catholicism, developed the related conception of a network of corporations. The place of the latter is at least touched on in the treatment, given in Reading 8, of another question – the evolution in the attitude of the Catholic Church towards workers' self-determination.

The later decades of the nineteenth century were not a time of actual progress towards workers' self-management. At the same time, several new movements developed with a bearing on the subject, all within the ample matrix of socialism. In Britain, the Fabian Society founded in 1884 was a small group which engaged in intellectual propaganda for the gradual advent of a specifically English form of socialism in government. The Fabians' strongest impetus was for the organs of local and regional government to undertake projects for the common good; thus the government or the state would become a major employer. The consumers' cooperative movement was supported by Fabian socialism, and especially by its leading spirits Sidney and Beatrice Webb who were concerned with trying to integrate it into a socialist pattern for England, although they strongly opposed and criticized producers' cooperatives, which they felt were undemocratic and wrongly motivated by profits. Thus workers' participation was excluded from the Fabian programme in two ways: by its positive aim of introducing socialism through the organs of government rather than through organizing workers; and by the negatively critical attitude towards producers' cooperatives.

By contrast, the Guild Socialist movement in England, represented by G. D. H. Cole in Reading 3, had as its chief concern a socialist economy through workers' organization. On the one hand, the Guild Socialists harked back to the Christian Socialists, and even farther, to the medieval craft guilds. On the other, they intended – as more suited to modern conditions of production – a broad vertical integration which would eventually band the workers of the nation in a given trade or industry into a single guild, which would then be the controlling power in that industry. By this method they sought to introduce what was variously called economic democracy, self-government in industry or sometimes workers' control. It was indeed an advocacy of workers' participation. After the First World War some guilds were organized, especially in housing, but the movement ended abruptly in a few years, a victim of the more general economic crisis.

Cole presents a moving rationale for the aims and vision of the Guild Socialists: he also contrasts to some extent their programme with that of another contemporaneous movement. For 'workers' control', slogan of the Guild Socialists, was also that of the syndicalist (or revolutionary syndicalist) movement in France and other continental countries in the decades before the First World War. What the syndicalists meant by workers' control was markedly different, for they wanted the labour union movements to expand their power so that the syndicates would finally not only control industry but also do away with the power of the capitalist state. As part of their way to power, the syndicalists believed in the efficacy of strikes and above all else the general strike. In this they were revolutionary, but in their longing to do away with the prevailing mechanisms of government they were profoundly anarchist. Even as advocates of the proletariat, the syndicalists had no deep interest in participatory self-management; their goals were primarily political.

More relevant for us are developments in Germany after the First World War. There, in addition to 'works councils' which had been organized 'from above' as early as the 1890s and which gave workers some small measure of codetermination along with management and entrepreneurs, the greater power of 'workers' councils' was obtained in the 1918 revolutions in German cities. Their existence was brief; the Weimar Republic reverted to the works councils, but the experiment formed the basis on which German *Mitbestimmung* (workers' codetermination) could develop after the Second World War. Similarly, in Italy, in 1920 the workers 'occupied' some northern factories and made their own organization of production, but their movement did not last even a few months before it was subdued by political and economic pressures.

In Russia at the same time, workers' self-determination was the principle by which factories were organized in the early days after the October revolution of 1917. The Bolsheviks were apparently turned from this path by the exigencies of wartime production, and the Soviet authorities took control of the factories. From the point of view that concerns us the situation has remained substantially unchanged ever since.

Thus we come to recent decades and what we may consider the present period in the debate over workers' control or participation in management. The outstanding event of this period is the adoption of self-management as the new economic system of Yugoslavia at the moment of its departure from the Soviet bloc, though not from socialism. As the basic statement of this arrangement, we include excerpts from the Yugoslav constitution (Reading 4) and also a piece by an important contemporary Yugoslav economist, Branko Horvat, who offers us an amalgamation of his experience of the Yugoslav reality and his vision of an ideal participatory, or ideal socialist economy (Reading 9).

In the West and in developing countries, the debate over workers' participation continues. An important question for industrialized countries is the role of trade unions under a system of labour management. One side holds that industrial democracy is desirable, but can best be sought through the trade unions and collective bargaining, akin to an opposition party in politics. It is represented here by an important British exponent, Hugh Clegg (Reading 5). Opposing this position rather convincingly is the American sociologist Paul Blumberg (Reading 6).

In Reading 7, another English exponent, Ken Coates, gives a valuable inside account of the dynamics of the transition to full self-management in the context of the British setting and configuration of labour union, business and political forces. For him, workers' control – which we may think of as another concept in terms of our general categorization of the preceding section – is a strategy of transition, or instrument of liberation. The role of the labour union here is liberating, without the unions' countervailing (opposition) power itself being the ultimate bliss and final solution.

We conclude Part One with a paper by an American progressive writer, David Ellerman, representing a group of young intellectuals in America and abroad. He examines the philosophical foundations of appropriation, and the resolution of his problem leads him to self-management as the only logical alternative. His paper is controversial; many agree with it, at least in principle if not in detail, while others tend to dislike it. Whatever may be the case, his bringing in the moral dimension where it generally has been lost is refreshing.

3 Cases of self-management and participation in the world of today

In Part Two of the volume we turn to some significant real cases of self-management and participation as they occur in the world of today. In this section we will briefly outline the papers included in the volume dealing with these cases. We will use the categorization proposed in section one and indicate in its terms the nature of each particular situation.

Our first reading is a comparative study of worker participation in Europe. It bears on what is probably the best known form of participation in the world today, the cases of partial, and often very limited, forms of influencing the affairs of the enterprise by its workers and employees. The term most often associated with these forms is that of codetermination (*Mitbestimmung*) linking it to the developments in Germany.

In terms of our categorization in section one, codetermination can be seen as a more or less mild alteration of category 2 in the direction of category 1. Thus we can employ for the case at hand the notation 2(1)–viii, if the firms are private, and 2(1)–i, if they are public. As is shown, in different countries the codetermination assumes many different forms and varies according to the size and other characteristics of the enterprises. In the predominant number of cases, as for example in Germany or the Netherlands, it is established through national legislation. In some other situations, various forms, often very weak ones, are established by agreement between the employer and the workers on the level of a national union or otherwise. The situation is constantly changing: David Garson supplies a picture of participation up to the middle of 1973.

In the second reading of Part Two, Jacques Gouverneur addresses himself to the workers' participation which was instituted in Peru, in the industrial sector and subsequently in some other sectors of the economy, under the new revolutionary government after 1969. As in the case of codetermination, the formula used by the Peruvians is one giving the workers and employees only partial control in their firms. However, the formula is different in the sense that participation in management and income is linked to share ownership, the share being acquired by the so-called industrial community, that is, the total working collective, defined as a single legal person.

While this formula of co-ownership is, in 1973, the predominant form of labour participation, it is not the only one in the minds of policy-makers. A new sector referred to as Sector of Social Ownership is to be developed embodying a large number of characteristics of an optimal, or ideal, participatory economy, of the type outlined in the concluding section of this chapter. In terms of our categorization in section one, this new sector of social ownership could be most closely described as 1–ii, iv(a) (self-managed, national ownership combined with individual claims by members of the working collectives). On the other hand, the Peruvian reforms based on the industrial community, which are the principal concern of Gouverneur's article, would fall under the classification 2-viii, iii(a), that is, controlled by private capitalists together with the working collectives. The Peruvians have also introduced, in particular in the nationalized sugar estates, a more conventional producers' cooperative devoted to growing of sugar cane and sugar production. This cooperative can most closely be characterized – at least in its final state when the entire value of assets will have been paid for to the government – as 1-iii(a) (self-managed collective of all participants). Some might prefer to substitute 2 for 1 in this description on grounds of some fairly serious imperfections, in particular, occasional use of non-member labour and democratic representation which is not based on the rule of full equality.

Proceeding further, we find in Reading 13 Carl Bellas's discussion of the American plywood cooperatives. We have placed it here because for the first time we encounter a situation where a productive organization is entirely controlled and exploited by its workers. However, it is still a quite imperfect form because among other flaws, it involves control, ownership and exploitation by less than the entire working collective. As such, Bellas's plywood cooperative can be identified as 2-iv(b) (capital-controlled, individual ownership by only some participants).

The plywood cooperative and Bellas's analysis of it teach us a good deal about possible imperfections of producer cooperatives which may be so serious as to cause failure or transformation of these productive organizations into other forms. It is precisely these imperfections that must be avoided if one wants to design a viable and efficient self-managed firm. In addition to hired nonmember workers, another imperfection and cause of difficulties in the plywood cooperatives is the fact that the general manager often is also a hired employee and not a member. Perhaps most important is the position of capital in the enterprise. Membership, as in common stock companies, is defined by a share ownership instead of by the simple requirement of active participation. Especially in successful cooperatives where the capitalized value of individual shares can become extremely high, it becomes virtually impossible for a young worker to 'buy his way' into the cooperative. Thus there will be a general tendency for the average age of the members to increase; and when most of the members come close to retirement, there will be a strong inducement to sell the whole enterprise to capitalist interests, and the cooperative will disappear even if the enterprise survives. Note that this has absolutely nothing to do with any inefficiency in the firm . In fact, it is the most efficient cooperatives with the highest accumulation that are most liable to undergo this transformation or degeneration. Without going into any detail of the requirements for efficiency and viability, let us only note one universal principle underlying all such optimality conditions. The principle is that in all possible respects a self-managed firm should be defined and operated under the humanist principle of active participation and not on the principle of capital or capital ownership. Quite clearly, if this principle is adhered to, all the difficulties arising from the second-class citizenship of workers or managers, the difficulty of the disappearance of the cooperative once all of its shares are sold (even if many workers would like to be employed in the firm) and many others, will disappear.

In principle, a very advanced and perfect cooperative form is encountered in the Israeli kibbutzim, described in Reading 14 by Haim Barkai. In fact, in many kibbutzim the participatory principles are carried well beyond the mere participation and exploitation of the enterprise. Unfortunately it seems that some of the kibbutzim have been experiencing one serious difficulty in more recent years (as have the American plywood cooperatives). That is the weakening of the democratic and egalitarian principles through admission of nonmember hired workers. In my view we again have here a flaw resulting from the non-separation of membership from ownership (collective or individual). The crux of the matter is that a substantial portion of members' incomes in fact are land or capital rents and the existing members tend to be unwilling to share these rents with the new members. Thus there will be a tendency, if this is legally possible, to hire workers under a wage contract excluding such rents. (By law this is not possible in Yugoslavia.)

According to our categorization, then, the ideal form of the kibbutz appears as 1–iii(a) (a self-managed collective of all participants). In the weakened and less democratic form just discussed, alternatively, we have 2–iii(b) (a collective of only some participants, capital-controlled).

Next we turn to what is probably the best known and most successful self-managed firm in England today, the Scott Bader Commonwealth. This firm, discussed in Reading 15, has resolved some of the fundamental problems inherent in other self-managed firms. First, all workers and employees are equal in their rights to participate in the control and management of the firm. Second, the firm is owned, so to speak, by itself and cannot be sold to anyone, so that, as stated in the paper, 'the company is on a permanent footing'. A third highly desirable feature is that the basic statutes of the firm provide for a mandatory share of the surplus to be allocated to accumulation. This principle of mandatory accumulation in somewhat modified technical form (see section six of this introduction) is probably the single most important condition for a successful self-managed firm or economy.

Reading 16 bears on another participatory case from England, which can also be broadly characterized as 1–iii(a), like the Scott Bader Common-wealth. Instead of being taken as an example of success and growth, it is rather offered here as an instance of the deeply human significance of the participatory form of production, and more specifically a demonstration of its ability to survive under duress, even in an alien environment. It is a small cooperative of miners who, disabled by it, had to leave their former profession. In fact this ability to survive is a very important feature of labour-managed and cooperative forms of production, and it has been demonstrated in numerous instances. Perhaps the clearest substantiation of this is that many self-managed firms in existence in the western world today were born from bankrupt or nearly bankrupt capitalist firms; their very existence was preserved by being taken over by the workers and they survived and often did very well in their new form.

Reading 17 is a substantial portion of a chapter of a book dealing with self-management in Yugoslavia by my late brother, to whose memory this volume of readings is dedicated. Unfortunately my brother, who gave most of his active life to research and writing on self-management and participation (largely unsigned as an official of the International Labour Organization), did not live to see his book published.

As we have noted already, the philosophy of the Yugoslavs is that no scarcity-reflecting charge should be levied on capital, and that all net income of enterprises should be claimed by those who work in them. At the same time, Yugoslav law scrupulously links membership and the right to self-management to active participation, on a basis of absolute equality of vote. For this reason we chose to use for the Yugoslav case the term 'worker-managed', and to categorize it as 1(a)–i (self-managed with capital income to the workers and social ownership of capital).

The case of Yugoslavia is today by far the most significant instance of self-management in the world. For that reason, our single selection on the Yugoslav firm might be taken as an underrepresentation, but the reader will be reminded that the case of Yugoslavia is dealt with in different contexts in four other places in this volume (Readings 4, 9, 23 and 27).

Reading 18 bears on the Czechoslovakian experience with self-management in its two different phases. The first occurred when in the early stages of Czechoslovak socialism workers' councils were used to wrestle power from capitalist owners, only to be deprived of their power soon afterwards – a well-known tactic in Communist strategy. The second, of greater importance for the purposes of our study, is the short, but vigorous effort of the Czechs to attain industrial democracy during the Dubcek era – so spontaneous that it could be quenched only by a Russian occupation of the country. The Czechoslovakian case was not given time to develop enough for us to be able to categorize it exactly now, but there can be little doubt from the spirit of the reforms that it would have come somewhere under our category 1 or 1w, that is, self-managed.

Reading 19 comes the closest to the notion of labour management, that is, category 1. It is found in the experience of Mondragon, Spain. In its fully democratic structure, charging of real return on capital, and predominant funding from sources other than collective retained earnings, it also comes closest to the optimal design of a labour-managed system as developed in section six. A fundamental message of Mondragon to all efforts for self-management is the role of education in bringing about economic self-determination and liberation. Particularly for the many Latin American countries which are actively or potentially interested in self-management, Mondragon may prove a significant inspiration and example.

4 On performance

The comparative youth of the formal science of self-management is reflected in the scattered and incomplete state of the literature evaluating the performance of the system. An enormous amount of work is needed to complete and stabilize the picture and there is hardly a more useful and fruitful field of research for the economist or, for that matter, the industrial psychologist and sociologist.

However, this limitation notwithstanding, a definite and favourable picture is beginning to emerge from the more recent efforts, and the evidence is remarkably consistent among alternative approaches, and inconsistent with, or contradicting, traditional preconceptions and historical judgements.

Following the initial optimism of the fathers of self-management and production cooperation (like Buchez and the Rochdale Pioneers) founded more in philosophical hope and optimism than in theoretical and empirical evidence, a certain accepted position of those in authority can be discerned. This position is roughly stationary and ranges from mixed to outright condemnation. The latter position is well illustrated by the attitude of the Webbs referred to in section two. The mixed view was that producer cooperation is a way through which to obtain a more humane and pleasant working atmosphere at the cost of some sacrifice in terms of efficiency, and consequently in output and income.

It is safe to say this lukewarm-to-negative attitude towards self-management which lasted through some hundred years – well into the 1950s and 1960s – was largely the result of superficial judgement based on a few concrete cases, and of the objective fact that self-management never developed into a substantial *modus operandi* of any economy. The fact that self-management might not have developed significantly for other reasons than inefficiency or basic human undesirability was hardly given a serious consideration. It was only most natural in the best *laissez faire* tradition to expect that if any socio-economic arrangement were good it would have taken a hold by itself, through the operation of free-market competition and the 'invisible hand'.

Our first selection in Part Three is a scholarly theoretical piece by Abram Bergson entitled *Market Socialism Revisited*. While only its smaller second part is devoted explicitly to the self-management solution, we reproduce it in its entirety because it allows the reader to see the whole problem at hand in a broader context of other forms of market socialism. While more scholarly, Professor Bergson's piece is quite characteristic of the accepted position that we have noted above. Guarding himself against any very precise statements, Bergson nonetheless leads the reader towards a set of fairly negative conclusions. While he would give an edge to market socialism over nonmarket socialism within the socialist category, the cooperative variant would appear as inferior. The comparison between the capitalist-market solution and the socialist-market solution is fuzzy and probably inferior for the socialist alternative, hence, by implication, considerably inferior for the participatory solution.

While the other three selections arrive at significantly different conclusions, and ought to be left to make their own points, I consider it appropriate to call the reader's attention to several facts. The outcome of Bergson's analysis is conditioned to a considerable degree by the very narrow frame of reference quite typical of modern, western, and especially American, economics. The market inefficiency of possible income differentials between different firms or industries (which Bergson adopts from Ward) is for the most part Bergson's principal piece of negative evidence, and it is theoretically correct. This need not arise however, and will not do so in a correctly organized labour-managed economy. If it does arise, its quantitative effects may be quite insignificant. Above all, the evaluation is based on a possibility of loss of physical amounts of output. No true positive value is ascribed to the fact that in the labour-managed solution, the working man is the absolute master of his own affairs during the eight hours a day in which he produces, whereas he is dominated and controlled by others whether in the capitalist solution or in the other socialist market or nonmarket alternatives. It can be said that for a human being, the specific forms and modalities of his employment are as much a source of dissatisfaction as the goods that he consumes, and that the freedom of choice in both areas can equally contribute to his welfare. And yet, the theory through whose eyes Bergson sees the working man, neglects one-half of the relevant spectrum.

Bergson's brief remarks on Yugoslavia in his concluding section are also noteworthy. He says, '. . . but the Yugoslav case hardly conflicts with what

I have said thus far . . .'. What Bergson has to say is quite unfavourable, as we have noted already; but at just about the time that he was writing, Yugoslavia completed, under labour management, a period of some twelve to fourteen years of rates of growth which were among the highest in the world. This was the case in spite of some major difficulties that were being experienced by Yugoslavia since it was experimenting with a completely new system without precedent. In the absence of such difficulties – primarily traceable to serious but avoidable flaws of the capital market – the success of the Yugoslav reforms would have been even more dramatic.

The many work-related dimensions of man neglected by Bergson and most other western economists are well illustrated by our second selection by Blumberg, a sociologist. In fact, it is thanks to the sociologists and the industrial psychologists that we know something more definite about man as producer. As much as the western capitalist system itself, the western economist always tended to look at man primarily as a consumer, degrading him on the side of his producing function to not much more than a useful machine, substitutable more or less on the basis of equality for capital, land or other factors, according to a well-defined production function.

Blumberg's contribution is to summarize a large number of experiments on participation and its effects on human behaviour. The results are quite conclusive and the fact that they are taken from a number of different authors and situations is reassuring. Unfortunately, the size of this volume did not permit more detail; however, we have included Blumberg's bibliography underlying his summary table. Together with the more detailed chapters of Blumberg's work, it should be useful to the interested reader.

Our third paper in Part Three, like the second, is empirical in nature; but instead of looking at individual cases of experiments, its authors study and compare the performance of whole economic sectors in different countries. Balassa and Bertrand, in their interesting paper, attempt to perform basically two key comparisons. One is a comparison between the socialist, self-managed economy of Yugoslavia and other socialist economies adhering to central planning. The other comparison is between the decentralized, market and self-managed economy of Yugoslavia and other economies which adhere to capitalist control and management rather than to self-management. As indicated in their Table 1, the results are consistently highly favourable for Yugoslavia in both comparisons. More specifically, for total productivity, which is probably the most standard and widely accepted criterion, the figures of 4·5 or 4·7 annual increase in total productivity are not far below the double of comparable average figures for either of the two groups of reference. We recall again that we are comparing an entirely untried and new system with the capitalist and centrally-planned socialist systems, tried for many decades in many countries.

In the fourth and last reading we have attempted to summarize the efficiency conclusions of a more extensive theoretical study of mine. The conclusions are considerably more favourable than those of Bergson, among other reasons because the analysis is more general, covering a broader spectrum of the dimensions of self-management.

We may conclude with a set of key notions emerging from recent research. Self-management and participation, and more generally economic self-determination, are a very efficient *modus operandi* for firms and economies, both humanly and economically. As more and more experience is acquired in that area, considerably further gains can be expected. However, the participatory form needs a certain shelter, and in its absence, it is unlikely to develop on its own. This holds true especially for the environment of modern capitalist economies where those who hold economic power – the entrepreneurs, top management and most union leadership – feel fundamentally threatened by self-management. A whole body of doctrine, that of most western economics for the entrepreneurs and that of union bargaining for the union establishment (Clegg, Reading 5) has been developed to defend the *status quo* This doctrine is by no means the only instrument of defence.

Development and transformation of other economies into more democratic forms will require a shelter, in the form either of direct political protection and stimulation as in Yugoslavia, or of the conscious action of large and sufficiently strong social groups who have rejected on moral grounds the profit motive and capital domination of men, or some semi-official amalgamation of the two. In the absence of these, as in the past hundred years, the participatory form is likely to remain marginal. On the more subtle plane, as indicated in the last selection of this volume, a truly perfect functioning of the labour-managed system will also need the shelter of the working man from himself as a collective capitalist or owner of his capital assets. These assets must not be generated from a collective operating surplus and must be hired by the participatory firm whose only foundation is cooperation through work and *not* through ownership.

5 Formal theory of labour management

Stimulated primarily by the Yugoslav experience, we have witnessed over the last twenty years the development of a formal economic theory of labour management. In Part Four of this volume we present what are considered to be the key selections in that area. In this section we will attempt to introduce the Readings and integrate them into a more coherent framework.

In a broad sense, the objective of the formal theory of labour management is to explain the behaviour of self-managed enterprises and of entire systems composed of such enterprises, using modern tools of exact economic analysis. More precisely, the objective thus defined falls into four distinct tasks. Task one consists of selecting assumptions describing as closely as possible the self-managed firm or system. The most significant part of this is to describe correctly what is actually the moving force, the objective function, or simply the objective of the self-managed firm. Only once such an objective is known can the remaining three tasks be carried out. Task two is to examine the nature of equilibria to which the objective function and other assumed conditions lead and task three is to study the mechanics of the labour-managed firms or systems resulting from the equilibrium conditions identified under task two. Specifically, the problem here is to find out how the labour-managed firms, sectors or systems will react to changes of economic environment such as changes in prices, technology and economic policy of all kinds. The remaining task (four) consists in using all the results obtained under the first three headings and studying the objective efficiency of the labour-managed firm, and more generally of the labour-managed economic system. One major problem here is the efficiency of resource allocation – that is the capability of the labour-managed solution to produce from given productive resources of labour, capital and land the maximum of output, and more important, of human satisfaction. A second problem, equally important, even if less extensively dealt with, is the distributive or distributional efficiency of self-management. The question here is, how well does a labour-managed firm or system tend to allocate the incomes, or resources produced, to different members of society?

Under the first heading, task one, at least five different objectives have been suggested, all of which (perhaps with one exception) are fundamentally related to each other, and in that sense form a continuum ranging from the most narrow to the most general. The first objective may be referred to as the individualistic maximization of income per worker within the working collective. The term individualistic is used here to indicate that maximization will be pursued at all costs, even if under changing economic conditions it implies the expulsion of some of the members. Under such conditions the income of the members expelled would be minimized rather than maximized. The second objective proposed in the literature is similar, but it attempts to take care of the anomaly of expelling fellow workers under certain conditions by postulating maximization of income per man of all members of the collective. By contrast to the first, individualistic type, the second objective of maximization of income per worker may be referred to as a social objective.

The third objective is similar, but postulates, probably under the influence of the Marxist theory of value, maximization of income not only per worker actually employed in the enterprise, but also per unit of embodied labour, that is, labour which was used at some earlier date in producing the capital used by the labour-managed enterprise. The fourth objective, while recognizing the merits of the second, pushes the notion of social motivation a good deal further and postulates that besides income per worker, there is a whole spectrum of other objectives which enter the working collective's preferences. Among such additional objectives may be listed: the intensity of work; collective consumption; effects of the activities of the enterprise on its environment; and even objectives of an altruistic nature such as service to the broader community outside the enterprise.

Compared to the first four objectives which can be termed man-centred, the fifth objective can be seen as somewhat of a retrogression in the direction of a capitalist firm. The postulate here is that workers year after year fix a certain wage rate, and having done so, maximize profit in the same way as a conventional capitalist firm. If the objective is supplemented by the supposition of investment of all retained earnings, it also boils down to the objective of maximization of accumulation under the restriction of the prescribed wage level.

The pioneering paper analysing the behaviour of a self-managed firm using the first objective is Benjamin Ward's 'The firm in Illyria' (1958). It was later critically reviewed and extended by Evsey Domar. Because the Domar paper contains the results of both contributions, we use it as our first selection of the theoretical part. Both contributions study the labour-managed firm under our tasks two and three outlined above. Ward's principal and most surprising result is a backward-bending supply function in the short run, and Domar's important contribution is that that elasticity will be turned into positive if possibilities of alternative employment of labour are introduced.

Using the first objective and then developing the social objective of the working collective, I developed in my *General Theory of Labor-Managed Market Economies* (1970) a comprehensive microeconomic and macroeconomic theory of the labour-managed system, going beyond the theory of the firm offered by Ward and Domar and covering the areas of formal theory of industry and general equilibrium and the macroeconomic theory of national income determination. In that study I also dealt extensively with problems of economic policy, planning and system implementation and attempted to tackle the more complex theory arising from the multivariate fourth objective. It will be recalled that the key results, especially those with reference to the evaluation of efficiency of the labour-managed system, are summarized in the last chapter of Part Three of this volume.

The broader formal theory of labour management is dealt with by James Meade in the second reading. He does so referring extensively to my work, contributing valuable criticism and systematic comparison with the theory of the capitalist market economy.

The third type of objective function, relating to returns not only to employed labour but also to labour embodied in capital assets, is developed by Yugoslav authors, particularly Professor Korac. Their work is discussed by Deborah Milenkovitch in the third reading in Part Four. Unfortunately, Korac's presentation is somewhat unclear and he, as most Yugoslav authors, has not gone beyond the statement of the objective into what we have referred to above as tasks two, three and four.[2]

The introduction of objective four without any doubt renders the theory of labour management more realistic. But at the same time it considerably increases the complexity of the analysis and in a significant sense takes it out of the realm of economics into adjacent spheres of psychology, industrial sociology and even political science. At least an illustration of the sociological dimensions of self-management is contained in Blumberg (Reading 21). Remaining on the plane of economics, a 'reduced' case of multidimensionality is dealt with in the fourth Reading of Part Four. In it, an attempt is made to introduce variability of productive effort and corresponding income earned in the context of less-developed societies living close to subsistence conditions. Using that analysis in evaluating the self-management solution and comparing it with other organizational forms, it can be shown that the self-management alternative can be significantly superior. In addition to the obvious human advantages of economic self-determination, the self-managed solution can produce growth and development in many instances where under capitalist conditions there could be no progress.

As can be seen in the Milenkovitch selection, at least two Yugoslav authors have adhered to the motivating principle number five, that is, that the Yugoslav self-managed firm maximizes profit. Of the two, Todorovic and Horvat, the latter is somewhat more precise, postulating that the working collective first fixes its wage rates and proceeds to maximize profit. However, neither of the two elaborates in any detail the implications of this assumption for the labour-managed firm. For one thing, a complete theory would also have to include postulates about the process through which the wages are actually fixed in a world where a labour market does

2 However, a dissertation was produced at Cornell University by Dr Daniel Mahoney analysing the results obtained from the Korac postulate. In summary, the results are that while some of the optimal efficiency of the labour-managed system obtained on the other objective functions are preserved, some others disappear and lead to suboptimal solutions.

not exist and hence there is no objective process of determining the wage rate. This lack of elaboration together with the fact that a profit-maximizing (that is, capitalist) firm has been extensively studied are the reasons why we have not explicitly introduced selections in this domain.

This brings us to the last selection of Part Four, which may have the greatest practical significance. Following the established traditions of the theory of the firm, most of the writings on the labour-managed enterprise either neglect the problem of how capital is procured by the firm, or make a standard conventional assumption that capital as much as other non-human factors of production is a factor rented at a given price in a competitive factor market.

In practice, as can be noted from the selections in Part Two and also from the doctrine of self-management, in an overwhelming majority of cases the postulate of external funding at a constant price of capital does not obtain. Thus the conclusions regarding the high degree of efficiency of the labour-managed solution are also put in question. My paper on the fundamental theory of financing of labour-managed firms shows how dramatic the departure from efficiency can be if the conditions of external funding at a meaningful price are not fulfilled, but substituted for by internal collective funding. This in turn can provide a sufficient explanation for why full industrial democracy and labour management did not develop over the years into a significant form of productive organization. The collective inalienable patrimony of productive assets, found in Buchez's doctrine and the cooperative practice, together with the natural unwillingness of the democratic associations to depend on a hostile and economically undemocratic environment, constituted a serious impediment which prevented the flourishing of the participatory principles in production. More than just explaining the comparative failure of producers' cooperation in the past, the last Reading of the volume also, we hope, points to a way out of the impasse.

6 Fundamental rules for efficient labour-managed systems

Economic self-determination and self-management have historically assumed a variety of forms, and a number of other modalities can also be conceived of in theory. Some of these forms can be very efficient, indeed the most effective forms of economic organization of any kind, but others, as is amply demonstrated by history, can be ineffective, sometimes to the degree of dooming to failure all efforts to introduce producer cooperation and self-management.

In this concluding section, we will summarize in twelve separate points the necessary conditions of an optimal and viable self-managed economy (or, implicitly, of an isolated self-managed firm). Of course, we cannot go into the full justification and reasoning behind each of the points but, by and large, this is contained or implicit in the various chapters, both empirical and theoretical, of this volume.

These necessary conditions are:

1 All control, management and income (after payment of all costs and taxes) should always remain in the hands of those who work in a given enterprise, whatever their number; the underlying operational principle being a fully democratic rule on the basis of equality of vote. The philosophical and moral basis of this must always remain the work in common of a group of men and nothing else, in particular not, as was often the case with traditional producer cooperatives, some kind of ownership of shares or basic contributions. This is nothing but an expression of a fundamental humanist principle upon which any viable self-managed economy must be based.

2 Whenever, on grounds of static or dynamic economies of scale, division of labour and cooperation among two or more men in an enterprise are necessary,[3] funding of capital assets other than through collective retained earnings must be brought about. Funding should preferably be based on national ownership, administered by a shelter agency, or otherwise as explained in point 8 below. Of course funding does not imply control, which by condition 1 above remains in the hands of the working collective. If members of the self-managed enterprise contribute through their savings, this should be done freely, and in some way retain the individual claims of the savers.

3 While capital, or more precisely the source of financial capital, does not command any right of control, it is entitled to adequate remuneration at a rate reflecting the relative scarcity of that factor in the economy. Such a rate in real terms can be quite high in developing countries, perhaps well in excess of ten per cent.

4 Conditions 1, 2 and 3 are equally applicable to productive land, which for all practical purposes can be treated as capital. The only exception here is that the payment of rent or income of land should be conditioned by the attainment of necessary minimum subsistence of those who work on the land.

5 The returns on capital and land should in their entirety or at least predominantly be earmarked for accumulation – that is, creation of new capital assets – and not for individual consumption of any kind. In this

3 Collective exploitation of land is sometimes justified in developing countries by such dynamic economies of scale; modernization and technological change are impossible on traditional, very small, and sometimes fragmented, individual holdings.

way the fundamental problem of accumulation facing especially the developing economies is resolved, while at the same time the objection to personal capital income (non-labour income) on distributional grounds is eliminated.[4] It can be shown that the rates of accumulation attainable through this method are quite considerable. In case of an isolated self-managed firm, it is imperative that the firm itself perform on its own behalf this accumulation function, at a fixed rate of return to capital.

6 In principle the returns charged on capital should be the same for all users. This guarantees an optimal allocation of capital resources.

7 It is imperative to establish a shelter organization or institution on the national level (which can be decentralized according to need), whose express function would be to fund and promote the self-managed sector or economy. More specifically, this agency would be charged with the supervision but not the control of the capital market, the promotion and expansion of new firms or sectors according to national plans, the coordination and spreading of information regarding alternative investment projects, technical and other assistance to new groups desiring to form self-managing firms, and supervision designed to secure in the long run the equalization of income per worker (of course, of equal skill) among industrial branches. The shelter organization is the active arm of the national planning agency or ministry, if such a thing exists. Its fundamental objective must be the promotion of the social good of the participatory sector and of the whole economy. In the absence of a nationally endorsed self-management policy, in a western economy, the shelter organization can assume the form of one or more nonprofit supporting corporations. Such corporations can then be given the additional task of accumulating and using for investment pension funds within the sector and other savings of individuals belonging to the self-managing sector.

8 To minimize the need for the services of the sheltering institution, it is advisable that existing firms be given the priority of using the funds which they are paying as interest on capital for the purpose of their own expansion or creation of new firms. The projects must pass accepted criteria of viability, and funds thus re-invested must yield the normal rate of return as all other investments.

9 In general, but especially in young countries interested in rapid accumulation and the efficient flow of resources, the depreciation allowances

4 A significant exception to this rule can be permitted if capital assets are generated through workers' own savings and not through inheritance. A case in point here is one which played an important role in many successful self-managed firms where old-age insurance (pension) funds are used as a source of investment funds, and at retirement paid out together with accumulated interest income.

of the self-managed firms should also be collected and added to the national investment fund and allocated according to optimality criteria. To protect the interest of the firms contributing their depreciation allowances, the authorities and the shelter organization must guarantee automatic availability of the real value of these funds when actual replacement of plant and/or equipment (on which the depreciation allowances were paid) is called for.

10 The optimal form of the self-managed economy or sector is one based on the market mechanism, in the sense that all firms act to the best advantage of their working collectives and whoever else they may be concerned with, while using prices in all product and factor markets[5] as objective signals in their decision-making. But of course, the authorities, planning institute or the shelter organization can and ought to exercise influence over the individual firms of the participatory sector by means of nondiscriminatory tools (tax policies of all kinds, price ceilings and other price controls). Price regulation in particular should be used whenever a significant degree of monopoly power exists in a given industry.

11 At all times, but especially in its early stages, the effort of introducing self-management must be accompanied by an educational effort focusing on both the basic philosophy of economic self-determination and the specifics of self-management. This effort should be cooperative to the greatest possible degree as much as self-management itself.

12 On the political plane, especially in countries having or aspiring to political democracy, it is most constructive, honest and effective to place the struggle for self-management on the philosophico-ideological base of *fundamental rights of the working man*. These rights, which must be guaranteed by society, are broadly defined as economic self-determination and include, most importantly, the right to employment and the right to self-management. To use the traditional platforms and categories of socialism–communism–capitalism can be most divisive and can frustrate efforts for democratization in the economic sphere for many years. It is not good to pour new wine into old skins.

References

VANEK, J. (1970), *The General Theory of Labor-Managed Market Economies*, Cornell University Press.
WARD, B. (1958), 'The firm in Illyria: market syndicalism', *Amer. econ. Rev.*, vol. 48, pp. 566–89.

5 Note, however, that the labour market is no longer a market in the traditional sense, labour remuneration being given by the performance and effort of each particular firm.

Part One
Doctrine

1 R. Reibel

The Workingman's Production Association, or the Republic in the Workshop

From R. Reibel, 'Les idées politiques et sociales de P.-J.-B. Buchez', 'L'association ouvrière de production ou "la république dans l'atelier" ', in R. Reibel and P. Róngère, *Socialisme et Ethique*, Presse Universitaire de France, Paris, 1966, pp. 45–51.

It seems that Buchez conceived very early the idea of a workers' association. If we can believe his disciple Feugueray, 'since before the July revolution, he had proposed it to his friends and collaborators', in 1830 he must have submitted the idea to the republicans of the 'Society of the Friends of the People'. Finally, the plan received all the publicity to be desired in *The European* of 17 December 1831 under the title, 'A means of ameliorating the condition of urban wage-earners'.

Buchez does not indicate his sources to us. Certainly, Fourier before him had spoken of association, but his ideas, which are more or less utopian, have nothing in common with the plan of Buchez, which is much more limited, more exact and able to be applied immediately. The school of Saint-Simon had thought of an 'association of labourers' to resolve the state of struggle and antagonism in which society found itself; but what a difference between what was really a 'collectivist, hierarchic organization of production' and the true workers' association, conceived to introduce democracy on a broad social base. Buchez's notion thus remains entirely original and Armand Cuvillier can rightly say that it 'is at the roots of the whole French tradition of the producers' association'.

The idea of Buchez is not taken from pure theory; it sums up the aspirations of a whole generation of workers. The theory of workers' association took its definitive form only in the course of repeated contacts with workers themselves. Buchez recognized this:

We have talked with these men in sweaters and heavy working boots, . . . of rude speech and simple language, of things which certainly would have been unintelligible to many gentlemen of the salon. Even better than that, from several of them we have received memoirs, written in bad French to be sure, but full of ideas which would make the fortune of an economist.

The evolution of Buchez's ideas

In 1831, Buchez believed that two schemes which were immediately realizable were capable of 'improving the lot of urban wage-earners', according to the category into which they fall. For independent craftsmen, 'such as carpenters, construction workers, masons, shoemakers, lock-smiths ... [who] do not need expensive equipment, [and whose] ability is their main capital', the most apt way of improving their lot is through association. On the other hand, for factory and manufacturing workers he speaks only of 'organizing' their labour. It is impossible to withdraw capital from the hands of its owners; only the government can intervene here to improve the condition of the workers.

The goal of association, wherever it is possible, is to eliminate the entrepreneur, a useless intermediary, a 'pure parasite' who merely provides capital. The existence of this intermediary results in cutting off the worker's gain to a considerable extent, and as well in making the consumer pay usurious prices.

To create a 'producers' association' a certain number of workers in the same trade join together in an enterprise based on articles 1842 of the Civil Code and 48 of the Code of Commerce, the terms of the contract being as follows.

The associates, joined together as entrepreneurs, choose one or two representatives to have the legal signature. Each associate continues to be paid as is customary in the trade, by day or by piece, and according to his skill. The amount representing the contribution of the entrepreneur is set aside and divided in two parts at the end of the year: '20 per cent would be taken to form and increase the social capital; the rest would be used for help when needed or distributed among the associates, proportionately to their work.' The social capital which thus increases each year by one-fifth of the profits is inalienable; belonging to an association which is itself perpetual since it is continually admitting new members, it is not liable to inheritance.

The social capital, inalienable and indivisible, is the 'important fact' in the association:

It is the factor by which this type of society creates a better future for the working classes. If it were otherwise, the association would become just like any other corporation; it would be useful only to its founders and harmful to everyone who was not part of it from the first; for it would end up by being in the hands of the former, a means of exploitation.

The great difficulty which would prevent associations from multiplying is the lack of credit. Buchez believes that with respect to this it would be easy to set up special banks, branches of a 'General Fund for Public Credit'. Not only would these banks liberate the working class with respect to capital, but they could also 'regulate production' and prevent 'these terrible periodic crises from which European industry still suffers today' (Buchez thus already envisioned the possibility of a 'directed economy').

Since the association was not applicable to factory workers, Buchez provides for them the following reforms: the creation of bodies of equal representation for workers and management, the establishment of a minimum wage and of funds for assistance.

From this initial reform plan of 1831 to the one to be found in the *Treatise on Politics*, the ideas of Buchez must have evolved quite a long way. This evolution is in the direction of generalizing the association. In the final form of his thought, Buchez no longer distinguished between two categories of workers, but rather between 'transitional' and 'definitive' means of resolving the social question.

The transitional means are three in number: a minimum wage, fixed by region and by profession, 'below which it would not be permitted to anyone to offer, nor to accept work'; an institution permitting the poor to live at the expense of the Administration (in return, they would accept any employment whatsoever and would have the position of 'industrial soldiers'); and finally, a sizeable expansion of public assistance.

As for the definitive solution of the social problem, it consists in the 'general extension, or rather in the universality of the workingman's association', but this goal can be attained only in the rather distant future. To reach it, there will have to be a 'revolution of ways and of morals' which Buchez believes would be as great as that by which mankind passes from slavery to freedom.

In effect, two major difficulties exist. On the one hand, Buchez does not want a violent dispossession of owners and capitalists; the credit institution which is supposed to make possible buying back the instruments of labour will obviously not be able to do it all in one day. But there is an even greater obstacle (Buchez had realized this in 1835; see the Preface to volume 32 of the *Parliamentary History of the French Revolution*). Men are not yet qualified to receive the workers' association as he conceives of it:

It seems at first glance that this type of association, where everything profits the worker, should not meet any obstacle in propagating and multiplying itself, at least on the part of those who are called to take part in it. However, just the opposite happens: and according to the forceful expression of one worker, it is easier to find 100 000 francs than to find a man who, on entering a community of this sort, would absolutely renounce the hope of becoming the boss, and of having someday other wage-earners under him. . . . Association in work is not possible if each one does not reject egoism, and does not forget himself to think of others. *Before joining together in association, men need a fundamental change of spirit.* Such a change is not a matter of one day, nor even of one generation. It required several centuries to make men understand the idea of national associations; will not some years be needed for them to comprehend the industrial community?

In fact, the workingman's association demanded an extremely developed spirit of charity, especially on the part of its founders. In setting up an indivisible capital, the first associates were working for those generations to come. This clause, which imposes so much self-denial, is nonetheless indispensable in the conception of Buchez. This gives the 'revolutionary' value to the association by making it the instrument of liberation of wage-earners. Feugueray could even write that to remove from an association its common, indivisible capital 'would be to castrate it; it would mean transforming it from an institution that is pre-eminently socialist to one that is capitalist'.

The universal extension of association will result in an *organization of industry* which Buchez (1835) qualifies as *Christian* and which he describes thus:

We can imagine that the earth would be covered with communities – agricultural, manufacturing, and so forth – each one dedicated to a specific work, all of whose members would be associates in the sense that they would all contribute to the common work, and that they would use to this end the capital of the community. ... Each community would no doubt have a manager, but he would be no better paid than the least of the labourers, since what would decide the level of material recompense would not be the importance of the work, but the degree of good will that each one would bring to it. Therefore, he who can give only the work of his hands, and gives it, is worth as much morally as he who can give his intelligence and puts it at the service of others. We suppose also that all the communities would be united by an *industrial administration* where the law of hierarchy would be arranged in a way inverse to what prevails today, that is where the greatest power rebounds to him who agrees to sacrifice most of well-being and liberty. ...

Such a scheme runs the risk of being called utopian, 'but it is scarcely conceivable how Christian morality would ever be a political reality if something similar does not come to pass among us'.

We should note that such an organization corresponds perfectly to the very restrictive notion which Buchez posits for the rights of property: land to be held in common; severe limitation on inheritance; in short, right only to the product of work. It is likely, moreover, that Buchez developed such a bold conception (1866, book III, ch. 7) only to justify *a posteriori* the universality of association.

The workers' association in the ideology of 1848

What was the influence of the associationist doctrine of Buchez? It was manifested in two ways: on the one hand, some very limited attempts to bring it to fruition; on the other, a considerable influence on the cooperative movement in general, and especially on the ideology of 1848.

The associations drawn up on the Buchezian model were never very numerous. On 10 September 1831, a 'Contract of Association of Carpenters' was signed but it was never applied. Other associations were founded subsequently and succeeded in eking out existence for a certain time, but only one made its mark, that of the *Jewelry-workers in Gold* which, founded in 1834 by one Leroy, continued until 1873 with clear results. The story of this association, although most interesting, will detain us here only for the manner in which it attempted to put into practice the doctrine of Buchez.

It wanted above all to make of itself an example and a model, and therefore demanded of its members not only a high professional capacity, but also to 'practise the morality of the Gospel'. Its discipline was rigid; under pain of fine, all members were obliged to attend weekly general assemblies, at which 'one of the managers read aloud a chapter of the Gospel, in order to show clearly that the Association was founded to seek before all else the Kingdom of God and its justice'.

Feugueray (1851), from whom we take these details, praises highly this moral austerity 'drawn from the school of M. Buchez', as well as the 'scrupulous prudence' which the association applied both in the choice of its members and in the administration of its affairs. While thinking that the association would never increase very fast, he added: 'It is certain that it will not perish. It is founded on granite.' Even though this was showing somewhat too much optimism, forty years of existence demonstrated that the association of Buchez was not a Utopia.

The associationist idea received a new impetus starting in 1840. *L'Atelier* (*The Workshop*) was founded primarily to defend and diffuse it, but it reached only a rather narrow circle.

Far more important was the influence of Louis Blanc. Feugueray attributes to him the merit of giving to the theory of association, thanks to his literary talent, a 'great reverberation throughout the intellectual world', but at the same time finds fault with Blanc's eclecticism. Starting from Buchez's idea of indivisible capital, Louis Blanc would have added to it the suppression of competition, which brought the association into the hands of the State, and in the end confused association with community. The Buchezian journal, the *Revue Nationale*, on 27 April 1848 had already hurled strong criticism at the national workshops:

One of two things, either the national workshops will function freely at their own profit, and then the ruin of the State is ever imminent, or else the State will be manager, supplier, buyer, seller, and will have to share in the profits in compensation for its risks. From there to monopoly is only one step, which would be soon taken. Thus France would be nothing more than one vast administration, all of whose citizens would be public functionaries. It would be a new Paraguay, where nothing could enter and whence nothing could leave at anyone's will, and of which M. Louis Blanc would probably want to be the Dr Francia. Away with these enormities!

What may we think, then, of the opinion of Cuvillier, who, citing several authors, accuses Louis Blanc of having purely and simply plagiarized Buchez?

The statutes of the Carpenters' Association show us that in 1831 Buchez, before anyone else, was opposed to the idea of competition. A single association, established in each sector, should progressively draw to itself all the workers (see Corbon, 1863):

The first association to be founded should be considered as the kernel of the universal association. It should be very absorptive, and unique insofar as possible within a given profession; and all of them, converging toward the same goal, ought to maintain a strict solidarity. .... Our theory from the very first was distinguished from that of the pure communists in only one sense, that, outside the workshop, each one disposed as he wished of his possessions.

It is the earlier conception which Louis Blanc must have adopted, even while carrying it further, since unity was to be realized by the intervention of the State. Buchez and his friends of the *Atelier* were following an opposite evolution during this time, which led them to recognize the necessity of a certain amount of competition among associations. The whole error of Louis Blanc, then, was in remaining with positions which Buchez had long since abandoned.

Whatever may have been the case, cooperative and associationist theories had an important role to play in the 'ideology of '48'.

From the twenty-fifth of February, the provisional government recognized that 'workers ought to join together in associations (*s'associer entre eux*) to enjoy the legitimate profit of their labour'. The Constitution itself – in a climate already completely different – would still affirm in Article 13 that 'society favours and encourages voluntary associations'. Moreover, a decree of 5 July 1848 determined to distribute a credit of three millions among the workers' associations. In the 'Council of Encouragement' that was set up to distribute the funds, the influence of the Buchezians was at first predominant, then it yielded to the conservative element which used the credits for 'disguised payments to owners who had their workers participate in profits' (Duroselle, 1951). Let us note that the numerous associations founded at that time understood for the most part nothing of the stipulation of indivisible capital. Those which had introduced it into their statutes looked only for how to get rid of it as soon as possible. This did not prevent the *Atelier*, before ceasing publication, from proudly writing:

The idea that we would have been happy to make penetrate, little by little, in our class, has indeed penetrated so well that there is scarcely a street in Paris today where the passers by cannot read on the door of some shop: 'Fraternal Association of Workingmen'.

If the cooperative movement of 1848 was defeated in the end, it was for political reasons. Beginning in 1849, and even much more under the Second Empire, the government showed itself openly hostile with regard to the workers' association. One may wonder whether, applied loyally and under the best circumstances, the idea of Buchez would not have contributed to improving notably the condition of the proletariat.

Cuvillier, who rightly sees in Buchez the 'founder' of the workingman's production association, has shown that his influence was profound on the cooperative movement in general, in England as well as France. On this subject we can only refer to his studies.

In committing the working class to liberate itself of itself, in showing it how the association could contribute, Buchez was one of the first to seek to introduce democracy throughout the society. Out of the workingman's association, he wanted to make a small Republic in which 'as in every good democracy, there is not one function which is not conferred by election and is not revokable or at least temporary'. According to the memorable phrase of Feugueray, 'the workingman's association is the Republic of the Workshop'.

However, it was with the small Buchezian republic as with the large one: one had to devote oneself to it body and soul. The first generations of associates had to impose great sacrifices on themselves to augment the capital and thus put the instruments of work at the disposition of future generations, so that the latter might finally enjoy the entire fruit of their labour. Here is Buchez's asceticism put into practice; Feugueray was exhorting the workers to see in the association not so much the possibility of an immediate increase in well-being, as the instrument of the 'future good' that will bring to pass Justice and the Kingdom of God in the industrial world. The working class would thus have the extraordinary merit of having realized by itself, without violence, 'the greatest social transformation to be effected on earth since the abolition of slavery'. He was forgetting that all men are not saints. . . .

Anthime Corbon, former editor of the *Atelier*, had to abandon this illusion as did the others. In his interesting book, *The Secret of the People of Paris* (1863), he criticized the ideas of Buchez of which he had been an enthusiastic propagandist. Indivisible capital and the perpetuity of the association seem to him contrary to the theory of Progress, 'which demands mobility of institutions'; but above all, he refuses to see the association as a 'religious, socialist order instituted in the midst of civil society to regenerate it'. According to his picturesque expression, this is only some 'gaudy finery' which decorates and dissimulates the real value of a good idea; for he continues to believe in the workers' association, and this is in fact a last homage he gives to his master:

Either democracy will never be more than nominal, or the workingman's association will be the great institution of the future. Insofar as the worker is not owner of all or part of the instrument of his labour, liberty and equality will be only dreams for him; and democracy would be only a decoy if it did not end up one day, by the efforts of the workers themselves, in bringing about in most working-places, if not in all where there used to be a boss and wage labourers, henceforth a manager and associates. ... Democracy in the political order, and a nearly absolute Monarchy in the workingplace, are two things that cannot long coexist.

References

BUCHEZ, P. J. B. (1831–2), *L'Européan.*
BUCHEZ, P. J. B. (1835) *Histoire Parlementaire de la Révolution Française,* preface to vol. 32.
BUCHEZ, P. J. B. (1840), *L'Atelier.*
BUCHEZ, P. J. B. (1847–8), *Revue Nationale.*
BUCHEZ, P. J. B. (1866), *Traité de Politique et de Science Sociale.*
CORBON, A. (1863), *Le Secret du Peuple de Paris,* Paris.
CUVILLIER, A. (1948), *Buchez et les Origines du Socialisme Chrétien,* Paris.
DUROSELLE, J. B. (1951), *Les Débuts du Catholicisme Social en France,* Paris.
FEUGUERAY, H. (1851), *L'Association Ouvrière, Industrielle et Agricole,* Paris.

2 R. Selucky

Marxism and Self-Management

First published in this volume.

Contemporary Marxists are strongly divided (among others) into two groups: the first one tries to prove that the only legitimate Marxian concept for socialist economy must consist of the self-government of the producers, while the second one identifies the only truly Marxian concept of socialism with a command-planning system. Both groups are aware that it is very difficult to find any consistent chain of authentic evidences indicating Marx's willingness to subscribe to either system. Marx and Engels were vague enough as far as organization of the future socialist economy was concerned. Both strongly believed that any prediction of this kind must necessarily consist of some utopian elements and they did their best to avoid such an unscientific approach to the problem. Both Marx and Engels have commented occasionally on the basic principles of a future socialist society, but their comments were not only very marginal but often very general too. The supporters of the self-managing socialism usually quote the famous paragraph from Marx (1968a), 'The communal *régime* once established in Paris and the secondary centres, the old centralized government would in the provinces, too, have to give way to the self-government of the producers', while their adversaries quote a no less famous paragraph written by Marx: 'The national centralization of the means of production will become the natural base for a society which will consist of an association of free and equal producers acting consciously according to a general and rational plan', or from Engels (1968), that 'the proletariat seizes political power and turns means of production in the first instance into state property'. These two quotations are to support the thesis that centralized economic management is fully compatible with the association of free producers, and that the form of the ownership of socialized means of production must be defined in terms of state property.

It would be possible to go on with enumerating less clear and less important quotations supporting the first or the second Marxist concept. It seems to me, however, that such a method would be quite useless and unscientific – or, if you will, quite *anti-Marxist*. The quotation is no argument. Even more so: Marx himself did believe that what counts is a methodology, and this was confirmed by Engels (1969b), 'but all concepts of Marx (*Auffassungsweise*) are not doctrines but methods. They do not provide complete doctrines but starting points for further research and methods for that research.'

The purpose of this paper is to examine the Marxist approach to the future socialist economy from the point of view of its methodology as well as from the point of view of its concept of the market and that of the state. I take it for granted that the main political goal of both Marx and Engels was the liberation of man from both economic exploitation, different forms of alienation and material dependence.[1]

Marxist concept of the market

Every Marxist would probably agree with the suggestion that the market has at least three basic shortcomings. As it operates spontaneously and organizes the proportions of the production *ex post*, it periodically causes disharmony between supply and demand, creates an economic imbalance and gives rise to economic crises. The second shortcoming of the market mechanism is that it leads to social inequality and increases it, while its third failure is that it encourages only such economic activity which yields profits and is advantageous for the producers. It is unable to stimulate production of goods and services which, though needed by the community, are not subject to the criterion of profit or material advantage. This is true particularly about social and public services, including the infrastructure, the development of which must be supported by modern society, and particularly by any socialist society, even at a loss.

There are at least six other characteristics of the market which have been generally accepted by the Marxist theory:

1 The market is a product of the social division of labour and of autonomous producers.

2 It organizes economic processes and regulates the exchange of labour among men.

3 It is a mediating link and, at the same time, a feedback between production and consumption.

1 'Relationships of personal dependence (which were at first quite spontaneous) are the first forms of society in which human productivity develops, though only to a slight extent and at isolated points. Personal independence founded on material dependence is the second great form: in it there developed for the first time a system of general social interchange, resulting in universal relations, varied requirements and universal capacities. Free individuality, which is founded on the universal development of individuals and the domination of their communal and social productivity, which has become their social power, is the third stage. The second stage creates the conditions for the third' (McLellan, 1971, p. 67).

4 It creates objective criteria and control mechanism for comparing the social costs of production.

5 It is the medium of communication and cooperation among the carriers of economic activity.

6 It operates spontaneously, has no internal aim and regulates production and exchange only *ex post*.

The market is not a product of capitalism; it came into being and it developed concurrently with the origins and development of the social division of labour. In pre-capitalist production forms, the market existed only insofar as it found the two prerequisites of its existence: the social division of labour as well as autonomous producers. It could therefore not be applied *within* the relationships of patriarchalism, slavery or feudalism; if it existed and developed in pre-capitalist societies at all, it did so only parallel with these relationships, not within them. Only in the capitalist society did the market become the universal regulator of economy, and market relations extended over the entire society, composed – again for the first time in human history – of autonomous and personally free men. Thus capitalism is the only known social and economic system in which market relations are universally valid and are the basis of all social relations.

The Marxist critique of commodity, market and money relations has three sources: moral, philosophic and economic. Money as a universal commodity, and gold as its material substance are at the same time a universal form of the existence of the capital which is the wrongdoer of exploitation and the cause of human misery; the fetish of gold – even more obvious than the fetishism of commodities – is an expression of the dominance of things and conditions over people. The moral condemnation of money as a universal commodity, as a measure of values, as a hoarding, as an instrument of accumulation and element of exchange, was expressed by Marx in words as fiery as those used by the utopian socialists; and Lenin, one of the interpreters of Marxian teachings, prophesied a similar fate for gold as Thomas Moore assigned to it in his Utopia: 'It shall be used, after the victory of the world proletarian revolution, as building material for public lavatories.'[2]

Nevertheless, the moral condemnation of commodity, market and money relations is irrelevant from the theoretical point of view, and it should be noted that it does not represent the substance of the Marxist critique of market society. The philosophic and economic condemnation is of much greater importance. The basis of the philosophic condemnation

2 Compare with Marx (1964, 1968b) and Lenin (1968).

is Marx's theory of alienation of labour. The alienation stems from three sources: one is the very existence of commodity and market relations; another is the existence of division of labour in detail, for instance within the factory; the third is the existence of capital relations of exploitation.[3] Alienation of labour caused by the universality of commodity and market relations lies in the fact that the producer ceases to be concerned with the use-value which he has created, with the concrete existence of his product, with its meaning, significance and usefulness, and is concerned merely with its exchange value, primarily from the quantitative point of view. Thus the aim of his labour and its content is alienated from the producer; human labour is reduced to a mere abstract quality which forms the exchange value.

In a market society, the only links between people are things (goods), through the exchange of which people obtain the means of their existence. The fate of the producer depends on whether or not a thing (commodity) can be exchanged. A thing, quite simple as long as it was a mere thing, turns into a mystery and a fetish as soon as it becomes a commodity.[4] The mystery is not its use-value but its exchange value as the only form of its substance, i.e. value. Why is it that the same thing yields an equivalent in one instance and fails to do so in another? Why are some things (commodities) sometimes exchangeable and sometimes not? Why does man's fate depend on their fate in the process of exchange? Why is his work sometimes recognized as social labour and sometimes not? Why does it not depend on the producer himself and on the specifics of his work? What does it actually depend on? On the conditions which prevail over people, on things which change into commodities – to which man no longer feels as intimately and immediately bound as he used to, and which appear to him as alien, unknown, mysterious and all-powerful forces.

This alienation grows even deeper as the division of labour works its way into the workshop, the manufacture, the factory and transforms the worker (the immediate producer) into a *detail* worker who no longer creates the whole (final) product but only a part of it and carries out

3 Some official interpreters of Marx later made the first and third sources of alienation identical, thus denying that alienation of labour could exist in a socialist society. The second source of alienation is being generally overlooked by the overwhelming majority of official Marxists in both socialist and capitalist countries.
4 'For instance, the form of wood is altered when we make a table of it. Nonetheless, the table is still wood, an ordinary palpable thing. But as soon as it presents itself as a commodity it is transformed into a thing which is transcendental as well as palpable. It stands with its feet solidly planted on the floor; but at the same time, over against all other commodities, it stands on its head; and in that wooden head it forms crotchets far stronger than table-turning ever was' (Marx, 1967, p. 44).

several tasks or even one partial task in which he specializes and acquires a degree of virtuosity. If human labour had a meaning earlier (man was the maker of the use-value, of the final product), that meaning is now lost. The immediate producer is not interested in what he is producing; what he is interested in is the fact that labour has become the source of his livelihood and thus a prerequisite of his existence. Man is not interested in his profession; he is merely interested in his *job*. It is alienated labour since it has ceased to be an inner need of human self-expression and self-fulfilment; it stands apart from the man, since he carries it out not because of a need to create but under the pressure of necessity, in order to make a living. So the alienation of man from the results of his labour goes hand in hand with the externalization of man and his labour; it dehumanizes labour as the basic feature which distinguishes man from the rest of animals.

There is, however, the third dimension to the alienation of man from his labour. As far as wage labour is concerned, the worker creates values not for himself but for the capitalist who has purchased his working power and who appropriates the result of his work in the framework of the capitalist relationship of exploitation. The product of exploited labour – the surplus value – is alienated from the worker because it does not belong to him but instead to the capitalist and is changed into profit; but even the working time is alienated from the worker, and thus also his labour, because during his working hours, under the supervision of the capitalist and for the capitalist's benefit, he creates not only the equivalent of his wages as the basis of his existence but also the surplus value for the capitalist. The capital relations loom as a superstructure over the commodity and market relations (in the Marxian concept, the worker sells not his labour but his working-power whose specific use-value lies in that it is capable of producing in any given day a greater value than that which it has by itself). Without the market relationship in which the worker sells his working power to the capitalist, no capital relationships could either exist or reproduce; thus, the specific capitalist form of wage labour and exploitation could not exist without market relations. This is why Marx is able to say that the working time is a part of the worker's alienation from the entire capitalist system, that the worker becomes himself only when he is back home, after work, in his spare time, i.e. outside of his labour which is both alienated and stolen from him. Only when the capital relationship is abolished will the capitalist form of alienation vanish; only when the market relationship is abolished and commodities again become products without mystery, will the market form of alienation disappear; and only when things cease to rule over men will the market form of the externalization of man disappear.

Marx's economic condemnation of the market relations is based on the fact that the market determines the proportions of production factors, both spontaneously and *ex post*, that is, not only blindly but, above all, uneconomically. The market determination of proportions *ex post* means wasting social labour; in the conditions of capitalism, it is accompanied by crises. Marx (1967, p. 92) sees their theoretical possibility already in the most elementary act of exchange, commodity–money–commodity; in short, it is a most irrational way of regulating the economic processes.

This critique of commodity and market relations appears and reappears throughout the entire body of the work of Marx and Engels (1968). The conclusion that Engels draws from it is that 'no society can remain in command over its own production indefinitely, or control the social consequences of its production process, unless it abolishes exchange among individuals'.

Then, if commodity production and market organization of national economy work as obstacles of a rationally functioning society, humanistically organized and developing without crises, there would seem to be no way out but abolishing the market and replacing it by a direct distribution of production factors, and instead of its function of an *ex post* regulator of proportions introducing the plan as an external regulator of the economy which operates *ex ante*. However, in order to abolish the market, it would be also necessary to abolish its material and social prerequisites: the social division of labour and the autonomy of producers.

As far as the social division of labour is concerned, the situation is quite hopeless. This naturally changes in the course of human history concurrently with the development of applied technology and science and with the changing human needs; but its substance – specialization of producers – remains. It could actually be stipulated that the development of society deepens the professional division of labour: new professions keep emerging with new branches; new specializations become necessary with the growing volume of human knowledge of the external world; relations among producers grow increasingly complicated, their mutual communication and cooperation becoming more and more complex and unmanageable. All this tends to strengthen rather than weaken the need for a self-regulating mechanism, capable of reducing the varied activities of men, and their varied economic interests to a common denominator. This happens for at least as long as the economic sphere remains an area of objectified action and until it changes into a sphere of creative activity, satisfying the human need of self-realization.

If, therefore, the social division of labour as the foundation of commodity production and market relations cannot be changed by a conscious intervention, it becomes necessary to change the position of producers in the system of national economy. If their professional differentiation and their functional specialization cannot be abolished, it becomes necessary to abolish their *autonomous* position as independent elements of the economic processes. The only way of abolishing the autonomy of producers is to socialize the means of production and to liquidate private property in the process of a socialist revolution.

Thus a solution does exist; but what must be done about the social division of labour which has not disappeared? What is there to replace the market relations and ties among the producers? How can a new system of communication and a new feedback between production and consumption be created?

Here, too, a way out seems to offer itself which appears to be, from the quantitative point of view, very persuasive. The division of labour exists not only within society but also within every unit of production, starting with the manufacture. If the links among the producers are those of the market, the links of those within an economic unit are deprived of their market content which is replaced by a direct control of the production process according to a unified plan. This respects the technological basis of both the labour and production process. The organization of work in a shop is direct, not mediated: the hierarchy progresses from the top downward. Marx compared the capitalist owner of a production unit to a commanding general, technicians and engineers to officers, foremen and supervisors to noncommissioned officers, workers to soldiers. The comparison of the workshop with an army is not accidental. Not only because at the time when Marx lived the industrial organization within plants was really based on a hard military type of discipline through which the former independent peasants or private craftsmen were to be taught the necessary industrial order, the coordination of work and the orderly dovetailing of one production process with another, but also because, given the specialization of work and the compartmentalization of the work process in detail operations, the end effect depends on a coordinated effort and on a united interest of all the participants of the production process. Only the end product as the result of the activity of various individuals and various machines gives a meaning to the common work, only the final use-value of the jointly produced commodity can be realized on the market as an exchange value. The shop, the factory or the plant always represent a production community in which there has to be both the directing work and the directed work; it requires both those who lead, organize and provide the common effort with form, features and aims, and those who only fulfil the orders or carry out limited functions. Without such organization, without mutual dependence of one member of the collective on another (and one detailed work operation on another) the desired goal could not be reached. Thus the links between people within a production unit are different from those within society, operating not through the medium of the market and exchange but managed directly. Only the production unit as a whole can face other production units as one independent producer faces another. While the only authority for production units is the market, on which the exchange is carried out and thus the result of economic activity is realized, the authority within a production unit is its owner or his employee who directs and organizes the production unit by his power and in his interest, acting in a manner which translates the activity of the production unit into material advantage for himself. In order to make his employees interested in this aim of his, he may apply various methods of economic enforcement. If a production unit is to assert itself successfully on the market, the necessary prerequisite is that the interests of the production become the interests of all its employees, that the production unit as a whole appears *vis-à-vis* other production units as a representative of a particular interest *vis-à-vis* other particular interests.

If the division of labour within a production unit is supported by the authority of the organizer, by direct management of the work process, by an exact plan and by a conscious coordination of employees with the exclusion of intermediary market mechanism – why should it not be possible to apply these features of enterprise management in the whole of society? Both Marx and Lenin give a positive reply to this question: such management is possible in the framework of the entire society, provided that the autonomy of production units is abolished, the means of production are taken over by the state and social economy is organized in a manner similar to the organization of an enterprise or trust. Marx (1964, p. 356) says:

The *a priori* system on which the division of labour, within the workshop, is regularly carried out, becomes in the division of labour within the society, and *a posteriori*, nature-imposed necessity, controlling the lawless caprice of the producers, and perceptible in the barometrical fluctuations of the market-prices. Division of labour within the workshop implies the undisputed authority of the capitalist over men, that are but parts of a mechanism that belongs to him. The division of labour within the society brings into contact independent commodity-producers, who acknowledge no other authority but that of competition, of the coercion exerted by the pressure of their mutual interests; just as in the animal kingdom, the *bellum omnium contra omnes* more or less preserves the conditions of existence of every species. The same bourgeois mind which praises division of labour in the workshop, life-long annexation of the labourer to a partial operation and his complete subjection to capital, as being an organization of labour that increases its productiveness – that same bourgeois mind denounces with equal vigour every conscious attempt to control and regulate the process of production socially, as an inroad upon such sacred things as the rights of property, freedom and unrestricted play for the bent of the individual capitalist. It is very characteristic that the enthusiastic apologists of the factory system have nothing more damning to urge against a general organization of the labour of society, than that it would turn all society into one immense factory.

Lenin (1967, vol. 2, pp. 344–5) adds that 'the whole of society will have become a single office and a single factory, with equality of labour and pay'. He goes on to say that 'all citizens become employees and workers of a *single* countryside state "syndicate"'.

From the theoretical point of view, the concept has at least two obvious shortcomings. The first is that it identifies the division of labour within society with the division of labour within a production unit enterprise, and if it sees any difference at all between these two types of the division, then it is merely a difference of quantity and location and not one of quality. It is not only a theoretical error but a methodological one, confusing social microstructures with the social macrostructure. The second shortcoming is that the concept overlooks the entirely different *quality of interests* induced by the division of labour in detail, for example, division within an enterprise, particularly division of labour within a branch, division of labour in general and within the whole of society.

These then are, in a very brief outline, the three sources of the Marxist critique of the market and of the market mechanism, as well as an outline of an attempt at overcoming the market form of regulating the economic processes by a direct, planned social management. It must be noted, however, that elsewhere in their writings Marx, Engels and Lenin spoke of an overcoming of the negative features of the market mechanism itself much more cautiously. In particular, they differentiated between state ownership and the actual socialization of production. The young Marx saw nationalization or cooperative ownership of the means of production as bringing about no particular change in the nature of human labour. He pointed out that state ownership is a mere legal, formal act, only a step in the direction toward a real emancipation of men which should be followed by important changes in the internal structure of economy, in the development of the material base of society and, particularly, in the social division of labour. Also, the new society begins only when men have abolished labour as drudgery and a mere means of making a living and have transformed it into creative activity. This of course requires changing the social division of labour in such a manner that men no longer have to perform tedious, mechanical and purely functional tasks and can transform labour from a mere wage-earning activity into a creative one in which the capabilities of each individual will be utilized. Even Lenin realized at times that a change in the nature of labour does not depend on the nationalization of the means of production alone but above all, on the development of the production forces and on a change in their structure; that the abolition of autonomous producers is a matter of a high degree of socialization of the production rather than of a forcible act of power politics or legal measures.[5]

However, Lenin was also convinced that socialization of labour, production and management in large capitalist corporations confirmed his idea on the weakening and withering away of market relationships in the monopoly–oligopoly stage of capitalism. In *Imperialism as the Highest Stage of Capitalism* he says that 'although commodity production still "reigns" and continues to be regarded as the basis of economic life, it has in reality been undermined' (Lenin, 1967, vol. 2, p. 684).[6]

What is the cause of Lenin's error? Above all the fact that he saw commodity production and market relations as being conditioned not only by the social division of labour but also by the existence of *private* autonomous producers whose autonomy status is the result, in his view, of their being scattered, not knowing about each other and producing for an unknown market. In this sense, large corporations are neither entirely private nor entirely autonomous; they are, by virtue of their position in a country's national economy, social producers, even though their ownership is either private or in the form of a stock company.[7] In this analysis, Lenin certainly proceeded in a more Marxist manner than some of his contemporaries and disciples since he was deducing the socialization of production from actual changes in the material-technical basis of pro-

5 '... even the greatest possible "determination" in the world is not enough to pass *from* nationalization and confiscation *to* socialization' (Lenin, 1967, vol. 2, p. 692).
6 In Lenin's terminology, such corporations are called monopolies; from the point of view of their actual position on the market, however, they are mostly oligopolies. It should be noted, therefore, that Lenin makes no distinction between a monopoly and an oligopoly. When, in his *Imperialism as the Highest Stage of Capitalism*, he speaks of the contradiction of monopoly and free competition, the assertion is valid only where it concerns an absolute monopoly solidly established with a long-term prospect; one cannot, however, speak of an absolutely contradictory nature of oligopoly and free competition (Lenin, 1967).
7 Typical of this point of view is the following passage in Lenin's *Imperialism*: 'When a big enterprise assumes gigantic proportions, and on the basis of an exact computation of mass data organizes according to plan the supply of primary raw materials to the extent of two-thirds or three-quarters of all that is necessary for tens of millions of people; when the raw materials are transported in a systematic and organized manner to the most suitable places of production, sometimes situated hundreds of thousands of miles from one another; when a single centre directs all the consecutive stages of processing the material right up to the manufacture of numerous varieties of finished articles; when these products are distributed according to a single plan among tens and hundreds of millions of consumers ... then it becomes evident that we have a socialization of production and not mere "interlocking" [i.e. of private and social interests]' (Lenin, 1967).

duction and not merely from the form of ownership. On the other hand, however, he failed to distinguish between two entirely different phenomena: the market mechanism of the nineteenth-century capitalism as a *transitory form* of the capitalist commodity production, and the capitalist commodity and market production as such. He saw the transformation of this form as a withering away of commodity production and of the market although it was a mere modification of commodity and market relationships. The error is not important in itself; but it did acquire tremendous significance as an argument for the construction of the noncommodity and nonmarket model of socialism in the Soviet Union in the 1920s.[8]

According to all known marginal remarks of both Marx and Engels any future socialist society should be based on a nonmarket economic system. It is quite explicitly stated in *Critique of the Gotha Programme*:

Within the cooperative society based on common ownership of the means of production, the producers do not exchange their products; just as little does the labour employed on the products appear here as the value of these products, as a material quality possessed by them, since now, in contrast to capitalist society, individual labour no longer exists in an indirect fashion but directly as a component part of the total labour (Marx, 1968b).

I am not going to discuss the correctness or validity of this concept. I would like merely to suggest that rejection of the market is, by definition, incompatible with the concept of self-managing socialist economic system. If the market is abolished, the autonomy of economic units disappears. If the market is abolished, horizontal relationship (i.e. exchange) among economic units also disappears. If the market is abolished, the information coming from the consumers (demand) is either fully cut or at least quite irrelevant for producers. Then, the central plan is the only source supplying producers with relevant information for decision making. If this is the case, the structure of economic system must be based on the prevailing vertical type of relationship (i.e. subordination and superiority), with decision-making centralized in the planning board, without any outside control of central decisions. Self-managing system, even if formally introduced, is a

8 Viewed qualitatively, the market of the Ricardo or Marx era was a market of small commodity production rather than one really typical for an industrialized capitalist country. The difference between a market of small-commodity production and a market of capitalist industrialization is primarily quantitative; the difference between the market of capitalist industrialization of mid-nineteenth century and the market of advanced capitalist countries of the twentieth century is primarily qualitative. Nevertheless, the *substance* of the economy – the universality of commodity production and the functioning of the market as a self-regulating mechanism – remains, even though it is overshadowed by the state's intervention in the economy, planning, market, wage and price regulation, in short, conscious influencing of the economic processes (Lenin, 1967).

foreign body within any nonmarket, vertical and centralized economic structure. Even if self-managing organs are formally granted authority to make decisions, the only source of their information is the central plan since the market has been eliminated. Any consistently nonmarket economy must be by definition:

Centralized;
Run by the command plan;
Controlled by a handful of planners rather than by workers themselves;
Based on manipulation of producers by the planning board.

Since any workable model of self-management or worker's participation requires decentralization of microeconomic decisions, an indicative rather than command central plan, information coming both from the plan and consumers, control of macrodecision-making from the bottom and real autonomy of enterprises and self-managing bodies, it is quite clear that any concept of self-managing socialist economy would require a revision of the Marxist rejection of the market socialist economy. Apart from what Marx and Engels have said about self-government of producers or about centralized planning, their antimarket concept for future socialist economy implicitly puts any variant of self-management out of question. In order to interpret Marxist concept of socialist economy as a self-managing one, it would be necessary to start with the basic revision of the Marxist attitude to the role of the market in a socialist society. On the other hand, in order to interpret Marxist concept of socialist economy in the same way as it was done by Lenin and Stalin does not require any substantial revision of Marxist concept of the market. This is what leads us to the conclusion that if Marx's concept of the market had been meant seriously, it by no means favours any self-managing economic socialist system.

Marxist concept of liberation of man

Whoever quotes the famous sentence from Engels (1968, p. 429) that, 'the proletariat seizes political power and turns the means of production into state property', should quote also the following idea:

The first act by virtue of which the state really constitutes itself the representative of the whole society – the taking possession of the means of production in the name of society – this is, at the same time, its last independent act as a state. State interference in social relations becomes, in one domain after another, superfluous, and then dies out of itself; the government of persons is replaced by the administration of things, and by the conduct of processes of production. The state is not 'abolished'. *It dies out* (Engels, 1968, p. 430).

Elsewhere Engels (1969a, p. 63) is even more specific: 'Society which will newly organize production on the basis of a free and equal association of producers, will put the state machinery where it belongs: in a museum, along with the distaff and the bronze axe.'

The state, simply speaking, is a historical phenomenon, a product of class antagonism, both a political organization of society and at the same time a machinery for the oppression of exploited classes. Once the proletariat seizes political power and expropriates expropriators, there is no further need for the existence of the state: since the class society has been overcome, there is no need for any oppression, there is no reason why the state should stay above the society as an external force alienated from the people.

If it is so, one legitimate question arises: what organization will replace the state? What would replace the state in its capacity as the owner of the means of production, means of communication and as the organ of economic planning and management? If there is no room for the existence of the state in a socialist society, which other body will replace the state in all its political and economic functions?

There is no explicit answer to all these questions either in Marx or Engels. It was a matter for the far future and therefore never dealt with in their writings. Implicitly it seems to be quite clear that the only type of social organization which could replace the state both in its economic and political functions is a self-government of producers. In the economic sphere it is, by definition, a self-managing system, based on the direct participation and control of free associated producers, without any interference from the outside.

It seems to be quite logical and consequent to suggest, that according to classical Marxist theory, the development of socialist economy must go through different stages. The first stage, as indicated in both *Communist Manifesto* and *Anti-Dühring*, is the period of the dictatorship of the proletariat lasting during the transition period between capitalism and socialism. Once the social restructuring of the society is completed, there is no need for the further existence of the state. The state-owned economy must be replaced by the social-owned economy; the state ownership of the means of production is transformed into the public (or common) ownership of the means of production. All functions of management (e.g. planning, allocation of resources, distribution of wealth, etc.) should be taken over by direct producers.

Although not explicitly stated, this concept is implicitly present in the Marxist thesis that the proletariat is to be liberated not only from capitalist exploitation, but also from its lot to perform merely directed functions. Provided that the national economy is centralized, centrally run and planned from one centre, the working class cannot emerge as the ruling class: according to the existing industrial division of labour it can but carry out orders of the plan. The only possibility for the working class to become a *ruling* class is its real participation in both political and economic decision-making. It is theoretically conceivable to assume that its participation in political decision-making can also be guaranteed by the traditional representative democracy. This is possible only under one condition: that the existence of the state (and of indirect, representative democracy) is extended *ad infinitum*. As far as economic decision-making is concerned, the only possibility of the proletariat being able to take part is in the introduction of self-managing system. Self-management alone provides working people with the access to the control over economic processes, even without any transformation of the traditional industrial division of labour.

If the first provision of the Marxist political theory (i.e. that the proletariat should be elevated to the position of the ruling class) has ever been meant seriously then the only way it will materialize is through the introduction of economic self-management and political self-government. If we add to it the theory of the withering away of the state after the socialist revolution, the dying out of state organs and state machinery makes this a necessity. The first stage of a 'state socialism' should be followed by the second one, that of self-managing socialist economy and self-governing socialist politics.

This leads us to the conclusion, that apart from what has been written by Marx or Engels about the future socialist economy, according to their concept of liberating the proletariat from exploitation, alienation and manipulation; according to their concept of elevating the proletariat into the ruling class; and according to their theory of the withering away of the state, a self-management of socialist economy and a self-government of socialist society is the only legitimate Marxist concept of socialism. In order to interpret this concept in a different way, it would be necessary to start with the basic revision of the whole of Marxism as a socialistic, revolutionary and political doctrine.

Conclusions

The concept of self-management could not be either accepted or rejected without a substantial revision of the original Marxist theory. In order to accept the concept of self-management, it would be necessary to revise the Marxist concept of the market. In order to reject the concept of self-management, it would be necessary to revise the Marxist concept of the historical role of the proletariat; the Marxist concept of socialist revolution; and finally, the Marxist concept of state.

If we compare the significance of the Marxist concept of the market with that of the historical role of proletariat, socialist revolution and state, we can easily find the way out of this dilemma. The Marxist concept of the market is far less important for the whole doctrine than is the Marxist concept of revolution. Moreover, Marx himself was no economist in the strict sense of the word: he was merely a critic of the political economy, the first sociologist (and social scientist) to analyse the capitalist economy of the nineteenth century in order to justify (both historically, politically, economically and ethically) a socialist revolution. If we accept his doctrine as a whole rather than the marginal or polemical remarks and footnotes, it seems to us that any interpretation favouring self-managing socialism is more legitimate than any interpretation favouring the nonmarket centralized-state socialism of the Soviet type. In order to overcome this key contradiction within the Marxist theory, a revision of original Marxist doctrine is unavoidable. Admitting this we suggest that the revision of the Marxist concept of the market is less harmful to the whole doctrine than the revision of the rest.

References

ENGELS, F. (1968), 'Socialism: Utopian and scientific', in K. Marx and F. Engels, *Selected Works*, vol. 1, International Publishers, New York.

ENGELS, F. (1969a), 'Anti-Dühring', in B. Horvat, *An Essay on Yugoslav Society*, International Arts and Sciences Press, New York.

ENGELS, F. (1969b), 'Letter to W. Sombart, 11 March 1895', in B. Horvat, *An Essay on Yugoslav Society*, International Arts and Sciences Press, New York.

LENIN, V. I. (1967), *Selected Works*, vols. 1 and 2, Foreign Language Publishing House, Moscow.

LENIN, V. I. (1968), *Collected Works*, vol. 33, Lawrence and Wishart.

MCLELLAN, D. (1971), *Marx's Grundrisse*, Macmillan.

MARX, K. (1964), *Economic and Philosophic Manuscripts of 1844*, International Publishers, New York.

MARX, K. (1967), *Sochinenia*, vol. 13, Foreign Language Publishing House, Moscow.

MARX, K. (1968a), 'The Civil War in France', in K. Marx and F. Engels, *Selected Works*, International Publishers, New York.

MARX, K. (1968b), 'The critique of the Gotha Programme', in K. Marx and F. Engels, *Selected Works*, International Publishers, New York.

3 G. D. H. Cole

Collectivism, Syndicalism and Guilds

From G. D. H. Cole, *Self-Government in Industry*, Bell, 1920, pp. 26–35, 39–42, 45–7.

In the society of today the State is a coercive power, existing for the protection of private property, and merely reflecting, in its subservience to capitalism, the economic class-structure of the modern world. The trade unions are today merely associations of wage-earners, combining in face of exploitation to make the conditions of their servitude less burdensome. Out of these two – out of the capitalist State and the trade unions of wage-earners – what vision of the future society can we Socialists conjure up?

Realizing rightly that the structure of our industrial society finds its natural and inevitable expression in the class-struggle, and preoccupied ceaselessly with the demands of our everyday warfare with capitalism, we are too apt, despite our will to regenerate society, to regard the present characteristics of the State and the unions as fixed and unalterable. Some regard the State as essentially the expression of capitalism, and hold that with the rise of the worker to power, the State and all its functions will disappear automatically. This is anarchism, to which one kind of syndicalism approximates. Others, again, regard the trade union as essentially a bargaining body which, with the passing of capitalism, will have fulfilled its purpose, and will at once cease to exist or become of very minor importance. This is the attitude of pure State Socialism – of collectivist theory, as it has been commonly misunderstood, both in Great Britain and abroad.

Both these views rest on false assumptions. One side presupposes that the State must be always much as it is today; the other assumes that its narrow conception of the function of the trade union under capitalism includes all the functions the unions ever could, or ought to, assume. Both views are one-sided in that they accept the possibility of transforming one of the two bodies in question, and deny the possibility of transforming the other. But nothing is more certain than that both State and trade union, if they are to form the foundation of a worthy society, must be radically altered and penetrated by a new spirit.

A stable community, recognizing the rights and personality of all sections of consumers and producers alike, can only be secured if both the State and the trade unions take on new functions, and are invested with control in their respective spheres. Collectivism which is not supplemented by strong trade unions will be merely State bureaucracy on a colossal scale; trade unions not confronted by a strong and democratized State might well be no less tyrannous than a supreme State unchecked by any complementary association.

The proper sphere of the industrial organization is the control of production and of the producer's side of exchange: its function is industrial in the widest sense, and includes such matters as directly concern the producer as a producer – in his work, the most important and serviceable part of his daily life. It has no claim to decide 'political' questions: for its right rests upon the fact that it stands for the producer, and that the producers ought to exercise direct control over production.

The proper sphere of the State in relation to industry is the expression of those common needs and desires which belong to men as consumers or users of the products of industry. It has no claim to decide producers' questions or to exercise direct control over production; for its right rests upon the fact that it stands for the consumers, and that the consumers ought to control the division of the national product, or the division of income in the community.

Industry, in the widest sense, is a matter of both production and use. The product has to be produced, and it has to be determined who shall have the right to consume it. On the one hand, the decision of the character and use of the product is clearly a matter primarily for the user: on the other, the conditions under which work is carried on so vitally and directly concern the various sections of organized producers that they cannot afford to let the control of those conditions remain in the hands of outsiders. The old collectivist claimed everything for the democratic community, and maintained that the workers would find their grievances adequately ventilated and their interests thoroughly safeguarded by means of a reformed Parliament and under democratic control. He looked forward to a future society in which the State and the municipalities would employ all the workers much as they now employ men in the Post Office, the Government dockyards, or on the tramways, with the difference that the goodwill of the whole body of consumers would secure for the worker decent wages, hours and conditions of labour. The new syndicalist claims everything for the organized workers; he would have them so organize as to secure the monopoly of their labour, and supplement this first principle of economic power by the provision of economic resource, and then he would have them, by direct action, oust the capitalist from the control of industry, and enter themselves into complete possession of the means of production and distribution.

There is in this more than a clash of policies; there is a clash of funda-mental ideas. The collectivist, immersed in the daily struggle of the worker for a living wage, has thought only of distribution. High wages under State control have been the sum of his ambition; he has dismissed, as artists, dreamers, or idealists, those who, like William Morris, have contended that no less fundamental is the question of production – the problem of giving to the workers responsibility and control, in short, freedom to express their personality in the work which is their way of serving the community. The problem of Socialist theory in the present is the reconciliation of these two points of view; for either, alone, is impotent to form the framework of a noble ideal. Political democracy must be completed by democracy in the workshop; industrial democracy must realize that, in denying the State, it is falling back into a tyranny of industrialism. If, instead of condemning syndicalism unheard, the Socialist would endeavour to grasp this, its central idea, and harmonize it with his own ideal of political justice, col-lectivism and syndicalism would stand forth as, in essentials, not opposing forces, but indispensable and complementary ideas.

A close analysis of the syndicalist demand points the way to the only real solution. That absolute ownership of the means of production by the unions to which some syndicalists look forward is but a perversion and exaggeration of a just demand. The workers ought to control the normal conduct of industry; but they ought not to regulate the price of com-modities at will, to dictate to the consumer what he shall consume, or, in short, to exploit the community as the individual profiteer exploits it today.

What, then, is the solution? Surely it lies in a division of functions between the State as the representative of the organized consumers and the trade unions, or bodies arising out of them through industrial unionism, as the representatives of the organized producers.

These bodies we call National Guilds, in order both to link them up with the tradition of the Middle Ages and to distinguish them from that tradition. We who call ourselves National Guildsmen, look forward to a community in which production will be organized through democratic associations of all the workers in each industry, linked up in a body representing all workers in all industries. On the other hand, we look forwards to a democratization of the State and of local government, and to a sharing of industrial control between producers and consumers. The State should own the means of production: the guild should control the work of production. In some such partnership as this, and neither in pure collectivism nor in pure syndicalism, lies the solution of the problem of industrial control.

Naturally, such a suggestion needs far more elaborate working out than can be given here, and, in particular, much must be left for decision in the future as the practical problems arise. We cannot hope to work out a full and definite scheme of partnership in advance; but we have everything to gain by realizing, even in broad outline, what kind of society we actually desire to create. We need at the same time to satisfy the producers' demand for responsibility and self-government, and to meet the consumers' just claim to an equitable division of the national income, and to a full provision of the goods and services which he justly requires.

Some sort of partnership, then, must come about; but there is a notable tendency nowadays for persons to adopt the phrase without intending to bring any effective partnership into being. The partnership, to be worth anything, must be a partnership of equals, not the revocable concession of a benignant and superior State, and, to make it real, the guilds must be in a position to bargain on equal terms with the State. The conditions upon which the producers consent to serve, and the community to accept their service, must be determined by negotiation between the guilds and the State. The guild must preserve the right and the economic resource to withdraw its labour; the State must rely, to check unjust demands, on its equal voice in the decision of points of difference, and on the organized opinion of the community as a whole. As a last resort the preservation of equality between the two types of organization involves the possibility of a deadlock; but it is almost impossible to imagine such a deadlock arising in an equalitarian society.

I have stated my ideal very baldly, because it has already been stated well and fully elsewhere, and I do not desire to go over again the ground which others have covered. I must, however, state briefly the fundamental moral case both against Socialism as it is usually conceived and in favour of the ideal for which I am contending.

What, I want to ask, is the fundamental evil in our modern society which we should set out to abolish?

There are two possible answers to that question, and I am sure that very many well-meaning people would make the wrong one. They would answer *poverty*, when they ought to answer *slavery*. Face to face every day with the shameful contrasts of riches and destitution, high dividends and low wages, and painfully conscious of the futility of trying to adjust the balance by means of charity, private or public, they would answer unhesitatingly that they stand for the *abolition of poverty*.

Well and good! On that issue every socialist is with them. But their answer to my question is nonetheless wrong.

Poverty is the symptom: slavery the disease. The extremes of riches and destitution follow inevitably upon the extremes of licence and bondage. The many are not enslaved because they are poor, they are poor because they are enslaved. Yet socialists have all too often fixed their eyes upon the material misery of the poor without realizing that it rests upon the spiritual degradation of the slave. . . .

The Collectivist is prepared to recognize trade unionism under a collectivist regime, but he is not prepared to trust trade unionism, or to entrust it with the conduct of industry. He does not believe in industrial self-government; his 'industrial democracy' embodies only the right of the workers to manage their trade unions, and not their right to control industry. The National Guildsman, on the other hand, bases his social philosophy on the idea of function. In the industrial sphere, he desires not the recognition of trade unions by a collectivist State, but the recognition of a democratic State by National Guilds controlling industry in the common interest.

Those of us whose hopes of working-class emancipation are centred round the trade unions must be specially anxious today. When the war [1914–18] broke out, trade unionism was passing through a critical period of transition, and it is just at such times that external shocks are most dangerous. Weary of their long struggle to secure 'reforms', weary of trying at least to raise wages enough to meet the rise in prices; weary, in fact, of failure, or successes so small as to amount to failure, the unions were beginning to take a wider view and to adopt more revolutionary aims. Mere collective bargaining with the employers would, they were beginning to feel, lead them nowhere; mere political reforms only gilded the chains with which they were bound. Beyond these men began to seek some better way of overthrowing capitalism and of introducing into industry a free and democratic system.

The first effect of this change of attitude was seen in the more militant tactics adopted by the unions. The transport strikes of 1911 and the miners' strike of 1912, little as they achieved in comparison with the task in prospect, served as stimulants throughout the world of Labour. The Dublin strike and the London building dispute quickened the imaginations thus aroused and set men thinking about the future of trade unionism. If there were comparatively few syndicalists, syndicalist and industrial unionist ideas were having a wide influence throughout the movement, while the new doctrine of National Guilds was slowly leavening some of the best elements in the trade union world. In short, wherever the unions were awake, the thoughts of their members were taking a new direction, and growing bodies of trade unionists were demanding the control of industry by the workers themselves.

This idea of the control of industry, which was forced to the front by the coming of syndicalism in its French and American forms, is not new, but is a revival of the first ideas of working-class combinations. It represents a return, after a long sojourn in the wilderness of materialism and reform, to the idealism of the early revolutionaries. But this time the idealism is clothed not only with a fundamentally right philosophy, but also with a practical policy. The new revolutionaries know that only by means of trade unionism can capitalism be transformed, and they know also by what methods the revolution can be accomplished. They aim at the consolidation of trade union forces, because beyond the trade union lies the guild.

Out of the trade unionism of today must rise a greater unionism, in which craft shall be no longer divided from craft, nor industry from industry. Industrial unionism lies next on the road to freedom, and industrial unionism means not only 'One Industry, One Union, One Card', but the linking-up of all industries into one great army of labour. But even this great army will achieve no final victory in the war that really matters unless it has behind it the driving force of a great constructive idea. This idea Guild Socialism fully supplies. The workers cannot be free unless industry is managed and organized by the workers themselves in the interests of the whole community. The trade union, which has been till now a bargaining force, disputing with the employer about the conditions of labour, must become a controlling force, an industrial republic. In short, out of the bargaining trade union must grow the producing guild. ...

We can only destroy the tyranny of machinery – which is not the same as destroying machinery itself – by giving into the hands of the workers the control of their life and work, by freeing them to choose whether they will make well or ill, whether they will do the work of slaves or of free men. All our efforts must be turned in that direction: in our immediate measures we must strive to pave the way for the coming free alliance of producers and consumers.

This is indeed a doctrine directly in opposition to the political tendencies of our time. For today we are moving at a headlong pace in the direction of a 'national' control of the lives of men which is in fact national only in the sense that it serves the interests of the dominant class in the nation. Already many of the Socialists who have been the most enthusiastic advocates of State action are standing aghast at the application of their principles to an undemocratic society. The greatest of all dangers is the 'Selfridge' State, so loudly heralded these twenty years by Mr 'Callisthenes' Webb. The workers must be free and self-governing in the industrial sphere, or all their struggle for emancipation will have been in vain. If we had to choose between syndicalism and collectivism, it would be the duty and the impulse of every good man to choose syndicalism, despite the dangers it involves. For syndicalism at least aims high, even though it fails to ensure that production shall actually be carried on, as it desires, in the general interest. Syndicalism is the infirmity of noble minds: collectivism is at best only the sordid dream of a business man with a conscience. Fortunately, we have not to choose between these two: for in the Guild idea, socialism and syndicalism are reconciled. To it collectivism will yield if only all lovers of freedom will rally round the banner, for it has a message for them especially such as no other school of socialism has had. Out of the trade union shall grow the guild; and in the guild alone is freedom for the worker and a release from the ever-present tyranny of modern industrialism.

4 The Constitution of the Socialist Federal Republic of Yugoslavia

From *The Constitution of the Socialist Federal Republic of Yugoslavia*, Belgrade, 1974, pp. 55–60, 63–5.

Part two

The socialist social system of the Socialist Federal Republic of Yugoslavia is based on the power of the working class and all working people and on relations among people as free and equal producers and creators whose labour serves exclusively for the satisfaction of their personal and common needs.

These relationships are based on the socio-economic status of the working man which ensures him that, by working with socially-owned resources and by deciding directly and on an equal footing with other working people in associated labour on all matters concerning social reproduction under conditions and relations of mutual interdependence, responsibility and solidarity, he shall realize his personal material and moral interests and the right to benefit from the results of his current and past labour and from the achievements of general material and social progress, and that on this basis he shall satisfy his personal and social needs and develop his working and other creative abilities.

In conformity with this, man's inviolable status and role shall be based on:

the social ownership of the means of production which precludes the return of any kind of system of exploitation of man, and which, by ending the alienation of the working class and working people from the means of production and other conditions of labour, ensures self-management by the working people in production, in the distribution of the product of labour, and in guidance of the development of society on self-management foundations;

the emancipation of labour as a means of transcending the historically conditioned socio-economic inequalities and dependence of people in labour, which shall be ensured through the elimination of antagonism between labour and capital and of any form of wage-labour relationships, the all-round development of productive forces, a rise in labour productivity, a reduction in working hours, the development and application of science and technical achievements, the increasing provision of higher education for all, and a rise in the culture of the working people;

the right to self-management, on the basis of which every working man, on an equal footing with other working people, shall decide on his own labour and on the conditions and results of labour, on his own and common interests, and on the guidance of social development, and shall exercise power and manage other social affairs;

the right of the working man to enjoy the fruits of his labour and of the economic progress of the social community in keeping with the principle: 'from each according to his abilities – to each according to his labour', provided he ensures the development of the economic foundations of his own and social labour and contributes to the satisfaction of other social needs;

man's economic, social and personal security;

solidarity and reciprocity by everyone towards all and by all towards everyone, based on the awareness of the working people that they can realize their lasting interests only on the basis of these principles;

free initiative in the development of production and other social and personal activities for the benefit of man and the social community;

democratic political relations which make it possible for man to realize his interests, the right to self-management and other rights, to develop his personality through direct activity in social life, and especially in bodies of self-management, socio-political organizations and other social organizations and associations, which he himself sets up and through which he exercises an influence on the development of social consciousness and on the expansion of conditions ofr his own activity and for the attainment of his interests and rights;

equality of rights, duties and responsibilities of people, in conformity with constitutionality and legality.[1]

The socio-economic and political system stems from this position of man and it shall serve him and his role in society.

Any form of the management of production and of other social activities, and any form of distribution that distorts social relationships based on the above defined position of man – be it through bureaucratic arbitrariness, technocratic usurpation or privileges based on the monopoly of management of the means of production, or the appropriation of social resources on a group-property basis or any other mode of privatization of these resources, or in the form of private-property or particularist selfishness, or through any form restricting the working class in playing its historic role in

1 Constitutionality = conformity of statutes and other enactments with the Constitution; legality = conformity of all enactments of lower rank with statutes [translator's note].

socio-economic and political relations and in organizing power for itself and for all working people, shall be contrary to the socio-economic and political system laid down by the present Constitution.

Part three

Social ownership, as an expression of socialist socio-economic relationships among people, shall be the basis of free associated labour and of the ruling position of the working class in production and in social reproduction as a whole; it shall also be the basis of personal property acquired through one's own labour and serving for the satisfaction of man's needs and interests.

Socially-owned means of production, being the common, inalienable basis of social labour and social reproduction, shall exclusively serve as a basis for the performance of work aimed at the satisfaction of the personal and common needs and interests of the working people and at the development of the economic foundations of socialist society and socialist relations of self-management. Socially-owned means of production, including the means for expanded reproduction, shall be managed directly by associated workers working with these means, in their own interests and in the interests of the working class and socialist society. In performing these social functions associated workers shall be responsible to one another and to the socialist community as a whole.

Social ownership of the means of production and other resources shall ensure that everyone becomes integrated, under equal conditions, into associated labour working with social resources, and that, by realizing his right to work with social resources, and on the basis of his own labour, he earns income for the satisfaction of this personal and common needs.

Since no one has the right of ownership over social means of production, nobody – not socio-political communities,[2] nor organizations of associated labour, nor groups of citizens, nor individuals – may appropriate on any legal-property grounds the product of social labour or manage and dispose of the social means of production and labour, or arbitrarily determine conditions for distribution.

Man's labour shall be the only basis for the appropriation of the product of social labour and for the management of social resources.

The distribution of income between the part which serves for the expansion of the economic foundations of social labour and the part which serves for the satisfaction of the personal and common needs of working people in conformity with the principle of distribution according to work performed, shall be decided upon by the working people who generate this

2. The term 'socio-political communities' (*drustveno-politicke zajednice*) relates to the Federation, Socialist Republics, Autonomous Provinces, Districts and Communes as electoral-political units [translator's note].

income, in compliance with mutual responsibility and solidarity and with socially-determined fundamentals of and criteria for the acquisition and distribution of income.

Resources earmarked for the replacement and expansion of the economic foundations of social labour shall be the common basis for the maintenance and development of society, i.e. for social reproduction realized on the basis of self-managemement by the working people through all forms of pooling of labour and resources and through mutual cooperation among organizations of associated labour.

The basic organizations of associated labour, which are the fundamental form of associated labour in which workers exercise their inalienable right by working with social resources to manage their own labour and conditions of labour and to decide on the results of their labour, shall be the basis of all forms of pooling of labour and resources and of self-management integration.

By realizing the results of their joint labour in terms of value on the market under conditions of socialist commodity production, workers, through direct linkage, self-management agreements and social compacts concluded by their organizations of associated labour and other self-managing organizations and communities, and by planning work and development, shall integrate social labour, promote the entire system of socialist socio-economic relations, and control the blind forces of the market.

Part four

In the Socialist Federal Republic of Yugoslavia all power shall be vested in the working class in alliance with all working people in towns and villages.

In order to create a society of free producers, the working class and all working people shall develop socialist self-management democracy as a special form of the dictatorship of the proletariat; they shall ensure this through:

the revolutionary abolition of and constitutional ban on any form of socio-economic and political relations and organizations based on class exploitation and property monolopy, or on any kind of political action aimed at the establishment of such relations;

the realization of self-management in organizations of associated labour, local communities, self-managing communities of interest and other self-managing organizations and communities, and also in socio-political communities and society as a whole, and through the mutual linkage of and cooperation among these organizations and communities;

the free and equal self-management regulation of mutual relations and the adjustment of the common and general interests of the working people and their self-managing organizations and communities by self-management agreements and social compacts;

decision-making by the working people in the realization of power and in the management of other social affairs in the basic organizations of associated labour and other basic self-managing organizations and communities, through delegations and delegates in the managing bodies of self-managing organizations and communities, and also through delegations and delegates to the assemblies of the socio-political communities and other bodies of self-management;

keeping the working people informed on all questions significant for the realization of their socio-economic status and for the fullest and most competent possible decision-making in the performance of functions of power and management of other social affairs;

the public character of work of all organs of power and self-management and of holders of self-management, public and other social function;

personal responsibility of the holders of self-management, public and other social functions, responsibility of the organs of power and self-management, recallability of the holders of self-management, public and other social functions, and restriction of their re-election and re-appointment to specific functions;

realization of supervision by workers and other working people and of social control in general over the work of the holders of self-management, public and other social functions in self-managing organizations and communities and in socio-political communities;

realization and protection of constitutionality and legality;

socio-political activity by socialist forces organized in socio-political organizations;

free and all-round activity by people.

Self-management by the working people in the basic organizations of associated labour, local communities, self-managing communities of interest and other basic self-managing organizations and communities shall be the basis of a uniform system of self-management by and power of the working class and all working people ...

5 H. A. Clegg

A Retreat

From H. A. Clegg, *A New Approach to Industrial Democracy*, Blackwell, 1960, pp. 27–9.

The source of the principles

One of the central principles of modern democracy is that concentration of power is to be feared so much that opposition must be positively encouraged. We therefore welcome the party systems which have grown up to operate our electoral systems, whatever our opinions of the individual parties. We may take a strong dislike to the policies of any one, or, indeed, of all of them, but nevertheless, we treasure them, for if there was no more than one of them, democracy would cease to exist. Or if it did not suffer immediate destruction, there would be no guarantee of its continued existence.

Conversion to this view has been one of the signs of maturity in Western Socialist parties. In their early years they had looked forward to a society in which political differences would have ceased to matter and there would be no need for parties or party conflict. Differences over important general issues would have been settled by the general acceptance of Socialism, and the remaining differences over matters of administration, relations between individuals and personal preferences could be settled without the cumbersome mechanisms of party government. Few but Marxists now hold this view. Most other Socialists reject it, and hold that opposition is and always will be essential even under a Socialist Government; that if a Socialist Government had no opponents it would be necessary to create them to avoid the corruption of Socialism.

The need for opposition is closely related to the principles of trade union independence and of sole representation. Independence is necessary for opposition to be real. One of the main tasks of trade unions is to limit and control those persons and institutions who wield direct authority over industry. If trade unions were too closely connected with industrial management they would not be able to do that job. In the government of countries we do, of course, allow temporary coalitions, bi-partisan policies and agreed legislation, but all these can be allowed only because they are exceptional. If two parties became so closely bound that they could not take an independent stand on the next issue that arose, there would no longer be a sufficient guarantee of democracy.[1] Henceforth they should be treated as a single party, and a new and independent opposition would have to be found.

Industry provides a close parallel. Trade unions may negotiate with managers and sign agreements with them, hold discussions with them and try to foster good relations with them, but they must not take this beyond the point where they can choose to act independently if they wish to, for at that point they have ceased to be able to limit and control management; they have become a part of management.

If opposition is so important in politics that our constitutions are drawn up to give it positive encouragement even when the differences which they foster may seem stupid and unnecessary, then it is important for society to foster and encourage trade unions even when the unions seem to be obstructing enlightened managements and upholding stupid restrictions. For they must be ready to apply their powerful checks on management when those checks are needed. Hence the principle of sole representation.

The necessity for opposition also supplies the link between democratic theory and the third principle. Public ownership may have profound effects on the management of industry, but if the essence of democracy is *opposition*, then changes in *management* cannot be of primary importance to industrial democracy.

Their consequences

The doctrines which have been set out in this chapter constitute a practical and empirical creed, the creed of democracy achieved, of trade unionism which has arrived. They are fine doctrines to encourage men to protect what they have achieved from the corruption of Fascism or Communism. They may be useful guides to show how democratic society should be reconstructed in countries liberated from dictatorship, or constructed for the first time in underdeveloped countries. But they have little in common with the visionary doctrines of the early industrial democrats, for visions are not tough, nor practical, nor empirical.

The new theories are both pessimistic and traditional. They are rooted in distrust – distrust of power. They argue that the political and industrial institutions of the stable democracies already approach the best that can be realized. They return to traditions of liberal thought which preceded the rise of Socialism.

Earlier generations of Socialists thought that it would be possible to

1 The post-war coalition in Austria has shown remarkable stability, but for most of the time in the exceptional circumstances of occupation. If it were to survive for another decade or so without degenerating into authoritarianism this part of my thesis would be disproved.

improve upon the political institutions of a capitalist democracy. Modern Socialists fear that the changes that were then proposed might, if applied, have accomplished the destruction of democracy, not its improvement. To this extent they agree with the former opponents of Socialism. Similarly the syndicalists, the industrial unionists, the guild Socialists and even supporters of joint control all thought they had a means of creating a far better order in industry than capitalism could ever offer. Now we think we know better. Their proposals would not have led to an industrial democracy. On the contrary they would have undermined the existing institutions of industrial democracy, already developed under capitalism.

6 P. Blumberg

The Case Against Workers' Management: Hugh Clegg's World of Industrial Democracy

From P. Blumberg, *Industrial Democracy, The Sociology of Participation*, Constable, 1968, pp. 139–52.

The recent discussions of industrial democracy by Hugh Clegg – one of Britain's leading industrial relations experts – are extremely important for the entire subject of workers' management. In essence, Clegg's views represent the culmination of an ideological and political retreat from the idea of workers' control, an idea which reached the peak of its influence in Britain between 1910 and 1922 with the influence of syndicalism in British unions, the rise of guild socialism, and the development of the shop stewards' movement. What Clegg offers is the latest, most contemporary, and most sociologically sophisticated refutation of workers' management, a refutation which has been embraced by the Centre and Right of the British Labour party and used as a justification for opposing any extension of workers' management in the nationalized sector. Clegg directs his theses both at and beyond the British industrial scene and stresses that his arguments against workers' management have near-universal applicability. It is therefore crucial to assess these arguments here.

Before offering a critical appraisal of Clegg's theory of industrial democracy, I should like to sketch out his argument as it has developed in two books which he has written since 1951. The theories I shall discuss here were developed in his *Industrial Democracy and Nationalization* (1951) and were later repeated and elaborated in *A New Approach to Industrial Democracy* (1960).

Underpinning this new view of *industrial* democracy, according to Clegg, is a changed definition of *political* democracy, especially among socialists. Clegg argues that the conception of political democracy held by nineteenth-century social democrats was both naïve and fallacious. For the most part they believed that socialism would abolish not only class conflict but political conflict as well. Once the opportunity for economic exploitation was removed, then political exploitation arising out of the class struggle would also disappear. In the new society checks on political power would be unnecessary because a workers' government would naturally rule in the interests of the workers.

However, under the impact of twentieth-century totalitarian socialism, democratic socialists have had to revise their previous views drastically. Now it is recognized that it is indeed possible for political exploitation to be superimposed upon a socialist economic base, as in the Communist world. Democratic socialists, according to Clegg, have come to realize that political pluralism, meaning the existence of an opposition to the government, organized and ready to replace it by peaceful means, is the *sine qua non* of democracy today, under capitalism or socialism. As Clegg (1951, p. 14) says:

Democracy is not only a matter of choosing who shall govern, it is a matter of making that choice more than formal by allowing opposition between parties, so that the electorate may choose between men and parties. . . . We now believe that the dangers of power are so great that even when a socialist government is in office every opportunity must be given to its opponents to bring about its defeat – so long as they use democratic methods.

Standing at the root of his argument, then, is the assertion that opposition is a necessary condition of political democracy as we know it and that opposition is as vital in a socialist as in a capitalist framework to prevent abuses of political power which will otherwise inevitably arise.

Now, from this premise, Clegg goes on to make a direct analogy from politics to industry. He claims that just as political democracy is based on the existence of an opposition, so therefore industrial democracy is also contingent upon the existence of an opposition within the industry to the prevailing power of management or ownership. What constitutes an effective industrial opposition for Clegg is a strong trade union organization. The trade union within the factory is to management what the opposition political party is to government in power. According to Clegg (1951, p. 131), 'the most important function of a trade union is to represent and defend the interests of its members. Trade unions owe their existence to the need felt by the workers for an organization to oppose managers and employers on their behalf.'

As political or – in this case – industrial pluralism tends to be his prime criterion for democracy in any system, Clegg's definition of industrial democracy tends, therefore, to be quite modest and bland, especially when compared to the ambitious dreams of socialists of a previous generation who viewed industrial democracy as a system of complete workers' management, administered either by trade unions or by other forms of elected workers' representatives. Not so for Clegg, however. In fact, armed with his new theory of democracy, Clegg believes that the key elements in any system of industrial democracy are merely:

1 The existence of a trade union strong enough to oppose management;
2 A management which accepts trade unionism as a 'loyal opposition' and

is willing to compromise and come to terms with it in the interests of industrial harmony and unity.

As Clegg (1951, p. 121) says:

... industrial democracy consists, in part, of the opposition of the trade unions to the employer, and, in part, of the attempt of the employer to build his employees into a team working together towards a common purpose....

Now, it is not clear in this early work whether Clegg believes that industrial democracy is attainable in private as well as in publicly-owned industry. Indeed, logically it should be, for if industrial democracy consists of no more than trade union opposition and a management which accepts this opposition, then certainly this kind of 'industrial democracy' has been attained and is compatible with private ownership of industry. However, in this work, Clegg, a prominent Fabian, does not go quite this far; he refers occasionally to 'capitalist authoritarianism' and it is clear that he still retains a sentimental, if not a logical, attachment to socialism. Indeed, perhaps it was sentiment that caused Clegg to delay for nine years what seemed an obvious logical jump, for example to realize that if industrial democracy consists primarily of the existence of trade union opposition, then capitalism offers this as well as does socialism; and if this is so, then nationalization is actually unnecessary because the dream of industrial democracy – Clegg's version of it anyway – is already fulfilled under capitalism. Clegg, in fact, does ultimately reach this conclusion in a later work, *A New Approach to Industrial Democracy* (1960), and we shall examine its major hypothesis later.

Having established to his own satisfaction the argument that the major purpose of trade unions is to act as an industrial opposition, he goes on to argue that for several reasons trade unions should never attempt to share the job of management with management itself. First of all, Clegg (1951, p. 73) disputes the technical ability of trade unions to administer industry, and believes that they could not do so even if they chose. 'To take a serious part in the planning of large-scale industry,' he argues, 'requires a high degree of technical knowledge, or briefing by technical experts. Hardly any of those who represent the workers have either of these advantages.' Elsewhere (1960, p. 5) he asserts that 'trade unions have not the technical, administrative, and commercial experience to run a large-scale industry'.

A second argument against extending trade union power into the management of industry pertains to the question of democracy within the trade unions. Clegg argues that as a fighting organization, a trade union must be granted a certain amount of indulgence for its frequent violations of democratic procedure, but one should be fully aware that penetration by unions into the realm of managerial responsibility means that these undemocratic practices are sure to accompany the unions as their power spreads. Clegg argues that an undemocratic voluntary organization (such as a trade union) is far more tolerable in a free society than one which is not voluntary as trade unions would be if they assumed total responsibility for industrial management.

Finally, we come to Clegg's primary reason for opposing trade union encroachment into management and it is a reason which stems from his initial discussion of the nature of industrial democracy. If, as Clegg asserts, industrial democracy is defined in terms of the existence of organized and autonomous trade unions, then any act or policy which would jeopardize the independence of trade unions from management or which would deflect union policy from its proper role as opposition, would to that degree undermine industrial democracy. As Clegg (1951, p. 131) says:

> The trade union cannot . . . become the organ of industrial management; there would be no one to oppose the management, and no hope of democracy. Nor can the union enter into an unholy alliance for the joint management of industry, for its opposition functions would then become subordinate and finally stifled.

If the trade unions were to participate in management, they would inevitably be drawn into an organizational role conflict, with the workers as the ultimate losers, for the workers' primary need is to have a force behind them which is in every respect free and independent of management, which bears no responsibility for management's decisions, and which is not in any way obliged to defend management policy. For this reason, according to Clegg (1951, p. 133), 'the conception of trade union leaders getting together with the board of a nationalized industry round a table which has no sides in order to solve together all the problems of industry, is both false and dangerous'.

In addition, unions in a managerial role would inevitably begin to share the managerial *Weltanschauung* and would take on new concerns for productivity, profit margins, and the like. Clegg argues (1951, p. 91), for example, that the acceptance of wage restraint by British unions during Labour's first post-war government 'led them to use arguments about inflation, about prices and profits which they would have scorned even so recently as during the last War. . . .'[1]

Clegg also discusses and quickly dismisses the proposal that another group of workers' representatives, outside of the trade unions, should assume managerial authority. In such a case, Clegg asserts (in a vastly

1 It is paradoxical that the Labour Government, which implicitly shares Clegg's views, is now attempting 'to integrate the trade unions in the machinery and ethos of plan capitalism', via wage restraints, increasing labour productivity, and so on, in order to lift the performance of the lagging British economy.

oversimplified way) that there would be a struggle to the death between the two organizations as both would claim to represent the workers. Confronted by this threat to its power as the sole voice of the workers within the plant, the trade union would undoubtedly attempt to capture control of the workers' management organs by getting its nominees placed. If this were successful there would be a reversion to trade union management and all the disadvantages mentioned above. If unions were unsuccessful in capturing workers' management bodies, then, according to Clegg, union power would be smashed and there would, again, be no effective workers' opposition to management.

Clegg argues, therefore, that any attempt by modern-day 'industrial democrats' or enthusiasts of workers' control to extend the influence of workers or their unions or other workers' representatives into the realm of management threatens to destroy the very basis of industrial democracy as it exists today, the autonomous trade unions. Advocates of workers' control would create an industrial despotism, not an industrial democracy, because they would destroy independent trade unions which are the bulwark of industrial pluralism, which in turn is the essential component of industrial democracy. Clegg (1951, p. 139) believes that the kinds of complete workers' control envisaged by those firm believers in total industrial self-government is possible only 'if industry is operated by small independent groups of free associates'. Unfortunately, however, such workers' control is incompatible with the irreversible large-scale organization of industry today. But this should not be a cause of concern. Rather, Clegg advises that, like Molière's *bourgeois gentilhomme* who never realized he had been speaking prose all his life, those contemporary worshippers of workers' control should realize that industrial democracy need not be a remote aspiration, but rather is an accomplished fact, and lies in the existence of a free trade union movement whose activities are accepted by modern management.

If industrial democracy operates imperfectly in the public sector today in England, then Clegg's remedy is not to scrap the entire machinery of the public corporation in favour of thoroughgoing workers' participation, but rather a few very modest proposals to improve its operations such as methods to improve selection of industrial leaders, reform of promotion, hiring, and educational policies and improvement in the joint consultation machinery.

We place our hope . . . in the eagerness of boards to build up good relations, in the wide use of their powers of appointment and promotion, in the democratization of promotion and training systems, and in the extension and improvement of schemes for educating managers in new methods for democratic leadership (1951, p. 126).

I find Clegg's arguments both logically and empirically weak, and thus desperately in need of correction. First of all, his definition of democracy is simplistic and inadequate, for he tends to believe that the mere existence of an opposition has certain magical properties which guarantee democracy wherever it is found. The truth of the matter, however, is that opposition, though one means of achieving democracy, is neither a necessary nor a sufficient condition of democracy. For example, there are historically many circumstances where opposition has existed but where political democracy was completely absent. Medieval society saw conflicts between rival royal and aristocratic elites for power and was thus partially pluralistic, but certainly not democratic in any meaningful sense. In England before the second Reform Act which extended suffrage widely, there was political opposition, political rivalry between Whigs and Tories, but little democracy as far as the vast majority of the population was concerned. (Harrison, 1960, p. 34).

On the other hand, there are numerous examples of democracy, mainly on a small scale, which have flourished without any organized opposition – the town meeting, the dissenting chapel, the trade union lodge, the consumers' cooperative. Modern Mexico has achieved a measure of political democracy without the presence of a meaningful opposition political party.

I believe, therefore, that to define democracy exclusively in terms of opposition is a mistake; democracy is much more appropriately defined as the *accountability* of leadership to an electorate which has the power to remove that leadership. In this sense, the role of opposition is to make accountability effective by facilitating the selection of alternate sets of leaders. It should be made clear, however, that the mere existence of political opposition, without accountability, does not assure democracy.

Clegg (1951, p. 41) himself realizes the importance of accountability to democracy when he discusses nationalized industry, and he argues correctly that industries must, if they are to be democratically organized at all, be accountable in some fashion to the public. With respect to the socially-owned sector, he argues that '... we must have some means of public accountability and control'.

Now, if we are correct in arguing that democracy is best defined in terms of accountability, rather than in terms of opposition, then surely one must conclude that there is very little democracy – industrial or otherwise – in the ordinary trade union-organized factory as Clegg claims there is. For although the trade unions do constitute an opposition, nevertheless the employer is only minimally accountable to the union or the workers for decisions which lie outside the immediate job area. Thus, trade union opposition in itself does not constitute a sufficient condition for genuine industrial democracy.

But suppose we grant Clegg's definition of democracy as being synonymous with the existence of organized opposition. Even if we do so, his argument fails and the analogy he has made from politics to industry will not stand. Remember that Clegg has argued that in government the 'essence' of democracy is organized opposition and that in industry the same is true, so that the existence of trade union opposition is sufficient to guarantee industrial democracy. However, the crucial condition of any true multiparty system, or any system where political opposition exists, is that one or more parties is always ready and able to *replace* the party in power. An 'opposition' whose role is confined to protesting, making suggestions or criticizing, but which can never itself *assume power*, is not an effective or a genuine opposition at all.

Now, it is obvious that British trade unions, in the public as well as the private sector, can never 'replace' their employer and become the ruling power in industry as, for example, the Labour party may replace the Conservative party in government. Clegg (1951, p. 22) himself is quite aware of this, for he admits parenthetically, 'The trade union is thus industry's opposition – *an opposition which can never become a government.*' Further on (p. 24), he states the idea again, but this time more explicitly:

The aim of parliamentary opposition is to defeat and replace the government. A trade union can never hope to become the government of industry, unless the syndicalist dream is fulfilled [which Clegg believes is impossible].

What Clegg does not seem to realize is that with this admission his analogy between political and industrial democracy completely breaks down and his entire argument lies in ruins. If trade unions have no power to replace the present government of industry but are merely able to challenge management in a carefully delineated sphere of its activity – the job area – then in terms of Clegg's own definition, there is no pluralism, no choice, no alternative, and no opposition – in short, no democracy. Nowhere does Clegg meet this issue.

In summary:

1 Clegg's definition of democracy is faulty. He defines it in terms of the formal existence of an opposition rather than in terms of the accountability of leadership to the led. As employers are not accountable to their employees or to trade unions for the vast majority of their decisions, industrial democracy cannot be said to exist in the ordinary trade union-organized enterprise.

2 Even if we accept Clegg's definition of democracy as synonymous with the existence of opposition, industrial democracy is still absent in public and private enterprise, for the trade union does not constitute a genuine

opposition in the full sense of the word, i.e. one that is ready and able to assume power and replace the present leadership. If this is true, then industrial democracy is something still to be attained and not, as Clegg argues, something to be cherished as an accomplished fact.

Nine years after *Industrial Democracy and Nationalization* (1951) appeared, Clegg published his *New Approach to Industrial Democracy* (1960) which contains an extension and elaboration of the arguments set forth in the earlier volume. In the years which intervened between the publication of these two volumes, Clegg's views on industrial democracy changed basically in two ways. First, he no longer looks to joint consultation in Great Britain, whether voluntary (as in private industry) or compulsory (as in the nationalized sector) as a fruitful means of enlarging industrial democracy. He claims (1960, p. 36) that in recent years joint consultation has proved itself a failure on all counts – increasing productivity, raising the standards of labour relations, interesting the workers in the decision-making process, or improving the wages and conditions of workers. In short, Clegg (1960, p. 91) has now turned against joint consultation, claiming that it 'can be written off as an effective instrument of industrial democracy'.

More important than this, however, is Clegg's new position on the role of socialized industry in creating the preconditions for industrial democracy. Clegg's view in this later volume, which provides further ammunition for the Right wing of the Labour party, is that the ownership of property is now *irrelevant* to industrial democracy, that industrial democracy can be achieved just as readily with private as well as public ownership of the means of production.

As we mentioned earlier, this shift from his 1951 work was not particularly unexpected as it follows from all the premises of his previous discussion of industrial democracy. Nevertheless, it took Clegg nearly a decade to make the short logical hop from his earlier position to this later one. In the earlier work, as we have said, he talked of industrial democracy almost solely in terms of opposition, but he still stressed the importance, or at least the desirability, of public ownership. In the later work, however, he 'realized' that if trade union opposition is all that really matters, then the locus of ownership has nothing to do with industrial democracy, in which case it is sentimental foolishness to continue arguing for public ownership. This rather obvious logical jump is finally taken early in his *New Approach* (1960, p. 29), 'Public ownership may have profound effects on the management of industry, but if the essence of democracy is *opposition*, then changes in *management* cannot be of primary importance to industrial democracy.' This argument, which we shall discuss later, is part of a codification of principles of industrial democracy which Clegg sets forth early in the volume. These principles are as follows (p. 21):

The first is that trade unions must be independent both of the state and of management. The second is that only the unions can represent the industrial interests of workers. The third is that ownership of industry is irrelevant to good industrial relations.

These principles he spells out in a chapter entitled 'Return to Tradition' which, for Clegg, is a euphemism for a retreat from socialism into the waiting arms of the *status quo* and political liberalism. As Clegg (1960, p. 29) himself admits, these principles assume 'that the political and industrial institutions of the stable democracies already approach the best that can be realized. They return to traditions of liberal thought which preceded the rise of Socialism.'

Of these three principles, the first, trade union independence from management, is a clear carry over from the earlier volume, while the second and third are inferences readily made from the arguments presented in that book. All three are so clearly based upon this theory of industrial-democracy-as-opposition which we have already described that they need no further explication here; however, further criticism is definitely in order.

Clegg argues that these principles, which constitute the basis for his new approach, have been applied successfully in many western countries including Britain, the United States, Scandinavia, Holland, Switzerland, Canada, Australia and New Zealand, and he proceeds to examine the industrial relations systems of other countries (West Germany, France, Israel and Yugoslavia) in order to test and validate the principles he sets forth initially. The book is interesting methodologically, for it is really a deviant case analysis of several countries whose industrial relations systems do not adhere to Clegg's three principles. But unlike most successful deviant case analyses which, as the textbooks say, suggest new lines of inquiry, qualify and enrich the original hypothesis, this deviant case analysis drives his original hypotheses into a full-scale retreat and in the end we have nothing or nearly nothing. The deviant cases prove so formidable and contradict his initial hypotheses so blatantly that Clegg immediately begins to hedge, retreat, qualify, modify, offer *ad hoc* excuses and explanations, so that by the time his analysis of the deviant cases is completed, his original principles lie in shambles and, in his attempt to salvage them, they become so watered down as to be meaningless.

Clegg's approach, as we have said, is to state his principles boldly and then turn and run from them as the contradictory evidence pours in. His first principle, for example, is that trade unions must always remain independent of both the state and of management if they are not to compromise their essential freedom to oppose which would jeopardize industrial democracy. 'This principle', according to the author (1960, p. 22), 'seems to prevent unions from sending direct representatives to serve on the boards of nationalized industries. That would compromise their independence.' Then Clegg (1960, p. 22) examines at some length the West German experiment in codetermination in which labour representatives are accorded one-half of the seats on the Supervisory Boards[2] in the steel and coal industries and one-third of the seats on the Supervisory Boards in most other German industries. In the steel and coal industries both the union federation (DGB) and the appropriate industrial union (Metal Workers or Mine Workers Union) directly select many of the labour members of the Supervisory Boards. In addition union officers are very frequently selected to sit on these boards. Data collected in the 1950s from thirty-five mining and twelve steel enterprises revealed that sixty-three of the 252 labour representatives on the supervisory boards were union functionaries, from local, industrial unions, and the federation. An additional 105 were plant workers, of which 99 were representatives of the plants' works council, a workers' defence organization with collective bargaining functions. Undoubtedly most of the 105 plant worker representatives were also trade unionists.

In all probability, the proportion of trade unionists on supervisory boards has increased since these data were collected, for in the early days of codetermination there was a great shortage of qualified union personnel due to the Nazi decimation of trade union leadership and the initial lack of training and preparation of trade unionists for board positions (Blumenthal, 1956, p. 29). The unions also play a large role in the selection of the Labour Director in each coal and steel company who is one of three members of top management. These labour directors are very frequently old trade unionists (Shuchman, 1957, p. 152).

Now, reasoning *a priori* from Clegg's first principle, one would conclude that such an arrangement would deal a death blow to German trade union independence and thus to 'industrial democracy' in that country. But is this the case? According to Clegg (1960, p. 94) himself, this is emphatically *not* the case and he readily admits that '... it cannot be shown that the German unions have lost their independence under codetermination'. He adds that (1960, p. 55), 'Above all, no widespread unofficial movement has been called into being to protect the workers against representatives who can no longer represent them because they have "gone over to the other side".' This is true 'despite the considerable salaries, fees and other perquisites which go with membership on the

2 The German Supervisory Boards are roughly comparable to American corporate boards of directors.

boards [and to an even greater extent to the labour directors in top management, Clegg might have added] and the responsible way in which the workers' representatives have exercised their managerial authority' (1960, p. 55).

If codetermination has not weakened trade union independence and industrial democracy among German unions as a whole, then perhaps it has done so in the Metal Workers and Mine Workers Unions which play a larger role in codetermination than unions in other industries. But Clegg (1960, p. 54) concedes that this also is not the case.

There is certainly no evidence that codetermination has weakened the metal workers and mine workers in comparison to other unions in the *Deutsche Gewerkschaftsbund*. On the contrary, they are two of the strongest links in its armour.

Forced to admit that worker and trade union representation on supervisory boards and in positions of top management 'appears to contravene the rule enjoining trade union independence' (1960, p. 56), and that in general 'it is difficult to reconcile codetermination with the three principles' (1960, p. 56) stated early in the book, he casts around for an explanation of why codetermination has 'done no obvious harm'. He asks rhetorically (1960, p. 98):

Why has it not undermined the independence of the German unions? If British unions with their greater strength, longer traditions and more continuous progress fear that the acceptance of joint responsibility with management for the running of industry would undermine their independence and destroy their value as unions, then surely the weaker and less stable unions of West Germany ought to have suffered badly from codetermination. But they have not.

Trying to turn a rout into a strategic withdrawal, Clegg attempts to explain the anomaly. In brief, his explanation is that codetermination gives unions only a partial share in management; a larger share would certainly be dangerous. According to this explanation, however, we would expect the German Metal Workers and Mine Workers Unions which have a greater voice in management than other German unions to be less independent than other unions, but we have seen that this is not the case.

A more convincing rebuttal to Clegg's argument is apparent when we turn from the experience of West Germany to that of Israel where trade union participation in management is not partial at all but *total*. But even here, according to Clegg (1960, p. 67) himself, the Histadrut 'appears to have maintained its independence', even though it is inextricably tied into ownership and management. The Histadrut, again in Clegg's words (1960, p. 69), 'has not realized the fears of those [i.e. Clegg himself!] who think trade unions cannot avoid corruption if they lose independence from management'.

P. Blumberg 87

In need of another patch to mend his badly tattered hypothesis, Clegg (1960, p. 102) tries one that he hopes will do the job. He begins tentatively by allowing himself to hope that 'perhaps this state of affairs [successful Histadrut management combined with maintenance of its autonomous trade union functions] cannot continue'. He goes on:

Israel's experience as an industrial country is very brief. [But Histadrut has managed and owned enterprises for forty years or more.] It is very difficult to believe it [trade union independence] could continue if Histadrut's share in industrial ownership expanded to include the great majority of industrial undertakings. [But he does not explain why he believes this is so, and it is certainly not self-evident.] But for the moment it is so, and an explanation must be found.

Clegg (1960, p. 102) eventually 'finds' an explanation for Histadrut's success, but it is, to this writer at any rate, *ad hoc*, vague, and unsatisfactory.

Although Israel's own trade union movement is relatively young, many of the men and women who built it had long experience of the working and tradition of labour movements in other countries. Some of them had been amongst the most capable, the most trustworthy, and the most independent-minded in those labour movements. Consequently, far greater strength and self-reliance were implanted into the Israeli trade unions than could have developed if they had been a purely indigenous growth. It is this which has enabled them to bear the strain of a power and responsibility which otherwise would have broken them.

So, although this principle of industrial democracy was initially based upon rigid and inflexible structural imperatives, now we see that it can be easily contravened by trade unionists who are 'experienced', 'capable', 'trustworthy' and 'independent-minded', and thus able to build up a strong trade union movement which can weather the storm of managerial responsibility. But if this can be done in Israel, then why not elsewhere, and if it is possible elsewhere, then why the need for strict trade union independence from management? And in that case, what has become of Clegg's cardinal principle of industrial democracy?

Not quite satisfied with this explanation of Histadrut's success in Israel, Clegg (1960, p. 67) invokes an alternate hypothesis:

. . . in the past Histadrut has left the boards of its own concerns to run their own firms, and has been able to do so because the Israeli movement threw up a number of dynamic entrepreneurs eager for industrial expansion and very ready to accept responsibility. Consequently Left-Wing circles attacked the Histadrut industry on the grounds that it was no better than private industry – not that the Histadrut management had the Histadrut unions and shop stewards in their pockets.

It is indeed true that trade union enterprises in Israel traditionally have had considerable autonomy from the Histadrut. Clegg, in pointing to this independence, treats it as a curiosity or a quirk; he does not realize that in managerial autonomy lies the key to the successful trade union management of industry. Clegg has correctly pointed out that in trade union management there is a great danger of the development of conflicting loyalties and of a general undermining of the traditional role of the trade union as a workers' defence organization. Any trade union, then, which seeks active participation in management, must carefully *isolate* its trade union functions from its managerial functions, and in this way the autonomy of each can be protected. The Histadrut did just this long ago by creating the *Hevrat Ovdim*, the separate holding company for Histadrut enterprises, and in giving considerable managerial autonomy to the boards of the enterprises and to their directors. With this done, the trade union as a defence organization is not endangered and meaningful collective bargaining between the 'two halves' of the organization remains possible.

References

BLUMENTHAL, W. M. (1956), *Co-determination in the German Steel Industry*, Industrial Relations Section, Department of Economics and Sociology Research report series no. 94, Princeton University.

CLEGG, H. A. (1951), *Industrial Democracy and Nationalization*, Blackwell.

CLEGG, H. A. (1960), *A New Approach to Industrial Democracy*, Blackwell.

HARRISON, R. (1960), 'Retreat from Industrial Democracy', *New Left Review*, no. 1.

SHUCHMAN, A. (1957), *Co-determination: Labor's Middle Way in Germany*, Public Affairs Press, Washington D.C.

7 K. Coates

Democracy and Workers' Control

Ken Coates, 'Democracy and workers' control', in *Towards Socialism*, edited by the *New Left Review*, Collins, 1966.

Part one

The term 'workers' control' is commonly used to cover two quite distinct concepts. One maintains, in the words of the German socialist Thalheimer, that 'control over production signifies the management of the industries by the workers', and usually appears in discussion as an attempt to outline an ideal norm of administration for socialized industries. In this tradition, one finds that in Britain, throughout the 1930s, speakers in TUC debates on the popular administration of nationalized industries almost invariably used the term in this sense. But another tradition has evolved a quite different concept which speaks of 'workers' control' in those contexts where militant Trade Unions have been able to wrest some, or most, of the prerogatives of management from the unilateral disposition of managers.

It is misleading to use the same term to speak of two such different conditions. To do so implies that an unbroken continuity of democratic advance stretches between the imposition of a Trade Union veto on dismissals and the ultimate overcoming of capitalist property relations. This is a naïve view, because it completely ignores the deforming power of these property relations in the generation both of ideology and of social forces beyond democratic control. In a climate in which all human relationships are founded on cash-values, the most flagrantly anti-social and irresponsible acts of capital appear as 'natural' events, beyond the scope of social control.

What appears to be 'fair' in such a structure is very remote from what would seem so in a society uncluttered by the domination of institutions of property. Even active Trade Unionists, who will respond most vigorously to changes in their conditions of work when these appear to be unfair, very seldom break through the given standards of our society to form any conception of the incomparably richer and more human standards which a classless society would create. Within the compass of this ideology, generated by it and constantly reinforcing it, lies the power of the state. This power, far from giving expression to democratic initiative, inhibits and frustrates it. Nowhere is this more clearly to be seen than in the field of industrial relations, in which the state has consistently intervened to contain or transmute pressures for democratic control into harmless experiments permitting the sovereignty of property institutions to survive unimpaired.

Even if these things were not true, and the continuous encroachment of democracy in industry were assured, we should still require at some point in its progress the recognition of a qualitatively different set of problems. It seems incorrect to speak of 'workers' control' where ultimate authority is supposed to rest with the workers, because 'control' is a term which implies a more or less involved apparatus of checks, or even vetoes, by one party on the behaviour of another. The demand for workers' control, thus literally interpreted, becomes a demand, explicit or implicit, for a reversal of roles in a class-divided society. The workers wish to limit the scope of the action of other *persons*, of managers or owners, and not merely, as is often implied, to 'control' inanimate objects such as their machines and raw materials. Inanimate objects appear to be at stake, because reification is at work; what the machines do is not the result of any will of their own, but of the outcome of a tussle of wills between people, whose relationships have been refracted through things and camouflaged in the process. Whether at the level of shop control of hire-and-fire, and agreements on 100 per cent Trade Union membership, or at the level of detailed Union inspection of a firm's account books and a workers' veto on investment decisions and the distribution of profits, workers' control in this sense involves a balance of hostile forces, a division of authority between rival contenders.

Once property and its taboos are overcome, this mobile, dual relationship ceases to exist. The new problem becomes one of democratic self-regulation. This is a very different concern from that which faces the labour movement this side of the socialist transformation of private property into common wealth. A recognition of this fact is implied in the interesting experiences of – among others – the Yugoslavs and the Algerians. The Algerians invariably speak of the administrative system of their nationalized concerns as 'auto-gestion', while the Yugoslavs use the term 'self-management' to describe the government of their socialized sector. Following this usage, it seems sensible for us to speak of 'workers' control' to indicate the aggressive encroachment of Trade Unions on management powers in a capitalist framework, and of 'workers' self-management' to indicate attempts to administer a socialized economy democratically. While insisting that there is most unlikely to be a simple institutional continuity between the two conditions, it seems quite clear that workers' control can be a most valuable school for self-management, and that the notion of self-management can be an important stimulus to the demand for control. Between the two, however it may be accomplished, lies the political transformation of the social structure.

Part two

After resting dormant for two generations, the movement for workers' control in Britain has once again begun to stir, reshape itself, and gather force and insight. Already it has become sufficiently explicit to appear as a demand on Union conference agendas, in the utterances of important Trade Union leaders, and in resolutions approved at the Labour Party Conference and Trade Union Congress in 1963.[1] Numerous articles and papers on it have begun to circulate in the socialist and Trade Union press,[2] and well-attended seminars of academics and Trade Unionists have convened to discuss it.[3] The interest which it arouses is not, naturally enough, very easily visible in the popular press, or through the other means of communication which are among the perquisites of capital. But neither do the formal commitments of the big Trade Unions, or statements by their

1 See *Labour Party* (1963, pp. 189–90), *TUC* (1963, pp. 276, 420) and *TUC* (1964, pp. 321, 446, 489). The TUC discussions involve 'workers' participation in the nationalized industries'. This is an ambiguous term, which can mean anything from Joint Consultation (as it does, obviously, to many members of the General Council) up to full workers' management of nationalized enterprises.
2 Among other interesting examples is an Editorial by Sid Hill (1963), leader of the National Union of Public Employees (215 000 strong) and member of the General Council of the TUC.
  The most radical and coherent appeal yet has come from Ernie Roberts, Assistant General Secretary of the AEU. In a broadsheet issued with the Autumn 1964 issue of *Voice of the Unions*, he puts forward a comprehensive plan for the administration of the steel industry after nationalization. This would have the effect of bringing 'participation' up to the point of workers' management: 'Each shop would have its own elected Shop Committee which would send delegates to a central Works Council. The Shop Committee would also elect its supervision, and the Works Councils would appoint higher management. The Board of the enterprise would have representatives from the State agency, charged with implementing the plan, and representatives from the Works Councils, responsible for details of production.' Unions would negotiate with this Board about the distribution of the surplus and conditions of work, just as they would today. Such a scheme would have the dual effect of popularizing nationalization, which is generally construed as a bureaucratic monster, and, at the same time, ensuring that the nationalized industry did not simply subserve the private sector, but made its own pace. *Voice of the Unions* has announced a campaign in the steel producing areas around this platform: its outcome could be extremely important for the advance of British socialism.
3 One, at Nottingham, attracted 140 participants drawn from most Unions and a number of universities. Reports of it have appeared in *Tribune* (May 1964), *New Left Review* (1965), *Anarchy* (1964), and *The Week* (1964). *Hull Left*, published by Labour Students at Hull University, reproduced a number of papers which had been submitted for the consideration of the seminar.

leading personalities, give an adequate idea of the huge powder-keg of workpeople's daily concern about it which could eventually be set off by the lightest, most sensitive of trigger actions.

The basic change in the economic condition of Britain, like that of Western Europe as a whole, is the near-full employment which underpins not only the successes but also all the major problems of neo-capitalism. The social effects of this change have, until recently, been noted simply in the shape of obtrusive and often misleading marks of affluence. Up to the beginning of this decade, affluence was almost universally equated with working-class apathy, enervation, and depoliticization. The election result of October 1964 has provided it sown commentary on this view of things. There is some evidence that the Labour victory was the result of a major renovation of traditional working-class loyalties, resulting in a large working-class poll. By and large the middle strata stayed shy of the Labour Party (*Observer*, 1964). This working-class feeling came as no surprise to more thoughtful analysts. The Cambridge sociologists Goldthorpe and Lockwood (1963), in their paper 'Affluence and the British Class Structure', concluded that insofar as the traditional communal solidarity of some sections of the British working class has become attenuated, and 'instrumental collectivism' has come to replace it, this in no way underwrites the conservative cause, although it may from time to time assist it. Quite possibly the more calculating, rationalistic assessment of interests implied in the new outlook may result in a radicalization of working-class politics. To the extent that workers expect improved living standards to be accompanied by improved status, a strain is thrown on the received social structure. If that structure cannot adapt to allow recognition of new status, then something will give. That something may not be the aspirations of the workers.

Unquestionably, the main battlefront of the real status war is not the suburb. There, problems of social standing have little direct political significance; they are trivialized into the tensions of competing snobberies. The place where status has teeth is beyond all doubt the factory, the office, the enterprise. Here all the brutalizing implications of power, from the petty but often infuriating forms it takes in the workshop to the subtly extended and carefully veiled realities at the summits of industry, work into men's souls. The shape of hierarchy in industry was known and felt all too clearly before the war: but it could not become a political issue in any open way while the disciplinary weight of mass-unemployment existed to grind down any protest. Even the socialist case for nationalization before the war rested almost entirely on grounds of efficiency, and was angled solely at the abolition of unemployment. A job was a goal in such circumstances. Only when stomachs were filled, and relative security established, could people afford to notice the real indignities of their position. Before the war, not only did the worker in work watch his step and count his blessings (the shop stewards' movement disappeared immediately after the First World War, only to show up again in the late thirties, in an aircraft industry whose war contracts provided islands of guaranteed work amid the general insecurity) but the worker out of work, or on short time, aspired above all to a regular job. Post-war workers have not faced these troubles, in the overwhelming majority of cases. Far from being chastened by short-time working, most workers have consistently averaged several hours of overtime[4] a week since the late forties. True, a series of recessions, each one tending to become more pronounced than the last, have served to remind Trade Unionists of earlier days; while areas of limbo have continued to exist in the north, and in Northern Ireland, providing a dismal exception to the normal story. Yet the ordinary worker has come to form expectations based on continuing full employment, and these are by no means limited to simple economic appetites. Above all, he has come to experience, day in, day out, the taste of capitalism working as nearly as possible to its ideal performance. This is not a sweet taste. Indeed, soothing though it may be to certain directors, for whom things are at their best imaginable, it is becoming increasingly brackish to large numbers of workers.

Their feelings can even be dimly discerned in a book like Ferdinand Zweig's *The Worker in an Affluent Society* (1961). One of his chapters begins: ' "Home and work don't mix." This is a phrase which often circulates among working men. It means that "you should leave home at home and work at work", or, "once you leave work, forget it". As one man said, "when you clock out, clock out your mind". . . . Work matters are rarely mentioned at home. . . . Work means tension, and home is for relaxation. Men say "I never mention work at home, otherwise I would never relax . . ." ' (p. 84). And, towards the end of the book, he writes 'When I asked "Do you like your job?" a generalization was put forward such as "No one really likes his job"; or to a question "Do you work only for money; does the job give you something else from money?" The answer might be "We all work for money, there is nothing else in the job" ' (p. 199).

This is the *quiet* response of workers to the working capitalism they have come to know; it is one of dissociation and it is suitable for interviewers. There is a harder response as well.

Faced with psychological withdrawal, and apprehensive about unnecessary aggravating aspects of the industrial power structure, some leading industrialists have sought ways of mitigating the feel of sub-

4 Many of which have been unnecessary, according to H. A. Clegg (1962).

ordination which is basic to factory organization as far as employees are concerned (see Brown, 1965). Thus the practice of clocking in, the anomalies of differentials between increasingly routinized clerical workers and shop-floor operatives, the more blatantly inefficient effects of piecework – all of these have been quite sternly debated not only in the schools of human relations, but among the more perceptive industrial executives themselves. Yet movement is slow. The inertia of British businessmen is perhaps nowhere more recognizable than in this field, where their own interests might be thought to spell out a certain liberalization. But perhaps this conservative resistance to change is not entirely stupid, since a thaw might produce a greater flow beneath the ice than could be contained within acceptable channels. One thing is very clear: for all the labours of industrial liberals, things are constantly called by their right names on the shop-floor. It is still extremely common for a new recruit to be told upon engagement, by the brisk, sergeant-majorly figure who signs him on, that 'When you start here, it is to work, not think: we pay our own thinkers, and they don't need your help.' Even where the notion that workers are hands, not brains, has been expunged by managerial fiat from the vocabulary of supervision, its reality remains no less painfully obvious. The proliferation of work study and method study techniques serve not only to increase the rate of return per man employed, but also, and perhaps far more damagingly to the man concerned, to strip away with increasing efficiency the last remaining areas of independent decision and initiative which had hitherto survived in the workshop. That such techniques do not necessarily serve to increase productivity (see Friedmann, 1955, 1961) seems to present no noticeable obstacle to their advance: it seems clear that they owe at least as much of their popularity to their disciplinary advantages as to their productive merits. The growth and decline of formal means of communication, including suggestion schemes, has done nothing whatever to ameliorate the fact that in modern industry workers are used as mere means to ends formed independently of their will. At best such devices have exposed workers to the unilateral adoption of *their* ideas by others; they provide no long-term assurance that the application of these ideas may not be to their own detriment. The remorseless division of labour which polarizes the factory into a small corps of decision-takers on one side, and an army of subordinates on the other, does not simply alienate the labour force. The concentration of decision-taking power, untempered by any effective responsible controls, tends to produce a succession of organizational crises, in which expensive blunders are followed by brutal reshuffles, as the left hand of management vainly gropes after even the rudiments of knowledge about the movements of its right hand.

Were data available, there can be little doubt that the present incidence of managerial waste would stagger everyone. As things are, it is seldom documented, and almost never openly discussed, but unless the Nottingham area is completely exceptional, it must run into millions every year. Its human cost is unmeasurable, because mistakes that are tiny in terms of revenue can be cataclysmic in their effects on people. In one enterprise in Nottinghamshire, workers were recently engaged to build an annexe, which was subsequently discovered to be in the way of other developments, and therefore scheduled for demolition. This, so far, is a common enough story, but on this job, the demolition gangs moved in to start work while the decorators were still at their task, making habitable the barely completed building. So, while the painters were busily finishing their work on the fourth wall, the other three were being removed by the heavy squads. Some of the workers concerned claim that they were compelled to wait because demolition had to be suspended until the painters finished and got out of the way. Countless similar stories will be retailed to anyone who talks to groups of workers about the problem of waste. In the nationalized industries the record is no better: I personally have several times been involved in quite large-scale works which were demolished on completion, and have innumerable experiences of installing expensive machines which did not work, or walking past other expensive machines which had lain idle and forgotten for months on end in very damaging conditions. None of these things would be permitted if workpeople were assured of both an interest in production as a whole, and sufficient powers to uphold it. If this is true where a firm's income is at stake, it is even more true where men's dignity and self-respect are involved. One small example of the kind of tragedy that often happens was recorded in the Nottingham press a year ago. It concerns an engineering plant, in which a man was seriously injured by a jet of steam that had been discharged through a grating as he was walking over it. Inquiries revealed that this discharge was the result of a mistake. Another employee had, more than twenty years previously, been detailed to open a valve at certain fixed times of the day, in order to lower available steam-pressure. Many years ago this operation had been made completely unnecessary, because the plant had been adapted in order to make it safe. But no one had ever informed the worker concerned. Year in, year out, he had continued to perform an unneeded task, which was dangerous to others, until an accident interfered to redress the organization of his work. The feelings of this man, placed in such a situation, are not difficult to imagine. In fact, his workmates reported that he was utterly demoralized by the discovery that he had for years been paid to perform a completely useless and damaging operation. Such instances could be extended indefinitely, but the point should already be clear: the deprivation of responsibility which workers suffer in this sort of situation does not merely damage them personally, as individuals; it is also socially destructive, and constantly undermines the development of productive powers. However vigorously employers seek out means to overcome these difficulties, they are fighting a losing battle. While the product itself remains beyond the control of the workpeople who produce it, their self-protection impels them not merely to suffer such absurd failures of 'organization', but even to conspire to prevent their alleviation. If you are alienated from the product of your work, such forms of ca'canny as are involved in protecting management from attaining accurate self-knowledge, and sometimes more radical forms of resistance as well, are by no means stupid. You are aware that augmented productivity may turn out to be a weapon for use against you, rather than a straightforward development and extension of your powers. On the national scale, crusades for productivity were summed up in the early months of 1963 by special postage stamps exalting additional effort, while the unemployment figures were mounting week by week.

The main device which has been employed to sidetrack the frustrations which the authoritarian control of industry induces in its workpeople, and the recurring problems of production which stem from the necessarily abortive attempt to restrict or abolish the initiative of workers, is that of joint consultation. Born in the First World War, an uncertain changeling, it did not survive very long. Between 1918 and 1939 the dole queues provided most employers with all the consultation they felt they needed. But the Second World War brought about a strange reincarnation. Bevin's elevation to the Ministry of Labour coincided with a bizarre turn of fortune, in which the most militant goading force in the Unions, the Communist Party, was soon to come out of opposition, and play a major role in the crusade for war-production. Effective pioneer of the reborn shop-stewards movement, the Communist Party found itself also pioneering at the rebirth of joint consultation. It demanded the setting up of joint production committees and activated their members. Huge conferences of stewards were held in the glare of enthusiastic press publicity to consider ways of expanding production. All of this had the effect of creating a certain ambivalence among shop-stewards, which did not wear off with the war effort. But the rationality of joint consultation was not ambivalent. The new situation of the early forties required new practices by management, if it was to continue managing for long. Seldom has the argument for these been presented with more disarming frankness than by Walpole in *Management and Men* (1944), published as a guide to joint consultation:

What joint consultation does for industry is threefold in character. It provides the higher management with an additional source of information, warning and advice – particularly valuable because it covers a field in which conventional channels of information and advice are too often biased or ineffective. It also provides the means for transmitting to employees information and explanation without which their attitudes towards their work or their management is liable to be prejudiced. Thirdly, on the psychological side *it canalizes the legitimate aspiration of labour to have a voice in the industry to which it contributes so much* [my italics] (p. 43).

This canalization was furthered and consolidated after the election of the post-war Labour Government by the simple device of writing joint consultation procedures into the nationalization acts governing those industries which Labour took into public ownership. (At the same time, a few eminent Trade Union leaders found themselves on the boards of these new corporations – in this way ended all the declamatory 'workers' control' talk of the TUC during the thirties.) The net effect of such consultation, whether in public or private sectors, will surprise very few people. For private industry, it has recently been summed up by Llewellyn Davies (1962), in a study entitled *Formal Consultation in Practice*. His view is: 'The general impression gained is that the majority of firms do not fully believe in and practise formal consultation and all that it implies, but use it rather as a forum for company pronouncements and the airing of employee irritants.' Even when the employers *do* 'believe in' consultation, of course, all that this can ever mean is that they may seek employees' opinions before they tell them what to do. Such procedures may provide a certain soothing balm during those honeymoons in which competition leaves management free of the need to make sharp turns in policy, with all the consequent upheavals in working conditions which these so frequently involve. But overall, there is no doubt whatever that in recent years they have become increasingly irrelevant.

As evidence of this, we may consider a number of facts. The growth rate of shop-steward representation in the Amalgamated Engineering Union doubled in the period 1957–61, as compared with the period 1947–56 (cf. Marsh and Coker, 1963). Anthony Topham (1964), in a valuable study published by *New Left Review*, points out:

Associated with this very rapid rate of expansion of stewards, has been a decline of one-third in formal Joint Consultation Committees, and a corresponding rise in 'domestic' (i.e. plant-level) bargaining. Related to this again, the number of work stoppages has increased in federated establishments [in the Engineering Industry – K.C.] by 23 per cent and the number of working days lost as a result rose by 82 per cent.

Direct workshop representation is, in other words, replacing 'the concessionary management device of joint consultation'. In this atmosphere the 'legitimate aspirations' of workpeople to have a say in the control and direction of the enterprises in which they work are less and less capable of being 'canalized', and more and more likely to erupt into their own consciously formulated demands. Until now these demands have tended to remain close to the present experiences of workers, and, as a result, to take on a partial, regional or local significance. This tendency has been reinforced by the whole post-war tradition of the shop-stewards' movement, which began its evolution towards the present state of affairs during the Attlee Government's 'wage-freeze', which in Britain was paradoxically responsible for the initial growth of the phenomenon of wage-drift (or the widening gap between basic rates of pay, usually nationally negotiated, and actual earnings, including locally negotiated piece-work and bonus increments and overtime), which has recently triggered off such complaints from the National Incomes Commission. As local managements found the need to bid up wages in competition for scarce labour, and shop-stewards discovered both the need to fend for themselves and the possibility of doing it rather well, decentralization of wage-bargaining set in with a vengeance. Socialist militants have frequently registered the results of this with some pleasure, because it tends to feed the image of an activist rank and file and a lethargic bureaucracy dominating the central apparatus of the Unions. This image is by no means without its reference point in reality, but it is often very over-simplified. The price of this decentralization was high, both in terms of apathy (if local strikes are not 'a private solution to public problems', then at least they are often a less-than-public solution of them), and in terms of fragmentation and loss of political consciousness. It is strange that more attention has not been paid to this phenomenon in relation to the Labour Party's crisis during the fifties – it is no coincidence that Labour's revival came after a number of fierce attacks on the Unions by the Conservative administration of 1959–64.

Be that as it may, Topham documents a remarkable change in the character of the shop-stewards. He quotes the findings of Professor Turner (1963) on the causes of strikes, as given by strikers themselves: between 1940 and 1960, if one excludes strikes in the mining industry, which is still a separate universe in these matters, the proportion of strikes about wage matters *other than* demands for increases', or about 'working arrangements, rules and discipline', rose from one-third to three-quarters of the total. This gives us a measure, not simply of the extent of the 'drift', but also of the changing mood of the workers. There is additional evidence on this score. In 1960 the TUC General Council published their report on 'Disputes and Workshop Representation' (pp. 125–6) which analysed the results of four separate questionnaires, covering the cost of dispute pay to affiliated Unions between 1956 and 1959, details of both official and unofficial strikes in 1958 and 1959, and details of stoppages in which one Union found its members unable to work because members of other unions were on strike. One hundred and forty-seven Unions representing seven and a half million workers replied, and this response proved completely unambiguous: only 32 per cent of strikes during that period had been directly about money, and these included cases in which workers had been resisting attempts by employers to reduce wages; 29 per cent were about dismissals, 20 per cent were caused by disciplinary dismissals of stewards or other members, and 9 per cent concerned redundancies. The remainder were about recognition, non-unionism, breach of agreements, changes in work systems, demarcation and dilution, bad working conditions or complaints about supervisors. When the Unions concerned were able to differentiate between 'underlying causes' as opposed to stated causes, this had the effect of still further reducing the proportion of disputes over wages. The power of shop-stewards was originally fostered and extended by the growth of local negotiations about wages. The strike-record makes it clear that their power is now firmly rooted, and able to burgeon into very much wider fields.

If one accepts that strikes are still relatively uncommon occurrences in British industry, and moves on to examine the normal working of shop-stewards in less turbulent conditions, this story is sharply confirmed. According to Clegg, Killick and Adams (1961), in their survey *Trade Union Officers*, which contains a comprehensive study of the role of stewards in the working of the Unions, the average steward spends six hours a week of his working time and five of his own on a whole range of Trade Union duties. By far the most important of these concern negotiations with foremen and managers. Following these in importance, as a proportion of stewards' time, comes the item 'consultation with constituents and discussions with other stewards'. Together these took up 69 per cent of the time spent on Union business by stewards covered in the survey (pp. 149–80). When the same stewards were asked to define the priority of their Trade Union aims (p. 262), 23 per cent of them thought that first was 'better wages and conditions'. But 21 per cent thought that the main thing was 100 per cent organization, 14 per cent that it was 'creating unity between workers', and 10 per cent that it was 'fullest use by the rank and file of the democratic procedures of the Union'. With the 5 per cent who put 'creating political consciousness' first, this amounts to 50 per cent who saw their main Trade Union aims as turning around the development and consolidation of workpeople's *power*. Of course, this power will lever pence out of the employers: but it also poses them with deeper problems, to which cash offers no immediate solution. Even when one looks at the 19 per cent who put first the priority 'effective consultation with the management', one may suspect that this does not always mean quite what the official propagandists of consultation expect.

The sum of these developments has been calculated and expressed by a whole number of close observers of the industrial landscape, many of whom are very far from being disaffected radicals. Speaking of 'something like a revolution in our industrial relations', Arthur Marsh (1963) notes that full employment has extended the Trade Union expectations of craftsmen to all the workers, who, since the war, have 'been able to rely more on the fact that employers have been competing for labour of all kinds, that they have been reluctant to lose workers, and unable and unwilling to back their authority by large-scale or selective dismissals. *Work group sanctions against management have gradually become effective, and "management by consent" generally necessary.*' To this picture, Alan Flanders adds in a paper on 'The importance of shop stewards': 'The steward's formal role under our traditional system of collective bargaining was largely that of watchdog and policeman. Earnings drift has rendered that view of their role totally unrealistic. Today they are negotiators in their own right, *rule makers as well as rule enforcers.*'

It would be wrong to find in these signs an omen of immediately impending upheaval. Shop-stewards are – contrary to the Press image of them – responsible men. Their average age is in the forties. They have family responsibilities which weigh as heavily on them as on their workmates. The political implications of their situation do not confront them in clear, lucid prescriptions, but are refracted through a fog of local prejudices, overlapping and at times conflicting group interests, irrational organizational boundaries. At the head of their Unions often stand, not the kind of men who can see over all the territory and pierce its obscurities with the insight drawn from a live movement of many thousands of people, but anxious, timid and purblind intriguers, who try to chart their paths through an alien countryside (which they imagine they know well) by landmarks which have long since ceased to exist (and which they recreate in their imagination, hazier each time, day by day). Beyond these structural deformities in the vision of the labour movement, lies the mystery of capitalist property relations itself.

Today, the problems which capital itself has created are fiercely sharpening the outlines, and settling the fog. Neo-capitalism is forced to 'plan', to rationalize itself, and above all to constrain and discipline its labour force; in doing so, it precipitates new problems and objectives for the Unions. The pace at which this has occurred has noticeably increased in the past few years. Indeed, the election of a Labour Government is only one early result of its gathering force, and by no means the ultimate one. Having created the wage-drift, and reactivated the Trade Unions on a local, fragmented basis, neo-capitalism is now in the process of recentralizing them, and giving them new, more integrated and probing policies.

But just as the rise of stewards' power was not the result of an act of will by the employers, even though many of them individually fed it and contributed to it, so this new coordination is not likely to fall into the set patterns which would enable the established powers to approve it. To be sure, there are now many strange new advocates of industrial Unions, as the business Press begins to evaluate the effects of 'anarchy' in the Unions on the new planning machinery which is being established. But the Unions have not up to now proved amenable to such schemes: if they are to regroup, and streamline their organizations, then very many of their members will insist that this must be under their own banners, in pursuit of their own objects. Paradoxically, this process has been assisted by the very attacks which have been launched to inhibit Trade Union powers. The effect of pay pauses, National Incomes Commissions, rationalization schemes of the Beeching variety, and even the notorious Rookes versus Barnard judgment which placed the right to strike itself in jeopardy, has been to stimulate political consciousness and to turn Trade Union activists away from narrow sectionalism. Clearly the pursuit of political answers to some of the most urgent problems faced by shop-stewards does not in the least imply any retreat from gains won locally. At the local level, the Unions will remain combative, jealous of their powers, and anxious to develop their strength. New political tasks do not in the least imply that one should let go of control of hire and fire, or give away rest breaks, or abandon any of the powers which have been wrested away from the formerly unchallenged disposition of management. On the other hand, the defence of such gains itself comes to insist that a larger view of the world be taken, and that effective nationwide resistance be offered to the concerted probes which have recently been undertaken to test whether any of the Unions' gains can be recouped from them. The most serious of these probes is beyond any doubt the sustained pressure for an incomes policy, which has simultaneously taken shape in almost every country in Europe in the last few years, and which threatens *all* the major Union advances in a very direct manner.[5]

The campaign for an incomes policy poses on a new plane the very old problem of how capital can co-exist with a powerful Trade Union movement. Beneath all the trimmings of welfare in which neo-capitalism is bedecked, this basic conflict has in no way been resolved. Now, however, neo-capitalism faces many closed doors which were at one time open to its forerunners. Above all, the pre-war disciplinary force of sustained un-

5 Some useful documentation on this appears in *International Socialist Journal*, no. 3, June 1964. The issue includes a general analysis by Vittorio Foa, Deputy Secretary of the Italian CGIL, and reports on the state of play in England, France, Italy and Federal Germany.

employment, running into millions, is not an option today. Meanwhile, international competition demands that margins be considered ever more tightly, and basic costs be budgeted over longer periods within narrower limits of fluctuation. Hence the overriding concern about inflation, and the constant pre-occupation with the 'stabilization' of wage-costs. Wages must be brought under control if the cutting edge of capital is not to be dulled to a degree intolerable to its masters.

Those spokesmen of the labour movement who are closest to the acceptance of neo-capitalism pure and simple have already drawn an appropriate moral from this. They see the role of the Labour Government as being that of rationalizer-extraordinary to a system which is short-winded, queasy and directionless. To liberate the power of efficient and well-directed greed, they will happily treat with the Unions, offering to exchange such meagre cash-benefits as they can afford against a surrender of power. So, well-known Fabians write of a controlled war against wage-drift, which of course involves quite simply an offensive against the powers of shop-stewards (cf. McCarthy, 1964): they speak of the 'relegation of collective bargaining machinery to a secondary place in the structure' (cf. Stewart and Winsbury, 1963): and they discuss the price which Unions may or may not demand as compensation for loss of powers in this realm (McCarthy, 1964).[6] In all this can be discerned a pattern of authoritarian paternalism, which assumes a standard of 'fairness' in income distribution which has only to be announced, and then applied by civil servants, to produce universal harmony and rocketing economic advance. In fact, no such standard is possible: while the overwhelming majority of goods are distributed on the market, and not by means of welfare services, 'fairness' will always be determined in the course of argument and the interplay of rival interests, unless totalitarian edicts are to prescribe its limits. More: far from representing a drag on productivity, this argument is generally a stimulus to it. Certainly, under capitalism, Union demands represent a continual goad to technological advance, indeed, they often pose the most serious questions of organization that are ever faced by an increasingly lethargic economic directorate. This point was made, in a heavy-handed way, by Charles Babbage as long ago as 1832, and it has lost none of its force with the concentration of industrial power and the growth of bureaucratic forms of administration. Paternalist Fabianism is in great danger when it plays with these types of policy. Its advocates seldom show any awareness of the extent to which all the freedoms that they empirically support, are underpinned by the existence of an independent Trade

6 Others, including, rather terrifyingly, Ray Gunter, have allowed themselves to discuss this matter in more brutal terms. A heated controversy on Gunter's views broke out in the AEU Journal in mid-1964.

Union movement. The statification of Union powers clearly demands fierce inroads in the freedom of movement of Unions, above all at local level. In the last analysis, Unions do not exist anywhere else than at local level. If apathy and demoralization set in at the root, the leading Trade Union 'planners', who flit from office to office in Whitehall in order to discuss guesses about production levels and fiats about wages, will become increasingly empty poseurs.[7] Without active and politically alive shop-stewards behind them, they can be discarded by any government commission which tires of them. As for the Labour Party, without enthusiasm in the factories it is a shroud for unattained dreams.

A heavy responsibility rests, then, on Trade Union activists under a Labour Government. Confronted with crisis on a dozen fronts at once, the Labour Government will insistently press for agreement on an incomes policy. This places the Unions between two perils. If they agree, their vital powers are at stake. If they refuse, they must fear the fall of the Government, which cannot be seen as an advantage to the workers. What, then, is to be done?

It is here that the traditional demand for workers' control takes on a new meaning, gathering a hard relevance that can turn it from a concern of a few militants into the central strategic demand of the day. The Unions can hardly refuse to negotiate with their own Government on incomes policy. But they can set their own price for starting talks, provided it is reasonable. And the elementary price for beginning a discussion on incomes policy is hard information about what incomes *are*. The employers will enter talks on this matter furnished with data which can tell them to the last halfpenny what the incomes of the workpeople are. They know all about wages, because they control the payment of them, but the workers know the next best thing to nothing about the incomes of the employers. A point which is commonly made in discussions of tax problems is almost inevitably forgotten when this matter is at issue: it is that rentier incomes can be camouflaged, split, hidden in themselves, in a thousand and one ways. Professor Titmuss (1962) has shown in spellbinding detail some of the devices which can be used to convert personal incomes into capital or to lose them in a variety of separate identities. The same sort of analysis, applied to corporate evasions and manoeuvres, would be doubly instructive. Today, complaints are heard on all sides that the balance-sheets which are prepared for public consumption do not even allow share-holders to form any intelligible picture of the real financial health of their companies (cf. Rose, 1963). Lurking in a hundred special reserves, or depreciation allowances, may lie endless delights in store for those who

7 As Frank Cousins wisely pointed out to the 1963 TUC: compare with TUC (1963, p. 399).

have the power to manipulate, shunt, dissemble and simply 'lose' the revenue of large firms. Where were the mistakes I discussed above, in the balance-sheets? Were they really mistakes, at all? Did some of the planning snags arise purely for the benefit of the tax men? If such suspicions are merely uninformed socialist prejudices, libellous to boot, no doubt the British Employers' Confederation will be pleased to recommend to its members that they open their accounts to Trade Union inspection, thus allowing the Trade Union movement to judge for itself on what basis it needs to negotiate about incomes policy.

Of course, any incomes policy which the Unions even begin to consider must be redistributive. It must take from the haves, and give to the have-nots. Even the most timid, paternalistic supporters of conformity in the Unions will agree to this. The policy will be judged in the light of its ability to reduce rentier incomes and add to the sector of wages and salaries. But it is impossible to uphold even the status quo in this field, once you approach the problem through a centralized decision, unless you have the necessary prior information. If the employers' accounts are not open to them, the Union leaders will be blindfolded. Only fools or men who want to lose play such delicate games as these blindfold. Supposing the General Council tells the Labour Government that before it can negotiate an incomes policy, it must see the books? Then we shall see an immediate strengthening, rather than enervation, of the Trade Unions at local level. The national leadership of Unions cannot effectively inspect the accounts of all the firms with which they have negotiating connections, and even if they could see them all, they could never decipher them. But the shop-stewards *can* unravel their own employers' mysteries, given a modicum of professional advice, which many of them could afford to secure at the drop of a hat. Once the accounts are open in sufficient detail, then depreciation claims come home to shop level, and the experience of the workers concerned will be ever liable to discover any snags or contentious areas which may exist. Questionable allowances will be delimited by such grass roots inspection, and if necessary the inland revenue can be called in to adjudicate. Since no one objects to Pay As You Earn when applied to employees, it is difficult to see on what ground such an innovation can be rejected by employers.

If the Unions stand out for this right before starting talks on incomes policy, they will neither weaken their own powers nor threaten the Labour Government. The ball will be in the employers' court, and if they prove hesitant or petulant about the matter, this will present Labour with an excellent campaigning issue. An election fought on such a matter would not be a difficult one for the Left. Of course, if such data are secured by the Unions, it may still not result in an acceptable policy on incomes: and they may be compelled to stand their ground on other issues. But at least they will know the score, talks will be conducted on an almost equal footing (almost, because workers' inspection of the accounts only adds to the *risk* involved in distorting them, and will in any case vary in efficiency and rigour) and judgements will therefore lack the perilous, gambling uncertainty with which they will otherwise undoubtedly be fraught.

This approach would remove some of the shibboleths engendered by the dominance of private property over men's minds. The present pattern of rewards, and the absurd tolerance of the private appropriation of the results of public effort, will come to seem less and less 'natural'. When they see precisely how far 'self-financing' has become the norm in private industry, workers will begin to wonder why the results of their effort cannot be invested in their own name rather than to the credit of some rentier. Clause Four of the Labour Party's constitution will cease to be an inspirational icon. From an intensification of the campaign for workers' control, we shall prepare for the leap towards new political and social forms, to self-management.

Part three

The transition to socialism in Britain is not necessarily a matter of decades. The weight of the problems of capitalism is so heavy and their effect has so disoriented the political guides and leaders of the system, that it seems clear that it is only the inertia and lack of insight of the Labour Movement that allows the whole system to continue. To develop a strategy of advance is the crucial task of the Left today: but this cannot be done if we are not prepared to discuss socialism itself. The goal will cast its own shape on the path we beat towards it.

To say that duality of power ceases to exist once industry is socialized would be a truism, were the word 'socialized' to refer not merely to the juridical ownership of plant, but also to the product. If socialist, or welfare, forms of distribution were general, many present conflicts would be inconceivable. These conflicts arise essentially between opposed interests, which generate opposed ideals, appealing to property and democracy respectively. Although the antithetical natures of private property and democracy are often obscured, deliberately, by ideologists who offer verbal resolutions of the real contradiction, and as a reflex response by people who are thinking within a climate in which it appears as 'natural', nonetheless it is constantly reasserted in the struggles which take place every day in almost every enterprise. On workpeople's side, the development of democratic ideas under capitalism is inseparable from the development of solidarity. Yet this solidarity is not to be interpreted, as it has been on many occasions, as a founding charter for monolithic discipline in *socialist* factories. The problem of self-management begins with a recognition that each worker has a complex of interests, often divergent ones, involving him as consumer, as producer and as citizen. These must persist as long as the division of labour itself compels men to adopt fixed roles during formative parts of their lives. Such interests will align him with some other men into shifting groups and lobbies, and oppose him to some other men at every major turn of the decision-making process. Either these interests will achieve open and satisfying expression, or they will be muffled, frustrated, and thwarted, thus producing an inhibiting apathy which will drive them further and further underground, sterilizing the creative force which they represent.

Yet those who have witnessed this process at work in countries in which the democratic process has been paralysed over long periods, frequently identify it with the dehumanization of labour under capitalist relations of production, and then telescope all problems of dehumanization together, locating them all in the problem of the popular administration of industry. This is mistaken. The traditional socialist answer to the search for the source of the dehumanization of labour under capitalism involves an integrated critique of the force of the market and the division of labour which it produces: these phenomena express themselves in forms of property. Unless the constrictions of private property can be overcome, we cannot begin to get to grips with the problem of overcoming the tyranny of the market, and with it the division of labour itself. This means that for a socialist the problem of the market can never be a secondary one. Our strategy can never be limited to moves designed to ameliorate the labour process (desirable in themselves though these may be), because our problem is that of overcoming the compulsion to labour itself, and abolishing with it the whole preformed and viciously mutilating division of labour which aligns men into classes and divides classes into castes, stamping rank on the faces of people and dissolving their common humanity. How far can labour be humanized by democratizing industry? The answer is complex: but some things about it are very simple indeed. If we speak of humanizing labour,[8] we are speaking of developing the labourer's freedom. This freedom is a capacity for self-realization, or it is nothing. But we are members of one another. Our selves are not contained in our skins, but learnt from the people around us in reciprocal human action. For this reason, the division of labour, having opened doors to freedom, becomes a cruel barrier to it. A democratically-run sand-foundry is a far better place than one run by order: but in a world where some men ride round the moon or sing in *Fidelio*, a foundryman is not a *free* man. To secure an explosion

8 If we do, strictly speaking we are erring. The humanization of *work* involves the *abolition* of labour, as Marx was concerned to point out again and again.

in the amount of free time, in which men can travel, work, design or speculate by turns as their wish takes them, we must liberate a technological and productive explosion which can underpin it. Of course, this requires a planned, coordinated effort. But precisely here, in the pursuit of the goal of freedom, we find the commonest alibi for ignoring what remains a vital question, that of self-management.

For self-management is essentially a problem of democratic planning. It would be foolish to assume that this is solved, even at the blue-print stage. Whilst we can learn something important from experiments which have already been made, we have most of the work to do ourselves. Even in Yugoslavia, the problem is so far from being solved that it is not impossible that we may yet regard that country as an object-lesson in pitfalls, rather than the brave pilot which it looked like being in the beginning. The Yugoslav assumption that the encroachment of bureaucracy can only be combated by decentralization and increased sensitivity to the demands of the market, tends to reduce the question of democratic control to one of an increasingly meaningless local autonomy, and gradually replaces a central, conscious, willed network of decisions by impalpable and unseen economic pressures. The market calls out for power to repair the damage done by the market, and a complex of incentives invades even hospitals and schools in a vain attempt to check bureaucracy by increasing differentials. All this feeds the fragmentation of workpeople, and multiplies their apathy. This makes it increasingly difficult to evolve corrective policies. One hopes this pessimistic picture will be falsified. But the Yugoslav experience reinforces the view that the key to the problem of democratic planning involves the discovery of means by which we can institutionalize, and thereby legitimize, conflicts about the priorities of the master plan itself. Such conflicts are bound to be serious even in the most advanced countries, where they are extremely unlikely to be resolved in appeals to charismatic forces and individuals 'above the battle'.

To see these difficulties is not to solve them. The solutions will not be easy, and are unlikely to be reached by a process of speculation. Men will hammer out their institutions on the problems that they face with the forces that they have. It is a very practical process, and it gets into books after it has happened. But we have half a century of warnings about some of the problems of the transition we will soon be entering, and we would be fools to ignore them.

We can clear the way for action. In less than a generation we *can* see, if we wish it, the beginnings of a new style of men, who will have miles to grow and universes to subdue, but who will never have taken an order, or been afraid of other men, or done an action without knowing why.

References

Anarchy (1964), no. 40, June.

BROWN, W. (1965), *Piecework Abandoned*, Heinemann Educational.

CLEGG, H. A. (1962), *Implications of the Shorter Working Week for Management*, British Institute of Management.

CLEGG, H. A., *et al.* (1961), *Trade Union Officers*, Blackwell.

FRIEDMANN, G. (1955), *Industrial Society*, Collier Macmillan.

FRIEDMANN, G. (1961), *The Anatomy of Work*, Heinemann Educational.

GOLDTHORPE, J. H., and LOCKWOOD, D. (1963), 'Affluence and the British class structure', *Soc. Rev.*, vol. 11, no. 2, pp. 133–64.

HILL, S. (1963), 'Editorial', *Public Employees Journal*, Winter.

LABOUR PARTY (1963), *Conference Report*, Labour Party.

LLEWELLYN DAVIES, D. (1962), *Formal Consultation in Practice*, Industrial Welfare.

MCCARTHY, W. E. J. (1964), 'The price of wage restraint', *New Society*, 5 March.

MARSH, A. (1963), *Managers and Shop Stewards*, Institute of Personnel Management.

MARSH, A. T., and COKER, E. E. (1963), 'Shop steward organization in engineering', *Brit. J. Indust. Rel.*, vol. 1, no. 2.

New Left Review (1965), no. 25, pp. 13–16.

Observer (1964), 'A study on the election', 18 October.

ROSE, H. (1963), *Disclosure in Company Accounts*, Eaton Paper, Institute of Economic Affairs.

STEWART and WINSBURY, R. (1963), *An Incomes Policy for Labour*, Fabian Society.

TITMUSS, R. M. (1962), *Income Distribution and Social Change*, Allen & Unwin.

TOPHAM, A. (1964), 'Shop stewards and workers' control', *New Left Review*, no. 25, p. 5.

TUC (1963), *Trade Union Congress Report*, TUC.

TUC (1964), *Trade Union Congress Report*, TUC.

TURNER, H. A. (1963), *The Trend of Strike*, Leeds University Press.

WALPOLE, G. S. (1944), *Management and Men*, Cape.

The Week (1964), vol. 2, no. 4, July.

ZWEIG, F. (1961), *The Worker in an Affluent Society*, Heinemann Educational.

8 K. Skalicky

The Catholic Church and Workers' Participation

First published in this volume.

To trace the Catholic Church's position on worker participation we can do no better than to begin with that champion of the rights of workers, Leo XIII. In a classic passage (1960) he discusses the low estate to which working men had been reduced by Liberal Capitalism:

In any case we clearly see, and on this there is general agreement, that some opportune remedy must be found quickly for the misery and wretchedness pressing so unjustly on the majority of the working class: for the ancient working-men's guilds were abolished in the last century, and no other protective organization took their place. Public institutions and the laws set aside the ancient religion. Hence by degrees it has come to pass that working men have been surrendered, isolated and helpless, to the hard-heartedness of employers. . . .

What especially made this possible, the Pope goes on to say, was that:

the hiring of labour and the conduct of trade are concentrated in the hands of comparatively few; so that a small number of very rich men have been able to lay upon the teeming masses of the labouring poor a yoke little better than that of slavery itself.

With these grave and prophetic words Leo XIII denounces these evils of liberalism: first, the fragmentation of society (the result of an exaggerated individualism, which is, in the last analysis, only the consequence of the assumption of the absolute autonomy of man – a fundamental postulate of bourgeois philosophy); secondly, that the individual worker becomes a victim of the free play of the laws of supply and demand (with the consequent degradation of human labour to the level of mere merchandise); thirdly, that the society is split into two opposing classes, capitalists on the one hand and proletariat on the other, with mediation between them difficult if not altogether impossible. In fact, 'The discussion is not easy, nor is it void of danger,' notes Leo XIII (1960) concerning the problem of the workingman: 'It is no easy matter to define the relative rights and mutual duties of the rich and of the poor, of Capital and of Labour.'

The setting for this decisive and profound division of human society – a division which seemingly excludes any possibility of mediation, thus threatening to destroy community among men – is *the enterprise*. It may seem paradoxical that it is precisely the enterprise – that is, that union of men and material things which requires, by its very nature, collaboration, agreement, and harmony – which became the breeding place for so profound and potentially destructive a division as that of classes. But in fact enterprises, especially medium and large, as a creation of liberalism and capitalism, are marked by a clear separation between workmen and entrepreneurs; between those who work and the possessors of the means of production who direct them there in a relationship of dependence. Between these two classes the wage system is almost always in force. The enterprise is not in any sense a place where one can breathe the free air of democracy, even though liberalism championed democracy in civic life against the hierarchic feudal society. By advocating democracy in politics without admitting it in the life of the enterprise (economic democracy), liberalism ran into an incurable contradiction and became incapable of overcoming the unpromising division of society into two classes, having perforce deprived itself of any principle to support its mediation. It seems logical to believe that the overcoming of this division will not be realized in any other setting than that from which it sprang, that is, in the enterprise itself; and that political democracy should be carried into the enterprise through what is called workers' participation in the enterprise.

What was the attitude of the Catholic Church toward the social problem of class divisions, and what principles did the Church emphasize with a view to possible solutions (which are not within her competence) and more precisely, with respect to workers' participation in the life of the enterprise?

The harbingers of 'Rerum Novarum'

Before any pronouncement was made by the highest authority of the Church, it was of course the faithful themselves who confronted the problem on their own account. Certainly the best of the Catholics had not waited for Marx. In fact, as Daniel Rops (1964) writes, the awakening of Catholics to social problems can be dated to 1822, recalling the voices of Lamennais in the *Drapeau Blanc* and of Chateaubriand in the *Mémoires d'Outre Tombe*. Through the action of Abbé Lowenbruck arose the 'Society of St Joseph' for working-class youth (dissolved in 1830 by the French government) and later the 'Society of St Nicholas', which founded in Paris the first professional school. In the *Avenir* Charles de Coux and Abbé Gerbert from 1831 on scored 'the great barons of industrialism, those who fix the rates of salaries by their own caprice'. Viscount Alban de

Villeneuve-Bargemont in 1834 published a *Grand Traité d'Économie Politique Chrétienne*. From the pulpit of Notre Dame, Lacordaire, beginning in 1835, pronounced his celebrated lectures vibrant with social connection. Frédéric Ozanam founded in May 1833 the noted Society of St Vincent de Paul. It was Wilhem E. Von Ketteler, the 'fighting bishop', who awoke Germany to social awareness, and with him Canon Leming, the former-shoemaker priest Adolf Kolping, and the former official and land-proprietor Baron Burghard de Schorlemer Alst.

In his time, the most original Catholic thinker on social questions is probably Buchez (1796–1865), who can be considered the first theoretician of workers' associations. The bourgeoisie, according to him, had applied the principle of association to capital: the workers ought to apply it to labour. In joining together to found a workers' association, they take on themselves two obligations:

1 To bring together a common capital which will be the instrument of labour and which must remain inalienable and indivisible, and will be destined, by virtue of annual contributions, to increase continually.

2 To join forces to put the capital to use through their work, under a direction that they themselves should name.

To these two obligations correspond two rights:

1 To receive a sufficient salary;

2 To receive the portion of profits which is distributed among the workers, in proportion to their work done, setting aside a portion to increase the common capital.

Besides Buchez, Frédéric Le Play (1806–82) also confronted, in *La Réforme Sociale*, the problems of spreading pauperism, taking inspiration from Christian morality and relying mainly on solutions which strengthened the family. The ideas of Le Play influenced La Tour du Pin (1834–1924), who however found the key to the solution not so much in the family as in the restoration of corporations. He did not have in mind the medieval corporations which were local and aristocratic. Those he proposed were to exist on a national scale and be democratic. Such corporations, however, do not predetermine, according to La Tour du Pin, the management of the enterprise, which remains in the hands of the owner; their function would be mainly social.

In 1894, Bishop Mermillod of Friburg created the Union of Friburg which was, during its seven years of life, of great importance in the elaboration of Christian social doctrine. La Tour du Pin and Albert de Mun took part in its work. In 1887 the Union brought out this indictment (quoted in Lefranc, 1966) of the capitalist regime:

The capitalist system depends on the idea of the productivity of capital and of money, on the concept of money as the general and supreme producer which must always bear fruit. It is not a question of bringing charges against any one act of capitalism: rather it is the system itself which is usurious in its very essence, because in its totality it is based on the interests of unproductive values.

In 1888 Bishop Mermillod introduced a delegation of the Union to Pope Leo XIII, who requested a memorandum explaining the views of the group. The ensuing text presented to the Pope stresses three points:

1 Working conditions should be such as to safeguard the dignity of man;
2 The right to property does not imply the right to abuse the same;
3 The organization of corporations.

In Italy at that time there was no lack of men sensitive to social problems. We may recall the names of Father Taparelli, D'Azeglio, Father Liberatore, Cardinal Zigliara and Guiseppe Toniolo. Vincenzo Gioachino Pecci (after 1878 Pope Leo XIII) was an attentive observer of social evils. While still Archbishop of Perugia, he denounced them implacably in his pastoral letters. As soon as he was elected Pope, he decided to confront the social problem with all the weight of his high office. He conceived the idea of the first social encyclical. The drafting of such a document understandably required more than one year, and three drafts preceded the definitive version: the first worked out by Father Liberatore, the second by Cardinal Zigliara; the third is the Liberatore draft modified and completed by Cardinal Marella and Father Liberatore himself. During all this time Leo XIII occupied himself actively with the drafting of the encyclical, and his participation may be clearly discerned in the various phases of its preparation (cf. Antonazzi, 1957).

Principles of Leo's social teaching

What are the main lines of the Leonine social teaching on which later popes based themselves in confronting more directly the question of workers' participation in economic management? They are:

1 The preservation of private property, understood as the fruit of labour and an extension of the person. This principle must be coupled with the equally true one (Van Gestel, 1965) that: 'The earth, even though apportioned among private owners, ceases not thereby to minister to the needs of all.' This is the social function of private property, which is founded on the fact that God gave 'the earth for the use and enjoyment of the whole human race' (*Rerum Novarum*, p. 9).

2 The reconciliation of the two classes cannot be attained simply by abolishing private property. In fact, it is not even fundamentally a question of abolishing classes ('. . . it is impossible to reduce civil society to one dead level') (*Rerum Novarum*, p. 14), since they have a good reason for existing ('. . . Social and public life can only be maintained by means of various kinds of business and the playing of many parts') (*Rerum Novarum*, p. 14). What is essential is that they discharge their duties one to the other, because the one cannot exist without the other ('so . . . is it ordained by nature that these two classes should dwell in harmony and agreement, so as to maintain the balance of the body politic. Each needs the other: Capital cannot do without Labour, nor Labour without Capital.').

3 Human work has two characteristics logically distinct but inseparable in reality. It is *personal*, because it is inherent in the person and entirely proper to him who exercises it: and *necessary*, because it serves for the maintenance of man's life. From this derives the fact that the amount of a wage is not determined by 'the free agreement of the parties concerned' only (the liberal position). Rather, given that the wage is the compensation for labour contributed and that labour is human activity ordained to provide for the needs of life and especially for its preservation (the necessary aspect), the workman – under the first (personal) aspect may agree to a compensation less than what is just, while under the second (necessary) aspect he cannot live because he has the duty to preserve his life, and, for a poor man, his wages are the only means of doing so. Furthermore, no matter what the agreement may be between the supplier of a job and the worker, there is always an element of natural justice, anterior and superior to the free will of the contracting parties: this is that the amount of compensation must not be inferior to the worker's normal sustenance.

4 Leo XIII commends the creation of 'working-men's Unions' and does not hesitate to say that 'it is gratifying to know that there are actually in existence not a few associations of this nature, consisting either of workmen alone, or of workers and employers together' (*Rerum Novarum*, p. 36). (The former type of association or syndicates succeeded, but not the latter!)

The Leonine encyclical, however, does not touch directly on the problem of workers' participation in economic management, but posits certain principles concerning property, the class struggle, the nature of work, and workers' associations which bear on it indirectly. *Rerum Novarum* represents without doubt a great step forward in the Church's position on the social question (deciding in favour of 'Social Christians' against liberal

Christians and giving a start towards Christian trade unionism). But it failed to touch the causes of the birth of the proletariat. In fact, 'neither the paternalism of benevolent proprietors, nor the syndical action of the workers, nor the intervention of the state, nor corporate organization brought about any real change in the actual relations between owners and workers, because they do not touch them where they are born, formed and interwoven, that is, within the very heart of the factory' (Van Gestel, 1965).

The teaching of the encyclical 'Quadragesimo Anno'

On the fortieth anniversary of the encyclical *Rerum Novarum*, 15 May 1931, Pope Pius XI published another social encyclical, *Quadragesimo Anno*, which beyond clarifying the Leonine doctrine in 'some of its points', aimed systematically 'to expose the root (*radicem*) of the present social disorder' (*Quadragesimo Anno*, p. 15). We are thus dealing with a *radical* encyclical.

Between the two encyclicals, however, a new situation had arisen: the further concentration of capital, the development of Christian unionism in many countries of Europe, the First World War, and breaking up of the united Socialist movement and the birth of communism, the Bolshevik revolution, and the great economic crisis that broke out in October 1929.

What is the encyclical's most original contribution? Analysing capitalism in its more developed phase, that of imperialism, the Pope finds the root of the evil above all in the unequal relationship between capital and labour. In capitalism, labour is considered as merchandise; the worker sells his labour to the entrepreneur, receiving a price (wage) according to the laws of supply and demand. Pius XI (*Quadragesimo Anno*, p. 83) observes: '... as things are now, the wage system divides men in what is called the labour market into two sections, resembling armies, and the disputes between these sections transform this labour market into an arena where the two armies are engaged in fierce combat.'

Confronted by this problem, what position does the Pope take? Let us consider only his fundamental principles:

1 Recalling the doctrine of Leo XIII, Pius XI (*Rerum Novarum*, p.15) emphasizes the principle that 'capital cannot do without labour, nor labour without capital', concluding (*Quadragesimo Anno*, p. 53) that, 'it is therefore entirely false to ascribe the results of their combined efforts to either capital or labour alone'.

2 Human labour cannot be considered as mere merchandise: 'Labour, indeed, as has been well said by Our Predecessor in his encyclical, is not a

mere chattel (*Rerum Novarum*, p. 16); the human dignity of the working-man must be recognized in it, and consequently it cannot be bought and sold like any piece of merchandise' (*Quadragesimo Anno*, p. 83).

3 Even though labour is not merchandise, it does not follow that the system of compensation based on a labour contract or wage-contract is unjust, as was claimed by Weiss and the representatives of the Austrian radical school (*Quadragesimo Anno*, p. 64): '. . . those who hold that the wage-contract is essentially unjust, and that therefore in its place must be introduced the contract of partnership, are certainly in error.'

4 The wage-contract is not unjust on one condition, namely that remuneration of labour be calculated on more than one consideration. As in the case of property, so labour has in addition to its personal and individual aspect a *social character*. The principal factors in the determination of wages are: (a) the sustenance of the workman and his family; (b) business conditions of the firm; (c) the requirements of the common good.

5 Having established these principles regarding the wage system, the Pope makes this affirmation of capital importance (*Quadragesimo Anno*, p. 65): 'Nevertheless, in the present state of human society, we deem it advisable that the wage-contract should, when possible, be modified somewhat (*aliquantum temperetur*) by a contract of partnership, as is already being tried in various ways to the not small gain both of the wage-earners and of the employers. In this way wage-earners and other employees participate in the ownership or the management or in some way share in the profits.'

With these words comanagement and participation in profits became sanctioned, at least in principle, and the way was opened for further evolution of doctrine. This time the Pope, even if only in passing, touched the problem at its root.

At first, however – as Father Van Gestel notes – these words did not find an immediate echo; the main theme of *Quadragesimo Anno*, the idea of professional organization, was at that moment occupying the whole attention of socially minded Catholics, and the economic crisis then raging created an environment that was not very favourable to the realization of structural reform. Even less propitious were the years of the Second World War which followed.

The imperative of Pius XII

The War was not altogether finished, when Pope Pius XII treated the problem in his radio message of 1 September 1944. Stressing once again the right of private property correctly understood as a limited right inasmuch as it is subordinated to the common good and rejecting 'those excessive concentrations of economic goods, which, often hidden under anonymous forms, succeed in shirking their social obligations', the Pope admits in this case that the state may 'decree expropriation, given a suitable indemnity, if it pronounces in favour of "small and middle-sized property in agriculture, in the arts and crafts, in commerce and industry," '. He then continues: 'Where the large enterprise shows itself to be still more productive today, there should be offered the possibility to temper the labour contract with a contract of partnership' (see *Quadragesimo Anno*).

At first sight, the Pope merely repeats the teaching of Pius XI, but there is a notable difference: his statement is not conditional, it is imperative and unconditional: '. . . there *should* be offered the possibility. . . .'

Now, serious difficulties do not arise regarding co-ownership or participation in profits, but when we turn to participation in management, the problem becomes more thorny. Apart from various imperfect forms of participation – such as the right of information (*mithören*), the right of discussion (*mitsprache*), the right of deliberation (*mitberatung*), the right of collaboration in the execution of measures taken (*mitwirkung*) – the right of decision (*mitbestimmung*), which alone fulfils co-management in the full sense of the word, can be double: it can be of a *social* nature or *economic* nature.

These two forms of participation in management result from the ambivalent conception of the firm, for it can be thought of as either solely the *working community* (which brings together only one of the elements of production, men), or as the *unit of production* (which is formed from the joining together and organizing of the various factors of production). If then, participation in management refers uniquely to the working community, its role is by nature *social* and *personal* (as for example the regulation of conditions of work, relations between the direction and personnel, the taking-on and discharging of employees and so forth). If instead the firm is referred to as the unit of production, participation acquires an *economic* character.

Against participation in its social character there can be no basic objections; it is co-management in its economic sense that meets resistance and serious objection. This problem emerged at the 'Catholic Day' of Bochum (Germany) at the end of August 1949, where a resolution was approved which among other things stated: 'Catholic workers and employers are agreed in recognizing that the participation of all collaborators in decisions concerning social and economic questions of personnel is a natural right in conformity with the order desired by God.'

Further clarifications of Pius XII

The affirmation that participation in management is a matter of natural right and therefore willed by God was undoubtedly a serious matter, and aroused the reaction of Pius XII.

The Pope, in fact, had already spoken out on these problems several months before the Catholic Day at Bochum, on 7 May 1949, on the occasion of the ninth conference of the 'Union Internationale des Associations Patronales Catholiques'. In his allocution he said:

Neither would it be true to state that every private enterprise is by its nature a society such that the relationships among the participants are determined by the rules of distributive justice, so that all without distinction, whether or not owners of the means of production, would have a right to their part of the property or at least to the profits of the enterprise. Such an idea draws its origin from the hypothesis that every enterprise pertains by nature to the sphere of public right. But this supposition is inexact. No matter whether the enterprise be constituted in the form of a foundation or an association of all the workers as co-proprietors, or as the private property of an individual who signs a labour contract with all his workers, it belongs to the *private* juridical order of economic life. Everything we have just said applies to the juridical nature of the enterprise as such; but the enterprise may include a whole category of other personal relationships among the participants. These also must be taken into account, including relationships of common responsibility.

Some months after the 'Catholic Day', the Pope returned to the subject in his address to the participants at the International Congress of Social Studies (3 June 1950). In warning against the dangers of nationalization which consists in withdrawing disposal over the means of production from the personal responsibility of the private owner (individual or corporate) to transfer them to the responsibility of anonymous collective forms, Pius XII declared:

The same danger appears when it is demanded that the wage earners belonging to a firm have the right of economic codetermination, especially when the exercise of this right is in fact called for, directly or indirectly, by organizations guided from outside the enterprise. Now, neither the nature of the labour contract, nor the nature of the firm include necessarily and *per se* a right of this kind.

Then referring to the above-cited words of Pius XI (*Quadragesimo Anno*, p. 65), the Pope continues:

There the intrinsic necessity that the labour contract conform to one of the partnership is denied. This is not to disregard the usefulness of what has been attained up to now in this direction, in various ways, to the common advantage of workers and owners; but for reasons both of principle and of actual fact, the right of economic participation in management that is being claimed remains outside the field of possible realizations (Pius XII, vol. 6, p. 127).

From these limiting affirmations, however, we should by no means deduce that Pius XII was negative towards economic codetermination. This is seen in other statements of his. On 7 July 1952, on the occasion of the 'Thirty-Ninth Social Week of France', he said (Pius XII, vol. 12, pp. 100–101): 'Moreover, if owners and workers have a common interest in the healthy prosperity of the national economy, why would it not be legitimate to attribute to the workers a fair part of the responsibility in the formation and development of this economy?'

On the one hand, then, Pius XII holds that in the case of the large enterprise (and only there) 'should be offered the possibility to mitigate the labour contract with a contract of partnership', on the other hand, he rejects the opinion which holds that the very nature of the labour contract or the nature of the enterprise (or even human nature) includes necessarily and *per se* a right to economic codetermination. What then is the foundation of the pontifical imperative: '. . . should be offered . . .'?

The opinions of Catholic scholars and the letter of Monsignor Montini

With this question we enter into the field of the debatable. One can say, however, that even then, the most authoritative Catholic specialists were inclined to maintain that the right of economic codetermination could be based in some way on human nature. But it was not always easy to uphold this opinion when Pius XII – especially under the influence of the postwar European political situation – seemed to abandon his original openness towards workers' participation in management, and expressed himself against any natural right to codetermination. Naturally, these restrictive statements of Pius XII provoked an understandable feeling of delusion and even indignation in many Catholics who concentrated too much on their negative side. This was the motive that led Monsignor Pavan, one of the most authoritative specialists on this subject, to take on the task of interpreting the affirmations of the pontiff (Pavan, 1950) more positively in his article in *La Documentation Catholique*, in which he says among other things:

It must nevertheless be affirmed, according to the teaching of the Pope, that, even if the personnel cannot have recourse to a natural right for the economic codetermination of enterprises, they may still aim at this participation as an ideal and that in consequence, they have the right to make use of all legitimate means to attain it.

Likewise, Constant Van Gestel (1965, p. 412), referring to this interpretation and following the conclusions of the Union of Malines (29 October 1953) regarding codetermination, writes:

Economic codetermination, while not a requirement of natural law, might become a positive right, whether by agreements freely arrived at, or by legal dispositions taken and respecting private ownership of the goods of production, might hold it useful for reasons of the common good to make a profound transformation of the relationships between labourers and employers within the firms.[1]

More decidedly in favour of the natural right to codetermination is Oswald Von Nell-Breuning (1950). This leading Jesuit maintains that:

Codetermination and the right of codetermination are not institutions of natural law like the family, the state, or property; nevertheless, codetermination and the right of codetermination may be in specific circumstances required in view of the common good; if this is so, they are demanded by natural law.

The same position is taken by Eberhard Welty (1958):

Codetermination does not necessarily result from the common nature of man, nor from the nature of the labour contract and of the firm. Therefore, it does not enter into the sphere of the unchanging precepts of natural law. . . . The right of codetermination may result from the particular properties of human nature, that is, it may enter into the sphere of 'new forms of natural requirements' (Pius XII), which are conditioned by changes in the economic and social situation and are essential to the established order of the common good and the society. These natural requirements are a true natural right, even though of the 'second order'. They derive not only from human arrangements and agreements; they are also something more than mere 'high natural suitability', because they are founded on changeable, it is true, but interior necessities or aspirations of human nature.

Monsignor Pavan (1950) defends this opinion and strengthens it with a more penetrating exposition. His judgement is all the more significant because it is not merely a 'Roman voice', but the voice of one of the future collaborators of the encyclical *Mater et Magistra*. In his work *L'ordine sociale*, Monsignor Pavan asks the question if there are signs today that spur us on to think that historical evolution is oriented towards a progressive surmounting of the wage system or at least towards new ideas and attempts at new contractual forms. His reply, based on various considerations – metaphysical, psychological, moral, economic, historical and socio-political – is positive. His conclusion (1950) is:

The supreme teaching of the Church in these recent times has clearly said, as is expressed above, that in workers there is no natural right to directive responsibility in the complex enterprise of today; but it without doubt conforms to the teaching of the *Magisterium* to maintain that the assumption of the said responsibilities can be cherished by the workers as a legitimate ideal and thus actively pursued by every licit means; it is not at all forbidden to think that the evolving attitudes in the workers themselves, the more acute social sensitiveness in the entrepreneurs or directors, and the exigencies of the common good in a given moment of the evolution of social relationships urge and demand that that ideal

1 Roughly similar is Eberhard Muller (1950).

should have a juridical expression, and on the historical plane, should rise to the dignity and effectiveness of a right.

Among the voices of these authoritative specialists that in general agree in admitting that there is a certain kind of right to economic codetermination, is another document that because of its authority cannot be ignored. That is the letter which on 21 September 1952, Monsignor Montini, at that time Vice-Secretary of State of Pope Pius XII and to become Pope Paul VI, addressed to the 'Social Week' of Italy, where he says (*Observatore Romano*, 1952):

The Holy Father Pius XII, then, has several times referred to the juridico-social position of the workers in enterprises, specifying what pertains to the sphere of natural law and what is part of the aspirations of the working class, which can hence be pursued as an ideal by licit means. Generally speaking then, there is not a real right of the worker to participate in management; but that does not deny the entrepreneur from letting the worker participate in some form and measure, as it does not prevent the state from giving to labour the faculties for letting its voice be heard in management, acting in certain factories and given cases in which the excessive power of anonymous capital abandoned to itself manifestly harms the community.

As is seen, the distinction between the right and the ideal, drawn some time before by Monsignor Pavan in the article quoted above, in which he gave a more positive interpretation to the restrictive statements of Pius XII that was apparently not very pleasing to the pontiff, now echoes in the letter that Monsignor Montini wrote as Secretary of State to the same pontiff.

Codetermination in 'Mater et Magistra' of John XXIII

The hesitant and ambivalent position of Pius XII echoed in the letter of Monsignor Montini does not represent the last word on the matter. Once again the question of workers' participation was taken up by the highest authority of the Catholic Church, this time by Pope John XXIII in his encyclical *Mater et Magistra* (15 May 1961).

What greatly impresses us in his words is the spontaneous and free way in which he confronts the problem of the right to codetermination, without so much concern to limit it, through denial of its ties to human nature. Referring to his predecessors, the Pope says: 'We, no less than our predecessors, are convinced that employees are justified in wishing to participate in the activity of the industrial concern for which they work.' The Pope realized that it is not possible to predetermine the means and degrees of such participation, they being dependent on the concrete situation of each enterprise. Nevertheless, the Pope states his conviction that 'We are in no two minds as to the need for giving workers an active share in the business of the company for which they work – be it a private or public one. Every effort must be made to ensure that the company is indeed a true community of persons, concerned about the needs, the activities and the standing of each of its members.' Such 'humanization' of the enterprise supposes, according to the Pope, that:

... the relations between management and employees reflect understanding, appreciation and good-will on both sides. It demands, too, that all parties cooperate actively and loyally in the common enterprise, not so much for what they can get out of it for themselves, but as discharging a duty and rendering a service to their fellowmen. All this implies that the workers have their say in, and make their own contribution to, the efficient running and development of the enterprise (*Mater et Magistra*, pp. 91–2).

Then, citing the words of Pius XII: 'the economic and social function which every man aspires to fulfil demands that the carrying on of the activity of each one is not completely subjected to the will of others', John XXIII (*Mater et Magistra*, p. 92) continues:

Obviously, any firm which is concerned for the human dignity of its workers must also maintain a necessary and efficient unity of direction. But it must not treat those employees who spend their days in service with the firm as though they were mere cogs in the machinery, denying them any opportunity of expressing their wishes or bringing their experience to bear on the work in hand, and keeping them entirely passive in regard to decisions that regulate their activity.

Having established this, the Pope adds an important statement which demonstrates clearly that he does not share Pius XII's anxiety over the natural right to codetermination. He says (*Mater et Magistra*, p. 93), 'We would observe finally, that the present demand for workers to have a greater say in the conduct of the firm *accords not only with man's nature*, but also with recent progress in the economic, social and political spheres.'

It can thus be concluded that the imperative ('. . . should be offered . . .') with which Pius XII pronounced in favour of codetermination in large undertakings, though not supporting it as found in nature, becomes, for John XXIII, an imperative squarely based on 'man's nature'.

Workers' participation and Vatican Council II

The popes in their encyclicals have not been the only ones to concern themselves with this question. Vatican Council II confronted it in one of its two most authoritative documents, that is, in the pastoral constitution on *The Church in the Modern World* (*Gaudium et Spes*). It is precisely this rank of constitution (not merely decree or declaration) that confers on the text on participation the highest authority. The text, it is true, does not say much more than the popes had already said, and compared with the statement of the encyclicals, it may seem rather generic, but the fact that the text is found in the conciliar constitution engages the whole Church in quite a special way.

The Council states in this solemn document (*Gaudium et Spes*, 1966): 'In economic enterprises it is persons who work together, that is, free and independent human beings created to the image of God. Therefore the active participation of everyone in the running of an enterprise should be promoted. This participation should be exercised in appropriately determined ways. It should take into account each person's function, whether it be one of ownership, hiring, management, or labour. It should provide for the necessary unity of operations.'[2]

In the debate within the council which preceded the final formulation of the text, two trends emerged; one group wanted more specific statements, the other advised remaining more in the generic. The first group is well exemplified by the statement of Bishop Franic of Split in Yugoslavia:

Moreover, the third chapter, for example, appears less solid and dynamic in some places than certain documents of recent popes. . . . The text speaks so timidly of the participation of workers in the life of the enterprise, without which all structural reforms would remain ineffective. Man has become aware that work is part of his person and that it cannot therefore be bought or sold like any other object (Caprile, 1965, p. 158).

The second direction, more moderate towards codetermination, was expressed by Cardinal Siri (Caprile, 1965, p. 155), archbishop of Genoa. 'The complexity of technical matters,' said the cardinal, 'indicates that we should limit ourselves to simple general affirmations, understood to urge an ever wider participation in social and economic management without entering into the particulars. Participation in economic administration on the part of many, even of all, may be wished for, but never at the detriment of the freedom of initiative and of the rational and human ordering of society.'

As may be seen from these two positions, it was not a matter of giving a 'yes' or 'no' to participation, but only a matter of degree; in other

2 The text presented for the conciliar debate, the so-called Aricia text, originally drawn up in French and dated 26 June 1965, was more eloquent. Its paragraph 80 read: 'Dans les entreprises de production, les propriétaires (individus, groupes, collectivités y compris l'Etat dans les cas où le bien commun le requiert) aussi bien que ceux qui, sans être propriétaires, détiennent effectivement le pouvoir économique, ne sauraient jamais se conduire en maîtres absolus. Les entreprises doivent au contraire tendre à devenir, dans toute la mesure du possible, des communautés de personnes, c'est-à-dire d'êtres libres et autonomes, créés à l'image de Dieu. Selon des modalités adaptées, tous les membres de l'entreprise doivent donc pouvoir participer à sa vie, à sa gestion et à ses fruits.'

words, the question was one of how far the Council ought to go in giving concrete specifications on the subject. If one appraises the relevant statements, it seems that the Council, for obvious reasons, wanted to stay more in generalities, and not to engage itself in questions that were too technical. In fact, Father Lebret (Giammancheri, 1966), commenting on the conciliar text, writes:

It is in place to note that the definitive text on the role of workers within the enterprise was weakened in comparison with the French text of 26 June 1965. . . . The term '*gestione*' posed such serious problems that the subsequent text, distributed at the beginning of the fourth session, became '*in inceptorum negotiis eorumque curatione et fructibus*'. The Council did not want to use a formula that appeared for the episcopate of certain countries, excessive. It skirted around the delicate question of participation in management. . . .

His statement that the Council avoided the question of codetermination does not seem to us precisely correct. It is true that the expressions in the text of Aricia, '*à sa vie, à sa gestion et à ses fruits*' (in the Latin version, '*negotia inceptum eorumque administrationem et fructibus*') were replaced with '*in inceptorum negotiis eorumque curatione et fructibus*' and finally with the simple '*omnium actuosa participatio in inceptorum curatione*'. From that fact, though, that the term '*administratio*' was replaced by the term '*curatio*' it cannot be deduced that the question of codetermination was set aside.

It seems to us that a more adequate explanation is given by Monsignor Ferrari-Toniolo. 'The Fathers,' he writes, 'in choosing the term *curationis*, wished to exclude participation in the other two aspects expressed with the terms *dominium* or "property" and *de lucris participatio* or "participation in profits". These two hypotheses are rather to be linked to the criteria given for the just remuneration of labour according to the degrees of productivity and of income, as well as the associated problem of adequate participation in ownership. . . .' Monsignor Ferrari-Toniolo (1966) then concludes that of the three meanings that codetermination may assume – participation in ownership (*condominium*); participation in profits; participation in the economic and financial direction of the enterprises – the Council's declaration intended to refer to the third possibility only, that is, to authentic codetermination.

Von Nell-Breuning (1966) explains the text in this same way. Pointing out that the Council recommends not only active participation in the life of the enterprise but *also* (*etiam*) in the choices regarding the institutions of a higher order, where decisions are taken on general social and economic conditions, he draws the following conclusion: 'if . . . the word "also" is to have any meaning, it can be only this: economic codetermination at the level of the enterprise implies economic decisions, and therefore what we call "economic codetermination" should be achieved also at levels higher than the enterprise.'

This judgement is confirmed by Rahner and Vorgrimler (1966), in their short commentary on the conciliar documents, and by J. Y. Calvez (1967), who referring to the meaning of the term *curatio* in the encyclical *Mater et Magistra* of John XXIII (cited in a note to the conciliar document), adds: '. . . it is difficult to maintain that John XXIII's expression would exclude participation in management in economic matters. "The activity", "running and development", "a greater say in the operation of the firm" (*Mater et Magistra*, pp. 91, 92, 93) are broad expressions which certainly imply economic decisions and the economic aspects of decisions.'

We may therefore conclude that the Council by the term '*curatio*' (management) means economic codetermination, and that this codetermination, in the words of the Council, 'should be promoted'.

Concluding evaluation

The Church, as we have seen, has placed the root of social evils in the degradation of human work, by virtue of the principles of liberalism, to the value of mere merchandise; from this devaluation ensues the system of wage-earning which splits society into two classes, sellers of labour (workers), and buyers of it (capitalists). Without condemning the system of wage-earning as such, the Church in its official declarations insists on the need to integrate it with elements of a contract of partnership (Pius XII), which later leads on to the affirmation of the necessity (at least in large enterprises) of participation in management (Pius XII) and to grounding this necessity on human nature (John XXIII). The Council later makes this doctrine its own, reaffirming it – at least in general – in one of its two most authoritative documents, the pastoral constitution *Gaudium et Spes* (*The Church in the Modern World*).

An evaluation of this position might characterize it as 'reformist'. The system of wage-earning is not rejected as such, but the demand is expressed that it 'should . . . be modified somewhat'. It may be objected that 'this is a hybrid position, neither fish nor fowl'. One may agree, I think, with this judgement to the extent that the official position of the Church does not basically reject capitalism (the wage-system), but wants only to 'humanize' it. One might go so far as to say that the Church has hereby postulated a 'capitalism with a human face'. Before judging this 'hybrid' position, one should realize that the radical negation of capitalism (or what believes itself such), that is, Marxist–Leninist socialism or communism, has also revealed itself in need of a 'human face'; and the Church in socialist countries has demonstrated, not with official declarations but with its silent work and above all with its hidden suffering that it does not want to condemn socialism but to humanize it, that it stands for a 'socialism with a human face'.

If then one were to put to the Church today the question, 'Tell us what you are for – socialism or capitalism?' it would in my opinion reply, '*I am for the human face of both.*' Are we to say that this is a hybrid position? Perhaps. But when all is said and done, what matters is not whether something is hybrid or not, but whether it is *human*. After all, is not man himself the greatest of all hybrids?

Yet, it may be that the real solution to the present social problem will be found only in the line of an authentic realization of worker participation, which, precisely because it is authentic, will bypass the capitalist–socialist dialectic and advance towards a solution thus far without name and for which new technical forms must be sought – inevitably tentative and imperfect – the whole moving forward towards participatory society.

References

ABBOT, W. M. (ed.) (1966), *Gaudium et Spes*, in *The Documents of Vatican II*, Guild Press.

ANTONAZZI, A. (1957), *L'enciclica Rerum Novarum, testo autentico e redazioni preparatorie dai documenti originali*, Rome.

CALVEZ, J. Y. (1967), 'La vie économico-sociale', in *Vatican II, L'Eglise dans le monde de ce temps*, vol. 2, Paris.

CAPRILE, G. (ed.) (1965), *Il Concilio Vaticano II*, vol. 5.

FERRARI-TONIOLO, A. (1966), 'La vita economico-sociale', in *La Chiesa nel mondo contemporaneo*, Turin.

GIAMMANCHERI, E. (ed.) (1966), *La Chiesa nel mondo contemporaneo, commento alla constituzione 'Gaudium et Spes'*, Brescia.

JOHN XXIII (1961), *Mater et Magistra*, Catholic Truth Society.

LEFRANC, G. (1966), *Histoire des doctrines sociales dans l'Europe contemporaine*, vol. 1, Paris.

LEO XIII (1960), *Encyclical letter 'Rerum Novarum'*, Catholic Truth Society; first published 1891.

MULLER, E. (1950), *Recht und Gerechtigkeit in der Mitbestimmung: ein evangelischer Ratschlag*, Stuttgart.

Observatore Romano (1952), 22–3 September.

PAVAN, P. (1950), 'L'ascension économique et sociale des classes ouvrières', *La Documentation Catholique*, vol. 47, pp. 1143–7.

PAVAN, P. (1956), *L'ordine sociale*, Turin, pp. 99–107.

PIUS XI (1931), *Quadragesimo Anno*, Catholic Truth Society.

PIUS XII (1944), *Speeches and Radio Messages (Discorsi e Radiomessagi)*, vol. 6.

RAHNER, K., and VORGRIMLER, H. (1966), *Kleines Konzilskompendium*.

ROPS, D. (1964), *Storia della Chiesa, VI*, vol. 1, Turin.

VAN GESTEL, C. (1965), *La dottrina sociale della Chiesa*, Rome.

VON NELL-BREUNING, O. (1950), *Mitbestimmung*, Girth, Landshut.

VON NELL-BREUNING, O. (1966), 'Die wirtschaft in Urteil des II. Vatikanischen Konzils', *Theologie und Philosophie*, p. 199.

WELTY, E. (1958), *Herders Sozialkatechismus*, vol. 2, Freiburg.

9 B. Horvat

An Institutional Model of a Self-Managed Socialist Economy

B. Horvat, 'An institutional model of a self-managed socialist economy', in *Eastern European Economics*, vol. 10, no. 4, 1972, pp. 369–92.

Defining self-management socialism[1]

Strictly speaking, 'self-management (or "associative") socialism' is a redundancy, for without self-management there is no socialism. Nevertheless, the term 'self-management' (or 'associative') is necessary for precision and to avoid misunderstanding. 'Socialism', like all frequently used words with marked emotional content, is used to mean so many different things that it has become completely indefinite as a scientific concept.

In its original meaning – which I also accept as the meaning with the most sense – socialism is a socio-economic system based on equality. In fact, capitalism was also founded on equality – in relation to feudalism, whose basis is inherited status – and that is what makes capitalism so vital.

However, the equality of liberal capitalism is defined formally and negatively: it is a matter of freedom from state or some other compulsion; and it is freedom of action *within the framework* of a market system that is accepted as natural, and hence the consequences of that freedom of action are not questioned. Equality in socialism is defined essentially and positively: the system is regulated by social action so that real equality is guaranteed to all members of society. It is worth noting that equality does not mean sameness; people are not the same, and therefore their positions in society are not the same. This is one of the defects of socialism that can be mitigated to some extent (especially in the noneconomic sphere), but cannot be eliminated. This defect is objectively conditioned, and this must be kept in mind if one does not wish to fall into frivolous utopianism.

Man has three basic roles in social life: he appears as a producer, as a consumer, and as a citizen. Consequently, equality should also be defined in terms of these three roles. *Equality in production* means guaranteeing

---

1 The model presented here is not a description of the Yugoslav institutional structure, although based upon it, but rather should be conceived as a proposal for its reform.

to all who wish to work the possibility of using the means of production under the same conditions. This implies:

1 Social ownership of the means of production;

2 The right to work;

3 The right to manage production (performing the entrepreneurial function, which involves making decisions about the quantity and assortment of production, purchases and sales, prices, investments and distribution of income). Individual labor and individual initiative represent a special case of equality in production (defined positively). In that sense individual labor is equal both to socialist and collective labor. (See Horvat, 1969, ch. 15.)

Social ownership should be interpreted as an economic, and not a legal, category. Legal private ownership (of land, a handicraft shop, etc.) that does not provide its owner with distinct income above and beyond the income of labor represents economically socialized ownership. Conversely, constitutionally legal social ownership can permit a high degree of privatization if the collective using it exploits its monopolistic position and extracts monopoly incomes that are not the result of work. Consequently, social ownership in the economic sense can be defined only according to the manner of distribution and appropriation, and not according to the formal legal title of ownership.

Equality as a consumer amounts to distribution according to work (which refers to distribution according to the results of work, and not according to some physical expenditure of labor power). It is obvious that producer and consumer equality are two sides of the same self-management coin, and that without producer equality there is no consumer equality. The latter also requires that the conditions of economic activity be equalized by social regulation. Unequal conditions of economic activity exclude distribution according to work. Polemics often occur over what equalized conditions of economic activity ought to mean. It follows from the above that equality of conditions of economic activity is measured by the degree to which the postulate of distribution according to work is satisfied. Distribution according to work implies two requirements:

1 Income differentials must result from the autonomous decisions of work collectives, which evaluate the differences among various categories of work;

2 An individual worker should obtain the same reward for the same work regardless of the branch of market or non-market production in which he is employed (but the reward can vary substantially from enterprise to enterprise depending on business efficiency). (See Horvat, 1964 and 1968.)

Equality as a citizen implies political democracy. A high degree of political democracy is impossible without equality of producers and consumers. In capitalist society, both political democracy and market equality are defined formally. In reality, however, the citizen is to a large extent an object of manipulation by hierarchically organized bureaucratic structures. Such structures can be eliminated – or at least more effectively controlled – in a situation in which there is equality in production and distribution. This explains the order in which I presented roles in social life. However, it would be a mistake to forget that there are also strong feedbacks. The absence of effective political democracy can prevent, or at least hinder, the development of socialist relations in the sphere of production and distribution. The latter represents the contemporary Yugoslav situation. (See Horvat, 1969, chs. 19 and 20.)

To the extent that equality of producer, consumer, and citizen is achieved, we can speak of socialist society. To the extent that there are defects in the three spheres, the given socialism is also defective. If the defects are great, then – in the sense of the well-known principle of the transition of quantity into quality – there can be no talk of socialism. In that respect it is irrelevant whether, from the formal legal standpoint, private ownership is expropriated or not. This three-dimensionality of socialism makes measurement of the extent of socialism somewhat more complicated and does not permit the construction of any sort of simple index (for example, the percentage of nationalization) as a reliable instrument of measurement. In principle, however, it is not impossible to arrive at a quantitative measure of socialism (for example, by using discrimination analysis).

The three dimensions of equality are not, of course, a goal in themselves. They represent operationally defined spheres of man's positive freedom in contemporary conditions of production. Socialism is both desirable and historically necessary, for it represents an essential broadening of individual freedom. That is why self-management autonomy is the essential definition of socialism.

In this paper I shall be concerned with only the first two (economic) dimensions of socialism. I shall examine the simplest institutional model which makes it possible to satisfy the postulates of producer and consumer equality.

Types of linkages in coordinating the economy

Every economic system – precisely because it is a system – achieves a certain coordination of the activities of economic decision-makers. This coordination can be accomplished by various types of linkages. In fact, economic systems can also be classified according to the dominant type of link by which the coordination of economic activity is achieved.

1 Historically, the first form of economic coordination was the *laissez-faire market*. The free market served as the means for integrating the earlier fragmented feudal economy into a unified national economy. In principle the state is outside the economy and its role is to protect property and permit unlimited private initiative. Since one can sell only what someone wishes to buy, everyone who wants to make a profit must orient his activity so that he satisfies social needs as well as possible. It is from such reasoning that Adam Smith drew his theory of the *invisible hand*: motivated exclusively by their personal interests, private producers nevertheless produce in the social interest, for they produce precisely those commodities that are necessary, at the lowest costs of production.

2 The 'invisible hand' did not prove to be especially efficient. Periodic crises of overproduction and unemployment alternated for an entire century and a half. Growth was relatively slow (about 2 per cent annually, compared to the world average today of 5 and 10 per cent in the most rapidly growing contemporary economies). In addition, monetarily effective demand is not identical with social demand – in fact, it can greatly differ from social needs. Consequently, the socialist critics of the capitalist market oriented themselves toward the *visible hand* as the instrument of coordination. State initiative replaced private initiative, and *central planning* replaced the market.

3 The great economic crisis at the beginning of the 1930s brought the capitalist type of economic coordination to the verge of complete collapse. Central planning and expropriation of private property were obviously not acceptable alternatives in the capitalist countries. Besides, central planning had severe defects when conceived and implemented as administrative planning. An escape was found by introducing the state only partially into the economy, as an organ of *economic policy*. We may call this solution the *indirect hand*.

4 The development of economic statistics, economic analysis and the technology of gathering and distributing information enabled economic decision-makers to obtain incomparably more relevant information than hitherto. The more the market represented an information system, the more this technological progress represented a perfecting of the market. This improvement had two aspects: up-to-date and comprehensive economic statistics offer economic decision-makers complete information about the economic situation without delay (whereas the old market gave partial information belatedly); and modern forecasting methods permit

the reduction of uncertainty about future events, and thereby the earlier *ex-post* decisions are elevated into *ex-ante* decisions. Both mean that economic decision-makers obtain a rather complete collection of the parameters important in making correct decisions, i.e. those that will lead to the production of precisely those commodities which can be sold. We can call such improvement of the operation of the market by *organized informing* of economic decision-makers the improvement of the 'invisible hand'.

5 Finally, the 'visible hand' can also be improved. *Agreement, consultation* and *arbitration* constitute a non-market means of coordination which, however, is different from administrative orders of the state.

These five types of economic coordination – *laissez-faire*, administrative planning, economic policy, production of information, nonmarket-nonadministrative coordination – developed historically in the order just cited. But historical sequence does not mean either hierarchical order or evolution in the biological sense. Individual types are complementary and it is a question of attaining the organizational optimum. Different socio-economic systems allow different degrees of efficiency of economic organization.

Liberal capitalism was based on the free market, which means that *laissez-faire* was the dominant principle of macroeconomic coordination. Administrative planning is the basis for étatism, in which the state bureaucracy replaces individual entrepreneurs as organizers of production. The Keynesian revolution in the theory of economic policy made possible the submission of market instability to the efficient control of the state as an organ of economic policy. Together with the creation of state (public) corporations and the ever-greater use of *ex-post* and *ex-ante* information systems, this led to the so-called *mixed economies* (or 'welfare states') characteristic of the contemporary highly developed capitalist countries. Finally, a *socialist economy* should be characterized by optimal use of all five types of linkages in order to maximize the welfare of the members of the social community.

The federation

An economic system consists of a certain number of subsystems that are in constant interaction. For the purposes of this work we shall distinguish four basic subsystems with precisely defined functions. These are: (a) the federation, (b) the republic, (c) the community, and (d) the enterprise (work organization). However, I will consider only three of the subsystems because I do not know the fourth, the community, adequately.

The federation's task is to integrate the work of the subsystems and thus to ensure the aggregate functioning of the entire system. In the economic sense, this task reduces to permanently solving the following three components: (a) equalizing conditions of economic activity; (b) achieving short-run equilibrium; and (c) achieving long-run equilibrium. Task (a) means creation of the preconditions for distribution according to work, (b) means eliminating cyclical fluctuations, and (c) means attaining the maximum rate of economic growth.

All three tasks require making uniform decisions for the entire economic territory of the country. Consequently, in this context the 'federation' represents a synonym for making uniform, or centralized, or general social decisions. But the uniformity of decisions does not predetermine the way in which they are made, which depends on the political system and organizational solutions. That way can be autocratic, oligarchic, or democratic and participative. In particular, the federation, as I define it, is *not* identical with the federal government, nor are centralized decisions with official arbitrariness (which is in large measure characteristic of Yugoslav practice, because of which sharp reactions occurred). What is more, it is desirable, whenever possible, to exclude the state from federal economic regulation, or at least to limit it as much as possible. It can be established as a general organizational principle (a) that in making decisions the relevant interests must be directly represented; and (b) that the decision-maker must bear full moral-political responsibility for carrying out decisions.

In considering an institutional model of the federation, we can again conform to the historical order of the appearance of coordinating links. We proceed from the complete autonomy of the enterprise in the free market and a state that stands outside the economy and concerns itself exclusively with public administration. Since the market is inherently unstable, regulation is necessary, which is the concern primarily (but not exclusively) of the state. Hence the state establishes a certain number of its organs that specialize in various aspects of economic policy. These organs are connected by administrative political links and are obliged to execute the directives of the political center. How that center ought to look (the government, legislature, presidency, etc.), and how it should make decisions, is a matter for political science and lies outside the framework of this discussion. It is sufficient to state that such a center exists, so that we may move on to the analysis of the regulation that should be accomplished.

The social plan represents the basic social agreement in the area of the economy. Once the plan is accepted, it becomes an *obligation* for governmental bodies. The plan is not an obligation for enterprises, which should retain full independence and freedom in determining their actions.

The theses just presented once appeared – and to many appear also today – contradictory. Hence a dilemma was and is talked about: plan or market. But that is a false dilemma. The market is only one – and until now the most efficient – of the planning mechanisms, and the plan is the precondition for the proper functioning of the market. Contemporary economic theory, quantitative analysis, and information technology make it possible for planning forecasts to be essentially more efficient than *ex-post* market solutions and for planning goals to be reached by non-administrative methods, along with the full autonomy of enterprises. In this context, the state political center emerges as the source of regulatory impulses which reflect the constant, previously anticipated rules of the market. On that basis economic decision-makers obtain reliable parameters for their decisions and, seeking to maximize their incomes, carry out the intentions of the plan by their own initiative. In that way the plan and its adequate fulfillment represent the necessary condition for the autonomy of enterprises. Since only federal (i.e. central, or general social, or nationally uniform) regulation can achieve this, this is a necessary condition of self-management. In a situation in which the plans or economic policy or both are inexpertly formulated, in which the rules of economic activity are constantly changed, in which the obligations of the state are not performed, the economy is extremely unstable and uncertainty in decision-making is extreme – all of which are characteristic of the contemporary Yugoslav economy; the business success of enterprises depends more on chance, the force of circumstances, speculative activities, or arbitrary decisions by the state than on productive contribution. When one's position does not depend on one's own work, then only the form of self-management remains. In essence it disappears, and this arouses massive frustrations and the false sense that 'self-management is responsible for the disorder in the economy'.

The federal government establishes *economic ministries* to carry out economic policy measures. In a market economy, one segment of the market – the money market – has special significance, and a separate institution, the *National Bank*, which has a certain degree of independence from the ministries, is founded for its control. The National Bank regulates the functioning of the system of commercial banks, which enter directly into the market, by means of the instruments available to it. (See Horvat, 1971.) The lawfulness of the activity of enterprises and institutions is controlled most simply by the control of money flows. This function is performed by the *Social Accounting Service*, which alone among the federal institutions we have considered establishes direct administrative contact with economic decision-making units. This contact occurs because of the SAS's character as inspector; hence this administrative contact does not represent command, but rather verification. Simultaneously, the SAS is an exceptionally important source of information about monetary flows.

The market would still not function well with the cited bodies. The economy is constantly subjected to certain shocks that create disturbances which individual enterprises and their associations are not able to eliminate. Consequently, general social, i.e. federal, intervention is again necessary, the most suitable form of which is interventional funds.[2] The *Office for Agricultural Raw Materials* smoothes out fluctuations in the supply of agricultural products by means of its reserves. In addition, it conducts a program of protective and guaranteed minimum prices for agricultural products, by which stable and equalized conditions of economic activity are created for farmers (who currently represent about half the Yugoslav labor force) in spite of the extreme instability of production (which in Yugoslavia fluctuates in the interval of plus or minus 20 per cent). The *Office for Industrial Raw Materials* has a similar task, except that in this case it must eliminate disturbances that arise because of fluctuations of prices and supply conditions on the world market. Both Offices function as compensatory funds. Once the regulations of these funds are determined and several principles adopted, all the rest is for the most part routine work. Both Offices have functioned well until now, and hence there have been no objections to their work – if delays in making decisions, for which political bodies and not the Offices bear responsibility, are excepted.

The work of the third interventionary fund, the *Fund for Exports*, is much more delicate. Here the possibilities of favoritism, discrimination, and arbitrariness are much greater, and it is therefore necessary to work out the organization of this fund's management very carefully. However, the necessity of the fund's existence is undisputed. Yugoslavia already exports a fifth of its production, and that percentage must be further increased. Expansion of exports represents the main constraint on the acceleration of the economy's growth. The world market is under the control of mammoth multinational corporations,[3] international cartels, and state and intergovernmental organizations. Under such conditions, Yugoslav exporters can emerge as equal partners only if they are supported by the concentrated economic power of the entire Yugoslav economy and the political power of their government.

In order for the system described to function well, one more institution is needed to eliminate the possibility of abuses by monopolies – whether state bodies or individual enterprises – which inevitably occur in the market. This institution is the *Arbitration Board for Incomes and Prices*,

2 For an analysis of interventional funds as well as of various policies which the federation can employ, see Horvat *et al.* (1971).
3 The largest of them, General Motors, has a larger annual turnover than the gross national products of every country of the world except the twelve largest.

which upon the demand of interested parties will decide on proper incomes and prices. The Arbitration Board functions like the Constitutional Court and is composed of representatives of the economy, trade unions, institutions of higher learning and the government, who are appointed by the Parliament for a limited period and whose decisions are definitive and binding on all, including the government. The Arbitration Board is the guarantee that government bodies will in fact act to equalize the conditions of economic activity. If the government adopts measures which discriminate against some industry, that industry will turn to the Arbitration Board, which will make an estimate of the damages. If policies applied in the market put an industry in an unfavorable position, and the government does not undertake the necessary corrective measures, the Arbitration Board will determine the facts and designate a deadline for resolving the problem. The Arbitration Board is also a suitable body for determining the level of compensation. If the government has to carry out some important but unpopular measures, it can seek the prior judgment of the Arbitration Board, and with its consent can overcome the resistance of privileged groups much more effectively than at present. The Arbitration Board will determine the level of protective and guaranteed minimum prices in agriculture and representative income differentials according to qualifications. In short, arbitration will make it possible to avoid political pressures, unprincipled compromises and irresponsible decisions, which occur when the solution of the cited problems is left exclusively to government bodies. The Arbitration Board will rely in its work on an expert body like the present Price Bureau.

From all that we know about the contemporary market economy in general, and the Yugoslav one in particular, the battery of institutions just described would allow for the irreproachable stabilization of the market. But economic growth would be slow. To accelerate economic growth it is necessary to carry out *ex-ante* harmonizing of economic decisions to use science to the maximum in developing modern technology and in managing the economy (and society), and to ensure the necessary proportions in productive capacities, both regionally and according to individual industries. The latter is technically the easiest to do, but it has been the most politically abused and today evokes resistance to the point of complete prevention of its use. We begin, therefore, with the problem of harmonizing the structure of investments.

A large part of investment has an activization period of under two years. If, therefore, some plants are not built on time and the economy is growing slowly, the insufficiency of supply will be covered without great difficulty by increased imports. However, for construction of a large hydroelectric power plant or steel mill, or for the opening of a sizeable mine, five to seven, or even more, years are necessary. In addition, for such projects and for the transportation network large investment funds are needed. If the funds are not assured on time, if construction is not begun on time, and if the economy is growing rapidly, there will appear such disproportions in the material balance of the country that the balance of payments will be unable to bear them and the unavoidable result will be powerful inflationary pressure along with a slowing down of growth. Still other very negative consequences will follow. On the one hand, the lack of large concentrations of capital will lead to the construction of atomized, unprofitable plants. On the other hand, attempts to achieve sufficiently large concentrations of capital will lead to the formation of production and financial monopolies outside of social control. All these phenomena are well known in Yugoslav experience.

A solution should be sought in the formation of an *Interventionary Investment Fund*, whose task would be (a) to participate in financing those projects that require an exceptionally large concentration of capital and/or long period of construction; and (b) to intervene in eliminating disproportions in capacity – at the moment the best illustration of such a case is the two million deficit in production of cement that was once permanently on the list of exports – whenever for any reason the market does not sufficiently succeed in balancing supply and demand. Investments also have their regional aspect. Economic growth can always be accelerated if pockets of insufficiently employed human and natural resources are eliminated, or in other words if the development of the underdeveloped regions is accelerated. This aim is served by the Fund for the Insufficiently Developed Regions, which, however, should not be a mere redistributor of funds collected by taxation, but which should function like the corresponding international institutions for economic development. It is hardly necessary to mention that this fund has a purely social function besides its economic one; economic equality is impossible in conditions of excessive differences in the degree of economic development, and therefore these differences should be reduced as fast as possible.

The *Federal Bureau for Economic Planning* is responsible for *ex-ante* coordination of economic decisions. Its function is primarily informational. The federal government has two factories of information: the *Federal Bureau of Statistics*, which produces information about the past, and the *Planning Bureau*, which produces information about the future.

It is unnecessary to emphasize separately the role of science in a modern economy. The central government – as well as all other bodies – should directly rely in its work on the work of scientific institutes. A *Council of Economic Advisers*, composed of outstanding economists, could play an exceptionally important role in introducing science into the formation of economic policy. A *Bureau of Programming Scientific Research*, together with a corresponding fund, would ensure an orientation toward those types of research which from the standpoint of the country are most fruitful.

The list of federal institutions is thus exhausted. The economy, on its side, also creates some institutions which fill the gap between the market and the federal political center. These are first of all *cooperative chains*, which represent market subsystems and which lead to a more lasting structuring of the market. Then there are *business associations* with the usual integrative functions. The tasks of *chambers of commerce* are to harmonize the interests of industries and to influence current economic policy as a representative of the economy in consultations with the government. Finally, 'industries' in my scheme represent a particular type of business association, whose task is the integration of certain functions along with the preservation of the individuality of enterprises. It is obvious, that is, that a modern economy does not tolerate atomization and demands integration. It is also obvious that integration by means of administrative merger means the creation of large concentrations of economic power, the creation of monopolies and the liquidation of self-management. Therefore, I see a solution in enterprises preserving their business independence and integrating only those two functions for which direct coordination is essential: (a) basic research and development work, which is the precondition for constant modernization of technology in all the areas of the given industry, and (b) forecasting supply and demand and effective entry into the domestic and foreign market. With regard to (a), the development bureaus of industries are directly linked to the Bureau for Programming Scientific Research; with regard to (b), the planning and analysis bureaus of the industries are linked to the Federal Planning Bureau.[4] These links are informational and consultative, enabling all parties to be fully informed and to continually harmonize the majority of decisions or uncover areas of disagreement. With respect to the latter, the chambers of commerce and executive state bodies undertake the task of finding a satisfactory solution. In that way the system of permanent planning is completed.

The republic

Once we have defined socialism in the sense of self-management, that definition implies maximum decentralization from the organizational point of view. Maximum decentralization means that, in principle, decision-making is carried out on a lower level and that only those

4 It would probably be most consistent to form industry economic–technical bureaus, which would perform the two cited functions. The precondition for good performance of these functions is financial independence.

decisions are reserved to a higher level which otherwise would lead to damage to the interests of some individuals or groups by other individuals or groups. Honoring that principle, entire areas of decision-making should be brought down below the level of the federation. This demands territorial decentralization, which again should be carried out not only in harmony with types of decisions but also by taking into account historical development, cultural heritage, and tradition. In a multinational state, it is natural for such territorial decentralization to be implemented by forming national republics.[5]

A republic is also a state, and therefore the republican political center has a structure similar to the federal one. With respect to specific state affairs, there is a division of labor between the republic and the federation, in the sense that the federation is primarily responsible for foreign relations (foreign affairs and national defense) while the republic is responsible for domestic affairs (justice and public order).

Since the majority of federal institutions in the sphere of the economy are engaged in equalizing the conditions of economic activity and stabilizing the market – which can be achieved for the country as a whole, assuming a unified market, only by centralized decision-making – the republic is freed of these activities, with the result that its institutional structure in the sphere of the economy is much simpler. In the area of economic development, the basic task of the republic is to achieve even development over its territory. An *Interventionary Investment Fund* serves this purpose. The republic can also hasten the development of the economy in its territory to a certain extent by attracting investors from other areas and from abroad by tax exemptions and favorable treatment (by solving communal problems, training labor and participation in loans).

In the area of market stabilization, the republic can intervene by creating a *Mutual Reserve Fund*, which is used to cover losses and reorganize unprofitable enterprises. It would be necessary, however, not to stop at redistribution of funds, but to form alongside the funds personnel exchanges, or special bureaus for business organization, which would function by offering the struggling enterprise complete financial, technical, and personnel aid, including replacement of the entire management.

While the function of the republic in the sphere of the economy is in the nature of things relatively modest, it is basic in the sphere of nonproductive services. Consequently, only councils which have the role of informative-coordinating bodies remain for the federal level. Republican bodies formulate and carry out policy in the fields of education, culture,

5 In this work a general institutional model of a socialist economy is examined, along with suitable illustrations from Yugoslav practice. In a specifically Yugoslav model, besides republics, autonomous provinces should also be considered.

health, etc. The task of the federation, aside from coordination, is only to ensure financially (by supplementary funds from the federal budget) and legislatively certain minimum health and educational standards for the population of the underdeveloped regions.

In an effort to separate the state from the sector of nonproductive services in some way – to avoid the patronage of political forums, which in our conditions have always been a very negative influence – *interest communities* were formed. The Parliament by a political decision allocates funds to individual types of services. Interest communities receive these funds and pay them out, on behalf of consumers, for the services provided by schools, hospitals and museums. This solution, although it has many drawbacks with respect to concrete organization, appears to be correct in principle. These effects are achieved by:

1 Separation of the state from the final users of funds prevents the dictatorship of the administrative-political apparatus in this delicate sphere.

2 Work collectives in the sector of nonproductive services in principle are placed in the same position as work collectives in the productive sector.

3 Replacement of budgetary financing by contractual agreement develops consciousness of the economic aspects of the educational, health, and similar processes and can lead to more efficient use of the available funds.

4 In contrast to the productive sector, where distribution according to work prevails, in consumption of nonproductive services distribution according to needs prevails on the whole. In a socialist society, a young person should be educated and a sick person cured regardless of their property standing. This communist principle of distribution and market stimuli to efficiency in the production of services can be harmonized by the system of interest communities, or quasi-market system.

There are also direct links between the productive and non-productive sectors. At present these links are still very weak and sporadic, consisting of direct purchase of services provided by the nonproductive sector, the founding by enterprises of nonproductive service organizations, participation by the productive sector in the interest communities, and occasional patronage. However, it can be expected that these links will be extended in time, and to the extent that this happens the independence of work collectives providing nonproductive services will be strengthened.

Universities, education, culture and health are of fundamental importance for the life of a people and are of equally fundamental importance for the building of socialism. Technology is the same in all social systems. Equal or differentiated opportunity for education and health protection distinguishes the nonclass from the class society. For this reason, while it is the task of the federation to maintain the good performance of the overall system, the daily task of the republic is to instill socialist content into the system. This conclusion would be still firmer if we had also included the political component in the analysis.

The enterprise

In a more complete treatment it would be worthwhile to analyse the work organization in general. For the purposes of this study, however, I shall limit myself to consideration of the dominant type of work organization, the enterprise, and in relation to the enterprise I shall limit myself to a basic institutional analysis, since I have written more about this elsewhere (Horvat, 1971, part III).

Like the federation and the republic, the enterprise in a self-management society also represents not only an organizational but a political (sub)-system, although *sui generis*. This political component is so essential that failure to comprehend it leads to complete confusion in the institutional foundation of the self-managed enterprise. In fact, the most complete self-management – direct democracy – is possible just in the enterprise.

The basic problem in constructing the organization of the self-managed enterprise is maximizing democracy in making decisions along with maximizing efficiency in carrying them out. In poor organizational solutions, these two goals turn out to be mutually contradictory, which is quite a frequent occurrence in Yugoslav practice. Adequate organizational solutions not only harmonize these two goals but make them complementary – just as effective planning is the precondition of the self-managed autonomy of enterprises in the socioeconomic macrosystem.

It is important to determine as precisely as possible what is understood by maximizing democracy and efficiency. At first glance it might appear that maximizing democracy ought to mean that the opinion of each member of the collective has a weight in making relevant decisions that is determined exclusively by the objective value of that opinion, and that is therefore independent of the personality that has presented it. It is obvious that in this case maximal democracy and maximal efficiency would coincide. But reality rarely permits redundancies of abstract reasoning, and that holds also in this case. In practice, that is, these two questions are immediately posed:

1 Who will judge the objective value of some position?

2 What is the objective value of value judgements?

The answer to these two questions should be sought in the determination of the extent of democracy by the *way* in which decisions are made, and not by the *quality* of the decisions. Then democracy and efficiency are not only not identical, but it is obvious that there exists the possibility of conflict.

Maximal democracy is attained in a collective of one member. With the rise in the number of codecision-makers, the democracy of decision-making is reduced, for each individual opinion is limited by the opinions of all the others. In addition, there is always the possibility, often used, of manipulating opinions, of forming coalitions and cliques – in short, of deforming the 'true' opinion of the group. The majority's decision is not necessarily the best decision, for even in ideal conditions it can represent the outvoting of someone's legitimate minority interest. Accordingly, the first principle in the organization of a self-managed enterprise will be the *creation of sufficiently small and sufficiently homogeneous work groups*, which allow direct participation of all the members in making decisions and where decisions are sufficiently transparent. Homogeneity reduces the possibility of forming a majority on the basis of minority interests, and participation and transparency reduce the possibility of manipulation and the imposition of opinions. This is, after all, the explanation for the formation of work (economic) units in our enterprises. A system of decision-making with the cited characteristics is called polyarchy, in contrast to democracy where decision-making is by a majority regardless of the implications.

Maximal efficiency means (a) the making of correct decisions and (b) their efficient implementation. From that follow the next two organizational principles:

1 *The bodies or individuals who make decisions bear responsibility for them,* which is ensured by suitable sanctions;

2 *Execution of decisions is a matter of expertise and not democracy.*

The separation of responsibility from decision-making – which is characteristic of our entire present social organization – necessarily leads to irresponsibility, to inefficiency and, as a consequence, to the negation of self-management. Execution of decisions requires the possession of special knowledge and specialization in the social division of labor, and therefore can be entrusted only to those who fulfill these conditions. Thus, principle 2 implies the next organizational principle:

3 *Separation of the value, interest sphere from the sphere of expertise; of political authority from professional authority; of decisions about policy from the field of administration.*

In the first sphere each has only one vote; in the second, weights depend on the particular expertise which is sought for the given work. The judgement about what spread of personal incomes is desirable depends upon subjective value judgements; the judgement about the suitability of some machine for production of a good depends on expert knowledge. For the former, political polyarchy is relevant; for the latter, expert hierarchy. In practice, difficulties appear in that it is not always possible to separate the political from the professional sphere – in fact, these two spheres often partially coincide; and the possession of special knowledge can be misused for the destruction of polyarchy (and the establishment of oligarchy).

4 A practical solution to this problem lies in *institutionalizing control* over enterprise management. But this control cannot be arrived at – as individual political forums continually advise workers – by including workers in business operations and expert decisions.

This naïvely conceived control in fact means:

1 A reduction of efficiency, because it delays operational decisions and because correct operational decisions require that full working time be devoted to them, and not only sporadic meetings of an hour or two.

2 The illusion and deception that control is exercised, when it is in fact lacking because of inadequate expertise or insufficient information (full information requires full working time); and

3 The irresponsibility of people in the operational apparatus, who obtain without difficulty the cover for each of their dubious actions of self-management bodies entangled in operations.[6]

We shall now apply the above principles to the organization of the self-managed enterprise. Just as Yugoslavia represents a federation of work units, so also the enterprise represents a federation of work units. The analogy goes further, and the member-firms of a large merged enterprise correspond to republics. All decisions that concern the direct daily life and labor of workers – and that do not impinge on the interests of other workers – are made in the work unit with the direct participation of all interested parties. In order to be able to develop effective self-management autonomy, the work unit must coincide with an economic unit. In other countries there have already been developed accounting-organizational systems which make possible relatively great autonomy of economic

6 As an illustration I cite a drastic, but not atypical, case relating to an economic court, which is precisely the institution responsible for protecting norms of business behavior. *Ekonomska politika*, no. 949, 24 May 1971, states: 'The District Economic Court in Nis paid 16 500 dinars to an enterprise, paying a bill for painting that was not done. The Economic Court later recovered its money by charging an intermediary enterprise for old paper that it did not deliver. Attorneys for the accused former chairman of the District Economic Court in Nis said that in the given situation the Court resorted to a way of coping used by other enterprises and institutions to obtain funds – and the District Court in Nis freed the former chairman of the Economic Court of this complaint, for the actions with the imaginary painting and the imaginary paper were approved by the Workers' Council.'

units with the objective of improving the efficiency of the entire enterprise.[7]

Work units join together in the enterprise, work groups in the *collective*, and the collective makes some exceptionally important decisions of interest to all members by means of a referendum. The chairmen of work units enter into the *workers' council*. The other elected members of the workers' council become the chairmen of various committees or of the Supervisory Board. In that way *every member of the workers' council is personally responsible for a sector of work*. He periodically presents a report on his work, just as the entire workers' council periodically presents an accounting to the collective. The workers' council makes decisions on the basis of proposals of *committees*. The *Executive Board* is also one of the committees of the workers' council, the committee responsible for operations. The workers' council, on the basis of the director's nominations, appoints the Executive Board, consisting of specialists for individual aspects of business operations. The heads of economic units enter into the Executive Board. In that way, work units are represented in the worker's council by a political line, and in the Executive Board by an expert-organizational line. A procedure can be envisioned whereby the managers of a work unit are elected on the basis of an agreement between the director and that work unit.

A collective rather than individual management is probably more suitable for the self-managed enterprise. In order for that management to be able to function efficiently, its members must be mutually compatible. Hence the need to treat the director as the mandator for the composition of the Executive Board. The Executive Board periodically submits reports on business activity to the workers' council. At the end of the year it submits an exhaustive report on business in the course of the year to the workers' council and the collective. If that report is not accepted, this means a vote of no confidence, and the Executive Board automatically resigns, the workers' council elects a new director, and the latter proposes a new Executive Board. If everything is all right, the Executive Board proposes a program of work for the forthcoming year (or years). Once that program – with possible modifications – is accepted, this means *that the Executive Board has a free hand to carry it out and the workers' council is obliged to provide full support in its implementation*. The workers' council can replace the director – and thus the entire Executive Board – but it cannot interfere in the operational implementation of a program once adopted (except, of course, with the consent of the Executive Board), for the Executive Board bears full responsibility for operations, and therefore must have full freedom of action.

7 Gudman Leman (1967) gave a comparative analysis of the solutions of Yugoslav enterprises and German accounting theory.

Since the Executive Board can abuse its authorization, or since doubts (justified or unjustified) can appear concerning the correctness of individual decisions, institutional control is necessary. This function cannot be performed by the workers' council, for its members do not have all the necessary current information or the necessary knowledge. Hence the workers' council forms its *Supervisory Board*, which checks business operations quarterly and reacts to all complaints or warnings in that sphere. At the end of the year the Supervisory Board engages a specialized consulting firm to audit the entire business, and on the basis of the audit findings submits its report to the workers' council. *Without this report the annual report of the Executive Board cannot be accepted.*

The work units and various committees enable every worker to participate directly in management if he wishes. In addition, the committees make possible a certain combination of expertise and democracy. Committee chairmen are rotated periodically, for they must be members of the workers' council. However, there is no reason whatever for not re-electing committee members who carry out their work well. Thus it will happen that people with relatively modest formal qualifications, who have spent several years in the committee for income distribution or the committee for development, and so forth, will acquire valuable experience that will enable them to propose mature and effective measures to the workers' council.

The interaction of the workers' council and the Executive Board transforms political directives into professional, and value judgements into expert, administration. Directives begin in the work units and end in the work units. In that way the open hierarchical pyramid of a capitalist or étatist enterprise is replaced by the closed organizational structure of a self-managed enterprise. The closed form of the organizational structure together with the mechanism for transformation of political decisions into professional ones is precisely the *differentia specifica* of a self-managed organization.

References

HORVAT, B. (1964), *Towards a Theory of Planned Economy*, International Arts and Sciences Press, New York, ch. 6.

HORVAT, B. (1968), *Ekonomska nauka i narodna privreda*, Naprijed, Zagreb, ch. 8.

HORVAT, B. (1969), *An Essay on Yugoslav Society*, International Arts and Sciences Press, New York.

HORVAT, B. (1971), 'Yugoslav economic policy in the post-war period: problems, ideas, institutional developments', *Amer. econ. Rev.*, pp. 136–7.

HORVAT, B. *et al.* (1971), *Ekonomske funkcije federacije*, Institute of Economic Studies, Belgrade.

LEMAN, G. (1967), *Stellung und Aufgabung der ökonomischen Einheiten in den Jugoslawischen Unternehmungen*, Berlin.

10 D. Ellerman

Capitalism and Workers' Self-Management

D. Ellerman, 'Capitalism and Workers' Self-Management', in G. Hunnius, G. D. Garson, and J. Case (eds.), *Workers' Control: A Reader on Labor and Social Change*, Random House, 1973.

Introduction

The purpose of this essay is to examine the property-theoretic basis of capitalism. What is the moral basis of property? How is property rightfully appropriated? Certainly chattel-slavery violated inalienable natural rights. Does capitalism do the same? If so, how can the rights be satisfied?

We will approach these questions with a concrete example. Suppose that a criminally inclined entrepreneur hires a number of people at a fixed wage to rob a bank. Suppose further that he rents a car to escape in and that the car owner is not otherwise involved. The car owner is not a co-conspirator or co-worker with the entrepreneur and his employees. After the crime, the bank robbers are caught. In court, the hired criminals assert that they are just as innocent as the car owner. They inform the judge that they and the car owner are owners of certain services (labor-services in the one case and the services of the car in the other) which they sell as commodities on the market and which will then be used by the buyer. If the buyer uses these services to commit some crime, that is not the fault of the original factor owner.

Naturally the judge would reject this defense and hold that, unlike the car owner, the hired workers were responsible for the crime together with the entrepreneur. Why the distinction? The car owner, like the others, is a moral agent, but he only sold the entrepreneur the services of a natural agent (his car) and he was not involved himself as a moral agent. The hired workers, on the other hand, sold the entrepreneur the services of moral agents, i.e. themselves. The labor contract does not somehow turn the workers into machines like the car which can be used by others and which would have no responsibility for the results of the services provided. Thus the judge would correctly look beyond the superficial labor contract and hold that all those human agents who committed the crime were responsible for it. We might also suppose that, as a last resort, the hired criminals produced another contract they had made with the entrepreneur which 'absolved' them of all responsibility for their actions and 'transferred' it to the entrepreneur. The judge would, no doubt, be unmoved by this final gesture and would point out that their responsibility resulted directly from the fact that they deliberately performed the actions. Moral responsibility for one's actions cannot be 'transferred' or 'alienated' by consent or contract.

All this is rather clear and obvious in the case of hired criminals, but how, from the moral viewpoint, can it be any different in the case of ordinary hired labor? When the employees of an ordinary productive enterprise produce something of net positive value, do they *then* suddenly become like machines which are 'used' by their employers and which have no responsibility for the results of their services? Or is this case of productive hired labor simply the case where the propertied class finds it profitable to treat the workers as if they were such machines by instituting a special capitalist property system which gives the *legal* responsibility for the results of productive labor to the owners of capital?

Property appropriation

The above example makes a number of points which we may now explore at a more abstract and general level. The basic principle used is that people have the moral responsibility for the positive and negative results of their deliberate actions. If certain people act cooperatively as a group, then they have as a group the responsibility for the results of their actions. When their actions result in the creation of material goods, then their responsibility for these goods means, in property-theoretic language, that they rightfully appropriate the goods. If they are responsible for using up or destroying certain goods, then they rightfully are liable for those goods. These are the property-theoretic consequences of their moral responsibility for their actions and thus these rights of appropriation are moral or natural rights. The legal rights assigned to people in a specific legal property system may or may not coincide with their natural rights. In any case, people have the natural right to the results of their actions, i.e. to the assets and liabilities that they create. Furthermore, since these natural property rights result from the agents' moral responsibility, they are inalienable, because moral responsibility cannot be 'transferred' or 'alienated' by consent or contract (as we noted in the example). Of course, material goods that have been rightfully appropriated can then be exchanged or transferred, but it was one's non-transferable responsibility which accounted for one's rightful appropriation of the goods in the first place.

Consider a human enterprise such as an economic firm (or an institution such as a university or a hospital). All who work in the enterprise – be they called 'white-collar', 'blue-collar', 'management', or 'labor' – cooperatively perform the work of the enterprise. The legal role assigned by the legal system to 'employees' does not somehow turn them into automata which are 'used' by their 'employers' and which have no responsibility for their actions. Thus, regardless of the legal superstructure:

1 All those who work in an enterprise have, as a group, the moral responsibility for their productive activities. If they utilize and create material goods, then these material results of their activities can be represented by a list of positive and negative quantities $X = (x_1, x_2, ..., x_n)$, where the positive quantities represent the amounts of the commodities produced and the negative quantities represent the amounts of the commodities used up by the enterprise during a given time period. We will call the list X the *whole product* of the enterprise during the given time period, and the positive quantities will be called the *liabilities incurred*. One must be careful to note that *both* the assets and liabilities created in production are included in the whole product. This whole product is the material result of the productive activities of the workforce in the enterprise. Since they have the moral responsibility for the results of these activities:

2 The workforce has the natural right to appropriate the whole product of production. Furthermore, for the reasons given above, these natural rights are inalienable. If a legal property system is not to violate these moral rights, then it must recognize and guarantee in law: (a) that the workforce in an enterprise has the collective legal responsibility for its productive activities, i.e. that the workers have the right to self-manage their work, and (b) that the workforce in an enterprise has the legal right to appropriate its whole product. This form of production might be called *laborist production, labor-management, or workers' self-management*.[1] If the means of production or any of the material goods used in production are owned by absentee owners (e.g. by the workers who produced intermediate goods or by the community in the case of land and natural resources which are not the products of labor), then the workforce of the enterprise will have to satisfy its prospective liabilities by obtaining the owners' consent. This would usually require the payment of rent, interest, use tax, or simply purchase price.

The natural rights of an enterprise workforce to the self-management of its work and to its whole product are not even recognized, much less guaranteed, in the capitalist property system. The legal rights to the management of production and to the whole product are essential components in the bundle of legal rights called the 'firm'. In the capitalist

1 The property theory sketched here is essentially a development of the classical labor or natural rights theory of property. The labor theory of property was the foundation of the classical libertarian critique of capitalism by Proudhon and the early laborist school of 'Ricardian socialists'. This laborist tradition continued in the cooperativist, guild socialism, and anarcho-syndicalist movements.

system, these legal rights are typically attached directly to capital. In a corporation, the owners of the 'firm' are the owners of the capital assets of the enterprise – the stockholders. These extra 'divine rights of capital' – the rights to management and to the whole product – vastly extend the usual legitimate rights to receive rent or interest for the use of one's capital and they are defining characteristics of the peculiarly capitalist property system.[2]

These natural rights of an enterprise workforce are also not recognized in a state-capitalist or state-socialist system where the government legally appropriates the whole product and manages production. Under state socialism, the workers, far from being self-managing producers, are essentially changed from being privately owned commodities rented on the labor market to being socially owned resources drafted into the industrial army. Many socialists seem to implicitly accept the capitalist principle that the legal rights to the management of production and to the whole product are correctly attached to the ownership of the means of production. They are only against the '*private* ownership of the means of production'. This form of left-wing statism is against both the private management of an enterprise by capital and the private self-management of an enterprise by the people who work in it.

Professor Jaroslav Vanek, in his excellent book *The General Theory of Labor-Managed Market Economies* (1970), correctly isolates the capitalist principle that is shared by state socialists. He shows the inadequacy of the usual 'spectrum' of 'possible economic systems', where they are classified according to the degree of state intervention, but where they all assume the capitalist principle.

It is interesting to note that the almost universally accepted principle is that the right to manage – or more broadly, to control – an economic enterprise derives from the ownership of the capital assets used by the enterprise. The principle is equally applicable in western capitalism where the owners are private individuals; in Soviet-type socialist countries where the owner is society, or more operationally the state; and even in many traditional producer cooperatives where control has been linked to shares of joint ownership of the participants. The principle of labor management is entirely different, not having anything to do with ownership of productive assets. Rather, it postulates that in a productive activity where a

2 Analogous remarks apply to non-profit institutions. For instance, the legal rights to the management of a university are typically attached to those who have trusteeship over the capital assets of the university. The natural right of all those who work in a university (i.e. the faculty, students, and staff) to the self-management of their work is not recognized by the legal system. But in spite of these private economic and educational oligarchies based on 'property rights' and 'legal charters', most legal systems now acknowledge the inalienable right of the whole community to the self-management of its *public* affairs.

group of men cooperate in a joint effort, the right to control and manage that effort rests with all the members of the group.

It is important to note that the principle of labor management is in conflict with the principle of control and management by capital, i.e. by the owners of capital – but not with the principles of private or social ownership of productive assets. Capital assets still can be owned by individuals or anybody else outside the enterprise, but the owners cannot decide on the complex of human activities which constitute the production. The owners can only expect an adequate compensation for the use of the assets, established through market forces or in any other manner (pp. 4–5).

Capitalism and chattel-slavery

In order to elucidate the relationship between the systems of capitalism and chattel-slavery, we will present a parallel analysis for their deliberate actions. As they have this responsibility, it is their natural right to make their own decisions. This is the person's natural right to individual self-management and self-determination. As this moral responsibility cannot be 'transferred' by consent or contract, the right is inalienable. A legal system can violate peoples' inalienable rights in two ways, i.e. by not recognizing them at all and by recognizing them only as alienable rights. Chattel-slavery involved both violations since certain peoples' natural rights were not recognized at all – much less guaranteed: they were legal chattel. The legal rights to own and govern this chattel were not even initially held by the slaves but by other persons who had satisfied certain legal prerequisites. This was the historical case of involuntary chattel slavery.

A more illuminating case, from the theoretical viewpoint, would be a system of voluntary chattel-slavery. In such a system, certain individuals' right to self-determination would be recognized only as an alienable right. By undertaking a certain voluntary legal performance, e.g. by voluntarily signing a certain 'chattelhood contract', one could for a specified period of time extinguish one's legal agency and become, in the eyes of the law, a chattel under the government of another person. One should, of course, distinguish this sort of 'contract' from an ordinary contract wherein one does not give up one's legal personality but chooses to bind oneself to exercise it in a particular fashion. As noted before, such 'contracts' which would purport to 'transfer' inalienable rights would be moral nonsense. The signing of contracts, the solemn pronouncements of judges and the establishment of an entire legal superstructure to enforce the extinction of the slave's legal personality would not change the reality of the slave's moral agency, i.e. his capacity for moral responsibility. A person is not somehow changed into a brute beast even though he may voluntarily enter into such concocted 'chattelhood contracts'. Of course, there can be social systems in which a certain segment of the population is maintained in such a state that they will voluntarily enter into that type of 'contract'. However, these 'contracts' would provide no more of a sufficient moral reason for a legal system to extinguish their legal personality than would the color of their skin. Chattel-slavery, voluntary or involuntary, constitutes a legally sanctioned institutionalization of kidnapping and murder – not the murder of biological individuals but the annihilation and transformation of legal persons into legal chattel.

The capitalist property system is entirely parallel. It does to 'labor' (i.e. to the workforce of each enterprise during its time of productive work) what involuntary chattel-slavery did to certain persons. The capitalist property system does not recognize even as alienable rights the workforce's natural rights to the self-management of its work and to the ownership of the whole product, and much less does it guarantee them as inalienable rights. The corresponding legal rights are not attached to the workforce in an enterprise and they may be acquired by anybody who has satisfied certain legal prerequisites (e.g. the acquisition of corporate stock). Since these legal rights are not attached, even initially, to labor, labor enters a productive enterprise on a par with the productive services provided by machines and animals, i.e. as a 'productive service' sold to the owners of the whole product by the 'factor owners'. Thus labor becomes legally a commodity – a marketable productive service – just as the slave was legally a chattel. The wage contract sets the terms of the market transactions in the commodity 'labor', just as the contracts on the slave market set the terms of the traffic in persons.

'But,' it will be protested, 'the worker is a free man who sells his own labor by voluntary contract whereas the slave is owned and sold by others against his will.' Yes, capitalism and chattel-slavery are not identical. The essential difference derives from the fact that *all* the natural rights of the slave were legally denied. His whole person was thus considered legal chattel and he had no residual legal personality eligible to own that chattel. Thus slaves were legally owned and sold by *other* persons. However, in the case of the workers in a capitalist enterprise, it is only their natural rights resulting from their work which are legally denied, so it is only their labor that thus becomes a legal commodity (and not their whole person). They can maintain a residual legal personality as a 'factor owner' of their labor-commodity (and, of course, as a consumer and a citizen). The two legal roles of 'commodity-owner' and 'commodity', which were of necessity held by different people under chattel-slavery, are played by the same person under capitalism.

This difference between the systems has had enormous apologetic and obfuscatory consequences. It is a veritable mainstay of capitalist thought (not to mention so-called 'right-wing libertarianism') that the moral flaws of chattel-slavery have not survived in capitalism since the workers, unlike the slaves, are free people making voluntary wage contracts. But it is only that, in the case of capitalism, the denial of natural rights is less complete so that the worker has a residual legal personality as a free 'commodity-owner'. He is thus allowed to voluntarily put his own working life to traffic. When a robber denies another person's right to make an infinite number of other choices besides losing his money or his life and the denial is backed up by a gun, then this is clearly robbery even though it might be said that the victim is making a 'voluntary choice' between his remaining options. However, when the legal system itself denies the natural rights of working people in the name of the prerogatives of capital and the denial is sanctioned by the legal violence of the state, then the theorists of 'libertarian' capitalism do not proclaim institutional robbery, but rather they celebrate the 'natural liberty' of working people to choose between the remaining options of selling their labor as a commodity or being unemployed.

As before, we can hypothetically consider a voluntary form of the institution. In 'voluntary capitalism', the natural rights of the workforce in each enterprise to the self-management of its work and to its whole product would be legally recognized, but only as alienable rights. These rights would not be attached to capital at the outset, and capital would have to depend on its bargaining power to transfer these rights in its direction. The legal transfer would be accomplished by means of a new 'commodity-hood contract' (analogous to the previously considered 'chattelhood contract'). As in the case of voluntary chattel-slavery, this 'contract' would annihilate the legal personality of the party in question, which in this case is the workforce of the enterprise. The legal agency of the enterprise work-community would be extinguished and they would be transformed, in the eyes of the law, into an assemblage of 'commodity-owners' who sell their labor-commodity to the new owners of the 'firm'. Such a 'commodity contract' is quite different from an ordinary contract. When a self-managing workforce made an ordinary contract, it would not be annihilating its legal agency. Rather the workforce would be choosing to bind itself to *exercising* its self-management rights in the particular fashion specified by the contract. For instance, they might choose to sell part of their future produce to retailers at a specified price as insurance against price fluctuations, or they might contract to produce certain goods in a specific 'custom-made' manner.

'Voluntary capitalism', like voluntary chattel-slavery, is a hypothetical system of only theoretical interest. It is of interest because some economists have inexplicably held that a 'commodityhood contract' is 'implied' in the wage contract. It is said rather vaguely that the workers 'give up' their rights to the ownership of the product in exchange for the 'security' of a wage. One is left in the dark as to the identity of these legal rights to the product which the workers are said to 'give up'. This is, to say the least, a rather wilful interpretation of the wage contract since it can hardly be said that the managerial rights of stockholders are 'transferred' to them by labor in the wage contract. However, for the sake of argument, we have considered a hypothetical system of 'genuinely' voluntary capitalism. It, like voluntary chattel-slavery, flounders on the rock of *inalienable* natural rights. The moral agency of human action (whether the agents be productive workers or criminals – as in our first example) cannot be somehow annihilated by a legal performance like the signing of a 'commodityhood contract'. Moral responsibility cannot be alienated by consent or contracts. This being the case, there is no sufficient moral reason for a legal system to recognize and enforce such concocted 'contracts' by annihilating the corresponding legal agency of the one contracting party and by transferring their legal responsibility for their actions to the other party. That is why the rights are inalienable.

As the capitalist property system does not recognize or guarantee the inalienable rights of the workforce to the appropriation of its whole product and to the self-management of its work, the system constitutes a legally sanctioned institutionalization of theft and tyranny (in the workplace). In short, as Proudhon pointed out in his famous passage, slavery is murder and the capitalist property system is theft, 'the second proposition being no other than a transformation of the first'. Chattel-slavery was abolished by recognizing and guaranteeing the inalienable natural right of each person to individual self-determination so that all people became free self-governing agents. Similarly, capitalist production would be abolished by recognizing and guaranteeing the inalienable natural rights of the work-community in each enterprise so that all enterprises would become free associations of self-managing producers.

Capitalist political economy

We can now consider the highpoints of the relevant parts of preclassical, classical and neoclassical capitalist political economy as represented, respectively, by John Locke, John Stuart Mill and John Bates Clark. Locke is often considered the originator of the labor or natural rights theory of property, but that opinion does not stand up under critical scrutiny. The labor theory is a theory of appropriation and Locke did not even have a theory about the creation of property rights. Instead, he assumed an 'original position' of *existing* property rights, with human labor treated as one form of property among others (owned by the agent in the original position), which could then be transferred by voluntary exchange. One could exchange one's labor with Nature for the 'fruits of one's labor', or one could exchange one's labor for a wage so that the new owner could then enjoy the fruits of 'his' labor. Note that this involves the play on words between 'one's labor' in the morally relevant sense of 'one's moral agency', and 'one's labor' in the sense of a commodity that was bought.

Thus, the Grass my Horse has bit; the Turfs my Servant has cut; and the Ore I have digg'd in any place where I have a right to them in common with others, become my *Property*, without the assignation or consent of any body. The *labour* that was mine, removing them out of that common state they were in, hath *fixed* by my *Property* in them (Locke, 1960).

If Locke rents a horse (i.e. buys its services from its owner) and uses these services to produce something, then he has the sole moral responsibility for the results as the horse is not a moral agent at all and the agency of the original owner is not involved. Locke also thinks that he may rent a man (for instance, buy his services from their owner) and that the fruits of these services will be the fruits of the '*labour* that was mine' (Locke's). However, as the man is a moral agent, these fruits are not the result of only Locke's moral agency (unlike the case of the horse). Locke's gambit is to treat human labor as another form of property that can be bought on the market like the services provided by animals and machines and which can be used by others without the original owners incurring any moral responsibility for the results of the services. Locke's gambit is the commoditization of labor. Locke's 'natural right' is the 'natural right' of each person to the original ownership of their labor-commodity.

The classical tradition tried to preserve a rather vague form of the labor theory of property and it is instructive to consider the attempts to reconcile it with capitalism. John Stuart Mill begins with a brief statement of the labor theory: the foundation of property is 'the right of producers to what they themselves have produced', but he immediately sees that there may be difficulty involved in the capitalist property system.

It may be objected, therefore, to the institution as it now exists, that it recognizes rights of property in individuals over things which they have not produced. For example (it may be said), the operatives in a manufactory create, by their labour and skill, the whole produce; yet, instead of its belonging to them, the law gives them only their stipulated hire, and transfers the produce to some one who has merely supplied the funds, without perhaps contributing anything to the work itself, even in the form of superintendence (Mill, 1970, p. 368)

After such a clear statement of the peculiar prerogatives of those who have 'merely supplied the funds', one would expect Mill to give a justification of these specific features. Instead he only argues for the usual right to have something paid for the capital funds and capital goods used in production, i.e. for the 'fruits of previous labour'.

If the labourers were possessed of them, they would not need to divide the produce with any one; but while they have them not, an equivalent must be given to those who have, both for the antecedent labour, and for the abstinence by which the produce of that labour, instead of being expended on indulgences, has been reserved for this use (1970, p. 368).

Although Mill considers this a sufficient 'answer' to the objection, it is inadequate since capitalism is not the system in which laborers appropriate 'what they themselves have produced' and in which they 'need to divide the produce' in order to satisfy the liabilities they have incurred. Instead, capitalism is the system in which '*the law* gives them only their stipulated hire, and *transfers* the produce to some one who has merely supplied the funds' (italics added). Mill does not attempt to justify these peculiar prerogatives of capital which are quite additional to the usual right to receive interest, and which are given to capital by 'the law' in the capitalist property system.

Mill's strategy is to misrepresent the laborist argument as holding that the laborers should receive as *net* income the total revenues from the assets produced and should somehow not also be responsible for the liabilities incurred in production. Hence he can 'answer' the laborist straw-man by showing that interest, rent, or purchase price would need to be paid for the funds and goods used in production. But the labor theory implies with perfect symmetry that, for exactly the same reason, labor is also responsible for the costs incurred – the intermediate goods used up – in production and the theory hardly implies that the workers who produced these intermediate goods are supposed to give away their product – the 'fruits of previous labour' – for free. Thus Mill's apology fails and the plain logic of the libertarian principle that natural property rights are created only by labor (and transferred only by voluntary exchange) drives one to the conception of production wherein the workers appropriate 'what they themselves have produced' and wherein they 'need to divide the produce' in order to cover the liabilities they themselves have incurred; the logic drives one to the conception of laborist production. The consistently libertarian economists of Mill's time, such as William Thompson, Thomas Hodgskin and the others in the laborist school, drew essentially that logical conclusion.

The modern neoclassical treatment of the difficulties involved in the capitalist property system is very simple and yet quite sophisticated. Basically the idea is to completely *evade* property-theoretic questions in favor of concentrating solely on price-theoretic questions. There is associated with the whole product list $X = (x_1, ..., x_n)$ the list of product and factor prices $P = (p_1, ..., p_n)$. The property-theoretic part of political economy should consider the question: 'How is and how should the appropriation of the whole product X be determined?' Price theory considers the question: 'How is and how should the magnitude of P be determined?' Orthodox economic theory typically begs the property-theoretic question by assuming the prerogatives of capital and the status of labor as a marketable productive service, and then it concentrates on price theory. But it is the answer to the logically prior ownership question which determines whether labor may be treated as a factor at all – to be bought at a certain price by capital – or whether labor should always take the form of self-managing producers renting or owning the capital they use. Also the orthodox treatment of the problems of 'distribution' does not consider the basic structure of the distributive process as determined by the capitalist property system (i.e. who appropriates the whole product and controls industry, and thus who does the distributing). Instead, capitalist economists treat, in great detail, the 'allocative efficiency' of the price system and, sometimes, they voice individual opinions about the 'equity' of property ownership. Reforms, such as effective progressive taxation, lump-sum redistributions, and a guaranteed minimum income are suggested, which will perturbate the final distribution of ownership, but there is no questioning of the capitalist principle embodied in the basic structure of the distributive process. Property theory is the unopened Pandora's box of capitalist political economy.

While the fundamental strategy of modern capitalist theory is a strategy of evasion of basic property questions (banalities about 'the' private property system notwithstanding), this does not mean that price theory is free of ideological content. John Bates Clark, the American developer of marginal productivity (MP) theory, tried to give an appropriation-theoretic interpretation to the MP theory of factor prices. Clark, like Locke, Mill and many others, wanted to develop a theory which would apologize for capitalism and, at the same time, co-opt the intuitive moral force of the labor theory of appropriation. Clark's ploy was to take the labor theory and for 'moral agent' substitute 'productive agent' (anything that is causally efficacious in production – moral agents *and* natural agents such as machines, animals and raw materials), for 'responsibility' substitute 'productivity' (causal efficacy), and for 'actions by moral agents' (labor) substitute 'productive services of productive agents'. Clark assumed, of course, that the whole product was appropriated by capital (not to mention the status of labor as a commodity) and then he interpreted the factor payments made to the owners of the productive agents as their appropriation of their contribution (as measured by the productivity of the services they sell). The factor owners would be paid according to the principle: 'to each what he [sic] creates'. It is the 'natural law of distribution'. This theory has now become a solid part of the 'conventional wisdom' or 'folklore' engendered by capitalist economic theory.

Naturally there are a few difficulties involved in this 'marginal productivity theory of appropriation'. Firstly, not all productive 'agents' are moral agents and it is absurd to attempt to derive normative consequences from the causal efficacy of natural agents, e.g. to impute the blame for a crime to both the criminal and the 'tools of his trade' – to each according to 'his' productivity. The human owner of a natural agent incurs no responsibility if he is not in any other way involved. His ownership only implies that those who are involved in the productive activities are liable to him for the use of his property. Secondly, even if we restrict consideration to the moral agents involved, their responsibility is not determined by their 'marginal productivity'. For instance, criminals cannot avoid all responsibility for their actions by using redundant labor (so that the marginal productivity of their labor would be zero). They share, as a group, the responsibility for the results of their actions and, of course, the same holds for other, more productive, cooperative human activities. Thirdly, the MP theory of appropriation does not answer the ownership question even if it could be given a moderately plausible interpretation. That is, it does not determine who is to be the owner of the whole product and, thus, who is to be the residual claimant. The theory only tries to *paste* an appropriation-theoretic interpretation onto the factor payments made by the owners of the whole product in order to justify the specific magnitudes of the factor prices in the price list P. Evidently the only way that working people can be wronged is to be paid too low a price for their labor-commodity. Aside from the implausibility of the interpretation itself, this is rather like trying to close the 'barn door' after capital has already walked off with the legal rights to the whole product and the management rights over production.

Although Clark's ploy thus fails, he had some awareness of the problem (1899, p. 9):

A plan of living that would force men to leave in their employers' hands anything that by right of creation is theirs would be an institutional robbery – a legally established violation of the principle on which property is supposed to rest.

Quite so, but one should note that even this matter of posing the possibility of institutional robbery maintains the usually ideological subordination to the capitalist principle – it is a matter of how much the workers 'leave in their employers' hands' (Ellerman, 1972).

The dehumanization of labor
One can consider a hypothetical system in which labor has been suitably dehumanized so that the legal treatment of labor as a commodity – a

marketable productive service – would be permissible. In order to do so, we must borrow from science fiction some scheme wherein electrodes would be inserted in the brains of working people so that computers could drive them independently of their volition and cause them to perform their normal tasks. During nonworking hours they would be 'unplugged' so that they could lead their usual lives as consumers, citizens, and labor-sellers. In such a system, human labor would genuinely be devoid of moral agency. Labor would then truly be a commodity, like the services provided by a machine or animal which may be bought from their owners and used by others without the original owners incurring any moral responsibility for the results of the services. Although labor would then be devoid of moral agency, the causal efficacy of these services need not be changed, so the concepts of marginal productivity theory would still be applicable. Since a worker would only be run as a human tool on a part-time basis (during the work hours), he would maintain a residual moral personality as an owner of these labor services, as a consumer, and as a citizen. Since this residual agency is all that the capitalist legal system recognizes in the first place, that legal system would then be adequate. Since the original owners of these labor services would no longer have the moral responsi-bility for their use or the results of their use, the capitalist property system's denial of the rights of labor would then be accurate. The labor-sellers would still, of course, combine into unions to collectively bargain about the wage rate and to set up grievance procedures for the workers who do not like the way their labor was being used. Labor law would scrupulously guard the usual rights of labor-sellers and it would humanely curb abuses of labor by the employers. Philosophers would celebrate the natural right of each individual to the original ownership of his labor services. Slavery would be abolished and each person would exercise his natural liberty to sell his own labor services by voluntary contract to the highest bidder on the labor system.

In short, this system would be the same as normal capitalism, except that it would not violate the humanity of people during their working lives since that humanity would have been eliminated. By so turning working people into part-time human tools (or 'worked people'), labor would be rendered morally safe for capitalism. Since this system, which employs actually dehumanized labor, requires the same institutions as normal capitalism, it shows why normal capitalism is intrinsically dehumanizing. The basic legal and property structure of the actual capitalist system treats working people *as if* they already were such part-time human tools – just as the system of chattel-slavery treated the slaves *as if* they were full-time or complete human tools. That being the case, it is no surprise when the workers in this system feel alienated from their product as if it were not the results of their actions and when they think of their work as if it were just so many hours taken out of their lives. The attempts, by apologetic economists and philosophers, to describe the status of 'free labor' in the capitalist system in terms of the ideals of humanism and libertarianism does not require further comment.

Conclusion

Many persons talk of admitting working-people to a share in the products and profits; but in their minds this participation is pure benevolence: they have never shown – perhaps never suspected – that it was a natural, necessary right, inherent in labor, and inseparable from the function of producer, even in the lowest forms of his work (Proudhon, 1970, p. 112).

These words are as true today as when they were written – two decades before America had even abolished chattel-slavery. Today, a century and a quarter later, we continue to have a flourish of 'new' participation, profit-sharing, and job enrichment programs. These programs may well help to mitigate the dehumanizing impact of capitalist production, just as similar programs might have helped the 'attitude' and 'productivity' of 'maladjusted' and 'alienated' slaves. But most reformers have never realized – 'perhaps never suspected' – that capitalism, like chattel-slavery, *structurally* violates the inalienable natural rights of working people. Chattel-slavery was legalized kidnapping and murder whereas the capitalist property system legalizes theft and tyranny in the workplace. As in the one case, so in the other: the institutional wrongs can only be righted by basic changes in the property system. This requires the abolition of the unnatural prerogatives of capital and the refounding of private property appropriation on the natural basis of labor. It requires that the legal system recognize and guarantee in law the inalienable natural rights of the working people in each enterprise to the self-management of their work and to the appropriation of their whole product. All enterprises would then be free associations of self-managing producers. Then people could have human dignity and sovereignty in their working lives as well as in their lives as consumers and citizens. Then justice would mean more than 'a fair day's wage for a fair day's work'. Then democracy would no longer stop at the factory gates.

References

CLARK, J. (1899), *The Distribution of Wealth*, Macmillan Co., New York.
ELLERMAN, D. (1972), 'Introduction to Normative Property Theory', in *Rev. Radical polit. Econ.*, vol. 4, no. 2, pp. 49–67.
LOCKE, J. (1960), P. Laslett (ed.), *Two Treatises of Government*, Cambridge University Press.
MILL, J. S. (1970), *Principles of Political Economy*, Penguin.
PROUDHON, J. (1970), B. Tucher (trans.), *What is Property?*, Dover.
VANEK, J. (1970), *The General Theory of Labor-Managed Market Economies*, Cornell University Press.

Part Two
Actual Cases

11 G. D. Garson

Recent Developments in Workers' Participation in Europe

Talk prepared for the Seminar Series of the Program on Participation and Labor-Managed Systems, Cornell University, 2 November 1973.

In the late 1960s, Charles Levinson, Secretary-General of the International Federation of Chemical and General Workers' Unions, stated in an OECD report that 'History will record, I believe, that 1968 was the year that industrial democracy advanced to the center of the industrial relations stage' (Levinson, 1969, p. 6). While the movement for workers' participation in management was gaining ground in the late 1960s, employers' organizations mobilized to oppose such democratization, as in the resolution by UNICE of 28 October 1967 (Van Gorcum, 1972, pp. 2-3). More generally, employers sought to define social policy relating to industry as a national matter inappropriate to be dealt with on a European-wide basis (Casserini, 1969, p. 10).

Management resistance has proved inadequate to stem the growing sentiment in favor of work democratization. Since the Second World War, an intergenerational shift in attitudes has occurred, de-emphasizing traditional values like order and security in favor of new emphasis on free speech and participation (Inglehart, 1971). The report of a European management experts' meeting in 1971 stated that 'there can be no doubt that the assumptions as to the attitudes of the work force on which present day industry has been built are becoming less and less valid'. The experts' report went on to warn, 'It may well be that if industry does not make adjustments to accommodate changing attitudes, alienation will increase; it will become more and more difficult to recruit for industrial work; there will be more and more friction in industrial relations and it will be hard, to say the least, to maintain economic growth' (OECD, 1972).

Correspondingly, in recent years union demands have increasingly raised worker control issues, both through collective bargaining and through labor legislative programs. As participation in management has found its way into law, management attitudes have shifted. Formally, UNICE remains opposed to worker participation in managerial decisions. Informally, however, many executives have come to feel some change is inevitable; the question becomes one of embracing an acceptable version of democratic reform. A Conference Board survey (1973) cites, for example, a Swiss executive who 'comments that "it is very likely that some concessions will have to be made"', and a French businessman who states that because of European-wide changes, 'we shall be perhaps induced . . . to extend somewhat French law'.

Worker participation under the law of the European company

A strong inducement to change national laws regarding labor participation in management has come through the effort of the European Economic Community to develop a statute for European companies. Such companies, to be incorporated by the EEC, represent one aspect of the trend toward multinationalism in the world economy (ICFTU, 1971). The draft statute for the European company provides for a 'checks and balances' multi-tier organization: a board of directors or management board (no labor participation), a board of supervisors (partial labor representation), a shareholders' general meeting and a European works council in each enterprise incorporated under EEC authority.

As submitted to the Council of the European Communities on 30 June 1970 (European Commission, 1970), the proposed statute provided for worker representatives constituting one-third of the members of the supervisory board, which appoints and oversees the management board (*Trade Union News from the European Community*, 1970). The International Confederation of Free Trade Unions (ICFTU) objected to this minority, 'watchdog' role assigned to labor and called for an alternative system of one-third labor representatives, one-third employer representatives and one-third selected by agreement of labor and employer delegates. This alternative was endorsed in spring 1973 by the Legal Committee of the European Parliament, although it has yet to be approved at the Commission level (Gundelach, 1973, p. 6).[1]

Even at the one-third representation level, though less than generally demanded by various European unions, labor representation would be greater than attained anywhere in Western Europe outside Germany. In addition, Title V of the draft statute would establish a European works council in each European company and a group works council for European companies which are part of an integrated group. Such a works council would have rights of information and consultation over hiring, firing, seniority, vocational training, health and safety, social facilities, wages, hours, and vacations (*European Community*, 1970b, pp. 4–6). Actual working conditions, however, would be established through collective bargaining with trade unions (Article 146), though the works

1 On 11 April 1973, the Committee on Social Affairs voted to reaffirm the original proposal (one-third labor representation). The European Parliament has yet to vote on the matter; after it does so the Commission will come to a determination.

council may make collective agreements with the management board where these do not conflict with trade union agreements (Article 127.1). Both union and works council collective agreements have priority over agreements made by works councils established under national law (Article 127.2). The works councils would be composed exclusively of worker representatives.

These works councils under national law include German *betriebsrate* (established in 1952), Belgian *ondernemingsraden* and *conseils d'entreprise* (1948), French *comités d'entreprise* (1945), Italian *commissioni interne d'azienda* (1966), Luxembourg's *délégations ouvrières principales* and *délégations d'employés* (1962) and Dutch *ondernemingsraden* (1950), as provided in Article 102. Generally, these organs of worker representation are not changed in functions or powers by the proposed statute of the European company, though they are assigned a key role in the process of election of worker representatives to the European works councils.

Most major European unions have adopted or reaffirmed support for the principle of labor representation on supervisory boards and other levels of corporate decision-making, albeit with criticism of the merely symbolic reform proposals commonly advanced by management and government (Barry-Braunthal, 1972a, b). To press for better labor interest on this and other European-wide issues, attempts began in summer 1971 to join national unions in a European Confederation of Syndicates (CES), a purpose accomplished on 9 February 1973, in a founding convention in Brussels at the 'Maison de Huit Heures', a memorial to the struggle for the eight-hour day (Barry-Braunthal, 1973; Coyle, 1971; *Trade Union News from the European Community*, 1972). Such efforts toward multinational unionism have centered primarily on metalworkers, automobile workers and electronics workers, but internationalism is spreading among virtually every segment of European labor (MCI, 1972). In confronting the multinational corporation, European unions have come to look upon codetermination and labor participation in supervisory boards as a key part of their strategy. As one ICFTU report states, 'The European company will surely be a test case in seeing if it is possible to realize some partial democratization on this supranational level' (Asplund, 1972, p. 63).

However, as Brian Childs (1973, p. 4) has noted, the unions' 'conditional acceptance of worker participation goes no further than the Eurocompany. . . . The non-Communist unions' fundamentally positive attitude does not filter through to their stand on participation at other levels. They regard the Eurocompany as an exception that has nothing to do with management–worker relations at the national level.' Childs noted Belgian union support for workers' control, Italian and French unions dropping their support for codetermination, and the fact that even the Christian unions, in their last congress, placed comanagement in the context of progress toward worker control. Although there is some unity among non-Communist unions in supporting participation in the European company, the complex attitudes of various European unions toward worker participation and workers' control must be discussed on a country-by-country basis.

West Germany

The West German model of 'codetermination' has provided the most influential European model of worker participation to date, though radical demands to transcend its limited version of worker participation in favor of 'full' workers' control are now on the ascendant. Tied to Allied efforts to restructure German industrial power, codetermination originated in steel in 1947 and was extended to coal in 1951. In steel and coal, labor representatives constitute half of the board of directors (which then mutually selects a neutral director) and the personnel director of the enterprise is controlled by labor through his or her appointment. The Works Constitution Act of 1952 established works councils in all enterprises over five workers and economic committees in those over one hundred workers. The Act also prescribed one-third labor representation on boards of directors outside steel and coal.

Under the Codetermination Act (1951, for coal and steel), worker directors are chosen in part by the company works council and in part by unions bargaining with the enterprise, if any. In practice unions dominate selection of worker representatives. In contrast, the Works Constitution Act (1952) forbids nomination of unionists not directly employed by the company.

Management is required by law to appoint a finance committee to meet monthly with the works councils to consult on 'financial matters' such as cutbacks and closings, new technology and investments, and production and marketing matters. In 1972 revisions of the Act gave the works councils stronger influence in hiring, firing and other plant operations (Conference Board, 1973, pp. 12, 14). As the OECD (1972, p. 22) management experts' report noted, this new legislation 'will open up new possibilities of political discussions between management and labour, enabling unions to investigate whatever they wish, such as decisions by management about terms of employment'. The revisions also empower unions to suggest new methods of work as well as receive information about past performance. Among the anticipated consequences are use of outside experts in establishing standards of work within the enterprise.

Although primarily vested with rights of information and consultation, the works councils also have the following powers: regulation of daily working hours and breaks; the time and place for payment of remuneration; the preparation of the leave schedule; the carrying out of vocational training; the administration of welfare services; disciplinary matters; fixing of job and piece rates; principles of remuneration; introduction of new methods for remuneration; major alterations involving substantial disadvantages for the staff; and since 1971, greater power over unjustified transfers, regroupings, and dismissals (Asplund, 1972, p. 23). Additional areas of jurisdiction are questions of propriety and behavior on the job, determination of rates for piece-work, and application of social security provisions, as well as recruitment, redeployment, transfers, and dismissals, all handled through codetermination.

The codetermination rights of the works councils mean, in essence, that management decisions in these areas are not binding until approved by the works council. In cases of disagreement, the issue is submitted to arbitration. In other areas the councils have consultation rights only (that is, management must consult works council views prior to decision, but no council approval is necessary): safety regulations, construction and production planning measures, manpower requirements planning and factory arrangement planning. Finally, in some areas the councils have only rights of information, not including consultation or codetermination: plans for new buildings, work sites, information on job-procedures plans, manpower planning and the economic affairs of the company. In addition, the councils have the prerogative of inspecting personnel records and the right to demand dismissal of employees who constitute disturbing influences (MCI, 1972, pp. 99–101).

German employers found the 1972 extension of codetermination a bitter pill to swallow. Employers charge that full (50–50) codetermination as in coal and steel does not necessarily ensure labor peace or effective decision-making, and is not of significant interest to rank-and-file workers (Conference Board, 1973, p. 21). Academics (Blumberg, 1968, pp. 2–3; Schauer, 1973) and European unionists (Asplund, 1972, p. 26) also cite the clearly limited effects of codetermination on the average worker. Nevertheless, its grant of powers is sufficiently meaningful that German unions are pressing strongly for full codetermination in all industries (West German Trade Union Federation, 1973) and have influenced Chancellor Brandt to make codetermination a major domestic issue. Similarly, employers find it sufficiently a threat that they are active in opposing these pressures. Contrary to the academics who rightly note the limited nature of codetermination but then wrongly dismiss it as without significant effect, Van Gorcum has cited evidence showing that codetermination gives unions a considerable influence over the climate of the enterprise, over social policies, as well as information through seats on the boards of supervisors (Van Gorcum, 1972, p. 12). It also aids in the spread of unionism to non-union firms, is increasing in popularity as an experiment, and seems to have established expectations leading to demands for more extensive forms of worker participation in management.

Great Britain

In contrast to German unions, the British labor movement has traditionally emphasized shop-floor powers exercised through a strong shop stewards' movement. Given this orientation the British Trades Union Congress (TUC) responded to the EEC draft statute on the European company with a resolution favoring 50 per cent representation of labor on boards of supervisors, but opposed to the application of works councils provisions to Britain at this time (TUC, n.d.). Moreover, the TUC favored worker delegates being selected by the Trade Unions without recourse to works councils. This antipathy toward the concept of works councils reflects the unsatisfactory nature of joint participation in Britain's wartime Whitley councils, the strength of the shop stewards movement, and the influence of the workers' control movement among British unionists.

Left-wing unionists and the Institute for Workers' Control have attacked the EEC draft statutes, including the 50 per cent representation versions of it, as a proposal for the cooptation of labor and ineffectual administration along the lines of the National Coal Board (Coates, 1971). The plan was further criticized for failing to include a method of holding worker representatives accountable to their constituents, and for failing to give the working collectives veto power over such important matters as investment decisions.

In July 1973, the TUC issued an interim report on the subject, which, while not going over to the leftist position, marked the further radicalization of that body. Topham and Coates (1973), leaders of the English workers' control movement, have contrasted the 1973 position with that of 1953. Where in the earlier period the TUC accepted joint consultative machinery in a purely advisory capacity, its recent position condemns 'spurious joint consultative machinery' as inadequate to protect worker interests. In line with this, the TUC urged the following changes in the EEC proposed statute:

1 Where the proposed statute makes all directors, including worker directors, responsible to the shareholders, the TUC recommends the supervisory boards be the supreme authorities of the companies, able

to override the shareholders' general meetings as well as management board decisions.

2 Where the current proposed statute provides for only one-third labor representation, part selected by unions and part by councils, the TUC recommended 50 per cent representation, all appointed through union procedures, subject to recall and re-election under rules devised by the unions.

3 Works councils were seen as inappropriate to Britain.

The TUC proposed these principles be adopted in a new Companies Act, long discussed by both major parties in Britain (Topham and Coates, 1973, p. 9).

The more recent and more militant TUC proposals reflect a long evolution away from voluntary consultation. The Whitley councils of the First World War and the consultative bodies of the Second World War were mild concessions made for the interests of national unity. By comparison with the influence of guild-socialist concepts of workers' control in the early twentieth century, such consultative machinery seemed almost an adjunct of management. For its part, the British union movement went the way of collective bargaining rather than guild socialism.

During the debates over the Nationalization Acts of 1945–49, unions had, for example, gone along with the idea that unionists selected to serve on the boards of nationalized corporations should resign their union positions in the interest of maintaining union autonomy from management. Although the National Joint Advisory Council recommended continuing joint consultation machinery on a voluntary basis after the war, British labor spokesmen have tended to expect such consultation to be merged into the regular collective bargaining process eventually (Winchester, 1973, pp. 15–16).

Given this disinterest and the tradition of voluntarism, it is not surprising that the use of joint consultation machinery has declined in Britain. Whereas a study in the late 1940s showed nearly three-quarters of all manufacturing establishments to have such bodies, a recent study showed only one-third so constituted. As the table overleaf illustrates, this recent study showed consultation to be more common in larger firms (Clarke, Fatchett and Roberts, 1972, pp. 72–3).

About 25 per cent of firms had joint disciplinary committees, as under the National Dock Labour Board, while many more (52 per cent) had joint safety committees (Clarke, Fatchett and Roberts, 1972, pp. 179–80). Workers were also frequently involved with the administration of suggestion schemes committees and other special-function bodies.

By the 1960s a reaction had set in among unionists against consultation. Hugh Clegg (1960) shifted from support of consultation to a conservative doctrine equating collective bargaining with industrial democracy. On the other hand a movement for the radical extension of workers' control also emerged, manifesting itself in Labour Party and TUC resolutions and in the formation of the Institute for Workers' Control (Coates and Topham,

Table 1 Consultative committees by size of firm

Number of employees	Joint consultation bodies	
	Number of firms	Consultation (%)
1–99	19	12
100–499	54	22
500–999	30	47
1000–1999	35	52
2000 and over	69	62

1970). An early demand of the movement of the 1960s was 'opening the books', a demand finding its way into the 1971 British Industrial Relations Act, which requires large and medium-sized firms to disclose information required for purposes of collective bargaining (MCI, 1972, p. 12). Groups were also formed to press workers' control demands in specific industries, such as motors, aircraft, engineering, docks, mining and steel (Coates, 1968; Roberts, 1973, ch. 9).

In 1968, two significant strides occurred. First, the British Labour Party was induced to issue a call for opening the books. Second, an effort was made to establish workers' councils with powers of oversight in nationalized steel. The relative weakness of the movement was illustrated in the eventual 'compromise' plan, which provided for the usual consultative works councils and, as an innovation, a number of appointed worker-representatives on the board of directors. The latter experiment seems to have proved acceptable to management (Winchester, 1973, p. 16) but union reaction has been mixed, with advocates of workers' control deeming the experiment a failure in view of the lack of influence and even account-ability of the worker-directors (Roberts, 1973, pp. 165–8). The works councils, on the other hand, have fallen increasingly under union influence in steel, and labor attitudes are correspondingly more hopeful. The limited or doubtful benefits of the steel experiment underlie the TUC's decision in 1973 to insist on parity and accountability of worker-directors under European Corporate Law.

Since 1969 the workers' control movement in England has emphasized direct demonstrations and calls for government action to resist layoffs and closures (Kendall, 1972). By 1971, the Tory government's incomes and industrial relations policies had set a tone of militant confrontation and resistance in British labor. The 1971 Industrial Relations Act represents a national departure from voluntarism and collective bargaining, with the government intervening to determine worker–employer relations under law (Robinson, 1973). The new Act establishes a system of Industrial Tribunals and a Code of Industrial Relations Practice, introducing arbitration of many disputes and calling on unions to discipline shop stewards.

The TUC has sought to refuse cooperation with the Act, incurring penalty fines in its fight to prevent what is perceived as a drive to destroy the power of the shop stewards, impose rigorous discipline on workers and undermine collective bargaining, fining or imprisoning those who do not cooperate (Roberts, 1973, p. 98). Massive demonstrations against the Act were called by the TUC, in spite of the new labor rights (e.g. information) granted under the Act. In 1972, twenty unions were suspended for refusing to deregister under the Act, leading to their expulsion from the TUC in 1973. (On the other hand, the 1973 TUC convention narrowly turned back left-wing proposals calling on unions to cease relations with the pay board and the National Industrial Relations Court.)

Ironically, the Tory Industrial Relations Act shifted labor orientations to the left. In particular, it became apparent to management and unions alike that simple repeal of the Industrial Relations Act was impossible. Since the Act had made void much previous protective labor legislation, its repeal would leave unions unprotected. Consequently the unions, in their demand to repeal the Industrial Relations Act, were also impelled to consider a basic reformulation of British company law. In this context, the workers' control movement was in a more favorable situation to press its program as part of such a new set of legislation (Benn, 1973; Hughes, 1973; MCI, 1972, pp. 110–11).

Momentum has been added by other developments. In June 1971, Upper Clyde Shipbuilders collapsed, partly under the effects of Tory government policy. A press conference by UCS shop stewards announced their intentions to keep all Upper Clyde yards working. Subsequently the Scottish TUC supported the Clyde workers and demonstrations of unprecedented size were held in Glasgow (Graham, n.d.). Through a work-in by 700 employees who would have been made redundant, the UCS stewards were able eventually to secure a government agreement to keep all four Clyde yards open (Roberts, 1973, p. 144).

Similarly, in May 1971, Plessey (an electronics manufacturer) announced plans to close its works at Alexandria near Dumbarton due to 'falling international demand' (Graham, n.d., p. 7). Rather than leave, the fired workers voted to take over the works, which they did. After a twenty-week occupation, an agreement was reached whereby a new joint company was formed to develop the Alexandria works as an industrial site. Neither Clyde nor Plessey led to workers' control, but both raised control issues and intensified labor militancy on such issues as assertion of the right to veto plant closings.

In this situation, recent management opinion has increasingly regarded greater worker participation as inevitable (Conference Board, 1973, p. 2). The next developments may well lie in the areas of nationalized industries and stock ownership. With regard to the former, the TUC passed a resolution in September 1973 endorsing the demand for 50 per cent representation of directly elected trade unionists on boards of directors of nationalized industries, in line with its position on European company law generally (*Economist*, 1973). At the same time both major parties have put forward plans for worker participation in stock ownership. The Conservative proposal to Parliament would give workers the option of buying stock in their companies at a discount off the market price; the Labour Party plan would 'open the door to eventual worker control through majority ownership of stock' (*US News and World Report*, 1973).

France

Walter Kendall (1970a), prominent in the British workers' control movement, has written of the French Communist Party, 'Revolutionary in words, thoroughly reformist in deeds, and the most slavishly pro-Soviet of the major Communist parties in Europe, the Party's sclerotic grip on French working-class life is a prime cause of the weakness and sterility of French unionism and socialism today.' Ironically, the former Catholic union federation, now renamed the *Confédération Française Démocratique du Travail* (CFDT) is more militant than its Communist counterpart, the *Confédération Générale du Travail* (CGT). A socialist splinter from the CGT, the *Force Ouvrière* (FO), trails far behind. Altogether, union enrolment is still low.

The CFDT and the FO have long demanded workers' participation in decision-making at all levels in the Common Market (*European Documentation*, 1969), but the CGT has resisted 'collaboration with management'. French labor difficulties are as much a function of such internal divisions as of capitalist opposition (OECD, 1972, p. 20). Although the CFDT favors worker participation, as a slogan 'Participation' is associated with the Gaullists, not with the left.

As in Britain, the Second World War left France with a system of works councils (*comités d'entreprises*, established in 1945). As in Britain, these have declined from an estimated 21,000 in 1954 to about 10,000 in 1964, the most recent date for which figures were found (Asplund, 1972, p. 30). Though the councils enjoy certain legal rights, notably the right to receive certain accounts and have them interpreted by an accountant at the firm's expense (MCI, 1972, p. 12), their function is consultative if they are utilized at all. Labor, particularly the CGT, regards them as a failure in general.

Liberation also brought the concept of tripartism to nationalized enterprises, in the form of *conseils d'administration*. Worker representatives are appointed by the state from lists submitted by the union, though sometimes the union appoints directly and yet other times the lists are submitted to the state by the *comités d'entreprises* rather than the unions (Verdier, 1973). Representatives of the state and of the employers also serve on the administrative councils. In addition there are more specialized joint bodies, such as those on personnel (*commissions du personnel*). Except on questions of discipline, the unions seem to have had little influence through these bodies, though the national railways (SNCF) are studying a plan to extend the powers of the tripartite councils (Verdier, 1973, p. 11).

Recent developments in worker participation have come either from the government or from the rank-and-file, rather than from the unions. As part of its efforts to secure industrial peace, the government undertook in 1967 to make profit-sharing obligatory in enterprises employing more than one hundred workers. Far from pressing for this scheme, the CGT and FO took the position that much more was to be won through collective bargaining than through profit-sharing. In a 1971 joint statement the profit-sharing law was said not to alter the wage earner's share, except in a statistical procedural sense: 'About his firm the only things [the worker] knows are the content of his wage-packet and – if his works council is efficient – the company's overall output and balance-sheet. What happens in between remains – and is deliberately kept – a mystery to the man on the factory floor. If this is so, how can one talk of participation, of sharing in management, or whatever the current slogan is?' (Asplund, 1972, p. 50).

The French government apparently projects a three-stage industrial relations process, of which profit-sharing was the first stage. The second stage was marked by the passage in December 1969 of a bill enabling workers in the nationalized Renault automobile factories to hold stocks in the company. Again, the CGT opposed the measure. A future third stage would involve some form of participation in management responsibilities (*European Community*, 1970). But as one French executive put it, given CGT ideology, 'I do not believe that in the short term (fifteen years, for example) there will be a serious risk of seeing a *real* participation of workers in management' (emphasis in original, Conference Board, 1973, p. 34). Part of the government program involves the extension of collective bargaining and union organizing rights at national, company and plant levels, as in the labor legislation of 1968 and 1971 (MCI, 1972, pp. 149–51).

The other major dimension of advance toward workers' control has been in the form of relatively spontaneous factory occupations, most notable in the revolt of May 1968, and finding its theoretical articulation in the writing of André Gorz. Gorz (1967) views workers' control demands as 'nonreformist reforms': reforms which tend to accelerate beyond the capacity of capitalism to absorb them. In terms of strategy, he foresees an accelerating series of wildcats and industrial crises in which more and more extensive worker control demands are pressed. During the crisis of May 1968, the CFDT called for 'economic democracy'. 'Democratic structures,' they wrote, 'based on "autogestion" (self-management), must be substituted for industrial and administrative monarchy' (Hoyles, n.d.). The CGT denounced such views as leading to cooptation by the capitalist class. Since 1968 there have been smaller plant occupations, notably the 1973 takeover of a watch factory after its bankruptcy. There the workforce of some 1300 maintained plant operations, financing themselves through the accumulated inventory of the firm, selling watches at forty per cent off the pre-takeover price (IWC, 1973). In general, however, the dead hand of the CGT impedes any substantial moves toward workers' control in France.

Scandinavia

Scandinavia has traditionally been marked by voluntaristic approaches to industrial relations, exemplified by joint employer–labor cooperation in experiments such as that at Volvo. In recent years, however, a tendency toward formalizing workers' rights in law has emerged.

Sweden

Codetermination legislation has been introduced in Denmark, with the balance tipping in that direction in Norway and Sweden (Karlsson, 1973; Robinson, 1973). In 1972 the Swedish parliament passed an act requiring all firms over 500 employees to place two worker-directors on their boards of directors.[2] Such directors were not accountable to a worker constituency, however, and their minority position was such that this move was perceived as a mere token among Swedish unionists. In fact, union opposition to the limited nature of the plan was a source of significant friction between the labor movement and the Social Democratic administration.

2 The law, which became effective in 1973, applies only to firms in which a majority of employees are unionized. Worker-directors are designated by the unions (US News and World Report, 1973, pp. 76–7).

Joint consultation organs ('cooperative committees') date back to 1946 in Sweden and were long thought to epitomize a national, cooperative approach to labor–management relations. In 1970, however, 'the peace of industrial Sweden [was] shattered by an outburst of exhausting strikes, leaving the nation caught in an uneasy truce, with youth frequently rejecting industry as a way of making a career' (OECD, 1972, pp. 19–20).

Swedish works councils, like others, have 'rights' of information and of submitting suggestions. More specialized joint committees such as those on improving working conditions seem to have provided a more meaningful milieu of participation (Conference Board, 1973, p. 19). Rights of information and consultation extend to production matters, personnel matters and questions of shutdowns and cutbacks. Surveys conducted by the Swedish Labor Federation (LO) in 1968 and 1969 show unionists decreasingly believe in their ability to influence management through works councils, in spite of some reforms, especially in larger firms (Asplund, 1972, pp. 30–31). In 1971 the LO Congress adopted a resolution calling for the strengthening of the works councils. Similarly, the head of the Salaried Employees Union (TCO) federation issued a statement in 1971 calling for a move from rights of consultation to actual decision-making powers for such joint consultation bodies (Asplund, 1972, pp. 35–6, 59). Management seems to be coming to accept the likelihood of increased worker participation in management (Conference Board, 1973, pp. 2, 32).

The wildcat strike wave of 1969–70 brought a crisis to Swedish labor, with criticism in part directed against the LO's half-hearted interest in industrial democracy. In response the LO undertook an investigation of 'Democracy in the Firms', and in its 1971 Congress made commitments to move forward on this front, shifting from voluntary cooperation and consultation toward legally-instituted rights of codetermination (MCI, 1972, pp. 129–30). In part, this move represents a shift of priorities away from joint LO–employer efforts in the 1968–72 period toward work humanization, encouragement of self-steering work groups and experiments of the Volvo and Saab types. The limited nature of work democratization involved in these experiments is detailed in Karlsson (1973).

As in Britain and France, the government has introduced legislation providing for 'worker-participation' in the form of stock ownership. New legislation allows the social security pension fund (directed by a board of eleven on which unions have five members) to purchase stock in private companies. Although management has been upset by this move, the LO has opposed the introduction of capital-sharing schemes in recent years. As with the 1967 law providing a new constitution for cooperatives, this is a lesser development in Sweden. The central developments for the future will involve the extent to which Swedish labor will follow the recent TUC example of insisting on a more radical form of codetermination than the present token version.

Norway

As in Sweden, Norway has works councils (*bedriftsutvalg*) dating back to 1945 and more recently has led in voluntary experiments in self-directed work teams and like experiments, as at the Nordsk–Hydro fertilizer plants. The councils have the 'rights' of advice and information, including the right to require management to give an opinion on any questions raised by the councils. The scope of these limited rights includes questions of change in production plans, product quality, product development, expansions and cutbacks, health and safety, vocational training, economic information (the same as provided to stockholders) and social matters (Asplund, 1972, p. 18).

As in Sweden, the unions have been critical of the works councils. The Norwegian Federation of Trade Unions (LO) has urged recently that a new organ be created between the board of directors and the shareholders. This body, to be called the enterprise advisory assembly, would include one-third worker representation and would elect the executive board and appoint the general manager of the enterprise (Asplund, 1972, p. 44). At the same time the LO has been concerned with increasing shop-floor participation, and has been involved with voluntary experiments in this area encouraging self-directing work groups (Asplund, 1972, p. 60; Conference Board, 1973, p. 27).

T. U. Qvale (1973, pp. 2–3, 5) has reported on an interesting aspect of such experiments under the joint Norwegian Trade Union Confederation/ Confederation of Employers, in their 'Norwegian Industrial Democracy Programme', when working as part of a team led by Einar Thorsrud:

Our experience clearly demonstrates that the workers usually become more involved and committed to their work when their level of decision is extended. They also tend to expand their area of interest beyond the immediate shop floor level . . . the need for further change usually develops as a result of learning: the workers tend to get bored again once they control most variance on their jobs, workers and managers get ideas for further improvements, and so on.

In other words, voluntary experimentation itself may lead to radicalization of demands for worker participation. In this light Qvale concludes by raising the question of 'how far the area of mutual interest may be stretched'.

Thus it is not surprising to find Norwegian labor, like Swedish, now in the process of transcending voluntarism in favor of some more formal and extensive version of worker rights in management decisions. As in Sweden, the Norwegian parliament adopted a limited version of the German minority board representation model in 1972 (Conference Board, 1973, p. 3). Effective in 1973, this legislation accepts the LO's program by creating a new organ, a Board of Representatives, in all firms over 200 employees. The boards, one-third worker and two-thirds shareholder representation, elect the company's management board and have final authority over all important investment decisions and major reorganizations affecting workers. The law also requires smaller firms to provide for a majority of workers electing one-third of the management board, with a minimum of two representatives. Such legislation reflects the shift in top union and Labor Party thinking away from voluntarism; that shift has made worker participation a major national issue in Norway and momentum is gathering on a number of fronts. Worker stock-ownership is not one of these, it may be noted in conclusion, for as in Sweden, Norwegian labor has opposed this line of reform as not constituting a genuine advance in influence over management decisions.

Denmark

In contrast with the Norwegian situation, the Danish Federation of Trade Unions (LO) adopted a program in their 1971 congress calling for systematic acquisition of stock under a fund controlled by the unions. Endorsed by the Social Democratic Party and its leader, Danish Premier Anker Jorgensen (a former union leader), the proposal was being debated in parliament in October 1973, and, if passed, will go into effect in 1974 (*Wall Street Journal*, 1973). It is a model for legislation being proposed by the British Labour Party. Management opposition and inflationary problems may delay this stock-ownership plan, however.

The more traditional dimension of worker participation, as throughout Europe, has been through works councils (*samarbejdsuvalg*) established in 1947 and revised periodically since, last in 1971. These 'councils of co-operation' have powers of 'codetermination' and 'co-influence'. 'Co-determination' is used in a different sense from the customary German-model usage; it refers only to a non-binding obligation of both labor and management to strive for an agreement. Differences need not be resolved by arbitration. Codetermination matters in this sense include matters of work organization, safety and welfare. 'Co-influence' refers to the councils' right to have good opportunities to exchange ideas and make suggestions prior to management decisions. Co-influence rights include matters of day-to-day production and major alterations in the enterprise. In addition the councils have rights of information only over matters relating to the enterprise's 'economic situation and future prospects' (Asplund, 1972, p. 17). As in Norway, the unions have criticized the limitations of the councils and have successfully fought for the (slow) expansion of their powers. Again, however, the major thrust is not in this area but that of codetermination in the sense of worker-participation on boards of directors. On union initiative, the government has introduced a plan to give workers a minimum of one-third of the seats on boards of directors.

Finland

Under the label of 'business democracy', the Finns also have a system of joint consultation bodies. These production committees have 'powers' of advice and information over the promotion of productivity, discipline, safety and 'industrial peace' (Conference Board, 1973, p. 13). According to the Confederation of Salaried Employees, 'these committees do not have the power to decide anything' (Asplund, 1972, p. 36). A new reform is being planned within the labor movement which would create councils consisting solely of workers as well as the joint cooperation committees. Although labor representation on management boards has received attention in the Finnish press, the movement toward greater worker participation and control is, of all the North European states, weakest in Finland.

The Low Countries

The Low Countries have all been heavily influenced by the neighboring German model of codetermination, but there the commonality ends for some (Luxembourg) have been drawn toward imitation of the model while others (Belgium) have been strong in reaction against it.

Belgium

The Belgian labor movement is fairly evenly divided into Catholic (Confederation of Christian Trade Unions, CSC) and socialist wings (Belgian General Confederation of Labour, FGTB), with minor federations for the public services and other purposes. The FGTB is a militant confederation advocating a classless society and workers' control (Coates, 1971). By workers' control the FGTB means just that: it is opposed to codetermination and sharing of control with management. In this sense close to the usual Communist position, the FGTB nonetheless has visions of certain immediate reforms toward workers' control, particularly in the areas of control over the Committees of Safety and Health (rights of information, investigation, veto over dangerous processes, reform of work inspection and research leading to setting of standards), Factory Councils (rights to detailed information on costs, prices, relations with other economic groups, orders, sales, investments, research plans, forecasts, productivity matters, advertising and debts and profits), yet avoiding codetermination at the level of representation on the boards of directors. In addition the FGTB calls for reforms allowing union cadres to sit with employees on the factory councils.

The CSC has been more favorable toward codetermination at the board level, as well as toward the joint consultation committees formed in 1948. As of 1970, a new union–employers' organization agreement increased the rights of these councils, giving them rights of information, consultation and limited codetermination, with authority to make decisions on labor regulations, criteria for hiring and layoff of hourly workers, vacation and rotation schedules and administration of employee facilities subject to management veto. However, employers retain the crucial right of veto in all areas, leading to 'reduced respect for the works councils' (Asplund, 1972, p. 37).

In spite of FGTB criticism of consultation, codetermination and stock-participation schemes, unions do have representation on a number of economic bodies, including the Price Commission, the Central Council of the Economy, the National Council of Work, the Gas and Electricity Board and the National Bank of Belgium to name a few. The FGTB looks at its participation on such bodies primarily in terms of 'placing statistics in the use of the working class' and of the eventual integration of such bodies under some future national planning in a more radical form of government.

In practice the works councils have extensive powers in social matters, but not in economic. Originally meant to provide industrial peace, their function was utterly disrupted during the French crisis of May 1968, which spread to Belgium. Extreme left-wing groups such as All Power for the Workers, the Revolutionary Workers' League and the Third World Movement arose and wielded surprising influence. This in turn led to a National Collective Agreement in May 1971, whereby company-level union delegations were granted increased powers in the hope of restoring union control at the shop-floor level (MCI, 1972, p. 188). Thus, as in France, the revolutionary rhetoric of the unions (the FGTB) involves practical resistance to any form of codetermination and the *de facto* role of control over spontaneous rank-and-file rebellions raising worker control issues. Moreover, management experts expect Belgium will eventually go along with codetermination under European company law (MCI, 1972, p. 200; Van Outrive, 1972).

Netherlands

Dutch unions, in contrast, have been successful in winning legislation creating legal penalties for failure to establish enterprise councils, the right of council members to be assisted by experts and the protection of council members from management pressures (van Gorcum, 1972, p. 15). The 1971 Works Council Act reflects the tendency of such limited-participation bodies to shift questions at the shop-floor level (Drenth, 1972). The 1971 Act, following a strike wave in 1970, required councils in enterprises over a hundred, and gave the councils the right to be consulted in advance on mergers, significant changes in organization, size, or ownership, and the right to joint discussion of the company's annual report and the general situation of the firm.[3] In addition, unions, led by the metal-workers, are beginning to press for a union presence on the shop floor.

This greater acceptance of joint consultation in the Netherlands compared with Belgium is rooted in the semi-corporate system that developed after the Second World War under which unions cooperated closely with employers and government to promote harmony and restrain wages. Since the late 1950s, however, independent unionism has emerged, forcing the traditional unions to adopt a more militant stand. In addition, though small, Holland is one of the few European countries in which syndicalist groups are still significant in working-class attitudes (Kendall, 1970b). Nevertheless, it appears that most workers regard the works councils as an improvement over prewar conditions, especially in larger enterprises (Asplund, 1972, p. 27).

Since 1967 the three major union federations (NVV, NKV and CNV) have been considering plans for German-type codetermination. After the passage of the 1971 Works Council Act, the three federations issued a joint statement calling for further amendments 'to extend the right of codetermination of the works council and to clarify the position of the elected members as representatives of the personnel' (Asplund, 1972, p. 37). Dutch labor has favored a system of board representation under which one-third of the directors would be elected by shareholders, one-third by works council members and one-third selected jointly.

In addition, the Dutch unions support capital-sharing schemes and experiments in various forms of industrial democracy. Occasionally such experimentation emerges spontaneously from the rank-and-file. A recent meeting of European management experts noted 'some striking illustrations ... from countries whose citizens are often regarded as models of obedience, if not submissiveness or docility: a group of Dutch workers who drew a thick chalk line around their corner of the factory and then opposed the entry into it of any staff or other employees unless they could give a satisfactory explanation of their mission' (OECD, 1972, p. 19).

Far more attention has focused, however, on codetermination reforms. This is particularly so given the limited nature of works-council consul-

3 Prior to the 1971 law, half the firms covered by the 1950 statute on works councils had failed to comply with the law (MCI, 1972, p. 144).

tation, even after the 1971 changes. A Dutch international corporate executive noted recently that when it is all said and done, 'decision-making rests wholly with the employer. In fact, he does not have to ask for advice at all if he can give good reasons why this is in the company's interest (though in the case of a dispute a legal verdict may follow)' (Conference Board, 1973, p. 13).

In 1971 Holland adopted a board representation law, to go into effect in 1973. Under this law, works-council members may nominate supervisory board members, along with nominations from management and shareholders. However, employees and unionists dealing with the company or employed by it are excluded from nomination. Actual selection of board members is by a self-perpetuating system of cooption by the board itself. Power to name the managing directors of the enterprise is transferred by this law from the shareholders to the supervisory board (Conference Board, 1973, pp. 9–10). This reform thus excludes direct rank-and-file participation and does not make board members accountable to labor in any way; in fact, the opposite is its explicit intent. Although the works council may veto any board-member nomination, even this veto can be overridden by the National Social and Economic Council.

Thus, in spite of the two major labor acts of 1971, worker participation in Holland remains very limited. The relatively moderate union movement favors a more extensive version of codetermination, but the most radical and far-reaching tendencies toward workers' control in Holland remain with the rank-and-file. At Breda, for example, workers used sit-in tactics in 1972 to take over the ENKA factory, successfully forcing the firm to change its plans for mass lay-offs. This spontaneous form of workers' control, while not leading directly to new participative institutions, is accelerating the slow leftward drift of Dutch unionism.

Luxembourg

Like Belgium, the Luxembourg union movement is split into socialist (*Confédération Générale du Travail*, CGT, with strength in railways, civil service and transport) and Christian (*Letzeburger Chreschtleche Gewerkschaftsbond*, LCGB) wings. The CGT advocates a classless society as its goal, but, unlike the French CGT or Belgian FGTB, it advocates workers' codetermination at the level of the board of directors. It is, however, basically critical of capital-sharing schemes.

During 1973, in what was described as 'an obvious effort to attract workers' votes at the next general elections' in June 1974 (*Business Europe*, 1973), Prime Minister Pierre Werner, leader of the Christian Democrat–Liberal coalition government, submitted a bill providing for codetermination in Luxembourg. The bill is anticipated to pass as it is supported by all political parties and all the non-Communist unions. Although less than the unions' goal of 50 per cent representation, the act would give labor the right to designate one-third of the members of boards of directors of all firms over 1000 employees and all firms in which the state has over a quarter of the equity. Such worker-directors would have to be company employees, in direct contrast to Holland, except in the steel industry where the national unions are allowed to appoint other delegates.

In addition, the act would establish mixed work councils in all stock companies with over 250 employees or manufacturing firms over a given level of value added. These councils, formed on a fifty-fifty labor and management basis, would have the sole power to authorize performance evaluations, health and safety measures, and hiring, firing and promotion policies. In addition the councils would have the right of advance consultation in plant operations and production processes having a substantial impact on employees. Finally, the councils would have certain rights of information, including receipt of comprehensive reports prepared specially for their use.

Switzerland

The Swiss Labour Federation (SGB) has also called for a shift to transform the works councils from consultative to codetermination organs. It is now conducting a drive for a national vote on the issue of labor representation on boards of directors. In addition, the SGB favors capital-sharing schemes as a vehicle for increasing workers' share in management decision-making, though this strategy is not considered as important as the demand for codetermination. In fact, the codetermination issue has forged unprecedented unity between the SGB and the two Christian Trade Union Federations (Asplund, 1972, pp. 39, 58). In part, the turn toward worker participation as a major issue may be a union effort to counteract the trend toward decreasing union membership in Switzerland, and has been perceived as such by management (Conference Board, 1973, pp. 31, 32). As elsewhere, this focus on codetermination has eclipsed the traditional vehicle of works councils and specialized committees (dealing with remuneration, working conditions, production planning and social welfare), though the unions are interested in extending worker-participation at all levels, not just the board level.

Austria

Austrian works councils go back to the early twentieth century, though the modern form was initiated in 1947 and strengthened in 1971. Council powers are limited to information and consultation on wage rates, incentive rates and plant shutdowns and cutbacks. Its strongest aspects include the right to call for a state investigation of a company's economic affairs, limited right to veto dismissals and codetermination of work rules (Asplund, 1972, p. 23). Like Germany and in contrast to practice in Scandinavia and the Low Countries, the Austrian works councils are composed of workers, not workers and employers. Works councils in the public sector, called 'personnel representation councils' (*personalvertretungsgesetz*), were established at union initiative in 1967, but political influences are more prominent and the few decision-making powers absent – theoretically on the principle of maintaining parliamentary sovereignty through the ministers (Tomandl, 1973).

Since 1971 the Austrian Federation of Trade Unions (OGB) has favored capital-sharing through a central fund akin to the Danish model. As elsewhere, however, more attention has centered on OGB demands for representation on supervisory boards along the lines of the German coal and steel model with fifty per cent representation (Asplund, 1972, p. 42). Austrian labor has more recently advocated the passage of a compromise measure giving one-third labor representation on boards of directors, but the strength of employer-opposition makes passage of even this plan speculative (*U S News and World Report*, 1973, p. 77). Existing law allows workers' councils to nominate two representatives to the supervisory boards (which elect the managing boards and supervise them). The increase of this representation to one-third is sponsored by the ruling socialist party.

On a very different front, the Ministry of Higher Education in Austria has drafted a new organizational plan which would increase student participation in university affairs. Student groups are demanding that professors, students and assistants each have one-third representation. The draft plan would reduce the faculty from a majority to a minority position in decision-making organs of the universities. No similar plans are prominent in other public sector institutions (Tomandl, 1973, p. 13).

Spain

Even in fascist Spain tendencies toward workers' control are emerging, favored by the diverse traditions of syndicalism and of social Catholicism, c.f. worker cooperation in control of manufacturing at Mondragon (see Reading 19). Current Spanish law allows workers to elect one member to the board of directors for every seven management members (through the '*jurado de empresa*', not through independent unions). However, as a Spanish executive noted recently, 'greater participation is inevitable because of the pressures that unions and socialistic organized groups will have upon corporations and industries in the future ... new laws are moving towards greater freedom' (Conference Board, 1973, p. 32). As with much else in Spain, rapid changes may occur with the death of Franco; and even at present, the demands for greater worker-power are becoming more intense.

Italy

Italy bears some similarities to France: the opposition of the Communist union federation to workers' participation, a recent social crisis (1969) marked by intense strikes, raising rank-and-file demands for workers' control, and the raising of 'Participation' as a common political slogan since then not just in industrial relations but also in regard to education and government. While strikes are more intense in Italy than elsewhere in Europe and unions extremely militant in pressing demands, the pervasive Communist negativity toward class collaboration through worker-participation has squelched most moves in this direction.

Consequently workers' control has been most associated with split-offs from the Communists, such as the *Il Manifesto* group and *Lotta Continua*. The groups of the revolutionary left, as in the French strategy (Gorz, 1967), seek to work through wildcat strikes and other workers' struggles to press control 'reforms' beyond the capacity of the capitalist system to make concessions. The wage concessions of 1969, the repression of 1970 and the continuing industrial turmoil have constituted a major negative example, impelling other countries toward greater worker-participation on the theory that its relative absence in Italy underlies much of these troubles (*Radical American*, 1973).

Although the Communist CGL remains in opposition, the Italian Confederation of Workers' Unions (CISL) advocates extension of the powers of works councils but agrees that workers' codetermination 'must be realized through their participation in trade union activities' (Asplund, 1972, p. 38). The CISL also agrees on opposing capital-sharing plans as being cooptive. Instead the CISL is much more interested in utilizing a 1970 law guaranteeing trade union rights to hold factory meetings. Through factory meetings, it is believed, a decentralization and strengthening of labor at the factory level can take place. This strengthening, of course, refers to the union position in collective bargaining, not to assumption of direct powers of decision by workers.

Overall, the CGL, CSIL and the largely socialist UIL have been moving toward unity since 1969. The above-mentioned Workers' Charter of 1970 reflects this in part. The 1970 law seems associated with the 're-markable upsurge in collective bargaining at the plant level' (MCI, 1972, p. 182). This emphasis on the plant level, also apparent in France, in-directly favors the raising of specific workers' control demands that tend to get 'ironed out' in favor of general economic demands in national-level agreements. Similarly, a sharp radicalization of union activity at the shop-floor has taken place in which 'the unions question the whole organization of work within industry' (MCI, 1972, p. 183). This radicalization has served to strengthen the role of workers' delegates on factory committees, constituting a 'delegates movement' with vague analogies to the 'shop stewards' movement' that is a basis of the British workers' control movement.

Thus, while the Italian situation demonstrates a radical movement toward workers' control (as opposed to workers' participation), such powers as have been won in the recent struggles are by and large not institutionalized in law. It is an open question as to whether significant advances toward workers' power will actually be effected if the current militant mood fades without (barring revolutionary shifts in government) specific and necessarily more limited reforms being legislated.

Conclusion

Without exception, every West European country has experienced major developments in workers' participation in management during the past decade, particularly in the last five and even more specifically, in the last two or three years. These developments are rooted in intergenerational attitude changes associated with increasing standard of living and changes in the nature of the workforce, as discussed by Inglehart (1971) and others. It has been precipitated in many countries by the intense, world-wide wave of social ferment that developed in the late 1960s.

No country has seriously entertained genuine workers' control of management along the lines of Yugoslav self-management. The most revolutionary unions and the Communist unions have, in the name of opposing class collaboration, opposed many of the developments toward greater worker-participation. Yet their function in raising the vision of full workers' control has been important in delegitimating the systems of joint consultation formed after the Second World War.

Some countries, such as Austria, are only now moving toward minority labor representation on boards of directors and strengthening of works-council powers. Some, such as Norway, have recently attained this level, while others, such as Britain, have not reached that level but are considering even more radical plans of fifty per cent board representation. The development of EEC company law will probably provide at least one-third labor participation, and quite possibly one-third plus an additional third jointly selected with management or shareholders. Scandinavian abandonment of a voluntarist philosophy is a major move toward acceptance of codetermination. It is difficult to predict whether the German, British and other union demands for parity will become a general

European labor position among non-Communist unions, but in all countries the trend is in this direction. In addition, many examples exist of autonomous work-group experiments, experiments in capital participation, and increases in powers of shop-floor and company-worker organizations.

It is a mark of changing times that in the European context, the moderate position on worker participation usually envisions at least one-third worker representation on boards of directors, frequently combined with concessions increasing works council powers and worker-participation in capital. Only a few years ago this would have been regarded as the most that might be expected in European labor relations; today it seems the least. If present trends continue, board parity and strong shop-floor organizations (whether council or union delegations) will be the primary issues for this coming decade, although work-group and capital experiments will also increase in importance. After that, one may only speculate on whether labor will seek to move from a parity position compatible with capitalism toward a majority position involving major structural changes creating self-management. If this seems utopian today, present developments seemed utopian a decade ago.

References

ASPLUND, C. (1972), *Some Aspects of Workers' Participation*, International Confederation of Free Trade Unions, Brussels.

BARRY-BRAUNTHAL, T. (1972a), 'Labour *v.* management in Europe', *European Community*, no. 156, pp. 14–16.

BARRY-BRAUNTHAL, T. (1972b), 'The Trade Union movement in the European Community', *European Studies, Trade Union Series*, European Communities Press and Information, Brussels.

BARRY-BRAUNTHAL, T. (1973), 'Multinational labour: European workers unite', *European Community*, no. 167, April 1973, p. 22.

BENN, T., *et al.* (1973) *Workers' Control: How Far Can The Structure Meet Our Demands?*, IWC pamphlet no. 36, Institute of Workers' Control.

BLUMBERG, P. (1968), *Industrial Democracy: The Sociology of Participation*, Constable.

Business Europe (1973), 'Codetermination is coming to Luxembourg', 1 June 1973, p. 171.

CASSERINI, K. (1969), 'Multinational companies and collective bargaining', report II–5 of the Trade Union seminar, *New Perspectives in Collective Bargaining*, Social Affairs Division, OECD.

CHILDS, B. (1973), 'Workers, bosses clash on Eurocompany plan', *European Community*, March.

CLARKE, R. O., FATCHETT, D. J., and ROBERTS, B. C. (1972), *Workers' Participation in Management in Britain*, Heinemann.

CLEGG, H. (1960), *A New Approach to Industrial Democracy*, Blackwell.

COATES, K. (ed.) (1968), 'Conditions and plans in specific industries', in *Can The Workers Run Industry?*, Sphere.

COATES, K. (ed.) (1971), *A Trade Union Strategy in the Common Market: The Programme of the Belgian Trade Unions*, Spokesman Books, London.

COATES, K. (1973), 'Codetermination in Britain', *Bulletin of The Institute of Workers' Control*, no. 10.

COATES, K., and TOPHAM, T. (eds.) (1970), *Workers' Control*, Panther.

Conference Board (1973), *Worker Participation: New Voices in Management*, Conference Board.

COYLE, D. J. (1971), 'Eurounions', *Interplay*, February.

DRENTH, P. J. D. (1972), 'The works council in the Netherlands: an experiment in participation', *First International Sociological Conference on Participation and Self-Management*, Dubrovnik, mimeo.

Economist (1973), 'The TUC tries to live up to its friends', *Economist*, 8 September, p. 16, and also see October issues of the *Economist*.

European Commission (1970), 'Proposed statutes for the European company', *Bulletin of the European Communities*, no. 8, pp. 87–122.

European Community (1970a), 'Renault workers to get stock', no. 135, June, p. 12.

European Community (1970b), 'European company law', no. 136, August.

European Documentation (1969), 'The Trade Union Movement in France', p. 4. Distributed as part of *European Studies* (1972).

GORZ, ANDRE (1967), *Strategy for Labour: A Radical Proposal*, Beacon.

GRAHAM, A. (n.d.), *The Workers' Next Step*, Independent Labour Party.

GUNDELACH, R. (1973), 'Intervention and the European company', speech to *Legal Committee of European Parliament*, 13 April, xerox.

HOYLES, A. (n.d.), 'General strike, France, 1968', in *Insurgent Worker*, Chicago.

HUGHES, J. (1973), 'After the Industrial Relations Act', *Bulletin of the Institute of Workers' Control*, no. 10, pp. 8–13.

ICFTU (1971), *The Multinational Challenge*, International Confederation of Free Trade Unions, Brussels.

INGLEHART, R. (1971), 'The silent revolution in Europe: intergenerational change in post-industrial societies', *Amer. Polit. Sci. Rev.*, vol. 65, no. 4, pp. 991–1017.

IWC (1973), 'Lessons of the LIP occupation', *Bulletin of the Institute of Workers' Control*, October, p. 14.

KARLSSON, L. E. (1973), 'Experiences in employee participation in Sweden: 1969–1972'.

KENDALL, W. (1970a), 'Labour Union in France', *European Community*, no. 135, June.

KENDALL, W. (1970b), 'Labour Unions in the Netherlands', *European Community*, no. 137, August, pp. 15–16.

KENDALL, W. (1972), 'Workers' participation and workers' control: aspects of the British experience', *First International Sociological Conference on Participation and Self-Management*, Dubrovnik, mimeo.

LEVINSON, C. (1969), 'Collective bargaining in perspective', Report 1B of the Trade Union seminar on *New Perspectives in Collective Bargaining*, Social Affairs Division, OECD.

MCI (1972), *European Labour Relations in the '70s: An Overview*, Management Counsellors International, Brussels.

OECD (1972), *The Emerging Attitudes and Motivations of Workers: Report of a Management Experts' Meeting, Paris, 24–6 May 1971*, OECD.

QVALE, T. U. (1973), 'Participation and conflict: some experiences from the Norwegian industrial democracy programme', *International Industrial Relations Association, 3rd World Congress*.

Radical American (1973), 'Working class struggle in Italy', special issue, vol. 7, no. 2.

ROBERTS, E. (1973), *Workers' Control*, Allen & Unwin.

ROBINSON, J. (1973), 'Giving workers a say in owning the firm', *European Community*, March.

SCHAUER, H. (1973), 'A critique of codetermination', in G. Hunnius, D. Garson and J. Case (eds.), *Workers' Control*, Random House.

TOMANDL, T. (1973), 'Labour relations in the public sector of Austria', *International Industrial Relations Association, 3rd World Congress*.

TOPHAM, T. and COATES, K. (1973), *Catching Up with the Times: How Far the TUC Got the Message About Workers' Control*, IWC pamphlet no. 37, Institute of Workers' Control.

Trade Union News from the European Community (1970), 'Worker participation in the European company', no. 4, p. 14.

Trade Union News from the European Community (1972), 'New Trade Union structures for the community', no. 9, pp. 3–5.

TUC (n.d.), *EEC Proposals on Aspects of Company Law: Application to Britain – TUC Comments*, TUC, mimeo.

US News and World Report (1973), 'What are foreign firms doing to fight the "blue-collar blues"?', 23 July.

VAN GORCUM, O. H. (1972), 'La participation des travailleurs dans une SA de droit Européen', *First International Sociological Conference on Participation and Self-Management*, Dubrovnik, mimeo.

VON OUTRIVE, L. (1972), 'The Belgian Christian and Socialist Trade Unions: their participation in neo-capitalist concentration economy and their strategies in the sense of self-management', *First International Sociological Conference on Participation and Self-Management*, Dubrovnik, mimeo.

VERDIER, J. M. (1973), 'Les relations de travail dans le secteur public en France', *International Industrial Relations Association, 3rd World Conference*.

Wall Street Journal (1973), 'Unions in Europe press for co-ownership', 29 October, p. 6.

West German Trade Union Federation (1973), 'Codetermination in the Federal Republic of Germany', in G. Hunnius, D. Garson and J. Case (eds.), *Workers' Control*, Random House.

WINCHESTER, D. (1973), 'Labour relations in the public sector in the United Kingdom', *International Industrial Relations Association, 3rd World Congress*, mimeo.

12 J. Gouverneur

The Labor Communities in Peru: A Way to Labor Management?

Jacques Gouverneur, 'La réforme de l'entreprise au Pérou', in *Cultures et Développement*, University of Louvain, 1972, vol. 4, pp. 707–29 (revised version).

Of all the reforms undertaken by the Peruvian military government, in power since October 1968, the most original is unquestionably the creation of the 'labor communities' in the production enterprises. This is in effect a complete revision of the traditional relationship between workers and capitalists, by making the workers participate not only in the profits, but also, collectively, in the ownership and the management of their enterprise. Since the system in operation is relatively complex, we shall begin by describing it in some detail. After this, we shall attempt to make an appreciation of the scope of this reform, whose ambiguous nature gives rise to as many doubts as hopes. When making this appreciation, it will be necessary to mention the very recent creation of enterprises of a new type with equally original features, the 'social ownership' enterprise.

The labor communities

The system of worker participation in profits, ownership and management of enterprises came into being with the publication, on 27 July 1970, of the 'General Industries Law'. Its basic principles have subsequently been applied again in the 'General Fisheries Law', the 'General Mining Law' and the 'General Telecommunications Law', which have moreover perfected the system by introducing a certain measure of compensation between workers in enterprises of unequal profitability.[1] In order to understand these more complex variants, we must begin by examining the simplest and most general case, that of the industrial enterprises.[2]

1 The sectors of energy and services in general (commerce, transportation, etc.) have not yet been affected by the company reform, but ought to be in the coming months. We know, in particular, that a 'general law on trade' is being prepared, which is also to reaffirm the principle of a 'trade community'. As for the agricultural sector, it has been the object of a far-reaching reform, the effects of which are seen at the level of the enterprise in the disappearance of capitalist farming concerns and the setting up, alongside individual farms, of various forms of cooperative enterprises.

2 Let us note that the participation schemes that we shall describe do not concern 'small businesses' in the various sectors. In the industrial sector, the 'small business'

Participation in industrial enterprises

First of all the law provides for direct participation of the workers in the profits of their company, known as 'cash' participation. Each year a sum equal to 10 per cent of the company's net profit is distributed among all the full-time workers. This sum is shared out among them half in equal parts and half in proportion to individual earnings.

More important is the progressive participation of the workers in the ownership of their company, called 'ownership' participation. This participation is to be effected through the 'industrial community' (IC), a body that groups together all the full-time workers of the company. Before examining how this 'industrial community' comes to share progressively in the capital and the management of the company, let us say a few words about its internal organization.

We can distinguish two authorities within the IC: the general assembly and the council. The general assembly brings together all the (full-time) workers, with equal voting rights. Among other functions, it elects and discharges the chairman and the members of the community council. The council is the executive body of the IC. Neither workers owning shares in the company nor trade union leaders may be council members. It is the council that delegates from among its members the community representative(s) to the Board of Directors.

How does the IC's share in ownership build up? Each year the company must set aside 15 per cent of its net profit for this purpose. Normally, this 15 per cent of net profit must be reinvested by the company and bring about the issue of new shares; it is these new shares that the company must transfer to the IC. But if the company has no reinvestment program, or if its reinvestment program is not approved by the competent ministry, the 15 per cent of the net profit will be used by the community to acquire existing shares from the owners of the company.

Participation in the capital of the company gives the community proportional participation in the profits and the management of the enterprise. If, for example, after x years, the industrial community owns 20 per cent of the company's shares, it is entitled to 20 per cent of the profits which will swell its general fund. This fund is used in part for the IC's own purposes (social, cultural, administrative activities), the other part having

---

is closely defined as one employing a maximum of five workers and having a gross annual income of less than one million *soles* (43 *soles* = $1). In the fishing and telecommunications sectors, the small business is one whose gross annual income is less than one million and three million *soles* respectively. With regard to mining, the small business is defined by means of more complex criteria which are essentially concerned with the area exploited and the gross income.

to be distributed among the workers according to the following formula: one half in equal shares, the other half in proportion to years of service in the company. Thus the workers have a two-fold participation in profits: one direct (the annual 10 per cent mentioned above), the other indirect (its percentage depending on the share of the capital held by the IC and also on the policy of the IC). As for participation in management, the law provides that from the day it comes into being the industrial community is entitled to one representative on the Board of Directors, and this representation must increase in proportion to the numbers of shares owned by the industrial community; it is laid down, moreover, that the various representatives of the industrial community must always vote the same way.

The industrial community's participation in the capital and in the management of the enterprise must grow year by year by the process of acquisition, with the 15 per cent of the annual net profit, of shares in the enterprise. According to the law, the process is to continue until the community attains ownership of 50 per cent of the company's capital. What happens when this stage is reached? On the one hand, the industrial community will continue to receive 15 per cent of the annual net profits. However, this money will no longer be used to buy shares in the company, but securities of COFIDE (the State Development Finance Corporation). Thus participation in the capital and in the management of the enterprise remains limited to 50 per cent.

On the other hand, having reached the 50 per cent capital holding, the industrial community shall issue shares of its own representing its participation in the capital and shall distribute them among its workers on the basis of their length of service in the company. This distribution of shares involves a change in the workers' participation in the income shared out by the community. Up to now income distributed by the community was shared out according to the formula: half in equal parts, then the income to be divided on the basis of seniority in the firm. Once the community has reached 50 per cent of the capital and distributes its own shares, then the income to be handed out will be divided according to the number of shares in the community owned by each worker; since these shares will themselves be distributed in proportion to length of service in the company, then the *total* of the income shared out by the community will be divided among the workers in accordance with their seniority in the company.

Let us note, finally, that the company must always hold back 10 per cent of its annual net profit for the direct participation of the workers in the profits (this 10 per cent is shared out half in equal parts and half in proportion to individual earnings); but as the industrial community increases its participation in the capital of the enterprise, so direct participation in the 10 per cent will lose its relative importance by comparison with in-direct participation, which varies according to the I C's share in the capital of the enterprise.

Variants of the participation scheme described

The participation scheme described thus far was in relation to *capitalist* enterprises in the *industrial* sector. In the other sectors affected by the company reform (mines, fishing, telecommunications), the system has been completed by the creation, within each of these sectors, of a 'compensation community' whose role is to redistribute part of the profits and of the shareholding – but not of the management rights – among the various labor communities. Furthermore, as well in the industrial sector as in the others, certain categories of enterprises – particularly *state* and *mixed companies* – also reveal some variants of the participation system described.

The 'compensation community' is a private entity which groups to-gether, on an equal footing, all the labor communities of a specific sector (mining communities, fishing communities, telecommunications com-munities, as the case may be).[3] Let us examine its redistributing role, taking as our example the fishing sector.[4]

As regards the workers' direct ('cash') participation in profits (as opposed to that arising from the fishing community's participation in the ownership of the enterprise), the system laid down is as follows.

Each company must set aside 8 per cent of its annual net profit for the 'cash' participation of the workers. But the sum representing this 8 per cent is not distributed directly among the company's workers; one-half is handed over to the fishing community (FC); the other is passed to the fisheries compensation community (FCC), which redistributes all the cash contributions among the various FCs in proportion to the number of man-days worked in the corresponding companies. The total sum received by each FC (either directly from its company, or through the FCC) is then shared out among all the workers of the FC according to the same proportions as in industrial enterprises: one-half in equal parts and the other half in proportion to individual earnings.[5]

3 However, communities of companies attaining a net income below the minimum laid down by regulation are excluded from the compensation system. The regulation of the 'General Fisheries Law' stipulated that the net income of the enterprise must be at least 1 per cent of the average net income for the sector. The regulation of the 'General Mining Law' stipulates that the net income *per worker* must be at least 10 per cent of the average for the sector.
4 The principles are the same for both the mining and the telecommunications sectors. Only certain percentages differ, as will be shown hereafter.
5 In the mining sector, each company must set aside 4 per cent of its annual net profit for the workers' 'cash' participation; of this sum one-fifth is passed on to

As for community participation in ownership, it is laid down that every year the company must hand over 12 per cent of its net profit in the form of shares in the company.[6] But here too, each of the communities only receives half of these shares directly; the other half is passed to the compensation community, which issues shares of its own representing the total stock contributions received from all the FCs and distributes these shares among the various communities in proportion to the number of man-days worked by each one.[7] As we can see, the community's share in ownership therefore consists, on the one hand, of shares in the company and, on the other, of shares in the compensation community. This shareholding logically confers the right to participation in profits and in the management of the company, but a distinction must be drawn between these two forms of participation.

Just as each community only receives directly half of the shares made over by the company whilst the other half goes to the compensation community, which proceeds to a redistribution, so also each community shall only receive directly the income attaching to shares which it possesses in reality, the compensation community receiving the income from the shares it centralizes and redistributing it among the various communities according to the number of shares in the compensation community that each one holds. The income to which the communities are entitled through their ownership participation is thus redistributed in part.

On the other hand, the rights to a share in management attached to the ownership participation of the various communities are *not* redistributed. The community's management rights (number of votes at shareholders'

---

the mining community (MC) and four-fifths to the mining compensation community (MCC). In the telecommunications sector, each company must set aside 10 per cent of its annual net profit of which one-half goes to the telecommunications community (TC), the other half to the telecommunications compensation community (TCC). The rules for the subsequent redistribution and the percentages are the same as in the fishing sector.

6 As in the case of industrial enterprises, the shares handed over to the community are *new* shares issued as the result of the (normally compulsory) reinvestment of this part of the profits, or *existing* shares if the company has no reinvestment program approved by the competent ministry.

7 In the mining sector, each company must deduct 6 per cent of its annual net profit for the community's participation in ownership; one-fifth of the shares handed over is given directly to the mining community (MC) and four-fifths are transferred to the mining compensation community (MCC). In the telecommunications sector, each company must set aside 15 per cent of its annual net profit for 'ownership' participation; one-half of the shares is given to the telecommunications community (TC) and the other half passes to the telecommunications compensation community (TCC). The rules applied subsequently are the same as those in the fishing sector.

meetings, number of representatives on the Board of Directors of the company, etc.) are determined by the percentage of the capital of the company represented by the total value of the shares that the company has had to hand over as the community's participation in ownership, *no matter* whether these shares are in fact held by the community itself or by the compensation community: thus we have here a case of separation of participation in management of the company from participation in its ownership.

Thanks to the annual transfer of 12 per cent of the net profit, the community's share in ownership (either direct or through the compensation community) must increase year by year until it represents 50 per cent of the company's capital. The principle is therefore the same as in the case of the industrial sector, just as the provisions laid down once this proportion has been reached. On the one hand, the fishing community will issue shares representing its shareholding and will distribute them among its workers according to their seniority in the company. On the other hand, the company must continue to set aside for the community 12 per cent of its net profit (in the form of shares in COFIDE) and 10 per cent for the workers' direct participation in profits. The difference from the industrial sector lies in the fact that the system of compensation between companies continues to operate, one part of the shares and profits passing by way of the compensation community which then redistributes them among the various individual communities.

Other variants of the participation scheme described

These other variants, relating to certain types of enterprise, concern the community's participation in ownership and its share in management. They do not affect the workers' 'cash' participation nor the possible compensation schemes between different communities.

The first of the variants in question relates to *basic industries*. Under the 'General Industries Law', basic industries (closely defined by the law itself) are in principle reserved to the state, but they can be left to the private sector for a limited period of time. Whether it be a state-owned or a private company, the industrial community's *participation in ownership* does not consist of shares in the company: the 15 per cent of the net profit of the company set aside for the IC must be used for the purchase of the company's bonds or, failing these, for buying stock in COFIDE. In this case, the IC, instead of receiving dividends from the company, will receive the income attaching to the bonds or stock purchased. Furthermore, with regard to *participation in management*, the situation varies according to whether it is a state-owned or a private company. In *state-owned* enterprises in the basic sector, the IC will always be represented by *two* members on the directing bodies of the company. On the other hand, in *private* companies in the basic sector, the number of representatives of the IC on the directing bodies increases in proportion to the relative size of the IC's shareholding, according to the usual principles. However, since in this particular case the holding of the IC does not consist of shares in the company in which it operates, there is, here too, a dissociation between participation in the ownership and participation in the management of the company.

The other variant has to do with *state-owned* and *mixed* companies in the *mining* sector, and also with *state* companies in the *telecommunications* sector. Their case is similar to that of state companies operating in the basic industries. On the one hand, the portion of the net profit that the company must hand over as the community's share in ownership has to be used to buy bonds (not shares) in the company, or, failing these, stock in COFIDE.[8] On the other hand, the labor community, in these companies, is always represented by *two* members on the company's directing bodies.[9]

The problem of time requirement

How long will it take for the community's shareholding, purchased with a certain percentage transferred from the annual net profit of the company, finally to reach 50 per cent of the company's capital? There are obviously three basic factors that influence this time requirement:

1 The value of the company's capital;

2 The amount of its net profit;

3 The percentage of this profit which must be passed on to the community.

As the former two factors determine the rate of profit, we may say that the time requirement in question will be fundamentally affected, on the one hand, by the rate of profit of the company (and its development in the long term, bearing in mind especially the re-investment policy adopted) and, on the other, by the percentage of the profits laid down by the law for transfer to the community.

Let us begin by considering the simplest case of an industrial firm that does not increase its capital. Let us imagine, for example, that its capital is 1 000 000 (represented by 1000 shares valued at 1000) and that the net profit is 200 000 (thus the rate of profit is 20 per cent, and we shall assume that it remains constant from year to year). The company must assign

8 Under the compensation scheme studied above, part of this stock and of the income attaching to it is transferred by way of the compensation community.
9 The case of *mixed* companies in the *telecommunications* sector is similar to that of private companies operating in the basic industries: the community receives no shares in the company, but its share in management increases in proportion to the relative size of its shareholding.

15 per cent of its net profit, that is to say 30 000, towards the community's share in ownership: the community therefore receives 3 per cent of the firm's capital. In these circumstances, the community will come to own half of the company's capital after seventeen years.[10]

Let us suppose now that our industrial enterprise proceeds to reinvest and as a result to increase its capital. It is self-evident that the greater the reinvestment, the longer it will take the community to reach 50 per cent ownership of the capital. Does this mean that the capitalist can at will delay the workers' participation by investing to the utmost? Not at all, for there are several factors that have to be taken into account.

On the one hand, the very share in the capital held at any given moment by the community entitles it to a corresponding share in the new investment that the company has decided upon. If, for instance, a company has a capital of 1,000,000, 20 per cent of which belongs to the industrial community, and if furthermore this company makes a profit of 200,000 and decides to reinvest the whole amount, then the community will increase its holdings by a sum equal to $200,000 \times 15\% + 200,000 \times 20\%$, that is to say, 70,000 (instead of 30,000 if it were not taken into account that the community already holds 20 per cent of the capital).[11]

On the other hand, the capitalist operating in Peru is not free to reinvest all the profits he makes in his own company. First of all, we know that a certain percentage of the net profit (10 per cent for industrial enterprises) must be distributed among the workers as *'cash' participation*, which *ipso facto* reduces the maximum percentage for reinvestment.[12] Secondly, the *size of the market* constitutes yet another limit: the capitalist cannot afford to create over-capacities such that his rate of profit would be lastingly compromised. Finally, the law stipulates that all investment and reinvestment must, indeed, *be approved by the competent ministry*. Thus in

10 Under the conditions of this example, but taking account of the differences in the statutory percentages (12 per cent for the fishing sector and 6 per cent for the mining sector), the time lapse would be twenty-one years for a fishing community and forty-two years for a mining community. For a mining community to reach 50 per cent of the share capital within a space of time comparable with that of an industrial community, the rate of profit in the mining company – all other things being equal – would have to be double what it is in the industrial enterprise.

11 This principle, which springs from the community's ownership rights, is explicitly laid down by the 'General Industries Law' (article 24, paragraph 3). The fact that it is not explicitly stated in the laws relating to the other sectors cannot fail to give rise to conflicting interpretations.

12 If we further consider that a fraction of the net profit must be allotted to technological research (within the company or in a national center), the maximum percentage for reinvestment is 88 per cent of the net profit in the industrial and telecommunications sectors, 90 per cent in the fishing sector and 95 per cent in that of mining.

theory the government has at its disposal a direct means of preventing reinvestments and increased capitalization which arise not from any economic motive but solely out of a concern to delay the community's participation.

If the capitalist cannot act as he wishes with regard to the variable 'capital', is he not much freer to regulate the variable 'profit'? Can he not artificially reduce his net profit in such a way as to reduce indirectly the community's share in ownership? The legislator has provided for two types of check in this respect, but he has also left an important loophole uncovered. The first check consists of stipulating that any payments outside of remunerations for actual services shall not be counted among the company's costs and therefore shall not reduce the amount of net profit. The second check, more general in nature, is placed in the hands of the community. The community council can in fact examine all the accounts and documents of the company in order to determine whether the net profits declared are 'genuine'. This examination of the accounts and documents is carried out by the community's representatives sitting on the Board of Directors, with, if the need arises, the assistance of any member of the community and/or a specialist in accountancy. Any conflict between the community and the company would be settled by the competent ministry.

However, nothing prohibits the capitalist from cutting down his profits by extending the scale of remunerations. By raising the salary of the senior personnel (manager, administrative staff, technicians) or by engaging expensive foreign staff in preference to local employees, the capitalist can kill two birds with one stone: not only does he hold up the community's advancement, but also he divides the workers, among whom the community is intended to promote cohesion. Faced with this capitalist tactic – which did not take long to appear in practice – the workers are without defence. In order to protect them against this manoeuvre, the government would have to adopt an 'income policy' providing, in the immediate future, for the fixing of a ceiling to the highest salaries or for their reduction. But up to now, no majority has emerged within the government to impose such an income policy in the private sector.[13]

The meaning of the labor communities

For many observers of the Peruvian régime (both in Peru and abroad) the creation of the labor communities is nothing other than a measure for the

13 During a recent seminar on the labor community organized for businessmen, the government announced that it was going to take a series of measures to stop manoeuvres that hold up the advancement of the labor community. These measures seem to be intended to make more explicit the two checks mentioned above but without, for all that, introducing an 'income policy' (see *Oiga*, 3 November 1972, no. 499, p. 40).

modernization of capitalism, and at the same time a fraud committed against the workers. The arguments generally put forward in support of this thesis can be grouped and synthesized in a few basic points. The creation of the community rouses the Peruvian capitalists from their lethargy; it encourages them to reinvest in their companies, to increase production and productivity. This objective is all the more essential since the founding of the Andean Common Market is going to strengthen the competition from neighboring countries (like Colombia and Chile). At the same time, the hope of participating in the profits, ownership and management of the enterprise stimulates the efforts of the workers, which contributes towards precisely the object in view. But the reform is ultimately nothing but a fraud. Does not the length of time required for the community to reach a 50 per cent capital holding prove that the legislator has no wish to promote a true company reform? What is more, the new laws specify that upon reaching its 50 per cent holding, the community shall distribute individual shares to the workers; do we not, from that point on, fall into the trap of a kind of 'people's capitalism'?

The argument relating to increased production and productivity is undeniable. This aim can clearly be seen in the whole preamble to the various laws, as well as in certain clear-cut provisions. For example, the profits and the shares transferred by the company to the compensation community of the sector are redistributed by the latter in proportion to the number of man-days worked by each community. Likewise, in the mining sector, companies in which the average income per worker is below 10 per cent of the average for the sector are excluded from the benefits of the compensation system. These are, without any doubt, measures intended to discourage strikes (which are frequent in the mining sector) and to raise the production indexes.

But is the company reform, for all that, a measure intended to deceive the workers? Let us leave aside for the moment the question of time requirements and concentrate on the argument concerning dispersed worker-shareholding upon attainment of the 50 per cent participation. In our opinion, only a superficial reading of the dispositions relating to the labor communities can suggest this argument. A careful reading must lead us to dismiss it for several reasons. First, what the community issues and distributes to its members, once it has reached 50 per cent of the company's capital, are shares representing participation in the community itself and not shares in the company. This distribution of individual shares does not therefore give the workers any entitlement to share directly in the management of the company; this right belongs to the labor community as such. Second, the number of shares in the community held by the various workers does not even affect their individual power of decision within the community; at the general assembly of the community, the principle remains 'one man, one vote'. Third, as regards the community's participation in the direction of the company, the community's representatives (who at that time will have 50 per cent of the votes and possibly the chairmanship of the meetings of shareholders and on the Board of Directors) must continue as in the past to vote as a group; there can be no question therefore of buying the votes of 'new little capitalists' acting independently. In fact, the shares in the community owned by the workers will be no more than material evidence of their right to a proportional share in the income to be distributed by the community. These shares, moreover, will not be transferable, and on a worker's leaving the community or dying, they must be bought back by the community.

If one can, therefore, accept, on the basis of the texts of the laws, that the company reform is to lead to true joint management, there remains to be considered the delicate question of the length of time required to achieve all this. The previous discussion on this point was limited to an analysis of the various theoretical factors affecting this time requirement. In practice, it is impossible obviously to give a single uniform answer; in the most favorable cases (very profitable enterprises with limited reinvestment, as in the fishing sector), the time required could be from seven to ten years; in unfavorable cases, it could be forty years and more. Bearing in mind all the factors mentioned above, it seems plausible to assume that for an 'average' company the time required would be twenty to twenty-five years. How must we interpret such a lapse of time? Does not such a slow advance constitute a dilatory measure, barely disguising a concern to prevent any real company reform? Although this theory cannot be refuted by categorical arguments, it does seem possible to put forward some objections to it and to offer an altogether different interpretation.

If the régime in power had no intention of undertaking a true company reform, if its only concern was to gain the collaboration of the workers and to stimulate their productive effort, it is difficult to understand why it would have burdened itself with such a complex reform as the gradual participation of the labor community in company management. Was it not much simpler to decree a much higher profit-sharing (for example, three times what is at present laid down), whilst retaining the compensation system now in force (and introducing a similar compensation scheme in the industrial sector) which indirectly penalizes strikes and excessive unprofitability? In the mind of the workers, the result would have been much more tangible. A substantial share in the profits, direct and immediate, attracts them much more than gradual and far-off participation in the management of the company. In the mind of the capitalists, the response would also have been much better. The existence of the labor community has been a constant bone of contention between the government and the industrialists. The latter never tire of repeating that they are prepared to distribute 25 per cent of their profits to the workers, instead of 10 per cent to the workers and 15 per cent to the community, and knowing that they are indispensable to the carrying out of the development plans, they have sought, with great persistence, to gain the abolition of the community using the weapon of non-reinvestment.[14]

If the government wanted a real company reform, could it not devise a scheme setting up *immediately* a management structure shared equally between community and capitalists? Such a radical reform could not have been enacted overnight, and indeed never could be unless one or other of the following hypotheses were to be made true: either the 'private sector' is willing to accept the reform and collaborates with the new régime; or else, failing this collaboration, the government can rely on alternative solutions: state management of enterprises (nationalization), or management entirely by the workers themselves (self-management). It so happens that none of these hypotheses holds true. The businessmen in the private sector have given sufficient expression, as we have just said, to their opposition to joint-management even in the distant future. If they choose to stay in Peru, it is in the hope that the present government will soon have to stand down or to modify its policy with regard to private enterprise. If the government had imposed joint-management without a pause, there is little doubt but that a large number of them would have preferred to leave the country immediately. Alternative solutions, furthermore, do not exist for the immediate future. On the one hand, the state does not have the organization and staff which would enable it to take over the full responsibility for industrial development; this is so much the case that in July 1972, the public sector (to which the basic industries are reserved) had not yet started on even one of the industrial projects provided for in the 1971–5 plan. On the other hand, there are very few companies in which the workers' representatives could in actual fact take over the management of the business and ensure the required levels of production and productivity.[15] In these circumstances, the government's policy with regard to private enterprise could not but be ambiguous. Capitalists are granted generous incentives to expand (notably substantial tax reliefs), they are declared to be essential to the development of the country and told they can rely upon the support

14 Two years after the promulgation of the 'General Industries Law' – and in spite of all the incentives provided for therein – reinvestments in the private sector were still limited essentially to the modernization of existing companies, with very little founding of new enterprises (see *Oiga*, 21 July 1972, no. 484, p. 13).
15 Similarly, those companies are few where, at the present time, even joint-management could be a concrete reality and not just a facade.

of the government. In order to appease them, it is suggested that the community answers the need to modernize the company, that joint-management will not come overnight, that the dynamic company head will, when that time comes, be the owner of a half-company which will be bigger than the enterprise of which he is the sole owner today. At the same time, the government refuses to give way on the principle of community participation in company management. It relies on the fact that this reform, precisely because of its gradual application (added to the incentives of which we have spoken) will be assimilated little by little by an increasing percentage of the businessmen in the private sector.[16] It takes for granted also that the experience gained within the labor communities, together with the new training opportunities offered by the recent and radical educational reform, will gradually permit workers really to assume their share of the responsibilities of the company.

If it is possible to explain the gradual nature of the company reform by reasons of circumstances, may we not also suggest that the government's objective might go even beyond joint-management? Might not the ultimate goal be the setting-up of self-managed enterprises? One must recognize first of all that joint-management does not seem to constitute anything but a temporary solution; the duality of powers that it involves makes it scarcely viable in the long run. On the other hand, it is difficult to see why, if the workers are capable of truly assuming their role in joint-management, they could not go a step further and manage their enterprises completely. A number of signs give us leave to presume that, in fact, the government has always given consideration to the formula of self-management. Have not several ministers or highly-placed civil servants, for example, expressed more or less openly their approval of self-managed enterprises? One of them, the previous Minister for Industry, spoke of it with so much spirit and animosity towards the capitalists that he brought relations to a complete standstill between the government and the private sector. His successor did not let the reform already undertaken fall into oblivion, nor, as we shall see, the idea of self-management. Furthermore, has not the government proceeded to take action in the agricultural sector, handing over to the workers the management of the great agro-industrial complexes taken over by the agrarian reform? It is significant that this reform, which was not expected so soon, should have been decided upon in consequence of various public disturbances provoked by an earlier hybrid management

16 Let us note in this connection that some heads of average-sized firms have decided as of now to transfer 50 per cent of their shares and to institute a system of joint-management. Also let us note that the idea of joint-management (or even of self-management) makes more rapid headway – quite logically – in the mind of business executives than in that of capitalist owners.

scheme.[17] It is likely that it will serve as a precedent some years from now when the labor communities (or simply a good number of them) have reached a substantial share in the management of industrial enterprises. As for the legislation on labor communities, does it not establish officially more than one principle characteristic of a true labor-managed enterprise? Let us recall in particular the following: the separation of management from ownership (in many cases, the community has rights in management without the corresponding right to ownership); the separation of trade union activities from involvement in management (a union leader may not be a member of the council, the executive body of the community); the principle of 'one man–one vote'.

The most interesting factor for consideration is, however, the recent decision (28 July 1972) to set up 'social ownership' enterprises, whose future cannot fail to influence the existing labor communities. These enterprises, from what we know of them, correspond fairly closely to the characteristics defined by Professor J. Vanek, the founder of the economic theory of labor-management (1970, 1973).[18] Two essential features of this new type of enterprise are:

1 The absence of ownership rights on the part of the enterprise;

2 The exclusive management by those working in the enterprise.

A state agency provides all the financing needed (self-financing is excluded). The firm pays the state agency a substantial (fixed) rental for the finance and land[19] – as well as a depreciation charge – and 'usufructs'

17 The agrarian reform (June 1969) had transformed the big agro-industrial complexes into 'cooperatives', the management of which was carried out jointly by delegates of the government and workers' representatives. The latter, even beyond the fact that they were elected in an undemocratic fashion, were granted only very minority representation; this was indeed fixed in proportion to the capital which the cooperative had repaid to the state, which was financing the purchase of the land. Since April 1972, this system has been replaced by management exclusively by the workers' democratically-elected representatives.

18 These works demonstrate the higher efficiency (especially in comparison with the capitalist system) of a system combining labor-management in enterprises with central planning (preferably 'indirect'). Professor Vanek has stayed in Peru on several occasions and the government commissioned him, in 1971, to study the concrete possibilities of setting up a participatory economy in Peru. We must note that the creation of 'social ownership' enterprises was already provided for in the 'General Industries Law' of July 1970 (articles 6 and 3), but at that time nothing was specifically laid down concerning the concrete form of these enterprises, nor their relative importance in the economy.

19 One reason for fixing high 'rentals' for financing and land is to guarantee that the labor-managed firm will always use a comparatively large number of workers for every unit of capital and land (in contrast to the natural trend in the traditional

the assets it uses. All money made over and above the payments is regarded as income (rather than profit) and is distributed to the workers in the form of money or collective consumption. Workers have the exclusive right to take part in management, each of them having equality of vote. The basis of the new type of enterprise is therefore 'work in common' rather than 'ownership in common'.

The first 'social ownership' enterprises are to be set up in 1973. According to repeated official statements and law provisions, this new type of enterprise will receive full state support in technical assistance and financing, and should eventually become the leading type in the Peruvian economy. The government also stresses that the creation of the new enterprises will not be at the expense of existing forms; the 'pluralistic' economy will include, at the same time, both an important state-owned sector and the private sector of companies 'reformed' by the labor community. But it may be safely argued that the policy towards these private companies will be greatly influenced by the degree of success attained by the labor-managed enterprises: the better the performance of the 'social ownership' sector, the stronger will be the pressure to speed up the advancement of the labor communities and introduce self-management.

The problem, at that stage, would be to know what kind of self-management would be involved: with or without private ownership of the means of production? For social reasons and for economic efficiency, the second solution should be retained; once the labor community attains a controlling share (be it 50 per cent or any other figure) in the ownership and direction of the enterprise, the enterprise should be transformed into one of 'social ownership'. Otherwise, if self-management were to be associated with private (though common) ownership, 'common selfishness' could simply replace 'individual selfishness', and self-financing would lead to inefficient allocation of resources as in capitalist systems. Actually, the implementation of a truly 'participatory economy', socially satisfying and economically efficient, requires that:

1 The 'social ownership' firms really become the most important sector, both through the direct creation of new firms and through the transformation of enterprises with labor communities.

2 Some kind of 'National Labor Management Agency' finance and promote the labor-managed firms and serve as an instrument of national planning.

cooperatives and enterprises with labor communities towards increasing mechanization and restricted membership). Another reason is that high 'rentals' will ensure the availability of funds to the state agency for reinvestment in new labor-managed enterprises.

3 The workers and all people in general play an effective part in determining the objectives of the national and local plans and the means of reaching them.

These goals are not attainable overnight and imply definite political choices, but they show the general direction in which various recent reforms and institutions must progress if the Peruvian 'development scheme', which is certainly very original in many respects, is to ensure its prosperity in the long run.

References

VANEK, J. (1970), *The General Theory of Labor-Managed Market Economies*, Cornell University Press.

VANEK, J. (1973), 'Some fundamental considerations of financing and the form of ownership under labor management', in H. C. Bos (ed.), *Economic Structure and Development*, North Holland, Amsterdam.

13 C. J. Bellas

Industrial Democracy Through Worker Ownership:
An American Experience

First published in this volume.

Industrial democracy

Industrial democracy is an elusive concept and there is no one acceptable definition for it.

Any discussion of 'industrial democracy' runs into difficulties because of a vagueness in the concept and the many different meanings injected into the term. Interpretations have changed in the course of time and are as numerous as the different political systems and ideologies (Waldenstrom, 1968, p. 59).

Democracy, in the political sphere, is associated with government by the people, or rule by those being ruled, through elected representatives.

When we transfer this idea [democracy] directly to the industrial sphere, the concept of industrial democracy takes on the meaning that the employees in an industrial enterprise should select, by majority vote, the board of the company, its managing director and other important company officers, and determine business policy. In principle, the board and management would be responsible to the employees for the administration (Waldenstrom, 1968, p. 59).

Political systems in which the rights of direction and control accrue to the owners of an enterprise, find it impossible to apply the democracy defined above to industrial organizations. The worker-owned plywood mills (or cooperatives) discussed here attain democracy through ownership and therefore they do not violate the fundamentals of the capitalist system in which they operate. One cannot determine to what extent industrial democracy will be achieved in the future, with or without worker ownership, and therefore the existence of the plywood cooperatives, operating under the definition of industrial democracy quoted above, is truly a remarkable and noteworthy phenomenon.

Production cooperatives

The cooperative has been a successful form of business ownership in the areas of retailing, marketing and electric utility operation, yet there have been few successful worker or production cooperatives, in which the employees themselves own the instruments of production. Most of the attempts have failed because of:

1 The lack of adequate capital;

2 The difficulty of maintaining discipline and productivity in an enterprise in which all workers are at the same time co-owners;

3 The absence of business experience;

4 The fact that many of these societies are inspired by a syndicalist ideal to establish the whole economy on the basis of the worker function;

5 The difficulty of selling the goods produced (International Labour Office, 1944, pp. 56–7).

When not one firm but a group of worker-owned firms is able to overcome the aforementioned problems, the occurrence is rare and worthy of examination. Specifically, twenty plywood manufacturing firms in the Pacific Northwest represent the only known group of manufacturing co-operatives in the United States today.

History

The first plywood cooperative and the sixth plywood mill in the United States, Olympia Veneer Company, was organized in 1921 at Olympia, Washington. Organization apparently resulted from the efforts of workers with Scandinavian backgrounds and strong cooperative traditions. A new, labor-intensive industry and access to good quality timber were distinct advantages for a cooperative organization. Job skills were relatively easy to learn, little status differential existed among jobs and with the emphasis on productivity and quality the owners were able to overcome startup difficulties and turn the firm into a successful operation.

The formation of new plywood mills all but ceased during the Depression but began again in the late thirties and early forties, spurred by wartime demand. By 1942 three more cooperatives had begun operations, encouraged by the success of Olympia and the return its worker-owners had realized on their initial investment. By this time the plywood industry had acquired characteristics that helped overcome additional problems that production cooperatives have historically faced. Homogeneity of product and industry grading standards allowed for relatively easy entry. The sales function was being handled by agents, therefore a firm needed no marketing organization. Finally, the booming demand created by the increased use of plywood in home construction generated a volume of sales adequate to pay off initial loans and secure future credit.

The remainder of the cooperative mills organized between 1945 and 1955 were organized by promoters acting for their own personal gain.

Typically they collected large fees for their services which involved either setting up a new cooperative with new facilities or forming a cooperative to purchase an existing operating company from its owner. The promoters were assisted by the favorable reports generated from the early cooperative successes. The promotion of cooperatives halted rather abruptly as several promoters were prohibited from further sales by the Securities and Exchange Commission which subsequently filed criminal indictments. The unfavorable publicity made any future formations virtually impossible. The tragic part of the episode was that many new cooperatives had used all of their capital to purchase outdated and overpriced plants, and others had been induced to enter into contracts with the promoter calling for exorbitant fees for management services. Some of these cooperatives failed, some have never financially recovered from the effects of their formation, but some have recovered and prospered. Records indicate that a total of twenty-eight cooperative plywood mills have existed. Three of these, including Olympia, have sold out to larger firms, five have closed, and the rest remain in operation.

Size

In terms of output, the size of the worker-owned mills ranges from twelve million to 135 million square feet per year. At a hypothetical net price of eighty dollars per thousand feet, net sales for the mills would range from approximately $0·96 million to $10·8 million. Average cooperative mill output is slightly higher than the industry average. Employment ranges from a low of seventy to a high of 450.

The mills are primarily sanded plywood producers. Sanded plywood requires more direct labor than sheathing or rough plywood. Companies whose production mix consists of more than 85 per cent sanded plywood account for 16 per cent of the total industry plywood output. Of this approximately 90 per cent is produced by the worker-owned mills. Much of this sanded plywood is supplied to the large wood products firms such as Georgia–Pacific.

Organization and operation

The plywood cooperatives were organized along similar lines yet each has variations peculiar to itself. It is possible therefore to describe a typical cooperative; yet differences do exist among firms.

The underlying principles of organization are:

Each owner has only one vote regardless of the number of shares he holds;
Income or surplus is returned to the owners as workers and not as dividends on capital;

Available work is distributed among all owners who wish to work;
All worker–owners receive the same hourly wage rate;
Final authority resides in a general meeting of the membership.

The owner of a share (or some multiple thereof designated as a working share) is entitled to a job in the enterprise, if a job is available. If full-time employment is not available for all owners, then the bylaws usually provide that rotation shall occur among all workers so that they share equally. Nonowners may be hired, especially in the larger mills, but their jobs are the most vulnerable when employment is cut back. Owners may sell their shares, but the company usually has the right to purchase the offered share at the market price. Dismissal of an owner is extremely difficult because the owners have protected their rights as workers by putting restrictive dismissal provisions in the bylaws.

Membership on the board of directors is limited to owners. The occupants of certain positions such as superintendent, general manager, or log buyer are often prohibited from board service. The organizations are willing to sacrifice the expertise of certain individuals rather than allow anyone to build up excessive power in the organization.

The top operating officer is the general manager, usually not an owner. His position is extremely vulnerable and manager turnover is high. When compared to managers of conventional plywood mills of the same size the cooperative managers are better paid but indicate that their security, autonomy and self-actualization needs are much less satisfied.

Cooperative boards have the wide power given to boards of conventional corporations, however they usually are limited in the capital outlays they can authorize; anything over a specified dollar amount must be submitted to a vote of the general membership.

The cooperatives attempt to maintain a unitary wage scale for all owners regardless of job, but owners in key managerial positions are often paid at a somewhat higher wage. Certain jobs which are best handled on an incentive basis are frequently assigned to nonowners to preserve equality. It is difficult to maintain both high productivity and wage equality without a great deal of personal commitment to the organization. Where this occurs, results indicate that any possible loss of incentive or status has not decreased organizational effectiveness.

The cooperatives are constantly under pressure from owners to pay the highest hourly wages possible and this also serves to lessen income and reduce corporate taxes. Any surplus is divided among the worker–owners on the basis of hours worked. The plywood industry is notorious for price fluctuations and these wide shifts are transmitted to owners' wages. The magnitude of the effect of the fluctuations usually depends on the financial position of the company.

Performance and its associated variables

The worker-owned plywood mills are a phenomenon resulting from a unique combination of location, industry and individuals. It is highly probable that they will all eventually succumb due to various conditions, but until that happens, these cooperatives can provide us with much valuable information.

Within the group there appear to be wide deviations in performance. It is our intent to compare the performance of the cooperative mills and try to explain the differences. One of the key variables that merits investigation is worker–owner participation. Advocates of democratic organizations believe that legitimized participation should result in healthier organizations which will be better performers over the long run.

Performance

Performance, as the term is used here, is related to the goals of the organization and the extent to which they are achieved. The plywood cooperatives currently in operation exhibit very little cooperative idealism but rather exist to further the welfare of their owners. The goals of the worker–owners are income and job security. Security is a function of the nature of the organization and of the level of income. Except in rare cases, an owner who wants a job is entitled to one. If the wages or hours available make working in the mill economically unattractive, the income goal is not attained and neither, therefore, is security. By focusing our attention on the income goal we in effect consider the security goal.

Worker–owners receive payment at an hourly rate. Depending on the legal nature of the firm's organization these are designated as wages or advances on the owner's share of retained earnings. At year's end, additional distributions may be made on the basis of hours worked. Other earnings are placed in employee trust or retirement funds. The income or return to the worker–owners is the sum of all these payments.

It is unrealistic to measure a firm's performance solely on direct return to owners because an irrational payout could undermine future ability to continue operations. An owner has a financial stake in the firm by virtue of the share that he owns. Any depletion of the physical assets and/or closure of the plant would cause almost total loss of his investment. Invested earnings that increase productivity or assure raw material supply will increase the book value of his share and also improve the chances of increasing his direct remuneration. For this study, both the long and short run returns to owners were incorporated in the measure of performance.

The measure of performance or effectiveness for a worker-owned mill has for this research been defined as the total return to an average working owner over a given period of time plus the net change in the book value of his share over the same period. The inclusion of immediate returns and increase in share value considers both short and long range performance. The time period used here was the five year period, 1963–7. This covers several high and low plywood price periods.

The difference in the average five year return between worker–owners in the highest and lowest performing mills was approximately $35,000 or $7000 per year. The mean return for the eighteen mills studied was approximately $43,000. This wide disparity indicates that industrial cooperation, as practised in the plywood industry, can be successful or unsuccessful.

The hourly wage rates of the highest performers are consistently higher than the industry average, and the lowest performers, wage rates are consistently lower. The availability of considerable amounts of overtime work undoubtedly raises the annual wage of the worker at a low performing cooperative above the industry average.

Participation

The participation measure is an index constructed from variables that involve not only the actual participation of the worker–owner, but also his felt participation. The latter is influenced by: the opportunity to participate, whether or not this opportunity is taken, and the amount and character of organizational communication. The participation index comprises:

1 The percentage of working owners that have served on the board of directors in the past five years;

2 The percentage of working owners serving on committees;

3 The number of board meetings held each year;

4 The number of general meetings held during the year;

5 The effectiveness of methods used to communicate minutes of board meetings to the worker–owners.

Other variables

There are certain factors that restricted the selection of operating variables for inclusion in the study. Technical operations vary widely from plant to plant, and these differences make comparisons difficult if not impossible. Many firms keep disorganized records and others are reluctant to divulge key operating data. A key variable such as productivity is virtually impossible to measure. Nevertheless, many comparable variables were available including those relating to size, output, production and raw material costs, sales prices and margins.

Results

The participation and performance variables correlated at 0·005 level of statistical significance, a strong indication of an underlying relationship between the two. Of the operation variables, only the average total capital variable was correlated with performance at a statistically significant level of 0·05 or above. The investigation has uncovered a large difference in the performance of the cooperative mills, but it has uncovered little in its operations that explains the relative success and failure. This writer believes that the inability to identify certain operating variables associated with performance focuses attention on the results of the participation analysis. There is apparently an *esprit de corps*; a sense of pulling together – 'cooperation' – that surmounts obstacles presented by the environment and enables a cooperative enterprise to succeed. Certain economic factors may assist the operation but they appear insufficient to overcome the lack of participation and involvement.

The instability of the system

The plywood cooperatives demonstrated that the readily accepted reasons for past cooperative failures can be overcome under the proper conditions. What is of greater importance is that this type of cooperative is inherently unstable. Instability can result in organizational failure, even with financial success.

The instability is a product of the organization's primary objective which is not maximization of profit, but maximization of worker–owner income. It is this objective, and the decisions supporting it that determine the survival of the organization.

Figure 1 illustrates the critical decisions concerning the allocation of anticipated retained earnings as an intersection of two feedback loops – one positive, the other negative. In some form these exist in conventional firms, but it is the group making the allocation decision that is unique here.

At the time of formation there is a low level of investment in sophisticated plant and equipment. In the positive feedback loop an increase in retained earnings makes more money available for investment, this lowers production costs and increases earnings. In the negative loop, an increase in retained earnings makes more money available for owner returns (in the form of wages), this increases production costs, and decreases earnings. The crucial decision for the employees is to decide the amount of the anticipated profits to allocate to themselves and the amount to reinvest in the firm – a conflict between the desire to receive maximum return for their effort and the long run survival of the firm.

The simple system of Figure 1 is complicated by the impact of market prices upon retained earnings. A conventional firm fights lower prices and reduced demand by furloughing employees. The cooperative adjusts by

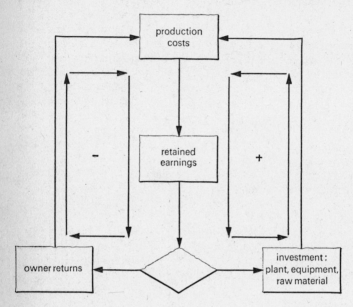

Figure 1 The basic allocation decision

rationing the available work and/or cutting wages to working shareholders. As one can well imagine, shareholders resist reduction in their wages. The financially stable cooperative can ride out price fluctuations without adjusting wages, but the financially weak are continually in a state of adjustment. This constant readjustment hinders long range planning, including investment programs.

More than merely allocating adequate funds for investment, a careful balance must be maintained between it and owner returns. In the early stages of growth, emphasis must be placed on the positive feedback loop of reinvestment to lower production and/or raw material costs. Firms that have failed to emphasize this have been unable to achieve a stability or growth of income to the owners. However, once a firm has reduced debt, upgraded facilities and secured raw materials, it can increase returns to owners and still invest, perhaps in other related ventures (see Figure 2). Excessive investment, expansion, and vertical or horizontal integration result in a larger organization, one that is difficult to operate demo-

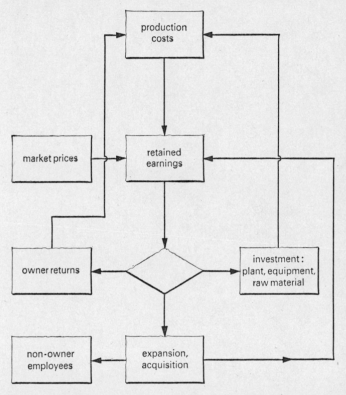

Figure 2 The allocation decision complicated by prices and growth opportunities

cratically. The owners, unwilling to dilute ownership, characteristically do not admit the workers from an acquired firm to ownership. The democratic nature of the organization begins to deteriorate, and it may eventually resemble a conventional corporation.

Conclusion

When owners are interested in maximization of worker income at the expense of profit or company survival, survival *as a cooperative* is impossible. It is this problem which limits producer cooperatives of the current variety and which must be overcome if similar attempts are to succeed.

The plywood firms studied operate successfully with a work force of as many as 450 men, 90 per cent of whom are owners. Even though ownership could be extended to 1000 workers, the participation mechanism so necessary to efficient operation would be difficult to achieve.

Producer cooperatives have not been successful, and where apparently successful as reported here, still possess characteristics which signal their eventual demise. Under their current methods of operation, the key to longevity appears to be in their ability to reach peak operating efficiency while rejecting over-expansion. Decisions therefore must be made with much more 'fine tuning' than in conventional organizations. Unfortunately, the shareholders possess neither the talent nor experience to accomplish this delicate task. It is questionable whether any individuals or groups could do so.

What will happen to these firms in an industry that is becoming highly mechanized? The poor performers will eventually dissolve. The shares of the successful firms have attained values that make sale by a retiring owner to a potential worker–owner almost impossible. As this condition increases, the successful cooperative can either 'go public' or sell out to a major producer. The relatively uncomplicated nature of the latter seems more likely.

The problems confronting the plywood cooperatives are not necessarily characteristic of other self-managed firms. Worker ownership proved to be an effective way to revive a troubled conventional firm or to start a new one, yet this same organizational form may be inadequate once an enterprise has achieved a measure of success and growth. This may indicate that while worker management is workable and desirable, there are better models than worker ownership for achieving long-run success with full worker participation.

References

BELLAS, C. J. (1972), *Industrial Democracy and the Worker Owned Firm*, Praeger.
BERMAN, K. (1967), *Worker-Owned Plywood Companies*, Washington State University Press.
BOGARDUS, E. (1952), *Principles of Cooperation*, Cooperative League of the USA, Chicago.
International Labour Office (1944), *Cooperative Organizations and Post-War Relief*, Montreal.
JONES, B. (1894), *Cooperative Production*, Clarendon Press.
STURMTHAL, A. (1964), *Workers' Councils*, Harvard University Press.
WALDENSTROM, E. (1968), 'Works councils', *Columbia J. World Bus.*, vol. 3.
WEBB, S. and B. (1968), 'Democracies of producers', in K. Coates and A. Topham (eds.), *Industrial Democracy in Great Britain*, MacGibbon & Kee.

14 H. Barkai

The Kibbutz: An Experiment in Microsocialism

Adapted from Haim Barkai, 'The kibbutz: an experiment in microsocialism', in *Israel and Arabs: Views from the Left*, Bantam, 1972, pp. 69–100.

Factual background

Kibbutzim are familiar landmarks in Israel's landscape. The roughly 230 kibbutzim founded since 1910 have put their imprint on the geography of the country. Their impact on the ideology and the politics of Zionism and on the evolving institutional and social structure of the Jewish community in Palestine and later in Israel is presumably even more significant. The world fame of the kibbutz, not to mention its standing as a household word in the country, bears ample witness to its extraordinary position at the frontier of action and the focus of politics in Palestine and Israel, and to its unique features as a socio-economic entity.

This position of eminence, it is important to remember, was reached and maintained even though each kibbutz is a rather small community, and the kibbutz movement as a whole has always been a minority phenomenon. The average kibbutz has a population of 400, and a membership of about 200 – only three kibbutzim have a population of over 1000. Total population grew from about 500–600 in the early 1920s to close to 100,000 in the early 1970s, and was always a rather small fraction of the Jewish, and *a fortiori* the total population. By the middle 1920s (1927) when existing kibbutzim were already more stable entities, kibbutz population was about 2·5 per cent of total Jewish population. By 1970 it was about 3·6 per cent, after reaching a peak of nearly 6 per cent in the late 1930s.

Population and membership grew rapidly by any standard. Even if we take 1927 as the base year instead of 1921, these figures imply an annual average growth rate of about 10 per cent for the forty-five years ending in 1971. Population growth slowed down considerably in the 1950s and 1960s, in which it was close to only 1·5 per cent. However, compared with the growth rates of rural communities in industrial societies, which are usually negative, this is still rapid growth.

Though the principles of the collective do not permit the use of differential material benefits as work incentives, kibbutzim are amongst the more efficient production units in the country. This allows the kibbutz population to enjoy a living standard which is about equal to the country average.

It also means that the kibbutzim are in the upper third of the total population ranked by per capita consumption levels. Annual per capita income and consumption growth rates of about 5 and 4 per cent respectively (in the 1950s and 1960s) underline the dynamics of this process. This rapid increase means that towards the end of the 1970s, kibbutz living standards will be close to the present consumption levels of Western and Northern Europe.

Structure and organization

It is the nature of the kibbutz as a collective that lends particular interest to these facts. A sketch of its structure and government may help to clarify how this intricate organism, guided by socialist principles, organizes production and distributes income. Figure 1 attempts to convey the most essential elements of kibbutz structure and links in formal terms.

The inherently democratic nature of the kibbutz is underlined by the position of the general assembly at the top of the chart. Yet as production and distribution grew in magnitude and complexity, the kibbutzim were forced to give up the innocent belief in decision-making and direct control of every aspect of communal life by all members, meeting in the general assembly. The initial attempt at direct control gave way to a more indirect technique of decision-making and control. This led, step-by-step, as the need arose, to the development of the elaborate network of offices, committees and functions outlined in Figure 1, which represents the machinery of the kibbutz as it is today.

The general assembly, which meets weekly, is the central deliberative organ and the ultimate source of power. A council composed of twenty to thirty is, in the larger kibbutzim, empowered to discuss in depth most of the subjects which come up to the general assembly, make its recommendation to the assembly,[1] or take a final decision (subject to appeal). The secretariat, also meeting weekly, is the main decision-making organ. It is composed of the principal office holders: the general secretary, the economic coordinator, the labor coordinator, the treasurer, the coordinator of education and several lay members.

Most of the details are, however, studied and decided by the various subsidiary committees, such as the economic, labor, housing, welfare and education and culture committees, to mention only the most important amongst them. A cardinal function of these committees is their role in the process of selecting and nominating members for administrative and mana-

1 For example, the granting of membership to candidates is a delicate matter, and is usually carried by the general assembly with little deliberation on the basis of the council's recommendation. It is in the council that each candidature is given a thorough airing.

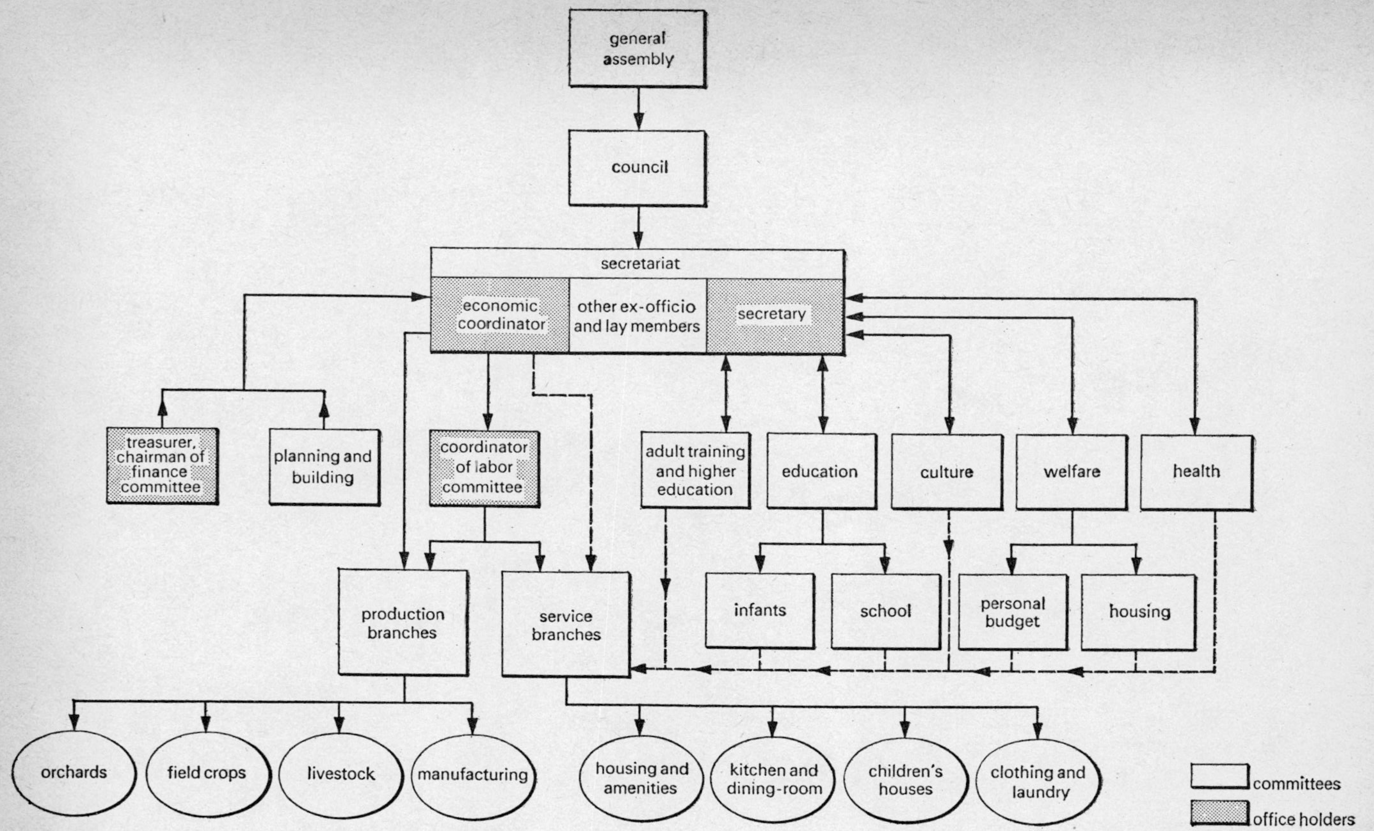

Figure 1

Legend:
- committees (white boxes)
- office holders (shaded boxes)

Chart structure:

general assembly → council → secretariat

Secretariat contains: economic coordinator, other ex-officio and lay members, secretary

From secretariat/economic coordinator:
- treasurer, chairman of finance committee
- planning and building
- production branches → orchards, field crops, livestock, manufacturing
- coordinator of labor committee
- service branches → housing and amenities, kitchen and dining-room, children's houses, clothing and laundry

From secretary:
- adult training and higher education
- education → infants, school
- culture
- welfare → personal budget, housing
- health

gerial functions. Thus, the economic committee nominates branch co-ordinators, the labor committee decides on who is to work where, the education committee decides who will be the school principal and who is going to be in charge of, say, baby houses.

This elaborate system of committees and managerial functions means that a significant part of the adult population has a responsible position of one sort or another. If we add to this also branch coordinators, and taking duplication into account, the number of members involved in one or the other of these capacities can reach eighty to 100 in a kibbutz of average size. This means that 40–50 per cent of members take part in running the affairs of the kibbutz. Since rotation is as a matter of principle an integral element of the kibbutz system of government, almost everyone is expected sooner or later to serve in one capacity or another.

The specific contribution of kibbutzim to human experience is un-doubtedly their attempt to translate socialist principles into everyday practice within communities based on voluntary membership. This led them, by means of an evolutionary process, to adopt and adapt a set of rules of action and behavior, which may be summarized as follows:

1 All kibbutz property is owned in common – the legal title being in the collective. Assets which serve in production are operated by the community. Some of the assets which serve consumption purposes are also operated and used on a communal basis. Others are, however, distributed for personal use.

2 The kibbutz abides by the principle of self-labor, which means that hired labor should not be employed.

3 Kibbutz manpower is at the disposal of the community. The allocation of time between work, study and leisure and the allocation of labor between alternative employment in production or services branches are determined by the relevant community organs.

4 The kibbutz maintains *equality* in the distribution of real income. First and foremost, this involves a severance of the link between an individual's contribution to production and the real income from which he benefits.

This set of tenets refers to the two facets of the kibbutz which make it into an integrated social and economic entity. On the one hand they set rules for running the production and services sectors in which kibbutz income is earned. On the other hand they imply the principles and thus set the rules for the distribution of real income among the individuals which make up the community. To gather an overall perspective of the way in which the kibbutz operates it might be helpful to try first to visualize the workings of the production side and afterwards to study its counterpart – the consumption facet.

The 'modus operandi' of the production sector

Production and the provision of services are organized in the form of separate units, or, in kibbutz parlance, 'branches'. Each branch, whether it is a production or a service branch, is run by a permanent team headed by a branch coordinator. If seasonal work is required the permanent staff is reinforced by temporary workers. Land, buildings, equipment, and the stocks required for their operation are put at the disposal of the branches. This, of course, means that production and service branches compete with each other for scarce resources: land, capital equipment, unskilled and skilled labor, and inevitably for entrepreneurial talent too. The function of the branches as the elementary cells of the economic structure is underlined by the fact that they are distinct accounting units.

The permanent team consists of a group of experienced members who work in a branch for a fairly long period of, say, several years. This informal group normally includes from four to eight persons and not more than, say, ten.[2] The running of a branch is therefore not burdened with formalities. An institution known as the 'branch meeting' exists though its responsibilities are not specifically defined. The branch coordinator who heads the team often 'emerges' from among its members. Formally, however, the branch coordinator is nominated by the economic committee in the case of production branches, and by the relevant committee in the case of service branches.

The permanent team shares responsibilities for the regular day-to-day running of the branch. It also usually initiates the adoption of new techniques and this usually involves changes in equipment and the product mix. More extensive development plans are also suggested and studied by the permanent team before being submitted for discussion and approval by the relevant committees, the secretariat and finally the general assembly.

The motivation of individuals to do their best at every production and service branch is evidently the *sine qua non* of kibbutz viability. This applies both on the entrepreneurial and the managerial plane and on the more humble plane of the man on the job – the tractor driver or the man in the dining room. The continuous growth and success of the kibbutz in terms of accepted success indicates that so far this problem has been satisfactorily solved. How this has been done, and particularly what is the social and institutional set-up which ensures that the efforts of individuals

2 The size of the permanent team in a manufacturing enterprise, which is one of several branches in many kibbutzim, may be larger. This point is taken up later.

will make the kibbutz tick, is probably the most interesting aspect of the matter.

The question of motivation however, is more easily raised than convincingly resolved. What we know is only what is not relevant to motivation in the kibbutz milieu. Differential material benefits, which are a major means for motivating individual performance in the nonkibbutz world, are ruled out by ideology and, for all purposes in practice. Nonmaterial benefits which are also relevant in the nonkibbutz world are, however, not excluded. Respect and esteem for a good day's work and for the success in managerial and entrepreneurial functions is undoubtedly an important factor in the attitude of individuals towards work and responsibility in the kibbutz environment. And *per contra*, the disfavor with which shirking is viewed is, in the closely knit communities which even the largest kibbutzim still are, a powerful sanction.[3]

The kibbutz expression 'work attitude' conveys in a nutshell that it is self-discipline which is expected to count most in this context. It is self-discipline sustained by the socialist maxim 'from each according to his ability', and by the concept of 'human fulfilment' through work.[4] These notions require each individual to make the greatest effort for the good of the community, even though he cannot expect to be rewarded personally. This is not to say that community disapproval, which is mainly informal, fulfils no function in maintaining work discipline.[5] Even informal disapproval affects behavior or may induce people who cannot adapt themselves to this self-imposed discipline to leave. Hence personal effort in a kibbutz depends ultimately on ideology and thus on the intellectual ability of members to understand, absorb, and turn into action a complicated set of abstractions.

Self-discipline sustained by ideology explains behavior on the plane of the individual. The kibbutz plane is, however, another matter. Rules for operating the various components which make up the whole and performance criteria to ensure optimal allocation of manpower and other

3 In this context we may mention again some of the relevant figures: mean kibbutz population in the late 1960s was a little over 400 and 95 per cent of kibbutzim had a total population of 800 or less. This, of course, means that kibbutz members know each other very well indeed. This is less so in the handful of settlements which have a population of between 1000 and 1500. Still, even there, direct personal contacts are strong by the standards of the nonkibbutz society.

4 The view that work is one of the more important values of human life has been accepted by all shades of opinion among the forerunners of the collective movement before World War One and its immediate aftermath. This view, from which they deduced that it is everybody's duty to work, has been strongly influenced by the Russian populist and revolutionary traditions from Kropotkin onwards.

5 A formal decision asking an individual to leave a kibbutz – which is the strongest sanction possible – is very rarely applied.

resources between competing production and service branches are obviously required. One may therefore ask what are the rules which guide the operation of each producer unit? And what are the principles of coordination of the medley of these units which make up the production sector of the kibbutz? Finally, how do these mesh with operations of the personal services sector to enable the system to work efficiently?

Consider first the problems faced by a production branch. How do the people in charge of a branch decide how much to produce, and on what basis do they determine the input combination – that is, the size of the various inputs to be used, such as labor, raw materials and fixed equipment? However, it is not only short-run and long-run factor combination that have to be determined. The size of the operation, which means the size of the output, has to be determined – and for the long-run this applies both ways, to the contraction or even the phasing out of a branch altogether, as well as to its extension.

The general rule to be applied by production branches is obvious – size and composition of output and the input combination should be set so as to maximize the differences between sales proceeds and (alternative) costs. This maximum net income condition is conceptually identical to the conventional rule for efficient production applied by a competitive firm. But under kibbutz conditions its application in practice involves a peculiar problem related to the use of labor.

The nature of this may become clear if we specify the relevant variables and parameters more precisely. Since the output of each kibbutz is small in relation to the size of the market, product prices are given. The sales proceeds of each branch thus depend on exogenous data – prices, and on the quantity produced – a decision variable. On the cost side, kibbutzim are also too small to affect input prices – the prices of raw materials, water, machinery – so that only the quantities of these inputs are variables whose determination is part of the problem.

This condition applies to neither kibbutz labor nor land. The latter carries a nominal rent, and wages are not paid to kibbutz labor, so that prices for these two major inputs are not exogenous market parameters as is the case with the other inputs. Yet, though there is no formal charge for the use of labor and land to any of the branches, the use of them is evidently not 'free' to the kibbutz, and therefore is not free to its branches. The scarcity condition is in this case imposed not by the conventional market constraint, price, but is a quantity constraint. The land endowment of each kibbutz is a given quantity. The size of the labor force in the short-run is also given. In the longer run, though, its size does change – it has been rising slowly throughout the 1950s and 1960s. Yet whatever the determinants of the long-run supply of kibbutz (self) labor, a wage rate as such is not one of the determinants of its size at any point of time. The employment of labor and the allocation of land to any production and service branch – given the full employment situation – which has been a reality since 1940, has inevitably an alternative cost in terms of the diversion of these resources from other existing or projected branches.

Though the quantity constraints on labor and land somewhat complicate the formal specification of the kibbutz model, this is merely a technical complication which can be dealt with in analytical terms. On the basis of information on the technical relationships in production and service branches (production functions), exogenous data on factor and product prices, institutionally specified demands for personal services and amenities, and finally the quantity constraints on labor and land, it is possible to deduce for each kibbutz the optimum solution for the size of its outputs and the allocation of inputs. This solution involves setting 'shadow' prices for land and labor. These shadow prices represent the alternative cost of land and labor from the point of view of the kibbutz.

Thus, given the prices of all factors, including the shadow prices of factors which 'belong' to the kibbutz, and the prices of products, each production branch is requested to follow a simple rule: it should produce a product mix, and use a factor combination which maximizes the difference between sales proceeds and the alternative cost of factors inclusive of labor and land. If the rule of maximizing this difference – defined as 'net branch income' – is followed by every production unit, net kibbutz income will be the highest feasible under the given set of technological, market, and ideological constraints.[6]

Modern techniques of analysis and data processing make an optimum

6 Calculations of branch profitability were introduced early in kibbutz history, and were supposed to serve as a yardstick of performance, but since wages as such were operationally meaningless, and also because of ideological considerations, the yardstick for performance which was specified and used was the 'income per labor-day'. This was defined as the difference between the value of sales, and the cost of raw materials plus depreciation divided by the number of labor days worked in the specific branch.

Since this yardstick implicitly attributes the whole value added to labor (which is consistent with the assumptions of the labor theory of value), the most capital intensive and land intensive branches always ranked highest in terms of income per labor days. This suggested, even in the 1930s and 1940s, that the extension of dry farming and animal husbandry and the elimination of labor intensive branches, like vegetable growing, is the optimum policy for kibbutzim. However, the restriction on the amount of land and the financing of fixed capital stock prevented this from being carried into practice. This underlined the inadequacy of the 'income per labor-day' criterion as a basis for decisions on the structure of the kibbutz production sector. Its failure as a tool for efficient management is evidently due to the fact that it ignores two cardinal economic constraints – the size of the land endowment and the price of capital.

solution along such lines not only conceptually meaningful, but also feasible in practice. Since the short-run labor supply is a known quantity it is evidently easier to reach an equilibrium solution for shorter periods. Yet this approach is also flexible enough to allow solutions for the longer run. The crucial difference between the long-run and the short-run is evidently the specification of the long-run supply function of labor. This cannot be expected to be a fixed quantity; kibbutzim have gained and expect to gain population and labor through natural increase and inflow, and have been losing population and labor through outflow. Inflow and outflow depend probably on internal factors such as expected living standards, and on exogenous factors such as the size and country of origin of immigration, the state of the economy, and last but not least, the ideological ramifications of the political situation. Birth rates, and hence natural increase, may also partly depend on some of these factors.

This difference in the nature of the supply functions means that the long-run shadow price of labor may be different from the short-run price. More specifically, in response to the rapid technological change and the expected growth of the capital stock, on the one hand, and an expected small expansion of kibbutz population and labor force, the long-run shadow price of labor is expected to rise. This, of course, suggests the adoption of policies for the phasing out of labor intensive branches and operations, hence far-reaching changes in the branch mix of the production sector, and a restructuring of the personal service sector to save labor intensive operations. In practice this was the most important feature of the evolving pattern of the kibbutz in the 1960s. The rapid extension of manufacturing, the introduction of (partial) self-service in dining halls and the tendency to shift from the local kibbutz school to the district school are obvious examples.

'Self-labor' – principle and practice

We have noted that the equilibrium set-up of factor allocation and product mix of kibbutz production depends crucially on the size of its labor force. The consistency of the optimum-output mix and input structure with ideology depends therefore on the application in practice of the self-labor principle. This means that the kibbutz labor force *per se* should consist of members and candidates to membership, the older kibbutz children and temporaries.[7] The common denominator of these three categories is the

7 This category includes groups who intend to form the nucleus of a new kibbutz and are getting their occupational and 'community' training as the 'Nahal' section of the army at an established kibbutz. It includes also youth groups and high-school children who spend part of their holidays in kibbutzim doing part-time work. These temporaries were 10–12 per cent of total population in the 1960s, and a smaller proportion of the labor force.

absence of a wage nexus between the kibbutz and the individuals who compose it. This constraint on the actual size of the labor force is effective only as long as the ideological inhibition against the employment of hired labor remains in force. This barrier is evidently more easily maintained the smaller the inducement to hire labor.

The analytical framework outlined above suggests at once the context in which economic forces would generate powerful pressures to hire labor. The equilibrium solution which specifies the optimum factor allocation and product mix for the kibbutz also involves the determination of the shadow price of kibbutz labor. Suppose that this price, which actually represents the productivity of labor (at the margin), is higher than the relevant market wage rates. If this is so, the kibbutz can evidently increase its total and hence its per capita income by hiring labor. Obviously, the greater the gap between the shadow price of labor and market wages the greater the temptation to overcome the ideological barrier which separates the kibbutz production sector from the general labor market.

In the 1920s, 1930s and, for most kibbutzim, 1940s, this was merely an academic question. The shadow price of kibbutz labor was low and this obviated any incentive to employ nonkibbutz labor. Disguised unemployment was the rule rather than the exception for most kibbutzim before the Second World War boom which, in Palestine, began in 1941. However, by the late 1940s the situation was changing, and from the early 1950s on almost all kibbutzim that had been established for, say, ten years, suffered labor shortages. In terms of price relatives this suggests a gap between the shadow price of kibbutz labor and the market wage rates of unskilled and semi-skilled farm and factory labor, to say the least. Since the number of new kibbutzim established after 1951 was small, most kibbutzim had passed into the phase of labor shortage by the end of the 1950s. This means that by the early 1960s the economic incentive to breach the self-labor principle affected almost every kibbutz.

The advent of the kibbutz industrial revolution around the mid-1950s had considerable bearing on this issue. Even small-scale manufacturing enterprises require a minimum of, say, ten workers per shift. A two-shift operation, which is what is usually required by efficiency considerations, means that such a manufacturing enterprise requires about 10–15 per cent of the labor force at the disposal of a kibbutz of average size. It goes without saying that if efficiency in some lines of production such as plywood, plastics and food, to mention some relevant examples, requires plants which may engage forty to fifty workers or more per shift, even a large kibbutz with a population of 800 would be hard pressed to supply the necessary labor. Kibbutzim are therefore inevitably on the horns of a dilemma – to reject a promising line of manufacturing, or to engage hired labor.

Finally, the general economic situation, particularly in the 1950s, also had some bearing on the issue. In the wake of mass immigration unemployment was a major problem, and most severe among new immigrants. Public opinion and government therefore applied (moral) pressure on the kibbutzim – which were short of labor – to forego, temporarily as it was then put, their principle of self-labor.

These factors succeeded in undermining the ideological barrier separating the kibbutz from the general labor market. By 1954 kibbutzim employed probably 2500 hired workers, about 8 per cent of total kibbutz employment in those days. But although the economic incentive to engage more hired workers grew significantly in the later 1950s and in the 1960s in view of rapidly rising labor productivity and an accelerating process of industrialization, the kibbutz movement succeeded in preventing a further significant rise in the relative size of the hired labor component. In the later 1960s there were 5500–5800 hired workers, 8·5 to 9·2 per cent of total kibbutz employment.

This further, though silent, erosion of the principle of self-labor is practically all due to manufacturing. The hired-labor intensity of this branch is of an entirely different order of magnitude from that of other production and service branches: in 1969 over 50 per cent of workers in kibbutz manufacturing enterprises were employees, as compared with only 14 and 4 per cent in farming and personal services branches respectively.[8]

This non-failure on the employment front, as kibbutz people would prefer to describe the containment of forces which were pushing up the share of hired workers in kibbutz employment, prevented the irrevocable erosion of the self-labor principle. The efforts to stave off what might have been a fatal blow to the kibbutz as a form of social organization, induced the rapid introduction of labor-saving techniques and the phasing out of labor intensive lines in the production sector. In personal services which demand a considerable slice of the labor force, it set on foot an

8 Several of the larger enterprises are by now only partially owned by kibbutzim. These have been organized as limited liability companies in which the other partners hold 50 per cent or somewhat less of the share capital. Partnerships with non-kibbutz interests have been established for several reasons. Yet an important consideration in favor of establishing such joint ventures has always been legitimation of the engagement of hired labor. When labor shortage forces a kibbutz to hire labor in order to maintain production at an existing plant, or the possible loss of a promising venture suggests basing production initially on the hiring of some labor, this is usually considered as a stop gap only. When the 'temporary' hiring of labor turns into more or less a permanent feature, kibbutzim, egged on by the executives of their federation, look for a way out, which partnership with nonkibbutz interests seems to offer. Whether this offers more than a formal escape from the dilemma is, of course, open to dispute.

extensive respecification of services provided, far-reaching reorganization and the substitution of more capital intensive techniques in their production.

The principle of equality

The severance of the link between an individual's contribution to production and personal benefits is the key that translates the socialist principle of equality into everyday reality: 'to everyone according to his needs *within the means of the community*.' The qualification added to Louis Blanc's well-known aphorism is an expression of the scarcity constraint, which is always relevant, and came very much to the fore in the heroic founding days of the 1920s, when real income was very low indeed and sometimes not much above starvation level.

We may note that the needs concept is specified in terms of individual choice, so that the kibbutz technique of income distribution, which has been evolving over fifty years, is required to satisfy three conditions simultaneously:

It should allow for differences in the tastes of individuals;
It should adapt living standards to real income;
It should ensure equality.

An obvious way to abide by these not necessarily consistent conditions is to adopt a technique which supplies 'free' goods and services to members, and yet maintains overall budgetary control.

Communal dining, which was the common practice in the 1920s, was initially introduced more in response to exogenous conditions than to ideological motives. This way of distributing food is obviously compatible with the collective way of life. The communal dining-hall has consequently evolved as the focus, in every sense, of kibbutz life – a point underlined by the central location and architectural eminence of kibbutz dining-halls. One of the most felicitous aspects of communal dining is the feasibility of realizing the principle of equality without recourse to overt rationing and its unsympathetic trappings, while allowing limited though growing variety, which means some freedom of consumer's choice.

It is evidently the device of communal dining which warrants the statement that as far as food is concerned, and this is a major item of the consumption basket, equality in the kibbutz is not only preached but also practised. Now, if this technique of distributing real income – collective consumption in kibbutz parlance – could be applied generally, it would be the optimum solution from the point of view of equality, on the one hand, and budgetary control, on the other. This, of course, means that all the other components of consumption – housing and furniture, clothing and footwear, health and education, holidays and sundries such as cigarettes – should be distributed by means of a similar technique.

Collective consumption, in the sense of free goods and services, which means that rationing is not applied at the individual level, is in fact applied to the distribution of some other consumer goods and services. But whereas food is at the 'private' end of the consumption range, these other goods and services which include the so-called Welfare-State items, are at the 'public' end of the range. Medical care, which is unlimited, is an obvious example, and so is retirement. It goes without saying that other insurance and Welfare-State items such as maternity leave, and the equivalent of full life insurance, which are the ultimate goal of the Welfare State, are, because of its very nature, part and parcel of the kibbutz way of life.

Child care and education from birth to the age of eighteen is also a communal service. It was the principle of sex equality, which requires equal treatment of every type of work, household jobs with those in production branches, which led to the introduction of communal living quarters for the children. This brought into being the system of communal child-care, probably one of the most characteristic features of the kibbutz and one of its most interesting contributions to human experience.

The technique of free distribution has never been applied to the whole range of goods and services which make up the consumption basket. Clothing and footwear, cigarettes and more expensive toiletries, and housing, furniture and (some) household equipment, as well as pocket money, are allocated to individuals by means of different rationing techniques.

The case of clothing and footwear suggests the reason for adopting rationing rather than the technique of free distribution in the above instances. The obvious point is the fact that these items are essentially individual ones. Thus, even if a uniform analogous to the monastic habit were adopted as the only apparel for kibbutz members, a common pool would still run into, for example, problems of size. Since the kibbutz was not conceived as a monastic order in the first place and has never been run as such, individual taste, which is of considerable significance as far as dress is concerned, is certainly relevant. Initially, kibbutzim did attempt to run the clothing store on a nonindividual basis. However, this was in the 1920s and early 1930s, when expenditure on clothing, footwear, and similar items was minimal owing to low incomes. The practice was soon restricted, though with some ideological misgivings, to working clothes and linen. It should not come as a surprise to anyone that it was the women who initiated and promoted the trend towards individual as opposed to communal choice.

Thus, by the end of the 1930s kibbutzim had adopted a system whereby each person was entitled to a clothing basket composed of specified items, which allowed some choice within the prescribed limits. This device, the 'personal budget', was similarly applied to footwear, cigarettes and pocket money which was minimal, even by the standards of the period. The clothing and footwear budgets worked rather like the points system perfected during the Second World War, while items such as cigarettes were rationed outright. The several budgets were specified in physical terms, which meant that they were kept in separate watertight compartments. Thus, not only does the community control how much is consumed, but to a large degree also what is consumed.

Housing is another interesting example of the intricate problems involved in applying equality in real life. Since, in most kibbutzim, children live in children's houses, the rule which requires similar housing conditions can, so it seems, easily be applied by allocating a similar amount of space to each family. Nevertheless, differences in the size and quality of housing units, which reflect mainly time of construction, exclude equal distribution of housing services to adults at any point of time. Some members live in better, indeed much better, apartments than others.

However, since housing is a major component of the standard of living, and since equal distribution of housing services is impossible, allocative devices based on the principle of equality had to be devised. This led to the development of a code for the allocation of housing and consumer durables based on what may be called the principle of 'potential' equality. It is in essence a points technique for calculating priority. Seniority in the kibbutz (and also in the kibbutz movement) and age are given the major weight in an individual's points endowment.[9] In special cases other factors, such as health, are brought in too. At any point in time a member's points ranking determines his housing standards and the composition and quality of the consumer durables put at his disposal.

With respect to this major component of the standard of living, equality is consequently not understood to mean equal consumer benefits at every point of time. It is rather interpreted in a less rigid sense to mean equal rights to a given level of real consumption to everybody whose ranking reaches a specified level in terms of the point system. This rank, one may note, is only to a very minor extent – via seniority – related to the *potential* (still not the actual) contribution to production.

9 For kibbutz-born members seniority is defined in terms of age minus eighteen. The seniority component of the points endowment has operational significance for adults only. Children of families joining a kibbutz are integrated at once within their age group, which means that they benefit immediately from every service and amenity given to it.

15 E. Bader

From Profit Sharing to Common Ownership

Ernest Bader, 'From profit sharing to common ownership', *Journal of Current Social Issues*, 1971, vol. 10, no. 1, pp. 4–15.

Let me try in a few words to indicate the motives which inspired me to introduce revolutionary changes in my firm, based on a philosophy which attempts to fit industry to human needs. The problem was two-fold:

1 How to organize or combine a maximum sense of freedom, happiness and human dignity in our firm without loss of profitability;

2 To do this by ways and means that could be generally acceptable to the private sector of industry.

At the time of heart-searching efforts within our community, I realized that – as years ago when I took the plunge and ceased to be an employee – I was up against the capitalist philosophy of dividing people into the managed on the one hand, and those that manage on the other. The real obstacle, however, was Company Law, with its provisions for dictatorial powers of shareholders and the hierarchy of management they control.

Therefore, taking the long view, the original purpose of forming the Commonwealth was to raise employees to the status of responsible owners; or, in other words, to liberate them from the wage nexus, as I had already liberated myself. The wage system takes almost everything for granted; it is all too common to speak of obligations and rights, of duties and hours of work. In a family, such a state of affairs would be strange since, ideally, whether rich or poor, there is a natural concern for all.

Mutual voluntary goodwill and solidarity of purpose form the basis for good human relations and when all things are held in common, management usually can rely on the full support of the employees. Valuable time is thus gained for the heads of enterprise to devote themselves to the tasks before them. The welfare of a human community, working together, is so much the greater, as each member contributes his best to the good of others, rather than to himself. This constitutes, as thinking people will agree, the fundamental law of a healthy society and through such recognition the idea of the Commonwealth was born.

The pretense of profit sharing

Since in the States there are powerful organizations propagating profit sharing as a panacea to the ills in industry, it seems useful to point out the inherent inadequacy of this practice.

The two conceptions of 'Profit Sharing' and 'Common Ownership' indicate basically two distinct approaches to industrial problems. One looks backwards and is based on results after the event. The other deals with the actual ongoing process in a working community. Profits issue from past results; Common Ownership indicates a state of permanent activity.

While it is feasible in both cases to manipulate the balance sheet, one does not need to be an accountant to know that one usually tries to reduce profits in order to save taxation. Lawyers and tax collectors talk of the distinction between 'tax avoidance' and 'tax evasion'. The former is legal and the latter is illegal. It is clear that Profit Sharing in these circumstances fails to function as a reliable method. Another reason for calling Profit Sharing a mere pretense is that it ignores the method of stock assessment and hidden reserves, as well as the usual yearly capital growth of the company. It can be seen, therefore, that Profit Sharing by itself is a totally unreliable basis for establishing just relations.

Admittedly, Profit Sharing was practiced in my firm from the day we started to make profits, when usually 20 per cent of the surplus was paid out as a Christmas bonus. The same norm of 20 per cent sharing in the yearly profits by everyone in the firm has been maintained in our present Commonwealth since it was formed in 1951. This new scheme was incorporated on 1 June of that year when the firm experienced a total metamorphosis of its former self. This event, its consequences, and the subsequent history form the main topic of this article.

Common ownership

It is interesting that the British Industrial Co-Partnership Association, which no doubt has collected more experience than anyone else, officially expresses the opinion that 'the logical final stage in making the employee a partner in his firm is to give him a share in the actual ownership of the business by a grant of stock'. Is it not remarkable that this body of big business corporations, prompted by enlightened self-interest and patronage toward their workers, has clearly recognized that the problem can finally be solved only by the making of free gifts of shares? Does this not plainly point our way? The closer the employer and employed come together, the greater their common interests, the better their profitability, and the further recession of the usual claims for more pay and less work.

Mankind's greatest stumbling block, the evil giants of Mammon and Mars, however, are still with us. The profit-seeking of capitalists and the pressure for higher wages on the part of the employed, leading to strikes and lockouts, still continue to increase inflation. We believe that Common Ownership undoubtedly offers the best solution for peace in industry. But what do we mean by Common Ownership?

I suggest that it means a fundamental reconstruction so that undertakings are communally owned and cooperatively run, and express that synthesis which is neither Collectivism nor Individualism, depending on leadership founded on approval rather than dictation, within a framework of freedom of conscience and obedience to God. This definition involves a self-divestment of privilege and power on the part of the present employers and shareholders; and on the part of the employees, the acceptance of their full share of responsibility for the policy, efficiency, and general welfare of the undertaking.

This calls for that unbounding generosity and goodwill on the part of those in control of wealth and power to which I have already referred. To palm off employees with employee shares – with their money incentive and subject to all kinds of conditions, reducing them to mere scraps of paper – does not help at all. For the reasons I have already explained, neither do Co-Partnership, Profit Sharing, or any other schemes based on individual shareholding. Besides, they, at best, would take years to build up and cannot meet the urgency of the times.

The crisis is with us *now* and calls for immediate, effective action. It is my belief that we must cut the Gordian knot, and do away with this wretched business of individual bargaining and dealing in stocks and shares, exploiting one another to get rich quickly. Instead of trusting in things that 'moth and rust destroy, and thieves break through and steal', let us put our faith in God and our fellowmen and build on common ownership. The possibility that there may be those of the extreme right and left should not deter us. The clash of ideas and personalities can be overcome if our schemes are sufficiently generous and of obvious advantage to all.

Common Ownership, or Commonwealth, is a natural development from Profit Sharing, Co-Partnership or Co-Ownership, or any scheme where individuals hold sectional interests in a common enterprise. They are on the way to owning things in common, and, as we shall see, Common Ownership has unique advantages.

The idea of Common Ownership itself suggests harmony and finality; in fact, it is ultimate realism in economics. Instead of investing in money, it means investing in people. When we have reached a state of organizing our lives on Common Ownership principles, we have reached economic emancipation – a society mature, free from the worst stresses and tensions.

Common Ownership embraces a philosophy that makes nonsense of our economic warfare and the struggle for power, and takes away all excuses for man's hostility toward his fellowmen. After all, we come into the world and leave it again entirely without personal possessions and under conditions which are common to us all. The wealth of all the earth is a common heritage to all humanity, whatever people do by economic strife and war to frustrate this fundamental fact. Not only politically, but also economically, our world is a unit and cannot be divided if we are to have peace. We must have hearts and brains big enough to embrace all humanity, and not merely think of the interests of our particular nation or personal well-being.

As Christians, we are bound to apply the Christian principles of positive and unqualified goodwill to all our problems, including that of overcoming war, and loyally to stand by the Prince of Peace against all contrary claims of the Prince of this World.

Situations like this have occurred in other countries, and I am reminded of the example in Japanese history. It was not until the stranglehold of a few feudal families on the economic life of the nation was broken that Japan could take her rightful place among progressive nations. Japanese history records that some fifty-five nobles and landowners led by Prince Ito started the reconstruction in the 1870s by divesting themselves of power and wealth and by giving their possessions to the nation. They literally sacrificed themselves for the common good. Something similar is now required in the Western world.

It is not only the deadly blow of rearmament but also the cumbersome bureaucratic machinery, combined with the stranglehold of stocks and shares on our national economy, that are our trouble. The futility of the above activities is clearly shown in the rise of unemployment, throwing on the scrap heap valuable human resources. Economic war has now reached its ultimate contradiction. Restlessness and tension in the world will continue until our ideals have been realized in the spirit of true Christianity. The attempt my firm is making is nothing less than to strive toward these ideals. How far we shall succeed, of course, remains to be seen.

Change in a complex economic organization does not come without detailed and sometimes painful rethinking of goals and routines. In a paper which draws on his experience with our company through 1964 entitled 'Problems of the Pioneer in Industrial Democracy', Roger Hadley, a social scientist, states:

Whether Christian or humanist in inspiration, the pioneer experiments in industrial democracy have in most cases grown out of broadly similar conceptions of human nature and the same fundamental criticisms of the values and structures of modern industrial society. Their theories of human nature conceive of man as potentially a self-actualizing being, capable of developing to high levels of creativity, through a responsible and loving relationship with his fellows. Although industrial society provides, for the first time in history, the material basis for a dignified life for all men, at the same time negative aspects of this society prevent its achievement. Human aspirations are distorted by the dominant emphasis on materialistic and competitive values, the life chances of most are restricted by the gross inequalities of wealth and power, and man is degraded in his daily work where usually conditions allow him minimal opportunities to develop his capacities and demand a child-like acceptance of authority.

The pioneers in the field of industrial democracy have a common belief that only fundamental changes in the ownership and control of industry, coupled with changes in the organization of work, can bring about the radical transformation in society that will allow man to develop according to their models. But in their own experiments, however ambitious their manifestos may sound, they seldom seek to establish miniature versions of a new society. Their more modest aim is to make sufficient progress toward new forms of human organization to convince others that more far-reaching change is possible. Their emphasis on democratic values implies that these new forms will be based on the sharing of power within the firm, the involvement of all employees in the business of management, and a policy of helping every individual to realize his human potentialities through his work.

The enterprise which is conceived out of a rejection of the values of the surrounding society and aims to develop and live by rival standards of the kind outlined above, is faced by the problem that the character of its major inputs – personnel, technology, and market – is largely determined by the surrounding society, and is likely to be antipathetic to the aims of the enterprise. Most of the workers and managers are likely to accept the values of the outside world. Normally, their conceptions of their work roles will have been shaped by the traditional divisions of labor and authority. Typically, workers will assume passive or defensive roles and managers will adopt active, authoritative roles. The goals of industrial democracy will be unfamiliar and hard to understand for both. The technology that the firm must use, and which will determine the limits within which the organization of work can be manipulated, has evolved to meet the demands of a system with totally different values. Finally, the enterprise must make its living by the methods used in the economic system of which it is part. The pressures of the market economy, in particular the constant challenge of competition and the fight for financial security, will make heavy demands on the time and energy of the business leaders in the firm and will constantly intrude the values of the hostile environment into the organization.

The only 'input' which can be regarded as working for the realization of the goals of the pioneer firm is the presence of the group of committed members who founded the venture or were afterwards attracted to it. Given the dominance of forces antipathetic to the values of the pioneer firm in the surrounding society, the proportion of such committed members at the outset is likely to be small.

The hostile forces arrayed against the pioneer firm, therefore, are formidable.

E. Bader 231

The success or failure of the firm will depend almost entirely on its capacity to devise *internal* structures and processes which are strong enough to neutralize them.

In devising their strategy in 1951, the founders of the Scott Bader Commonwealth had few examples of industrial democracy to draw on in the world around them and the reaction of their employees could not be forecast. In these circumstances the scheme they devised, while generous and visionary in conception, was cautious and partial in its practical formulation. In outline, their strategy relied on:

1 The introduction of common ownership through the transfer of 90 per cent of the firm's shares to the employees;

2 The creation of a limited number of changes in the structure of authority (notably, an independent judicial body and employee representatives on the Board);

3 The creation of a consultative system parallel to the command structure;

4 The improvement of the conditions surrounding work (notably, security of employment and full pay in sickness).

Ultimate control of the management of the firm still rested with its founders, the Bader family. They retained 10 per cent of the shares of the firm which carried over 50 per cent of the voting rights on key issues. . . .

In the early sixties, Scott Bader began to evolve new strategies for change. This is not the place to explore in detail the probable reasons for the new initiative. It must suffice to point out that the founders of the experiment, and others both within the firm and outside it who were interested in its progress, were acutely aware of the gap that existed between the aims of the Commonwealth and its current achievements. This awareness created a tension that could only be effectively relieved by the abandonment of the experiment *or* its further development. The most important of the changes introduced at this time was the transfer in 1963 of the shares still held by the founders to the Commonwealth, and the creation of the Board of Trustees to take over the reserve powers formerly vested in the founders. But other measures, less dramatic in their impact, were also taken at this period in an attempt to remedy the weaknesses identified in the original strategy for change.

The new scheme is based on two separate Limited Companies duly registered under Company Law. The industrial undertaking, as the parent Company, continues to function as before – with the difference, however, that the shares of the operating company are held by the second Company, which is the community organization, on behalf of the whole staff. These shares, which are called Membership Certificates of Mutual Security, were handed over as a free gift to an Association of the Employees, not for their members to become individual shareholders, but to hold their shares in common. We find that this is best achieved by establishing a Trust Company limited by guarantee, without share capital; this is legal under English Company Law. Private individual capital interests and the problem of personal inheritance being eliminated, the capital or shares are owned by the business itself. All the members together enjoy the privilege of ownership. The result is that the Company is on a permanent footing. The employees and workers know that the business cannot be disposed of or sold over their heads or come under a different management overnight. The business is theirs and it is their responsibility. They have every incentive to cooperate with the management to the fullest possible extent.

In accordance with the true Christian view of money and the ancient law against usury, the Founder Directors look upon themselves as trustees for the administration of their capital, and maintain that it is wrong to exploit the possession of money by demanding interest or dividends. They are in receipt of salaries (in the proportion of 1:7 between the lowest and highest basic pay) on the same basis of merit and responsibility in the discharge of their duties as any other employees.

Everyone benefits by the profits, in the form of bonus, and all the members in General Meeting decide on their distribution.

Another important aspect is that a sum equal to the amount the members decide to distribute annually as bonus is allocated for charitable objects which they choose at the Annual General Meeting. This does not mean that the members are expected to suffer by being over-generous to people less fortunate than themselves. They are given the right to choose, and they can be either thrifty or indulgent. Before the Annual General Meeting, all the members are given the Balance Sheet so that they can decide as to whether they should vote themselves a larger or a lesser share of any surplus that may be available. At present the arrangements are that they can, if they wish, vote a distribution of a maximum of 40 per cent of the annual surplus, of which one-half must be earmarked for charitable purposes, leaving them an equal share as bonus. This means that a maximum of 20 per cent of the annual profits can be distributed as bonus. The bonus is distributed equally to everybody acknowledging ownership rather than contribution.

In 1971, a further reorganization took place, and we validated the existence of the following four tasks in our Commonwealth:

1 The economic task: to secure orders which can be designed, made, and serviced in such a manner as to make a profit.

2 The technical task: to enable marketing, to secure profitable orders by keeping them supplied with up-to-date product design.

3 The social task: to provide members of the company with opportunities for satisfaction and development through their participation in the working community.

4 The political task: To encourage other men and women to change society by offering them an example by being economically healthy and socially responsible.

Figure 1 shows further refinement in the organization of work:

1 The Scott Bader Commonwealth Ltd, being the community and co-ownership organization of the enterprise, holds all the shares communally.

2 The Board of Management is the governing body of the Commonwealth and deals specifically with the distribution of monies to charity, acceptance of new coowners from among the employees and the broad 'philosophical' oversight for long-term development.

3 The Scott Bader Company Ltd is the operating Company.

4 The Board of Directors is the policy-making body of the Company and is composed of the chairman, six executive directors, two outside part-time directors and two employee (Commonwealth) directors.

5 The Managing Director's Committees deal with the execution of policy in the fields of resources (human, financial, etc.), production, marketing and development. The intention is that participation shall be developed by delegating authority down the line, ending up with the working groups in a semi-autonomous capacity. These are called managing groups.

6 The Community Council, elected by all sections of the company, from constituencies of twenty to thirty people each, is composed of sixteen people elected by secret ballot from the sixteen constituencies representing management and non-management alike. The Council performs the participation by representation, and deals specifically with the following functions:

The approval or otherwise of the appointment of any directors of the Company, the Chairman of the Board, and their remunerations;
The election of the two Commonwealth Directors from among their members;
Discusses any matter and makes recommendations to the Board;
Deals with any dispute or disciplinary action and arrives at a final decision.

In addition, the Council deals with the editorial policy of the international journal; the administration of a number of funds to help members buy houses, meet emergencies and organize sports and social functions. The Council meets every two weeks to deal with its business. In short, the Council is the standing committee representing the interests of the members and the staff of the company. The Trustees are trustees of the Constitution,

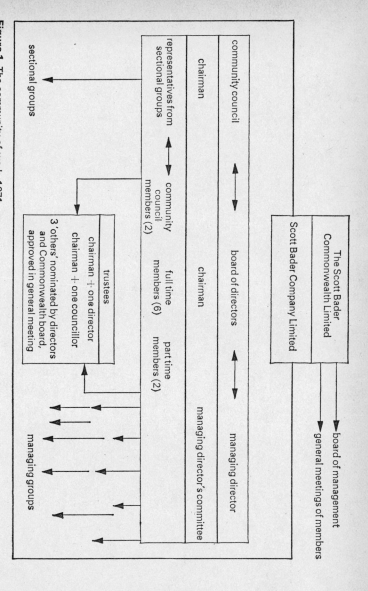

Figure 1 The community of work, 1971

without most of their previously held veto powers. They do, however, arbitrate between the Council and the Board on issues of fundamental policy.

The progress achieved during the last twenty years is shown in Table 1.

Table 1 Progress achieved in the last twenty years[a]

Year to 30 June	Sales based on 1951 = 100	Net profit before appropriation, percentage of sales	Percentage of Profits				Number of staff
			Taxation	Dividend to Commonwealth for charitable purposes	Cash bonus to employees	Plough back	
1951	100	11·6	50	2	8	40	161
1952	102	3·0	51·75	2·25	8	37	150
1953	65·6	9·7	40	10	10	40	138
1954	69	13·3	40	7	7	46	138
1955	71	3·0	47	—	—	53	162
1956	81·5	8·1	33	10	10	42	155
1957	140	10·0	40	10	10	40	177
1958	177	11·0	37	8	8	47	199
1959	189	8·6	39	8	8	45	209
1960	246	5·5	40	7	7	46	228
1961	236	4·7	42	5	5	48	250
1962	240	6·4	45	10	10	35	260
1963	260	7·2	40	8	8	44	262
1964	335	8·5	35	9	9	47	289
1965	405	6·3	29	5·5	5·5	60	312
1966	435	6·6	37	2	2	59	323
1967	465	6·0	42	6	6	46	320
1968	626	6·7	43	6	6	45	337
1969	756	6·1	42	7	7	44	357
1970	805	4·3	41	3	3	53	376
1971	801	6·0	35	8	8	49	379

[a]The Scott Bader Commonwealth has grown steadily since 1951 when it had a turnover of approximately £625 000, In 1970, its turnover approached £5 million.

A new Society

I am convinced that the new Society we are looking for is not based on coercion and force; it is free from such tensions, and this can only be achieved through freedom to follow the dictates of one's own conscience. We cannot profess faith in one thing, and be forced to do another without losing our peace of mind. What is morally wrong cannot be politically right. The State cannot be allowed to force us to do what we consider a crime, namely to participate in war and the 'rat race'. In any case, we detest the idea of making profits out of the misery of others, and while supplying goods which also have a peacetime purpose, we refuse orders for the manufacture of weapons of war.

We are anxious to remain an undertaking of limited size, so that every person among us can embrace it in his mind and imagination. This is also essential for the right spirit and relationship between us all. As an Association engaged in creative activity and consisting of men and women irrespective of class, race, nationality, politics or religion, we have bound ourselves together in a bond of friendship and mutual service. Gone is the privilege of position, money, or even learning. We wish to cut ourselves adrift from the snares of capitalism.

The experience gained during many years of effort to establish the Christian way of life in our business has been a great encouragement; it has brought us good results in our relations with one another, as well as in the quality and quantity of our production. Now we wish to press on and consummate what we have so far achieved, making a concrete contribution toward a better society in the service of God and our fellowmen.

16 R. Hadley

Rowen, South Wales: Notes on an Experiment in Workers'
Self-Management

Roger Hadley, *Rowen, South Wales: Notes on an Experiment in Workers' Self-Management*, The Society for Democratic Integration in Industry, 1971.

The significance of experiments in industrial democracy

This pamphlet describes the formation and first four and a half years
operation of Rowen Onllwyn Ltd., a small firm collectively owned and
controlled by its workers. The firm is a practitioner member of the Society
for Democratic Integration in Industry. The Society is committed to spreading the practice of co-ownership and democratic management in industry.
At present there are five other practitioner members: Scott Bader, Lands-
man's Caravans, Rowen Engineering, Trylon and Michael Jones. In
addition, the Society also has a substantial number of individual members.

The ideals of common ownership and democratic management have a
long history both in this country and abroad. To confine ourselves to
Britain and go back no further than the last century they found practical
form in the Owenite communities, in the self-governing factories set-up
by the Christian Socialists, and in the establishment of many cooperative
productive societies (see Webb, 1931). In this century similar ideals have
been pursued by the syndicalists and later the guild socialists (see Glass,
1966). For a period the goal of workers' control in industry found popularity in the Labour Party, although it was later supplanted by the doctrine
of nationalization and state control. Recently, industrial democracy has
found a new advocate in the labour movement with the founding of the
Institute for Workers' Control.[1] The strength of the response to the
Institute's lead together with the growing demand for participation in
many areas of industry and government give a new significance to the
practical experiments in self-management.

Although the philosophical systems of the various advocates of industrial
democracy are diverse, they share an important area of common ground.
All contain the assumption that men are of equal worth, that they should
have the right to self-determination, and that they have the capacity to
achieve this in a manner that respects the needs of others. The present

1 The Institute for Workers' Control was founded in 1968 at the Sixth National
Conference for Workers' Control.

industrial order is attacked because it operates from opposite assumptions. The hierarchical distribution of opportunities and rewards secures the satisfaction of the few at the expense of the many. The sub-division of work into minor, repetitive tasks, the low level of skill demanded by many jobs, the narrow definition of responsibilities, all combine to create stunted and dependent men.

The roots of the problem lie in the system of ownership and control. Private and state ownership are both usually associated with exploitive philosophies and systems of centralized and bureaucratic control. The exponents of common ownership and self-management believe that where the employees become the owners the system of control can be radically reformed and the alienating consequences of industrial work ameliorated or removed. Under these conditions workers of all 'levels' can share in management. Responsibility for decisions itself involves a broadening of experience, and the work tasks of the enterprise can be redesigned and reorganized to measure up to the needs of whole human beings.

Critics of industrial democracy have emphasized that however attractive the idea may appear in theory, there is little evidence that it could work in practice. It is variously argued that workers are not interested in self-management, or that they are not capable of it, or that if they are capable they would be likely to run their enterprises for their own selfish benefit and not for the good of the community.

The importance of the few practical experiments in common-ownership and democratic management that exist in this country is that they give us an opportunity to bring argument down from the realms of theory and to examine both the claims made for the system and the criticisms levelled against it in an empirical context. Of course, there are severe limitations in the general applicability of the experience of any single experiment. Not only are there likely to be many particular conditions such as the local environment, the type of business, the nature of the work force and so on, but the predominant character of the surrounding capitalist society must be regarded as hostile to the venture. Nevertheless, if man's true nature is striving for liberation, as the exponents of industrial democracy maintain, even the very limited changes possible in the isolated experiment should be sufficient to give some indication of the potential of the system.

How Rowen Onllwyn was founded

The formation of Rowen Onllwyn can be traced to four main factors: the inspiration of earlier experiments and in particular that of Rowen Engineering; the active promotion of the scheme by a number of able and energetic individuals; the support of important local and national organizations including the National Union of Mineworkers, the Society of Friends and the National Coal Board; the urgent need for new industry in the depressed areas of South Wales.

Rowen Engineering was established as a self-governing enterprise in Glasgow in 1963. From the beginning the firm had declared its intention of encouraging the establishment of similar organizations elsewhere and had commissioned a number of voluntary agents to search for suitable conditions in which to start new enterprises. One of these agents was Philip Seed, a lecturer in social studies in South Wales. In September 1964 he sponsored a public meeting in Cardiff to discuss the idea of setting up a worker-run factory in the area. Following this meeting and a subsequent meeting in November an action committee was set up to promote the scheme. The members of the group included Dai Francis, the Secretary of the South Wales National Union of Mineworkers.

The participation of Francis and the NUM turned out to be crucial. It resulted not only in the choice of area for the factory and the selection of the type of worker who should be recruited to staff it, but also led to the acquisition of buildings and the provision of a substantial part of the initial working capital. Dai Francis suggested that the factory should be set up in the Dulais valley. This was an area hard hit by pit closures and one in which, like so many declining mining areas, the problem of unemployment was aggravated by the problem of disablement. While the mines were still operating, disabled miners were whenever possible found surface jobs in the collieries, but when the pits were closed they faced the greatest difficulties in obtaining alternative employment. The double handicap of being both unskilled and disabled made them a poor employment prospect in an area where alternative sources of work were few enough.

Francis proposed that the new factory should employ as high a proportion of disabled miners as it could. In doing this it would be able to claim charitable status and would also gain the enthusiastic support of the NUM. He had even been able to find a suitable home for the factory in the disused office building of the recently closed pit at Onllwyn. The working party accepted his proposal and the National Coal Board gave generous backing, offering the pit offices at a nominal rent.

The project had made a promising start but several problems remained to be solved. A product or products had to be chosen, skilled management had to be found, and the capital for the project raised. The obvious choice for a product seemed to be the storage heaters which the Rowen factory in Glasgow had developed and was beginning to market with some success. Skilled help could be lent from the Glasgow factory to train the Onllwyn workers. Heaters could be made to the same specifications, and a joint sales organization developed. Even before any official fund raising had been started, money started to come in for the project, mainly from miners' lodges throughout South Wales. Some gave from their welfare funds, others arranged for a deduction from their wages. Within six weeks of setting up the action committee, £1400 had come from this source alone.

Although no firm decision was taken on the product and no manager or workers had yet been recruited, the committee decided to declare the factory open when they launched their official appeal for funds on May 1st 1965. A public meeting and press conference was called in the premises at Onllwyn and thousands of letters were sent out. An impressive list of sponsors including Bertrand Russell, Lord Robens, Emlyn Williams, the South Wales branch of the NUM, the Society of Friends and the United Nations Association backed the appeal. The response was good (eventually it was to reach nearly £10,000) and the action committee felt able to start looking for a manager for the enterprise.

The legal framework

It was decided that in the first year or so of its life the new firm should exist legally as part of Rowen Engineering (Glasgow). As soon as possible, however, Rowen Onllwyn would be established as a completely independent organization. In fact, although production began at Onllwyn in August 1965, it was two years before the articles of association for the firm were drawn up and approved. But from the start the South Wales enterprise was given complete freedom of action and the legal connection with Rowen Engineering remained a formality.

The formal organization adopted by Rowen Onllwyn was modelled on that of Rowen Engineering which in turn owed much to the design of the Scott Bader organization. Two companies were created: an operating company Rowen Onllwyn Ltd. and a holding company Rowen Community (South Wales) Ltd. Only the employees of the firm can belong to either company.

The managing bodies of the operating company, Rowen Onllwyn, are the Directors, the Management, the General Council and the General Meeting of employees. All appointments are made by the general meeting of the holding company, the Rowen Community, or in other words by the workers as a body.

The directors and managers of the firm are formally entrusted with the usual functions of such office. The General Council is a consultative and judicial body, composed of representatives of the Directors, Management and the Workers. It can discuss any aspect of the business and is the ultimate authority in the case of a dispute. There is also provision for a Departmental Committee (or Committees) in which employees can meet weekly to discuss any aspects of the running of their departments.

The holding company, the Rowen Community, is run by a management committee elected by its members. But the ultimate authority in the company is the general meeting of all employees. The company has charitable status because of its purpose to employ and rehabilitate the disabled.

Finally, the constitution provides for an Advisory Council. This is composed of the representatives of local miners welfare associations and the South Wales Society of Friends. Its function, in addition to giving advice on the general development of the enterprise, is to guard the constitution. To this end, it has veto powers which it must use if members of the firm try to:

1 Sell its products for military use;

2 Sell the business for their own profit;

3 Disband the Advisory Council without its consent.

The following account of the first four and a half years work in the firm makes it clear that the full apparatus of the formal organization has never been used. The Directors and Managers have seen their functions not as bosses but as 'coordinators', who, in the words of the present manager, 'represent the company to the outsider and bring together all the relevant information, details and statistics, necessary for the management committee to make their decisions'. Because numbers have remained small (no more than ten people have been employed in the firm at any one time) this committee has so far consisted of all members of the firm and there has been no need to form either the General Council or a Departmental Committee.

The first four years: 1965–9

The history of the first four years of the firm is dominated by the different phases in its economic life. There were four distinct phases:

1 The search for a satisfactory product;

2 The production of storage heaters;

3 The failure of the heater business;

4 The search for diversification and the beginning of production of outdoor furniture.

The search for a satisfactory product

The action committee found the man to manage the new factory in a Quaker, Frank Gregory. At the time he was Works Director of a furniture factory in Berkshire. He had long been interested in seeing democracy introduced into industry but his own efforts to promote the idea where he worked were limited by the fact that the firm was privately owned. He got in touch with Rowen in Glasgow, who in turn recommended him to the South Wales committee.

Frank Gregory started work in August 1965. His assets, apart from his own skills as a manager, were the premises at Onllwyn, let to the firm by the NCB at a peppercorn rent of £5 a year, an appeal fund which had already reached £3400 and was eventually to total about £10,000, and an almost inexhaustible supply of labour, amongst the disabled miners of the valley. He could also count on the goodwill of the NUM, the NCB, the support of many individuals sympathetic to the enterprise as well as the practical help and advice of the parent factory in Glasgow. But he faced numerous difficulties. It had been hoped that the factory would go straight into the manufacture of storage heaters, to the design developed at Glasgow, but sales of the heaters were not yet sufficiently established from the Glasgow factory to make this a viable proposition and an alternative product had to be found. The appeal money was still coming in but the final total could only be guessed. Further, while the supply of workers was unlimited, their skills were restricted to coalmining and their poor health limited the types of tasks they could undertake.

What was not in doubt, however, was the enthusiasm of the disabled miners of the area for the project and their strong desire to work. On his first visit to the old colliery offices in which the factory was to be housed, the new manager was accompanied by eight or nine of the miners who had expressed an interest in the scheme. On arriving at the building they took off their coats and prepared to start work immediately. The new manager's first task was to explain that opening a new factory was not like opening a new mine. The process was a slow one and it might be a long time before there would be work for more than two or three people.

Frank Gregory explored a number of possible products. Some were related to his previous work in the furniture trade, such as the idea for stacking chairs, and another for cupboards and kitchen units for a nearby manufacturer of factory built houses. Others, such as simple jewellery were suggested by students at the Swansea College of Art who were among the many enthusiastic local supporters of the factory. Some jewellery was produced, but the result was, in the manager's words 'amateurish', and the other proposals came to nothing. The work which finally launched the firm was the salvage of metal scrap and machinery from the many closed pits in the area. In October 1965, two disabled miners were employed in addition to Frank Gregory. One was sent on a special training course to learn the technique of metal reclamation. For the next nine or ten months this small team toured the NCB sites in the area, combing them for scrap.

Sometimes during the winter the search had to be made through a thick cover of snow. On many occasions the loads they brought back to their factory for breaking down turned out to be worth little more than the price they had paid for them. Other times they would come across a valuable metal such as copper or a piece of machinery in good condition and would realize a profit of 100 per cent or more. But overall, the business did little more than survive and it was evident that if it was to be put on a sound basis and employ a significant number of men, a more satisfactory product would have to be found.

The storage heaters

In the summer of 1966 when Rowen Onllwyn had been open for nearly a year, news was received from the Glasgow factory that the heater business was going well and it was proposed that the South Wales factory should tool up for production in the winter. The staff was now expanded to six by the addition of two more disabled miners and a skilled metal worker who was to be the foreman. The necessary machinery was obtained on hire purchase, and the slow business of producing the prototype begun. The new foreman had not only the technical problems to face, he had also to train his work force from scratch. None of the ex-miners on the staff were metal workers or had any other skill than that of mining. According to their manager they not only lacked skill but also had little confidence in themselves. Outside the pits they were regarded as labourers. With their disability classification and, in most cases a history of years of unemployment, they had little belief in their capacities to undertake skilled work. The early days were the most difficult. Men used to wielding pick and shovel found the demand that they should work to three thousandths of an inch a difficult one to meet. The struggle to master the techniques drove some men to the point of despair and more than once the learner threw the equipment to the floor and stormed out of the building. But with the careful and patient care of the foreman and manager, and the occasional training session from outside experts provided by the Ministry of Technology, the new skills were acquired. With them came a new self-confidence which was the first evidence of the powerful capacity of the factory to rehabilitate.

However, as the point was neared when the first heater would be completed, the venture suffered an unexpected set-back. Frank Gregory who had carried the main burden of launching the enterprise and keeping it afloat for the past eighteen months was taken seriously ill. At once it became apparent how much the staff had relied on his leadership for the immediate reaction of most of them was that the firm would have to close down. The survival of the firm over the next few months owed much to Frank Gregory's wife Pauline. With her acting as an intermediary between the works and her husband's sick bed, the workers finally produced the first heater. When this was achieved, there was renewed confidence. In the spring of 1967, Frank Gregory was able to come back on a part-time basis with his wife working as a volunteer in the office to help him out.

The heaters were made to a high standard and compared well with the product of the more experienced Glasgow factory. But production started too late for the firm to make many sales in the 1966–7 season. During the summer months the business was kept going by making for stock. Costs were kept to a minimum by concentrating work on the time-consuming part of the process, the manufacture of the metal-cases for the heaters, leaving the installation of the wiring and the bricks that stored the heat until the next sales season.

The prospects for the new season of 1967–8 were good. Orders were beginning to come in through the joint sales organization that was now formally established between the Glasgow and South Wales factories and the staff was increased to ten. As the business expanded it became evident that the factory building at Onllwyn was too small to allow further development. Frank Gregory proposed that the plant should be moved to larger premises which had become available in the pithead baths at the neighbouring village of Seven Sisters. This proposal led to the only serious internal conflict experienced in the first four years of the enterprise. The foreman felt that the existing premises were good enough and the move would be a mistake. A further cause of disagreement was his opposition to the suggestion that the firm should change the type of heater being produced in response to what its market advisers judged to be a shift in demand.

The minutes of the meetings of the company, attended by all staff, and the effective decision making body in the firm, faithfully record the stages of the discussion over four months and the search for a solution. From the start the large majority of the staff backed both of the manager's proposals. In the end, as the foreman remained adamant in his opposition, it was agreed both by him and the general meeting of the firm, that he must resign. He left the company as production moved into its busiest period but the response of the workers to this new situation provided further evidence of the success of the foreman's work in training them and of the capacity of the self-governing workshop to produce responsibility and self-confidence in the most difficult circumstances. It was decided that for the time being until a really suitable person could be found, production would go on without a foreman. The men had been instructed so competently and learned their work so well that they were able to maintain the same high standards for the next three months and with the help of their manager were able to carry collectively the organizing responsibilities the foreman had held. Their effort was rewarded when the firm showed an overall profit on the year's trading.

The new foreman, William Burnett, was recruited from Rowen Engineering in Glasgow. He was a young tradesman who had completed his apprenticeship in sheet metal work there. He joined the South Wales factory while it was still at Onllwyn. Soon afterwards, in June 1968, the move was made to the larger building in the pithead baths at Seven Sisters. With the new foreman's help production was switched to the new larger storage heaters. The firm was now making a regular monthly profit and the workers looked forward with some confidence to the coming season.

The failure of the heater business

Before the year was out, however, the firm had to face its most serious crisis yet and was brought to the edge of bankruptcy. Orders flowed in steadily during the summer months and in particular a good agreement was made with one retail organization. This company ordered increasing quantities of the Rowen heaters as the autumn went on but turned out to be a slow payer. Creditworthiness checks were followed up by application for references to the customer's bank. All reports said the firm was sound and deliveries were continued, but when money was still not forthcoming the company's accountant was contacted and pressed for an immediate payment. Half the sum was promised within a fortnight, but again nothing materialized, and it was found that two directors of the company had disappeared without trace, leaving a debt of £4700 to Rowen unpaid. The police were called in, but their inquiries have so far met with no success. Other firms were hit as well as Rowen, and the total extent of the fraud amounted to some £158,000. To a small company such as Rowen with few reserves, the loss was a serious blow. As if this were not enough, almost simultaneously another of the firm's major debtors was declared bankrupt and a further £2300 was added to its losses.

In December 1968, a general meeting of the staff was called to consider the position. It was clear to everyone that such large losses could not be absorbed and if drastic action was not taken, the firm would itself be declared bankrupt. The minutes of the meeting summarize the position baldly: 'We are faced with three alternatives: compulsory liquidation, voluntary liquidation, the possibility of fighting our way out.' One of the workers proposed that 'we try and keep the factory going even if manpower is reduced', and suggested that 'we keep on Frank Gregory and one other employee . . .'. The meeting was adjourned to discuss the position with the firm's accountants and the following day this proposal was accepted. Six of the eight workers employed were to resign immediately, a week before Christmas. They would be invited to attend future meetings in an advisory capacity. The two remaining employees would finish off all the partly completed heaters and endeavour to pay off all the firm's debts. The meeting then had to decide who should be the second man to stay on with the manager. The obvious choice seemed the most skilled worker, the foreman, but he was unhappy about the idea. He explained later, 'I didn't want to stay on in a firm for disabled miners when I wasn't disabled myself.' Nevertheless, the workers remained determined to give the firm its best chance of survival and minuted that 'the needs of the company should be the first consideration', in the selection of the second man to stay: they finally chose the person whom, after their foreman, they considered to have the most versatile range of skills.

During the next few months the manager and worker carried on together steadily completing and selling the heaters that had been started. By the summer of 1969 the bulk of the stock had been sold and outstanding debts squared. But the firm was left with no capital and no prospects.

Diversification: the outdoor furniture production

The experience of the first four years had convinced the manager that if the firm was to survive two conditions must be met: its production would have to be diversified so that the risk of the vagaries of the market could be spread, and a substantial part of its output must be in the area where steady sales could be guaranteed. Apart from the factory premises and the hard won experience, the firm was in a poor position to embark on a new period of activity. Its capital was exhausted and no suitable products had been found.

At this stage, another of the Demintry firms, Scott Bader, offered its help. Scott Bader is the largest and most prosperous of the firms in the Society, employing about 400 people in the manufacture of chemicals, and having a turnover of over £5 million in 1969. Their first move was to send down a sales manager to carry out a local market survey. Although many possibilities were explored, no suitable product could be found and the future for Rowen still seemed bleak.

At this juncture, a fortunate coincidence occurred. The furniture firm for which Frank Gregory had been working before he joined Rowen was taken over. Part of the business, making garden furniture, was sold off separately to two of the managers of the old firm. They found themselves with the machinery, sales organization, and customers of the business, but with no premises and no work force. They came to Wales to discuss the situation with their old manager, Frank Gregory, and were very favourably impressed with the factory premises at Seven Sisters and the additional premises in the old pithead baths at Onllwyn which were also available. Part of the metal working equipment used for making storage heaters could be used to make the metal frames for the seats. Frank Gregory's long experience in the furniture trade assured the skill necessary to manage the machining of the wood work. Tom Lupton, who had designed the furniture agreed to give his services free for the first year. As a result, various other products including wooden toys and shelving were also planned. Only the problem of capital remained. This was solved by the generous action of Scott Bader. From their charitable funds the Scott Bader employees made a gift of £2300. The firm made a further loan of £11,000. In addition, Scott Bader assisted Rowen in drawing up detailed budgetary plans for the first year of production.

In October 1969, Rowen began to come alive again. It was decided from the start that the economic viability of the organization must come first. This principle was followed in deciding which of the old staff to take back. The foreman was the first to come. Later, one of the disabled miners who had acquired considerable metal working skills was brought back. The rest of the staff were new to the firm. An apprentice was taken on to learn welding, and another new man, a disabled miner who was experienced in handling wood was brought in to work the wood machining plant which was installed at the new Onllwyn premises. It was decided that to put the firm on a sound organizational basis and to prevent the situation recurring where the manager had to carry all the administration of the business, an office manager would be recruited. The job was filled by an insurance office manager, who, with his children grown up, was looking for a more challenging occupation. Finally, to gain entrepreneurial skill a general manager was brought in from the furniture trade. With this team and an assured market the firm restarted production early in 1970.

Organization of work

Much has been made by recent studies of human relations in the factory of the influence of technology. The importance of the productive process cannot be ignored but Rowen provides an interesting example of the modifying effect of the system of ownership and control on the organization of work. The Seven Sisters factory, in which most of the production was being carried on, when this writer visited the firm, is a spacious plant with three large workshops. The various metal working machines were at that time concentrated in one of these but there was plenty of room between them. Probably the logic of production in a 'traditional' firm would lead to the specialization of workers, one to each machine or type of work. The worker might encourage such development since his special skill would give him a certain 'scarcity' value and he could not easily be replaced by any of his fellows, but he would pay a high price in the boredom of repetition and the segmentation of work. At Rowen, in contrast, it has been taken for granted that a man should learn all he can about as many work processes as possible. The visitor will see the men swopping jobs frequently in the course of the day, or moving from one part of the process to another. The effect of informal job switching of this kind might be to produce chaos in a more complex organization, or one in which the workers had no clear idea of overall organization of production, but at Rowen where the working group is small and management is genuinely collective, these difficulties do not arise. The workers are fully conscious of the advantage of this flexibility:

The foreman. The thing about workers' control is that the workers can control their environment. Usually they pick their own job at any time.

Metal worker. By changing your work from time to time, you make sure it is not monotonous. It also helps that you know the end product. You can see the point of what to do. It makes you keener to get the right finish ... On the heaters I learnt to do everything except the spraying, I couldn't do that because of my chest.

Office manager. They get a satisfaction in their jobs here. They get a go at all sides of the work. I sometimes go out and help them unload or carry things. I could get a go at welding if I wanted. My thoughts are spread out over everything they do. (He keeps overalls on the back of his office door.)

Day to day decisions are formally delegated to the foreman by the workers. In practice, however, once the pattern of work is established and the necessary skills acquired, little direction is needed. In the foreman's words, it was enough for him to 'let it be generally known what has to be done'.

All major decisions such as changes in production, wage rates, and the recruitment of new workers, are taken by meetings of all members. The meetings usually take place in tea breaks or over lunch. The Chairmanship is rotated amongst the members, a different person holding the office each month. The minutes of the meetings record few votes since issues are usually discussed until there is agreement.[2]

The members' experience of workers' control

Workers' control has an immediate and clear cut meaning for the people of this firm.

Wood machinist. It means a place that is run by the men. The men decide what's done.

Metal worker. The workers take the decisions.

2 Two matters on which votes have been taken, were the decision to ask the firm's first foreman to resign following his objection to moving to the new plant, and a decision to fix wages rates. Over the first four and a half years of operation (October 1965–January 1970) there were thirty-four meetings of the business Company. At nearly every meeting all the firm's workers were present.

Office manager. The employees have a satisfying feeling that they are sharing the responsibility for the factory ... There aren't two sides now – employers and employees. It's *us* now.

One of the main gains from this system which almost all the members of Rowen expressed was the sense of responsibility and involvement. This was apparent from their replies to the question: 'What is the main advantage of working at Rowen?'

Apprentice. You know what's going on around you. You have got a feeling of responsibility. You aren't just somone in a corner, where the boss doesn't know you.

Metal worker. (After describing the way in which the work was made more interesting by being varied.) In this system you use your own initiative. In here you have no one to lean on. In other factories there are other people to think for you. [Interviewer: Nevertheless, you still have a manager and foreman here?] They are to advise me not to dictate to me. I have picked up things. I sometimes advise ... [the foreman]. It's a funny thing about this place – it makes your brain more active. I think about work at home: 'Could we do this job better that way?'

Foreman. I feel that I'm working for the men – not just the employers ... My satisfaction is that I am working for other people.

Office manager [comparing this job to his previous job]. I am happier in this. You feel when you get here that you are helping towards this effort ... You feel an important fellow. I am part of it. Before, I was just allocating work ... Here you feel a key person. They depend on me for all the accounts matters.

Working conditions

The unique character of this firm is illustrated in the letter sent to each worker on joining. After setting out the hours, holidays, wages and minimum period of notice in accordance with the Contracts of Employment Act, it concludes: 'All other conditions of employment are determined by majority decisions of workers in Rowen Onllwyn Limited within the lines of its Constitution and Articles of Memorandum and Association ...'

In practice, all the conditions of employment are determined by the workers. They have decided to make their minimum rates for a forty hour week those for a surface worker in the mining industry, at present [1970] £15 a week. The foreman and managers are paid above this rate. At first the worker who was off sick was guaranteed full pay for an indefinite period. After two year's experience it was decided in the light of the firm's precarious finances to reduce the period to four weeks in any one year. The members have two weeks holiday a year, in addition to the usual Bank Holidays.

It could hardly be claimed therefore, that the workers at Rowen have been self indulgent in the conditions they have voted themselves, but their decisions do seem to reflect the realism of those responsibly engaged in managing their own affairs. There are no formal provisions for discipline at Rowen beyond the ultimate power of dismissal vested in the general body of the workers and the machinery of the General Council. In practice, the main disciplinary problems of traditionally organized firms, such as poor time keeping and discrepancies between managerial and worker definitions of a fair day's work, hardly arise. When a worker has been persistently late without good cause, the sarcasm of his fellows has been enough to solve the problem. As to work commitment, the pace of work is set by the employees themselves and is varied according to the requirements of the situation. Both the manager and the foreman feel that by comparison with their experience of conventionally run firms, individual application at Rowen is substantially superior.

Some lessons from the experiment

For those who want to see the extension of coownership in industry, the experience of the early years of the Rowen community at Onllwyn has some valuable lessons, both economic and social.

Economic experience

Five major problem areas can be distinguished: capital, market, product, labour, and management. The enterprise was undercapitalized from the start. This did not prove a major handicap in establishing the factory and getting the plant since the premises were made available at a nominal rent and machinery was bought on hire purchase, but it did mean that the firm had little in the way of reserves. This had two consequences: in the first instance it meant that the firm could not be too choosey about its customers. Thus the chance of falling in with bad payers, or even worse, non-payers, was increased. Secondly, it meant that when the firm did run into trouble, it had insufficient funds to fall back on to tide it over the difficult period.

Clearly, business of any kind is bound to involve some risk, however well financed, but the undercapitalized firm has to face far greater odds. If Rowen had started with funds of say £50,000 or more instead of about £10,000, the loss of £7000 through bankruptcy and fraud could have been survived. The coownership firm starting up in a capitalist society must be ready to cope with the hazards that characterize that society and in this particular respect Rowen was poorly prepared.

Rowen had no one solely concerned with sales work and the marketing of the firm's products was another task added to the burdens of the manager. This not only made it impossible to devote sufficient time to promoting sales, but also meant it was more difficult to establish a sensitive knowledge of changes in the market on which to base decisions to modify or change the firm's products.

A further problem faced by Rowen was the extent of its concentration on a single product. Although there had been experiments with a number of different products in the first year of operation, the firm came to rely almost exclusively on the sales of heaters. The only other product, a folding support for 'back' sufferers, was not developed until 1968. Although it found an immediate welcome in the medical world (see *District Nursing*, 1969), early sales were relatively limited. The success of the firm continued to depend on one product. If that failed, the firm failed.

As we have seen, labour was not a problem either from the point of view of the availability of would-be employees, nor of the commitment and enthusiasm of those who were taken on. The two major difficulties were those of skill and good health. The firm deliberately sought to employ those lacking both these attributes, but the experience of the first year showed the cost of such a policy when it was taken to the extreme. All those employed with the exception of the foreman had to learn metal working and electrical work from scratch. Much time in the first year of operation was spent in training workers. Although a Department of Employment grant was received towards the training, it was hardly an adequate compensation for the cost of missing the high sales of the first winter season. Similarly, the poor health of several of the workers restricted their contribution in certain areas such as paint spraying, and meant that much of the heavy work had to be handled by the two or three men who were sound in heart and lung.

Finally, this firm like so many small enterprises, faced the difficulty of having insufficient management resources. During its first year Rowen relied entirely on Frank Gregory for its managerial, administrative, accountancy and sales work. This resulted in an intolerable strain on him and doubtless contributed to the breakdown in his health. Later, a secretary was brought in to help with the office work, but all the managerial functions still remained his responsibility. In his own view, this was a fundamental weakness: 'We should have spent more time on getting the management structure right than we did. There should be someone who understands accountancy so that budgeting can be done . . . There should be a separate office manager to take over the administration.'

These lessons can now be summarized:

1 The enterprise must be adequately capitalized to survive the setbacks which can be expected in the initial period of business, and to enable it to choose its customers with the maximum regard to their creditworthiness.

2 Provision must be made for a salesman and for market research.

3 Production should be diversified to spread risk.

4 In a firm committed to the rehabilitation of the disabled, the proportion of disabled and unskilled in the work force should be restricted at the outset until the business is on a firm footing.

5 The success of the small firm depends even more than that of larger enterprises on skilled entrepreneurship. The management function must be strongly represented in the original work force, and must include financial and sales skills, as well as technical and human relations skills.

Rowen has learnt these lessons the hard way, in four years of struggle. The reorganized firm which started on the manufacture of garden furniture at the beginning of this year has been able to meet each of these requirements to an extent that was not possible before. Thanks to the arrangement with Orchard Seating all the equipment necessary for wood machining has been available. Further, the sales organization of the business is now at the service of Rowen. The market established by Orchard Seating should assure the business of a substantial ready-made outlet. The generosity of a fellow Demintry firm, Scott Bader, has resulted in an injection of capital to launch the new project. Plans for the diversification of production are well advanced and include a new type of shelving unit, and a range of wooden toys.

In building up the new staff, the economic needs of the enterprise have been regarded as paramount. Of the first seven staff, only two are disabled miners and both had acquired relevant skills to the manufacture of the new product. Management has been expanded, with the addition of an office manager and a general manager. The firm now seems well placed to construct a sound economic base for future expansion.

To a large extent Rowen has only been able to solve its problems with outside help. Without the support and advice of Scott Bader and the agreement with Orchard Seating, it is doubtful if the firm could have survived the failure of the heater business. What chance, then, have other similar small coownership enterprises if they cannot count on such support?

It has been recognized for some time that small firms are at a disadvantage in contemporary industrial society. As Bernard Hollowood (1970, p. 3) recently noted, they are 'handicapped by shortages of capital, information, research and marketing facilities, and consultative expertise, and every one of these shortages has been made more acute in recent years by the burgeoning indispensability of neotechnic know-how'. The same writer suggested (1970, p. 9) that these firms need government and union backed 'cooperatives in management, consultancy, marketing, industrial design and accountancy', to overcome their disadvantage. A special committee of the Board of Trade is currently considering the problems of the small business, and it may be that some kind of service on these lines will eventually be established although it seems unlikely that it will be as comprehensive or as well financed as Hollowood would like.

If a cooperative management service to small firms is established, it could clearly be of great assistance to new coownership ventures. However, it would be wrong to wait for its appearance, and naïve to expect that if it does appear, support on the scale given to Rowen would be available for all new ventures. The implication of the Rowen experiment for the co-ownership movement is that it must set up its own management services organization, to provide expert consultancy services, research, and finance to existing co-ownership firms and to groups considering setting up such firms. The Society for Democratic Integration in Industry and Rowen Industries (GB)[3] represent attempts to set up organizations which include aims of this kind. The long established cooperative productive societies set up an organization for the same purpose, more than eighty years ago.[4] It should not be beyond the wit of cooperators of these three breeds to pool their experience and energies in a single organization for the service of their members.

Social experience

Whatever the economic problems encountered by Rowen Onllwyn, its success as a social experiment has been considerable. A responsible self-governing community has been established which has been able to provide its members with satisfying and constructive work, and which has shown a remarkable capacity to rehabilitate the disabled. The history of the experiment provides ample evidence that, given the right conditions, workers can run their own business, that they can evolve common goals, and that they are capable of imposing their own discipline. The most striking evidence of the maturity of this community has been shown in the way it has faced the many crises encountered in its struggle to achieve economic viability. The response to the crises at the end of 1968, when the firm faced financial failure, was particularly revealing in this respect.

3 Rowen Industries (GB) was set up in 1967 to provide a central service body to the two existing Rowen factories and to other factories it is hoped to open in the future. Its services include common selling and design, as well as the promotion of new enterprises. Rowen Industries is owned by the various Rowen factories through a holding company, The Rowen Community (GB).
4 The Co-operative Productive Federation.

There were few recriminations, no one sought to save his own skin at the expense of others, and the overriding concern was the survival of the firm and what it stood for. Some indications that the firm had created conditions for a richer experience of work have been reviewed, but perhaps the most readily visible of the firm's social achievements has been its capacity to rehabilitate. Men who have joined the Rowen after years of sickness and unemployment, possessing no skills beyond those of the labourer, have left the firm with a training in sheet metal working, a record of continuous employment, and a new confidence in themselves that have enabled them to find permanent jobs in other firms which they could never have obtained before.

What is the basis of these achievements? In a short study of this kind any answer to this question must necessarily be tentative. However, two factors which would seem to have been particularly important are the enthusiasm and commitment of the work force as a whole, and the quality of the leadership of the firm's management. The enthusiasm of the workers for the experiment may be attributed in part to the new hope that employment in the firm offered to men who had been on the dole for many years. But this alone is insufficient to explain the sustained commitment and involvement which seems to have been typical of people who have worked in the firm since it was founded. The mainspring of this behaviour is more likely to be found in the special characteristics of the organization of work at Rowen. The experiment seems to have succeeded in creating a work environment which is relatively free from the major sources of alienation. These are commonly recognized by industrial sociologists to include the meaninglessness, powerlessness, lack of identity, and social isolation often experienced by the modern industrial worker (see Blauner, 1964). At Rowen, the worker is not likely to be subjected to any of these deprivations to a significant extent. He has power over his environment, both in terms of the immediate work task and the productive process as a whole. His work has meaning because of this control and his involvement with the managerial process. His sense of identity is developed and reinforced through the acquisition and practice of a variety of skills, and through the role he plays in the government of the enterprise. As a member of a self-governing group he is significant and integrated, not isolated.

The character of the leadership provided by the manager and foreman has probably been decisive in determining the social achievements of the firm. These two men have had a monopoly of the skills necessary to run the firm and were strongly placed to dominate the organization. Instead of exploiting this situation, it has been one of their main concerns to prevent power from gravitating to themselves. They have done their best to share their knowledge and involve the rest of the work force in management decisions. In particular, they seem to have developed the ability, indispensable to the democratic leader, of teaching and supporting without dominating.

In noting the very considerable achievements at Rowen, it would be wrong to exaggerate them by seeing them out of the context of the industrial world in which the firm finds itself. In particular, it must be emphasized that the enterprise is a very small one, a fact which has made it much easier to develop participation. (Even given this advantage, the manager and foreman both feel that members of the firm should share in decisions more than they do at present.) Evidence from other experiments in workers' self-management suggests that the most testing time for such ventures, when the number of members increases substantially and the ratio of managers is stepped up, still lies ahead for Rowen (see Meister, 1958, pp. 61–71). People in the firm are well aware of these difficulties and at present seem set on avoiding the problems of size by keeping numbers down to a maximum of forty. Whether it is desirable or realistic to do this is another matter. It is arguable that if the movement for industrial democracy is to make any serious impact in modern society then it must be shown that it can work in the large scale organization as well as the small. This question apart, it is also arguable that the optimum size of a firm in a competitive market will have to be determined by economic and technological factors rather than social factors. And even if Rowen remains relatively small and increases to no more than twenty or thirty members, it will still have to cope with the potentially divisive consequences of an increasing proportion of managers.

Whatever problems this small experiment may have to face in the future, it has already provided encouraging evidence of the potential of the self-governing enterprise to create a humane civilized work environment in which men can assume full responsibility for their own lives and find a measure of self-fulfilment.

References

BLAUNER, R. (1964), *Alienation and Freedom*, Chicago University Press.
District Nursing (1969), 'Back support for travellers', May.
GLASS, S. T. (1966), *The Responsible Society*, Longman.
HOLLOWOOD, B. (1970), 'The small business and the economic climate', *National Westminster Bank Quarterly Review*, February.
MEISTER, A. (1958), *Les Communautés de Travail*, Entente Communautaire.
WEBB, C., ed. (1931), *Industrial Cooperation*, Cooperative Union, Manchester.

17 Jan Vanek

The Worker-Managed Enterprise as an Institution

Excerpt from Jan Vanek, *The Economics of Workers' Management: A Yugoslav Case Study*, Allen & Unwin, 1972, ch. 4.

The Yugoslav worker-managed enterprise has very little in common with the concept of private or public enterprise of the Western countries or with that developed under Soviet central planning, although it clearly developed from the latter. Its two main distinctive features are that it is a public corporate body and that it finds within itself both the motivation for action and the corresponding decision-making structure. It is not a mere technical unit under the command of outside owners or authority. A combination of self-governing commune and producers' cooperative would seem to provide the closest analogy. It certainly represents a phenomenon of extraordinary complexity.

For our purposes, it is essential to recall here at least two major aspects of the Yugoslav firm:

1 Its actual status and internal structure;

2 The actual concrete dimensions of its existence, such as size, specialization, rate of change.

The self-governing enterprise is the basic agent of all economic activity and the only complete form through which such activity may be performed in Yugoslavia. The communes, banks, self-employed craftsmen or peasants are also – each in their own area – basic economic agents, yet their business or entrepreneurial activity is limited in various ways as compared with that of the enterprise. Like most Yugoslav institutions, enterprises are too complex to allow for a formal, even legal definition. The 1965 basic law on enterprises only suggests certain major elements of such a definition in its first article, which reads:

By freely combining their work on the basis of social assets and self-management, the working people in an enterprise organize and constantly expand production, trade, or other economic activities, so as to satisfy their individual and collective interests and the general interests of society.

Free combinations of workers, a self-governing decision-making structure, availability of the necessary productive assets and their social ownership, freedom to engage in productive or other lawful economic activities, the development imperative and the plurality of purpose appear as the major characteristics of the enterprise. The Basic Law contains 298 other articles, and there are several other major pieces of legislation (particularly those governing employment relations, the election of the workers' councils and other management bodies, and the management of enterprise assets), which all add new, and often essential, elements to such a definition. The main points may be summed up as follows.

The *work collectivity* comprises all those working in the enterprise: manual workers, technicians and managers alike, all enjoying equal rights as members. Within the limits of the law, the collectivity adopts rules and plans, defines the internal structure of the enterprise, elects collective management bodies and appoints individual managers. Wherever possible, the collectivity decides directly on all major issues in a general assembly, by way of referendum or in any other manner as may be provided by the enterprise's own by-laws (statutes).

Except in smaller enterprises (less than seventy workers) a permanent representative body, the *workers' council*, is elected to deal with all policy issues and other items reserved to it by law, the enterprise by-laws or other rules, including appeals against all other decisions. The workers' council comprises at least fifteen but often well up to a hundred members; half of these are elected each year, exclusively from the members of the work collectivity (other than the director of the enterprise). No immediate re-election for a second term is permitted.

Each year the Council elects its executive, the *Management Board*, which deals with current issues of a general nature, as well as specialized boards or committees required by law or the by-laws of the enterprise. Employment, discipline, grievances and suggestions, investment, social services and housing, are commonly reserved to such specialized committees (with a varying degree of decision-making autonomy).

The Workers' Council and the Management Board also appoint all members of higher management. There is a single executive Director (or General Director) of the enterprise, appointed by the workers' council for a four-year term, who may be re-appointed, according to a special statutory procedure. In brief, the selection process is regulated as follows: the conditions to be fulfilled by a candidate are defined by the enterprise by-laws; the vacancy is declared and advertised by the workers' councils; and the applications are examined by a panel, appointed half by the workers' council, half by the commune, which presents to the workers' council the name of one or several candidates. Should the council reject their recommendation, the whole procedure is repeated. The Director directs all current business and implements the decisions of the collective management bodies. He is also legally responsible for the observance of statutory provisions. Accountable to the council, he may be dismissed within his term for bad management or gross incompetence. In principle, the recall of the Director is subject to a procedure similar to that governing his appointment. In practice, however, once a resolution to recall the Director has been approved by the workers' council, it automatically stands as final. In most cases of major conflict, the resignation of the Director would precede (and thereby avoid) the formal vote of no confidence. In the case of a vacancy, the workers' council appoints the interim director.

In enterprises of a certain size, similar self-management bodies are also formed at the level of the various production and administrative units, and the process of decentralization may be repeated again within larger firms. Three-tier, and even four-tier self-management structures are by no means uncommon. The directors of the lower units are similarly appointed or elected by the work collectivity, or its self-management bodies, without any outside intervention. In a very large firm, several dozen self-management bodies of all kinds and levels, including specialized committees, may operate simultaneously and cooperate in the shaping of production and business activities. Hundreds of people may be directly associated with these activities within a single enterprise. There is a distinct tendency to pass down to the workshops, for direct decision by the workers themselves, as many issues as possible. (In one enterprise, for instance, the monthly share of income reached each workshop in a bulk sum to be shared out or retained as reserve according to the decision of the workers' assemblies.) The general management services (accounting, commercial, etc.) are themselves frequently endowed with self-management bodies and considered as autonomous service activities with their own funds and current income. As far as compatible with the enterprise's own plans and operations, any such autonomous section may accept outside contracts or commissions and develop its own business and investment policies. Indeed, under a new basic law on enterprise income, which came into force on 1 January 1969, such arrangements, formerly purely internal, and resting on the enterprise by-laws alone, received a full statutory basis as a typical form of work organization. They may be endowed with full legal personality comparable to that of the enterprise itself, and deal independently in their own name with customers and other outside persons and bodies, as well as with other similar units within the enterprise or elsewhere. Moreover, as we have already mentioned, the existing enterprises may themselves combine in similarly larger self-governing units. The earlier model of a single enterprise is thus deeply eroded and gives way to an infinitely more flexible concept of 'autonomous organization of associated labour'.

According to a special enquiry of the Federal Office of Statistics, in 1966 out of 516 enterprises employing 1000 workers or more, 408 had a two-tier, sixty-nine a three-tier and five a four-tier self-management structure, while no decentralized self-management bodies were found in thirty-four enterprises. The central workers' councils and management boards had 4228 and 700 permanent committees respectively; workers' councils were elected in a total of 5480 units, while 1692 others practised direct decision-making by members of the work units. The total membership of these bodies (not counting the direct decision makers at workshop level) amounted to over 120,000 (with possible overlapping where one person may hold two or more posts). Detailed breakdowns by region and sectors, as well as information on the skill, formal training, and age of members of such bodies, their chairmen, the enterprise directors, were also made available.[1]

All this amounts to an immensely complex decision-making process for which it is difficult to find an analogy or a precedent. According to most accepted management theories, it should paralyse all decisions, all action. Yet this conclusion is obviously incompatible with Yugoslav experience. There have certainly been cases where internal conflicts led to delays or inefficiency but, on the whole, there are few examples of actual paralysis of decision making within an enterprise. On the contrary, there are very few examples of collectivities as active and action-minded as the average Yugoslav firm. There seems no need to prompt the self-management bodies into activity: they meet more often than is legally required, and their agendas are mostly full to bursting. New projects, big or small, are actively pursued in all areas, especially investment, training, and social development. Directors often acquire extraordinary authority, others are sacked or not re-appointed and internal reorganizations and external co-operative arrangements are continuously under active consideration. The often nearly paranoiac rate of growth (rates of 30 or 50 per cent per annum are not uncommon for an enterprise or sector) would indeed be quite incompatible with inactive or unbusinesslike management. The particular success of foreign trade enterprises and export services generally seem to point in the same direction. Indeed, even the most outspoken critics of other institutional aspects of the Yugoslav system have hardly ever found the self-management bodies in the enterprises dormant or intrinsically inefficient. The extremely prompt reaction of the Yugoslav firm to even minor changes in fiscal or financial policy may be recalled as additional evidence. In nearly all cases the enterprises tend to 'over-act' as compared with what was expected by the law and policy makers.

Some explanations of this apparent 'activism' seem essential for an

1 Compare with Federal Office of Statistics (1967). Corresponding but less detailed data are also available for all Yugoslav enterprises in each issue of the Statistical Yearbook.

understanding of the operation of the self-management institutions. First, things appear infinitely less complex when seen from within a particular enterprise, for it does not operate scores of alternative institutional models but only one, its own, which has not been parachuted there by some outside benefactor, but represents the result of years of discussion and experiment, progress and setbacks. Its concrete features are thus largely familiar to the participants and carry very definite names and specific meaning. Written rules and informal models of institutional behaviour have formed with the passage of time and become known in very concrete terms to the members of the work collectivity.

Second, the self-management bodies actually *must* act. The 'must' rests not on some legal obligation to hold meetings at regular intervals, but on the fact that the enterprise cannot make a single move without the proper deliberation or decision of one of its collective management bodies. First of all, no action is possible unless there are properly approved rules and regulations governing the matter. We have already mentioned the enterprise by-laws, which may be likened to a works' constitution, but an enterprise would normally have a dozen or more specific rules and regulations (on employment, income sharing, personal incomes, output norms and bonuses, safety and hygiene, and many others including the rules of procedure of its councils and other bodies). Each requires from time to time to be amended, revised or completed. To deal with any new phenomenon, a general ruling by the workers' council is usually required, failing which an action may be void of legal effect and cause considerable financial damage or outlays.

An example at hand – among scores of others – is disciplinary discharge for a cause not specifically provided for under the enterprise works and regulations, where full damages for loss of earnings are always awarded by the courts. The latter tend also closely to review the process of adoption of such rules, particularly their publicity (the awareness by those concerned of their existence). In consequence, in larger enterprises both the draft rules and the final text to be published and distributed in printed form to all members of the work collectivity, are sometimes formally promulgated in the enterprise Official Gazette. All enterprise by-laws and rules are also subject to review by the constitutional courts (similarly to all other legislative instruments), either at the request of anyone concerned or under *ex officio* proceedings initiated by the Public Attorney. Price lists, where prescribed by the by-laws, rates of travel allowance, the granting of rights of attorney and similar items must be covered by similar rulings. Moreover, no capital spending, investment, borrowing, changes in inventory, or any other unusual expenditure (publicity, individual grants, etc.), not to speak of a reduction or increase in employment, can take place unless properly authorized and agreed to by the works' council or any other body as determined by the by-laws. Extracts, minutes or certified copies of relevant decisions form an essential part of documentation. Any request for an *ex post* validation of any unauthorized spending or other 'oversight' can be a most painful exercise for a director or executive. The advance approval of such varied items (as indeed the consideration of mission reports by the workers' councils) may be time consuming, yet there is no adequate alternative (save the setting up of an *ad hoc* committee). Indeed, we have noted even in most monotonous litanies of disparate objects a sudden upsurge of interest resulting in a change or a suggestion for future action.

The wide practice of such reserved powers, which cover scores of items not mentioned here provides perhaps the strongest motive force for the constant activity of the workers' management bodies. Another major factor is what may be termed 'outside changes' in legislative or financial and fiscal policy, in the market conditions, etc. It is in everyone's interest to follow them very closely, anticipating them as far as possible, for they may very soon affect the enterprise income, or else delay may cause a loss of possible advantage or additional income. If left unattended, a situation of this kind must finally affect the personal income of every member and is likely to lead to particularly lively reactions followed by an upsurge of activity. A particular contribution can be made by junior technicians or managers, as well as by qualified workers of some seniority for, whatever system of reporting is adopted, they often know well beforehand and can by-pass ordinary management channels.

This leads to another point which should be stressed. The unity of space, direct personal contact, local availability of means of implementation and relevant information considerably shortened the decision-making process. The advantages of not having to seek the approval of, nor to receive directives from, boards sitting in faraway capitals or anonymous services of a central ministry were often strongly emphasized by those who had shared in management responsibility under earlier systems. The concomitant risk of the workers' councils being too easily led into over-ambitious innovations by enthusiastic technicians or managers was, of course, quite considerable, particularly during the earlier period and offers an additional explanation of the relative instability and overreactiveness of the entire economy.

The last point to be recalled is that the self-management bodies are not alone within the enterprise. They may be asked to act on the suggestion of other organizations within the enterprise, or even by outside public bodies or individuals. Although rather infrequently availed of, it is the accepted practice that they would consider issues suggested by the League of Communists, the trade unions or the youth organizations. As public or social bodies they are bound to consider – although again by no means to adopt or to implement – recommendations of the local commune, or of any other higher State body or economic organization. They may have to consider reports of various public inspectorates (finance, labour, etc.), and may be approached by similar bodies in other enterprises or by individual firms within or outside their own enterprise.

Unlike other self-governing bodies, particularly above the local level, where such multiplicity and complexity of decision-making institutions may more easily lead to relative paralysis or inefficiency, the enterprise self-management bodies live with and work under constant pressure of economic, social and personal issues which require urgent solution. Delay or error may not only be costly in general terms (as, for instance, in the case of an oversight of a central bank, a customs authority or a social security agency), but the cost must also be borne by the decision makers themselves and their workmates. Complex decentralization thus appears necessary to expedite the decision-making process, placing it under direct pressure from those who bear the risk of, or stand to benefit from, the consequences of any particular decision.

There is an obvious possibility of *conflict* within such a highly decentralized, nonhierarchical structure of management. In many cases specific solutions are provided, as in the case already mentioned of appeals by individual workers. Where divergencies occur between a wider body (the workers' collectivity or council) and the executive (management board, director), the former's view would normally prevail both in law and in practice, except where the latter is backed by a specific statutory provision (or opposes an illegal decision). Where conflict arises between two equivalent bodies (for example, workers' councils), voluntary arbitration may be resorted to. Where no agreement is forthcoming, the question usually remains open, both parties having to face the economic consequences of their non-cooperative attitude. Such conflicts are comparatively rare – as compared, for instance, with conflicts with other enterprises or outside bodies – and recourse to internal arbitration is quite exceptional. The economic pressure to settle fast is indeed extremely forceful. Contrary to the views of some foreign observers, the work collectivity is not a stock market operator dealing with paper certificates and able to withhold them for an unlimited period, but a body of producers for whom any delay means not only loss of current income but also a much greater piling of indirect costs and other real or potential losses.

The work collectivity, in other words 'labour', is thus in command of the entire decision-making process within the enterprise. It is not entirely isolated from the outside world, yet forms a much more self-contained, self-regulating, self-directing and self-perpetuating microcosm than any other form of enterprise, private or public, which depends not only on the will or whim but also on the personal fortunes and philosophy of its owner, the responsible ministry, or another outside decision maker. It is as if it were its own causation, alone bearing the responsibility of its success or failure.

The *assets*, or *capital*, or *means of production* are in most cases (but not all) an essential part of the enterprise, but only as a sleeping partner, with no active rights or duties. The legal concept of social property, equivalent to absence of ownership, had already been developed in the fifties and raises no major practical problems. The analogy with a foundation or endowment offers a quite satisfactory approximation of the legal position of assets.

At the start, each enterprise (its work collective) has the right to receive such assets, in terms both of basic capital or fixed assets (physical means of production, buildings, etc.), and of circulating capital for current production, as are necessary in order to develop its normal activity. In the case of existing enterprises, this meant that such means or funds which were actually at their disposal were entrusted for management to the work collectivity at various times. As regards new enterprises, the assets are supplied by the founder, normally as a repayable grant under contract. They are formally taken over by the newly elected workers' council when the enterprise is ready to start productive operation. Should they appear insufficient, the work collectivity has a claim against the founder to cover the difference. Similarly, additional funds are normally set aside to cover possible losses arising from the early experimental phase of the enterprise operation. An inventory and balance sheet are established stating the original capital endowment of the enterprise subject to the assent of the workers' council.

From this point onwards the enterprise has no claim to acquire additional assets from others, nor can anyone deprive it of any part of its endowment capital. The latter must always be preserved at least at its original value (but not necessarily in its physical form). The work collectivity can use the assets in any manner compatible with the object of the enterprise, provided it observes the principles of sound business management. It is expected to create new productive assets through its productive activity (self-financing) and may also secure further funds through credit borrowed from the banks or other sources.

Assets which were part of the original endowment are subject to interest at a rate fixed by law (recently 4·5 per cent annually, with lower rates applicable in a number of instances). Similar payments are due in respect of assets or funds created by self-financing, while interest on borrowed capital is based on free agreement with the lender, subject to the maximum rates fixed by the National Bank (8–10 per cent annually in 1968). All fixed assets are subject to depreciation at the minimum legal rates (varying from 0–12 per cent), or by the enterprise itself (for example, for patents and licences). Higher rates, and even differentiated rates for identical items in various departments, may be introduced by each enterprise if it desires. Finally, because the enterprise is obliged to maintain the original value of its capital, it must replace from its current income the book value of any scrapped items of inventory or other losses on stock or inventory.

The enterprise may, of course, sell any items of its inventory provided it replaces them by others of the same or greater value. If it holds superfluous or unused capital assets, it may also escape the obligations relating thereto by transferring them free of charge to another enterprise or other social organizations which would accept the corresponding interest and depreciation costs. Such a transfer amounts to a reduction of capital in the former, and a corresponding increase in the latter enterprise, the global value of social assets held by the self-management sector remaining unchanged.

All decisions concerning the enterprise assets are within the terms of reference of the workers' council. Failure to comply with the legal provisions may entail the dissolution of the council and penal liability of the enterprise and the responsible members of management. If unable to meet the financial liabilities arising from the assets at its disposal, the enterprise is placed under a public receiver and, unless new credits or subventions are forthcoming, has to be wound up or reorganized.

The main purpose of all these provisions – which constitute a mere skeleton summary of the actual regulations governing the management of assets – is to ensure sound and rational management of the assets by the work collectivity and to equalize conditions between enterprises according to the volume of funds and assets at their disposal. The need for capital varies very considerably from industry to industry and from enterprise to enterprise. Some may work successfully with very little funds, or indeed none, while others may require and dispose of very considerable funds per head of worker. Similarly, one enterprise may operate departments or sections with widely differing levels of capital intensity. In both cases, the charges made against the available capital assets aim at making the work collectivity watchful over expenses attaching to the assets placed at their disposal, and at limiting their demands for additional investment to projects whose profitability is well in excess of the corresponding charges and risks.

The capital assets are nothing more than the result of past accumulated labour and the corresponding charges can be thought of as constituting a form of remuneration to those who in the past abstained from direct consumption, as well as an assurance that their past sacrifice will not be cast away by the present generation. The level of charges corresponds to the relative scarcity of such accumulated assets. As already mentioned, the interest payments on the endowment capital are presently credited to the

Fund for regional development. In other circumstances, they could as properly constitute a major resource of pension schemes and workers' compensation generally, while current development could properly be financed from current taxation and/or credit. The hardship suffered by the post-war generation now in their fifties – who have borne the full burden of the struggle for independence as well as of post-war reconstruction and early development – has been put forward as one of the arguments for reducing in their favour the age of retirement.

The *economic object of the enterprise* is of particular importance. Legally, each enterprise has a definite principal activity which is registered in court at the time of its formal constitution and spelled out in more detail in its by-laws. For statistical and related purposes, it is classified as belonging to the corresponding sector and branch of industry, and it affiliates to organizations and elects representatives along with other enterprises of the same branch and/or sector. The law provides that, in addition to various social or service activities, the enterprise may also engage in subsidiary economic activity other than that for which it is registered. It may also register other principal activities it may engage in at various times. Industrial enterprises always include transport and marketing of their products, including retail activities, among possible secondary operations. Moreover, any department or section of an enterprise, including its central services (for instance research, management organization and accounting) may engage in direct business or service relations with others, and such side-line operations may with time develop considerably. Formally, there is no obstacle to an enterprise moving rapidly from one type of activity to another according to its best interest and using any comparative advantage it may have. Financially, the possibility of freely allocating both the depreciation funds and self-financed capital make such rapid transfers perfectly feasible. (Depreciation and self-financing at the rate of 30 per cent per annum – quite modest by Yugoslav standards – makes it possible to develop entirely different operations of similar magnitude in less than three years.)

Very few enterprises, and certainly no branches or sectors, in Yugoslavia are therefore purely specialized in manufacturing, transport, or commercial. This applies to the 'confederate' or other agglomerated enterprises already mentioned, such as the agricultural–industrial combinates, and to most enterprises of a certain size and 'age' which have had time to meet with the need to diversify or transform their economic activity. There are numerous examples of such major changes prompted by various circumstances, including the transfer of secondary activities to more specialized enterprises, and changes in the geographical location of firms, to which there is no legal obstacle in Yugoslavia.

The Yugoslav firm is solely responsible for the development of *technology* and *skill*, which in a wide interpretation corresponds to what some authors refer to as the 'residual' or 'unknown' factor. These are obviously not open to any comprehensive statutory regulations nor can they be meaningfully expressed by any statistical or accounting data. Rules can obviously be set, and indeed exist, covering hundreds of specific items coming under this heading, and many corresponding statistical indices can be assembled and are available. No common denominator can however be found to cover all the extremely diversified possibilities and conditions.

Yet it is precisely in this area that the self-governing character of the Yugoslav firm may prove of particular value. For technology is only rarely a problem of finance or investment alone, but rather of the will to learn and to adapt. A minor investment can produce revolutionary progress, provided that it is backed by the will of all concerned to put it to full use. Failing such will, massive investments may prove of no avail. Often, indeed, no apparent costs are necessary in order to achieve significant results. Similarly, the importance of skill is obvious and widely recognized, yet it is not mainly a question of costs or aptitudes, but rather of will to progress – will to make full use of the available facilities and resources. A mass of quite imponderable elements enter into play and may have decisive impact: work and management organization, human relations and discipline, job security and satisfaction, career prospects and the active involvement of all concerned. With identical factor endowment, two enterprises – in Yugoslavia as anywhere else – may achieve quite different standards, both in quantity and quality of production and in terms of financial results, according to whether they have succeeded or not in solving satisfactorily problems arising in these various areas. As it alone is responsible for whatever ways and means it applies, the Yugoslav self-governing firm stands a good chance of adapting, rapidly and efficiently and with due regard to local customs and preferences, to the required skills and techniques. At the same time, should major strains develop within the work collectivity, it faces the danger of being left on its own for periods of time much longer than under a system of central planning (possibly until the time it faces bankruptcy). In all this crucial area of entrepreneurial responsibility, its behaviour and performance will differ vastly from those of any other form of enterprise, in view of the different and quite specific 'interest spectrum' of the work collectivity. In its concrete forms behaviour and performance in this area will of course vary widely from enterprise to enterprise, according to local circumstances and conditions.

A brief comment is required concerning the institutional forms governing the *setting-up* and *liquidation* of enterprises, as well as other cases of changes in their institutional status and identity (such as amalgamation or division). The *entry and exit of firms* is obviously of great importance for the behaviour of the system as a whole.

Institutional solutions were first introduced at the end of 1953 and, despite considerable subsequent changes in the relevant legislation, appear to be one of the most stable features of the system. Any public body, or institution, social organization, enterprise or group of citizens may appear as prospective founders of an enterprise, provided they find the necessary finance. This may vary from practically nothing in the case of a small workshop or consulting bureau, to hundreds of millions for a modern plant of considerable magnitude. Even productive enterprises of some size may be found with insignificant financial endowment in view of the operation of the depreciation system, whereby written-off but still workable equipment can be acquired at little or no costs, for example by a rural commune in a remote area, and operated at the start at very low levels of remuneration (e.g. a rural quarry, brick works or a small textile mill). Under the earlier system of public investment funds, the local and regional authorities, particularly the communes, played the role of principal initiators and sponsors of new enterprises. In principle, however, all prospective sponsors competed on equal terms for the allocation of the funds' credits. At present, this system is continued only for the benefit of the underdeveloped regions, while all other founders have to approach one or other of the business banks to secure such funds as may be necessary, this procedure being designed *inter alia* to give a better chance to projects sponsored by existing enterprises. Where no credits are required, the founder may proceed on his own (subject only to compliance with rules regarding technical standards, urban development or safety) and, provided complete documentation is submitted, is entitled to have the enterprise registered by the local court and put into operation. Where a longer period is necessary to develop the enterprise, provisional management is appointed and workers' representative bodies with consultative powers may be selected. When ready to start its operations, the enterprise is formally constituted and handed over to a newly elected workers' council, which then has to adopt the enterprise by-laws and rules and open a competitive examination for the appointment of the director. The founder may reserve the right to repayment of the invested capital, as well as legal interest. He may also reserve certain rights for a limited period (such as the exclusive purchase of production), but the new enterprise is entitled to renegotiate these, or to have them reviewed by the courts, should they be contrary to normal business practice or equity. No right to interfere in the actual management of the new firm can be reserved to or exercised by the founder.

New enterprises may also be formed by voluntary division of an existing enterprise or, more frequently, by the separation of a self-contained department or service, where the work collectivity prefers to take full responsibility in its own hands. This is the right of any such collectivity, provided existing conditions permit its operation as an independent enterprise. If such separation is not granted by the workers' council, the collectivity in question may petition the courts. It has the right to its share in the assets of the enterprise and must accept corresponding liabilities. A similar right of secession may also be exercised by the work collectivity of a productive or service department of an institution or organization, able to operate as an economic enterprise. For instance, the former publishing house of the Central Council of Trade Unions obtained its establishment as an independent enterprise, the parent organization setting up a new editorial service of its own.

Two or more enterprises are free to merge if they see fit. They determine their future relationship themselves, which may result in the complete disappearance of the existing enterprises or take the form of looser federal or confederal arrangements. The holding of a general referendum of a proposed merger seems mandatory in recent practice. In fact, such mergers have been widely encouraged in recent years, great emphasis being given to the advantages of cooperation and integration in all branches of the economy.

There seems to be no provision for a voluntary winding-up of an existing enterprise. The members of the work collectivity having no stake in the social capital, and being free to part at any time, subject only to a period of notice, such provision would indeed seem meaningless.

The cessation of activity is envisaged only where the enterprise cannot cope with its financial obligations, such as taxes, repayment of credits and interest, or if it is insolvent in current operations, or has insufficient income to provide minimum remuneration for work. The appointment of a public receiver may be requested by a creditor of the enterprise or effected directly by a commune called upon to advance funds to cover the minimum remuneration due to members of the work collectivity. The appointment of a receiver, if and when effected, automatically entails the recall of the director and dissolution of all the workers' management bodies, the receiver exercising all management authority. Again, all those affected by such a measure, be they the dissolved council or a group of workers, can and frequently do fight their case in the courts. There is a voluminous body of case law and legal opinion concerning the status and powers of the public receiver, which are neither arbitrary nor all inclusive, particularly as there is no succession to the regulatory powers of the workers' council.

If an arrangement is made with the creditors, or additional credits are secured, or the commune is ready to bear the deficit for a time, or if business conditions improve, the receiver will retain his powers with a view to reorganizing the enterprise and handing it back to the work collectivity within a period of one year at the most. If no alternative is found, a liquidator will be appointed and the remaining assets of the enterprise disposed of in the best interests of the creditors.

In some cases, the appointment of a receiver has been requested by the workers' council or collectivity even prior to reaching insolvency (and also as a vote of no-confidence in the director, who is thereby automatically removed from office). The enterprise is legally obliged to inform the commune in advance if possible, where it is likely that it might not be able to meet its financial liabilities (and not merely when it has actually become insolvent). While voluntary winding-up is not provided for, a request to have a receiver appointed where conditions or relations rapidly deteriorate seems a most logical and rational step if the work collectivity does not feel up to solving their difficulties themselves. Others in similar circumstances may grant extraordinary powers to the director and/or take radical measures themselves to revise their plans and their *modus operandi*. The institution of receiver proved unexpectedly successful as it succeeded in nearly all cases in reorganizing the enterprise and putting it afloat again. A recent survey of some 160 enterprises placed under a public receiver showed that only in one case did the procedure result in final liquidation of the enterprise, while all others recovered. This would seem to point to the non-economic origin of most of the difficulties, where the removal of the director or other key people was conducive to swift improvement. In some cases, also, the influx of new credits, and more concentrated attention by various public or social bodies to the specific problems of the enterprise, have been of help. Nevertheless the receiver is sometimes resented as an alien element within the system and removal of the institution has been formally proposed by certain trade union bodies. It seems difficult however to find a viable alternative.

The liquidation of enterprises is exceptional and usually only occurs in the case of minor shops or workshops with little or no capital resources. Much more frequent is the disappearance of enterprises as a result of mergers, which account for most of the slow but continuous decline in the number of enterprises for a number of years past.

Reference
Federal Office of Statistics (1967), *Bulletin*, no. 492, October.

18 R. Vitak

Workers' Control in Czechoslovakia

R. Vitak, 'Workers' control in Czechoslovak experience', in R. Miliband and J. Saville, *Socialist Register*, Merlin Press, 1971, pp. 245–63.

The discussion about workers' control or the general extension of industrial democracy raises for most socialists some fundamental problems of power in society; but not, it should be noted, for some of the more recent advocates of the idea. When Anthony Wedgwood Benn (1970), for example, came forward with his contribution he was quite explicit in his view that 'real workers' control' would fit comfortably within the existing relations of power:

Certainly there is no reason why industrial power at plant or office level should be exclusively linked to ownership of shares than that political power should have been exclusively linked to the ownership of land and other property as it was in Britain until the 'voters' control' movement won its battle.

When European managements, increasingly challenged by their trade union movements, insist that 'Involvement is the key to industrial relations' (*The Times*, 8 September 1970) and when Robert Carr talks about the men and women in industry wanting 'greater involvement in the decisions which affect their everyday working lives' (*The Times*, 28 January 1971), we do not, of course, expect them to question ownership rights. Commenting, however, on what he terms Mr Benn's 'fairly full-blooded form of workers' control' a *Times* leader writer (5 September 1970) puts his finger on the dilemma of power: 'Mr Benn does not pause to consider the implication of that for the provision of capital, innovation, and restructuring of industry.'

When we turn to the debates among socialists, although the realities of power in capitalist society are at least explicitly recognized, there is often some confusion about the objectives of workers' control demands. The starting point for all, and the end for some, is the assumption that 'once we have socialism all will be different'. As Bill Jones wrote in a discussion published in *Marxism Today* (March 1969, p. 96):

It is only when the workers win political power that we will see an end to our profit society and its replacement by a service society in which the skill, knowledge and ability of our working class is used to the full. Only in such a society will the talents of our people be fully used: only in a new society will we be able to control our environment and obtain the full fruits to which our labour, skill and knowledge entitles us. That, for me, is the meaning of workers' control.

These are certainly aims with which we can all agree, but merely to state them fails to advance the argument about how to achieve them or to clarify the concept of workers' political and economic power. A noteworthy feature in the debate is that those who display the greatest caution about using the slogan of workers' control in contemporary society tend to be equally sceptical about implementing it in a socialist economy. Bert Ramelson, a leading spokesman on the subject for the Communist Party, argued in the *Marxism Today* (October 1968, p. 299) symposium already referred to that industrial democracy was a relative and not an absolute concept:

Only in the sense that the workers as citizens have a political say in determining the economic and social policies of the state, in determining the main lines and indicators of the overall plan and in contributing towards the plant plan, can it be argued that workers' control becomes feasible under socialism.

The assumption here is, of course, that once the powers of ownership are in the hands of a socialist state, direct control, or 'self-management' by the workers at the point of production, might conflict with the national interest. Admitting that at this stage of socialism differences between management and workers cannot be expected to disappear, the article sees in the present-day countries of Eastern Europe 'a tremendous expansion of industrial democracy' thanks to the powers of the trade unions.

Unfortunately, events in some of the countries Ramelson had in mind hardly confirm this view; witness the accumulated problems, economic and political, that Czechoslovakia was trying to solve under Dubcek's leadership in 1968, and more recently, and more alarmingly, the unhappy events of December 1970 in Poland.

In Czechoslovakia especially, we have seen over the past two years not an expansion but an erosion of the industrial democracy which began to take shape through what has been known as the Prague Spring. The workers' councils set up at that time have now been abolished and supremacy of state power in the economy has been reaffirmed.

Rude Pravo wrote on 29 October 1970, that the socialist industrial manager

is empowered by the socialist state to direct and organize production in his enterprise in a qualified manner in accordance with the society-wide aims and in the interests of all members of the community. He performs his management functions within the socialist production relations which have abolished the contradiction between management and labour.

The job of the socialist manager, the article continues, is more demanding than that of his capitalist counterpart, for

whenever he makes an important decision he must consider not only the interests of the collective he leads, but also those of the entire national economy ... Creating a continual harmony between society-wide interests and the interests of the enterprise collective is the feature of the decision-making process of a socialist manager.

We have here an emphasis on decision-making at the top by a manager who has to 'master the art of leading and motivating people correctly and providing the preconditions for developing their working initiative'. It was this system of 'one-man management' under centralized state control – instituted under very different circumstances in the Soviet Union – that had already proved an unwieldy, undemocratic instrument long before 1968; and while the reference to the interests of the collective is perhaps a concession to criticism of rigid centralization, it is still the managerial and not the democratic voice that will decide. Therefore the dilemma of power still exists, and the whole experience of Czechoslovakia provides an interesting commentary on the realities behind the concept of 'workers' power'.

In the years between 1945 and 1948, when the Czechoslovak Communist Party was a member of a multi-party coalition and accepting a 'special road to socialism' the organized working-class movement turned as a matter of course to ideas and policies of workers' control in industry. A study of the economy (Acta Oeconomica Pragensia, 1968, p. 77) in the immediate post-war years, which was published in 1968, summed up the situation in these terms:

Nationalization as it was carried out in Czechoslovakia in 1945 ... was implemented by a people's democracy in which power rested with the popular masses ... the working class had a big say in the management of national enterprises, primarily through works councils and the revolutionary trade unions.

That these works councils were seen as an integral part of the change to public ownership is demonstrated by the fact that they were given official standing by a Presidential decree issued simultaneously with the decrees introducing nationalization in various sectors of the economy; they were set up by the trade unions and operated in many firms that were still in private hands. The trade union movement, through its Central Council, had a voice in appointing the directors of nationalized enterprises. Apart from the works councils the shop floor was represented on the managing boards that administered what came to be known as 'national enterprises'; one-third of the members of these boards were elected by employees, two-thirds were nominated by government authorities in consultation with the Central Trade Union Council. 'In the light of these circumstances,' the author of this study tells us, 'factories, mines and other nationalized enterprises can be regarded as having been in socialist ownership from October 1945.'

In those early years the works councils also played a revolutionary role in pressing for progress in nationalization. The miners of the North Bohemian coalfield, for instance, sent a delegation from their works councils to Prague in July 1945 with the message that they would not support a government that left the mines to private capital. The Ostrava miners called a strike on the issue, while employees of power stations, banks, and other concerns also demanded nationalization (Acta Oeconomica Pragensia, 1968, p. 13).

When, by February 1948, the Cold War tensions projected on to the domestic scene had plunged the democratic coalition into crisis, it was a national convention of works councils that voiced the working class demand for radical socialization of the economy. Yet these works councils which played such a powerful part in helping the Communist Party to emerge victorious from the crisis were not encouraged to go forward from their role of workers' control to socialist industrial democracy; in 1949 they were disbanded and the principle of one-man management, so emphatically reiterated in 1970, was rigidly applied, while the trade unions were gradually incorporated into the power machine.

Speaking in 1968, when the country was trying to bring power down from the abstract heights of 'ownership in the name of the working class', Professor Sik (in a television talk in Prague, 1968) described the consequences of that early departure from democracy:

The first ventures in progressive management were abandoned. Czechoslovakia went over to an administrative, centralized type of planning and management evolved in a different environment, under different conditions . . . Enterprises increasingly lost sight of their own wants and those of others, submitting meekly to the arbitrary directives, advice and orders from the top. The authorities at the centre literally confiscated all financial resources in the factories, doling them out as they thought best to investment, raw material supplies and wages. With their monopoly of wisdom they were the ones to decide what should or should not be left to the enterprises down below. And so, in time, the unhealthy principles that could at best be justified in time of war grew into a set and indisputable routine. Orders were passed down from the top about the size of the labour force, the level of gross output, the industrial branches to be given priority. The outcome was that the working people, who were supposed by law to be co-owners of socialist property, in fact lost this sense of ownership.

The image of socialism as a matter of growth rates, construction of heavy industry and of Five Year Plans heroically fulfilled by mobilizing the economy as one gigantic enterprise, and subjecting the economic processes to the indomitable will of the leaders, was born of the special conditions of the Russian revolution. 'Industrialization,' as the Czech Marxist Radovan Richta (1969, p. 50) pointed out, 'is one of the *preconditions* and *starting points*, rather than the goal of socialist progress.' In their study, which provided part of the theoretical basis for the 1968 Action Programme, Richta and his team showed how the industrial system with its separation of man and the machine, operative labour and management, perpetuated the gulf between the leaders and the led in both the economic and the political fields. The tragedy of Czechoslovakia was that although in 1949 she already possessed many of the preconditions for bridging the gulf, she was forced by the external circumstances of the Cold War and by Cominform pressure dictated by Stalin to take a step back. In the words of political economist Radoslav Selucky (1970, p. 28): 'Paradoxical as it may seem, Czechoslovakia – one of the world's ten most highly industrialized countries – underwent in this period 1949–63 a second phase of industrialization very similar in structure and methods to that of the Soviet Union in the 1930s.'

What came to be known as the iron and steel concept of the economy put a stop to the promising ventures in flexible planning and workers' control belonging to the 'special road'.

The Czechoslovak working class movement, however, embarked in good faith on the new course. The enthusiasm of the rapid and successful post-war reconstruction period was, for a time, injected into what seemed the surest road to the socialist goal. For this the workers were willing to put their faith in the advantages of centralized management, the mobilization of resources and manpower, and the planning by decree. They could not know what even the economists began to understand only when the operation failed to yield the promised fruits – that is, that this type of *extensive* growth (building more factories, recruiting more manpower) could not, in a relatively advanced economy, achieve what was required; as soon as the industrial potential had been created, only *intensive* use of capacities, technological progress and free play for 'the skill, knowledge and ability of the working class' could be effective. Nor could the Czechs and Slovaks know that, in addition to economic stagnation (which despite partial reforms in the late fifties was to be obvious to all by the winter of 1962–3), the course adopted, far from liberating the working class, would subject them to a political system matching one-man management in industry with one-man rule of the whole country, with both managers and the labour force figuring as cogs in the political and economic machine.

With the abolition of democratic control at the point of production one of the main ways of consolidating the dictatorship of the proletariat was seen to be the promotion of workers from the shop floor to positions in the economy and administration. One-year training courses were organized, but the majority received much shorter training for their new jobs, or none; it is estimated that during the early 1950s some 100,000 workers went into managerial, administrative and technical occupations (see *Revue dejin socialismu*, 1968). The subsequent decade was to show that despite this seemingly admirable and democratic move, the 'promotion' of individuals did not add up to workers' power – a discovery not surprising, perhaps, to British workers who have too often seen what can happen to trade unionists when, cut off from democratic control by their members, they are elevated to positions of power in industry and the administration. Although there were, of course, worker managers who did an excellent job, in many cases the efficiency which was supposed to be the reason for rigid one-man management was lost, for as economic difficulties continued lack of managerial skills proved a serious drawback; in 1953 some 60 per cent of enterprise directors had no special training for their jobs and less than five years experience in them, while by 1962 only 29·1 per cent of enterprise and works managers matched up to the standards of qualification which had, by then, been prescribed as desirable. And this ill-conceived 'working-class policy' deprived the country of one of its great initial advantages – a strong body of economists and technical intelligentsia willing to work for a socialist government (before February 1948, 35 per cent of the directors of industrial concerns had been members of the Communist Party) – men whose skill and experience were often wasted.

Bureaucracy flourished under this system, while the rank-and-file workers, despite the social prestige, job security and other undoubted advantages they enjoyed, were – as the most numerous section of the population – also the worst sufferers when the economic and other defects of the system made themselves felt; and both at work and as citizens they were excluded from the vital processes of decision-making. A report of 1969 (*Politika*, 13 March 1969, p. 15) shows that when the population was classified according to selected indices of social status, 'participation in management' (at work and through leisure-time political involvement) was confined almost exclusively to the two top strata (comprising respectively 2·3 per cent and 8 per cent of men of productive age) and these consisted of intellectual occupations with a strong emphasis on the middle-aged. (The top political and governmental office-holders were excluded from the survey).[1]

As another indication of the state of affairs in the late sixties we may

1 An account of the sociological and statistical methods employed in this survey is published in *Co-existence* (1968, vol. 4, pp. 7–16). The results quoted are from *Reporter* (15 May 1969, p. 24).

quote the findings of a poll carried out among leading Party and Government officials and directors of big enterprises in a district of southern Bohemia in April 1968 (that is, before the Dubcek reforms had got under way, but when people could speak freely). To the question whether power in the country rested with the working class only 54·4 per cent answered 'yes'; and 50·8 per cent agreed with the proposition that power was limited to the few, the working class worked but did not govern (*Reporter*, 6–13 November, p. 24).

As an epitaph on the era of 'socialist industrialization' the words of a worker speaking in 1968 are revealing; he was referring to proposals sent from his plant to the Communist Party's Twelfth Congress in 1962: 'When we steel workers pointed out that we were turning out steel for the scrap heap, they nearly put us in jail because, they said, we were throwing mud at our socialist industry. . . . When we protested again about the "steel concept" and showed it could only lead to bankruptcy, the people in Prague jumped down our throats; "Aren't you ashamed," they said, "you're steel workers and you criticize the steel concept. You're reactionaries." Only I don't have to be dumb just because I'm a steel worker. What's the use of a thriving steel industry if the whole Republic is going to rack and ruin?' (*Politika*, 31 October 1969, p. 35). That, of course, was the voice of a politically conscious man, and although there were many such in all spheres of life, indifference to what 'they' were doing in the seats of power was for many years an all too common reaction.

Tempting as it is to present the workers' council movement of 1968–9 as a political revolt against Stalinist bureaucracy, the reality is more prosaic. The primary concern was to make the economy work and the self-management idea was, in fact, a logical extension of the economic reforms first mooted in the early sixties.

By 1962 it had become painfully clear that extensive industrial growth and the rigidly centralized system of planning and management associated with it had led the country to a dead end. Economists set to work on proposals for radical change, involving a switch to intensive operation; the spokesman for the proposed reforms was Professor Ota Sik, then a member of the Communist Party Central Committee. Subsequently, some well-meaning critics on the Left had suggested that the measures involved 'a return to the market'; we should note in passing that nothing could be further from the truth. To bring dynamism into the system, the economists argued, it was necessary to allow *enterprises*[2] to operate as genuine undertakings in a market economy controlled by overall planning. In place of commands from the top the state would make extensive use of

2 Enterprises are the basic units of the Czechoslovak economy, often consisting of several plants and works.

indirect pressures designed to create an atmosphere in which the interests of enterprises would tend to coincide with the national interest. This concept was at the very heart of the endeavour not merely to revitalize the stagnant economy but, more fundamentally, to advance from the simple negation of capitalism, represented by state ownership of the means of production, towards ownership in the hand of the 'associated producers', to use the words of the *Communist Manifesto*. Perhaps only those who have lived in the system can fully appreciate what it means when 'there is no link between producer and consumer to transmit a positive or negative verdict on the expenditure of effort by millions of people' (Selucky, 1970, p. 38). As long as commodity production persists, that link is provided by the market as an instrument of the plan; without the existence of the socialist market as a democratic regulator, no amount of workers' councils or decentralized planning can bridge the gulf between the producers, consumers and the power structure.

The concept of enterprise operation in a socialist market economy – which, of course, is not comparable to the Soviet NEP because it applies to a fully socialized economy – goes back, in a sense, to the point in Czechoslovakia's history before workers' control was abolished and before decision-making was elevated to higher spheres. It presupposes a democratic political system which precludes bureaucratic dictation of the overall plan.

Although the political implications were not spelled out in the proposals advanced by the economists, it took no great theoretical knowledge for the Party leadership of the day to appreciate the danger to the monolithic structure on which their personal power rested. Forced, however, to take some steps to salvage the economy, they ultimately accepted a watered down version of the original proposals, to be introduced without undue haste. Full implementation was supposed to date from January 1967, but features of the old system were still retained.

The result was, not surprisingly, disappointing and did much to discredit the whole idea. Although the more forward-looking and politically active among the industrial workers and technical intelligentsia were determined, nonetheless, to try and make a success of the venture, for many workers this seemed to be just one more reorganization from above and there was quite natural concern about possible redundancies, stricter demands on skills and so on. Insofar as this compromise reform did delegate responsibility to the enterprises, it was managements and not the workers who had to make the decisions. However, all through the preceding discussions the feature of the proposals that had been universally popular had been the demand for improvement in management skills, replacing the politically reliable amateurs by trained men.

Progress already made during the sixties in improving the level of management had been generally welcomed, although many people grumbled when new brooms in the shape of the technical intelligentsia presumed to disturb the even tenor of their inefficiently organized labours. And the situation was complicated by the efforts of the regime to sow discord between the workers and the intellectuals – the working class being commonly identified with manual workers only, with 'origin' by birth holding pride of place. It is a tribute to the political maturity of the Czechoslovak workers that when it came to the point – in 1968 – they not only joined forces with intellectuals, but also refused to be baffled by the allegedly knotty problem of technocracy versus democracy, a matter we discuss below in describing the development of the workers' councils.

To understand both the limitations of the working class attitudes in those years of chronic crisis, and also the soil from which the experiment in self-management ultimately sprang, it should be realized that the dissatisfaction in the workshops was due not solely to a decline in the standard of living and the irritations of an ineffective economy; there was also a sense of frustration peculiar to a system that was socialist at least in name. Workers under capitalism faced with such a situation would have fought back against the bosses. But for the workers of Czechoslovakia there was no easily identifiable enemy who could be held responsible. The fact of socialization and the constant assurances that they were indeed the owners of the nation's wealth had kept alive some sense of involvement in the conduct of affairs and so, when things went wrong, many felt, over and above a natural concern about their own lives and jobs, a frustrated desire to help put matters right. The 'participation' through trade union committees, production conferences and so on, especially in the early years, had given thousands of devoted volunteers some insight into the problems of their everyday working lives – although as one who has experienced all this at shop floor level this author can confidently venture the opinion that shop stewards in capitalist Britain exert a greater influence on working conditions than Czechoslovak trade unionists did under the 'directive administrative' system of what purported to be socialism.

While these attitudes help to explain the widespread faith in skilled management as the cure for economic disorders, they were also a potential source of more direct action. It is interesting to note that when the first steps were being taken in applying the new economic measures some groping attempts were made by employees to take matters into their own hands at plant level. Thus in 1966, in a big Prague engineering works, the trade unions and Party committees were forced by pressure from below to go beyond the customary limits of formal participation to intervene in management, even setting up temporary bodies of a self-managing type to cope with a crisis threatening their enterprise (see *Odbory a spolecnost*, 1969).[3]

In the political atmosphere of the day, however, these were isolated ventures; at that time, as again after the fall of Dubcek (see *Rude Pravo*, 1970), anything which smacked of self-management was officially regarded as an attack on state power. The people of Czechoslovakia were learning to their cost that the reforms for which the economy was crying out were cramped and confined by the political interests entrenched in the seats of power, while it was equally clear that the most perfect democratic system would be doomed if it failed to cure the economic ills.

The opportunity to escape from the dilemma was offered in January 1968. Throughout the preceding year the political and economic pressures had been building up to crisis point and the target of criticism was the man who personified the 'one-man management' of society – Antonin Novotny, who since 1957 had combined the posts of President and First Secretary of the Communist Party. It was the decision taken by the Party Central Committee in January 1968 to replace Novotny in the post of Secretary by Alexander Dubcek that released the pent up opposition and precipitated the events now known as the Prague Spring.

Discussions that had been going on more or less quietly and discreetly were now conducted openly at meetings and through the mass media. While democracy in the political sense was the chief topic during the first exciting months, the economic reform was not ignored. Ideas about industrial democracy which the economists had seen theoretically as a necessary component if their schemes were to advance socialism, as they hoped, and some of the thinking that had been going on in the higher echelons of the trade unions could at last be confronted with the opinions current in the factories. At a pragmatic level the views coincided: if enterprises were to have powers of decision, the people who would feel the consequences in their pay packets should be able to take a hand in that decision-making. In these simple terms the point was made in the Communist Party's Action Programme of April 1968:

The economic reform will increasingly place the working communities of socialist enterprises in the position of bearing the direct consequences of good or bad management. The Party therefore considers it essential that those who bear the consequences should exert an influence. There is a need for democratic

3 This number of an official journal of the Czechoslovak Trade Unions was devoted to the subject of enterprise self-management. Much of the information in the latter part of the present article has been drawn from its pages, but to avoid a multiplicity of footnotes, references to the separate items are not given.

bodies in the enterprises with well-defined powers in relation to management. The directors and top executives should be responsible to these bodies for overall performance and would be appointed by them.

The debates before and after publication of the Action Programme touched on more fundamental issues as well, most important, that of ownership. Previously it had been the state, ostensibly in the name of the people, that had appeared in the role of owner of all nationalized enterprises (others, including cooperatives, had been so hemmed in by regulations that there had been little scope for 'group ownership' to assert itself). The directors of these establishments had been in effect civil servants answerable to the state, but the economists assumed that under the new system the state, which would exercise control, would have to be separated from the enterprise sphere. To whom, then, would the directors be responsible? Now a socialist enterprise, it was argued, like any other firm, consists of three parts – employees, management and owner (the owner being whoever bears financial responsibility and the risk of the undertaking). Insofar as the state relinquished the role of direct and exclusive owner its place could be taken in a nationalized concern either by management (the technocratic or managerial concept) or by a workers' council (the democratic concept). Whereas before 1968 the reform could not go beyond the technocratic measure of giving more power to managements, the Action Programme came out in favour of the democratic alternative, which was what Professor Sik and the other authors of the reform had had in mind.

If, however, the enterprises were to operate as self-governing units would this mean breaking up state ownership into group ownership? Would, in fact, the enterprises be handed over to enterprise ownership? This, in the opinion of many people, would mean relinquishing one of the advantages of socialism, that is, the concentration of the entire production process in public hands. Though finding much of interest in the Yugoslav system, Czechoslovak economists never set out to copy their model. In general, with differences of emphasis, the argument on this subject ran as follows: social ownership is never, even under the most rigid centralism, an undifferentiated whole, it can only be expressed through its parts. The reform would encourage elements of group ownership that would help to overcome the situation where property belonged 'to everyone and to no one', but the economy should not be split into separate units of enterprise ownership. Overall social ownership would operate through the groups to the benefit of the group and of society as a whole. Brought down to the realm of practical operation these considerations led to various proposals about the composition of the self-governing bodies. Some urged caution – and this was the official view – suggesting that it would be wise to have some outside members of enterprise councils (specialists, representatives of local and consumer interests, banks, the firm's suppliers) as guardians of the wider interests. There was disagreement between those who thought these members should be democratically elected by the enterprise personnel and those who favoured nomination by management or even governmental authorities.

The issue of democracy and expert management was hotly debated. The less democratically-minded suggested giving the managerial side a strong foothold in the workers' councils to prevent the untutored masses from riding roughshod over the province of the experts. Others, including many trade unionists, saw the solution in a careful definition of managerial and council competency. When ultimately the movement came into being, however, the prepared schemes were often swept aside.

For the trade unions the economic reform had meant something of an upheaval even before the events of 1968. As long as orders came from the top they had carried out their job as transmission levers in orthodox Stalinist style, with defence of their members' interests taking second place. Even the partial measures of reform, however, made this position more and more untenable. The unions found themselves under crossfire – on the one hand they were not serving their members (the question, 'What does one get out of it?' had long been heard among the rank and file), on the other hand they were accused of blocking progress by trying to protect established practices and inefficient concerns. It took political change and the infusion of new blood in the trade union leadership to bring clarity to the discussion.

Previously, while not turning down the idea of some kind of employee involvement in management, the official union view had been, as it is in Britain, that this would be the prerogative of the unions themselves. The new standpoint that emerged from the rethinking of the spring of 1968 was that the trade union branches and the workers' councils should each perform a different job. The argument for this is interesting because it ties in with the discussion on ownership mentioned above.

People working in a socialist enterprise, it was said, have a dual status – on the one hand they are employees, on the other they share in social ownership (whether in the group or the wider sense). The two sides cannot be satisfactorily represented by a single body. Therefore the employee status should be the concern of the trade unions, while the workers' councils would fulfil the ownership function. Implicit in this approach is the realization that what we call the workers' side in Britain could not withdraw from decision-making, should a conflict arise, to assume its defensive role in confrontation with management or employers. But the benefits of the trade union role in industrial democracy were not discarded; the unions did a great deal to prepare the ground for setting up workers' councils – indeed, some two-thirds of the preparatory committees for councils were formed on their initiative (see *Odbory a spolecnost*, 1969).

In the spring months of 1968, then, people in industrial and other enterprises began to explore the idea of setting up democratic bodies to take a hand in management; the move was seen as a necessary part of the economic reform which, it was hoped, could now be operated without the compromises imposed in the Novotny era.

Apart from the statement in the Action Programme, there was no firmly organized lead from the top, so that it was a matter of local initiative whether anything was done or not. Where interest existed preparatory committees were set up to sound out opinion in the workshops, examine the practical aspects and, if things seemed favourable, to arrange for workers' councils to be formed by due process of democratic election. Figures based on enquiries in ninety-three enterprises where preparatory committees had been formed during 1968 show that the trade unions were the initiators in about 65 per cent of the cases; Communist Party branches, 17 per cent; managements, 14 per cent; groups of technicians, 2 to 3 per cent; and groups of workers around 1 per cent.

In view of the conflicting attitudes on the role of the projected councils, official quarters tended to slow down these developments. Nevertheless, reports from government departments during the summer showed some 350 enterprises expected to be operating with workers' councils by January 1969. Interestingly enough, while the formation of preparatory committees had reached a peak in June and July and then showed a downward trend, the number of actual councils set up by these committees soared in the month following the invasion by the Warsaw Pact countries to a high point that was only exceeded by a new peak in December; many reports show that the feeling in the factories was that in the face of such a crisis it was even more important to assert their democratic rights. A decline in the graph of council formation after September is accounted for by a Government pronouncement in October calling a halt until legislation had been passed (with the fall of Dubcek in April 1969 this was shelved). The opponents of industrial democracy, especially among top-ranking bureaucrats, began to take courage and succeeded in scotching plans in some places or even in disbanding some existing councils. All the more remarkable, then, is the new rise in December, evidently due to the determination at trade union branch level, encouraged by a still progressive leadership. The net result was that at a conservative estimate (from trade union sources) 120 workers' councils were in existence by the beginning of 1969 and they represented some 800,000 employees, or about one-sixth of the labour force in the productive industries. At a delegate meeting held in

January, with notable lack of publicity or official support, there were 101 councils and sixty-four preparatory committees represented. A publicity black-out then prevented further figures being published, but repeated calls from Party and Government for a halt until legislation had been passed suggests that in the first half of 1969, at least, the movement had not been stifled. Finally, the article in *Rude Pravo* (22 July 1970), ringing the death knell of the councils, mentions the figure of 300 still operating in June 1969.

There was of course little time for the success of the venture to be judged in the field of performance, but surveys and statistical information on the election, membership and powers of the councils did appear in the first half of 1969. In reading the reports one is struck by the varied picture given, suggesting that this was a voluntary movement refreshingly free from regimentation, while also reflecting the divergent attitudes and the pressures at work. Most of our information is based on data from ninety-five workers' councils, sixty-nine in the manufacturing industries, twenty-six in other sectors. The bulk of the membership consisted of people elected from the shop or office floor, their share ranging from two-thirds to four-fifths of all council members. With many variations, the balance was made up of *ex officio* members from management and other departments within the enterprises, of people nominated by directors and, exceptionally, by government departments. Outsiders, specialists and others, were very much in a minority; in some cases they were nominated, but more often they were co-opted by the elected councils, and their voting rights on purely domestic matters were usually restricted. In brief, the evidence indicates that while considerations of expert know-how and of safe-guarding the wider interests were not ignored, the emphasis was on the democratic element.

A review of the conduct of the elections shows a degree of freedom remarkable to anyone acquainted with how such matters were handled in the past. Nominations came in from all organizations within the enter-prises – the trade unions, Communist Party branches, youth organizations – and directly from working groups on the shop floor, in departments, offices and so on. The latter and the unions each accounted for one quarter of the nominations, only 8 per cent coming from managements and 10 per cent from Party branches. No outside bodies were allowed to put forward candidates. From a total of 3622 candidates in the ninety-five cases investigated, 1421 were elected. Eighty-three per cent of the people eligible cast their votes.

Before looking at information on the membership of the councils it will be useful to see what powers they possessed. A survey of their constitutions, made in 1969, shows that in all cases they were responsible for appointing the enterprise director and top management staff; this in its very procedure was a more revolutionary step than appears at first sight because, in many cases, posts were advertised, candidates were interviewed and the selection made on merit – something unheard of in the days of 'cadre policy' dictated from the top. As an example we may cite the Skoda Works. When the wind of change was blowing in the summer of 1968 the General Director resigned and his place was taken by a member of the management staff. In September a workers' council was established. In *Rude Pravo* (18 December 1968) we read: 'The Workers' Council of Skoda, in accordance with its constitution approved by the Ministry of Heavy Industry, decided at a meeting on 31 October to advertise the post of General Director.' Ten applications were received – one from a Deputy Minister. The candidates submitted references and statements about how they envisaged doing the job, they were given psychological tests and interviewed by a special committee of council members. A short list of five having been drawn up, the candidates came before a full council meeting where they spoke and answered questions. The meeting then voted by secret ballot; by twenty-two out of twenty-nine votes the man who had been holding the post since August was elected and engaged on a six-year contract.

The councils also fixed the director's salary and the share of enterprise earnings that he and the executive staff should draw; they had powers of decision on such matters as mergers with other enterprises, dividing into smaller units or liquidating a concern. In general it was their business to decide the overall lines of development and the principles of operation (usually in the light of proposals put forward by the enterprise director), and to keep control of financial policy, including the distribution of profits after paying the prescribed charges to the state (an important attribute of ownership, entirely lacking under the old system when the bulk of enterprise funds were appropriated by the government). Some constitutions gave the workers' councils full powers of decision on these matters, others allowed for consultative powers on proposals put forward by management, in which case, however, they did have a right to veto projects that might conflict with the workers' interests. In short, the survey revealed two main trends in the constitutions, the one subordinating management to the democratic body on overall matters of policy, the other giving greater rein to management decision. The day-to-day direction of production was, however, always left to the qualified staff appointed by the councils. In general, we find here, too, a predominance of the democratic over the technocratic or managerial concept.

Moreover – and this is the most striking fact to emerge from an analysis of the elected membership of the ninety-five councils – the vexed question of whether interference by laymen might not run counter to efficient management was resolved in a remarkable way: 70·3 per cent of the council members turned out to be technicians, 24·3 per cent were manual workers and 5·4 per cent administrative staff. Since at least two-thirds of the voters were manual workers, many must have cast their votes for candidates who were technicians. Czechoslovak commentators said that this was a unique feature, not found in Poland or in Yugoslavia, and surprising in a country where, as we have noted, antagonism between workers by hand and brain had been diligently fostered by the Novotny regime; it was seen as a protest against the amateurism of the old system. Figures for skill and education follow the same pattern: of the worker members, 68 per cent were recorded as highly skilled (in the metal-working trades 85 per cent), while 55 per cent of the technicians were highly qualified; 26 per cent of council members were university trained, 26 per cent had higher secondary education.

There might be reason to fear an undemocratic or technocratic element in this and obviously one would want to see what the workers' electorate felt after, say, a year's operation. But in a country where the economic base for class distinctions between manual worker and technician had long since disappeared, where higher education was not the prerogative of a privileged class, and all were equally in the position of wage earners (with, moreover, surprisingly small wage differentials), it looks as if the voters knew what they were doing. In any case, most important was probably the democratic climate of opinion; in elections to trade union committees at plant level there had never been this emphasis on skill and education, yet in an authoritarian set-up they were only too often bureaucratic. People on the spot, evidently aware of the possibility that the workers' councils might, in their turn, become a new, self-managing bureaucracy, were already suggesting ways to ensure they should not become alienated from their constituents: by making certain, for instance, that there was a steady turnover of membership.

The election results also showed that people voted for candidates they knew well and who knew the enterprise concerned and its problems. By length of employment in the given enterprise the members were divided as follows: 72 per cent with 10 and more years' employment, over 50 per cent with 15 and more years in the firm and only 4 per cent less than 5 years. But age was not equated with wisdom and experience – 71 per cent of the successful candidates were between the ages of thirty-five and forty-nine years.

It is worth recording that the political composition of the councils also produced a surprise. There had been some idea that popular revulsion against the bureaucratic methods employed by the ruling party in the past might lead to a majority of non-Communists being elected. In fact, all eighty-three councils where the political structure was recorded included Communists, in forty-four they were a majority, in six the balance was even, and in thirty-three non-Communists predominated. In all, 52 per cent of members were Communist Party members, and only in the building trades (49 per cent) and agriculture (37 per cent) were the figures below the average, interestingly enough both sectors where a higher than average proportion of manual workers and a lower of the highly educated were elected.

Among the dramatic events of 1968 and 1969 the workers' council movement was not, of course, in the forefront of public interest and not everyone was informed about its purpose. Nevertheless, we have some pointers to the state of public opinion, including two polls conducted by the Institute for Public Opinion Research (see *Reporter*, 24 April 1969), one in July 1968 (nation-wide sample of 1610 people questioned), the other in May 1969 (sample 1603). To the question, 'Do you consider the establishment of workers' councils in the bigger enterprises would or would not be useful?' the affirmative answers were 53·3 per cent in the first and 59·1 per cent in the second poll; opinion against the councils was 9·9 per cent in the first and 3 per cent in the second, while the don't knows were 33·1 and 35·1 per cent respectively, the balance being made up of miscellaneous other views. We have given these results in some detail to bring out the interesting point that the swing between July 1968 and March 1969 in favour of the self-management idea was at the expense of the opposition which, as more detailed figures show, consisted in July 1968 in part of technocratically inclined people; many of the latter, after the shock of the August invasion, were to change their minds about industrial democracy. Support was strongest in Czechoslovakia's Black Country in northern Bohemia (70 per cent in 1969), followed by Prague (67 per cent), itself an important industrial centre.

It should be pointed out that the workers' councils established or in course of formation were in enterprises often comprising several factories or plants, some of them the biggest concerns in the country. For instance, the Skoda Works in Pilsen, a stronghold of the movement, elected from 113 candidates a twenty-nine-member council; this worked out at one member to 1500–2000 employees, and some had to travel from the firm's branches in faraway Slovakia to attend meetings. An analysis of the press reports, however, showed that it was clear that the pattern varied considerably according to the size and nature of the undertakings. The first council in transport (Czechoslovak Road Transport, Usti nad Labem) had twenty-four members elected by eleven depots with a total of 6200 employees.

Rude Pravo of 3 October 1968 published an interview with the chairman of the newly-formed workers' council, the enterprise director and the Party chairman at Slovnaft, the big chemical combine in Bratislava, Slovakia. Here they had taken time in preparing the ground – responding in April, to the idea put forward in the Party's Action Programme, they finally held the elections to their council at the end of September, after the August invasion. All employees at work that day – 4285 of them – cast their votes, electing fifteen council members from different departments (five manual workers, ten technicians); five co-opted members from outside the firm included the director of the other big chemical works in Bratislava; five members were to be appointed by government authorities – making a total of twenty-five. In its make-up, then, this council tended towards the official concept of limited or managerial democracy, and its chairman, too, spoke in the interview of partnership with management; there was to be joint decision-making on investment policy, technological development and so on. The first meeting had discussed and approved proposals from the directors of chemical enterprises in Slovakia for the development of the industry in the region. The feeling was that there would now be scope for new ideas and expansion that had been stultified under the old system.

There was a danger, of course – especially in the big enterprises or where the managerial concept predominated – that council activities would be rather remote from the shop floor. In late 1968 and early 1969, when self-management could still be openly discussed, the argument was being voiced that the next step would be to have councils at plant level, too, and although this was not the government view, the movement would probably have advanced in that way. For short-lived as it was, this was a genuine movement, enjoying, as we have seen, considerable public support. Of all the features of the 'Prague Spring', this essentially working class undertaking, though perhaps slow to develop, was among the longest to survive. Today we can only surmise what potentialities it possessed; but in the summer of 1968, when the prospects for both economic and political democracy seemed fair, Professor Sik, for instance, ventured the suggestion that the workers' councils might one day prove to be the nucleus for a new self-governing system in the political as well as the economic field – producer groups might be associated in a chamber of Parliament, thereby exercising more fully the power deriving from ownership.

Of course, as things are this is speculation. Nor, it should be noted, did the Czechoslovak experiment ever presume to offer a model for other countries. The workers' council movement emerged in the special circumstances of a country where the relations of production were entirely non-capitalist, but where owing to the bureaucratic barriers that were holding back an advance to fully socialist relations there was a tragic wastage of human potential. In examining the implications of workers' control both as an instrument of attack on capitalism and as a means for enabling the skill and talents of the working class in the broadest sense to be fully used in a future socialist society, socialists in other countries can learn much from the post-war history of Czechoslovakia. It should be borne in mind, however, that the course taken by Czechoslovakia cannot be attributed solely to Cold War pressures. It has been pointed out by Czechoslovak historians (see Belda, 1969) that whereas in 1945–8 there were ideas about a special *road* to socialism, no theoretical or programmatic statement was ever made suggesting that any model was envisaged at the end of the road other than that evolved in the very special circumstances of the Soviet Union. True, Yugoslavia did choose a different model, but it should not be forgotten that up to 1950 she was following the Soviet example far more rigidly than Czechoslovakia; it was the upheaval of the Cominform excommunication that led her to question the dogmas and begin dismantling her Stalinist structure. The special circumstances of a backward economy and a multinational state have made Yugoslavia's path exceptionally difficult. The strategy of socialist revolution aiming from the outset to overcome the tensions and contradictions inherent in industrial society and to place power truly in the hands of the workers by hand and brain has yet to be worked out.

References

Acta Oeconomica Pragensia (1968), *The Czechoslovak Economy, 1945–1948*, State Pedagogical Publishing House, Prague.

BELDA, J. (1969), 'Some problems regarding the Czechoslovak road to socialism', in *History of Socialism Yearbook*, Prague.

Odbory a spolecnost (*Trade Unions and Society*) (1969), no. 4.

Revue dejin socialismu (*Review of the History of Socialism*) (1968), 'Development of the structure and portion of Czechoslovak industrial workers and technicians in the 1950s', special number.

RICHTA, R. (1969), *Civilization at the Crossroads*, International Arts and Sciences Press, New York.

Rude Pravo (1970), 'Why the workers' councils were abolished', 22 July.

SELUCKY, R. (1970), *Czechoslovakia, the Plan that Failed*, Nelson.

WEDGWOOD BENN, A. (1970), *New Politics: A Socialist Renaissance*, Fabian Tract.

19 R. Oakeshott

Mondragon: Spain's Oasis of Democracy

R. Oakeshott, 'Spain's oasis of democracy', *Observer* Colour Supplement, 21 January 1973.

Although the idea of workers' participation in the control of industry is attracting an increasing number of adherents, Franco's Spain might seem inhospitable soil for it to grow in. But at Mondragon, in Guipuzcoa Province, a cooperative enterprise employing 10 000 has grown up, in which the directors can be fired by a general assembly of workers. It offers important lessons for advanced industrial countries.

Thirty years ago a young Catholic priest, Fr José María Arizmendi, came to the small town of Mondragon in the Basque country of northern Spain. He had supported the losing Republican side in the Spanish Civil War. The normal roads to progress – political or trade union activity – were closed. So Fr José María set out to find a different one. It led him first into technical education and then, in the middle 1950s, into cooperative industrial production. Today the cooperatives that he inspired – a group of linked enterprises employing roughly 10 000 people – are the largest producers of refrigerators in Spain, and among the largest producers of machine tools. They have their own bank. They have their own hybrid educational institution that turns out both machine operatives and craftsmen, and engineers with degree qualifications. At least in western Europe, this cooperative complex is *unique*.

'You can think of our dynamic as coming from *an alliance between the Catholic Church and technology*,' one of the most senior cooperators told me. It is an unusual combination to under-pin rapid economic growth. But this Basque enterprise is unusual in other ways too. Historically cooperatives have been fairly successful in the retail trade and to some extent in agriculture. With the odd exception in France, cooperative manufacturing, where it exists at all, is usually confined to low-technology activities like boot and shoe production. But production at Mondragon *is heavily concentrated on manufacturing and, within that, on capital-intensive, high-technology activities*. The average age of those involved is thirty-two.

Mondragon is set in mountainous country about fifty miles inland from the big coastal cities of San Sebastian and Bilbao. Today its population, swelled by immigrants attracted by the new employment opportunities, is probably close to 30,000. And economic advance has brought with it the inevitable depressing crop of high-rise blocks of flats. But an ancient flagstoned square, with a church on one side and a sort of mayor's parlour on the other, seems to have remained, as it must have been for centuries, the real centre of the community's life. On a saint's day during my visit the church was packed with a congregation of all ages. They sang each successive hymn as if it were the Hallelujah Chorus. In the evening the square was thronged with young people dancing to pop music.

The Mondragon cooperatives include a number of consumer societies – retail stores – an agricultural cooperative, and a few not very successful cooperative fishing boats. But manufacturing and construction account for more than 90 per cent of the group's operations, whether measurement is made in terms of jobs or value added. Construction is much less important than manufacturing – less than ten per cent. The cooperators of Mondragon do not aim to lead the world back to a rural Arcadia of cows, market gardens and cottage industries; nor do they reject modern technology with talk of ecodoom. They are engaged in an exciting attempt to reconcile modern industry with social justice and democracy. And most of them seem to be having rather a good time in the process.

Production started in 1956, when five graduates from a technical school started by Fr José María formed the nucleus of the first industrial cooperative. They made simple stoves and cooking equipment. Today there are a total of fifty-five producer cooperatives in the group, of which forty-seven are industrial. The largest unit, ULGOR, which produces mainly refrigerators, employs more than 2500 people. Total group sales last year are expected to exceed 10,000 million pesetas (£65 million).

Sales have been growing at an annual rate of over thirty per cent since 1966, and the increase in value added has been only slightly less fast. Another indication of the group's success is its high degree of self-financing. Over the five years from 1967 to 1971 it financed more than half its investments from ploughed-back profits. A recent study by the Bank of Spain showed that this figure was roughly twice the average for private Spanish industry as a whole. It is their cooperative structure – shared ownership and democratic control – that makes the Mondragon cooperatives so unusual and exciting.

Take wage and salary differentials. These are laid down in the constitution of each cooperative; all have a maximum pre-tax differential. Thus a managing director, or a professor who teaches in the Mondragon educational institution, or the top man in the co-op bank, cannot receive more than three times as much as the lowest-paid workers. As a result of the rather lightly progressive Spanish income tax the maximum after-tax differential comes down to roughly two and three-quarters to one. And since new recruits in the lowest paid grades can normally expect a twenty per cent wage increase at the end of one year, the difference in take-home money only rarely exceeds two and a half to one. This is, of course, very much narrower than is usually found in enterprises of a similar size, in Spain, or anywhere else. Because the rates for the lowest-paid are fixed just a little above the highest level for similar work elsewhere in the region, it follows that the top managers and professionals are receiving a good deal less than the 'market rate' for their jobs. There is a clear link between these economic differentials and workers' participation in control.

All the cooperatives are ultimately controlled by general assemblies of all their members – which normally meet once a year to elect boards of directors and decide basic policy. Voting in these general assemblies used to be weighted in proportion with wage rates. Thus an assembly-line worker might have one or two votes, compared with three votes for the tiny minority paid at the top rate. The system was replaced earlier this year by a simple one member one vote arrangement.

Ownership of the Mondragon cooperatives, like control, is distributed among all members. In this narrow sense – the sense in which it is something separate from control – ownership means participation in profits. Though a few people are occasionally taken on for temporary work, all who join the cooperative on a permanent basis must make a minimum contribution to their capital, which entitles them to a share in profits. No individual may own more than five per cent of the total capital.

The capital contribution required of new members seems relatively high. It has been changed from time to time, but was fixed at 100 000 pesetas (about £650) in the middle of last year [1972]. On the other hand only 5 per cent of this sum is required as an initial down-payment. The balance can be paid out of earnings over a period of years. It is worth pointing out that the average cost of creating a new industrial job in the Mondragon cooperatives is 800 000 pesetas – eight times the required capital contribution. In any case it was clear from conversations with both management and line workers that the contribution did not deter people from applying to join. 'Everybody these days,' I was told, 'can somehow lay his hands on 5000 pesetas.'

Capital is rewarded at a fixed rate of interest. The current figure is six per cent, though there is provision for some distribution above this, if profits exceed a certain level. The effect of these arrangements has been the reinvestment of a very high proportion of profit – and thus a very high rate of growth.

The system does not exploit members unreasonably, because the greater part of their contributions is paid back when they leave. A proportion of the payment – currently 12·5 per cent – is allocated to the reserves of the cooperative. This money is not paid back: nor does it earn a rate of interest, but the balance is normally repaid to the departing member under an equitable formula that takes into account changes in the retail price index and the real capital accumulation of the cooperative since the contribution was made. Thus, apart from the twelve and a half per cent, a member shares fully in any capital accumulation through ploughed-back profits, and his original stake is protected against price inflation. It is difficult to imagine a fairer set of workers' ownership arrangements.

In their wage and salary differentials and in their control and ownership structures these Mondragon cooperatives are clearly strikingly different from anything to be found under normal private or State capitalism. All the cooperatives have a fairly conventional management arrangement from top directors down to foremen. But election of top managers obviously makes for greater feelings of confidence and security among the workers. 'You aren't pushed around here in the way that happens elsewhere,' I was told by several young workers. Others referred to the right of appeal against disciplinary action or proposed dismissal. And a senior executive said: 'You can't give orders in the tone of a general around here, and you can't walk around as if you own the place – anyway not if you are hoping for re-election.'

Lively discussions about income differences take place continuously amongst the workforce. While I was at Mondragon some of the professionals were saying they intended to propose a widening of the differential limit – from three-to-one to five-to-one – at the next general assembly. Lower-paid and assembly-line workers took a different attitude. 'This three to one is already too large,' one spirited girl told me. 'It should certainly not be allowed to widen; if anything it must be narrowed.' A number of the younger professionals have left for private industry and higher salaries over the last year or two. However, there still seem to be enough who are ready to forego the chance of higher incomes in exchange for the non-financial satisfaction of working at Mondragon. And the probability is that, if the issue is raised at all at the next general assembly, a decision will be made to keep the differentials as they are.

One wonders what differentials would result in Britain if they were decided by even a partially democratic voting system, as at Mondragon. Sir Joseph Lockwood, head of EMI, was quoted some months ago as saying that 'the chairman of a major company cannot live on less than £50,000 a year'. That must represent a differential, before tax, of at least fifty-to-one, compared with the lowest paid.

A striking demonstration that Mondragon democracy has some 'teeth' came when the evening shift workers demanded a wage rise. They took their case to the general assembly. The management opposed the demand.

R. Oakeshott 293

But a majority of votes in the assembly awarded the evening shift an increase of five per cent compared with the day workers.

Even the most committed supporters of the experiment admit that there is still much to be done. For one thing, the general assembly's democratic working is hindered by the level of education of the majority of the workers. One man, after favourably comparing Mondragon's shop-floor conditions with what he had experienced elsewhere, said that ninety per cent of what went on in a general assembly meeting was quite incomprehensible to him. He was perhaps an extreme case. He was well above the average age and told me that his education consisted of 'ten years studying the Catholic religion'. Even a young woman who held a position of some authority on the assembly line said she could understand less than half of what was said at the meetings.

It is plain too that the two sides of industry have not disappeared at Mondragon. In February 1971 there was a widespread strike for higher wages that lasted a full day. Obviously the strikers did not stop work 'against themselves', so their action must have been directed against the management.

That the situation was still perceived as being one of two sides was made even plainer by management's reaction. An extraordinary general assembly was called. A new statute covering strike action was proposed by the board of directors and passed by a narrow majority. External or 'solidarity' strikes were to be treated with reasonable tolerance. But in the case of internal strikes, the new statute laid down that the 'instigators' would be sacked – though dismissal would be subject to appeal. Of course it may be reversed, and at least up to now it has never been used. But it obviously reflects the survival of traditional attitudes.

It would be wrong to make too much of the strike. For to do so would distract attention from the real successes at Mondragon in solving the two crucial and connected problems of social justice and economic growth – successes that are all the more striking because they have been achieved with virtually no help from outside experts or members of the financial establishment, but simply by ordinary people. Have 'special factors' also contributed to the success? Or would similar experiments elsewhere be similarly successful?

Historically the Basque priesthood has had close links with popular movements. And the association of the founders of the Mondragon co-operatives with the Church has obviously been a source of strength and popular support for them. But the fact that this support has been mobilized and channelled into constructive action is due more than anything else to the ideas and leadership of Fr José María Arizmendi. He set up a technical school in the early 1940s. And it was to him that a small group of graduates from the school came for advice when they started to think about setting up a cooperative enterprise in the middle 1950s.

Now aged fifty-eight, Fr José María has a thin face, grey hair, and wears spectacles. His appearance suggests an elderly don. He wears clerical dress on Sundays and major saints' days, but the day I saw him he was wearing a light grey jacket and trousers and a grey shirt buttoned to the top. He emphasized that he performed all his customary duties in church. But he put even greater stress on his non-clerical work. 'As a priest only the minimum of my work is in church,' he said. His key idea is that 'politics' and 'theory' must be rooted in productive work. Since this obviously requires skills and techniques, it is easy to understand why his first step was to start a technical school. There is the closest possible connection between his ideas and what he has done.

Three other ideas came across very strongly in our talk, and help to explain what has been developed at Mondragon. The first seemed to combine 'social obligation' and 'social justice'. He used the phrase 'educación social' and spoke both of the need for the more privileged to help those less fortunate, and of the need for systems like those at Mondragon, designed to satisfy people's demands for social justice and fairness.

Secondly, he repeatedly emphasized the importance of freedom. The democracy at Mondragon, even if imperfect, provided for the exercise of free choice. He insisted that people should be allowed the maximum of choice at all times. The issue came up in particular when we discussed an arrangement under which students at the Escuela Profesional Politécnica (Mondragon's educational institution) can contribute to their school fees, and earn themselves pocket money, by doing productive work. I asked whether he would object to this arrangement being made compulsory. His reply was unequivocal. Though nearly all the students in fact chose to take part in productive work, it would be totally wrong to force them to do so.

Thirdly, Fr José María emphasized time and again the importance of working with young people. That, as well as his insistence on the importance of productive skills and techniques, helps to explain why it was the technical school that he founded first. It also helps to explain his particular identification with the school – he has an office there – and why it has prospered and grown. Started in 1943 with an enrolment of twenty, by the middle 1950s – when cooperative production first started – its student population had grown to 200. Today's figure is around 2000.

The school's contribution to the development of the Mondragon complex has been enormous. For it has meant, in effect, that the enterprise possesses its own internal source of skilled manpower. It has meant too that the courses taught can be continually adjusted to meet the changing needs of production. So it has been able to bridge the gap between education and production. And it has been able to do so while continuing to satisfy official Spanish requirements for Government-approved qualifications.

The role of the Mondragon bank has also been crucial. It is called the Caja Laboral Popular, not succinctly translatable into English, but meaning roughly the 'savings bank of the people's labour'. Established in 1959, the bank had a total of fifty-four branches by the end of 1971. Its functions combine those of a savings and an investment bank. On the one hand it mobilizes private savings. On the other it has a key role in the planning and authorization of all new Mondragon investment. It is very proud of the growth rate achieved up to now and is very expansionist-minded.

Mondragon's achievements cannot be ignored by anyone who seriously advocates industrial democracy. Of course there are imperfections. The structures are not fully democratic; relationships between management and manual workers are not without friction. There is a big educational job to be done before a majority of the ordinary workers really understand what is going on. Some would argue too that the differentials, though probably the narrowest in Europe, are still too wide. On the other hand it is clear that in terms of both economic success and social justice, the men and women of the Mondragon cooperatives have advanced well beyond anything that is normal in western Europe. There are lessons here for the British Labour Party.

Some of the more imaginative leaders of the Third World, like President Nyerere of Tanzania, might also find something in the experience of the Mondragon cooperative to think about.

Part Three
Performance

20 A. Bergson

Market Socialism Revisited[1]

A. Bergson, 'Market socialism revisited', *The Journal of Political Economy*, vol. 75, no. 5, October 1967, pp. 655–73.

In the sphere of socialist planning, this is manifestly the era of reform. The era in a sense began in the early fifties when for the first time a socialist country abandoned, for a relatively decentralized system incorporating many market-type institutions, the notably centralized and bureaucratic working arrangements that had previously been virtually sacrosanct in the socialist world. But this was for long an isolated case, and reform has now become almost the rule. While working arrangements in Yugoslavia, the venturesome country just referred to, apparently are continuing to evolve in the direction already taken, other socialist states by all accounts are also veering from 'centralized planning' towards 'market socialism', though probably not always as sharply as has been reported. Even the USSR, the country that pioneered the earlier system, is not untouched by the strange new winds. Why are such changes being made? Will the trend toward market socialism persist? What of the possibility of further and even more basic changes in the future?

While posing these intriguing questions, for the economist recent events serve no less to draw attention to an issue long familiar in theory: the economic efficiency of market socialism. This question is also logically prior to the more topical ones just raised. Thus, in experimenting with novel working arrangements, those ultimately responsible for economic policy in the socialist world are clearly seeking greater efficiency. They are doing so with increased understanding of this desideratum and a greater willingness than they had hitherto manifested to subordinate to it conflicting concerns for ideology and politics. Though a more speculative matter than some suppose, the future evolution of socialist planning should turn in part on how efficient market socialism proves to be.

1 I am most grateful to Professor Herbert A. Simon for a searching review of an earlier version and have also benefited from comments by Professor Samuel S. Bowles and a number of other colleagues. Needless to say, however, responsibility for views expressed is my own. A preliminary draft served as the basis of a brief talk in a session on 'Convergence' that was jointly sponsored by the American Economic Association and Comparative Economic Association, December 1966.

On an abstract plane, the economic efficiency of market socialism came to the fore especially in the great theoretic debate on socialist economic rationality that was waged during the interwar period. I myself surveyed the pertinent literature in an essay first published in 1948.[2] A brief review, however, will permit me to take account of further theoretic analyses and also of further thoughts on a topic which is now increasingly important.

The competitive solution

As understood here, the market variety of socialism differs from that where centralized planning prevails chiefly in regard to working arrangements for determining inputs and outputs of production units. Thus, under centralized planning such inputs and outputs typically are controlled to a marked degree by superior agencies in a bureaucratic structure through use of extra-market devices, such as physical quotas. Under market socialism, determination of factor inputs and outputs typically is left to authorities immediately in charge of production units, though superior agencies may still exercise much influence through manipulation of prices and other financial instruments.

As so understood, market socialism might take very diverse forms, but in the theoretic debate on socialist economic rationality attention has been focused particularly on one of them. Moreover, while the famous Competitive Solution is notably abstract, for purposes of theoretical analysis it has the great merit that it has been elaborated relatively fully. Also, wherever appropriate it is not difficult to explore variants. In reviewing the possible efficiency of market socialism, therefore, we can do no better, I think, than to turn again, at least initially, to the Competitive Solution.

This planning scheme is chiefly the work of the late Oskar Lange. I shall refer especially to the construction he gave to it, though it will sometimes be of interest to refer also to the work of another principal architect, H. D. Dickinson.[3] Let us recall the bare essentials: in an economy which is still pecuniary, in the sense that transfers of goods and services between agencies and persons take place at established prices, households are allowed freedom of choice in respect of the work they do and the consumers' goods they purchase with their resultant earnings.

Managers of socialist plants and industries – the former responsible primarily for current operations, the latter for larger investments, especially introduction of new plants – are allowed similarly to determine autonomously inputs of factors and corresponding outputs. In the process, however, each is supposed to observe two rules: (1) to combine factors in

2 Bergson, 1948; to be cited hereafter as reprinted in Bergson, 1966.
3 See Lange, 1938; Dickinson, 1939; Bergson, 1966, pp. 217 ff., and other writings cited in the latter.

such a way as to assure that at the prices established for such inputs any given output is produced at a minimum cost, and (2) to fix the scale of output of any commodity produced at a point where its marginal cost equals the corresponding price.

While thus treated as 'parameters' by managers as well as households, prices are fixed by the Central Planning Board (CPB). Through a trial-and-error process, the Board endeavors to adjust prices so as to assure that, for each good, supply and demand correspond. The CPB also decides on the volume of investment and fixes the rate of interest so that the requirements for new capital on the part of managers of enterprises and industries correspond to the supply which it wishes to make available. The CPB also allocates a tax or dividend among households. In total, this corresponds to the difference between, on the one hand, the volume of investment (as this exceeds any voluntary savings) and outlays for government administration and other goods distributed communally without charge; and on the other, the sum of profits earned by enterprises, and interest and rental charges paid by them.

Except regarding investment, the system supposedly is responsive to consumers' demand. But, if for some consumers' goods the Board should wish to substitute its own preferences for those of households, it might do so simply by maintaining two prices for each such commodity, one to guide production and the other to guide their disposition to households.

The problem of a success criterion

How efficient might the Competitive Solution be? Income distribution apart, equilibrium under the Competitive Solution is supposed generally to correspond to that under capitalist 'perfect competition', and this, of course, does tend to conform to an optimum use of resources representing perfect efficiency. While such an equilibrium hardly is fully attainable anywhere in fact, proponents of the Competitive Solution consider that it might be approached relatively closely under this scheme. Moreover, externalities which would give rise to inefficiency even in the equilibrium of capitalist perfect competition, it is held, might readily be allowed for in an appropriate manner, while income distribution too can be expected to be relatively equitable. In sum, diverse sources of waste that are familiar under capitalism in the real world are largely, if not entirely, absent, and other sources that might come to prevail under socialism should not be very consequential.

In trying to judge how valid this reasoning is, we must consider that Lange nowhere provided any criterion for judging and rewarding managerial success. The rules themselves, it is true, might be viewed as such a criterion, but in order to gauge and reward success on this basis the CPB would have to probe deeply into the cost and other internal records of individual production units. This would vastly increase the CPB's responsibilities, which it is a cardinal concern of the Competitive solution to limit. The failure to establish any practical success criterion for managers, it was held previously (Bergson, 1966, pp. 220 ff.), represents a major deficiency of the Competitive Solution and one not easily repaired. And this I still feel is a valid criticism, but the deficiency now seems, if anything, more serious than before.

To begin with, the obvious test for success is profits, and use of this standard no doubt would often induce the manager to do what is desired of him. But he might often be led to behave otherwise. Thus, if the manager seeks to maximize profits he would, of course, tend to conform to the rules provided he also behaves competitively and takes prices as data. But he might not view prices in this way whenever his production unit is large in relation to the market supplied. In such a case the individual manager might be able, through his decisions on output, to influence the CPB's decisions on prices and so find it more profitable to violate than to observe the rules. Rather than behave competitively, the manager would be led to restrict output much as a monopolist does under capitalism. Hence, the Board, in order to assure conformity to the rules, might often have to examine internal records of production units after all.

So much was argued before, but – and this was not sufficiently taken into consideration – a test for success presumably is needed for the manager not only of a plant but also of an industry. For the latter reference to profits manifestly would be the more dubious. Thus, the manager of an industry would always have monopoly power, and if profits were the test of this success monopolistic violation of the rules might be very marked. It is sometimes suggested, however, that as he ascends a bureaucratic structure an executive tends to identify more with those at the highest level. If this is so, perhaps the manager of an industry could be counted on, to a greater degree than the manager of a plant, to conform to the rules without their being buttressed by a further success criterion. Otherwise, however, occasions where the Board would have to probe into the internal records of production units would be numerous indeed.[4]

To return to the plant manager, even if his output were not relatively large in any conventional sense, should profits be the test of success he would still be tempted to violate the rules provided either his suppliers or his customers for any reason remained more or less attached to him, even

4 Lange (1938, p. 81) was aware that managers might influence prices by their decisions on output but apparently felt that the CPB could compel the managers to treat prices as parameters by imposing such prices as an 'accounting rule'. How this would impel the managers to ignore their influence was not explained.

though prices were in some degree differentiated accordingly. As is rarely considered, even under socialism this must often be so. Customers who have become familiar with one plant's products, for example, might often be reluctant to shift to another plant's products of inferior quality, even at a reduced price. Given such an attitude, it would be still more difficult to assure conformity to the rules.

Under a planning scheme such as is in question, Dickinson (1939, pp. 213-19) acknowledged that profits could not always serve as an appropriate standard for appraising and rewarding managerial success. But the alternatives he proposes, including cost reduction and output increases, clearly would also have their limitations.

Given a satisfactory test of success, managerial incentives must still be related to it appropriately. Hayek argued [5] that such a result might not be easy to achieve. In practice, managers very likely would be reluctant to take risks. This is perhaps not inevitable, but the construction of a satisfactory incentive system now appears more difficult than I envisaged it to be previously.

Suppose that profits could be taken as the test of success. Even so, the manager is properly rewarded not for profits earned but for such earnings as are attributed to his own exertions. To arrange this can never be easy wherever ownership is divorced from management, but it could be more difficult where prices are fixed not by impersonal market forces but by a CPB. Even if the manager has no monopoly power, he must, in determining investment, estimate future prices just as the competitive firm does in a capitalist market. And like the latter he must often erf, but with prices fixed by the Board rather than by the market, responsibility for such error might easily become controversial.[6] Attribution of earnings to one or another manager must be further complicated when, as in the Competitive Solution, one manager introduces and another operates a new plant.[7]

Managerial behaviour under alternative technologies

The difficulties regarding the managerial success criterion that have been described must arise even if there should be no 'indivisibilities' in production, but they would be compounded if such indivisibilities are present.

5 Hayek, 1940, as reprinted in Hayek, 1948, p. 199. See also Bergson, 1966, p. 221.
6 Compare Hayek, 1948, pp. 197-8.
7 In the Competitive Solution, profits are supposed to tend to zero, and if profits were the test of success this might be felt to be discouraging to managers but differential earnings due to differences in managerial talent presumably would persist even in the long run. Assuming such earnings could be identified and paid to the managers responsible for them, they would become wages of management. The tendency of profits to zero for any other reason, therefore, should raise no further difficulty at this point.

This is by now familiar, but as was not made very clear in my earlier essay and perhaps is still not always understood, the further difficulties arising in the exploitation of an indivisible resource differ from those arising in its introduction. Suppose, for example, that plant capacity generally is subject to indivisibilities. Because of the large overhead costs that could result, observation of rule 2, which requires current output to be at the level where price equals marginal costs, may mean losses (see Figure 1, where

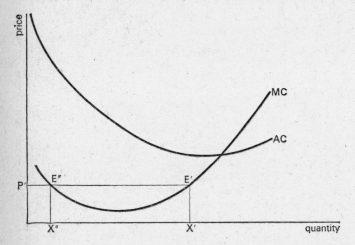

Figure 1

output would have to be at X'). For this reason, it might be especially difficult to establish a suitable managerial success criterion to assure conformity to rule 2, but the rule itself could still be applied meaningfully.

Where plant capacity itself is to be varied, however, this is no longer so. Not only does the variation in capacity affect price, but the effect must be considered in appraising the expansion in question. In place of rule 2, therefore, reference must now be made to 'consumers' surplus', where account is taken of the effect of the manager's decision on prices. Also, conformity to the consumers' surplus standard could not be assured through profit maximization, so use of profits as a success criterion is precluded.[8]

8 To return to the determination of the level of operation of the plant in Figure 1, price equals marginal cost, at two levels of output rather than one, but it was tacitly assumed above that the larger output, X', would be the one sought. Unless the industry manager had erred wildly in constructing the plant to begin with this certainly would be so, but such an error is possible. It should be observed, therefore, that X'' could also be an appropriate desideratum. Thus, suppose for simplicity that the plant in question is the only one in the industry and that the demand

While, as indicated, the Competitive Solution supposedly facilitates dealing with externalities generally, Lange (1938, pp. 77, 105) felt it was especially advantageous regarding external economies and diseconomies of scale of production, that is, external economies and diseconomies that are internal to the industry. In fixing output at the point where price equals marginal cost, the manager of the plant apparently considers only the costs he incurs when his output varies, but the manager of the industry is supposed to consider costs incurred by the industry. Hence, gains and losses which accrue to other plants due to the actions of any one of them are taken into account 'automatically'.

Externalities such as are in question, however, may give rise to decreasing costs for the industry, and as Hansen (n.d., p. 179) reminds us, here too profit maximization is inappropriate. And even if the manager (in this case, of an industry rather than a plant) could be counted on to observe rule 2, it evidently might now be difficult to approach equilibrium through a trial-and-error process, at least one of a sort applicable elsewhere.

The foregoing apart, to regard externalities as being taken into account 'automatically' seems rather dubious when we consider that, whether costs are decreasing or not, proper accounting for the externalities would require the CPB to fix two prices for the product of any industry, one for the

schedule for the industry's product passed through E''. In this case X'' might well be an appropriate output to produce in the short run. While losses are a maximum and the price would fall short even of average prime cost, the total consumers' benefits might still be large enough to warrant operating the plant rather than closing it down.

In sum, rule 2 by itself does not suffice to determine the level of operations of the plant in question. Moreover, while the ambiguity in this rule is removed if the manager is instructed to maximize profits, or minimize losses, this precept also excludes operation at X''. To exclude such a scale of output would no doubt ordinarily be in order, but conceivably it might not be, so here again the Board would have to consider that profits might sometimes be an unsatisfactory success criterion.

While reference has been to the case of an indivisible plant, price, of course, might also equal marginal costs for two levels of output when the plant is divisible. Profits might sometimes turn out to be a defective success criterion, therefore, in the latter case as well.

Given the ambiguity of rule 2 and the inappropriateness of profits as a success criterion, use of a trial-and-error process of the sort required in the Competitive Solution in order to induce the manager to settle at E'' would already seem precluded, but it should be observed that E'' falls in an area where marginal as well as average costs are declining. As will appear, given such decreasing costs, use of such a trial-and-error process would encounter difficulties even if there were only one output for which price equals marginal cost, and the manager could be relied on to produce at this output.

manager of a plant, which would correspond to his marginal costs, and the other for the manager of the industry, which would correspond to his marginal costs. Industry marginal costs would differ from plant marginal costs because of externalities, which somehow would have to be evaluated. The difference between the two prices, of course, would be the counterpart of the tax or subsidy which it has been urged should be established under capitalist competition in similar circumstances.

Hansen (n.d., p. 176) has also properly stressed more than I did previously the case of constant costs, for here even if the manager should seek to conform to the rules he would be in doubt how to behave, within whatever range costs are constant, whenever price equals marginal costs; and with price different from costs he would be impelled either to expand to capacity or to close down his plant. At some levels of operation by different managers in an industry total supply would still equal demand at the established price, but given constant costs such a situation would be difficult to approach under the Competitive Solution. While Hansen refers to the manager of a plant, constant costs would pose even more of a problem for the manager of an industry since here there is no capacity constraint. Moreover, in neither case would the difficulties be much diminished if costs should only be nearly, rather than precisely, constant. In the real world approximation to constancy must be the more usual case.

In order to grapple with the problem raised by constant costs under a planning scheme such as Lange's, Mirrlees (1966, p. 10) proposes that, in expanding capacity in response to current market conditions, the manager should be instructed to proceed cautiously. In other words, he should be required 'to adjust the proposed scale of production by quite small amounts from period to period'.[9] In this way, it is hoped to avoid the large errors and oscillations that otherwise might easily occur. Perhaps some such constraint on managerial behavior as is envisaged would sometimes be to the good, but in effect the manager would be required to subordinate his judgement of the market where this conflicted with the constraint, and the manager's judgement might often be nearer the mark.

I have been referring to a single-product firm or industry, but as Waelbroeck has drawn to my attention, a further related problem must arise in the case of a multiproduct firm, for transformations between products might often occur at constant rate. Hence, the Board would also find it difficult under the Competitive Solution to control satisfactorily the assortment and quality of products.

9 I am grateful to Mr Mirrlees for kindly permitting me to refer to the unpublished paper cited.

Price fixing and income distribution

Reference has been made to the way in which the trial-and-error process of the Competitive Solution might proceed in a single industry experiencing cost variation of one or another sort. The functioning of such a process has recently been examined by Arrow and Hurwicz (1960) and, as is more appropriate, in respect of the economy as a whole rather than only a single industry. For a very abstract but illuminating model, it is found, not very surprisingly, that adjustments of a sort that might be called for by the Competitive Solution would tend to converge to an equilibrium provided production processes generally are subject to diminishing returns. Such adjustments may not so converge, however, if returns are constant, and difficulties regarding convergence are compounded if returns are increasing.[10]

While convergence is of interest, as Waelbroeck has noted, of great interest too is its rapidity, for efficiency of resource use would depend on the latter (see Waelbroeck, 1964, p. 22; Marschak, 1959).[11] Lange (1938, p. 89) apparently considered that under the Competitive Solution convergence would in fact be relatively rapid, but here I still find myself more

10 Arrow and Hurwicz (1960) assume that the community seeks to maximize welfare as given by a single function, representing the relation of utility to the aggregate consumption of different final goods by the community generally. More particularly, a 'helmsman', confronted by varying shadow prices for different final goods, chooses for any set of such prices a mix of final goods which maximizes utility as so understood.

This may seem much too esoteric, but as Paul A. Samuelson (1956) has in effect shown the choices made by such a helmsman could correspond to the mix of final goods selected by different households in a competitive market, where the aggregate income of the households is continually allocated optimally among them through the use of lump sum taxes and dividends. The helmsman's choices could also be regarded as maximizing a social welfare function of the conventional individualistic sort, where social welfare varies positively with the utility of each household. By the same token, the helmsman's choices could also be viewed as corresponding to those for final goods generated by the Competitive Solution, for recall that here too households have freedom of choice in spending their incomes at established prices. Also, they apparently share in a total tax or dividend that is allocated in some manner deemed optimal.

In order to demonstrate convergence, Arrow and Hurwicz (1960, pp. 81–2) assume that the helmsman's indifference surfaces are convex to the axes and contain no linear or planar segments. Given optimal lump-sum allocations and reallocations of the community's tax or dividend, the choice of different households taken together, I believe, would generate aggregative indifference surfaces of this type.

The indifference surfaces of each household were shaped similarly (see Samuelson, 1956, p. 16), but it should be observed that this rules out the interesting case where the household's marginal rate of substitution between any two goods is constant for substitutions made along a given indifference curve.

11 Strictly speaking, what really matters is the time path of convergence.

in accord with Hayek (1948, pp. 187–9, 192–3) who argued that on the contrary the task of fixing prices for an entire economy, which Lange assigns to the Board, would prove formidable. Almost inevitably, the Board would find it difficult to respond quickly to continually occurring changes in supply and demand. It would also be unable to fix prices in sufficient detail to take into account almost endlessly diverse varieties of goods produced by a modern economy. Imbalances between supply and demand, therefore, might be large and persistent.

In fixing prices, the CPB admittedly might hire additional personnel. It might also establish a complex of subordinate agencies, including field offices, to assist it in its work. But such measures could be costly, and it is not clear to what extent the incongruities predicted by Hayek would be avoided. As the CPB expanded and proliferated agencies, it would also face a further and possibly demanding problem of directing and coordinating its own personnel. The Board's task in fixing prices should not be exaggerated, but its difficulties could be consequential.

They might be so even if the CPB confined itself, as Lange apparently assumed it should, to current prices. The difficulties would be greater if, as Mirrlees (1966, pp. 11 ff.) has suggested, the Board also undertook to project future prices. Probably, however, the Board, as Mirrlees argues, could predict prices for broad categories of goods more accurately than the individual enterprise. Because of the possible confusion of responsibilities, the issuance of such predictions might complicate further the task of appraising and rewarding managerial success, but perhaps such difficulties could often be avoided if it were understood that the managers need not rely on the Board's projections and would still be held accountable in any case for their own performance generally.

As indicated, Lange (1938, pp. 83–4, 99–103) considered that the Competitive Solution would not only be relatively efficient generally but quite equitable. In the absence of private ownership of productive assets, there would be no private income from such assets, which is a major source of inequity under capitalism. Also, given freedom of choice of occupation, wage differentials would tend simply to correspond to differences in disutility, and hence to be not really inequitable, while the tax or dividend might also be distributed according to some equitable criterion, such as family size. As I observed previously (Bergson, 1966, pp. 223–4), wage differentials in fact could be expected to correspond to differences in marginal utility only in equilibrium and there only for workers on the margin of choice between occupations. So far as there is disequilibrium or workers are intramarginal, their earnings have the character of rents, which by Lange's own standard would be inequitable. As Lange recognized, rents would be particularly great for persons with rare talents, though he hoped, surely rather optimistically, that these rents could be extracted by taxation without adverse effects on efficiency.

But I refer to income distribution again not to review this matter generally but to draw attention to one aspect which has tended to be neglected, I think quite improperly: managerial earnings. If profits should be a success criterion, and managers should be rewarded correspondingly, their earnings might be viewed as a kind of wage of management, and like wages generally such earnings might tend to be related to disutility. But, for managerial earnings, the relation to disutility might be particularly tenuous. Thus, from the standpoint of efficiency, the manager should receive any and all additional earnings which might result from and induce additional effort on his part. Under any likely incentive arrangements, however, an attempt to realize this principle would be bound to yield the manager rental returns, which would be difficult to absorb through taxes. Especially if the manager were talented, the resulting divergencies from disutility could be wide. Alternatively, a reluctance to sanction managerial rewards of the needed magnitude could easily be a further consequential sourse of inefficiency.[12]

Alternative arrangements

It is time to refer to forms of market socialism other than the Competitive Solution. These are potentially infinite, but only a few are of theoretical interest, and sometimes these do not differ markedly from the Competitive Solution. They do seem to represent significant elaborations of that scheme, however, at least as it was envisaged by Lange. None was considered in my earlier essay.

Mathematical techniques

Possible uses of these procedures in socialist planning have lately become a familiar theme. Regarding economy-wide applications which are of chief interest, reference is usually to centralized planning and Lange himself (1938, p. 88) clearly – indeed, emphatically – envisaged no corresponding role to speak of for such procedures in market socialism. Dickinson (1939, pp. 98–105) once held, however, that under the Competitive Solution the

12 Under the Competitive Solution, the taxes that must be resorted to in order to absorb rents to labor should ideally be of the lump-sum sort, but as the cited article of Samuelson (1956) has made clear, the true lump-sum tax is an even more esoteric device than has been assumed and hardly to be approached closely in practice. And this says nothing of the likely adverse political consequences of reliance on such a measure. By implication, an attempt to realize equity at this point almost inevitably would be at the expense of efficiency. (See Samuelson, 1956, pp. 8–19; also Bergson, 1966, pp. 78 ff., 186–8.)

Board might in fact be able to fix prices simply by solving pertinent equations. While Dickinson subsequently withdrew, or at least greatly qualified, this proposal, both Lange and he wrote before the age of electronic computers. Given this technology, could not the CPB, in performing its cardinal task of fixing prices, confute Hayek after all simply by using mathematical techniques? Thus, could it not in this way largely, if not entirely, avoid trial and error, or at least substitute trial and error on paper for that in practice?

The questions are in order, but, when applied on an economy-wide scale, mathematical procedures are perhaps still not quite as potent as is sometimes assumed. This seems true also of such procedures in the particular economy-wide application in question. With all the progress that has been made, the use of computers still entails a cost. This could hardly be a factor in regard to calculations of any conventional sort that the Board might wish to make, but there are reasons to think it might become so should the Board seek continually to elaborate the mathematical system employed.[13]

More important, should the Board seek to employ mathematical procedures in fixing prices comprehensively and in detail, its undertaking surely could become burdensome for managers of production units, who might be called on to predict and articulate in inordinately concrete detail

13 With successive elaborations of the mathematical system, such benefits as are realized might well tend to diminish. So far as additional computing costs continue to be incurred, therefore, such costs presumably could become a constraint at some point. Admittedly, a further question concerns the manner in which the costs might vary as the mathematical system is elaborated, and this unhappily is a complex matter about which it is difficult to generalize.

Costs of computing, and often also the manner of their variation, are apparently apt to depend not only on the number of equations and unknowns in the mathematical system considered but on the nature of the relations in question, particularly whether reference is to linearities or non-linearities, the nature and degree of interconnectedness of the activities represented, initial knowledge concerning the magnitudes of unknowns in the vicinity of the final solution, and the degree of novelty of initial programming work and the frequency of subsequent changes in the program adopted. In the case of a system of linear equations with random coefficients where nothing is known of the location of the solution, machine operating time varies not with the number of unknowns but with the cube of their numbers; at least this is so for a given apparatus and for linear systems of a size appropriate to it. On a general plane, however, it seems to say much more than this about computing costs.

But granting the complexities, I do not think I am doing any violence to the facts in considering computing costs as a possible limitation on application of highly elaborate systems far outside the conventional range. On this matter, I have learned from discussions with numerous colleagues, though it is only fair to say that some feel that I am inclined to stress it unduly.

the complex and ever changing constraints and opportunities that confront them, and on this basis to communicate to the Board such data on these matters as the Board would require; and for the Board itself, which promptly would have to digest such information and to communicate the results of its deliberations to the managers. The capacities of managers as well as of the Board to grapple with these tasks might often be enhanced by use of computers, but not always.

In fixing prices the CPB obviously would find it advantageous to employ mathematical techniques in some way. Thus, it should be to the good sometimes by use of such techniques to make trial calculations of a highly aggregative or selective kind, and very possibly the Board would also wish to experiment with one or another ingenious scheme, such as 'the two-level planning' of Kornai (1965) and of Kornai and Liptak (1965), which seeks to combine the virtues of decentralization with those of mathematical computation. But the Board could hardly dispose entirely in such ways of a task that, at least in a modern economy, is almost infinitely complex. In fixing prices, therefore, it would still have to resort to trial and error, and in practice as well as on paper.[14]

In using mathematics in the manner envisaged, the CPB evidently need not infringe on the autonomy of managers regarding inputs and outputs. The Board would simply seek by applying mathematical procedures to approach equilibrium levels of prices more quickly. The procedures in question, thus, could be applied under market socialism; and it is on this understanding that they have been considered here. Indeed, within the limits of market socialism the Board might even go a step further and publish the prospective outputs, which in its calculations were found to correspond to the prices that were expected to approach equilibrium levels. Without requiring that such outputs be in any sense compulsory on managers, the Board might hope in this way to provide further guidance

14 As envisaged by Kornai (1965) and Kornai and Liptak (1965), two-level planning entails decentralization of price-fixing and centralization of resource allocation at least as between sectors. This, of course, is a quite different situation from that under Competitive Solution, but considered as a game, such two-level planning might possibly be employed in the context of the Competitive Solution. Thus the Board might seek, through the completion of a number of trial adjustments of a required sort to approach more readily an equilibrium when it undertook to fix prices in practice. On the other hand I understand that under the Kornai–Liptak scheme convergence proceeds rather erratically. This could be an obstacle to the scheme's use in the manner suggested.

I have not found anywhere a systematic account of possible applications of mathematical techniques in national economic planning under market socialism, but reference may be made to the articles of Kornai (1965) and of Kornai and Liptak (1965), just referred to, to Hardt, Hoffenberg, Kaplan and Levine (1967), Marschak (1959) and Neuberger (1966).

for the latter. Such guidance might be especially helpful in the crucial sphere of investment decisions, where as Dobb (1939, pp. 723–7) observed long ago managers must be particularly prone to error. In appraising the possible efficiency of market socialism, then, we must consider that a commitment to this system does not preclude publication of a national economic plan, even one with physical targets, and that trial and error might be abbreviated to some extent in this way.

In sum, the Board might find it in order to engage in 'indicative planning', and so long as the planning remained indicative rather than imperative it would in no way be violating the principles of market socialism (Massé, 1965, pp. 265–6). Once having formulated and published a more or less detailed economic plan, however, the CPB might find it difficult to refrain from resorting to extra-market controls to enforce it, but the question posed regarding the effect of introducing such controls into market socialism is to be discussed below in a somewhat different context.

Decentralization of price fixing

Under the Competitive Solution, the task of fixing prices must be a most difficult one for the CPB even if it should employ mathematical techniques. What, however, if price determination should be decentralized along with the determination of inputs and outputs?

As Hayek (1948, p. 186) observed, even to embrace the Competitive Solution already implies abandonment of much that was supposed to be distinctive, and hence superior, about socialism. If price fixing generally should be left to the market, this process would be carried a step further.

Nevertheless, Lange (1938, p. 78) himself envisaged that the Board would not really be responsible for any and all prices. Rather it was to leave to the market the prices of consumers' goods and labor services. Dickinson (1939, pp. 98–105) too does not always seem to have been insistent that prices be fixed by the Board. One still cannot be sure, however, that they were to be left to the market.

In any event, under market socialism decentralization of price fixing is a possibility, but assuming the Competitive Solution prevails otherwise, what can be inferred as to economic efficiency is fairly evident.

Thus, while arbitrariness on the part of the Board would be obviated, the market prices too would often diverge from their equilibrium values. Also, the danger of monopolistic behavior referred to earlier must now increase. If there are trade unions, such behavior might not be avoided even in regard to wages, which Lange himself would have left to the market. But monopoly restrictions might tend to become pervasive if price fixing should be left to the market on any extensive scale. Perhaps such evils could be mitigated, however, if as is logical, an energetic antitrust division should be established in the Board in place of the division that was to fix prices. The possible effect on efficiency of decentralization of price fixing must be judged in the light of these diverse considerations.

Extra-market controls

While market socialism was defined as a system in which factor inputs and outputs are *typically* determined by authorities immediately in charge of production units, reference thus far has been to forms of market socialism where factor inputs and outputs are *universally* so determined. Mirrlees (1966, pp. 18 ff.) has analysed, however, an alternative planning scheme in which production authorities are allowed to determine factor inputs and outputs but with one notable exception. Production capacity is fixed finally by superior agencies.[15] For the individual enterprise, the pertinent superior agency might be an organization administering an industry or region. This is in itself not an essential departure from Lange, for recall that for the latter too large investment decisions are left to an industry manager. But for Mirrlees appropriate capacity levels are also imposed as quotas on the industrial or regional authority by the CPB. Price and other financial instruments, therefore, are supplanted generally in regard to production capacity.

It is perhaps in order to ask whether with such a major breach in market institutions the planning system in question should still be considered market socialism. But of more interest is the further question whether the introduction of extra-market procedures to determine capacity might be to the good, as Mirrlees apparently assumes.

This is difficult to gauge. Obviously, as Mirrlees urges, the market is not at its best in the determination of new production capacity. The Board, however, might find it difficult to do better through the imposition of quotas, for its administrative burden would be much increased. In a sense this would already be so even if the Board should engage only in indicative planning, but the errors involved in resorting to aggregation and other expedients assume quite a different aspect if the resultant targets are compulsory and not merely orientative for production authorities. One wonders too whether prices would not tend to become more dubious if the Board should no longer rely on them to bring about adjustments regarding capacity. How to arrange suitable success criteria for managers should also be no less of a problem here than in the Competitive Solution.[16]

15 While Mirrlees refers to 'scale of production' he clearly means here 'production capacity'.
16 The question at issue is related to, though evidently not the same thing as, that concerning the comparative efficiency of, on the one hand, a decentralized system where extra-market controls are entirely absent, and, on the other, a

The cooperative variant

Under the Competitive Solution, the manager of a production unit is supposed to follow certain rules, though how such behavior might be assured is an interesting question. Benjamin Ward (1958) has explored an alternative form of market socialism in which the organization of the production unit is approached rather differently. Administration is by a cooperative of workers. Assets are publicly owned, and the government levies a tax on the cooperative as a charge for their use, but otherwise all earnings, in excess of operating expenses for materials, accrue to the workers. In the simple model considered, fixed assets are nondepreciating. The cooperative firm supposedly is free to determine employment and output as it wishes.

As Ward may not consider sufficiently, such arrangements – I shall call them the Cooperative Variant – might have a favorable effect on workers' attitudes and in this way tend to increase productivity. But there is no basis otherwise to quarrel with his interesting conclusion that the firm envisaged might behave quite differently from a competitive enterprise under capitalism. Hence, the Cooperative Variant could be inherently inefficient.

To refer to a simple case of a sort considered by Ward, suppose labor is homogeneous and that net earnings are divided equally among employed workers, but that more senior workers are free to vary the employment of junior ones. Also, labor is the only variable input. The more senior workers presumably will seek to determine total employment and output in such a way that average earnings per employed worker or the per worker average of sales revenue net of the government tax (which is taken to be of

---

centralized one, where such controls are pervasive. In his pioneer article of 1959, Marschak examines the latter problem in a highly formal way for a model embracing three decision makers. Apparently, depending on the time required for reading and writing messages and for turning from one message to another, the centralized system might be preferable to the decentralized one at least according to one of two efficiency criteria employed.

This is clearly a plausible result, but in trying to appraise the possible merit of the two systems more realistically we must also consider a number of complexities from which Marschak understandably abstracts, including some that already have been mentioned, such as difficulties encountered by managers of production units in predicting and articulating pertinent constraints and opportunities and the problem of coordinating activities within the CPB itself.

To repeat, Marschak refers to two systems; one in which extra market controls are absent, the other in which they are general. On the still further question regarding the comparative efficiency of market socialism and centralist planning in the real world, see below.

a lump-sum sort) are a maximum. As is readily seen, such a position is realized when

$$P(MPL) = \frac{PX - R}{L}.$$ **1**

Here P is the going price of the product; X is output; L employment; R the lump-sum tax, and MPL the marginal product of labor. In other words, the value of the marginal product of labor must equal average net earnings per worker. This is so because, if the value of the marginal product of labor exceeds average net earnings, it would pay the more senior workers to increase employment until this ceased to be so; and similarly if the value of the marginal product of labor falls short of average net earnings, employment would be curtailed. The equilibrium position is illustrated. See Figure

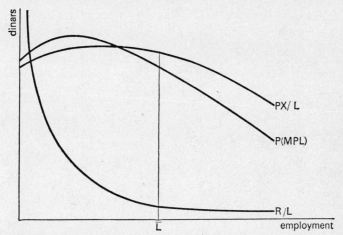

Figure 2

2, where at L, $(PX - R)/L$ is a maximum, and equals $P(MPL)$. Note that here the gradients of the PX/L and R/L schedules are equal.

Depending on the comparative stocks of capital and technologies employed in different firms, then, marginal workers might produce very different value products even among firms in the same industry. Depending too on the going prices, they might also produce different value products in different industries. Such divergencies in marginal returns to employment, which might prevail even in equilibrium, necessarily would betoken inefficiency.

For any firm, output would also depend on the tax, and, as Ward points out, by varying the amount of this levy independently for different firms the government conceivably could still assure that marginal returns to labor were the same everywhere. In effect, the government would simply be taking into its budget, in addition to interest charged at some uniform rate, any and all 'rents' and 'windfall gains' accruing to the different firms. But such a policy would not be easy to realize in practice. Given 'free entry', differences in marginal returns to labor might also be dispelled through establishment of new firms, but this could occur only in the long run.

Curiously, as the going price changes, it can be shown that the firm tends to vary its output in the contrary direction. Such a negatively sloped supply curve could be a source of economic instability, but reference is still to the case where labor is the only variable input. If, say, materials are also variable and are an important part of total cost, all is essentially as before, but the supply curve in this case might have a positive slope.

In contrast to the Competitive Solution, the Cooperative Variant as depicted by Ward assumes that determination of prices is left to the market rather than being made the task of a CPB. The analysis thus far, however, relates to a competitive firm which takes the market price as a datum. As Ward explains, should the firm have any monopoly power it would tend to restrict output below the competitive level.

To repeat, it is assumed that, say through operation of the principle of seniority, employment in the firm may be varied freely. In any more realistic case of working arrangements such as are in question, employment most likely could be varied upward more readily than downward, but, granting this, marginal returns to labor in different firms could still diverge material-ly. Hence the conflict between cooperation and efficiency, which Ward discovered, would still prevail.

The cooperative firm in Ward's analysis produces only one commodity. As Domar (1966) has shown, if the cooperative firm produces many products, the supply schedule for any one of them is more likely to have a positive slope than is that for all products taken together, for an increase in the price of any one product tends to cause a reallocation of inputs in its favor. Domar also elaborates Ward's model by introducing into the analysis a supply curve for cooperative labor, which apparently represents the amount of work members of the cooperative would wish to offer if their dividends were fixed at any given level. While as noted a cooperative should at least be able to increase, and hence also to refrain from increasing, its membership, Domar takes the number of members as given. The supply of labor may still vary, however, through changes in, say, working hours or outside activities. By juxtaposing the supply schedule with the sche-dule of average net earnings realized at different levels of employment ($[PX-R]/L$ in Figure 2), the equilibrium level of cooperative employment is determined. As it turns out, cooperative behavior may be rather different from that envisaged by Ward, though still not necessarily the same as that of a competitive firm under capitalism.

I agree that the Domar cooperative would behave differently from Ward's, but while Domar recognizes that his 'equilibrium' level of employment is not likely to be optimal for the cooperative, he is not entirely explicit as to just what is maximized in, and the determination of, the optimum. In the spirit of Ward's analysis, the cooperative presumably would seek to maximize the utility of its members, allowing for the disutility of their exertions. Given this, the cooperative's optimum must be

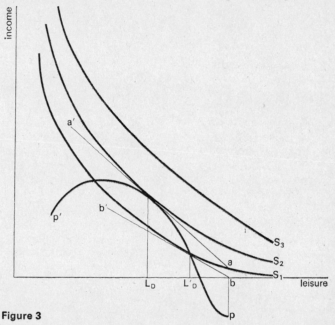

Figure 3

determined in accord with members' preferences between income and leisure and their 'production possibilities' in the manner illustrated (Figure 3).

For simplicity I refer to a cooperative whose members have similar tastes and are equally skilled. In the figure, S_1, S_2, S_3,..., represent any household's indifference curves in respect of choices between income and leisure and pp' its corresponding production possibilities. Variations in the household's employment are understood to typify variations in cooperative employment generally, while the income produced by the household is taken to be a pro rata part of the total cooperative income. With employment nil, income is negative because of the need to pay a tax to the government. The optimum level of employment for the household, then, is at L_D, where its marginal rate of substitution between leisure and income equals the corresponding marginal rate of transformation.

As for the cooperative's equilibrium, this might properly be taken to be the same as the optimum, for the cooperative presumably would seek to realize the latter. Moreover, it could actually approach this desideratum more or less closely depending on how well the management knew the members' tastes and production possibilities. With full knowledge of these aspects, the manager might fix working hours optimally without more ado.

Domar assumes, however, that the cooperative would recruit labor through money wage offers. If it did, the equilibrium might well be at L'_D, as his analysis suggests. Here the household is induced by a wage rate corresponding to the gradient of bb' to work $(b-L'_D)$ hours, while his total wages correspond in turn to his production possibilities. As Domar is aware, however, the cooperative might still approach the optimum more closely by resorting to discrimination – in the present case, between wage rates for successive hours of work. Moreover, the optimum could also be approached simply by use of an internal tax or subsidy. Thus, in the case illustrated, the cooperative might offer the household an internal subsidy, ab, in place of the tax, bp, that is actually paid to the government. The appropriate money wage rate is that corresponding to the gradient of $a'a$.

But in the Domar cooperative as in the Ward cooperative the marginal productivity of labor might still vary as between firms. This would be so whether the cooperative equilibrium is at L_D or L'_D. How a change in price of the product would affect output, however, would now depend partly on the nature of the members' preferences between income and leisure.[17]

Construed as a form of profit sharing under socialism, the Cooperative Variant has also been examined by Kornai and Liptak (1962). Using programming methods, the authors focus particularly on the determination of the volume and structure of a firm's output under two alternative incentive schemes, one inducing maximization of profits and the other inducing maximization of the ratio of profits to sales. While implications for economic efficiency are not explored, as is readily seen cooperative be-

17 Domar (1966) calls his provocative essay 'Soviet Collective Farm'. For this reason, perhaps it is improper to examine the cooperative's behavior in the spirit of Ward, but note that even if the cooperative should desire only to exploit its members the optimum would still be of the sort portrayed in Figure 3. Should the cooperative seek, for example, to limit any member to some minimum consumption standard given by, say 'S_2', it could still maximize the 'tax' realized from the member's activities by allowing the member to respond freely to some wage rate such as is given by the gradient of aa', and some accounting subsidy or accounting tax. In this way the member would still reach a position such as L_D.

havior under the second scheme, though not the first, turns out to be fully as strange as in Ward's analysis.[18]

Conclusions

What may be concluded as to the economic efficiency of market socialism? In elaborating the Competitive Solution, Lange was concerned with how efficient market socialism might be in theory, and in appraising his scheme and exploring possible variants I have focused on the same issue. What we wish finally to know, however, is how efficient market socialism is likely to be in practice. As is still not always considered, practice here is apt to differ widely from theory, and in innumerable ways.

Suffice it to observe that market socialism has been materializing, and in the future may continue to materialize, as a successor not to capitalism but to centralist planning under socialism. For this reason it surely will tend to be much combined with extra-market controls, and often with such as are not envisaged in theory. Accordingly, such controls are not very apt to serve the interests of economic efficiency.[19]

More basically, systems directors in the socialist world, as indicated above, are more understanding of and concerned with economic efficiency than they used to be, but it would be surprising if their understanding and concern should not still leave something to be desired. For this reason they may not only tolerate wasteful extramarket controls. They may also be led to adopt a relatively inefficient form of market socialism. For example, the Cooperative Variant seems distinctly less promising than the Competitive Solution, but it might still be favored if its limitations were not fully understood, or because of its ideological or political appeal.

18 If I may revert to conventional marginal analysis, we need consider only the determination of total output. Suppose profits are maximized. Since the concern is with total profits, rather than profits per worker, and prices and wage rates are taken as data, the firm would ordinarily observe the same rules as are established for the plant under the Competitive Solution. Where the profit–sales ratio is maximized, however, output must always be fixed at the point where marginal and average costs are equal, and without regard to price. Thus, the concern is to maximize $[PX - C(X)]/PX$, where $C(X)$ represents total cost, and P and X as before represent price and output. As is readily seen, if price is given this is a maximum when $C(X)/X$ is a minimum, or $C'(X) = C(X)/X$.

19 When introduced into market socialism, extra-market controls might take the form of the physical quotas which characterize centralist planning, but for practical purposes the consequences might not be very different if use should be made instead of financial instruments but in a discriminatory way. Thus authorities in charge of production units might be deprived of much of their discretion through imposition of discriminatory prices and other financial terms. Such discriminatory terms in effect violate the requirement of anonymity which Hurwicz (1960, p. 169) has established for a decentralized system.

The still limited understanding of and concern for efficiency may also affect the implementation of market socialism, whatever the form. Even should the Competitive Solution be accepted in principle, for example, one wonders whether a socialist Board would be likely soon fully to emancipate itself from Marxian skepticism of market processes and so to feel impelled to manipulate prices freely in response to changes in supply and demand; and this still says nothing of the need on the part of the Board politically to consider the 'vested interests' that might be affected by such price changes. The political concern for vested interests would be the greater if, as might be so, market socialism should be associated with some diffusion of power generally.[20] The departure from theory at this point, I believe, might be very wide.

While considering that under the Competitive Solution socialism could achieve notable efficiency, Lange (1938, p. 109) conceded that 'bureaucratization of economic life' is a 'real danger' in such a society. Schumpeter (1947, pp. 205 ff.) too stressed this problem. Such bureaucratization could mean many things, and in one sense what is involved presumably is the question of managerial incentives already discussed. But, given the likely pervasive importance of politics, there is further reason to wonder whether managers of bureaucratic public agencies will behave in the manner theory envisages.

Schumpeter (1947, pp. 210 ff.) also stressed, rightly, the importance of labor attitudes and discipline as a factor that might affect the economic performance of socialism. I doubt, however, that he would still consider the ability of this system to command the 'moral allegiance' of the workers as conferring an advantage on it. Also, under the market variety, socialism might not be as efficacious as Schumpeter assumed in supplementing voluntary with authoritarian controls. This is because of the possible diffusion of power already referred to. The worker should become more favorably disposed to the system, however, if he were allowed to share more fully in the fruits of economic progress. Where market socialism succeeds centralized planning, perhaps he will be allowed to do so.

I have referred to market socialism as it might be in theory and practice. In Yugoslavia, however, market socialism by all accounts has in fact been approached, if not realized. How efficient is market socialism there? Relevant as it is, I cannot pursue this question here, but the Yugoslav case hardly conflicts with what I have said thus far. Indeed, at a number of points I have already had just this case in mind. Suffice it to refer to the use by superior government authorities not only of market but often (especially

20 The need to consider vested interests in fixing prices presumably would arise in part because of the difficulties with lump sum taxes already referred to in footnote 12 above.

in regard to investment allocation) of extra-market processes for purposes of directing activities of enterprises that administer individual production units. Again, where, as often is so, prices are controlled by superior agencies, such agencies tend to postpone, or to limit, increases which manifestly might be called for by increases in demand. Last but not least, there is the famous system of workers' 'self-management', with its quasi-cooperative system of labor remuneration. On an abstract plane, Ward's cooperative firm is intended, of course, to represent just this form of organization.[21]

In sum, the reader will wish to judge for himself the possible upshot for economic efficiency of the many diverse aspects that have been explored. For my part, I suspect that with all its limitations, market socialism, where introduced, will tend to be more efficient than centralized planning might have been in similar circumstances but not as much so as is often assumed. Even one who is favorably disposed toward market processes may feel, therefore, that the more enthusiastic proponents of market socialism will sometimes be disappointed.

We wish to compare this system not only with centralized planning but with capitalism. Lange felt that socialism could be more efficient than its great rival, but even under the Competitive Solution there are reasons to think socialism might not perform nearly as well as he assumed, and the kind of market socialism adopted in any actual case could easily be inferior to the Competitive Solution. Under centralized planning, as is widely agreed, the proverbial claims of socialists regarding the economic superiority of their system over capitalism have yet to be vindicated. One wonders whether such claims are apt to be vindicated either under market socialism, though socialist economic performance may well improve under this variant.[22]

---

21 On Yugoslav planning, in addition to the previously cited article of Ward, see Ward, 1957; Neuberger, 1959; International Labor Office, 1962; Fleming and Sertic, 1962; Waterston, 1962; Economic Commission for Europe, 1965; Ward, 1965; Macesich, 1966.

22 In pondering this weighty issue, we must of course consider that economic performance under capitalism has also been improving. Capitalism is certainly functioning far better than it did in the thirties, and there are reasons to think it may continue to improve in the future: for example, through the further development of macroeconomic forecasting procedures; the continued improvement in information available to businessmen on the state of the market and in their techniques of interpreting this information; and the further extension and improvement of accounting and other internal controls, with or without the use of computers. In order for socialism to gain on capitalism regarding efficiency, therefore, the improvement realized under the market variety of socialism might have to be not merely absolute but relative.

References

ARROW, K. J., and HURWICZ, L. (1960), 'Decentralization and computation in resource allocation', in R. W. Pfouts (ed.), *Essays in Economics and Econometrics: A Volume in Honour of Harold Hotelling*, University of North Carolina.

BERGSON, A. (1948), 'Socialist economics', in Howard Ellis (ed.), *A Survey of Contemporary Economics*, Blakiston, Philadelphia.

BERGSON, A. (1966), *Essays in Normative Economics*, Harvard University Press.

DICKINSON, H. D. (1939), *Economics of Socialism*, Oxford University Press.

DOBB, M. (1939), 'Saving and investment in socialist economy', *Econ. J.*, vol. 49, pp. 713–28.

DOMAR, E. D. (1966), 'The Soviet collective farm as a producer cooperative', *Amer. econ. Rev.*, vol. 56, no. 4, pp. 734–57.

Economic Commission for Europe (1965), *Economic Planning in Europe*, United Nations.

FLEMING, J. M., and SERTIC, V. R. (1962), 'The Yugoslav alternative', *International Monetary Fund Staff Papers*, vol. 9, pp. 202–25.

HANSEN, B. (n.d.), 'A note on the rules of behavior for competitive socialism', in *On Political Economy and Econometrics: Essays in Honour of Oskar Lange*, Polish Scientific Publishers, Warsaw.

HARDT, J., HOFFENBERG, M. KAPLAN, N., and LEVINE, H. S. (eds.) (1967), *Mathematics and Computers in Soviet Economic Planning*, Yale University Press.

HAYEK, F. A. (1940), 'Socialist calculation: the competitive solution', *Economica*, vol. 7, no. 26, pp. 125–49.

HAYEK, F. A. (1948), *Individualism and Economic Order*, University of Chicago Press.

HURWICZ, L. (1960), 'Efficiency of decentralized structures', in G. Grossman (ed.), *Value and Plan*, University of California Press.

International Labor Office (1962), *Workers' Management in Yugoslavia*, International Labor Office.

KORNAI, J. (1965), 'Mathematical programming as a tool in drawing up the five-year economic plan', *Econ. Planning*, vol. 5, no. 3, pp. 3–18.

KORNAI, J., and LIPTAK, T. (1962), 'A mathematical investigation of some economic effects of profit sharing', *Econometrica*, vol. 30, no. 1, pp. 140–61.

KORNAI, J., and LIPTAK, T. (1965), 'Two-level planning', *Econometrica*, vol. 33, no. 1, pp. 141–69.

LANGE, O. (1938), 'On the economic theory of socialism', in B. Lippincott (ed.), *On the Economic Theory of Socialism*, University of Minnesota Press.

MACESICH, G. (1966), *The Market-Planned Economy of Yugoslavia*, University of Minnesota Press.

MARSCHAK, T. (1959), 'Centralization and decentralization in economic organizations', *Econometrica*, vol. 27, no. 3, pp. 399–430.

MASSÉ, P. (1965), 'The French plan and economic theory', *Econometrica*, vol. 33, no. 2, pp. 265–77.

MIRRLEES, J. A. (1966), 'The price mechanism in a planned economy', unpublished paper presented at Conference on 'Planning and the Market', Nice, France, August 31–September 6.

NEUBERGER, E. (1959), 'The Yugoslav investment auctions', *Q.J. Econ.*, vol. 73, no. 1, pp. 88–115.

NEUBERGER, E. (1966), 'Libermanism, computopia and visible hand', *Amer. econ. Rev.*, vol. 56, no. 2, pp. 131–44.

SAMUELSON, P. A. (1956), 'Social indifference curves', *Q.J. Econ.*, vol. 70, no. 1, pp. 1–22.

SCHUMPETER, J. (1947), *Capitalism, Socialism and Democracy*, 2nd edn, Harper & Row.

WAELBROECK, J. (1964), 'La grand controverse sur la planification et la théorie économique mathématique contemporaine', *Cahiers de L'ISEA*, no. 146, pp. 3–24.

WARD, B. (1957), 'Workers' management in Yugoslavia', *J. polit. Econ.*, vol. 65, no. 5, pp. 373–86.

WARD, B. (1958), 'The firm in Illyria: market syndicalism', *Amer. econ. Rev.*, vol. 48, no. 4, pp. 566–89.

WARD, B. (1965), 'The nationalized firm in Yugoslavia', *Amer. econ. Rev.*, vol. 55, no. 2, pp. 65–74.

WATERSTON, A. (1962), *Planning in Yugoslavia*, Johns Hopkins Press.

21 P. Blumberg

Alienation and Participation: Conclusions

Excerpt from P. Blumberg, *Industrial Democracy, the Sociology of Participation*, Constable, 1968, chapter 6.

We have now completed our survey on some of the most important research on participation conducted in the last two and a half decades. Table 1 summarizes the conclusions of the major studies. In this participation literature we have seen tremendous diversity on all sides – diversity in the academic background and theoretical orientation of the researchers, diversity in the conception, design and execution of the research, diversity in the settings in which this research has taken place, and diversity in the characteristics of the population studied. There is significance in this diversity. It is just this impressive diversity in the participation literature which makes the consistency of the findings, by contrast, even more profound, significant, and valid. *There is hardly a study in the entire literature which fails to demonstrate that satisfaction in work is enhanced or that other generally acknowledged beneficial consequences accrue from a genuine increase in workers' decision-making power. Such consistency of findings, I submit, is rare in social research.*

It is not really difficult to explain why participation 'works'; it is almost a matter of common sense that men will take greater pride and pleasure in their work if they are allowed to participate in shaping the policies and decisions which affect that work. But such common sense has long been ignored by sociologists. On the contrary, in fact, sociologists would much rather offer sophisticated empirical refutations of common sense beliefs than confirm such beliefs, despite the importance of the implications which might underlie them. The participation literature, however, does not refute but confirms elementary common sense. Yet this literature which has potentially such far-reaching implications has until very recently all but been ignored in industrial sociology. Although every industrial sociologist has long been familiar with the Lewinian studies of democratic versus authoritarian leadership, few of them, though their minds are trained to see and to make generalizations, saw any relevance of these and other studies to an industrial setting.

It is true that participation has lately become quite fashionable in management and business school thinking in the United States, having

Table 1 Partial summary of the participation literature

Senior authors	Setting of study	Subjects	Nature of experiment or survey	Major conclusions
1 Lewin, Lippitt, White	boys' clubs	eleven-year-old boys	authoritarian, democratic, and laissez-faire leadership compared	democratic (participative) leadership most highly associated with high work motivation, harmonious interpersonal relations among group members, and overall satisfaction
2 Bennett	introductory psychology class	psychology students	examined components of participation: group discussion; group decision; overtness of commitment to decision; strength of group consensus; compared effectiveness of each in stimulating action (volunteering for experiment)	group decision was more crucial in raising the probability of action than any other factor
3 Bavelas	garment factory	sewing machine operators	compared efficiency of workers who were allowed to discuss *and decide* upon production with those allowed to discuss only	the discussion-and-decision group was clearly the more efficient
4 Lawrence and Smith	garment factory	office workers and manual workers	replication of above; compared efficiency of workers who were allowed to discuss and decide upon production with those allowed to discuss only	the discussion-and-decision group increased its productivity to statistically significant levels over its own pre-experimental level and over that of the discussion-only group
5 Coch and French	garment factory	manual workers	compared morale and efficiency of groups who were given different degrees of authority to participate in decisions relating to changes in work organization	success in bringing about job changes – both in terms of productivity and worker satisfaction – was directly proportional to the amount of worker participation permitted. 'Total-participation' groups had highest productivity and morale; 'no-participation' groups, the lowest

Table 1 – *Continued*

Senior authors	Setting of study	Subjects	Nature of experiment or survey	Major conclusions
6 Morse and Reimer	large insurance company	office workers	in two sections of the company, workers' powers of decision-making were increased substantially; in two other sections, workers' powers of decision-making were decreased substantially	workers in the autonomous sections experienced these statistically significant changes from the pre-experimental situation: greater feelings of 'self-actualization' on the job; greater satisfaction with supervisors at all levels; greater satisfaction with the company; greater intrinsic work satisfaction; workers in the hierarchically-controlled sections experienced statistically significant decreases in all these areas
7 French	Norwegian shoe factory	production workers	experimental groups given power of participation in certain areas of managerial decision-making with respect to the production process; compared with control groups	experimental groups were not more productive than control groups but satisfaction with the company and attitudes toward labour relations tended to be higher; within the experimental groups, those whose attitudes had changed most tended also to believe that participation was a legitimate workers' right
8 Levine and Butler	factory	supervisory personnel	effectiveness of lecture and discussion methods compared with respect to correcting supervisor's error in evaluating workers	only supervisors in the discussion-participation groups showed any subsequent improvement in their ratings of workers
9 Babchuck and Goode	men's clothing department in large department store	group of clothing salesmen	workers spontaneously altered a management-imposed commission system which had created friction within the department; under workers' plan, all commissions were shared equally	friction eliminated, morale increased under workers' reorganization

Table 1 – *Continued*

Senior authors	Setting of study	Subjects	Nature of experiment or survey	Major conclusions
10 Strauss	toy factory	female manual workers	discontent of the workers convinced management to grant workers' request to allow them to regulate speed of belt and other more minor conditions of work situation	both productivity and morale increased greatly; however, when increased productivity 'unbalanced' the flow of work to and from other departments, supervisors re-established control over speed of belt; productivity fell drastically and six of eight girls quit shortly thereafter
11 Weschler	naval research laboratory	physicists, engineers, scientific aids, and clerical workers	comparison of job satisfaction and morale of personnel in two divisions, one headed by scientist restrictive in leadership, one by scientist permissive in leadership	job satisfaction was more prevalent in division headed by permissive leader
12 Baumgartel	medical research	medical scientists	compared three leadership patterns in different labs: 1 *laissez-faire* 2 participatory 3 directive	participatory leadership was found to be more effective than the other two types in producing high work motivation, high morale and satisfaction with leadership
13 Mann and Baumgartel	public utility company	field and office supervisors	assessed the factors related to supervisory concern with costs	supervisors who were delegated authority and allowed to participate in decisions to allocate funds were more likely to be concerned with costs than those not participating
14 Vroom	delivery service company	1st, 2nd, 3rd line supervisors	examined job satisfaction in relation to amount of perceived participation in decision-making of superiors and how this was affected by personal independence needs and/or authoritarian characteristics	positive correlation found between perceived participation and job satisfaction; correlation increased among supervisors with high independence needs and few authoritarian tendencies

Table 1 – *Continued*

Senior authors	Setting of study	Subjects	Nature of experiment or survey	Major conclusions
15 Wickert	telephone company	telephone operators and service representatives	compared girls who had resigned with those still on the job!	girls who remained with the company were more likely to believe that they could make decisions on the job; those who left tended to feel they could not
16 Ross and Zander	factory	female skilled workers	comparison between characteristics of workers who resigned subsequently and those who remained on the job!	those who stayed tended to be more satisfied with: their autonomy on the job; their recognition; and their sense of achievement
17 Fleishman and Harris	US truck manufacturing plant	foremen and production workers	workers' grievances and turnover related to supervisory style of foremen	workers under foremen whose supervision was characterized by 'consideration' (including an element of participation) had far fewer grievances and far less turnover than workers under foremen whose mode of supervision was characterized by 'structure'

Sources: see reference list at end of reading.

replaced the human relations approach which was considered too manipulative and thus self-defeating; and the new fad has given rise to concepts and approaches such as bottom-up (!) authority styles, theory 'Y', T-Groups and an assorted alphabet soup of participative and pseudo-participative techniques.

Our approach, of course, differs from all of these in that we do not see participation as a device to lower costs to improve quality, to increase productivity, to undercut trade union or workers' demands, or to give workers the illusion of power without its actuality, the more easily to guarantee jealously guarded managerial prerogatives within the framework of private enterprise. We are interested in the question of participation as it bears on the larger sociological and philosophical issue of the alienation of labour, and we are prepared to follow wherever this research leads.

Now that participation is slowly beginning to catch on among behavioral scientists, one is still left with a question and a paradox. Despite the almost unanimous evidence on the favourable effects of participation in general and in industrial settings in particular, almost no one in any of the related fields has raised the question: to what extent does private ownership and control of modern industry place sharp limits upon the amount of participation that is structurally possible? Given the demonstrated beneficial effects of participation, to what degree is its application inherently limited by the framework of private ownership? Is it true, as T. B. Bottomore has said, that the full development of workers' participation is possible only on the basis of social ownership?

These questions are never raised. But what happens when staid social scientists conduct perfectly conventional research only to find their results telling them that perhaps the old advocates of 'workers' control' had something there? What happens is that they draw the narrowest possible conclusions which allow them to stay safely within the confines of the here and now. Participation is praised but no one asks any basic questions. Instead, the present system of ownership and control is merely assumed to be universal, despite the obvious fact that economic experiments are everywhere to be studied. This is rarely done, and the current system is assumed to be given, then, within the accepted framework, minor adjustments (of supervisory techniques, for example) are urged.

We have said that common sense explains why participation is effective, and, as we have seen, research has confirmed these assumptions. Research since the days of the Mayo experiments indicates that satisfaction in work is just as dependent upon fulfilment of the employees' ego needs as upon satisfaction of their physical needs. Psychologists engaged in research on participation have argued that participation, power, and responsibility on the job tend to satisfy basic ego needs. Having the power of participation implies to workers that they are equal partners, collaborators in an enterprise, rather than passive, coerced, and unwilling subordinates. Participation strengthens the belief, or creates it, that they, the workers, are worthy of being consulted, that they are intelligent and competent. When workers make the frequently bitter remark that 'they don't pay you to think around here', they are really saying that their opinions are not valued, that they are not regarded as competent collaborators, but merely as living automatons, passive extensions of the machines they operate. Participation corrects this by gratifying the basic human needs for respect, appreciation, responsibility, and autonomy. Is it any wonder, then, in light of all the foregoing research, that Ralph White and Ronald Lippitt (1960), pioneers, along with Kurt Lewin in group research, have concluded that:

Of all the generalizations growing out of the experimental study of groups, one of the most broadly and firmly established is that the members of a group tend to be more satisfied if they have at least some feeling of participation in its decisions.

The participating worker is an involved worker, for his job becomes an extension of himself and by his decisions he is creating his work, modifying and regulating it. As he is more involved in his work, he becomes more committed to it, and, being more committed, he naturally derives more satisfaction from it.

A good case for participation can be made on other psychological grounds as well. It can be argued that the traditional forms of authority in economic enterprises, in which employees are allowed little or no rights of participation, directly contradict the psychological needs of mature adults. Borrowing from the work of contemporary psychologists, Chris Argyris (1957) has said that as a person develops from infancy to mature adulthood, he attempts to move: from passivity to *activity*; from a state of dependence to adult *independence* and *control* of his own behavior; from having a short, here-and-now time perspective to a *longer perspective* which takes into account both past and future; from having a subordinate role in family and society to having an *equal* or *superordinate role*.

Ironically, just as the mature individual strives for these goals, so they may actually be undermined by his day-to-day experience on the job. Without rights of participation, employees work under a system of authority, according to which they must, in exchange for a wage or salary, submit to conditions which subvert the creation and the sustenance of a mature personality. At work, an authority which is essentially not accountable to its subordinates controls, directs, coordinates, dispenses, orders, hires, fires, assigns, rewards and punishes.

The main thrust of the autocratic organization is to drive the mature adult back into childhood. The mature individual strives to take an active part in his world, but the chain of command at work renders him *passive*. He seeks to be independent and to control his own behaviour, but as an employee, he is rendered *dependent* and essentially lacking in control over his own behaviour. The mature individual strives for the long time perspective, but as he does not possess or have access to necessary information at work which would permit this, his *time perspective* is consequently *shortened*. He seeks to achieve relationships based on equality, but as a *subordinate*, he becomes just that, once again as in childhood. At every turn, the psychological needs of the mature individual are at odds with the demands of the autocratic organization. The consequences, as Argyris has pointed out, are dysfunctional, both for the individual and for the organization. The employees' principal reaction is frustration which may be expressed in any number of ways, most of which are detrimental all round: aggression, ambivalence, regression, apathy, restriction of output and otherwise subverting the goals of the organization.

It can readily be inferred from the foregoing that while the autocratic organization tends to undermine the employee's psychological maturity, the democratic organization tends to strengthen maturity by stimulating the very traits associated with it: activity, independence, control, egalitarian relationships, and the like.

Having given so much attention to studies which confirm the participation hypothesis, we should at this point examine the negative evidence. This is rather easily done, for the contrary findings are sparse and often inaccurate.

It does seem true and reasonable, first of all, that participation is less useful in *crisis* situations such as in combat or in classrooms where examinations are imminent, to take two contrasting situations. Persons living under conditions of stress and crisis often feel that there is insufficient time and opportunity to indulge in the 'luxury' of participation and may prefer faster decisions made by designated leaders. Valid as this is, it should be noted that these kinds of situations are not typical but, by their nature, extraordinary.

Robert Dubin (1965, p. 40), examining only a very small part of what we have called the participation literature, has argued that participation is effective only in certain types of technological settings – in unit or craft production. He claims, for example, that participation was important in Wickert's study of telephone employees only because 'these aspects of participation in work are mediated by the need for autonomy that comes from the technology employed'. It should be obvious after our extensive treatment of the participation literature here, however, that its applicability greatly transcends the narrow technological band stipulated by Dubin.

The same author argues further that participation is useful only up to a point, beyond which greater participation may actually lead to a decline in work satisfaction. His view is based on the alleged fact that when participation increases beyond the expectations and abilities of workers, they may not be able to handle the added demands and responsibilities and may react negatively. Here Dubin leans heavily on a point made originally by Rensis Likert (1961, pp. 31–2):

Available research findings indicate . . . that when . . . the amount of participation used is less than or very much greater than expected, an unfavourable reaction is likely to be evoked. Substantially greater amounts of participation than expected appear to exceed the skill of the subordinate to cope with it and produce a negative reaction because of the threatening nature of the situation to the subordinate.

The available theory and research findings suggest that the best results obtain when the amount of participation is somewhat greater than expected by the subordinate, but still within their capacity to respond to it effectively.

Dubin (1965, p. 42) concludes that this is a factor 'that is rarely given attention by those who urge participative management as the be-all and end-all of supervisory practice'. But while Dubin has made use of Likert's premises here, he has systematically ignored Likert's own conclusions. If participation goes beyond the expectations and abilities of subordinates, Likert's solution is not to limit participation to some small but supposedly optimal amount, but to *increase* participation *gradually*, which will permit a steady expansion in the subordinates' expectations, abilities, feelings of legitimacy for the new system, and the like.

For the same reasons, Likert (1961, p. 245) writes that when management goes immediately from very tight control from above to a system of participation, the short range reaction is often not appreciation at all, but resentment, hostility, and apathy. The reasons for this initial reaction: 'the need to release bottled-up animosity and the need to test the superior's sincerity'. Thus, the initial negative reaction should not be taken as proof of the undesirability or unworkability of participation.

In conclusion, then, Dubin's hypothesis that there is a curvilinear relationship between participation and satisfaction is based really on a premise which sees the workers' expectations and abilities *vis-à-vis* participation as static and incapable of growing and expanding gradually as the quantity and quality of participation is increased.

It has often been argued that worker participation is undesirable and unnecessary primarily because of the apathy of the workers themselves. This argument requires two answers. First, if apathy were sufficient grounds for dismantling the democratic process, then we might have to dispense with political democracy altogether in the United States, for Americans are notoriously apathetic when it comes to political activity. In the presidential election of 1964 in the United States, despite the overwhelming political saturation of the mass media, less than two-thirds of the eligible voters cast their ballots for president (63 per cent) and less than 60 per cent voted for congressional candidates. In no off-year election from 1922 to 1962 have so much as 50 per cent of the electorate come to the polls, and in some years, the proportion fell below one-third. Local elections make these turnouts seem enormous, and an incredibly small number of citizens actually work for candidates, contribute to campaigns or are thoroughly and intelligently aware of the major issues of the day.

Secondly, the charge of worker apathy to participation is an unfounded assumption, largely refuted by research which indicates that workers are often eager to participate, if given the opportunity, and that job interest, commitment and satisfaction are all generally heightened by the introduction of various forms of participation.

Further confirmation of this derives from an interesting study conducted among white and blue collar workers in Oslo, Norway (see Holter, 1965). Some 1100 non-supervisory employees at eighteen establishments in Oslo were interviewed in 1962. Among the enterprises were ten factories employing between 100 and 400 workers each, seven insurance companies, and one large-scale industrial enterprise. 30–40 per cent of the employees were selected from each enterprise, yielding a sample of 628 blue collar workers, the remainder white collar workers. While the survey was originally designed to measure age and sex differences in job attitudes and behaviour, some pertinent data on attitudes towards participation were uncovered.

The researchers asked their respondents: 'Do you feel that the employees in general participate sufficiently in decisions that concern the management of the establishment as a whole?' Significantly, only 17 per cent of the blue collar workers answered affirmatively, while 78 per cent said that employees do not participate sufficiently. Of the white collar workers (employed primarily for the insurance companies), only 37 per cent said participation among employees was sufficient, 59 per cent said it was insufficient. The researchers also asked the workers: 'Do you feel that you personally participate sufficiently in decisions made at your place of work, or do you wish to participate more in them?' Only 22 per cent of the blue collar workers said that they had 'no special interest in more participation'. Over half (56 per cent) said that they 'would like to participate more in decisions that directly concern my own work and working conditions'. And an additional 16 per cent said that they wanted to go beyond that 'to participate more in decisions that concern the management of the whole enterprise'. The response of the white collar workers was comparable, with only 20 per cent expressing no special interest in participation, and the remainder desiring more participation, either at the job level (67 per cent) or at the enterprise level (11 per cent).

While no firm generalizations can be made from the attitudes of Norwegian workers to workers in other countries, this study nevertheless further calls into question the traditional view of workers as interested in only the narrowest and most personal satisfactions on the job and totally indifferent to larger issues of participation.

For Henri de Man, as well as for more contemporary scholars (see Friedman, 1961), the crucial element in the definition of work is its *coercive* nature. One man may repair automobiles in a shop. This is work. Another may repair his own automobile in his garage at home. This is a hobby, a pleasure. What distinguishes work from non-work is not always the nature of the task, but the elements of compulsion, necessity, regimentation and unfreedom. Is it not reasonable to assume, then, that anything which gives the worker increased freedom and control over his work environment – which participation does – will make work seem less coercive, regimented and unfree, less like the work he has always known, in short, less work-like?

Postscript

So successful is participation as a device that it has been used with some success among groups of persons who might be considered the worst possible risks and who might be regarded as the least likely to appreciate it, to benefit from it, to avail themselves of it and to use its machinery properly. I am referring to imprisoned criminals.

Experiments in prisoner self-government have had a long, chequered and controversial history in the United States, going back at least as far as 1793. There have been cases where inmate participation has worked spectacularly well, where prisons have been almost literally turned over to inmates via elected councils, but there have likewise been cases of spectacular failure. Of the notable early experiments, the movement beginning in 1895, which attempted to organize training schools for delinquents into self-governing 'Junior Republics', is worthy of mention.

Begun by William George, these Junior Republics spread to many privately run institutions in the United States within a few years. Thomas M. Osborne, whose name is now closely linked with the philosophy of inmate self-government, extended the idea to adult institutions at Auburn, New York (1914), and afterwards to Sing Sing and elsewhere.

Inmate self-government was at that time far more thorough-going than it is today. According to Glaser (1964, p. 218): '... rules for inmates were established by an elected body of inmate representatives, internal surveillance was performed by inmate "police", and inmates who misbehaved were tried and punished by inmate courts.'

Some of these early experiments were extremely successful in generating prisoner trustworthiness and reliability, and instances are occasionally cited wherein prisoners in a self-governing institution, having gone on field trips, returned to the prison virtually unchaperoned. An early observer (Haynes, 1935) reported that inmate participation led to fewer escapes, fewer riots, fewer fights among prisoners, less recidivism, and higher productivity among working inmates.

Nevertheless, these successful experiments tended to break down after a short period. Baker (1964) attributes their failure to:

1 The adverse effects of giving to prisoners power to discipline their fellow inmates;

2 The dependence of the experiment upon single crusaders who did not have staff support and who fell victim to adverse publicity and the outrages of a public that was aghast at the idea of giving extensive powers to hardened criminals.

To this day the issue of inmate self-government generates considerable emotion and many prison officials condemn it in the most vehement terms, while others defend it and claim that it has been unjustly maligned. A few of those officials opposed to inmate participation have had bad experiences with them personally; more of them have heard bad things of them from others; and probably most share a *Weltanschauung* with administrative and managerial personnel in all walks of life, whose very status and role incline them against systems of participation from below, whether 'below' means factory workers, university students, or prison inmates. Nevertheless, as many experiments in inmate self-government have clearly failed, there are legitimate grounds for opposing them and these include the following: the inmate council may become dominated by 'model prisoners' and others who do not have the respect of the informal inmate leaders; on the other hand, the council machinery may be seized by aggressive criminals who may exploit the system for their own ends; cliques, ward politics and privileges for members of the inmate council may develop; there may be bullying of prisoners and excessive punishment where inmate councils control discipline; the council may facilitate inmate unity and provide them with an instrument for prison disorders; or the inmate councils may degenerate into so-called 'gimme groups', fault-finding bodies which make excessive and unreasonable demands of the prison staff.

Nevertheless, many wardens and prison officials remain convinced that inmate self-government, properly organized, can be of great value to the institution, the staff and the inmates themselves. A recent survey indicated that, in one form or another, inmate councils exist in eight out of thirty-two US federal prisons and in thirteen of forty-four state penitentiaries. Their powers are quite circumscribed compared with earlier, more radical experiments. Of the councils existing in state penitentiaries, most operate under a formal constitution and by-laws, are usually staff-sponsored, are elected by democratic ballot (subject to administrative approval), prepare their own agendas, and meet on the average of once a month. Many of the previous abuses have been corrected. Nowhere are prisoners allowed to discipline their fellows and membership on the councils is usually restricted to those with good conduct records, in order to keep them out of the hands of those who would corrupt them and turn them to their own personal advantage.

In a survey of the activities of councils in the state penitentiaries, Baker found them most often involved in matters of recreation and entertainment (talent shows, deciding on TV, radio, and movie programmes, planning holiday events), organizing blood bank and eye bank campaigns, taking charge of postage funds, charity drives, sanitation drives, and self-improvement programmes.

The inmate council systems at the Terre Haute (Indiana) and Leavenworth (Kansas) prisons have gone beyond the kinds of activity sketched above. Officials at Terre Haute began a bold experiment in 1960, based on the premise that inmates were to be considered part of the prison staff itself, responsible, along with the regular staff, for the administration of the prison. This new concept is symbolized by the inclusion of inmates in the contests for federal prison employees. Inmates' suggestions are considered along with those of actual employees, and prisoners are equally eligible for prizes.

Prison officials at Terre Haute provide the elected inmate council with financial information concerning the operation of the prison, plus other pertinent, non-personal administrative data. The warden has written that integrating the council into prison management is instrumental in creating a harmonious dialogue between staff and inmates. In typical prisons, for example, inmates often feel that the amount of funds administered by the staff is unlimited and when food and facilities are less than what the inmates feel is adequate, they tend to believe that funds are somehow being wasted, misused, or diverted to the personal enrichment of the staff. At Terre Haute, according to the testimony of the warden, the council knows the details of budget allocation and realizes that the food and facilities are commensurate with the funds available. The council is free to make suggestions as to a different allocation of monies, if they think improvements might result. There is, as a result, less discontent, less bitterness, less suspicion than there otherwise might be. Furthermore, knowing the financial situation, the prisoners more readily appreciate that waste and malicious damage hurt only their own welfare and this tends to create among them genuine group responsibility, manifested in spontaneous campaigns to cut down waste and damage. Having access to financial information, the prisoners are made aware that their own misbehaviour may produce public reaction with adverse effects on funds for the prison.

Agendas for the monthly council meetings at Terre Haute are generally open, and are set by what the staff and inmates wish to discuss. In recent years, the inmate council has been divided into several separate committees composed of both inmate and staff members, and these committees are the sole prison bodies for their particular area of competence. There are committees for sports, entertainment, food, sanitation, laundry, safety, and one designed to oversee and improve relations among inmates and between inmates and staff.

As compared to the single inmate council system which exists in many prisons, the Leavenworth experiment has broadened participation considerably among inmates by having some forty separate committees, each of which has a special jurisdiction. This system of involving as many persons as possible in participatory groups recalls the recent Yugoslav innovation which has divided the factory (or enterprise) work force into small, self-governing economic units.

In general, those in the field of corrections who continue to favour the idea of inmate self-government tend to believe it worthwhile for the following reasons:

1 It is often a good barometer by which to measure inmate morale;

2 It not only reflects morale but tends to raise it as well, undoubtedly for the same reasons that participation lifts morale in the factory, the office, and the laboratory;

3 It instils in the inmates a sense of responsibility;

4 It calls into existence machinery for communication in both directions, and especially permits inmates to gain direct insight into aspects of prison administration;

5 It creates a situation where staff and inmates are conceived as part of a cooperative unit in operating the institution;

6 Finally, it tends to encourage inmate identification with anti-criminal persons, a basic element in the rehabilitative effort.

References

ARGYRIS, C. (1957), *Personality and Organization*, Harper & Row.
BAKER, J. E. (1964), 'Inmate self-government', *J. Criminal Law, Criminology, Police Science*, vol. 55, pp. 39–47.
DUBIN, R. *et al.* (1965), *Leadership and Productivity*, Chandler.
FRIEDMAN, G. (1961), *Anatomy of Work*, Free Press.
GLASER, D. (1964), *Effectiveness of a Prison and Parole System*, Bobbs-Merrill.
HAYNES, F. E. (1935), *Criminology*, Macmillan Co.
HOLTER, H. (1965), 'Attitudes toward employee participation in company decision-making processes: a study of non-supervisory employees in some Norwegian firms', *Hum. Rel.*, vol. 18, pp. 297–322.
LIKERT, R. (1961), *New Patterns of Management*, McGraw-Hill.
WHITE, R. K., and LIPPITT, R. (1960), *Autocracy and Democracy*, Harper & Row.

References to Table 1

1   K. Lewin, 'Frontiers in group dynamics', *Hum. Rel.*, vol. 1 (1947), pp. 5–47.
2   E. G. Bennett, 'Discussion, decision, commitment and consensus in "group decision" ', *Hum. Rel.*, vol. 8 (1955), pp. 251–73.
3   A. Bavelas, 'Morale and the training of leaders', in G. Watson (ed.), *Civilian Morale*, Houghton Mifflin, Boston, 1942.
    A. Bavelas, 'Some problems of organizational change', *J. Soc. Issues*, vol. 4 (1948), pp. 48–52.
4   L. C. Lawrence and P. C. Smith, 'Group decision and employee participation', *J. app. Psychol.*, vol. 39 (1955), pp. 334–7.
5   L. Coch and J. R. P. French Jr, 'Overcoming resistance to change', *Hum. Rel.*, vol. 1 (1948), pp. 312–32.
6   N. Morse and E. Reimer, 'The experimental manipulation of a major organizational variable', *J. abnorm. and soc. Psychol.*, vol. 52 (1956), pp. 120–29.
7   J. R. P. French Jr, 'Field experiments: changing group productivity', in J. G. Miller (ed.), *Experiments in Social Process*, McGraw-Hill, 1950.
    J. R. P. French Jr *et al.*, 'Employee participation in a program of industrial change', *Personnel*, vol. 35 (1958), pp. 16–29.
    J. R. P. French Jr, J. Israel and D. Aas, 'An experiment in participation in a Norwegian factory', *Hum. Rel.*, vol. 13 (1960), pp. 3–10.
    J. R. P. French Jr, E. Kay and H. H. Meyer, 'Participation and the appraisal system', *Hum. Rel.*, vol. 19 (1966), pp. 3–20.
8   J. Levine and J. Butler, 'Lecture *v.* group decision in changing behaviour', *J. appl. Psychol.*, vol. 36 (1952), pp. 29–33.
9   H. Babchuck and W. J. Goode, 'Work incentives in a self-determined group', *Amer. soc. Rev.*, vol. 16 (1951), pp. 679–87.
10 G. Strauss, in W. F. Whyte, *Money and Motivation*, Harper, 1955, pp. 90–96.
11 I. R. Weschler, M. Hahne and R. Tannenbaum, 'Job satisfaction, productivity, and morale: a case study', *Occupational Psychol.*, vol. 26 (1952), pp. 1–14.
12 H. Baumgartel, 'Leadership, motivation and attitudes in research laboratories', *J. Soc. Issues*, vol. 12 (1956), pp. 24–31.
13 F. C. Mann and H. Baumgartel, *Absences and Employee Attitudes in an Electric Power Company*, Survey Research Center, University of Michigan, 1952.
14 V. Vroom, *Some Personality Determinants of the Effects of Participation*, Prentice-Hall, 1960.
    V. Vroom, *Work and Motivation*, Wiley, 1964.
    V. Vroom and F. C. Mann, 'Leader authoritarianism and employee attitudes', *Personn. Psychol.*, vol. 13 (1960), pp. 125–40.
15 F. R. Wickert, 'Turnover and employee feelings of ego involvement in the day-to-day operation of a company', *Personn. Psychol.*, vol. 4 (1951), pp. 125–97.
16 I. Ross and A. Zander, 'Need satisfaction and employee turnover', *Personn. Psychol.*, vol. 10 (1957), pp. 327–38.
17 E. A. Fleishman and E. F. Harris, 'Patterns of leadership behaviour related to employee grievances and turnover', *Personn. Psychol.*, vol. 13 (1962), pp. 43–6.

22 B. Balassa and T. J. Bertrand

Growth Performance of Eastern European Economies and
Comparable Western European Countries[1]

Extract from B. Balassa and T. J. Bertrand, 'Growth performance of Eastern
European economies and comparable Western countries', *American Economic
Review*, vol. 60, no. 2, May 1970, pp. 134–320.

Part one

The purpose of this paper is to compare the growth performance of the
centrally-planned economies of Eastern Europe with that of European
economies characterized by decentralized decision-making. The investigation covers five centrally-planned economies (Bulgaria, Czechoslovakia,
Hungary, Poland and Romania), four Western European countries (Spain,
Greece, Norway and Ireland), and Yugoslavia which has developed a
decentralized socialist system. The choice of the countries included in
the study reflects a desire to have a representative group operating
under different economic systems at comparable levels of development
although it has, to some extent, been constrained by the availability of the
data.

The study covers the time period 1953 to 1965; the initial year has been
selected to avoid the effects of postwar reconstruction in several of the
countries in question while the choice of the terminal year has been
dictated by data availabilities. The investigation is limited to manufacturing
industry where the most important structural changes have taken place.

As an indication of the relative level of economic development of the
countries in question, in Table 1 we present estimates of per capita gross
national product calculated by the use of purchasing power parities for the
year 1955. The results may be subject to considerable error and, due to
differences in the statistical sources, there is greater comparability in the
data among the centralized and among the decentralized economies than
between countries that belong to different groups. Nonetheless, it is encouraging that in the case of Yugoslavia – the only country that appears in
both sets of calculations – the two estimates are very close. In any case, it
would appear that the countries under study can be classified into three
groups according to their relative levels of economic development: low –
Greece, Yugoslavia, Bulgaria, Spain and Romania; intermediate – Ireland,

1 The authors would like to acknowledge assistance from Michael Claudon with
the research for this paper.

Poland and Hungary; and high – Czechoslovakia and Norway. The latter two groups will further be combined in distinguishing between 'less developed' and 'more developed' countries among those under study.

Table 1 Estimate of Gross National Product per capita of selected European countries in US dollars, 1955, derived by the use of purchasing power parities

Country	1	2
Bulgaria	515	
Czechoslovakia	1163	
Hungary	835	
Poland	755	
Romania	551	
Greece		336
Ireland		704
Norway		1394
Spain		516
Yugoslavia	444	427

Source: Column 1 derived from data in Pryor and Staller (1955).
Column 2 from Balassa (1964a), pp. 384 and 385.

Part two

International comparison of growth performance is a formidable task and we approach it with some trepidation. There are difficulties in obtaining comparable data for the different countries, and a summary measure cannot take account of all the relevant variables. Comparisons of growth rates of output disregard changes in inputs, marginal capital–output ratios neglect labor as well as capital accumulation in earlier periods, while labor productivity comparisons abstract from the capital factor.

In recent years, it has become popular to separate the growth of output attributable to:

1 The growth of factor inputs;

2 A residual presumably reflecting organizational changes, improvements in labor quality, and technical progress.

The residual – also called the growth of total factor productivity or, simply, total factor productivity – has been taken by some writers to be an indicator of growth performance (see Balassa, 1964b; Bergson, 1963).

The separation of factor inputs and total factor productivity as sources of economic growth assumes that:

1 There are no economies of scale;

2 Organizational changes, improvements in labor quality, and technical progress are independent of the growth of factor inputs;

3 Factor inputs represent purely a cost and their growth does not contribute to economic welfare.

We will initially accept these assumptions in calculating total factor productivity for the countries under study. Subsequently, we will remove assumptions 1 and 2 in order to estimate net factor productivity, defined as the residual growth rate that is obtained if one adjusts for both the direct and indirect effects on growth of increases in factor outputs. Finally, we will consider the question of the welfare significance of increases in factor supplies.

Part three

In calculating total factor productivity, we have first attempted to fit production functions of the form shown in equation **1** to data on industrial output O, employment L, and the capital stock K in manufacturing industries,

$$O = e^{\gamma t} L^{\alpha} K^{\beta}, \tag{1}$$

both with and without constraining the sum of the exponents to one. However, for various reasons, such as multicollinearity, the shortness of the period of observation, and the variability of the data, statistically significant results have not been obtained. We have therefore used equation **2**, obtained by differentiating the logarithmic form of equation **1**, to estimate total factor productivity γ.

In equation **2**, o, l, and k denote the rate of growth of industrial output, labour, and capital respectively,

$$o = \gamma + \alpha l + \beta k, \tag{2}$$

while α and β are the elasticities of output with respect to labor and capital. With perfect factor markets, α and β are the shares of labor and capital, and we can use estimates of factor shares to weight the factor inputs. But there are no capital markets in the Eastern European economies, and the valuation of capital is largely arbitrary. Accordingly, it has been necessary to make some assumptions concerning the rate of return to capital in these countries.

In the Western European countries under study, the share of labor is between 45 and 65 per cent and the gross rate of return to capital ranges from 18 to 22 per cent. If 5 per cent is deducted for depreciation, the corresponding net rate of return is between 13 and 17 per cent.[2] These rates have been used in evaluating the returns to capital in the Eastern European countries for which capital stock data are available in absolute terms: Hungary, Romania, Czechoslovakia and Yugoslavia. The resulting labor shares for these countries are all in the 45 to 65 per cent range. Given the uncertainties associated with the data, we have used both 45 and 65 per cent as an estimate of the share of labor in manufacturing industry.

Data on the growth of output, capital and labor are presented in columns 1 to 3 of Table 2 while estimates of total factor productivity calculated under alternative assumptions as regards labor's share in output are shown in columns 4 and 5. To avoid giving undue weight to initial or terminal years, growth rates of output and factor inputs have been calculated by regressing the relevant data on time. Growth rates of output and capital stock are in real terms although there is a suspicion that the Bulgarian capital stock figures have not been appropriately deflated. Data on the capital stock and, to a lesser extent, on output are subject to considerable error in the other socialist countries, too, and error possibilities exist also in regard to capital stock estimates for Western European countries. Sources of data are described in the Appendix.

The interpretation of the results is reasonably straightforward. Irrespective of the choice of input weights, Romania, Spain and Yugoslavia show the most rapid increases in total factor productivity among the countries in question. With an appropriate deflation of the capital stock figures, Bulgaria would probably also appear in this group. The results thus lend credence to the contention that among countries that have passed the take-off point, the possibilities for utilizing existing technological knowledge permit more rapid growth in countries at lower than at higher levels of development.

Greece, however, provides an exception inasmuch as it belongs to the first group of countries in terms of the level of development and the second in terms of growth performance. Within the latter group, Norway and Czechoslovakia appear to be in the lead, followed by Greece and Poland, with Ireland and Hungary at the bottom of the list. But the ranking of these countries is affected if different input labor shares are assumed in particular cases.

It further appears that unweighted averages of total factor productivity differ little between the centralized socialist economies and the decentralized

2 By comparison, a range of 8 to 20 per cent has been suggested by Bergson in regard to the Soviet Union (1963, p. 20).

Table 2 Rates of growth of output and factor inputs and measure of factor productivity in the manufacturing industry of selected European countries

Country	Period	Annual rate of growth			Total factor productivity		Net factor productivity			
							Case A		Case B	
		Output	Capital	Labor	$\alpha = 0.45$	$\alpha = 0.65$	$\alpha = 0.45$	$\alpha = 0.65$	$\alpha = 0.45$	$\alpha = 0.65$
Bulgaria	1953–65	12·5	11·6	7·6	2·6	3·4	−0·3	0·7	−2·3	−1·5
Czechoslovakia	1953–65	7·0	6·6	2·7	2·1	2·9	0·7	1·6	−0·3	0·6
Hungary	1953–65	6·5	7·3	3·0	1·1	2·0	−0·4	0·6	−1·5	−0·2
Poland	1961–65	6·6	6·5	3·0	1·7	2·4	0·2	1·1	−0·8	0·2
Romania	1953–65	11·1	8·3	4·1	4·6	5·5	2·7	3·8	1·4	2·6
centrally planned economies										
including Bulgaria[a]					2·4	3·0	0·6	1·5	−0·7	0·3
excluding Bulgaria[a]					2·4	3·2	0·8	1·7	−0·3	0·7
Greece	1951–65	6·9	7·1	2·8	1·7	2·6	0·2	1·3	−0·8	0·4
Ireland	1953–65	4·7	4·2	1·7	1·7	2·2	0·8	1·4	0·1	0·9
Norway	1953–65	5·4	5·1	0·8	2·2	3·1	0·7	2·4	0·6	1·9
Spain	1959–65	11·2	8·7	4·5	4·5	5·3	2·5	3·7	0·3	1·6
decentralized private enterprise economies[a]					2·5	3·3	1·0	2·2	0·1	1·2
Yugoslavia	1953–65	11·8	7·5	6·7	4·5	4·7	2·4	2·6	1·0	1·2
decentralized economies[a]					2·9	3·6	1·3	2·3	0·3	1·2

[a]Unweighted average.
Sources: see Appendix.

private enterprise economies. The situation changes, however, if we add Yugoslavia to the second group. Now decentralized economies seem to be ahead of centralized economies by at least one-half of one percentage point.

Part four

Using total factor productivity as an indicator of the country's growth performance reflects the assumption that the results are independent of the rate of growth of the inputs themselves. This assumption will not be fulfilled if the quality of productive factors of a later 'vintage' is superior to those of an earlier vintage or if there are increasing returns to scale. In the first eventuality, the average quality of factors will be positively related to the rate of growth of factor inputs; in the second, the rapid growth of factors will bring forth increases in output by increasing the scale of production. As to the former, the reduction in illiteracy, improvements in schooling, and the institution of training programs which may be associated with the rapid growth of labor in manufacturing, will raise the quality of the labor force while the capital stock is upgraded as new investments embody more advanced technology.

We have attempted, therefore, to divide the estimates of total factor productivity into two parts: a part explained by the indirect effects of the growth of productive factors and a residual termed 'net factor productivity' which may more adequately reflect the differences between countries in regard to their systems of economic decision-making and organization. To do this, it is necessary to quantify the relation between factor input growth and total factor productivity as defined earlier.

For US manufacturing, A. A. Walters has found evidence of increasing returns to scale of from 27 to 35 per cent (1963). But Walters's results may reflect improvements in factor qualities as well, and we have interpreted them as such. At the same time, one can assume that in countries at lower levels of development there is more scope for improving factor qualities and exploiting economies of scale than in the United States. The results obtained for US manufacturing industries therefore may represent a lower limit to the joint effects of the two influences as they operate in national economies that are less developed industrially.

At any rate, the US results derive from the experience of a single country, and greater confidence can be placed in the figures if inter-country comparisons are made. We have attempted to do this by estimating the relationship between the average growth of factor inputs and total factor productivity in a cross-country regression. In order to increase the number of observations available, we have used data for four-year sub-periods in the countries under study, with the exclusion of Bulgaria whose capital stock figures are suspect. The results are given in equations 3 and 4.

$$\gamma_1 = 0.09 + 0.54T_1 \qquad R = 0.50, \quad DW = 2.27, \qquad\qquad 3$$
$$(0.13) \quad (4.24)$$

$$\gamma_2 = 1.60 + 0.45T_2 \qquad R = 0.47, \quad DW = 1.61, \qquad\qquad 4$$
$$(2.76) \quad (3.96)$$

where T_1 and T_2 are the growth rates of factor inputs weighted by $\alpha = 0.45$, $\beta = 0.55$ and by $\alpha = 0.65$, $\beta = 0.35$, respectively, and t-values are shown in parentheses.

The results tend to confirm our suspicion that in countries at a level of development as those under study, the indirect effects of growth in factor inputs on the growth of output can be very substantial. Equations 3 and 4 show this to be from 45 to 54 per cent of the direct effect. It should be added that the t-values correspond to levels of significance exceeding 99 per cent while the exclusion of other variables from the equation limits the values taken by the coefficients of determination. On the basis of Walters's results and our findings, we have next adjusted the total factor productivity figures on the assumption that a 1 per cent increase in combined factor inputs yields case A, an added 0.3 per cent, or case B, an added 0.5 percentage point growth of industrial output. The resulting net factor productivity figures are presented in columns 6–7 and 8–9 of Table 2.

This adjustment favors countries where the rate of growth of factor inputs has been relatively low. Thus, Norway joins Romania, Spain and Yugoslavia among countries with the highest net factor productivity and the relative positions of Ireland and Czechoslovakia are also improved. Furthermore, the imbalance between the less developed and the more developed countries of the group indicated by comparisons of total factor productivity is greatly reduced. For instance, while the unweighted average of total factor productivity (with $\alpha = 0.45$) is 5.0 for Greece, Spain, Yugoslavia and Romania as compared to 3.0 for Czechoslovakia and Norway, the corresponding net factor productivities are 2.8 and 2.0 under case A and 1.4 and 1.2 under case B.

Using net factor productivity as an indicator of growth performance, the differences between Yugoslavia and the other decentralized countries also tend to diminish – significantly so if the higher labor share is assumed. In turn, decentralized economies now appear in a much more favorable light than the centrally planned economies. While the results for the latter group of countries are affected by the exceptionally poor showing of Bulgaria due in part to the previously noted data problems, even excluding Bulgaria net factor productivity is decidedly higher in decentralized than in centrally planned economies. Thus, the hypothesis that the comparable gains in total factor productivity attained in Eastern Europe are the result of more rapid growth in factor inputs appears to be supported by our findings.

Finally, it should be noted that factors other than the direct and indirect effects of input growth would seem to have a negative impact on the growth of output in five countries if the lower (0·45) value is assumed for the α-coefficient and the higher value (0·5 per cent) is used for indirect effects. This unlikely result may be interpreted as evidence that the higher values of α are more reasonable. With $\alpha = 0·65$ only Hungary and Bulgaria show negative net factor productivity, and Hungary is a special case because of the 1956 events, as is Bulgaria because of data problems. Of course, the results might also be interpreted as evidence that the indirect effects of factor input growth on total factor productivity are less pronounced than is assumed in case B.

Part five

Net factor productivity has been estimated under the assumption that part of the increase in total factor productivity is explainable by the indirect effects of the growth of factor inputs on output growth, when such indirect effects reflect economies of scale and improvements in factor qualities. There are few problems with the first assumption, but the second opens possibilities of error since it disregards possible differences in the rate of improvement of the quality of capital and labor. The resulting error will be the greater, the larger are differences in factor growth rates.

To remove this source of error, it would be necessary to estimate the extent of improvements in the capital stock and in labor over time. While 'embodied' technical progress has been much discussed in recent years, no reliable estimates exist and even less can be said of its numerical importance in the countries under consideration. Similar considerations apply to the extent of improvements in the labor force. At the same time, Walters's findings and our regression results suggest that the proportionality assumption made in this study does not involve substantial error.

The problem remains that we have considered factor inputs purely as a cost and thus have attached no welfare significance to increasing the rate of saving and reallocating labor from low-productivity occupations or from the ranks of the unemployed to manufacturing industry. Yet, while in Western Europe (although not in centrally planned economies) capital accumulation largely depends on individual decisions and the absorption of labor in manufacturing industry is predicated on the availability of labor, the growth of factor inputs is affected by the economic policies followed.

It has not been possible to incorporate such considerations in the present study, however. Apart from the difficulties of statistical measurement, these considerations raise intricate welfare problems. In this connection it may be recalled that the Soviet Union was strongly criticized for forced reductions in consumption (increasing the rate of saving) and forced collectivization (increasing the mobility of labor) during the 1930s. Today some would look differently at that period of 'initial accumulation' but any judgment would involve interpersonal and intertemporal comparisons which we have wished to avoid in this paper.

Part six

A further question is whether there have been significant changes over time in the growth performance of the countries under consideration. In order to deal with this question, we have divided the total period into two subperiods – 1953–59 and 1959–65. But instead of simply comparing estimates of factor productivity in the two subperiods, we have used a statistical test which involved calculating the value of the elasticity of output with respect to labor, α, that would equate factor productivity between periods in the three cases considered earlier.[3] A judgment as to whether the calculated values of α are reasonable or not permits us to conclude whether and in what direction factor productivity has changed.

In Table 3 we show the condition placed on α in order that factor productivity in the period 1959–65 is greater or equal to that for the period 1953–59. On the assumption that the actual value of α will be between 0 and 1, and, most likely between 0·45 and 0·65, we can conclude that: (a) an increase in factor productivity had definitely occurred in Spain, Hungary and Ireland while there has been a decline in Czechoslovakia and Greece; and (b) factor productivity also seems to have increased in Bulgaria and Norway and decreased in Romania and Yugoslavia.

There is some support in our findings for the hypothesis that in the more developed economies of the group, decentralized decision-making has been more successful in maintaining or raising factor productivity than central planning. Thus, an increase in factor productivity has occurred in Norway and Ireland while a decrease is shown for Czechoslovakia. The exception to this hypothesis provided by Hungary may in fact be just that: an exception explainable in terms of the retarding effects in the earlier period of the 1956 events. As far as the less developed countries are concerned, no unambiguous conclusions are suggested by the results since improved performance occurs in Spain and Bulgaria, while a decrease in total factor productivity is shown in Greece, Romania and Yugoslavia.

3 This technique of analysis is due to Kaplan and has been previously used by him to analyze changes in total factor productivity in the Soviet Union (1968).

Table 3 Conditional values of the elasticity of output with respect to labor for which total factor productivity industry in 1959–65 is as great or greater than in 1953–59 for selected European countries

Country	Comparison of total factor productivity	Comparison of net factor productivity	
		Case A	Case B
Bulgaria	$\alpha \geqslant 0\cdot34$	$\alpha \geqslant 0\cdot31$	$\alpha \geqslant 0\cdot30$
Czechoslovakia	$\alpha \geqslant 4\cdot03$	$\alpha \geqslant 3\cdot23$	$\alpha \geqslant 2\cdot88$
Hungary	$\alpha \leqslant 1\cdot86$	$\alpha \leqslant 1\cdot20$	$\alpha \leqslant 1\cdot01$
Poland	(n.a.)	(n.a.)	(n.a.)
Romania	$\alpha \leqslant 0\cdot36$	$\alpha \leqslant 0\cdot10$	$\alpha \leqslant 0\cdot01$
Greece[a]	$\alpha \leqslant 0\cdot96$	$\alpha \leqslant 0\cdot46$	$\alpha \leqslant 0\cdot23$
Ireland	$\alpha \leqslant 12\cdot47$	$\alpha \leqslant 4\cdot65$	$\alpha \leqslant 1\cdot66$
Norway	$\alpha \leqslant 1\cdot15$	$\alpha \leqslant 0\cdot92$	$\alpha \leqslant 0\cdot78$
Spain[b]	$\alpha \leqslant 1\cdot86$	$\alpha \leqslant 1\cdot34$	$\alpha \leqslant 1\cdot11$
Yugoslavia	$\alpha \geqslant 0\cdot98$	$\alpha \geqslant 0\cdot82$	$\alpha \geqslant 0\cdot75$

[a]1961–65 compared with 1951–61.
[b]1961–65 compared with 1957–61.

Part seven

In this paper an attempt has been made to compare the growth performance of five centrally planned economies, four Western European countries and Yugoslavia – the only country with a decentralized socialist system. The countries selected for the investigation can also be classified according to the degree of economic development: low (Greece, Yugoslavia, Bulgaria, Spain and Romania), intermediate (Ireland, Poland and Hungary), and high (Czechoslovakia and Norway).

Calculations of total factor productivity for the manufacturing sector in the 1953–59 period show the low-income countries other than Greece in the lead, with Ireland and Hungary at the bottom of the list. Average of total factor productivity for centrally planned economies and Western European countries are about the same but adding Yugoslavia to the second group puts decentralized economies ahead of centrally planned productivity.

The measurement of total factor productivity reflects the assumptions of constant returns to scale and unchanged factor qualities over time. These assumptions are not fulfilled in practice; indeed, our results indicate the existence of a positive correlation between the growth of factor inputs and total factor productivity. Adjusting for the effects of the former on the latter, we obtain estimates of net factor productivity. As this adjustment favors countries with a relatively low rate of growth of factor inputs in manufacturing, the relative positions of Norway, Ireland and Czechoslovakia improve while Bulgaria, Spain and Yugoslavia now rank lower.

It also appears that if we adjust for the indirect effects of the growth of factor inputs, differences in the growth performance of countries at lower and at higher levels of development are reduced; Yugoslavia's advantage over decentralized free enterprise economies disappears; and the latter group of countries has a decided edge over centrally planned economies. Such an advantage is also shown if we consider changes in factor productivity over time.

Apart from the conceptual problems and the statistical difficulties of the calculations, note should be taken of the fact that the procedure applied considers the growth of factor inputs as a cost and attaches no welfare significance to it. If instead we take a high rate of saving and increases in manufacturing employment to have welfare significance in themselves, the relative position of the socialist countries will improve. But against this we should set the relatively poor performance of agriculture in these countries which has not been considered in this study; yet increases in the capital stock and in labor have taken place in part at the expense of agriculture.

Appendix

Bulgaria. Growth of industrial output, capital stock and labor were derived from Lazarcik and Wynnyczuk, *Bulgaria: Growth of Industrial Output 1934 and 1948–1965*, occasional paper no. 27 of the Research Project on National Income in East Central Europe, pp. 4, 9.

Czechoslovakia. Growth rates of industrial output, capital stock and labor were derived from Lazarcik and Staller, *A New Index of Czechoslovak Industrial Output 1937 and 1947–1965*, occasional paper no. 24 of the Research Project on National Income in East Central Europe, pp. 24, 27. In estimating factor shares, payments to labor were obtained from Lazarcik and Staller, p. 49, while value of net capital stock was estimated as seventy-five per cent of full replacement value given in L. Alton and Associates, *Czechoslovak National Income and Product (1947–48 and 1955–56)*, Columbia University Press, 1962, p. 223.

Romania. Growth rates of industrial output, capital stock and labor were derived from Tables 36, 46, 47 and 49 in Directia Centrala de Statistica, *Anuarul Statistic al RPR*, 1968. Net capital stock and payments to labor used in estimating factor shares are from M. Montias, *Economic Development in Communist Rumania*, Massachusetts Institute of Technology Press, 1967, pp. 57, 58.

Yugoslavia. Growth rates of industrial output and labor were derived from Federal Institute for Statistics, *Statisticki Godisnjak*, 1968, pp. 164, 170. Growth rate of net capital stock was derived from I. Vinski, 'Fixed Assets, 1946–1966', *Yugoslav Survey*, November 1968, p. 88. Net values of capital stock and payments to labor used in estimating factor shares are from I. Vinski, p. 88, and Federal Institute for Statistics, *Interindustry Relations for the Yugoslav Economy in 1962*, Belgrade, 1966, respectively.

Poland. Growth rate of industrial output derived from data provided by Thad Alton, Director of the Research Project on National Income in East Central Europe. Growth rates of industrial capital and labor derived from Central Statistical Office, *Roznek Statystezny, 1968*, pp. 65, 100, 180.

Hungary. Growth rates of output were derived from a series prepared by L. Czirjak of the Project on National Income in East Central Europe. Data on the capital stock, labor, and payments to labor were obtained from the *Hungarian Statistical Yearbook* and other publications of the Hungarian Statistical Office.

Greece. Growth rates of output and data on payments to labor and capital are from United Nations, *Growth of World Industry*. Data on employment and the capital stock were made available by Professor Balopoulos, Director of the Centre of Planning and Economic Research in Athens.

Ireland. Growth rates of output and data on payments to labor and capital are from United Nations, *Growth of World Industry*, and manufacturing employment figures are from the International Labor Office, *Yearbook of Labor Statistics*. Capital stock in manufacturing was estimated for 1853–1959 in Edward Nevin, *The Capital Stock of Irish Industry*, Economic Research Institute, paper no. 17. We made adjustments for the apparent overestimation of depreciation on investment prior to the Second World War and extended the figures from 1959 on.

Spain. Growth rates of output and data on payments to labor and capital are from United Nations, *Growth of World Industry*, and manufacturing employment figures from International Labor Office, *Yearbook of Labor Statistics*. Estimates on the capital stock were made for 1965 in *La Riqueza Nacional de España*. These figures were adjusted on the basis of the gross investment figures provided in a private communication by Professor Lasuen of Madrid University and estimates of depreciation derived from national accounts statistics.

Norway. Growth rates of output and data on payments to labor and capital are from United Nations, *Growth of World Industry*, and manufacturing employment figures from International Labor Office, *Yearbook of Labor Statistics.* Capital stock data were made available by Odd Aukrust, Research Director of the Norwegian Central Bureau of Statistics.

References

ARROW, K. J., KARLIN, S. and SUPPES, P. (eds.) (1960), *Mathematical Methods in the Social Sciences*, pp. 89–104, Stanford University Press.

BALASSA, BELA (1964a), *Trade Prospects for Developing Economies*, Irwin, pp. 384–85.

BALASSA, BELA (1964b), 'The dynamic efficiency of the Soviet economy', *Amer. Econ. Rev.*, vol. 64, pp. 490–505.

BERGSON, A. (1963), 'National trends', in A. Gergson and S. Kuznets (eds.), *Economic Trends in The Soviet Union*, pp. 1–37, Harvard University Press.

KAPLAN, N. M. (1968), 'Retardation in Soviet Growth', *Rev. Econ. Stat.*, vol. 50, no. 3, pp. 293–303.

PRYOR, F. L., and STALLER, G. J. (1955), 'The dollar values of the gross national products in Eastern Europe', in *Economics of Planning* (1966), vol. 6, no. 1.

WALTERS, A. A. (1963), 'A note on economies of scale', *Rev. Econ. Stat.*, vol. 45, no. 4 pp. 425–7.

23 Jaroslav Vanek

Decentralization Under Workers' Management: A Theoretical Appraisal

Jaroslav Vanek, 'Decentralization under workers' management: a theoretical appraisal', *American Economic Review*, vol. 59, no. 5, December 1969, pp. 1006–14.

The purpose of my paper is to carry out a theoretical appraisal of a labor-managed economy of the Yugoslav type. In my opinion, it is this type of economy that represents, by and large, the true aspirations of reformers in Eastern Europe.

There is full justification for such an endeavor. On the one hand, the empirical studies which we have on the subject are not fully conclusive; on the other, even if quantitative results fulfilled some accepted criteria of statistical significance, we still might want to verify them through a theoretical evaluation. Moreover, it ought not to be forgotten that the Yugoslav experiment is unique and comparatively young. To compare its real performance with that of systems which have been tried in a large number of instances over long periods, is not quite fair. At least as a supplement to the empirical studies, it is thus necessary to compare the corresponding theoretical models.

Besides the direct and practical objective of my paper, related to the economies of Eastern Europe, there is also the more academic question of the theoretical literature on the subject at hand. The latter, although of excellent quality, is extremely limited. In fact, there are only two important articles on what I would call economics of labor participation – those by Benjamin Ward (1958) and Evsey Domar (1966). These authors do not make anything near a full evaluation of an entire economic system. And yet, the findings emerging from such a limited coverage often are taken as characteristic of the efficiency of the system. For example, Ward's perverse supply elasticity in the short run is taken by many as the proof of the absurdity of labor management. Perhaps the best and most authoritative illustration of the overall pessimism regarding the labor-managed economy is contained in Abram Bergson's more recent evaluation of market socialism (1967).

At this stage of the argument, I do not want to dispute any specific points regarding the labor-managed economy; that will be done explicitly or by implication later in our discussion. I only want to contend that to appraise an economic system it is necessary to consider all of its major aspects. And this is what I propose to do.

The task would be an impossible one if each point were to be fully explained or proven. Fortunately, I have produced a more complete analysis elsewhere (Vanek, 1970, 1971) and thus I can restrict myself here to the presentation of the main conclusions, supplementing these with brief indications of the underlying reasoning. I will further limit my analysis by concentrating on questions of global economic efficiency, leaving out, as much as this is possible, the mechanics of the system.

I will first consider what may be referred to as a dehumanized model where, as in conventional capitalist theory, labor is considered merely a factor of production, of constant quality, exogenous to the system. This is done in the first two sections. In the third, by contrast, I discuss some of the most important special dimensions which emerge from the participatory nature of labor management. The principal objective of the remaining section is an overall evaluation of the labor-managed system in comparison with other major world systems.

The pure model

In what I call the pure model, I make basically the same assumptions as those underlying the contributions of Ward and Domar noted above. They can be summed up as implying a perfect, competitive and smooth neoclassical world in which the moving force, contrary to the capitalist situation, is maximization of income per laborer. There is only one type of labor, perfectly homogeneous, and active only as a factor of production. The only characteristic emanating from labor management is income sharing and the behavioral principle of maximization just noted. It should be clear from the outset that an economy thus defined is far from the complex reality of Yugoslavia, or any other economy adopting labor management; however, in my opinion the assumptions capture the ideal form of the economy, and thus their implications should be studied as a first step in any comprehensive evaluation.

To de-emphasize the single firm approach used by Ward and Domar, it may be desirable to reverse the process, and start with the discussion of a complete full employment general equilibrium solution of the labor-managed economy (situations involving unemployment will be taken up in the next section).

Let our starting point be the ideal conditions of perfect competition and full employment. We may make the observation that when all firms of an industry use the same technology and free entry is guaranteed, the labor-managed economy will be Pareto optimal. In other words, just like its ideal capitalist counterpart, the labor-managed economy will be producing the maximum producible output from given resources, and the maximum social satisfaction for a prescribed distribution of income (described later). These conclusions follow from the fact that competitive labor-managed firms equalize factor marginal products to factor returns for all factors including labor, from competition in nonlabor factor markets, free entry of firms and identical technologies.

By contrast, as has been pointed out by Ward (1958), if technologies of different firms within an industry are different, the optimum solution will not be reached by the labor-managed economy because the equilibrium behavior will not lead to equalization of marginal value products of labor among firms. In this context the capitalist alternative appears as superior, on the assumptions made. Of course, if imperfections in the labor market are permitted, the differences in marginal productivities of labor among firms and industries may be just as important. In any case, the comparative inefficiency of the labor-managed case here discussed should not be too pronounced. In fact, the labor-managed firms are all bound to operate at a point of maximum factor productivities (where their technologies are linear-homogeneous), the comparative shortcoming being merely imputable to the fact that the more efficient ones do not produce enough. Moreover, as we argue later, labor-managed economies will normally be in a much better position to proliferate the best technology throughout the industry. Finally, even if in the case studied the labor-managed economy will produce less than the capitalist with identical factor endowments, it can be shown that it will generate a stronger demand for, and correspondingly higher returns to, capital. Thus accumulation and growth may proceed at a higher rate, leading to more output and more consumption over time.

While recognizing the abstraction and lack of realism of all the pure theory presented in this section, it may be said that the perfectly competitive model just discussed is the least realistic. Indeed, the requirements of product homogeneity and a very large number of sellers (producers) are satisfied only in a few industries. Much more frequent is some degree of monopoly power coupled with product differentiation and, in many instances, active sales promotion. It is in this context that, I believe, Ward's earlier conclusion of greater restrictiveness of labor-managed monopolies, while formally correct, is misleading when we want to evaluate the theoretical performance of the system.

It is true that if the government or some other external agent were to set the number of firms for each industry at one, such a monopoly would be, *ceteris paribus*, more restrictive and thus socially more harmful than a capitalist monopoly. But in the real world monopolistic tendencies and market power are hardly ever of this type. Rather, they derive from the fact that efficient production is consistent with only a limited number of firms given the size of the market, the desire of firms to accumulate and grow, the artificial creation of barriers to entry, etc.

If viewed in this more realistic context of the entire industry, one can make a case for labor management which is strong indeed. On grounds of several arguments, labor management can be expected not only to yield market structures more competitive than any other free economy, but also prevent a good deal of wasteful and harmful sales promotion. The first and perhaps simplest argument is that with an increasing scale of operation, the benefits from participation – incentives, identification and involvement – will tend to diminish.

Thus it can be expected that, all other things being equal, the point of maximum efficiency, which also is the point of long-run equilibrium for a labor-managed firm, will be reached for a lower level of output than for a firm operating with a hired labor factor. Figuratively speaking, there will be room for more firms in a given industry.

The next point also hinges on the most efficient scale of operation. The labor-managed firm will never grow beyond that scale, whereas a capitalist firm often will, its growth being governed, even after greatest technical efficiency is reached, by the desire for profit maximization. Two extreme situations may further clarify the essence of this argument. Consider an ideal firm operating under constant returns to scale and facing a constant price yielding positive unit profits under capitalism. The equilibrium level of operation of that firm, if capitalist, is (at least in theory) infinite, while if labor-managed, it is finite and indeterminate at any level of operation. The simple crux of this deduction is that while the first firm must grow indefinitely to maximize profits, the second maximizes income per laborer at any level of operation. The other extreme situation is similar to that just described except that the firms in question face a less than infinitely elastic demand function. In that situation the capitalist monopoly, as is well-known, will find its equilibrium where the marginal (and average) cost reaches the marginal revenue; whereas the labor-managed firm must operate at zero output, or, more realistically, with only one employee; indeed, as the reader will easily verify, under the assumed conditions income per laborer will be maximized with only one member of the labor-managed firm. Clearly, under the assumed conditions it would take a very large number of firms to fill the industry (with a reasonable return to labor), but by the time such a large number would enter, the market power of each firm would become very low or disappear altogether.

Probably the most significant comparative advantage of the labor-managed oligopoly arises in connection with product differentiation and sales promotion. It can be shown that the labor-managed firm will in equilibrium produce less and engage in a less intensive advertising campaign than an equivalent capitalist firm as long as the latter makes positive profits, a condition which obtains virtually without exception. Especially if we realize that it is precisely the more extreme doses of exhortational advertising that constitute the heaviest social costs, the advantage of the labor-managed alternative is considerable. Not only can we expect a significantly less concentrated industry, but the external diseconomies such as mind pollution, should be significantly reduced or completely eliminated.

The last point deserving mention is based on the simple notion that there is a far greater desire within democratic structures to decentralize than in nondemocratic ones. For example, even with very small or no economies of scale, a capitalist, or for that matter a Soviet-type, firm will tend to retain its centralized organization, whereas the labor-managed one will attempt to subdivide itself into autonomous decision-making and production units based on location or other functional characteristics. I am quite convinced that this tendency is present with the labor-managed alternative for other reasons than the stronger production-incentive of small groups.

Finally, before concluding this section, we ought to reconsider Ward's negative supply elasticity, and discuss that and related issues in the context of general equilibrium efficiency. It is true that if short-run reactions of competitive firms were as posited by Ward, the resulting inefficiency could be quite considerable, and what is equally important, at least some markets could become unstable. The contention which I want to argue below is that matters are far from being so bad.

First of all, we have the two arguments made by Domar: one, with more than one product by the firm, even short-run elasticities can be positive and quite high for an individual product; two, even with only one product the supply elasticity in the short run must be positive if the firm operates with an (active) external labor-supply constraint, reflected by a labor-supply function of finite elasticity (Domar, 1966). In addition, there is the problem raised by Joan Robinson (1967) in her critique of Domar. Using my own words to push the argument a step further, how can one reasonably expect that a working collective will mutilate itself (kicking out, say one-tenth of the membership), if it has already realized a significant gain from a price increase, say 10 per cent of income, for the sake of gaining an extra, say 1 per cent? Indeed, this sounds like an extract from a book of rules of capitalist conduct. While what underlies the above rhetorical question is certainly true, I would further like to point out that the elimination of the negative elasticity argument does not even call for any higher morals. In the short run, a single-product producer operating under perfect competition will have very little possibility of capital–labor substitution; in terms of

Ward's diagrams, the relevant stretch of the marginal productivity of labor will generally be very near a vertical line. Consequently, the normal short-run supply elasticity of a competitive labor-managed firm producing a single output can for all practical purposes be considered zero, even if group solidarity were absent.

Before leaving the short run, two observations are in order. First, let it be noted that the zero elasticity eliminates possibilities of instability, and reduces a good deal the loss of general equilibrium efficiency (note that in a world with only single-product firms a change in relative prices would now keep, in the short run, the point on the production possibility locus unchanged). Second, in the context of aggregate national income analysis, the zero short-run supply elasticity by no means is something to frown on; but this we will discuss in the next section.

Finally, a few words on long-run adjustments within the general equilibrium framework. Again, the introduction of an additional piece of information from the real world helps a good deal. It is reasonable to expect that with most firms the point of constant returns to scale (the point corresponding to the minimum of the long-run average cost curve) in reality is not a point, but a whole range (of 'efficient outputs') – a range the end of which is hard to establish empirically. Once in such a range, as we have noted already, the long-run equilibrium of the labor-managed firms becomes indeterminate. The firms now can arbitrarily determine their scale of operation, and the most logical is that given by the size of the working collective, more or less exogenously determined. As the reader will find easy to verify, under these conditions the long-run supply elasticities will be positive and can be quite high even with single-product firms, and the general equilibrium adjustment to changing demand conditions will be quite efficient indeed. Of course, the most efficient and full (Pareto) optimal adjustment will occur once labor incomes are equalized through entry and exit – or, with firms operating under constant returns to scale, through expansion or contraction of existing firms.

Macroeconomics

We now turn to the determination of aggregate variables such as income, employment and the price level. I feel that it will be most expedient first to summarize the principal results that can be obtained for the labor-managed economy and then, to the extent that space permits, to elaborate on some of them.

The first observation is that unemployment is conceivable in a labor-managed economy, but if it occurs it will be of an entirely different nature – because of different causes and different duration – than unemployment of the Keynesian type in a capitalist economy. A second important point is that variations in effective demand can be expected in the labor-managed economy to lead primarily to variations in prices and not much or not at all to adjustments in income and employment. A third and related point is that on the whole there will be little natural cause for secular inflation, although variations in prices may be wide if markets are entirely free. Fourth, even if unemployment arises there will always be natural forces to restore full employment after a while, provided that capital markets are competitive. Fifth, the macroeconomic general equilibrium determining simultaneously the aggregate variables must be stable provided that real cost of capital varies with the general price level, and almost certainly it will be stable even if the money cost of capital is constant.

The key to points one and two is the low or zero short-run supply elasticity of firms. If for one reason or another the existing number of firms at given product and factor prices is incapable of employing (in equilibrium) all the labor force, then unemployment will prevail, and the supply elasticity being low, short-run changes in demand will be translated into price level variations. Note that this has nothing to do with wage-rigidity. Such rigidity in fact is highly unlikely if not impossible in the labor-managed economy because of the residual nature of labor income and the direct managerial ability of labor to make choices between price reductions on the one hand and idleness and sales reduction on the other. Thus, contrary to a capitalistic situation, a symmetrical flexibility of prices, up and down, and no systematic inflationary tendency should be expected.

Point four is a logical consequence of the fact that if there is unemployment, the unemployed will be in a considerably favored position in competing with existing firms for capital funds for development of new projects. Indeed, with very low unemployment incomes those currently unemployed will be able to offer considerably better terms to the lender. Thus any significant degree of unemployment carries with itself strong, even if perhaps not overly speedy, self-correcting forces. The prime vehicle of the latter is entry, and perhaps also expansion of existing firms (often into new lines of production) operating under constant returns to scale, whose scale of operation is arbitrary. It should be noted here that no parallel remedy exists for Keynesian unemployment; here either entry or expansion of existing firms implies opening of a deflationary gap and the ensuing return to a less than full employment equilibrium.

Point five asserting stability of the macroeconomic system involves some slightly involved mathematics and consequently I omit its demonstration. Full proof is contained, however, in my *General Theory of Labor-Managed Market Economies* (1970).

We may sum up by taking the position of the policy maker in the labor-managed economy: he need not fear autonomous variations in demand as a cause of cyclical unemployment. Rather, he may look out for such variations in order to prevent fluctuations in prices. In this endeavor he will be greatly assisted by an open and competitive foreign trade sector. Full employment does not entirely disappear, however, as the policy-maker's problem, but he must be concerned with it as a matter of long-range strategy, primarily ensuring perfect functioning of the capital market with proper interest structures. More actively, he may want to take discretionary steps: market research and consulting, indicative planning and forecasting, to enhance the speed and efficiency of new entry and expansion. In the final analysis, however, he has a considerable advantage compared to his capitalist colleague in that matters are bound to improve even if perchance he fell asleep on the job.

Special dimensions of labor management

Even if the labor-managed economy can pass with flying colors the scrutiny of conventional micro- and macroeconomic theory, as presented in the preceding two sections, its greatest strength lies in what we may identify as its *special dimensions*, dimensions largely absent in other economic systems. They are all related to, contained in, or emergent from the managerial function of labor, that is, of all participants of the enterprise. The field of analysis opened by these special dimensions is so vast that it cannot be treated in a single section; consequently we will restrict ourselves here to the outline of a few of the most important arguments. In my larger study referred to earlier, I devote to the subject several chapters (Vanek, 1970, pp. 215–310) and even there, I certainly cannot pretend that my analysis is exhaustive.

The first and simplest consideration is that, contrary to the models studied in the two preceding sections, labor is not unique and homogeneous, but rather that in every enterprise a large number of individuals of different skills and qualifications cooperate in a common endeavor. One necessary task of labor management thus is to decide on the distributive shares among the different labor categories. The specific form of the distribution schedule, indicating whether the director gets four times the pay of the janitor for instance, will be the outcome of two sets of forces: conditions of the labor market or more precisely, of the quasi-labor market, because there is no conventional labor market in a labor-managed economy; and the collective will of the working community as it emerges from the democratic decision-making process of labor management.

Noting that the labor-managed firm in equilibrium (when maximizing income for each laborer) will equalize the income of each labor category to the corresponding marginal value product, the first set of forces will guarantee that the allocation of labor throughout the economy will be at least approximately consistent with maximum aggregate output.[1] The second set of forces, on the other hand, will guarantee a reasonable distribution of income, consistent with the generally accepted notion of justice for a particular segment of society, a particular community, or a particular period of time. This 'dual' optimization of social welfare, striking a balance between the mechanistic rules of efficient resource allocation and a collective expression of distributional justice, seems to be a solution superior to that offered by either set of criteria in isolation. The cardinally important thing is that the 'dual' system guarantees that major mistakes will not be committed in either the allocational or the distributional sphere.

The labor force in a labor-managed economy is not only diverse but also of variable quality, and this brings us to the second important *special dimension* of labor management. Without any doubt, labor-management is among all the existing forms of enterprise organizations the optimal arrangement when it comes to the finding of the utility-maximizing effort; the proper quality, duration and intensity of work, by the working collective. Not only is there no situation of conflict between management and the workers that might hinder the finding of the optimum, but the process of self-management itself can be viewed as a highly efficient device for communication, collusion control and enforcement among the participants.

This should be contrasted with a situation of most other enterprises where the worker normally will be furnishing a minimum effort consistent with the retention of his job. It is true that expectation of promotion or a raise may stimulate effort over the acceptable minimum, but recall that this factor should be equally operative in all firms, and thus it does not establish a comparative disadvantage of the labor-managed firm.

Our second special dimension may conveniently be summarized in terms of a diagram. In Figure 1 we measure effort E to the left of O along the horizontal axis, whereas on the vertical axis we find an (average) laborer's income Y. A typical transformation function for the labor-managed alternative between effort and income is indicated by the contour ab (note that with some fixed costs it takes some effort to generate zero income). By contrast, a typical transformation function in capitalist

---

1 In pure theory a frictionless system should generate perfect income equalization through entry and/or exit of firms. However, considering that in the real world there is never enough time to bring such an equalization process to completion, given imperfect information, attachments and loyalties of individuals to the working collective, etc., the competitive forces can be expected to produce only approximate results.

enterprise is indicated by the rectangular broken contour defined by point k. Its comparative deficiency is of two kinds:

1 Point k is below ab, on account of some residual profit normally not distributed among the members;

2 ab is continuous.

On account of both, (as the reader may verify by drawing a set of convex indifference lines) losses in individual and collective utility, that is, in real income, will occur in one type of undertaking as compared with the other.

Third, as shown by Figure 1, there is another special dimension, Z which should be understood as a summary index standing for a very large number of special dimensions – also entering together with income and effort, the utility function of the members of the working collective. As indicated by the three dimensional transformation locus in Figure 1,

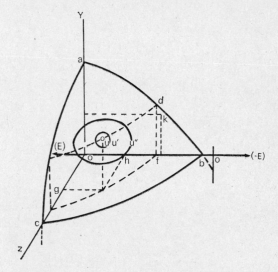

Figure 1

attainment of higher levels of Z involves an opportunity cost in terms of income and/or effort. Nevertheless, this new dimension further augments the number of choices of the working community and thus unambiguously (as shown by the equal-utility contours u, u', u'' and the maximum-utility point e) its real income. It is the comparison between point e and point k that should, in the context of our present analysis, be included in any comparison between a labor-managed and a capitalist, or for that matter, Soviet-type firm.

It would hardly be possible to be exhaustive in explaining all the variables for which Z actually stands. However, some illustrations should be helpful. For example, the working collective, or a subgroup of it, may prefer a conveyor belt to a traditional way of intraplant transportation, even if this should involve a reduction in money income. By contrast, a capitalist would perform such a substitution only if profit could be increased. Another example is training and education of some members of the community at the expense of the enterprise. Again, the corresponding motivation and decision-making is entirely different from what it would be in other firms. Still another example is collective consumption using part of the global income of the enterprise, including housing, recreation, etc. Moreover, the enterprise as a whole may undertake at its own expense social action directed toward the outside, the local community or other, and thus derive intangible real income – we may call it peace of mind – for itself.[2]

This last example brings us to a fourth category of special dimensions, related to Z, but not exactly the same, referred to as Z'. It resembles Z in all respects, including that it enters the utility index, except that it does not affect money income or effort of the working community. The transformation locus with Z' substituted for Z would thus appear as a cylindrical surface generated by lines parallel to the Z' axis. Normally, such a surface will be truncated at some finite level of Z' and, obviously, an equilibrium will be found (with indifference loci convex everywhere) at the corresponding ridge, at a level of collective utility again unambiguously higher than at a point such as d with two dimensions only. To give substance to this rather technical exposition, let us give at least one example; it is a significant one. We have noted in the first section that the long-run equilibrium of a competitive labor-managed firm operating under constant returns to scale – a condition encountered in many real situations – is indeterminate with respect to scale of operation. Under such conditions, total employment and output of the firm may become our Z' variable. The working community considers it a positive utility to maximize employment in the community; the external constraint, and the ridge line of our above discussion now are given by the full employment in the community.

In the opinion of the writer, the argument just made has a good deal of relevance, and when further generalized can become even more significant

2 Some will object that all this can be done by individuals or through nonbusiness-based grouping: this is true, but it holds even for the labor-managed system and thus the potential of action by firms, the primary generators of resources, still constitutes a comparative advantage.

especially in the context of less-developed countries. The generalization is based on the recognition that in most situations – especially in manufacturing – we cannot postulate perfect competition; some market power will always be present. In such situations, however, all it takes is to reclassify Z', a zero opportunity cost variable, into Z, a positive opportunity cost variable. But the absorption of unemployment in the community remains a positive good from the point of view of the working collective. Thus a solution involving higher employment than that dictated by strict income-per-laborer maximization still may be expected.

Concluding observations

Before attempting a summary evaluation of the labor-managed economy, two more matters ought to be taken up which normally enter the appraisal of an economic system. The first is the question of ability to mobilize national savings for accumulation. The second is the question of the capacity of generating technical progress and innovation.

Regarding the capacity to mobilize investment funds, the labor-managed economy, especially its socialist version, is in a very strong position. Noting that the labor-managed firms must pay for the use of capital the corresponding value of marginal product, and taking a reasonable set of estimates of national capital stock and marginal capital productivity, the economy can generate net savings of between twenty and thirty per cent of national income just by retaining capital income for reinvestment. These percentages, already among the highest currently encountered in the real world, can further be augmented through private savings, government surpluses, or as in Yugoslavia, through an obligation of firms to repay investment loans from current income.

With respect to the second question, the case for the labor-managed economy is somewhat less clear cut; but in the final analysis, it would be difficult to conclude that the system in question is at a comparative disadvantage. When it comes to 'small' inventive and innovative activity emerging as a side-effect of the productive process itself, the incentives, unity of purpose and ease of communication offered by labor-management (and by income sharing, which is an integral part of labor-management) are conditions unequalled by any other system. On the other side of the spectrum, with respect to basic research and major scientific developments the firms only rarely play a decisive role; thus in the present context the difference between alternative systems cannot be very important.

It is the middle of the spectrum, for 'medium size' incentive and innovative activity, that would seem the most important. Here the modern capitalist corporation almost certainly has a comparative advantage with its own low-cost – and often quite abundant – funds that it can employ in research and development. On the other hand, a socialist economy, labor-managed or other, is likely to have a distinct advantage in proliferating innovations throughout the whole economy.

Let us now try to make a summary evaluation of the labor-managed system. I realize that such an endeavor must always contain a certain element of subjective judgment. This is so because summary evaluation really means constructing an aggregate ordinal index based on a combination of several evaluations, not all of the same sign; clearly, some weights must be employed and these, to a degree at least, will be subjective.

With this in mind, and basing myself on ten years of intensive study more than on the present exposition, I cannot forego a set of strongly favorable conclusions; I cannot avoid them, even though I realize that I am contradicting the majority of our profession who have thought about the problem, and even though I may risk earning the displeasure of many.

In brief, the labor-managed system appears to me to be superior by far, judged on strictly economic criteria, to any other economic system in existence. In the sphere of allocation efficiency (concerning how well it utilizes its resources in national production), it is at worst equal to the western-type capitalist system in the context of a full-employment model (as discussed in the first section), while it is definitely superior in the context of the macroeconomic model (as discussed in the second section) and in the context of its special dimensions (as discussed in the third section). On the side of the system's capability to grind out an efficient pattern of income distribution, there are also strong reasons to believe that a socialist labor-managed economy will do a better job than other market systems. This conclusion is based not only on the argument of collective decision-making within the firm (as argued in the third section), but also on the fact that in the socialist economy the income share of capital, whether reinvested or not, will accrue to the society as a whole and not to a select group of individuals.

Compared to the Soviet-type command economy, the question of distributional efficiency really is empty of meaning because income distribution is decided by decree and not by some mechanism inherent in the economic system. As for allocational efficiency, far more important for our comparison because inherent in the system, we only have to recognize with Bergson (1964, p. 341) that the Soviet-type command economy is less efficient than market capitalism, and recall the above evaluation of the two market alternatives. In fact even the weaker postulate of approximate equality between the two major world systems would suffice here to establish a preference for the labor-managed alternative over that of a command economy.

Two remarks less strictly economic, and stemming much more from intuition than from careful analysis, may be in order before closing this discussion: first, it seems to me that the comparative advantage of labor-managed systems becomes even stronger once we leave the strictly economic frame of reference and replace it by one that takes account of broader human values. Second, taking a very long view of world events, it seems to me that if there is a meeting ground for the presently conflicting major world systems and ideologies, it is one not too far from the system discussed here.

References

BERGSON, A. (1964), *The Economics of Soviet Planning*, Yale University Press.

BERGSON, A. (1967), 'Market socialism revisited', *J. Polit. Econ.*, vol. 75, pp. 432–42; reprinted in this book as Reading 20.

DOMAR, E. (1966), 'The Soviet collective farm as a producer cooperative', *Amer. Econ. Rev.*, vol. 56, pp. 734–57; reprinted in this book as Reading 24.

ROBINSON, J. (1967), 'The Soviet collective farm as a producer cooperative: comment', *Amer. Econ. Rev.*, vol. 57, pp. 222–3.

VANEK, J. (1970), *The General Theory of Labor-Managed Market Economies*, Cornell University Press.

VANEK, J. (1971), *The Participatory Economy: An Evolutionary Hypothesis and a Development Strategy*, Cornell University Press.

WARD, B. (1958), 'The firm in Illyria: market syndicalism', *Amer. Econ. Rev.*, vol. 48, pp. 566–89.

Part Four
Economic Theory

24 E. D. Domar

The Soviet Collective Farm as a Producer Cooperative[1]

E. D. Domar, 'The Soviet collective farm as a producer cooperative',
American Economic Review, 1966, vol. 56, pp. 734-57.

Imagine that most of the obstacles facing Soviet kolkhozes (collective farms) today, such as output and delivery quotas, administrative interference, shortage of strategic inputs (materials, spare parts, fertilizer), depressed prices of outputs, etc., suddenly vanish, and the kolkhozes find themselves in a Lange–Lerner type of a competitive world where everything can be bought and sold at a market price, and where peasants are free to run their own affairs *provided the essential structure of the kolkhoz is retained.* How would Soviet agriculture, or for that matter any economic sector so organized, fare in such a wonderland?[2]

Freed from existing restrictions and abuses, the kolkhoz would presumably revert to its prototype – a producer cooperative which utilizes the labor of its members, purchases other inputs, sells its outputs, pays a rent and/or taxes, and divides all or a part of its net proceeds among its members. The presumed democratic nature of such a co-op and its freedom from capitalist exploitation has made it highly attractive to socialists and

1 The author is professor of economics at Massachusetts Institute of Technology. I am very grateful to Abram Bergson, Michael R. Dohan, John G. Gurley, Michael D. Intriligator, Nancy Nimitz, David McGarvey, and Egon Neuberger for their generous assistance and helpful comments. Questions raised by M. Neuberger made me rewrite the whole paper. David Conklin acted as my research assistant, and Martin Weitzman went over the mathematics. I had intended to include in the paper a brief survey of relevant recent Soviet literature, and James R. Millar of Cornell University kindly lent me three chapters of his dissertation (1965). This project was abandoned because of lack of space; besides, Millar's survey is more comprehensive and thorough than mine could have been. I am also grateful to the RAND Corporation for its facilities, encouragement and support. Some of the research was supported by the National Science Foundation as well. None of these persons or organizations is of course responsible for my conclusions or for any errors which may still be lurking around.
2 The question is not as academic as it sounds. Recent changes in Soviet agricultural policies represent another step toward that wonderland, though there is still a long way to go. See *Izvestia*, 27 March 1965, pp. 1–3; 11 April 1965, p. 2; 13 April 1965, pp. 1–2; *New York Times*, 28 March 1965, pp. 1, 6; *Pravda*, 7 November 1965, p. 2; 26 December 1965, pp. 1–2; 20 February 1966, p. 3.

social reformers for ages. But its popularity has not prompted its proponents to analyze it with the same loving curiosity that the 'bourgeois' economists have shown toward the capitalist firm. And yet it must have been obvious, at least to some of these proponents, that co-op members are likely to be ordinary human beings bent on maximizing the benefits from their participation in the co-op.[3] The first and only attempt to construct a model of a co-op that I have seen belongs to Benjamin Ward in a pathbreaking paper published in 1958.[4] But like many a pioneering work, it has not attracted much attention.[5]

The present study consists of three parts: in the first, Ward's creation, called here the 'Pure Model' of a co-op, is reworked with a generalized production function. The tenor of Ward's findings (based on a single-output, one-or-two-input function) is confirmed, but some of the results are made more definite, and one is reversed. In the second part, the co-op is faced with a supply schedule of labor; this makes the model much more realistic and reverses the paradoxical results of the 'Pure Model'. Finally, a summary and a few conclusions are presented in the third part.

List of symbols (*in order of appearance*)

R a fixed rent paid by the co-op ($R > 0$)

v ($-\pi/x_n$) – dividend rate or dividend per labor unit ($v > 0$)

x_n labor input ($x_n < 0$)

n number of outputs and inputs

π profit of the co-op gross of dividend payments ($\pi > 0$)

p_i price of x_i ($i = 1,..., n-1$)

x_i an output when $x_i > 0$, an input when $x_i < 0$ ($i = 1,..., n-1$)

p_n wage rate paid by the 'capitalist twin'; originally $p_n = v$

λ Lagrange's multiplier

3 I do not discuss here producer co-ops organized for essentially noneconomic reasons, such as by religious orders, Israeli pioneers, etc.

4 There have of course been a number of analyses of firms which do not maximize total profit in the usual way. See for example Scitovsky (1943); Lutz and Lutz (1951); Baumol (1959); Averch and Johnson (1962); and Westfield (1965). A very interesting book on cooperatives was published by Tugan-Baranovsky (1921). His conclusions were very similar to mine given in the third section of this paper. I owe this reference to Steven Rosefielde of Harvard.

5 In my sample of some forty or fifty reputable economists about a third of whom work in the Soviet and related fields, Ward's article had been read by three or four persons at most. Perhaps the paper's title gave the wrong impression that it pertained to Yugoslavia only. Or – who knows – this might have been the normal fate of an excellent paper.

$E_{x_i p_j} = (\partial x_i / \partial p_j)(p_j / x_i)$ elasticity of demand for, or supply of, x_i in response to change in p_j $(i, j = 1,..., n)$

$u_i = p_i x_i$ value of an output when $x_i > 0$, or of an input when $x_i < 0$

A few other symbols are defined when introduced.

An asterisk indicates that the expression pertains to the 'capitalist twin'.

The 'Pure Model' of a co-op

The following assumptions are made:

1 All nonlabor inputs are bought and all outputs are sold by the co-op at given (parametric) prices.

2 The production function of the co-op, if possessed by a profit-maximizing firm, would have all necessary and sufficient properties for a stable equilibrium under perfect competition (Allen, 1939, 1956).

3 The co-op pays a fixed rent $R > 0$ per year.[6]

---

6 Soviet kolkhozes do not pay rent as such, but the system of compulsory deliveries and differentiated zonal prices is directed against the richer farms and regions and allows the government to extract some rent. Until 1966, the farms paid a 12·5 per cent tax imposed on income net of nonlabor cost (excluding 80 per cent of income from animal products), but gross of dividend payments. The rate could be modified by regional authorities in favor of poorer and against richer farms (Shermeneva, 1963).

Beginning with 1966, the tax rate is set at 12 per cent, and the taxable income seems to exclude two items: (1) profit equal to 15 per cent of nonlabor costs, and (2) dividend payments not exceeding a certain average per member, to be set by the government (*Izvestia*, 11 April 1965, p. 1). If the post-tax dividend rate is indicated by v_t, it follows that

$$v_t = v(1-t) + Cet/L + wt$$

where t is the tax rate (12 per cent), e is the 15 per cent exclusion, w is the exemption per member, C is the nonlabor costs,

$$C = -\sum_{k}^{n-1} p_i x_i,$$

k is the first input and $L = -x_n$ (to avoid negative numbers). Now t, e and w are constants, but C/L is not. Hence the imposition of the tax in its new form will affect economic decisions in the kolkhoz. I am not sure, however, that my interpretation of this tax reform is correct (the official statement being rather confusing). For this reason and to save space, I will disregard the complexities of the tax law both before and after 1966, and mean by the word 'tax' a simple proportional levy on profits before dividend payments. But a further investigation of the effects of this new tax may be worthwhile.

4 Instead of paying wages, the co-op divides all (or a constant fraction) of its income net of all other costs and rent equally among its members or among homogeneous labor units in the form of a dividend.[7]

5 The objective of the co-op is the maximization of the dividend per unit of labor or of the dividend rate $v > 0$. There is complete certainty.[8]

6 The co-op is *actually able* to employ the optimum number of labor units maximizing the dividend rate. This assumption (used by Ward) distinguishes this model from those presented in the second section.

7 Finally, there exists a profit-maximizing firm, the 'capitalist twin', with the same production function and prices as the co-op, and with a wage rate initially equal to the co-op's dividend rate.

We are concerned in this model with a rent rather than with a tax because a glance at **1** below will show that neither an income tax (imposed on net income before dividends), nor a poll tax (per unit of labor) would affect the co-op's decisions in the context of this model: the optimum allocation of resources yielding the maximum dividend before the tax remains unchanged by the tax.[9]

The rent is assumed to be positive because an $R < 0$ (a subsidy) would induce the co-op to maximize the dividend rate v by reducing labor input to zero. Even an $R=0$ can produce this effect if v declines from the very beginning and has no maximum point. We shall assume that R is large enough to give us a meaningful problem but not to eliminate the co-op's net income or to convert it into a loss.

Note that in the generalized production function given in **2**, it is customary to express outputs in positive units, and inputs, including labor

---

7 Actually it is the Soviet practice to transform most of the labor of kolkhoz members into a homogeneous sum by a system of weights depending on the required skill and the nature of work. The weights vary from one kolkhoz to another, but the range seems to be around $2\frac{1}{2}:\frac{1}{2}$. If the relative weights correspond to the ratios of the values of the marginal products of the several kinds of labor this is a reasonable procedure. It would not matter if the co-op first paid uniform wages per labor unit (as Ward assumed) and then used the balance of income for dividends.

It should be also noted that a substantial fraction of the income of the kolkhoz is retained by it (the so-called 'Indivisible Fund') for reinvestment and improvements, and that this fraction varies from one farm to another and from one year to the next, depending on economic conditions and on administrative decisions.

8 No dynamic elements are considered either. Even though some comments about investment decisions will be made, the model essentially refers to the short run.

9 In models presented in the second section an income tax does affect economic decisions. A gross receipt tax would have the same effects as a proportional reduction in the price of every output. See note 6.

x_n, in negative. Hence many derivations in the mathematical Appendix have seemingly perverse signs, and a minus sign is attached to **1**.

Our basic problem consists of maximizing the dividend rate

$$v = -\pi/x_n = (-\sum_1^{n-1} p_i x_i - R)/x_n \qquad\qquad\qquad \mathbf{1}$$

subject to the production function

$$f(x_1, ..., x_n) = 0. \qquad\qquad\qquad \mathbf{2}$$

The solution of **1** and **2**, while not difficult, is somewhat involved, and can be safely relegated to the Appendix. It is shown there that the equilibrium position of the co-op is identical in every respect to that of its capitalist twin defined in assumption 7. On reflection, this is to be expected: for any given labor input the co-op simply maximizes total profit like the twin, and hence chooses the same outputs and nonlabor inputs. When it comes to labor, the attitudes of the two organizations differ: the twin hires labor until the value of the marginal product equals the wage; the co-op uses labor to the point where the value of the marginal product equals the dividend paid (a unit of labor contributing less than the going dividend rate will not be used).[10] But since the two schedules of the value of the marginal product of labor are identical and the wage paid by the twin initially equals the dividend paid by the co-op (by assumption 7), the labor inputs used by both organizations are identical as well.

The *reactions* of the two enterprises to changes in rent or in prices, however, are altogether different. An increase in R has no (short-run) effects on the twin because it changes neither the value of the marginal product of labor nor the wage rate. But it reduces the dividend rate paid by the co-op and therefore moves the point of intersection between the dividend rate ABC (on Figure 1) and the value of the marginal product of labor EBF further to the right, from B to B' because of the assumed negative slope of EBF. So, as Ward has shown, more labor will be used (OJ' instead of OJ) and, in the absence of Hicks's 'regression' (Hicks, 1946, pp. 96–8), output will increase as well.[11] But before the reader concludes that the best way to increase peasant participation in Soviet kolk-hozes is by imposing (or increasing) rents, he should take a look at the second section.

10 The schedules of the dividend rate and of the value of the marginal product of labor, as used here, are based on the assumption that equilibrium conditions are satisfied for all outputs and all nonlabor inputs all along the schedules. See, however, note 17.
11 See the Appendix, Section 3.

The effect of a price change on the co-op is more complex because both the dividend rate and the value of the marginal product of labor are affected.[12] If there is only one output x_1 and labor is the only input, the

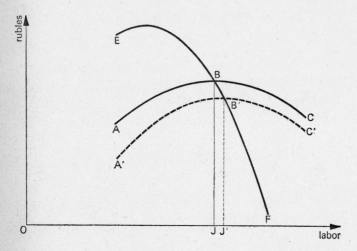

Figure 1

outcome is certain: a doubling of p_1 will double the value of the marginal product of labor, while the dividend rate, as shown by expression **1** rewritten for this occasion as

$$v = -\frac{p_1 x_1 - R}{x_n},\quad [13]$$

$$\qquad\qquad\qquad\qquad\qquad\qquad\qquad\qquad\qquad\qquad 3$$

will *more* than double. The intersection point of the curves *EBF* and *ABC* will now move to the left, from B to B' on Figure 2, and both the labor input and hence the output will contract, as proved by Ward.

With one output and several inputs the situation becomes clouded, but a plausible assumption (that the isoquants of the production function are radially parallel to each other) saves the day and preserves the re-

12 The values of the marginal products of other inputs will also be affected.
13 The relative increase in v is greater than in p_1 because R is subtracted from $p_1 x_1$ in the numerator. However, x_1 and x_n also change. It is shown in the last section of the Appendix that

$$\left(\frac{dv}{dp_1}\right)\frac{p_1}{v} = \frac{p_1 x_1}{p_1 x_1 - R} > 1,$$

if the production function consists of x_1 and x_n only. See also the Appendix, section 3.

374 Economic Theory

strictive conclusion just reached (Appendix, section 3). The solution of the general case of several outputs and inputs is given in the Appendix, (Appendix, section 3) the results being summarized in Table 1 overleaf.

On the whole, the co-op's reactions to an increase in p_1 are rather peculiar. When x_1 is an output, there is a general tendency to restrict operations; when x_1 is an input – to expand them. Even when the co-op

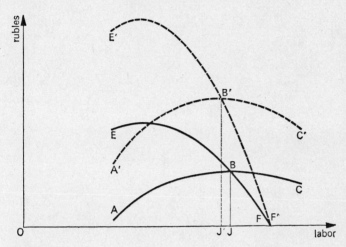

Figure 2

moves in the same direction as a capitalist firm, its response is usually more sluggish. For market stability, the picture is not particularly reassuring.

True enough, if x_1 is one of several outputs, a rise in its price is likely to *increase* its production; its own market can therefore be stable, contrary to Ward's expectations based on the one-output production function. But the input of labor is very likely to decrease and hence lead to a contraction of other outputs. Since many agricultural products are reasonably good substitutes for each other, the conditions which have led to a rise in the price of, say, wheat may very well raise the prices of rye and corn as well. The simultaneous rise in several prices, being similar to the rise in the price of some *important* single user of labor (see the first line of Table 1), can cause a general restriction of output. Although a negatively sloping supply curve is not a sufficient condition for market instability, it is too close to it for comfort.

Of course the undesirable negative effect of the rise in p_1 can be counteracted by an appropriate increase in rent. But such manipulations of rent

Table 1 Summary of the effects of an increase in p_1 on the magnitudes of outputs and inputs (in absolute terms)

Effect on	Usual capitalist reaction	Probable co-op reaction
	if x_1 is an output	
x_1	positive	positive, unless x_1 is a very important user of labor (or the only output)
$|x_n|$	positive	negative (except in a special case in the Appendix)
x_2 as all other outputs	positive, if x_2 is complementary to x_1. negative, if x_2 is competitive with x_1	negative if input proportions remain unchanged; otherwise, indeterminate. negative
$|x_2|$ as an input	positive	negative with high complementarity between x_2 and x_n indeterminate with partial complementarity
	if x_1 is an input	positive if x_2 and x_n are substitutes
$|x_1|$	negative	negative, except for constant proportions between x_1 and x_n when the effect is zero
$|x_n|$	negative if x_1 and x_n are complementary	positive, except for a zero effect if x_1 and x_n are used in constant proportions
	positive if they are substitutes	
x_2 as an output (or all output)	negative	indeterminate
$|x_2|$ as an input	negative if x_1 and x_2 are complementary positive if they are substitutes	indeterminate

in response to changing prices would require more knowledge and skill than are likely to be possessed by the Soviet or, for that matter, by most other governments. And besides, the whole idea of rent implies a sum fixed in advance for a reasonably long period of time. It would not help to replace it with a tax on net income because (as mentioned above) such a tax does not affect co-ops' decisions. Some other tax might, but it is hardly worth investigating in the light of the second section.

The model augurs little good for the allocation of resources among the co-ops. As Ward has observed, the labor market will be rigid. Indeed, if a rich and a poor co-op should each be in its respective equilibrium, no movement of labor from the poor co-op to the rich is possible (except through a merger) because any movement would reduce the dividend rates in both co-ops. Since the dividend rate in equilibrium equals the net value of the marginal product of labor, there is a definite misallocation of labor, and of course of other resources as well, among the co-ops. The hiring of the members of the poor co-op by the rich is the obvious solution, but it is not permitted in the present model.

The best measure both on equity and resource allocation grounds to be taken here is an increase in the rent paid by the rich co-op (or a relief for the poor one, if it pays any). Equity alone could be satisfied by a system of differential prices both for outputs and for inputs discriminating against the rich co-op,[14] but the equalization of the dividend rate so achieved would obviously not equate the social value of the marginal product of labor (and of other inputs) in the two co-ops.

All these equalizing measures can backfire if the wealth of the rich co-op is due not to its better natural conditions and location, but to greater effort and interest of its members not accounted for in the conventional measures of labor input. But these considerations are outside of the scope of this model and even of this paper.

In making investment decisions, each co-op will behave like its own capitalist twin paying a wage rate equal to the co-op's dividend rate. For the rich co-op labor is expensive, for the poor, it is cheap. Hence the former will prefer ready-made labor-saving machinery, while the latter will look for labor-using projects and be inclined, for instance, to use its own labor in construction. To the extent that the poor co-op is poor because of shortage of capital, it will be more inclined to invest than the rich. Whether it will have the means to do so is less likely.

The model with a supply schedule of labor

The 'Pure Model', for all its interesting and amusing (I hope) paradoxes, has one slight defect: it is unreal. It assumes that labor input can be varied with changing prices and rent in order to maximize the dividend rate (assumption 6), a highly unlikely situation once the co-op has been organized. Surely the co-op, by its very nature, cannot admit and expel members at will. Hours of labor contributed by each member can of course be

14 A standard remedy in Soviet literature and practice.

varied, but it is rather improbable that the members' welfare functions should call for a maximum dividend either per hour or per year irrespective of the number of hours worked.

Two possibilities will be considered here. First, the number of members is given (at least in the short run), and so is the number of hours contributed (according to some custom) by them. Then labor input is fixed, and the co-op simply maximizes total profit. Second, the co-op members may have other opportunities for employment and for leisure. In Soviet kolkhozes, they may cultivate their own plots, work in town, on a neighboring state farm, or even 'lie on the stove' and do nothing according to the age-old Russian custom. In other words, the co-op is faced with a supply schedule of labor, which will be assumed here to have the usual positive

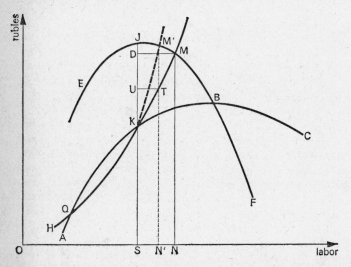

Figure 3

slope. The equilibrium position of the co-op is found in two steps: first the co-op maximizes total profit for every given labor input, and obtains the familiar dividend rate curve *ABC* on Figure 3. The latter now serves as the demand schedule for labor as well, and its intersection with the labor-supply curve determines the labor input contributed by members *acting as such*. It need not correspond to the highest point *B* on the *ABC* curve, where it is intersected by the marginal curve *EBF*.

The appearance of this innocent-looking supply curve of labor produces a drastic difference in the reactions of the co-op to changes in prices and in rent as compared with the 'Pure Model'. Also, an income tax imposed on the co-op's income gross of dividend payments, ineffective previously, becomes relevant here.[15] Depending on the position of the labor-supply curve in relation to *ABC*, three variations of the present model will be discussed.

Case 1: Moderate labor shortage

The supply curve of labor *HKM* in Figure 3 intersects the dividend-rate curve *ABC* at *K*, to the left of the maximum point *B*. If, to preserve the purity of the co-op, no discrimination among its members is permitted, the co-op has to reconcile itself to the situation and simply stay at point *K*.[16] But its paradoxical behavior disappears. Any improvement in the dividend rate, be it from lower rent or taxes, or from better prices, lifts the *ABC* curve, increases the employment of labor, and presumably raises output. In the light of this model, which is much closer to Soviet reality than the 'Pure' one, price reforms promulgated by Khrushchev and his successors are justified.

It is not clear what labor cost will be used in making economic decisions. The correct cost should be *SJ* – the net value of the marginal productivity of labor – but since no one is actually paid this rate, the management may not know what it is.

If it is possible to discriminate among members and to hire those with particularly attractive outside opportunities (or the laziest ones) between *K* and *M*, new possibilities open up. In treating its hired members, the co-op will behave *more or less* like a capitalist employer, depending on the standing of these members in the co-op and other circumstances. Consider:

(a) If the hired members have different skills (or if the co-op management is very adroit), the co-op may act as a discriminating monopsonist and pay each of them the wage indicated by the supply curve. The area *KJM* represents the profit so obtained; presumably it will be added to the dividend paid to the regular members.

(b) The hired members may persuade or force the co-op to hire all of them at the highest wage *NM*. A smaller profit equal to the area *DJM* is now made.

15 For practical reasons, we need not bother with a poll tax. In any case, its effects are similar (but not identical) to those of the income tax. Income or poll taxes *imposed on the members* (rather than on the co-op) are not considered here. See note 6.
16 Provided it gets to point *K* in the first place. Point *K* is stable in both directions, but *Q* is not. An upward movement from *Q* will bring the co-op to *K*, but unfortunately even a slight downward movement from *Q* can destroy the co-op altogether.

(c) As a compromise between these two extremes, the co-op may operate like any ordinary monopsonist, draw the dotted curve KM', representing the marginal labor cost, to its intersection with the value of the marginal product curve EBF, employ altogether ON' units of labor, pay a wage of $N'T$, and make a profit from hiring of $UJM'T$.[17]

In all these cases, the total employment of labor exceeds OS, output expands, and dividend rate rises over the original level of SK.[18] Everyone is better off provided the ordinary members are not consumed with envy. They need not be if the hired members do possess special skills. But if they are common members who refuse to work for the co-op more than the minimum required to retain their membership, the social situation can be rather difficult.[19]

The reactions of the co-op to changes in rent, income tax and prices now take still another turn and become more similar to those of a capitalist firm. An increase in rent lowers the average ABC curve but leaves the marginal EBF schedule intact. Hence, in cases (a) and (b) no reduction in labor input takes place, except that some members who were previously satisfied with dividends will now demand a wage. But output remains undisturbed. In case (c), however, the fall in the ABC curve has a special effect: now that hiring begins earlier (that is, to the left of point K) the curve KM' moves leftward and intersects EBF to the left of the old point M'. Hence, total employment of labor falls and so does output.

An increase in the income tax rate lowers both the average and the marginal curves (because it falls on profit *gross* of dividends) and thus reduces the employment of labor, while better prices raise both curves and have a positive effect on labor and on output.

17 There is some incongruity among the several curves in Figure 3. Schedules ABC and EBF are drawn on the assumption that the co-op is in equilibrium position in respect to all outputs and all nonlabor inputs for every given labor input, or that with every change in the labor input everything else is adjusted accordingly. The supply curve of labor HKM and the marginal cost of labor curve KM' indicate labor cost only, without allowing for these adjustments. I can take refuge in the approximate nature of Figure 3 used here for illustration only. A similar qualification applies to Figure 4 as well.

18 It will be above SK but somewhat below the corresponding point on the ABC curve because the latter implies that no members are paid a wage in excess of the dividend.

19 Strictly speaking, we assume either that the labor force is homogeneous, or that more skilled labor is transformed into ordinary labor according to some fixed weights, as it is done in Soviet kolkhozes (see note 7). So a refusal of a carpenter to work for the kolkhoz means his unwillingness to accept a multiple of the dividend rate paid to common workers.

, In the text, all members working for the co-op receive *either* the dividend *or* a wage. In reality, some combinations of the two are sometimes encountered (see note 20). But this paper is already too long to analyse such a situation.

Without the income tax, the wage rate paid to the marginal hired worker (or to all of them) in cases (a) and (b) equals the net value of the marginal product of labor. In case (c) there is the usual disparity created by monopsony. But the presence of the income tax creates a special gap between the social and private (as seen by the co-op) values of labor's marginal product in all three cases, and distorts allocation of resources.

So far only the hiring of its own members by the co-op has been considered. If the co-op can hire outsiders as well, as for instance a rich co-op hiring workers from a poor one, the allocation of labor may be further improved. The hiring co-op will simply behave like a profit-maximizing firm. We'll return to the hiring-out co-op in Case 3.[20]

Case 2: Severe labor shortage

When the supply curve of labor *HM* lies completely to the left of the *ABC* dividend curve, the co-op as such cannot function at all. And yet it *may* be possible to hire every member at the wage demanded by him and still pay a rent! The members may be divided into groups (by skill, for instance) and each group paid a wage demanded by its marginal member. Freedom in hiring certainly increases the flexibility of the organization. Perhaps this is one of the reasons why Soviet state farms who hire all their labor are doing better than the kolkhozes, and why some weak kolkhozes have been transformed into state farms[21] (Nauchno-Isseldovatel'skii Finansovyi Institut, 1963, p. 19).

20 In the actual operation of Soviet kolkhozes, some discrimination and hiring are permitted. The more skilled members are paid dividends at a higher rate (see note 7). In Abramov's delightful story about a kolkhoz (Abramov, 1963, pp. 109–37) carpenters are paid one rouble a day in addition to the dividend rate. In a *Krokodil* story, two neighboring kolkhozes hire each other's carpenters (presumably the carpenters have refused to work for dividends on either farm and demanded market wages). Finally, kolkhozes hire agricultural specialists and other experts and skilled workers. It seems that the richer farms even hire ordinary workers in busy times.

The Soviet Government has been recommending to the kolkhozes to pay their members a wage in money equal to some eighty per cent of the expected dividend (for the given type of work). But this was an advance payment of a dividend rather than a true wage. It seems that some of the kolkhozes who have tried to follow this recommendation became short of funds (Academiia Nauk SSSR, Institut Ekonomiki, 1963, pp. 54–6). New measures for alleviating the seasonal shortage of funds in the kolkhozes were announced on 5 January 1966 in *Pravda*, p. 2.

21 It seems that the definite wage paid by the state farms has a better incentive effect than the promise of an uncertain dividend. An official promise to investigate the possibility of 'guaranteed compensation of labor in all kolkhozes' was recently made (*Pravda*, 7 November 1965, p. 2). But there are many other reasons for the relative success of state farms, such as the payment of higher wages, and most important, access to the government budget. For that matter, not all state farms have been successful.

Case 3: An excess supply of labor

The supply curve of labor *HKM* intersects the *ABC* curve at *M* to the right of the optimum point *B* in Figure 4. The co-op may be either very rich or located far from other employment opportunities. The situation is analytically similar to Case 1. If it is impossible to get rid of some members or to reduce labor input by rationing, the co-op will simply stay at *M*. Any improvement in conditions, such as lower rent and taxes,

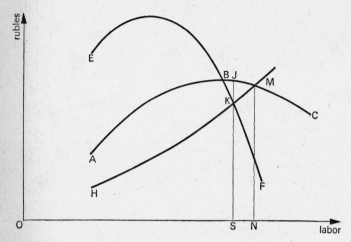

Figure 4

or better prices, will raise the *ABC* curve and increase the quantity of labor used, as in Case 1. But if each member between *K* and *M* can indeed take an outside job and earn a wage at least equal to the corresponding point of the supply curve, it will be better for all concerned to *hire out* the members in *KM*, and in fairness to them, collect their earnings and pay them the regular dividend. The members who are to the right of point *M* will prefer to remain on their own. In the absence of an income tax, the net value of the marginal product of labor will equal its supply price at *K*, which is good, but since the dividend rate paid to the members will be approximately equal to *SJ* rather than *SK*, there is a danger of over-evaluation of labor cost by the management.[22] The presence of an income tax creates the same distortions as in Case 1. When the

22 It will be somewhat higher than *SJ* because the *ABC* curve disregards the higher wages earned outside. See note 18. Perhaps a Soviet kolkhoz can act as a monopolist in hiring out labor. An analysis of this case is similar to that given in Cases 1b and 1c above. It should be noted that Figure 4 suffers from the same incongruity as Figure 3. See note 17.

hiring out of labor is permitted, changes in rent, income tax rates and prices in Case 3 will have the same effects on the total employment of labor by the co-op as in Cases 1a and 1b.

The (positive or negative) hiring of members improves the allocation of resources within each co-op, but so long as it is confined to its own members (as assumed here) the distribution of labor among the co-ops remains unchanged.[23] In contrast to the 'Pure Model' where the inequality of dividend rates among the co-ops indicated misallocation of labor (and of other resources) and where the transfer of labor from the poor to the rich units was clearly in the social interest, the present situation is ambiguous because the value of the marginal product of labor in each co-op no longer equals (except accidentally) the dividend rate: in Figure 3 it is above the dividend rate, in Figure 4, below it. In the improbable (at least among Soviet kolkhozes) case when Figure 3 depicts a rich unit, and Figure 4, a poor one, the transfer of labor from the poor to the rich co-op will be welcomed by all parties. But in the more realistic case when the poor co-op is to the left of the point B (as in Figure 3) and the rich to its right (as in Figure 4), both co-ops will object to this transfer because the poor co-op seeks more labor (so as to reach point B), and the rich less, while social desirability remains obscured by the differences (in opposite directions) between the value of the marginal product of labor and the dividend rate in each co-op.

Concluding remarks

The results of all our models are summarized in Table 2.

Table 2 The effects of changes in rent, tax rates and prices on the employment of labor by the co-op

Nature of change	'The Pure Model'	The Model with a supply curve of labor	
		Without hiring	With hiring
increase in rent	positive	negative	neutral, except in Case 1c
increase in income tax rate	neutral	negative	negative
improvement in prices	negative	positive	positive

I now turn to those aspects of Soviet agricultural policy to which this paper may be relevant. I think they can be fairly listed as follows:

1 To increase labor participation in the kolkhozes.

2 To improve resource allocation on the farms.

23 Except when the hired-out members of one co-op are hired by another.

3 To improve allocation of labor among the farms.

4 To bring about greater equality of income per member (or per labor unit) among the farms.

5 To siphon off the excess purchasing power which will be acquired by some peasants if agricultural prices are moved closer to their marginal costs.

All these (and other) aspects have been discussed in Soviet literature in recent years, with point 4 – the high degree of inequality among peasant incomes – receiving particular attention. I have not found a comprehensive distribution of peasant incomes, but it is fair to conclude from various sources that ratios of four to one, of six to one, and even higher, between rich and poor farms are not uncommon.[24] This inequality is attacked on equity grounds – unequal pay for equal work, the suggested remedy consisting of price manipulations in favor of the poor and against the

24 According to V. N. Starovsky, Director of the USSR Central Statistical Administration, '. . . in 1961 payments per man-day on about 30 per cent of the USSR's collective farms came to only one-fourth to one-fifth as much as on the 20 per cent of the farms where the pay was the highest' (*Kommunist*, 1962). It is not clear whether Starovsky referred to total or to money incomes only.

In the last few years many changes in Soviet agriculture have taken place, but it is hard to judge whether income inequality among the peasants has gone up or down. The following compilation of the official average kolkhoz money income per household among sixty-six provinces (*oblasti*) of the Russian Republic in 1960 and 1963 indicates little change (Tsentral'noe Statisticheskoe Upravlenie, 1964, pp. 316–18):

	1960	1963
ratio between the fourth and first quartiles of the distribution of the provinces	2·0	1·8
ratio between the means of the highest and lowest 25 per cent of the provinces	3·1	3·2
ratio between the highest and the lowest single provinces	8·4	8·6

Amongst the several republics comprising the Soviet Union, the richest one in the above terms – Turkmenia – had almost four times as large an income in 1963 as the poorest one – Georgia (Tsentral'noe Statisticheskoe Upravlenie, 1964, p. 347). A number of scattered sources indicates that ratios of two to one, three to one, and even higher within a republic or a province are quite usual. If so, income disparities between the richer and poorer farms become large indeed, and considerably larger than the ratios stated in the text above. On the other hand, a comparison of money income alone can exaggerate the advantage enjoyed by a cotton-producing area like Turkmenia, or by the seemingly rich Far Eastern provinces where the price level is likely to be higher than in the more central parts of the country. But it is important to note that these inequalities persist in spite of price differentials against the richer regions.

rich farms. That both the existing inequality and the remedy for it are linked with allocation of resources is hardly ever mentioned. Perhaps the discussion of these finer points in Soviet literature is premature, plagued as their agriculture still is with crude central planning, administrative interference and other problems.

In making the list of my recommendations based on Table 2, however, I shall retain our initial, though still unrealistic under Soviet conditions, assumptions that the peasants will be free to run the kolkhozes as they see fit (short of disbanding the kolkhoz system altogether) – there have been definite moves in that direction lately – and that relative price ratios will reflect real scarcities. Now a difficult (for an economic theorist) choice must be made between being original, if unrealistic, and being conventional and practical. For what could be more original and striking than recommendations derived from the 'Pure Model', namely that rent should be increased (or imposed) and terms of trade turned against the peasants in order to make them work longer and harder for the kolkhoz? This would indeed vindicate Stalin's agricultural policies, even though he had arrived at them without building any models.

Dismissing the 'Pure Model', we come to the following list of recommendations:

1 To allow the prices of material inputs and of agricultural outputs to move to their equilibrium levels as determined by demand–supply conditions, even at the expense of a sharp rise in peasant gross incomes.

2 To abolish the income tax paid by the kolkhozes.

3 To impose a rent on each farm related to its location, soil fertility, and other natural conditions.[25]

If this list is so conventional as to create an anticlimax, I apologize. Now and then conventional economic theory does give the right answers, even when applied to a Soviet kolkhoz, and – I almost forgot to make explicit a rather essential recommendation – provided that the kolkhoz be permitted to engage in as much positive or negative hiring of labor as it can

25 I do not mean to imply that these three measures are all that is required to create a healthy agriculture in the Soviet Union. Others, such as increased investment, may be as, or even more, important, but they are not relevant to this paper. Recent agricultural reforms (*Izvestiia*, 27 March; 11, 13 April 1965; *Pravda*, 7 November, 26 December 1965; 5 January, 20 February 1966) have raised prices in agricultural products, reduced prices on machinery and vehicles, cut taxes, promised more investment financed by the state, short- and long-term credit, and greater freedom to peasants in decision-making (see note 6). But there was no mention of the imposition of rent as such; since the Soviet constitution assures the kolkhozes of the free use of their land, the imposition of a formal rent would require a major change which would encounter ideological difficulties.

and wants. If this freedom brings it suspiciously close to a profit-maximizing capitalist firm, the similarity could be declared to be purely coincidental.

Two *caveats* are in order:

1 These conclusions have been derived from a model which proved to be highly sensitive to seemingly innocent changes in assumptions. If I think that my final creation is fairly realistic, so must Ward have thought about his.

2 Judged by strictly economic criteria the co-op has not come out well. But even on these grounds, it is quite possible that a co-op may be more efficient than a capitalist or a state-owned firm in societies where membership in the co-op, as contrasted with hiring out for a job, has a strong positive effect on workers' incentives (though hardly the case in Soviet kolkhozes). And so may the co-op's capitalist cousin – a firm with a profit-sharing scheme.

Mathematical Appendix to the 'Pure Model'

1 *Equilibrium conditions for the co-op*

Maximize 1 subject to 2

$$v = -\pi/x_n = (-\sum_1^{n-1} p_i x_i - R)/x_n,\qquad\qquad 1$$

$$f(x_1, ..., x_n) = 0,\qquad\qquad 2$$

and form with a Lagrange's multiplier

$$z = -\frac{\pi - \lambda f(x_1, ..., x_n)}{x_n}.\qquad\qquad 3$$

Equating $\partial z/\partial x_i = 0$ $(i = 1, ..., n)$ we obtain

$$\lambda f_i = p_i \ (i = 1, ..., n-1),\qquad\qquad 4$$

$$\lambda f_n x_n = -\pi.\qquad\qquad 5$$

To derive second-order conditions, take

$$dz = -\frac{x_n \, d\pi - \pi \, dx_n}{x_n^2},\qquad\qquad 6$$

$$d^2z = -\frac{-\pi x_n \, d^2x_n - 2x_n \, d\pi \, dx_n + 2\pi \, dx_n^2}{x_n^3},\qquad\qquad 7$$

on the assumption that x_n is the only dependent variable, so that

$$d^2\pi = \sum_1^{n-1} p_i \, d^2x_i = 0.$$

From **2** and **7**,

$$d^2z = \frac{\pi x_n \sum_1^n \sum_1^n f_{ij}\, dx_i\, dx_j - 2f_n\, x_n\, d\pi\, dx_n + 2f_n\, \pi\, dx_n^2}{f_n x_n^3}.$$ 8

From **1** and **4**,

$$d\pi = \lambda \sum_1^{n-1} f_i\, dx_i.$$ 9

Substituting **5** and **9** into **8**, we obtain

$$d^2z = (\lambda/x_n^2)\left(x_n \sum_1^n \sum_1^n f_{ij}\, dx_i\, dx_j + 2dx_n \sum_1^{n-1} f_i\, dx_i + 2f_n\, dx_n^2 \right);$$ 10

$$d^2z = (\lambda/x_n)\left\{ \sum_1^n \sum_1^n f_{ij}\, dx_i\, dx_j + 2\,(dx_n/x_n) \sum_1^n f_i\, dx_i \right\},$$ 11

which can be expressed as

$$d^2z = (\lambda/x_n)\,\{ f_{11}\, dx_1^2 + f_{12}\, dx_1\, dx_2 + \ldots (f_{1n} + f_1/x_n)\, dx_1\, dx_n +$$ 12
$$+ f_{12}\, dx_1\, dx_2 + f_{22}\, dx_2^2 + \ldots (f_{2n} + f_2/x_n)\, dx_2\, dx_n +$$
$$+ \ldots + \ldots + \ldots +$$
$$+ (f_{1n} + f_1/x_n)\, dx_1\, dx_n + (f_{2n} + f_1/x_n)\, dx_2\, dx_n$$
$$+ \ldots (f_{nn} + 2f_n/x_n)\, dx_n^2 \},$$

subject to $\sum_1^n f_i\, dx_i = 0.$ 13

Since $\lambda/x_n < 0$ (because $x_n < 0$), second order conditions for a maximum of d^2z require that the determinant

$$D = \begin{vmatrix} 0 & f_1 & f_2 & \ldots f_n \\ f_1 & f_{11} & f_{12} & \ldots (f_{1n} + f_1/x_n) \\ f_2 & f_{12} & f_{22} & \ldots (f_{2n} + f_2/x_n) \\ \vdots & \vdots & \vdots & \vdots \\ f_n & (f_{1n} + f_1/x_n) & (f_{2n} + f_1/x_n) & \ldots (f_{nn} + 2f_n/x_n) \end{vmatrix} < 0.$$ 14

Multiplying the first row by $1/x_n$ and subtracting it from the last, and performing the same operation on the first and the last columns as well, we reduce D to the well known 'bordered' determinant F,

$$F = \begin{vmatrix} 0 & f_1 & f_2 & \ldots f_n \\ f_1 & f_{11} & f_{12} & \ldots f_{1n} \\ f_2 & f_{12} & f_{22} & \ldots f_{2n} \\ \vdots & \vdots & \vdots & \vdots \\ f_n & f_{1n} & f_{2n} & \ldots f_{nn} \end{vmatrix} < 0.$$ 15

Thus the second order conditions for the equilibrium of the co-op and of the capitalist firm are the same.

In order to find the reactions of the co-op to changes in rent and prices, **2**, **3** and **4** are differentiated in the usual manner. The solutions of the resulting system of equations prove to be functions of the determinant F and of its co-factors (Allen, 1956, p. 615). So, of course, are the reactions of a capitalist firm to a change in price. Hence it is possible to express the reactions of the co-op in terms of the corresponding reactions of the twin, marked here with asterisks. As stated in the list of symbols,

$$E^*(x_i p_j) = (\partial x_i / \partial p_j) * (p_j / x_i) \quad i, j = 1, ..., n,$$

all indicating capitalist reactions. No asterisk is required for x_i because the twin and co-op are originally in the same equilibrium position.

2 The effects of a change in R

The differentiation of **2**, **4** and **5** in respect of R gives the system of equations

$$\sum_1^n f_i \frac{\partial x_i}{\partial R} = 0, \tag{16}$$

$$f_1 \left(\frac{1}{\lambda} \frac{\partial \lambda}{\partial R} \right) + \sum_1^n f_{1i} \frac{\partial x_i}{\partial R} = 0,$$

$$f_2 \left(\frac{1}{\lambda} \frac{\partial \lambda}{\partial R} \right) + \sum_1^n f_{2i} \frac{\partial x_i}{\partial R} = 0,$$

$$\vdots$$

$$f_n \left(\frac{1}{\lambda} \frac{\partial \lambda}{\partial R} \right) + \sum_1^n \left(f_{in} + \frac{f_i}{x_n} \right) \frac{\partial x_i}{\partial R} = \frac{1}{\lambda x_n}.$$

Multiplying the first equation by $1/x_n$ and subtracting it from the last we reduce the latter to

$$f_n \left(\frac{1}{\lambda} \frac{\partial \lambda}{\partial R} \right) + \sum_1^n f_{in} \frac{\partial x_i}{\partial R} = \frac{1}{\lambda x_n}. \tag{17}$$

Now the system of equations **16** and **17** is based on the matrix given in **15**. We can immediately derive

$$\frac{\partial x_n}{\partial R} = \left(\frac{1}{x_n} \right) \frac{F_{nn}}{\lambda F} = \frac{1}{x_n} \left(\frac{\partial x_n}{\partial p_n} \right)^*, \tag{18}$$

where F_{ij} is the co-factor of f_{ij} in F, and

$$\frac{\partial x_i}{\partial R} = \left(\frac{1}{x_n} \right) \frac{F_{in}}{\lambda F} = \frac{1}{x_n} \left(\frac{\partial x_i}{\partial p_n} \right)^*, \quad i \neq n. \tag{19}$$

Since $(\partial x_n/\partial p_n)* > 0$, $x_n < 0$, $\partial x_n/\partial R < 0$ and $-\partial x_n/\partial R > 0$.

If x_i is an output and $(\partial x_i/\partial p_n)* < 0$, $\partial x_i/\partial R > 0$.

If x_i is a nonlabor input, the sign of $\partial x_i/\partial R$ depends on whether x_i is complementary to or substitutable for x_n.

3 The effects of a change in p_1

Differentiate 2, 4, and 5 in respect to p_1, and using the same methods as in the preceding section obtain the system of equations,

$$\sum_1^n f_i \frac{\partial x_i}{\partial p_1} = 0 \tag{20}$$

$$f_1 \left(\frac{1}{\lambda}\frac{\partial \lambda}{\partial p_1}\right) + \sum_1^n f_{1i} \frac{\partial x_i}{\partial p_1} = \frac{1}{\lambda}$$

$$f_2 \left(\frac{1}{\lambda}\frac{\partial \lambda}{\partial p_1}\right) + \sum_1^n f_{2n} \frac{\partial x_i}{\partial p_1} = 0$$

$$\vdots$$

$$f_n \left(\frac{1}{\lambda}\frac{\partial \lambda}{\partial p_1}\right) + \sum_1^n f_{in} \frac{\partial x_i}{\partial p_1} = -\frac{x_1}{\lambda x_n},$$

again based on the matrix given in 15. Hence,

$$\frac{\partial x_1}{\partial p_1} = \frac{F_{11}}{\lambda F} - \left(\frac{x_1}{x_n}\right)\frac{F_{1n}}{\lambda F} = \left(\frac{\partial x_1}{\partial p_1}\right)^* - \frac{x_1}{x_n}\left(\frac{\partial x_n}{\partial p_1}\right)^*, \tag{21}$$

$$\frac{\partial x_n}{\partial p_1} = \frac{F_{1n}}{\lambda F} - \left(\frac{x_1}{x_n}\right)\frac{F_{nn}}{\lambda F} = \left(\frac{\partial x_1}{\partial p_n}\right)^* - \frac{x_1}{x_n}\left(\frac{\partial x_n}{\partial p_n}\right)^*, \tag{22}$$

$$\frac{\partial x_2}{\partial p_1} = \frac{F_{12}}{\lambda F} - \left(\frac{x_1}{x_n}\right)\frac{F_{2n}}{\lambda F} = \left(\frac{\partial x_1}{\partial p_2}\right)^* - \frac{x_1}{x_n}\left(\frac{\partial x_n}{\partial p_2}\right)^*. \tag{23}$$

By multiplying both sides of expressions 21, 22 and 23 by the proper variables, they can be expressed in a more convenient form,

$$E(x_1 p_1) = E^*(x_1 p_1) - E^*(x_n p_1), \tag{24}$$

$$E(x_n p_1) = u_1/u_n\{E^*(x_1 p_n) - E^*(x_n p_n)\}, \tag{25}$$

$$E(x_2 p_1) = u_1/u_2\{E^*(x_1 p_1) - E^*(x_n p_1)\}. \tag{26}$$

[To ease legibility $Ex_2 p_i$ is written as $E(x_2 p_i)$ etc.]

It is important to note that $u_i = p_i x_i < 0$ when x_i is an input.

Two assumptions are made here:

A given relative increase (or decrease) in all inputs in the twin results in a smaller relative increase (or decrease) in outputs taken as a whole, either because the production function has this attribute throughout the relevant range, or because the firm makes a profit (with $R > 0$) and hence operates to the right of the maximum average product point;

The absence of Hicks's 'regression', so that $E^*(x_i p_j) < 0$ if x_i is an output, x_j an input, and $E^*(x_i p_j) > 0$ if x_i is an input, x_j an output.

Actually, the presence of regression would weaken some results while strengthening others. It does not seem to me that the problem in hand is sufficiently important to warrant additional explorations of cases arising from the great variety of relationships among inputs and outputs possible in a generalized production function (even subject to the constraint given in **15**). Only the more probable cases are considered here.

One output, labor the only input. In **24**, $E^*(x_1 p_1) < E^*(x_n p_1)$ because of diminishing returns; therefore, $E(x_1 p_1) < 0$ and output contracts. So does the labor input.

One output, several inputs. The general case is indeterminate. We can establish the sign of $E(x_1 p_1)$ in **24** by making the plausible assumption that the isoquants are radially parallel to each other, so that a change in price p_1 of the output leaves input ratios unchanged, or that $E^*(x_i p_1) = E^*(x_j p_1)$ $(i, j = 2, ..., n)$.

From **2**
$$\sum_1^n p_i \left(\frac{\partial x_i}{\partial p_1}\right)^* = 0, \qquad 27$$

$$p_i \left(\frac{\partial x_i}{\partial p_1}\right)^* = p_i \left(\frac{\partial x_i}{\partial p_1}\right)^* \left(\frac{p_1 x_i}{p_1 x_i}\right) = \frac{u_i E^*(x_i p_1)}{p_1}. \qquad 28$$

$$\sum_1^n u_i E^*(x_i p_1) = 0. \qquad 29$$

If now $E^*(x_i p_1) = E^*(x_j p_1) = E^*(x_n p_1)$ $i, j = 2, ..., n,$

$$u_1 E^*(x_1 p_1) + E^*(x_n p_1) \sum_2^n u_i = 0, \qquad 30$$

$$E^*(x_n p_1) = -u_1 E^*(x_1 p_1) / \sum_2^n u_i. \qquad 31$$

The substitution of **31** into **24** gives

$$E(x_1 p_1) = \left(\sum_1^n u_i / \sum_2^n u_i\right) E^*(x_1 p_1). \qquad 32$$

Now $\sum_1^n u_i > 0$, $E^*(x_1 p_1) > 0$ and $\sum_2^n u_i < 0$,

because $x_i < 0 (i = 2, ..., n)$. Therefore $E(x_1 p_1) < 0$.

In 25 both $E^*(x_1 p_n) < 0$ and $E^*(x_n p_n) < 0$ but because of the presence of other inputs (and diminishing returns) $|E^*(x_1 p_n)| < |E^*(x_n p_n)|$. It follows that $E(x_n p_1) < 0$ (because $u_n < 0$). For the sign of $E(x_2 p_1)$ in 26 see below.

Several inputs and outputs; x_1 is an output

1 The sign of $E(x_1 p_1)$ in 24. If x_1 is a very important user of labor, diminishing returns may make $E^*(x_1 p_1) < E^*(x_n p_1)$ (though this also depends on the behavior of other inputs and outputs), and $E(x_1 p_1) < 0$, similar to the two preceding cases. But if x_1, being one of the several outputs, uses only a moderate part of total labor, then $E^*(x_1 p_1) > E^*(x_n p_2)$ and $E(x_1 p_1) > 0$.

2 The sign of $E(x_1 p_1)$ in 25. $E^*(x_n p_n) < 0$ and, by assumption, $E^*(x_1 p_n) < 0$. In the presence of other inputs (and diminishing returns), we can expect $|E^*(x_1 p_n)| < |E^*(x_n p_n)|$ and $E(x_n p_1) > 0$. But if wages constitute the major part of the cost of x_1 and if the value of the marginal product in the production of x_1 declines more slowly than in other uses of labor, it is possible that the sign of $E(x_n p_1)$ may be reversed.

3 The sign of $E(x_2 p_1)$ in 26, x_2 being an output. Let x_2 be at first all other outputs, or the only other output. Assume $E^*(x_n p_2) > 0$. If x_1 and x_2 are produced in constant proportions, the result is the same as if x_1 were the only output given above. If there is some, but not perfect, complementarity between x_1 and x_2 the result is indeterminate unless we assume that all ratios among inputs in the twin remain constant in spite of a change in p_2, in which case diminishing returns will give $E^*(x_2 p_2) < E^*(x_n p_2)$. Since $0 < E^*(x_1 p_2) < E^*(x_2 p_2)$, $E(x_2 p_1) < 0$. If x_1 and x_2 are competing outputs, $E^*(x_1 p_2) < 0$ and $E(x_2 p_1) < 0$.

In general, a rise in p_1 is likely to increase the output of x_1 and reduce the input of labor as shown above. Hence a reduction in other outputs taken as a whole is highly probable.

If x_2 is one of several outputs and is competitive with x_1, $E(x_2 p_1) < 0$. Otherwise, the result is indeterminate.

4 The sign of $E(x_2 p_1)$ in 26 being an input. Assume $E^*(x_1 p_2) < 0$. If x_2 is highly complementary with x_n, it is likely (but not certain) that $|E^*(x_1 p_1)| < |E^*(x_n p_2)|$ and $E(x_2 p_1) < 0$. If the complementarity is slight, the result is indeterminate. If x_2 and x_n are substitutes, $E^*(x_n p_2) > 0$ and $E(x_2 p_1) < 0$.

Several inputs and outputs: x_1 is an input.

1 The sign of $E(x_1 p_1)$ in 24. Here $E^*(x_1 p_1) < 0$. If there is some complementarity between x_1 and x_n, $|E^*(x_1 p_1)| > |E^*(x_n p_1)|$ and $E^*(x_1 p_1) < 0$, unless they are used in constant proportions, in which case $E(x_1 p_1) = 0$. If x_1 and x_n are substitutes, $E^*(x_n p_1) > 0$ and $E(x_1 p_1) < 0$.

2 The sign of $E(x_n p_1)$ in 25. With some complementarity between x_1 and x_n, $E^*(x_1 p_n) < |E^*(x_n p_n)|$ and $E(x_n p_1) > 0$. If they are substitutes $E^*(x_1 p_n) > 0$ and again $E(x_n p_1) > 0$. Only when x_1 and x_n are used in constant proportions $E(x_n p_1) = 0$. So the increase in the price of any non-labor input, even when complementary with labor, increases the use of labor (except for constant proportions).

3 The sign of $E(x_2 p_1)$ in 26, x_2 being an output or an input. Unless specific assumptions are made about the interrelationships among the variables involved, the result is indeterminate.

A comment on the effects of the magnitude of R on $E(x_1 p_1)$ and $E(x_n p_1)$ in 24 and 25. Since $p_n = v$, we obtain from 1

$$p_n x_n = -\left(\sum_{1}^{n-1} p_i x_i - R \right). \qquad\qquad 33$$

Differentiating both sides of this expression in respect to p_1 and taking advantage of $\sum_{1}^{n} p_i \, (\partial x_i / \partial p_1) = 0$, in equilibrium (Allen, 1956, p. 615) we find that

$$\partial p_n / \partial p_1 = -x_1 / x_n, \qquad\qquad 34$$

and therefore $\quad \left(\dfrac{\partial p_n}{\partial p_1} \right) \dfrac{p_1}{p_n} = \dfrac{p_1 x_1}{\displaystyle\sum_{1}^{n-1} p_i x_i - R}. \qquad\qquad 35$

Thus a larger R makes p_n more sensitive to a rise in p_1 and hence causes a greater reduction in labor input in response to a given rise in p_1. So $|E(x_n p_1)|$ is increased. But on $E(x_1 p_1)$ in 24, R does not have a clear effect, because a large R implies a small payroll for the twin and a reduction in the importance of labor cost. It is possible that the magnitude of R has no effect on $E(x_1 p_1)$ at all, and this is indeed the case with a Cobb–Douglas production function consisting of one output and several inputs, and subject to decreasing returns to scale.

References

ABRAMOV, F. (1963), *New Life – A Day on a Collective Farm*, Grove Press, New York.

Akademiia Nauk SSSR, Institut Ekonomiki (1963), *Material'noe stimulirovanie razvitiia kolkhoznova proizvodstva*, Moscow.

ALLEN, R. G. D. (1939), *Mathematical Analysis for Economists*, St Martins Press, New York.

ALLEN, R. G. D. (1956), *Mathematical Economics*, Macmillan.

AVERCH, H., and JOHNSON, L. (1962), 'The firm under regulatory constraint', *Amer. econ. Rev.*, vol. 52, pp. 1052–69.

BAUMOL, W. J. (1959), *Business Behaviour, Value and Growth*, Harcourt Brace Jahnovich, New York.

HICKS, J. R. (1946), *Value and Capital*, 2nd ed., Oxford University Press.

Kommunist (1962), 'The calculation of collective farm production costs' as reported in *Current Digest of Soviet Press*, 1962, vol. 14, 10 October, pp. 3–11.

LUTZ, F., and LUTZ, V. (1951), *The Theory of Investment of the Firm*, Greenwood Press, Westport, Connecticut.

MILLAR, J. R. (1965), *Income and Price Formation in the Soviet Collective Farm Sector since 1953*, unpublished doctoral dissertation, Cornell University.

Nauchno–Isseldovatel'skii Finansovyi Institut (1963), *Denezhnye dokhody kolkhozo i differentsial'naia renta*, Moscow.

ROZHIN, B. P. (1961), *Nekotorye voprosy pod"ema ekonomiki stabykh kolkhozov*, Moscow.

SCITOVSKY, T. (1943), 'A note on profit maximization and its implications', *Rev. econ. Stud.*, vol. 11, pp. 57–60; reprinted in G. J. Stigler and K. E. Boulding Irwin (eds.) (1952), *The Readings in Price Theory*, American Economic Association.

SHERMENEVA, M. K. (1963), *Finansy i kreditovanie sel'skokhoziaistvenykh predpriiatii*, Moscow.

Tsentral'noe Statisticheskoe Upravlenie pri Sovete Ministrov RSFSR (1964), *Narodnoe khoziaistvo RSFSR v 1963 godu. Statisticheskii czhegodnik*, Moscow.

Tsentral'noe Statisticheskoe Upravlenie pri Sovete Ministrov SSSR (1964), *Narodnoe khoziaistvo SSSR v 1963 godu. Statisticheskii czhegodnik*, Moscow.

TUGAN-BARANOVSKY, M. I. (1921), *Sotsial'nyia osnovy kooperatsii*, Berlin.

WARD, B. (1958), 'The firm in Illyria: market syndicalism', *Amer. econ. Rev.*, vol. 48, pp. 566–89.

WESTFIELD, F. M. (1965), 'Regulation and conspiracy', *Amer. econ. Rev.*, vol. 55, pp. 424–43.

25 J. E. Meade

The Theory of Labour-Managed Firms and of Profit Sharing[1]

J. E. Meade, 'The theory of labour-managed firms and profit sharing', *Economic Journal*, Special issue in honour of E. A. G. Robinson, March 1972, pp. 402–28.

One important problem in industrial economics which deserves more attention from economic theorists than it has received in the past is the effects of different forms of industrial organisation upon economic efficiency. To take one such question, what would happen if workers hired capital instead of capitalist entrepreneurs hiring workers? Professor J. Vanek has recently made an important contribution to this subject. Building on the work of two other economists (Ward, 1958, 1967; Domar, Reading 24), he has produced a full-scale textbook on the theory of labour-managed economies (Vanek, 1970). In this book he investigates the properties of a system in which workers get together and form collectives or partnerships to run firms; they hire capital and purchase other inputs and they sell the products of the firm at the best prices they can obtain in the markets for inputs and outputs; they themselves bear the risk of any unexpected gain or loss and distribute the resulting surplus among themselves, all workers of any one given grade or skill receiving an equal share of the surplus; their basic objective is assumed to be to maximise the return per worker. For shorthand we will in what follows refer to this as the Cooperative system.

Professor Vanek contrasts the micro-and macro-results of such a system with those of the textbook capitalist model in which an entrepreneur hires all the inputs (including labour) and sells all the outputs of a firm at market prices, bears the risks and runs the firm in such a way as to maximize the total surplus of revenues from the sale of outputs over costs of the purchase of inputs. For ease of reference I shall call this the Entrepreneurial system.

Many essential features of the contrast between the two systems are not basically affected by the question whether the capital resources of the community are privately owned or are socialized and owned by the State. In the case of a Cooperative the workers may be hiring their capital resources either in a competitive capital market fed by private savings or else from a central governmental organisation which lends out the State's

1 The author would like to thank Professors A. B. Atkinson, E. H. Phelps Brown and R. C. O. Matthews for many helpful comments in the preparation of this article.

capital resources at rentals which will clear the market. The contrasting features of the Entrepreneurial system are equally well portrayed by a system in which the managers of socialized plants are told to hire inputs and sell outputs at given prices, the managers operating so as to maximize the total surplus of the plant and the State setting the prices so as to clear the markets.

Section two

Let us start then with an enumeration of what appear to us to be the five main differences which Professor Vanek notes between the two systems.

Difference 1: incentives

A worker hired at a given hourly wage in an Entrepreneurial firm will have to observe the minimum standard of work and effort in order to keep his job; but he will have no immediate personal financial motive and, particularly in the case of a large concern, may well have little or no social participatory motivation to behave in a way which will promote the profitability of the enterprise. He may, of course, take a pride in his work; and he may well wish to stand well with his employer in order to achieve security and promotion in his job. But any extra profit due to his extra effort will in the first place accrue to the entrepreneur. It is difficult and in many cases impossible to overcome this problem by a system of piece-rate wages; and in any case the problem is not one simply of incentives to work harder and to produce more.

Let us go to the other extreme and consider a one-man Cooperative, i.e. a single self-employed worker who hires his equipment. He can balance money income against leisure and other amenities by pleasing himself over hours of work, holidays, the pace and concentration of work, tea-breaks or the choice of equipment and methods of work which will make his work more pleasant at the cost of profitability. Any innovative ideas which he has, he can apply at once and reap the whole benefit himself. And so on over a whole range of qualities and conditions of his working life.

The trouble is, of course, that there are economies of scale which mean that a one-man firm must normally be ruled out. In an n-man Cooperative the individual worker who shares the profit with his fellows will still get some direct benefit from any additional profit due to his own effort; but it will be only an nth of the result of his own efforts. If to reap the technical advantages of scale n must be large, then the direct advantage in financial incentives of the Cooperative over the Entrepreneurial firm may be small. But even in this case the sense of participation may be greater and thus provide a stronger social motivation to do the best for the firm as a whole, i.e. for the whole partnership of fellow workers.

This last consideration takes one out of the realms of strict economic analysis into those of the industrial and social psychologists and socio-logists; and it must be left to them to consider what is perhaps in fact the decisive question, namely whether or not there would be difficulties of disciplined administration in a self-governing Cooperative which would offset in part or whole the improved incentives which it would enjoy. One conclusion, however, may be reached. The most efficient scale for a Co-operative is likely to be smaller than for an Entrepreneurial firm; for in the case of the former but not of the latter a reduction in the number of workers increases the direct economic incentives for efficiency of the individual worker.

So much for difference 1. If we abstract from this difference in incen-tives and also from any differences due to the effects of risks, it can be shown that both the Cooperative and the Entrepreneurial systems will lead to the same Pareto-optimal equilibrium situations in the long-run, provided that there is perfect mobility of factors, including perfectly free and costless entry and exit of new firms in any industry and that there is perfect competition in the sense that no individual economic agent can by his own decisions affect appreciably any market price. Differences become apparent, however, as soon as we consider the short run, modify the assumption of free and costless entry of firms, or allow for monopolistic conditions. We will consider each of these three cases below under dif-ferences 2, 3 and 4 respectively. But before we do so, we must consider the long-run Pareto-optimal outcome of the two systems.

Let us do this first by considering a firm in an industry in which there are only two inputs – a homogeneous worker L who works a given number of hours at a given intensity, and a fixed capital good K, these two factors producing an output X with a production function $X = X(L, K)$ in which there is some substitutability between L and K.[2] Let P_x be the price of a

2 The firm's production function may be such as to result, with given prices of the two inputs, in either a U-shaped or an L-shaped long-run cost curve, as in the figure.

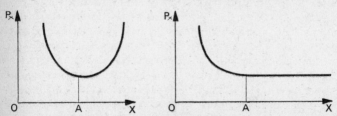

In order to rule out the one-man firm the cost per unit must at first fall because of economies of large-scale production, but in order that perfect competition should be possible the total demand for the industry's output must be many times the amount OA which, for an individual firm, is sufficient to lead to minimum cost per unit.

unit of X and W the market wage rate of labour in an Entrepreneurial firm. If the price of a machine (a unit of K) is P_k and if i is the market rate of interest, then iP_k is the rental paid for the hire of a machine. In an Entrepreneurial firm more (or less) labour will be hired if the value of the marginal product of labour $P_x(\partial X/\partial L)$ is greater (less) than the wage rate of labour W; and more (or less) machinery will be hired if the value of the marginal product of a machine $P_x(\partial X/\partial K)$ is greater (less) than the rental payable for a machine (iP_k). These relationships are shown in columns 1 and 2 of the Table.

In a Cooperative machinery is hired in the same way as in an Entrepreneurial firm and the same rule is, therefore, relevant. Machinery will be hired up to the point at which the value of its marginal product is equal to its rental. But the considerations governing the size of the labour force are different. If one more partner is accepted into a Cooperative, he will add to the revenue of the Cooperative an amount equal to the value of his marginal product $P_x(\partial X/\partial L)$; in a Cooperative he will receive the same share of the total surplus as do all the other partners, $(P_x X - iP_k K)/L$; if, therefore,

$$P_x \frac{\partial X}{\partial L} > \frac{P_x X - iP_k K}{L},$$

he will add to the surplus of the Cooperative something more than the existing surplus per head, so that the surplus per head can be raised for all the partners. Thus the existing partners will wish to build up the partnership until the value of the marginal product of labour is equal to the average earnings per worker. These relationships are shown for the Cooperative in column 3 of the Table.

It is now easy to see why both systems lead to the same long-run, free-entry-and-exit, and perfect-competition solution. As far as K is concerned, in both cases it is attracted from points where the value of its marginal product is low to points where it is high by a competitive process in which either the Entrepreneurial manager is attempting to maximise the surplus for the entrepreneur's or state's pocket or else the Cooperative partners are attempting to maximize the surplus for distribution between them. As far as L is concerned, in the Entrepreneurial firm the same competitive process will attract it to the uses in which the value of its marginal product is highest. In the Cooperative the process is different, but the final result the same. First, in each Cooperative L will be attracted until the value of its marginal product is equal to the average earnings of the existing workers in that firm. Second, if as a result of this the average earnings are higher in one industry than another workers will be attracted from Cooperatives in the industry of low earnings to set up new Cooperatives in

Table 1

Increase or decrease in K and L according to inequality	Entre-preneurial	Cooperative	Inegalitarian Cooperative	Joint-Stock	Inegalitarian Joint-Stock	Inegalitarian Joint-Stock Cooperative
$P_x \, (\partial X/\partial K) \gtrless$	iP_k	iP_k	iP_k	$\dfrac{P_x X - WL}{K}$	rP_k	rP_k
$P_x \, (\partial X/\partial L) \gtrless$	W	$\dfrac{P_x X - iP_k K}{L}$	E_0	W	W	E_0

the industry of high earnings; the output of the high earning product will rise and its price will fall, until earnings, and so the value of marginal products of labour, are equalised in all industries.

Difference 2: short-run adjustment

The short-run process of adjustment is, however, very different. Let us suppose that the capital is fixed in amount in each firm in the short run, but that the number of workers is variable. Suppose that we start in a full equilibrium and that then the demand price for the particular product X rises, while all other demand prices remain unchanged. In the Entrepreneurial system labour will be attracted into the X-industry, since the value of the marginal product of L is now higher in the production of X; and this is a Pareto-optimal process of adjustment, since L can be shifted from its low-valued to its high-valued uses, even though K is *ex hypothesi* not shiftable immediately from its low-valued to its high-valued uses.

But the short-run effect in the Cooperative system will be to reduce, not to increase, the levels of employment and output which will maximize earnings per head in the X-industry firms. A rise in the selling price of X will, of course, in itself raise both the value of the marginal product of labour and the average earnings per head in the X-industry firms; but it will raise the value of the marginal product of labour less than the average earnings[3] and it will thus mean that the average earnings could be still further raised if one worker was dismissed. The value of the reduction in the firm's output would be less than the amount paid by the Cooperative to the dismissed worker; and the remaining partners would gain by his dismissal.

This relationship is shown in Figure 1.

Measure the number of workers on the horizontal axis and money payments per worker on the vertical axis. Draw a rectangular hyperbola MN such that the rectangle $STUO$ has a constant value of $iP_k K$, the total rental payable for the hire of K. Then TU measures $(iP_k K)/L$ or the burden of debt payment per worker when the number of workers is OU. Draw a curve PQ such that its height measures $(P_x X)/L$ or the total value of receipts per worker, i.e. output per head multiplied by the price of output. Net earnings per head are then the excess of the height of the curve PQ over the height of the curve MN i.e. $(P_x X - iP_k K)/L$. These earnings are maximised

---

3 Suppose $P_x = £1$, $\partial X/\partial L = 1$, $X = 100$, $iP_k K = £50$ and $L = 50$.

Then $P_x \dfrac{\partial X}{\partial L} = £1$ and $\dfrac{P_x X - iP_k K}{L} = \dfrac{£100 - £50}{50} = £1$.

If P_x rises to £1.10, $P_x \dfrac{\partial X}{\partial L}$ rises to £1.10; but $\dfrac{P_x X - iP_k K}{L}$ rises to $\dfrac{£110 - £50}{50} = £1.20$.

at *CB*, where the slope of the curve *PQ* is the same as that of the curve *MN*. The optimum number of worker–partners is thus *OA*.

Suppose now that P_x rises by 10 per cent, then the curve *PQ* is replaced by the curve *RQ* which is 10 per cent higher than the curve *PQ* at every value of *L*. Consider now a volume of labour *OE* which is somewhat less than *OA*. Since *HG* = 10 per cent of *GE* and *DC* = 10 per cent of *CA* and since *GE* > *CA*, *HG* must be > *DC*. In other words the slope of *RQ* at *D*

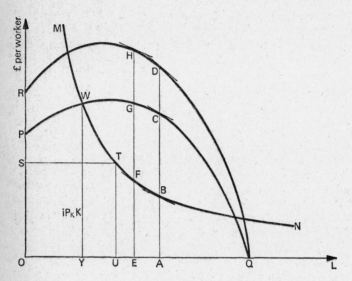

Figure 1

is steeper than the slope of *PQ* at *C* which is equal to the slope of *MN* at *B*. Since the slope of *RQ* is greater than the slope of *MN* with employment at *OA*, it will be possible by reducing the number of workers to *OE* (where the slope of *RQ* at *H* is equal to the slope of *MN* at *F*) to raise average earnings. The rise in P_x will itself raise earnings (*DB* > *CB*); but these can be raised still more if the number of workers is reduced (*HF* > *DB*).

The commonsense of this result can easily be seen in the following way:
1 With a fixed debt interest it is to the interest of the worker–partners to have a large partnership so that debt per head may be small.
2 With decreasing returns to labour applied to a given amount of capital it is desirable to have a small partnership so that the value of output per head may be high.
A rise in the selling price of the product or a fall in the rental of capital will

increase the importance of influence 2 relatively to influence 1 and will, therefore, work in the direction of a smaller partnership.[4]

Professor Vanek seems to assume tacitly in most of his analysis that the rules of a Cooperative would somehow permit the dismissal of a worker if it were to the advantage of the remaining workers, even if it were to the detriment of the dismissed worker.[5] In this case the short-run supply curve of X would be backward-sloping; and this would be highly perverse and inefficient. Pareto-optimality requires that in the short run the variable factor L should be attracted to, not pushed away from, its more highly valued uses.

At a later stage (Section five below) we will return to the question whether a rule which allowed the dismissal of a partner against his will is appropriate. But even if such dismissals are not allowed, there would be no mechanism inducing the existing partners to take the positive step of admitting more partners when the selling price of their product went up and when, in consequence, it would pay each existing partner to reduce rather than to increase the size of the partnership. The short-run supply curve of a Cooperative would at least be highly inelastic – certainly less elastic than the Pareto-optimal Entrepreneurial short-run supply curve.

The rather startling result that a rise in the selling price of a Cooperative's product will in the short run lead to a reduction in the amount produced and a reduction in the volume of employment rests upon the assumption that the firm employs only one variable input, namely L, to produce only one product, namely X. But, as Professor Vanek points out, if we allow for the fact that the firm may well produce more than one product (e.g. products X and Y) and may employ not only labour, L, but also a raw material, M, as a factor which is variable in the short run, these results may need to be modified.

4 As a *curiosum* it may be noted that if the production function were of a Cobb–Douglas variety with $X = K^{\alpha} L^{1-\alpha}$, then the backward-sloping short-run supply curve of X in terms of its price P_x would take the form of a rectangular hyperbola. In a Cooperative L is always adjusted until the earnings of labour are equal to the value of their marginal product; with constant returns to scale this means that what is left over (namely $iP_k K$) will be just sufficient to pay to each unit of capital the value of its marginal product; and with a Cobb–Douglas function in such an equilibrium capital will always be paid a constant proportion α of the value of the output; thus the equation $iP_k K = \alpha P_x X$ with $iP_k K$ as well as α constant in the short run provides the short-run supply curve for X, as depicted in Figure 2 (p. 402).
5 Professor B. Ward makes the assumption explicitly when he writes (1967, p. 186), 'Conflicts might arise in case the criterion by the workers' council would lead to layoffs. But as long as these amounted to less than half the work force (and less than half of the members of the workers' council) a majority decision would still follow the criterion.'
Professor Joan Robinson (1967) very pertinently queries this assumption.

The case of a multiproduct firm is easy to understand. If the price of
X goes up, the Cooperative may well shift from the production of the now
relatively unprofitable Y on to the now relatively profitable X. If X and
Y are very easy substitutes in the firm's production programme, a rise in the
price of X may thus well lead to an increase in the output of X even though,
for the reasons already discussed at length, the Cooperative were to reduce
the absolute level of its employment and total production.

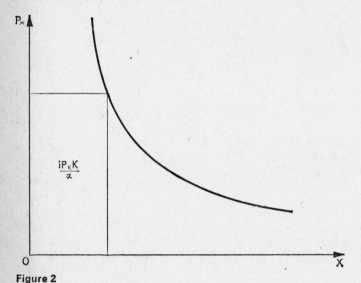

Figure 2

The case of a Cooperative which uses inputs of materials as well as of
labour needs a little more explanation. When the price of its output X
goes up, the Cooperative which buys its material M in the market will, just
like an Entrepreneurial firm, find that the cost-price of M is now less than
the value of the marginal product of M. For example, when the selling-
price of cars goes up, a firm assembling cars, whether it be a Cooperative
or an Entrepreneurial firm, will wish to purchase more components to
assemble because the profit margin on each assembled set of components
has risen. Suppose:

The marginal product of M does not fall at all rapidly as more X is
produced (that is to say, with the existing capital equipment K, a greater
throughput on the assembly line is fairly readily possible);
Labour L and materials M are rather highly complementary (that is to
say, it is difficult to reduce the labour per car assembled).

Then the possibility of extra profit because of the increased margin between the cost of M and the selling price of X may be more important in leading to an increased need for labour than the factors which we have previously examined can be in leading to a contraction in the labour force.

For these reasons with firms with many outputs and with many variable inputs the extreme paradoxical results of an increased selling price leading to reduced employment and output may disappear. But this in no way modifies what is the result of major importance which our previous analysis revealed. If the selling price of something produced by a Cooperative does go up, clearly the workers in that firm can improve their average earnings whether this is accompanied by a rise or by a fall in output or in employment. Moreover, the new level of employment which will maximize earnings per head will always be that which equates the value of the marginal product of labour to its average earnings. This bit of our previous analysis is in no way modified; one can always raise earnings per head by taking on one more worker so long as what he adds net to total revenue is greater than the existing level of earnings per head. Thus in the new equilibrium situation the average earnings and so the value of the marginal product of labour in the firm in question will be higher than before and will thus be higher than it is in the other outside occupations whose situation has not been improved. The Cooperative, unlike the Entrepreneurial firm, will, therefore, fail in the short run to attract the variable factor L from points in which the value of its marginal product is low to points where it is high. This is the essential point.

Difference 3: the importance of free entry

In the Cooperative system this situation is ultimately restored only by the free entry of new firms into any industry which has become exceptionally lucrative as a result of a rise in its selling prices. It is thus clear that the competitive pressures of free entry play a much more important role in a Cooperative than they do in an Entrepreneurial system. This can be illustrated in the following way. Consider a competitive industry with a large number of firms producing at constant returns to scale, i.e. firms with L-shaped cost curves of the kind shown in footnote 2 above, each producing an output appreciably greater than OA. P_x then rises. In an Entrepreneurial system firms take on more labour until the value of the marginal product of labour, $P_x(\partial X/\partial L)$, has fallen again to the ruling wage rate W partly as a result of the reduction in the marginal physical product of labour $\partial X/\partial L$ as more L is applied to the fixed amount of K and partly as a result of the reduction in P_x as more X is produced. The value of the marginal product of capital $P_x(\partial X/\partial K)$ will now be greater than the ruling rental iP_k because P_x will still be somewhat greater than before and the physical marginal product of capital $\partial X/\partial K$ will also have been raised because more L is now applied to the given amount of K. The Entrepreneurial firm will, therefore, invest in more K. The process will go on until P_x has fallen to its initial level (since the long-run cost curve is horizontal) and an increased X is produced by the use of more K and more L, both K and L being increased in the same proportion as X. The process does not in this case require the entry of any new firms, though new firms may come in.

In the Cooperative the first effect of the rise in P_x is to reduce L and X. This will go on until the marginal product of labour is so raised (as a result of the reduced application of L to the given amount of K) that the value of the marginal product of labour $P_x(\partial X/\partial L)$ has been raised once more as high as the amount of net average earnings per worker $(P_x X - iP_k K)/L$.[6] If and when a new equilibrium is reached, the earnings of workers will be equal to the value of their marginal products. With constant returns to scale what is then 'left over' as a return to capital (namely, $iP_k K$) will be just sufficient to pay to each unit of capital the value of marginal product $P_x(\partial X/\partial K)K$. The reduction in the amount of L will have reduced the marginal product of K until $P_x(\partial X/\partial K)$, which had been raised above iP_k by the rise in P_x, is once more reduced to equality with iP_k as a result of the fall in $\partial X/\partial K$.[7] The situation will then be that the existing Cooperatives are producing less X with the same amount of K and with less L in circumstances in which the value of the marginal product of labour is equal to the average earnings in the firms concerned but is greater than the value of the marginal product and the earnings of labour in other industries, and the value of the marginal product of capital is equal to the rental of capital, so that the existing firms have no incentive to invest in more capital. This is a Pareto non-optimal situation; restoration of the situation rests wholly upon the possibility of the free entry of new firms; and it should be emphasized that free entry involves workers who are unemployed as a result of the contraction of the firms in the X-industry getting together with workers in other industries who are earning less than the X-industry workers, and setting up new firms in the X-industry. The costs and institutional problems involved in such company promotion are not analysed in Professor Vanek's book.

6 We must assume that the demand curve for X is sufficiently price-elastic. If it were very inelastic, P_x might rise so quickly as the output X was reduced that, with a backward-sloping supply curve of X, the excess demand was not eliminated.
7 $P_x(\partial X/\partial L) = (P_x X - iP_k K)/L$ as a result of the adjustment in L. Since with constant returns to scale $P_x X = P_x L (\partial X/\partial L) + P_x K(\partial X/\partial K)$, it follows that $P_x(\partial X/\partial K) = iP_k K$.

Difference 4: monopolistic behaviour

A closely related difference is that in any given monopolistic conditions the Cooperative will always be more restrictive than the corresponding Entrepreneurial firm. The reason for this can be seen in the following way. Let us start with an Entrepreneurial firm making a positive monopoly profit of $M = P_x X - iP_k K - WL$. If this firm has maximized its monopoly profit it will be in a position in which a small reduction in L will cause no change in M. It follows that a small reduction in L will cause a rise in M/L but,

$$\frac{M}{L} = \frac{P_x X - iP_k K}{L} - W.$$

With W constant, it follows that a small reduction in L will cause a rise in $(P_x X - iP_k K)/L$, i.e. in the average earnings of L in a corresponding Cooperative. In other words in any given monopolistic situation the Cooperative will produce less than the corresponding Entrepreneurial firm.

A particular example of this tendency may be of interest. Consider a case of a monopolistic Entrepreneurial concern with an L-shaped cost curve facing a big demand, so that, as illustrated in Figure 3, it produces on the constant-cost part of its cost curve.

The Entrepreneurial firm produces OB where the marginal cost curve cuts the marginal revenue curve and sells the output at the price BC.

The Cooperative will, however, always produce less than OA (the output which is sufficient to make the average cost curve virtually horizontal), for the following reason. If there are constant returns to scale a 10 per cent reduction in L and K would reduce X by 10 per cent. But if P_x and iP_k were both constant, this 10 per cent reduction in L, K and X would leave $(P_x X - iP_k K)/L$ unchanged. But if as a result of the monopolistic situation P_x goes up when X is reduced by 10 per cent, then $(P_x X - iP_k K)/L$ rises when L, K and X are all reduced by 10 per cent. In other words, in order to maximize surplus per unit of L, there will always be in monopolistic situations, an incentive for a Cooperative to reduce output so long as there are constant returns to scale. Output will be reduced below OA, until the tendency for real costs per unit to rise as output is reduced offsets the tendency for a rise in the selling price of X to raise income per unit of factor inputs.

Professor Vanek concludes from this analysis that in conditions of monopolistic competition each Cooperative will tend to be smaller than the corresponding Entrepreneurial firm; but, he argues, in the Cooperative economy there will be more competing firms than in the Entrepreneurial

economy. This argument rests on the assumption that there will be full
employment in the Cooperative economy or, more precisely, that there
will not be more unemployment in the Cooperative economy than in the
Entrepreneurial economy. If there were the same number of firms but

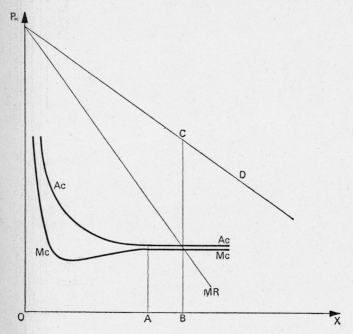

Figure 3

each firm were smaller then there would be more unemployment in the Cooperative economy. If these unemployed got together and set up new
firms, then there would be more, but smaller, firms in the Cooperative
economy.[8] This, in Professor Vanek's view, justifies the view that in a very
real and desirable sense the Cooperative economy will be more competitive than the Entrepreneurial economy. This is a somewhat paradoxical,
but to the present reviewer a convincing conclusion.[9]

8 This conclusion is reinforced by the argument (see p. 395 above) that because
of the effect on incentives the most efficient size of the firm is likely to be smaller
in the Cooperative than in the Entrepreneurial economy.
9 Professor Vanek also claims that there will be less expenditure on advertisement
in the Cooperative economy. The relevant question here is presumably not whether
the individual small Cooperative will spend less absolutely on advertisement than
the individual large Entrepreneurial firm, but whether advertisement expenditure

Difference 5: macroeconomic effects

As a result of the great difference in the short-run behaviour of firms (see difference 2 above), the problems of macroeconomic control of inflations and deflations of price and employment would be strikingly different. A fluctuation in the total money demand for goods as a whole would cause much greater fluctuations in price in the Cooperative than in the Entrepreneurial economy. In an Entrepreneurial economy an increase in total money expenditure engineered through monetary or fiscal policy may lead to some increase in prices, but if there is any considerable initial volume of unemployment, it will lead also, and importantly, to increased employment and output. In a Cooperative economy it will not give any incentive to existing firms to increase output and may indeed, for the reasons discussed in connection with difference 2 above, lead to a reduction in employment and output.[10] Prices are thus likely to fluctuate up and down much more in a Cooperative than in an Entrepreneurial economy, as total money expenditures fluctuate.

But Professor Vanek argues that at the same time it may be much easier in a Cooperative system to avoid a continuing upward inflation of money prices, since there can in a Cooperative economy *ex hypothesi* be no simple straightforward wage-cost inflation. Workers take what money earnings are left over after the firm has conducted its operations; they do not set money wage rates on which employers construct their cost prices. But may

---

per unit of total output will be smaller in the Cooperative than in the Entrepreneurial economy. After covering many sheets of paper with clumsy and inelegant differential calculus the present reviewer can find no plausible reason for giving an emphatic answer 'Yes' to the latter question. It seems to him that it might go either way.

10 Whether it causes an actual decline in output will depend *inter alia* upon the way in which the hire of K by the Cooperative workers is financed. For case (a), suppose that the existing K is financed by a long-term debt whose service is fixed in terms of money. In this case the workers will have a fixed sum (R) to pay in the service of debt. For case (b) suppose that the workers pay a rental of iP_k per unit of K, the terms i and P_k being adjusted from day to day to correspond to market changes in the short-term rate of interest i and the market price of a machine P_k. We start with a firm in equilibrium with

$$P_x \frac{\partial X}{\partial L} = \frac{P_x X - R}{L} \quad \text{in case (a)} \quad \text{and} \quad \frac{P_x X - iP_k K}{L} \quad \text{in case (b).}$$

If P_x and P_k are both inflated by 10 per cent while R remains unchanged the equilibrium is not disturbed in case (b), but in case (a) $P_x (\partial X/\partial L)$ rises less than $(P_x X - R)/L$ and there will be an incentive to reduce the size of the firm of the kind examined in connection with difference 2 above. Thus in case (b) a general inflation of commodity prices will leave output unchanged, while in case (a) it may actually cause a reduction in output and employment.

not this argument be too *simpliste*? In an Entrepreneurial system wage-earners push up money wage-rates; employers then push up prices to maintain their profit margins; and the government permits or engineers a rise in total money expenditures sufficient to maintain full employment at the higher money price level. In a Cooperative system may not workers push up their selling prices directly and the government then permit or engineer a rise in total money expenditures sufficient to equate demand to supply at the higher price level?[11]

But however that may be, the implications for employment policy are very far-reaching. To rely in a Cooperative system on Keynesian policies to expand effective demand in times of unemployment would be at best ineffective, and at worst might lead to a reduction in output and employment. Indeed, as a short-run policy to induce existing firms to give more employment it would be necessary to *decrease* total demand or to *increase* the fixed overhead cost which firms had to face, for example by *raising* some fixed tax on each firm. But it is pretty clear that such policies would be ill-advised. If the short-run elasticities of supply of existing firms are low, then employment cannot be substantially increased except by setting up new firms, a process which may take considerable time both because of the organizational–promotional problems involved and also because of the gestation period for the production of the necessary new fixed capital equipment.

In a Cooperative economy unemployment may well exist. If it does exist, its cure must be found in a longer-term structural policy aimed at promoting the institution of new firms by the unemployed in order to help them in their desire to enjoy the average earnings of an employed worker rather than the pittance of unemployment benefit. This relative short-run intractability of the unemployment problem may seem to be a serious disadvantage of the Cooperative system. But as Professor Vanek rightly points out one must set on the other side of the balance sheet the fact that if a long-run structure is achieved which gives full employment, then it will be much easier to maintain full employment than is the case in an Entrepreneurial system, since fluctuations in total demand will no longer lead to large fluctuations in output and employment. Prices, not output, will bear the brunt of the change.

So far only the macroeconomic effects of effective demand on output and employment, but not those of output and employment on effective demand, have been considered. We may perhaps assume that the consumption function (the effect of real income and employment on consumption) would be the same in both systems. As for the incentive to invest in new

11 With some possible adverse effect on total employment if the finance of fixed capital is by long-term fixed interest loans as in case (*a*) of the previous footnote.

capital goods by existing firms, perhaps we might also consider it to be the same, namely a function of the relationship between the cost of financing new capital goods and the value of the marginal product of new capital goods, investment by an existing firm being greater, the lower was iP_k and the higher $P_x (\partial X/\partial K)$.[12] If this is so, it points to a very fundamental difference in the workings of the two systems. Suppose that there is an initial increase in effective demand. As we have seen (p. 407) in an Entrepreneurial firm this will lead to an increase in output and employment and will also thereby lead to an increase in the value of the marginal product of capital in existing firms who will then (in the absence of any rise in the rate of interest) have an incentive to expand their capital equipment. In the Cooperative, however, there will be no increase in employment and, therefore, no rise in the physical marginal product of capital. Indeed, in the case in which labour can be dismissed from an existing partnership and in which there were constant returns to scale, employment and output would be reduced until the value of the marginal product of capital were equal to its rental (see p. 399). There would be no incentive to invest by existing firms as a result of an increase in effective demand.

But as we have seen, in a Cooperative we must rely much more on investment to set up new firms as a means for coping with unemployment. Suppose then that there is some automatic or government sponsored mechanism for promoting the setting up of new firms, such promotion being intensified as the volume of unemployment grows. Then if there were a reduction in employment and output, there would be a rise in the scale of investment to set up new firms to cope with the increased volume of unemployment.

But what a perverse universe this is! With the Entrepreneurial system a fall in effective demand reduces employment which reduces the marginal product of capital which reduces investment which reduces effective demand which reduces employment ..., a vicious circle of positive feedback. With the Cooperative system a rise in effective demand reduces employment which increases unemployment which increases investment to set up new firms which increases effective demand which increases unemployment ..., another vicious circle of positive feedback. The stability conditions of these two systems might be compared with some interest.[13] But on the face of it the devil seems to win whichever institutional arrangement we may adopt.

12 Professor Vanek (1970, pp. 168–72) discusses at length possible differences in the case of investment by Cooperative and Entrepreneurial firms. There is no space to discuss his views in this article.
13 The reader is referred to Professor Vanek's consideration of the stability of his labour-managed economy (1970, pp. 204–9).

Section three

So much for the main features of Professor Vanek's analysis. It is interesting to consider what are the basic institutional features which give rise to these differences in the workings of the two systems. We may ask whether the differences are due (i) to the fact that in a Cooperative the objective is to maximize a residual surplus per unit of a factor input (earnings per worker) whereas in an Entrepreneurial firm the objective is to maximize a residual total surplus (total company profit), or (ii) to the fact that in a Cooperative the factor which is variable in the short-run (L) is the hiring factor whereas in an Entrepreneurial system it is a hired factor.

We can answer this question by considering an institutional set-up in which owners of machines K get together, put their machines into a common enterprise, hire labour L and sell the output X on the best terms which they can obtain on the market, and run the concern so as to maximize the return per machine. This system which for ease of reference we will call a Joint-Stock system is exactly analogous to a Cooperative except that it is the factor which is fixed in the short-run (K) which hires the factor which is variable in the short-run (L) instead of the other way round. In conditions of perfect competition the management rules for maximizing the return per unit of K for the existing K-partners will be (i) to hire more labour until the value of the marginal product of labour is equal to the market wage rate and (ii), if possible, to expand the size of the partnership by getting more adventurers to put machines into the enterprise so long as the value of the marginal product of machines $P_x (\partial X/\partial K)$ is greater than the average return per machine in the enterprise as it exists at present $(P_x X - WL)/K$. These rules are shown in column 5 of the Table on p. 398.

As far as labour incentives are concerned (difference 1 above), Joint-Stock and Entrepreneurial firms are similar, since in both of these labour is hired at a given wage and told what to do. Moreover, in so far as the short period in which K is fixed is concerned, the objective of an Entrepreneurial firm to maximize a total surplus leads to exactly the same result as the objective of a Joint-Stock firm to maximize surplus per unit of the fixed amount of K. For this reason, as far as the short-run competitive behaviour of the systems are concerned (differences 2, 3 and 5 above), once more Joint-Stock and Entrepreneurial economies are similar and are to be contrasted with a Cooperative economy in which the variable factor (L) does the hiring.[14]

14 At first sight it seems very paradoxical that when P_x rises because of an increased demand for X, there should in the short run be an increase in the production of X if the fixed factor (K) hires the variable factor (L) but a reduction in the production of X if the variable factor (L) hires the fixed factor (K). But when one factor hires another factor, a rise in the selling price of the product by reducing

But so far as monopolistic behaviour is concerned (difference 4) a Joint-Stock firm is very similar in its effects to a Cooperative. A Joint-Stock firm and a Cooperative are more restrictive than an Entrepreneurial firm because they aim at maximizing a surplus per unit of a factor input instead of the total surplus of the firm. The similarity in this connection between a Joint-Stock firm and a Cooperative can be appreciated by simply substituting K for L and L for K in the analysis given above for difference 4. For example, a monopolistic Joint-Stock firm like a monopolistic Cooperative will always have an incentive to reduce output so long as it is producing with constant returns to scale. For if a 10 per cent reduction in K and L would lead to a 10 per cent reduction in X, then the return per machine $(P_x X - WL)/K$ would remain unchanged if the market prices P_x and W remained unchanged. But if P_x rose as X was reduced, $(P_x X - WL)/K$ would rise. Output would be reduced until the increase in real cost due to the low scale of operations offset the ability to raise earnings per machine by raising the price of the output.

In monopolistic conditions there is thus a real difference between an Entrepreneurial firm and a Joint-Stock firm. In what does this consist? An Entrepreneurial firm may be typified by a capitalist firm in which all the capital has been financed by the issue of fixed interest debentures, the entrepreneur being someone who simply bears the risk that the difference between the revenue of the firm and the total bill for interest and wages may be a high or low positive or negative figure. At first sight it might be thought[15] that a Joint-Stock firm could be typified by a capitalist firm in which all the capital was financed by the issue of ordinary shares and in which, therefore, the existing shareholders would wish to maximize surplus per existing share rather than total surplus and would issue new shares to finance an increase in K if and only if this would raise the return per existing share. For reasons which will become clear later, we will refer to such a firm as an Inegalitarian Joint-Stock firm.

In fact, however, this is not so: there is a world of difference between a

---

the real cost of the hired factor will induce each unit of the hiring factor to employ a greater amount of the hired factor. Thus when K is the hiring factor a rise in P_x will induce a rise in L/K which, in the short-run with K constant, means a rise in L. But when L is the hiring factor, a rise in P_x will induce a rise in K/L which, in the short-run with K constant, implies a reduction in L. In the long run, of course, in both systems if there are constant returns to scale L, K and X will all increase in the same proportion until the selling price of the product P_x has fallen once more to the old unchanged long-run cost of production.

15 The author of this paper presented this thought to a seminar at the Delhi School of Economics, but realized his mistake as he lay in bed that evening. He was thus fortunately able to correct his mistake when the seminar met again on the following day.

Joint-Stock firm in which the objective is the maximization of return per machine and an Inegalitarian Joint-Stock firm in which the objective is the maximization of return per share. Let us consider the rules which an Inegalitarian Joint-Stock firm must follow. Since labour is hired at a wage rate W, in perfect competition labour will be hired in the same way as in an Entrepreneurial firm or a Joint-Stock firm up to the point at which the value of its marginal product is equal to the wage rate, $W = P_x (\partial X/\partial L)$.

As far as capital is concerned, we assume that there is a perfectly competitive capital market in which there rules a price P_s at which the ordinary shares S of the firm can be sold. We are assuming that all capital is financed by the issue of ordinary shares, i.e. that all profits are distributed in dividends and none used for the internal finance of development. The yield on the ordinary shares S is thus $(P_x X - WL)/P_s S$; let us call this r. The total return per existing ordinary share $(P_x X - WL)/S$ can be raised by the issue of new shares to finance new capital equipment if the value of the marginal product of a machine $P_x(\partial X/\partial K)$ is greater than rP_k. For suppose that £100 worth of new shares are issued. This enables $100/P_k$ new machines to be purchased and this will add $(100/P_k)P_x (\partial X/\partial K)$ to total revenue at the current marginal productivity of machines. But the dividends which must be paid out to the new shareholders at the current rate of dividend per share will be $100r$.

If $\dfrac{100}{P_k} P_x \dfrac{\partial X}{\partial K} > 100r$,

i.e. if $P_x (\partial X/\partial K) > rP_k$, there will be some net gain which can be used to raise the dividend for all shareholders. These rules are shown in column 6 of the Table on p. 398.

It is clear that the rule for investing more capital in an Inegalitarian Joint-Stock firm is quite different from that for investment in a Joint-Stock firm but is very similar to that in an Entrepreneurial firm with the exception that we are concerned with the earnings yield on ordinary shares (r) instead of the rate of interest on debentures (i).[16]

16 This similiarity applies to monopolistic as well as to competitive conditions.

Let $P_x \left(1 - \dfrac{1}{ed}\right)$ represent the marginal revenue obtained from the sale of an additional unit of X. The Entrepreneurial firm will wish to invest in more K so long as the marginal revenue from the marginal product of K is greater than the rental for a unit of K, i.e. so long as $P_x \left(1 - \dfrac{1}{ed}\right) > iP_k$. The Inegalitarian Joint-Stock firm will wish to invest in more capital so long as the marginal revenue from the marginal product of K is greater than the additional dividends which must be paid on the value of the shares issued to finance the purchase of K, i.e. so long as

$P_x \left(1 - \dfrac{1}{ed}\right) > rP_k.$

Why is this so? The answer becomes clear when we substitute the value $r = (P_x X - WL)/P_s S$ in the expression

$$P_x \frac{\partial X}{\partial K} \lessgtr rP_k \quad \text{and obtain}$$

$$P_x \frac{\partial X}{\partial K} \lessgtr \frac{P_k K}{P_s S} \left(\frac{P_x X - WL}{K} \right).$$

There are now two influences at work tending to lead to an increase in K:
1 As in a Joint-Stock firm there is an incentive to increase K if the value of the marginal product of a machine $P_x (\partial X/\partial K)$ is high relatively to the existing return per machine $(P_x X - WL)/K$.
2 But now there is an additional incentive to expand K if the valuation ratio $P_s S/P_k K$ is high, i.e. if the market value of the share capital is high relatively to the market price of the machinery which it finances.

Point 2 means that while shareholders are treated equally, not all shareholders 'own', as it were, the same number of machines per £100 subscribed in money capital. Suppose that an Inegalitarian Joint-Stock firm is set up. The original shareholders purchase 100 shares at £1 a share and with the £100 so subscribed purchase 100 machines at £1 a machine. The company does well and the market value of a share rises from £1 to £2. Another 50 shares are issued raising £100 with which 100 additional machines are purchased again at £1 a machine. The company now owns 200 machines and has issued 150 shares. The first shareholders who own two-thirds of the shares 'own' as it were two-thirds of the 200 machines, i.e. $133\frac{1}{3}$ machines as a result of subscribing £100 which financed the purchase of only 100 machines; the second lot of shareholders own a third of the shares and thus 'own' as it were a third of the 200 machines, i.e. $66\frac{2}{3}$ machines as a result of subscribing £100 which financed the purchase of no less than 100 machines.

It should now be clear why we have nicknamed this an *Inegalitarian* Joint-Stock firm. Partners do not participate in the partnership according to the amount of real resources which they have put in. Early partners (the original shareholders) can determine the conditions on which new partners (the later shareholders) can come in; and if the early partners, having taken the first risks, find that they are on to a good thing they may admit new partners on less favourable terms than those which they enjoy themselves. It is interesting to see the effects of applying this principle to a Cooperative; and this we shall do in Section six.

Section five

Before we outline the structure of what we will call an Inegalitarian Co-operative it will be useful to consider in more detail some of the rules which are appropriate for the running of all forms of labour Cooperatives.

1 It is clear that in order to give some security to those owners of capital who lend capital to a Cooperative there must be some regulations governing the use of its real capital by a Cooperative. In this respect a Cooperative is in the same position as an Entrepreneurial firm. It must not be possible for a group of workers any more than for an entrepreneur to borrow money, use the proceeds for riotous living, and then go bankrupt. While the commercial decisions as to what is the most profitable form for the use of the borrowed funds must be left to the worker managers, there must clearly be some 'company-law' regulations which require the labour managers to make proper use of proper depreciation allowances to maintain the capital of the concern intact in some accepted accounting sense; and if the concern should go bankrupt, then the capital assets would revert to the ownership of those who had lent funds to the concern. The loans to the concern would be secured on the real capital assets of the concern, which the labour managers would be required by law to maintain intact in some accepted accounting sense.[17]

2 As for the rules governing the expansion of the number of worker-partners in a Cooperative, it would seem obvious that a new partner should enter the concern only if two conditions are fulfilled, namely (a) that the new partner wished to come in and (b) that the old partners wish to accept him.

3 The rules under 2 seem obviously fair and acceptable. We will now argue, what is not perhaps quite so obvious, that there must be two analogous conditions for the withdrawal of an existing partner from a Cooperative, namely (a) that the partner concerned wishes to leave and (b) that he should obtain from the remaining partners permission to withdraw.

17 This points to an important consideration concerning incentives. We have already argued (p. 410) that as far as labour incentives are concerned, Entrepreneurial and Joint-Stock firms are similar (in that labour is hired at a given wage and is told what to do), and are to be contrasted with a Cooperative (where labour manages itself). But economic efficiency depends not only on labour incentives, but also upon incentives to maintain the value of the real capital stock. In this respect Entrepreneurial and Cooperative firms are similar (in that those who receive the residual profit on the firm's operations have no direct interest in the wealth of the ultimate owners of the capital) and are to be contrasted with Joint-Stock firms (in which those who enjoy the residual profit themselves own the capital and have, therefore, a much more direct incentive to pay regard to the maintenance or improvement of its value).

Rule 3a is incompatible with the rule of the dismissal of partners by majority decision mentioned in footnote 5. There is presumably no absolute right or wrong about such a rule; but it would appear to the present reviewer that a fully participatory Cooperative must have a rule like 3a. In any case the following analysis is an analysis of what will occur if one does have such a rule.[18]

Rule 3b requires somewhat more discussion. Why should any individual worker–partner not be free to leave any Cooperative at any time if he so wishes without any cost to himself? Consider the following case in terms of Figure 1 on p. 400 above. Suppose the Cooperative to be confronted with the curve PQ for its average revenue per head $P_x X/L$. Suppose that it starts with the optimum size of the Cooperative (namely, OA) at which its average earnings $(CB = (P_x X - iP_k K)/L)$ are at a maximum. But suppose that the average earnings which partners might be able to get if they were free to join new Cooperatives in other industries were greater than the earnings inside the existing partnership, i.e.

$$E_0 > CB = \frac{P_x X - iP_k K}{L},$$

where E_0 measures the average earnings available outside the partnership. Some workers might be better able than others to take the opportunity of withdrawal to a more remunerative Cooperative. Suppose the size of the Cooperative is reduced to OE; then the remaining partners can earn only GF so that E_0 is now even greater than before relatively to

$$GF = \frac{P_x X - iP_k K}{L}.$$

This may go on until what may be called the starvation–bankruptcy size of the Cooperative is reached at a Cooperative size OV where the revenue is just sufficient to cover the debt interest and the remaining workers' earnings are zero.

The point is simply that as partners withdraw the remaining partners

---

18 Incidentally the existence of such a rule removes a serious problem which would otherwise arise from self-financing of Cooperatives to which Professor Vanek (1970, p. 307) draws attention. Consider a Cooperative which puts aside undistributed profits and thereby pays off the whole of its outside indebtedness. In terms of Figure 1 $iP_k K$ is reduced to zero and the curve MN collapses to coincide with the two axes. The size of a competitive partnership which will maximize earnings per head is now that which will maximize output per head, which, in the absence of any increasing returns to scale, would with any given amount of real capital involve the reduction of the partnership to one man. With no debt there is no incentive to enlarge the partnership in order to share the debt burden; and the remaining partner will be left endowed with an enormous equipment of real capital financed out of the savings of his previous partners who have been dismissed without compensation.

are left to hold the debt baby. If the debt obligation has been willingly incurred by all the partners, it is not a true participatory Cooperative if any individual partner can without any obligation just walk out and leave his other partners with the full debt burden. All must sink or swim together.

What then should be the rules for the closure of a Cooperative? What does bankruptcy mean?

One possibility would be that the partners could always in agreement decide to close down the concern leaving the debt holders with the ownership of the capital assets of the concern. Or, in the interests of the debt holders, it might be ruled that the existing partners could not take such action simply because they could do better elsewhere, but only if their earnings, after paying debt interest and maintaining capital intact, fell below some stated level. Indeed different rules, giving different degrees of security to the debt holders, might be freely negotiable between the partners and the debt holders when the partnership was first formed.[19]

Section six

Let us then consider a Cooperative with rules 1, 2a, 2b, 3a and 3b; and let us with these rules contrast the operation of a Cooperative (as described on p. 394) with that of an Inegalitarian Cooperative whose mode of working is as follows. Each individual L-partner on joining the partnership is allotted a share l in the total surplus $(P_x X - iP_k K)$ of the partnership. This share is such that it pays the new partner to come in and it pays the existing partners to let him in. A partner once in can (apart from death and retirement for reasons of age or ill-health) withdraw only if it pays him to do so and he can make it worthwhile for the remaining partners to release him. The shares allotted to the individual partners are not necessarily the same. They may differ because different partners with different skills and trainings may have different values to the partnerships, but they may also differ for partners with the same skills and trainings, because the partners have joined the partnership at different times.

The objective of the Inegalitarian Cooperative as it exists at any moment of time will be to maximize the return per share

$$a = \frac{P_x X - iP_k K}{l_1 + l_2 + \dots + l_n},$$

where $l_1, \dots, l_n$ are the shares allotted to individuals $l, \dots, n$ who make up the existing partnership. Given the distribution of the shares, it is a fully

19 Such rules would make schemes for capital reorganization possible. If the debt holders were as a result of a 'bankruptcy' left holding the real assets of some defunct concern, they might by cutting the debt interest (reducing $iP_k K$ and so the curve MN in Figure 1) bring the concern to life again with a different, or indeed the same, set of worker–partners.

participatory partnership in the sense that every partner has the same motive that the concern should be so managed as to maximize the return per share.

Let us consider the operation of rules 2 and 3 above for the expansion and contraction of such an Inegalitarian Cooperative.

The rules for expansion are straightforward. Suppose that

$$E_0 < P_x \frac{\partial X}{\partial L},$$

i.e. that the average earnings outside are less than the value of the marginal product of labour in the partnership. Then all that is necessary is for the existing partners to agree on a share l_{n+1} for a new partner such that

$$E_0 < al_{n+1} < P_x \frac{\partial X}{\partial L}.$$

The new partner will wish to join because $E_0 < al_{n+1}$. The existing partners will wish him to join because $al_{n+1} < P_x(\partial X/\partial L)$; for since the addition to the revenue of the concern as a result of his joining will be greater than his share of the surplus, the return to all existing workers will be raised.

The rules for withdrawal are a little more complicated. Let us suppose that $E_0 > P_x(\partial X/\partial L)$. Now there are three cases to be considered:

1 Suppose that some existing partner j has a share in the partnership l_j such that

$$E_0 > al_j > P_x \frac{\partial X}{\partial L}.$$

Then the partner will wish to withdraw because $E_0 > al_j$; and the existing partners will willingly let him go because $al_j > P_x(\partial X/\partial L)$, that is to say, they will lose less in revenue than they save on his share of the surplus.

2 But suppose that for all the existing partners

$$al > E_0 > P_x \frac{\partial X}{\partial L}.$$

The existing partners would like to see any individual partner withdraw because $al > P_x(\partial X/\partial L)$; but no existing partner will wish to go because $al > E_0$. However, there is a net gain to everyone concerned of

$$E_0 - P_x \frac{\partial X}{\partial L}$$

if one partner does withdraw, since that partner will earn E_0 and the existing partnership will lose only $P_x(\partial X/\partial L)$. In this case the existing partners might bribe one of their number to withdraw, perhaps by allowing him to retain some of his shares in the partnership even if he goes and works elsewhere. In this case L will be reduced so long as $E_0 > P_x (\partial X / \partial L)$.

3 Suppose that for all existing partners

$$E_0 > P_x \frac{\partial X}{\partial L} > al.$$

Then an individual partner will want to withdraw because $E_0 > al$, but the other partners will not want to release him since $P_x (\partial X / \partial L) > al$. But once again there is a net gain of $E_0 - P_x (\partial X / \partial L)$ and an individual partner should be able to purchase his release from his colleagues.[20] Once again L will be reduced so long as $E_0 > P_x (\partial X / \partial L)$.

An Inegalitarian Cooperative, in the same way as a Cooperative, will have an incentive to borrow money to expand its capital equipment so long as the value of the marginal product of machinery is greater than its rental $(P_x (\partial X / \partial K) > i P_k K)$. The resulting rules for an Inegalitarian Cooperative are shown in column 4 of the Table on p. 398.

For simplicity of exposition we have presented the argument without reference to the fact that not only the particular partnership which we have been examining, but also all the other concerns in the community, may be organized as Inegalitarian Cooperatives. Suppose this to be so and that the value of the marginal product of labour in one industry is greater than in another (e.g. $P_y (\partial Y / \partial L) > P_x (\partial X / \partial L)$). Then there is a net gain for everyone concerned of $P_y (\partial Y / \partial L) - P_x (\partial X / \partial L)$ if one unit of L moves from the X- to the Y-industry. There must be some bargain which will involve the choice of the share which the migrant worker will receive in the Y-industry and which may involve him in purchasing his release from his X-colleagues which improves the lot of everyone – the existing Y-partners, the migrant worker and the remaining X-partners. Thus labour will move from X to Y if $P_y (\partial Y / \partial Y) > P_x (\partial X / \partial L)$. The short-run adjustment process of the Inegalitarian Cooperative, unlike that of the Cooperative, becomes Pareto-optimal.

But this result is achieved only at the expense of a distributional principle which may involve two workers of equal age, sex, ability, skill, etc., working side by side at the same job at the same work-bench, but receiving

20 For example, if the withdrawing partner pays to the partnership the present value of earnings of $E = \frac{1}{2} \left(E_0 + P_x \frac{\partial X}{\partial L} \right) - al$, the gain will be shared equally between the withdrawing partner who will gain $E_0 - al - E = \frac{1}{2} \left(E_0 - P_x \frac{\partial X}{\partial L} \right)$ and the remaining partners who will gain $al - P_x \frac{\partial X}{\partial L} + E = \frac{1}{2} \left(E_0 - P_x \frac{\partial X}{\partial L} \right)$.

different shares in the product. As with the shareholders in the Inegalitarian Joint-Stock firm, the worker–partners in an Inegalitarian Cooperative who come in early bearing the initial risks in a concern which turns out to do well will earn more than those workers who come in later when the success of the enterprise is already established.

Section seven

There is no reason why one should not go the whole hog in participation and profit-sharing and apply the same principle both to those who supply the capital and to those who supply the labour. Such a set-up would be a combination of an Inegalitarian Joint-Stock firm (as far as the supply of capital was concerned) and an Inegalitarian Cooperative (as far as the supply of labour was concerned). Let us call the resulting structure an Inegalitarian Joint-Stock-Cooperative firm. Let S represent the number of shares issued to those who have subscribed capital. Let there be three skills or types of Labour (L, M and N) and let l_1, l_2, ..., m_1, m_2, ..., n_1, n_2, ..., represent the shares issued to individual workers L_1, L_2, ..., M_1, M_2, ..., N_1, N_2, ... Then the objective of the existing partners at any one time will be to maximize the return per share or

$$a = \frac{P_x X}{S + l_1 + l_2 + ... + m_1 + m_2 + ... + n_1 + n_2 + ...}.$$

This will be achieved by following the rules (which are summarized in column 7 of the Table on p. 398):

Increase or decrease S and so K as $P_x\,(\partial X/\partial K) \gtrless rP_k$,

Increase or decrease L as $\qquad P_x\,(\partial X/\partial L) \gtrless E_{ol}$,

Increase or decrease M as $\qquad P_x\,(\partial X/\partial M) \gtrless E_{om}$,

Increase or decrease N as $\qquad P_x\,(\partial X/\partial N) \gtrless E_{on}$.

Reductions in L, M and N must be associated, as far as is necessary, with bargains by which existing partners buy their way out or are bribed by the remaining partners to withdraw.

The analysis which leads to these results is exactly the same as that which has been given above for an Inegalitarian Joint-Stock firm and for an Inegalitarian Cooperative.

Nor is this the only possibility of combination of structures. There is nothing in the nature of things to prevent some capitalists and some workers getting together and forming a partnership (on Inegalitarian Joint-Stock–Cooperative principles), but nevertheless borrowing some additional capital at fixed interest and hiring some additional labour at a fixed wage (thus introducing Entrepreneurial elements into the concern). Or, as with the usual profit-sharing arrangement, we may find labour being rewarded in an ordinary company partly with a fixed wage rate and partly with shares in the concern, which introduces a Cooperative element into an Inegalitarian Joint-Stock firm. All sorts of participatory profit sharing combinations are theoretically possible.

There is no place in the present article to discuss the historical and empirical questions as to which of these structures have flourished in which conditions. But it is interesting to ask why the Cooperative structure is not more common than it is in fact in the free-enterprise world. Two factors spring to mind.

First, there is the basic, though not strictly economic question whether a workers' Cooperative organization is compatible with the maintenance of the discipline needed to ensure the efficient operation of a concern which employs a large body of workers.

Secondly, while property owners can spread their risks by putting small bits of their property into a large number of concerns, a worker cannot easily put small bits of his effort into a large number of different jobs. This presumably is a main reason why we find risk-bearing capital hiring labour rather than risk-bearing labour hiring capital. Moreover, since labour cannot spread its risks, we are likely to find Cooperative structures only in lines of activity in which the risk is not too great, and this means in lines of activity in which two conditions are fulfilled: first, the risk of fluctuations in the demand for the product must not be too great; and, secondly, the activity must be labour-intensive, in which the surplus accruing to labour does not constitute a small difference between two large quantities, the revenue from the sale of the product and the hire of capital plus the purchase of raw materials.[21] This may help to explain why such labour partnerships as do exist are usually to be found in labour-intensive services, such as lawyers, accountants, doctors, etc.

Section eight

Many questions remain unconsidered. Neither Professor Vanek nor the author of the present article have attempted to answer a very important question concerning risk, namely whether, if a workers' Cooperative did exist in any given situation, it would (in its decisions concerning output, price, investment, employment, etc.) react differently from an Entrepreneurial firm in the face of a given set of risks. Nor has any systematic attempt been made to compare the behaviour of a Cooperative system with that of Managerial Capitalism,[22] though Professor Vanek does claim (1970,

21 In terms of Figure 1 if the MN and the PQ curves were both raised substantially so as to leave the difference CB unchanged, a 1 per cent fall in the PQ curve would have a much more marked effect in reducing CB.
22 Of the kind described by such authors as Berle and Means, Burnham, Galbraith, and Marris.

p. 119) that the Cooperative system would be less prone to the temptations of 'gigantism' than any other economic regime.

In this article the author has made no attempt to argue for or against the institution of labour partnerships. Professor Vanek in his book which inspired this article professes himself to be a keen advocate of such participatory organizations; but in spite of this he maintains a most admirable scientific frankness in exposing the weaknesses as well as the strengths of such organizations. It has not been possible in this article to review all of Professor Vanek's arguments; his book should be read by all economists interested in the subject. The purpose of this article has been merely to analyse some of the implications of labour partnerships or profit-sharing structures. It may well be the case that the merits of participation should be so highly prized as to make the encouragement of such institutions a major objective of governmental policy. For governmental encouragement of one kind or another will almost certainly be necessary because of the natural tendency for risk-bearing capital to hire labour rather than the risk-bearing labour to hire capital.

If such governmental policies are to be devised, there are at least three main problems to be borne in mind.

First, as we have tried to show, the effective workings of labour partnerships will depend very much upon easy conditions for the formation of new partnerships to enter any profitable industry. But easy company promotion of this kind by unemployed or ill-paid workers will certainly be impossible without appropriate governmental interventions of a most extensive character – leading perhaps inevitably to a socialist ownership of the main capital resources of the community as in Yugoslavia.

Second, the labour partnership presents in its own special form a conflict between efficiency and equality. Some compromise rules on the distribution of the surplus among new and old workers must be found which does not introduce excessive inequalities on the one hand or excessive inefficiencies on the other.

Third, thought must be given to the extent to which labour partnerships involve workers risking all their eggs in one basket. Some compromise between the degree of participation and the degree of the spreading of risks would have to be sought.[23]

23 In this connection it would be helpful to encourage a wide distribution of the ownership of property (what the present reviewer has called a Propdem in another connection) so that the representative worker is also a representative property owner. A citizen could then at least spread his property in small parcels over a lot of other concerns, even though he had to concentrate his earnings from work on one particular concern.

References

DOMAR, E. (1966), 'The Soviet collective farm as a producer cooperative', *Amer. econ. Rev.*, vol. 56, no. 4, pp. 734–57.

ROBINSON, J. (1967), 'The Soviet collective farm as a producer cooperative: comment', *Amer. econ. Rev.*, vol. 57, no. 4.

VANEK, J. (1970), *The General Theory of Labor-Managed Market Economies*, Cornell University Press.

WARD, B. (1958), 'The firm in Illyria: market syndicalism', *Amer. econ. Rev.*, vol. 48, no. 4, pp. 566–89.

WARD, B. (1967), *The Socialist Economy*, Random House.

26 D. D. Milenkovitch

The Worker-Managed Enterprise

Excerpt from D. D. Milenkovitch, 'Plan and market in Yugoslav economic thought', in *The Worker-Managed Enterprise*, Yale University Press, 1971, pp. 187–96.

The 1965 economic reforms proposed to liberate the Yugoslav enterprise from a maze of interventions, and for the first time the question of how a Yugoslav enterprise responds to economic signals and incentives became relevant. The Yugoslavs are beginning to give this problem serious consideration. Previously, plan objectives had been attained by various policies that influenced the enterprises. The principal method of attaining the desired volume and structure was the almost complete control of investments. The economic reform drastically restricted the range of admissible policy instruments. More important, following the reforms the enterprises are expected to make investments in response to market forces. The outcome of reliance on market forces is uncertain and need not be the same as in the capitalist market system because the Yugoslav enterprise differs from the capitalist enterprise in a number of respects. The major analytical difference is that the workers in the Yugoslav enterprises are both managers and profit sharers, as well as workers. It is difficult to know in advance what effect this difference will have on enterprise behavior and how it will alter the enterprise response to a given policy. The Yugoslavs therefore require a theory of the worker-managed enterprise to serve as a basis for predicting the behavior of enterprises and their response to changes in policy instruments. Only then will it be possible to determine how enterprise behavior departs from policy objectives and to select policy instruments to correct the outcome.

Development of an economic theory serves still another purpose in Yugoslavia. As noted . . . there is some conflict between those Yugoslavs who consider the worker-managed enterprise as a (dispensable) *means* to attaining social objectives and those who see workers' management itself as an *end*, that is, an essential feature of socialism. In order to determine whether the system should be retained and whether there is any cost in terms of other social objectives, modified (and if so, how), or abandoned, the Yugoslavs must understand how this form of economic organization operates. Without such an understanding, the debate is doomed to remain mired in rhetoric and citationism.

In this chapter I shall consider first how the Yugoslavs view the worker-managed enterprise with respect to both its role and its maximizing principles and then I shall turn to the Western analysis of the producers cooperative as it applies to the Yugoslav firm. The last section of the chapter will treat the more complex, longer range questions of economic efficiency and the role of free entry, and the source of investment funds.

Yugoslav view of the enterprise

It is not possible to speak of a single Yugoslav theory of the enterprise. There is no generally accepted interpretation of the behavior of the worker-managed firm. In fact, until recently, Yugoslavs had put forward only a few explicit theories of the enterprise. It is possible, however, to cull from the various writings some of the implicit assumptions about enterprise behavior. Many of the earlier writings shared a common tendency to seek parallels between the socialist firm and the capitalist enterprise. The analogy was often carried too far and frequently obscured important differences. It was correctly applied to the *functions* of the socialist firm but it was not necessarily applicable to the *maximizing principles*. Others pursued a more fruitful line of inquiry and focused on the unique features of the Yugoslav enterprise. Although not satisfactorily solved, the economics of the enterprise is now recognized as a vital concern and recently has received greater theoretical and some empirical attention.

Function of the enterprise

Yugoslav authors readily recognized the crucial role of the entrepreneur in the capitalist system. In their view, the capitalist entrepreneur provides the 'motive force' that keeps the market economy moving. It is the entrepreneur who searches for maximum profits and who organizes production to this end. In the quest for profits he enters an industry in which supply is inadequate relative to demand. Finding a process for more efficient production or conceiving a new product, he puts it into operation. The capitalist entrepreneur continually scans the economic horizon, seeking to augment his income through perception of new investment and production opportunities. He invests, causing the economy to grow. The capitalist entrepreneur, in short, pursues with a single mind his own self-interest, but in so doing he also furthers the interests of society.

In a centrally planned economy, planners take the initiative in determining the character of the economy and in directing investments into specific activities. In Yugoslavia, however, central planning has been abandoned. The social plan, of an indicative character, is concerned with broad aggregates. It cannot provide a motivating force; it does not undertake to organize production or to direct investment into specific activities. The plan does not exert pressures for cost reduction, innovation, or product improvement. The economic logic of the Yugoslav system requires that the initiative for these tasks originate elsewhere. Decentralized socialism must have an agent to adopt new methods, produce new products, and establish new locations, in short, to select investments and to bear the risks in an uncertain world. In Yugoslav economic thought as well as practice, this function is assigned to the institution of workers' management (Bajt, 1968; Horvat, 1964; Korac, 1961; Lavrac, 1964; Todorovic, 1963a).

The management of the socialist enterprise legally lies in the hands of the workers. A few authors defined the function of management narrowly, virtually excluding entrepreneurial functions. According to Uvalic, for example, the worker-managers of social property are to be rewarded according to their success in carrying out specific tasks. He stated that 'the right of economic organizations to dispose of part of income is exclusively designed to enhance the productivity of labor and to stimulate collectives to exert maximum effort to fulfill their production targets' (Uvalic, 1964, pp. 140–47). This attitude toward the enterprise represented a minority opinion, even in the early sixties.

In function the Yugoslav working collective[1] is more than a manager, and most Yugoslav authors have properly recognized that the collective performs the function of the entrepreneur in their socialist system. The working collective of the enterprise establishes basic enterprise policy. The collective in principle makes all decisions about what to produce and how. The collective decides what portion of its earnings to invest, and how to invest them, or whether to lend them to other firms or to become shareholders in a bank. The Yugoslav collective makes these decisions from a private vantage point and pursues its own economic interests. Under the accounting system employed, the members of the collective receive residual incomes. From gross receipts, various contractual expenses, excluding wages, are deducted.[2] The remainder, a residual category, is the net income of the enterprise. The collective divides the income into two parts.[3] One part is retained for investment in the enterprise; the other is distributed to the workers as personal income. Most Yugoslav authors recognized the role of the residual part of income: 'This higher income realized by the enterprise is the indicator of, and remuneration for, risks successfully

1 The term 'working collective' is used to describe all the bodies of workers' management. For a more detailed discussion of the various management bodies in Yugoslavia, see chapter 5 [not included].
2 Contractual costs include the cost of materials, payment for services, depreciation, interest and principal payment on loans, and the capital tax.
3 Actually, into four parts: income, reinvestment, reserve funds, and enterprise-financed collective consumption of the workers. The present discussion ignores the latter two categories.

taken by the management of the enterprise ... a remuneration for the working collective as the manager of the enterprise' (Lavrac, 1964, p. 156).

Maximizing principle of the enterprise

The role of the enterprise in the Yugoslav economy is understood. It is a self-interested autonomous body that bears risks and receives rewards. What is not clear is the relevant maximizing principle. Extending the analogy of the capitalist enterprise, some Yugoslav authors attributed to the Yugoslav firm the same motives characteristic of the capitalist enterprise. This was particularly true in writings in the early sixties. For example, Rakic stated that 'the laws of commodity production and the market mechanism act in the same way as in an economy based on private ownership of the means of production' (Rakic, 1964, p. 130). Like the capitalist enterprise, the Yugoslav enterprise was assumed to maximize total profits. Similar conclusions were suggested by Samardzija (1960) and Hadji-Vasilev (1960).

Doubts about the similarity of capitalist and socialist enterprises grew over time and several authors began to distinguish different maximizing principles. Mijalko Todorovic, Miladin Korac, and Strasimir Popovic were among the first to note differences; their analyses, while incomplete, were more fruitful. Somewhat later France Cerne suggested several hypotheses about the objectives of the working collective. Finally, in 1968, Branko Horvat entered the discussion, taking note of the developments in the theory of producers' cooperatives in the West.

The Todorovic analysis (1962, 1963b, 1964) of the enterprise is not entirely valid, He stated several times in his long article (appearing in several parts, chiefly in late 1962 and early 1963) that the objective of the socialist as well as the capitalist enterprise is to maximize profits. 'In the enterprises in our country which are run by the workers themselves, it is also in the interests of the workers [that] $m/(c+v)$ [profit] be at a maximum' (Todorovic, 1963a, p. 46). The behavior of the socialist enterprise was presumed identical with that of the capitalist enterprise, and he concluded that the long run supply schedule of the cooperative and the capitalist enterprise were the same. Yet in his exposition he also recognized differences in the motivation of the capitalist and the socialist firm (Todorovic, 1963a, p. 46):

In contrast to the capitalists, the workers find it in their interests ... that the working collective ... number as few members as possible, because ... he must share the joint product with them. That is, the individual worker finds it in his interest to have the productivity of labor as high as possible.

Todorovic did not point out that profit maximization will normally be inconsistent with the interests of the workers to keep the number of profit sharers as small as possible. He did recognize, however, that the interests of the workers might mean their refusal to hire additional workers, which could contribute to unemployment. 'The desire of the worker to achieve a minimum [number of workers] conceals a contradiction existing among the direct producers themselves and can signify a tendency toward the creation of unemployment' (Todorovic, 1963a, p. 47). He also recognized that the entire labor force would be less mobile than in a competitive market system. 'The links of the worker with his collective and the commune manifest themselves through the *increased inertia of workers*, that is, through lesser mobility on their part' (Todorovic, 1963a, p. 51). He believed that the effect of the loss of mobility of already employed workers would be offset by the large number of new entrants into the market each year. Interestingly, he appeared to regard the reluctance of the working collective to hire additional workers as a desirable means for raising the average productivity of labor.

In contrast to Todorovic, Korac explicitly rejected the notion that the Yugoslav firm maximizes total profits (Korac 1961, 1962, 1963).[4] The maximizing principle of the socialist firm is 'contrary to the profit rate' (Korac, 1961, pp. 41–2). Korac constructed a model of the rational Yugoslav enterprise operating under the following conditions:

Means of production are owned by society and managed by the collective;
Competitive markets allocate productive factors and final products;
Enterprise retained earnings are the sole source of capital;
Enterprise can enter any branch of production.

Korac also assumed that workers wish to increase their incomes in the future. In his model, since the sole means of increasing future income is through reinvestment of retained earnings, there will be a positive rate of investment from undistributed earnings.

Korac's verbal statement of the enterprise maximizing principle was not clear. He asserted that 'the rate of income expresses the profitability of the socialist firm'. The collective seeks to maximize its present net income in relation to the capital and labor employed. 'The size of the rate of income depends, on the one hand, on the mass of realized income and the mass of engaged factors of production (or the value expression thereof) and, on the

4 His articles provoked extensive discussion about the normative price and allocation of resources that he and his followers asserted was the corollary of those theses about enterprise behavior. (See chapter 9 [not included] for a discussion of normative price.) Little new was said in later articles about the enterprise itself. His later article (Korac, 1966) has virtually the same theory of the firm.

other hand, on the organic composition of those factors of production' (Korac, 1961, p. 42).

In more specific form, however, the principle is either erroneous or unclear. Korac asserted that the rational enterprise would maximize its rate of income. The rate of income r was defined by him as

$$r = \frac{\text{realized income}}{\text{engaged means of production} + \text{newly created value}}.$$

Realized income here is the net income of the enterprise after taxes and all nonlabor expenses. Engaged means of production includes capital equipment and the materials employed (in Marxian terms, the means of labor and the objects of labor). Newly created value, by the assumption of equilibrium, has the same magnitude as realized income.[5] The rate of income so defined is allegedly the enterprise criterion for making short run decisions about what to produce, as well as decisions involving the investment of capital and possible moves into alternative branches of production.

This analysis of enterprise behavior has been attacked in the Yugoslav literature on several grounds. Strasimir Popovic (1963) was among the first to question whether the rational enterprise would behave in the manner Korac postulated. In the form in which Korac presented his criterion, there is no explicit mention of the number of workers in the enterprise. Popovic noted that the *rate* of income would be higher if the number of workers increased relative to a given stock of capital. In that way both realized income per unit of capital and the rate of income would be very high. Income per worker would not. He concluded that the Korac criterion would not be the objective of a rational collective. Todorovic was equally severe in condemning the income rate.

Popovic went on to state the explicit objective of the rational collective. He said openly what had scarcely appeared elsewhere in Yugoslavia: that the rational enterprise would want to *maximize income per worker*. 'To achieve larger income per worker . . . is the basic motive.' The criterion for decisions in the first instance depends on the effect on 'income per worker

5 Newly created value is a Marxian category. The total value (Marxian sense) of a commodity at any given stage of processing is composed of the value of the initial raw materials in it, the value added by previous labor, value transferred from the capital equipment that processed it in the present stage, and the newly created value added only by human labor in the present stage.

Realized income, a price and accounting category, could deviate from newly created value primarily for the same reasons – market fluctuations – that price deviates from value in Marxian analysis. Deviations could also result from any conscious policies of the state affecting prices directly or indirectly, as well as the existence of monopoly, etc. In simple commodity production, in long run competitive equilibrium, realized income would be identical with newly created value.

remaining for free distribution'. Popovic also perceived that this behavior might be undesirable for resource allocation but he did not extend his analysis of the problem.

These early discussions about the enterprise took place before 1964. Attention turned again to the theory of the firm after the economic reform of 1965, which made the problem more urgent.

References

BAJT, A. (1968), 'Drustvena svojina-kolektivna i individualna', *Gledista*, vol. 9, no. 4, pp. 531–44.

HADJI-VASILEV, M. (1960), 'Drustveno-ekonominska sustina socijalisticke vasplede prema radu', *Socijalizam*, vol. 3, no. 6.

HORVAT, B. (1964), *Towards a Theory of Planned Economy*, International Arts and Sciences Press, New York.

KORAC, M. (1961), 'Teze za teorige socijalisticke robne proizvodnje', *Socijalizam*, vol. 4, no. 1.

KORAC, M. (1962), 'Tcorije socialisticke robne proivzvodnje', *Nasa stvarnost*, vol. 16, no. 12, pp. 563–613.

KORAC, M. (1963), 'Socijalisticki robni proizvodjac u procesu drustvene reprodukeije', *Ekonomski pregled*, vol. 14, nos. 10, 12, pp. 1027–75.

KORAC, M. (1966), 'Zakon vrednosti kao regulatet raspodele dohotka u socijalistickom sistetnu robne privrede', *Ekonomski pregled*, vol. 17, no. 10, pp. 548–79.

LAVRAC, I. (1964), 'Competition and incentive in the Yugoslav economic system', in R. Stojanovic, *Yugoslav Economists on Problems of a Socialist Economy*, International Arts and Sciences Press, New York.

POPOVIC, S. (1963), 'Prilog gradji o ekonomiskom sistetnu Jugoslavije', *Nasa stvarnost*, vol. 17, no. 5, pp. 522–49.

RAKIC (1964), in R. Stojanovic, *Yugoslav Economists on Problems of a Socialist Economy*, International Arts and Sciences Press, New York.

SAMARDZIJA (1960), 'Problem cenu u socijalistickoj privendi', *Nasa stvarnost*, vol. 14, no. 12.

TODOROVIC, M. (1962), *Socijalizam*, vol. 5, no. 6.

TODOROVIC, M. (1963a), in *Socialist Thought and Practice*, no. 9, January.

TODOROVIC, M. (1963b), *Socijalizam*, vol. 6, nos. 1, 2 and 3.

TODOROVIC, M. (1964), *Socijalizam*, vol. 7, nos. 11–12.

UVALIC (1964), in R. Stojanovic, *Yugoslav Economists on Problems of a Socialist Economy*, International Arts and Sciences Press, New York.

27 Jaroslav Vanek and Juan Espinosa

The Subsistence Income, Effort and Development Potential of
Labour Management and Other Economic Systems

Vanek, J., and Espinosa, J., 'The subsistence income, effort and development
potential of labour management and other economic systems', *Economic Journal*,
vol. 82, 1972, pp. 1000–1013.

Introduction

In a recent study one of the present authors (Vanek, 1970) argued that
one of the significant advantages of labour management is the capability
of that system to produce efficient allocations – or combinations – of real
income on the one hand and effort (producing that real income) on the
other.[1] In developing the argument the situation envisaged was one of an
advanced economy where the incomes earned and produced are far in
excess of what we might call subsistence income.

When thinking about the developing countries where incomes – especially
the incomes of those who have not yet been incorporated into the modern
developmental sector – are usually very low, not far from subsistence levels,
the entire problem changes a good deal and deserves special attention. In
fact, real income, subsistence, effort and incentives may be the variables
most central to the question of economic development, and the choice of
an economic organization for development should depend heavily on them.

In this paper we will attempt to show that if labour management is a
suitable system from the standpoint of choosing an optimum of labour
effort in general, its comparative advantage with respect to other economic
systems is even greater in the context of developing countries. To show this
we will first develop a set of short- and long-run *subsistence effort functions*

1 We define as labour-managed an economy where:
Workers control and manage democratically the operation of their firms;
Workers distribute among themselves all net income;
Workers pay for the use of capital assets;
The economy is a market economy;
There is perfect freedom of employment.
A one-man (or one-family) owner-operated firm is also a labour-managed firm,
even if it is owned by its operator (the payment to capital, our third defining
characteristic, now being an imputed payment from and to the same person).
Consequently all the conclusions obtained in this paper also pertain to an individual
firm or to an economy composed of such firms.

in the second section, relating various levels of real income to maximum effort producible consistent with that income. In the third section we will then combine that analytical tool with the effort–income possibility locus[2] in showing the long-range adjustment of a labour-managed firm in typical developing countries. In the fourth section we contrast the solutions shown for the labour-managed firm (or economy) with solutions likely to occur under capitalist conditions.

The subsistence–effort loci

The key notion on which we should like to elaborate in this section is that what we usually refer to loosely as the subsistence minimum wage or subsistence minimum income, in the context of developmental analysis, that is by no means an unambiguous and easily observable or determinable magnitude. Our primary emphasis is on the fact that the subsistence minimum or the real income necessary to keep a human being alive will depend heavily on the amount of effort which he is supposed to supply. A man who can be completely idle can survive on real income far below that of a man who is supposed to work hard for eight hours a day.

This notion is by no means new, not even in economic theory where normally the real world penetrates with a considerable time lag.[3] For our purposes we will distinguish between the *short-run* (or short-range) subsistence–effort locus and the *long-run* (or long-range) subsistence–effort locus. We will elaborate the distinction later at the end of this section when a precise definition of the lengths of the time period will make more sense. For the moment let us simply remember that the short run is significantly less than the long run.

In Figure 1 along the vertical axis we measure real income y, while from the origin O to the left we measure the amount of effort supplied, by a representative individual. The distance between the two vertical axes is the maximum effort that ever could be supplied by the individual. The locus marked Φ dividing the shaded from the unshaded area we will refer to as the *long-run subsistence–effort line* or locus showing for each prescribed level of real income (such as y_1, y_2) the maximum amount of effort that a person living on such a level of real income *for long periods of time* can supply *over long periods of time*.

The shaded area below our locus Φ is a 'no man's land' or impossibility

2 We have used such a locus, comparable to the traditional production possibility function, in deriving the equilibrium output of a labour-managed firm.
3 For example, it underlies Professor Koopmans's consumption set of his First Essay (1957). Also it has been used in a seminar at Cornell University by Professor Mirrlees. It is his presentation which has helped us in the extension of the earlier work (Vanek, 1971, refs. 3, 5, pp. 30–31) and we should like to express our gratitude to him.

zone in the sense that any person forced to supply an effort in excess of that given by Φ for a given real income could not survive for more than a short time. Clearly locus Φ starting from point a_1 corresponding to the subsistence minimum for complete idleness is upward sloping as we move to higher and higher levels of effort, that positive slope itself increasing with E and reaching very high levels in the vicinity of the y axis.

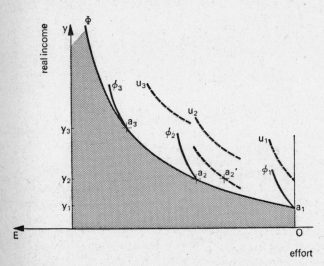

Figure 1

In addition to the long-run subsistence effort locus we have drawn in our diagram three short-run subsistence effort loci ϕ_1, ϕ_2, and ϕ_3 originating at points a_1, a_2 and a_3, respectively. The meaning of these loci can be understood in the following manner. Suppose that the individual considered has been at a_2 for a considerable period of time – i.e. working at the level of income y_2, and supplying the corresponding maximum amount of effort. If he is now expected to increase his supply of effort he can do so if his income is raised, but in the short run he will not be able to proceed on Φ but will have to proceed along a much steeper path such as ϕ_2.

If such increments become lasting, of course, over long periods of time, he will be able to supply an increased amount of effort and could eventually reach points on the long-run subsistence effort locus Φ – though he would *prefer* to go to a point above that locus if it were open to him to do so. As we have pointed out already, we leave it for a later stage of our argument to specify more exactly what is meant by these short or long periods of time involved in constructing the two types of loci.

Another set of questions remains to be discussed in this section. Clearly loci Φ and ϕ_i are reminiscent of the more conventional indifference curves, used in economic analysis. They also represent alternative combinations between which a man is indifferent. Thus the locus Φ is the ultimate or extreme range of possible combinations between income and effort beyond which life ceases and along which one might appear to be indifferent in the long run in the sense that one can survive. More generally, in the unshaded area to the right of Φ, it is possible to think of alternative indifference maps – we should think of them as short-run indifference maps – corresponding to or defined by alternative levels of real income experienced over a long period of time.[4] Thus, for example, the locus marked u_2 corresponding to an entire convex non-intersecting indifference map is conditioned by a long range experiencing of real income y_2. Of course, only points at the level of real income y_2 on the second indifference map can continue indefinitely to be relevant to the problem of income–effort allocation. Points a_2 and a_2' belonging to the second indifference map are such consistent or long-run feasible points.

In a sense the short-run indifference maps corresponding to the three levels of real income are linked to (or germane to) the short-run subsistence–effort loci which also are conditioned by the long range experience of such levels of real income and which should be thought of as the ultimate short-run indifference curves.[5] As the loci ϕ_i move to the left upwards, so do the indifference maps. This merely expresses the fact that as our individual moves to higher and higher levels of real income – each level being experienced over a long period of time – his marginal rate of substitution between effort and income in the short run is declining at any given point in the sense that an extra unit of real income becomes worth more and more of additional amounts of effort.

It may also be interesting to note that as we would move to higher and higher levels of real income, that is, from the zone of developing countries

4 Formally, what we are postulating here is a short-run utility function of the form $U = U(y, E, Y)$ where Y is some average income experienced in the past over a long period of time. Alternatively, and more precisely, Y could stand for income of the preceding period, that is, y_{t-1}. Still another interpretation of Y would be for income of the distance of the actual point in the yE plane from the Φ locus. But with any of these interpretations, the findings for very poor countries would essentially remain the same as those obtained in this paper. As a referee of this paper has suggested, corresponding to all the short-run maps, we have one long-run map each member of which envelopes an infinity of short-run contours at the levels of income defining them.

5 Professor Koopmans (1957, p. 19) draws his nonintersecting curves reaching the frontier of the consumption set at an angle. But it would imply preference of points with considerable excess of income and noneffort (or leisure) above subsistence over situations just on the brink of death by starvation.

considered here living near subsistence, to the zone of advanced wealthy countries with incomes some ten or twenty times higher, where the whole subsistence effort locus becomes irrelevant except for 'inhumanly' extreme levels of effort, the short-run indifference maps would just about merge with each other within the relevant levels, and become the same for all real incomes. And thus with no significant change in the short-run maps as we move from one level to another of real income (all incomes being very high in comparison with the incomes considered in Figure 1), the single (common) map becomes a long-run map corresponding to all high levels of income experienced over long periods of time. In our opinion it is this unique short- and long-run indifference map which has become, culturally, the standard tool of western economists. It just so happens that academic economists have traditionally been members of rather opulent income groups to whom the multiplicity suggested here for the neighbourhood of starvation levels of income never occurred as a real possibility.

It remains now to define more precisely our concepts of short and long run. In fact two distinct sets of interpretations are possible, both highly relevant for our analysis. First, it is possible to argue that what we have referred to as the short run is a period of some one or two years whereas the long run is a time span considerably longer than that, perhaps five or ten years. Thus it can be said that what we have termed in Figure 1 the short-run subsistence effort locus ϕ_1 indicates that within one or two years an idle man living at subsistence cannot increase the level of his effort beyond that locus. If, however, he is allowed to stay at the income y_2 on ϕ_1 for some five or ten years, his overall health, strength, familiarity with the job and also his acquisition of better skills will allow him to reach maximum levels of effort as high as those corresponding to a_2 in Figure 1. Of course it is another matter that he may never need any more to live at the subsistence effort locus Φ.

While the analysis of this paper can be understood in terms of such short and long runs, of some one and five years respectively, the concepts can be given entirely different interpretations and our analysis can still make a good deal of sense, perhaps more sense on this alternative interpretation than on the first one suggested. Suppose that what we have called short run corresponds to a generation and what we have called long run corresponds to intergeneration transitions and movements. What we have termed the short-run indifference maps now would largely correspond to different groups of individuals (that is, different generations).

This intergeneration interpretation of our concepts of short and long run seems to make a good deal of sense in view of the many biological and medical findings obtained for populations living under subsistence conditions. Children born in families living under subsistence conditions in the Andean mountains or in India will at best be able to increase effort in relation to real income according to a locus such as ϕ_1 in Figure 1 and not along the long-range intergeneration Φ.[6] If, however, two or more generations of families can live at the income y_2, such a living standard would permit them to supply a maximum effort corresponding to a_2 on Φ.

The labour-management solution of production in the light of the subsistence–effort function

In the preceding section we have laid down and explained the analytical concepts regarding the absolute ability to supply effort and also regarding the preferences in effort and real income: to summarise, we can say that we have discussed the conditions of labour supply. In this section we will expand the analysis to introduce demand for effort, or more generally to introduce the production possibility resulting from alternative levels of effort.

In Figure 2 we find first of all the long-run subsistence effort locus Φ together with some short-run loci for selected levels of income. In addition we have now introduced the concave locus P,[7] comparable to a conventional production possibility function and expressing the maximum level of real income producible by an *average* or *representative* worker using alternative levels of effort E. To simplify our analysis we assume that in the production process considered the capital per worker is fixed at the level K_o, and so is the rental of capital p_K. Consequently, if our representative does not supply any effort, his maximum attainable real income will be the negative amount $p_K K_o$ indicated in Figure 2 by the point e_o. Regarding the number of workers in the enterprise (for the scale of operation), it can either be assumed that it is fixed or that it is optimally adjusted for each level of E.

As the representative worker moves towards higher and higher levels of effort, the value of real output per man will be increasing. In our diagrammatic representation we have postulated that such increases will be at diminishing rates so that the possibility locus P is strictly concave to the left. However, this assumption is by no means essential for our analysis and we could just as well have postulated the locus P to be a straight line or even a locus slightly convex to the left.

Let us now move to the central point of our argument and examine how

6 An excellent substantiation of this is offered by Marcelo Selowsky (1971).
7 The locus has been discussed in more detail and the concept of effort defined elsewhere (Vanek, 1971, ch. 12, ref. 3). Normally one can think of effort as of some index combining the three main attributes of labour, namely duration (in hours per day), intensity of work and quality of work. The concavity of P is not necessary. To avoid complications we have only to postulate uniqueness of equilibria, a considerably weaker requirement.

in the short and in the long run a labour-managed firm will adjust, or keep adjusting, in finding its equilibrium level of operation and output. Let us re-emphasise that because we are dealing throughout with situations in the vicinity of the subsistence effort locus, the case that we are discussing is one most closely approximating conditions in poor countries. Leaving aside

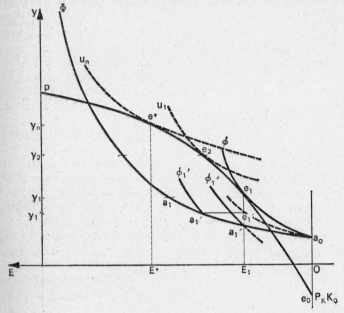

Figure 2

problems of income distribution among the various members of the labour-managed firm and problems of collective decision-making within such a firm which we have discussed elsewhere (Vanek, ch. 12), we postulate that the *representative* worker faces a possibility locus P.

To start from the most rudimentary and in some sense most destitute conditions (conditions which are experienced by many millions in the developing countries), suppose that at first our representative man is unemployed, supplying zero productive effort and is kept alive – at least temporarily – at the level of real income given by the point a_0 through government subsidisation, alms-giving, or the charity of his relatives or acquaintances. Because he has been living in this state of destitution for a long period of time, his short-run ability to increase effort is rather limited and any increases of effort would require a considerable increase in real income.

All this is reflected in Figure 2 by the short-run subsistence effort locus ϕ_o originating at point a_o. As we have drawn the locus, at point e_1 it is just tangential to the possibility locus P. In more human terms this means that in a world of labour management there is hope for our unemployed and destitute man. With some organisational and institutional assistance from some national or local labour-management agency [8] he can start producing at point e_1 in Figure 2, while paying his fixed capital cost, and in fact producing well above the long-range subsistence minimum for the corresponding equilibrium level effort E_1.

But this will be only the first step in the process of our man's advancement. If he would stay at e_1 for a substantial period of time, not only would his maximum producible effort eventually move to point a_1 but he would acquire tastes for real income and effort given by a new short-run preference function characterized in Figure 2 by the short-run indifference curve u_1 corresponding to real income y_1. And this in turn in our labour-management setting, where the workers can decide on their effort–income combination, would lead to an optimum solution at e_2. From the shifting of preference fields with increasing real income explained in the foregoing section it follows that the point e_2 must be at a higher level of real income and a higher level of effort than was the initial point e_1. Moreover, e_2 is well above the long-run subsistence effort locus or any short-run locus corresponding to that level of real income. Figuratively speaking, the income–effort combination has taken off from the runway of subsistence given by the Φ function.

But obviously at point e_2 and real income y_2 the preference map will again shift in the northwest direction and the process of readjustment just described will keep repeating itself, but repeat itself in what we may term a converging manner. It follows from the configuration of the Φ and P functions and the fact that the ϕ_i functions are also nonintersecting short-run indifference curves, that:

The process of readjustment will converge until at a specific point the equilibrium levels of effort and income determined by the short-run indifference map will be exactly consistent with the long-run level of real income determining the specific indifference map;
The solution will be above Φ.

In our diagram this has happened at the point e^* for equilibrium level of effort E^*. The corresponding income y_n now is precisely the income conditioning the short-run indifference curve u_n. And the final equilibrium is

8 This type of agency and its functions have been discussed elsewhere (Vanek, 1970, ch. 15, ref. 3).

far above the initial state e_1 which constituted the original and in fact sole opportunity of our destitute representative man.

Although we have started our 'narrative' from point a_o, it is descriptive of the labour-managed situation of any intermediate solution. For example, if we had first observed a labour-managed firm operating at the level of effort E_1, in Figure 2, the firm would have been producing at e_1, and proceeded therefore to e^*, as described already.

The capitalist solution

Let us now change the assumption of economic organization from labour-managed to capitalist. More specifically, workers now are not free producers deciding on the alternative levels of effort and income but rather they are hired by a capitalist entrepreneur who, within limits to be specified presently, determines some of the key production variables.

We assume that the P curve is unaffected, despite the change in organization. It has been pointed out to us that this is a very strong assumption, since the curve might be moved substantially for such reasons as:

1 There may be a change in the efficiency with which work is organized, when the workers' committee is replaced by a capitalist boss. Thus the time and effort which the workers previously put into running the committee will be available for production, and decisions may be guided by a more single-minded desire for efficiency; on the other hand, the better working morale and intra-firm communication may increase productivity considerably when workers are participating in the management.

2 Capital may be hired more cheaply (or more easily) by a capitalist entrepreneur than it could be by the workers' cooperative – although in certain countries the position may be reversed.

Nevertheless we make this assumption as being the simplest, and as providing a standard of reference.

We will start again from zero, considering a representative man who finds himself at the subsistence point with zero effort a_o in Figure 2. We assume that the optimal employment is known to the employer in advance, and that the representative man characterizes that situation.

The nature of the initial situation is the same as it was in the preceding section, that is we have a possibility locus P and an initial subsistence effort locus ϕ_o. Quite obviously – and this is our first important finding – a capitalist entrepreneur cannot engage in production under such conditions. At best he could produce a point e_1 where he would have to disburse all of his net income (after allowing for the 'hiring' of capital) to his workers and there would be no profit left for him. In fact, under realistic conditions, with the considerable degree of uncertainty and scarcity of entrepreneurial talent which is likely to prevail in developing countries, the entrepreneur would be unwilling to engage in production even if the locus ϕ_o were somewhat below the position shown in Figure 2.[9]

It would be only at the position indicated by the broken line passing through e_1', with a profit margin per worker (over and above the 'hiring' of capital) equivalent to the distance $e_1 e_1'$ that the capitalist entrepreneur might contemplate entering production.[10] In the short run, he would be paying his workers a real income y_1' for an effort per labourer equal to E_1.

In the long run, if the workers kept receiving income at the rate y_1' operating at the point e_1', the maximum attainable effort per worker, as we have argued previously, would increase, moving as high as the level corresponding to a_1' in Figure 2. In other words, in the long run, the point e_1' would no longer be at the subsistence effort.

Four alternative further solutions now are conceivable:

Solution 1

The entrepreneur, realizing that there are large numbers of unemployed around (under the windows of his factory, as Marx would say) might threaten workers with dismissal unless they increased their effort while receiving the income y_1'. Thereby he might get his entire working force operating in the long run at the point a_1' and this, as the diagram indicates, would give him a considerably increased profit. Realizing that what we are calling effort here has at least three composite dimensions – length of working hours, quality of work and intensity of work – it becomes quite obvious that many instances of this type of adjustment could be found in history, in early stages of industrialization.

Solution 2

Using very much the same threat or argument as in Solution 1, the entrepreneur, alternatively, over longer periods of time, could seek to depress the real income of his workers from the level y_1' as low as the level consistent with the long run subsistence–effort line, that is, to the point a_1''. Any combination of results between or outside points a_1' and a_2'' would be conceivable, including, at least as a possibility, the one where the capitalist's profit is maximized. A solution on Φ in the third quadrant remains the most likely because the entrepreneur does not know the locus Φ

---

9 It is also important to realize in this connection that entrepreneurial *excess* profits by those in business already are normally far above zero in developing countries.
10 We have drawn the diagram in such a way as to have the capitalist's profit at maximum for E, but this is by no means essential for our argument.

nor is it in the interest of the workers to reveal it to him. Under such conditions it is most likely that starting from e_1' the entrepreneur will try to maximize the return from his threats, and move in the southwest direction.

The important characteristic of all such solutions is that eventually the entrepreneur gets to the long-run subsistence effort locus and realizes considerably increased profits. Some might call it an increased rate of exploitation. Analytically, the most important fact is that wherever the long-run point of production on Φ may be, at a_1', a_1'' or anywhere else, none of the dynamics of expansion described in the preceding section can occur for the simple reason that the decision maker, that is, the capitalist entrepreneur, is completely oblivious of the preferences of his workers and is simply concerned with maximization of his own profit subject only to the life-and-death frontier Φ of the workers. The fact that he considers his workers as any other factor of production, that is, raw labour force, backfires in the social sense by stifling development, expansion and advancement for men at a very rudimentary level of existence, such as that corresponding to the range a_1', a_1''. Moreover, the workers (the majority of the population) live at subsistence, that is, under very difficult conditions. Some might argue rather cynically that the high profits made by the entrepreneur can serve the development effort through accumulation. But let us not forget that under both capitalist and labour-management systems there is the amount $p_K K_o$ which represents the cost of use of capital: under certain conditions this can constitute considerable resources for investment and capital accumulation.[11] Also it must be noted that even in the labour-management solution discussed in the preceding section, the income earned by the representative worker might be diminished from the very high levels indicated by the locus P by appropriate taxation, proceeds of which then would be used for accumulation. But let us now turn to the third possible solution.

Solution 3

Especially in situations of modern underdevelopment – as contrasted with the underdevelopment in industrialized countries some hundred or two hundred years ago following the industrial revolution – we often find a solution conditioned by the existence and considerable power of labour unions which have been introduced partly as a result of an international demonstration effect and partly as a result of a desperate attempt to combat situations like those described in our Solutions 1 and 2. That solution is one where the workers through power of their labour union resist over

11 The importance of such resources in the national economy has been considered elsewhere (Vanek, 1970, ch. 18, ref. 3).

long periods of time a movement from e_1' in Figure 2 towards a_1' or a_1'' and thus retain the position at e_1'.

Staying there over longer periods of time of course makes their condition somewhat less deplorable than in the first two situations. However, the inefficiency – let us refer to it as the stifling effect – still is present, the production remaining frozen in the initial point, and the changing preferences and ability to work of the workers with an increased living standard has no effect on further adjustment of the equilibrium of the firm.

While the situation is frozen in Solution 3, as we have seen, one might argue that solutions at points such as a_1', a_1'', in Figure 2, could not be solutions of long-range equilibrium because, given the locus ϕ_l the private entrepreneur is not maximizing his profit. But such an objection is not correct. Take, for example, the situation where the entrepreneur has in the way explained before reduced the real income of his workers to the absolute minimum and is operating at the point a_1''. In the short run, which normally will be the more relevant time horizon for him, he can increase the effort of his workers only along a locus such as ϕ_1'' and this would not add much if anything to his profit. On the contrary, in the 'good' capitalist tradition of the nineteenth century, he might try even to reduce real income below a_1'' taking the broken prolongation of ϕ_1'' below Φ mistakenly as the relevant locus. But sooner or later he would have to admit his mistake and thus remain on Φ at a_1'' or somewhere in its vicinity.

Solution 4

Referring to Figure 3, the essence of our argument in Solution 3 was that the primary purpose of the union is to resist employers' attempts to move the workers towards the long-range subsistence effort line Φ.[12] In many cases it can be said that the task of the union thus would be accomplished and therefore point e_1 would truly become a frozen point from which no further movement would take place.

If, however, a more subtle behaviour of the union is envisaged whereby it attempts to increase the utility of its members, even if this would involve gaining in terms of income and losing in terms of effort, or vice versa, then the point e_1 in Figure 3 need not be a frozen point. It is only in the case where the short-run preference map u_1, corresponding to income y_1, coincides with the short-run subsistence effort locus ϕ_e at e_1 that that point will be frozen. In that case, as is apparent from the locus P' (parallel to P and below that locus by the distance equivalent to the profit per worker in the initial short-run equilibrium accruing to the capitalist), there

12 Especially in countries experiencing high inflation rates, the prevention of a retrogression towards a_1'' in Figure 2 will be by far the most important preoccupation of a labour union.

is no movement from e_1 which would improve at the same time the profit per worker of the capitalist and the social utility of the union members.

If such a coincidence shown in Figure 3 by the equality of loci ϕ_0 and u_1 does not hold, there will be a small zone in the effort-income plane wherein starting from point e_1 the members of the union and the entre-

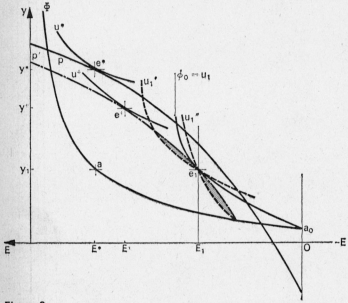

Figure 3

preneur can improve their respective positions. For example, when the preference function corresponding to y_1 passing through e_1 assumes the position u_1', then we will have the shaded zone defined by u_1' and P' in the diagram. Alternatively, in the case where the indifference curve at e_1 is steeper than ϕ_1, we have the other shaded zone pointing from e_1 in the southeast direction. Movements into these respective zones would improve conditions of both the entrepreneur and the union and thus they can be thought of as zones of collective bargaining.

It may be useful to note at this point that indeed the locus P' gives the maximum income, for each level of effort, that our entrepreneur would ever have to pay under pressure from the union because he always has the option to realize the profit corresponding to point e_1 in Figure 3 by hiring those who are unemployed according to the short-run subsistence effort line ϕ_0.

Now, of the two shaded areas that we have termed the collective bargaining zones, the one pointing in the northwest direction should be considered the most likely and, on our strict assumptions, the only possible outcome. This is so because, with an increasing real income from that corresponding to a_o in Figure 3 to the level of y_1, we expect flattening of indifference curves at any given point and thus, since ϕ_o is also an indifference curve corresponding to the initial level of income given by a_o, the indifference curve at e must assume the position given in the diagram by u_1'.

Of course, it cannot be overemphasized at this stage of our argument that the collective bargaining zones may be rather imperceptible and may be neglected by a labour union whose primary purpose is to prevent movements from e_1 in the southwest direction. If, however, the subtle mechanism of moving into the collective bargaining zones is accepted, it can be argued that a similar type of movement and gradual readjustment of real incomes through collective bargaining can take place as the one leading the labour-managed firm from the initial solution to a point such as e^* described in the third section. Clearly, if the union through collective bargaining moves from e_1 in Figure 3 into the collective bargaining zone northwest of that point, this will increase the real income of the union members and make their short-run preference functions or indifference curves alter in the direction explained in the second section. And this process again will continue until at some level of real income such as y^+, at e^+ and u^+ in our diagram, no further bargaining can take place because the collective bargaining zone has vanished.

We can sum up the principal findings of this section in the following manner. In developing countries where there is a substantial pool of employed and unemployed men living at subsistence, the capitalist solution is – on the assumptions made in this article – far inferior to the labour-managed solution because of two different stifling effects. The first is that in many cases production will not even be started or undertaken under capitalist conditions, where it would have been under labour management. The second stifling effect is that even if production is started by capitalist firms, our assumptions imply that the production solution becomes frozen at a rather rudimentary level of effort and output, although under labour management a long-range expansion, advancement and self improvement would have been a necessary result. Existence of a labour union under capitalism is likely to improve the lot of the working man, but can never, on our assumptions, produce anything like the labour-managed solution.

References

KOOPMANS, T. C. (1957), *Three Essays on the State of Economic Science*, McGraw-Hill.

SELOWSKY, M. (1971), 'Infant malnutrition and human capital formation', presented at the Research Workshop on Problems of Agricultural Development in Latin America, Caracas, Venezuela.

VANEK, JAROSLAV (1970), *The General Theory of Labor-Managed Market Economies*, Cornell University Press.

VANEK, JAROSLAV (1971), *The Participatory Economy: An Evolutionary Hypothesis and a Strategy for Development*, Cornell University Press.

28 Jaroslav Vanek

The Basic Theory of Financing of Participatory Firms

Jaroslav Vanek, 'The basic theory of financing of participatory firms', Working Paper no. 27, Cornell University, Department of Economics, Ithaca, July 1971.

Introduction

In an earlier study entitled 'Some Fundamental Considerations of Financing and the Form of Ownership under Labor Management' (Vanek, 1973) I have assembled a large number of arguments to explain in simple terms – primarily to the non-economist or practical policy maker – the desirability of having labor-managed firms always financed from the outside and not through self-financing and collective ownership. The purpose of this paper is to provide a unified theoretical basis on which the argument for external financing and against self-financing and collective ownership is based. We will primarily concentrate on the latter aspect, namely, the analysis of the drawbacks of self-financing, the advantages of the opposite form of financing through a capital market external to the firm being quite self-evident by implication.[1]

The arguments which follow are of considerable real relevance. All the actual forms of self-management that we encounter today in the world, be they the Yugoslav worker-managed firm, an Israeli kibbutz, a Western industrial producers' cooperative, or a Latin American farm cooperative, are much closer in their design and actual operation to the case of self-financing and collective ownership than to that of external financing. That these productive organizations rely heavily on their own funds, primarily in the forms of initial contributions or retained earnings which are largely irrecuperable (except in some instances, and only partially, at retirement) is not difficult to understand. Not only are – especially in the Western world – banks and other external creditors unwilling to finance the totality, or even a major portion of a labor-managed firm's assets, but, and this is more important, the firm itself will generally not want such financing because this would jeopardize its autonomy and thus undermine its very nature and *raison d'être*.

1 Into our concept of external funding we also include redeemable savings deposits of members, bearing a market rate of return paid, as to other creditors, prior to the distribution of labor incomes. To the extent that our analysis comes out in favor of external funding, it also favors this type of individualized funding by members.

In my opinion (with which some will disagree) the arguments presented hereafter are so powerful in explaining the shortcomings of traditional or conventional forms of producer cooperatives and participatory firms, that they offer an ample explanation of the comparative failure of these forms in history, ever since they were first conceived of by the writers of the eighteenth and nineteenth centuries. The development of this analysis was to me personally most gratifying. It had always puzzled me how it could have been possible that a productive organization based on cooperation, harmony of interests and the brotherhood of men, so appealing and desirable on moral and philosophical grounds, could have done so poorly when subjected to a practical test. It seems to me that we now have both an explanation and a way of remedy.

Assumptions

As customary in theoretical arguments, we will consider in most of this discussion a 'pure' or 'extreme' case, where, if a firm wants to invest, it must do so from its own resources, as a matter of a collective saving effort, the title to which remains in the hands of the working collective and not in the hands of individual members who would earn a given return on the capital and could recuperate the principal part of the investment at some point.[2] Later at the end of the fourth section we will generalize this discussion and permit some degree of external financing.

To simplify the analysis further, we will speak about a single firm, labor-managed, selling its product x at a constant price, for simplicity equal to unity, and using only capital K and (its members') labor L. Capital has an infinite durability, and thus there are no problems of depreciation. The production function is of the smooth neoclassical type. We will consider two cases: a linear-homogeneous function

$$x = Lf(K/L) \qquad\qquad 1$$

and a conventional increasing-diminishing returns function

$$x = x(K, L). \qquad\qquad 2$$

For simplicity, we also assume that all members of the firm have the same time preference R.[3] More explicitly, in a simple case involving only two periods, each worker is willing to save and surrender from his current consumption one dollar provided that next year he will be able to receive in return at least $1+R$ dollars.

2 In fact, this situation in many respects would approximate that of a capital market external to the firm.
3 R can be thought of also as an average taken over all the members. In that case, however, our analysis would not be perfectly rigorous because of some structural problems of decision-making which might arise.

We further postulate that the working community acts in its own self-interest and the interest of its individual members and not in the interest of those not belonging to it. This may be an incorrect assumption in some cases, where altruistic, religious or family considerations prevail. But we will not consider such conditions here, because they are rare and because their implications for our argument are quite obvious.

The case of constant returns to scale

The essentials which we need for our analysis are summarized in Figure 1. The function $f(K/L)$ expressing output per laborer (both in physical terms and in terms of value) is plotted against the capital–labor ratio and, as is well known, this must be strictly concave on the assumptions made. It can also be easily established that the slope at any given point, such as the slope A of dc at c, measures the marginal product of capital, the segment bc measures the income share of capital per laborer if capital is paid its marginal product, and the segment ab measures the wage rate provided also that labor is paid its marginal product.

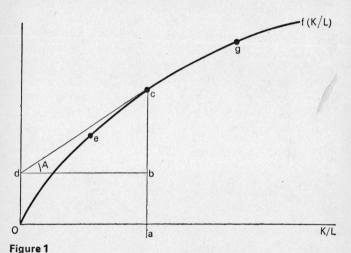

Figure 1

Suppose now that a firm finds itself temporarily or permanently at a point where its capital–output ratio equals a. The firm may have reached that point through an initial investment by those working in it, either through a transition from another type of firm (e.g. nationalization as in Yugoslavia) or through prior self-financing based on current income.

When the firm finds itself at that point, the income per worker actually earned is equivalent to the distance *ac*. The segments defined by point *b* and explained earlier are irrelevant because the community owns collectively its assets and does not pay for them.

Let us analyse the dynamic forces which will act on that equilibrium. First (at least on the assumptions made) there is the force that can be termed that of *self-extinction*. Irrespective of whether the point *a* is one for which the firm would be in equilibrium, given the time preferences of its members, there will be a natural tendency to reduce the number of members, for the given capital stock, and thereby move to the right of point *a*, to higher levels of income per laborer. Obviously, the working community will try to prevent this happening through prohibiting the expelling of members. But through attrition, retirement or voluntary withdrawal, it will always be possible to reduce numbers in the long run. The full compensation of departing members which would also mitigate this self-extinction force will generally be impossible, both because of a basic unwillingness to compensate a voluntarily retiring member and because of a lack of cash with which to do so.

This first force would thus tend to move the solution point indefinitely to the right in Figure 1, through a reduction in membership with a constant capital stock. It would be terminated only at the point of a single member adhering to the firm.[4]

Suppose now that the initial points *a* and *c* in Figure 1 actually correspond to an equilibrium of time preference in the sense that the community did not have any desire to invest or disinvest over time. As the self-extinction force sets in, as explained above, and the capital–labor ratio increases (we move to the right in Figure 1) the marginal productivity of capital, the slope of $f(K/L)$, diminishes and thus there will be a desire on the part of the members of the firm to return to the equilibrium point *a* through gradual disinvestment and capital consumption on the part of those who remain in the enterprise. We can now refer to this as the *second self-extinction force*, reserving for the other the term *first self-extinction force*.

But let us now turn to the forces determining the equilibrium of the firm as related to the time preference *R*. The first important conclusion, based on what we may refer to as the underinvestment force, is that if the time preference of the community is *R*, its equilibrium production will correspond to a point where the marginal productivity of capital is well above that magnitude at a level A^*, above *R* by a positive magnitude *D*, such that

$$A^* = R + D, \quad D > 0. \qquad 3$$

4 As we will see later for the case of our second technology, $x(K, L)$, this extreme situation will disappear, but its basic and undesirable character will remain.

This must be so for the following reason. If a member of the community invests a dollar, his total return from the investment will be only the increased future current incomes and *never* the recuperation of the amount itself invested, on grounds of the collective nature of the investment. Supposing that the net addition to his income is the marginal product of capital A of $i = 1, ..., T$ years preceding his expected retirement, we have as the criterion for investment, for the (subjective) present value V of all these returns.

$$V = A \sum_{i=1}^{T} (1+R)^{-i} \geqslant 1. \qquad\qquad 4$$

On the other hand, if the member could have recuperated the principal part of his investment, he would have decided in favor of an investment W provided that

$$W = A \sum_{i=1}^{T} (1+R)^{-i} + (1+R)^{-T} \geqslant 1. \qquad\qquad 5$$

By definition of subjective time preference, we know that in this case (equation **5**), $W = 1$ for $A = R$. We thus can write **4** as

$$A \sum_{i=1}^{T} (1+R)^{-i} - R \sum_{i=1}^{T} (1+R)^{-i} - (1+R)^{-T} \geqslant 0, \qquad\qquad 6$$

from where by inspection, it immediately follows that in order to invest under the criterion of **4**, the return A must exceed A^* which itself exceeds R by an amount

$$D = (1+R)^{-T} / \sum_{i=1}^{T} (1+R)^{-i}, \qquad\qquad 7$$

a decreasing function of T. If $A = A^*$ no investment or disinvestment will take place and thus, in connection with what we have called the *underinvestment force*, the firm will be in equilibrium. Obviously, this equilibrium is one of underinvestment because the marginal productivity of capital A^* exceeds the subjective rate of time preference. This differential D can be extremely significant especially when the membership time-expectation T is low. In the extreme case where all members are to retire in one year, we have $D = 1$. When $R = 10$ per cent, D then is 1000 per cent of R and A^*, the critical level of the marginal productivity of capital equal to $R(100+1000)$ per cent, i.e. 110 per cent. With that A^*, of course, hardly anyone would ever invest. With $T > 1$, the results become less extreme, but still highly significant, the realistic ranges for A^* being somewhere between twice and four times the time preference rate R.

The next effect, which is just as undesirable as the preceding ones, we will refer to as the *never-employ effect*, deriving from its corresponding *never-employ force*. With reference to Figure 1, suppose that the firm finds itself at point e, whereas the equilibrium level of the marginal productivity of capital A^* corresponds to point c; at point g, finally, the slope, that is the marginal productivity of capital, is equal to the time preference of the working community R. Because at e the marginal productivity of capital is more than A^*, the members of the community will desire to invest and expand production with increasing K/L, as long as K/L falls short of the level indicated by a in the diagram. On the assumptions made, in particular self-financing and constant returns to scale, this is the only situation where growth of the firm occurs, of course, assuming that the membership of the firm is constant and the first self-extinction effect inoperative. But it will be noted – and this we have referred to as the never-employ effect – that under no circumstances will the firm admit new members into the community, as such action would necessarily reduce the capital–labor ratio and consequently the income per worker.

It takes only a little reflection to realize that with external financing through a competitive capital market, at a rate equal to the time preference R, all four undesirable effects would disappear, and an equilibrium at point g in Figure 1 would be established. The first self-extinction effect would be absent since by reducing the membership of the community the K/L ratio would increase above that corresponding to g, and with constant payment R per unit of capital, the return per worker would decline. The desire to reduce the capital stock would *ipso facto* also disappear, because this would disturb the equilibrium from its position at g, and thus the second self-extinction effect also vanishes.

The underinvestment effect disappears, so to speak by definition, as the equilibrium now is at g, precisely at the point where the marginal productivity of capital equals the rate of time preference R. Finally, the never-employ effect also disappears in the sense that at any point the community can invest together with increasing employment *pari passu* without worsening anybody's condition. Actually, it is the very property of constant returns-to-scale technology that proportional increases in both factors, with unchanged prices of capital, leave labor's condition unchanged.

The case of increasing-diminishing returns

In the preceding section we have developed a simple theoretical model of a participatory firm operating under constant returns to scale, shown the equilibrium and disequilibrium behavior of that model and indicated four important drawbacks – or negative effects – of self-financing and collective ownership of participatory (labor-managed) firms. In this section we will make a major step in the direction of a more realistic model by relaxing the assumption of constant returns to scale. Instead, we will assume that the technology employed by the participatory firm is that given by 2 above, subject to increasing and then diminishing returns to scale. In fact, our analysis will also cover the case which is perhaps the most realistic of all, where increasing returns at first are followed, for higher levels of output, by constant returns to scale.[5] This is so because, as we will see presently, such firms can never grow to a point outside the increasing-returns range of the technology.

To start our discussion, let us turn to the capital–labor input plane of the firm in Figure 2 and identify in it some significant loci. First we observe the contour *EE*; it is the locus of maximum physical efficiency[6] along which, for prescribed K/L ratios, both average factor productivities are maximized. It may be useful to recall that a participatory firm which is externally financed will always, in the long run and under competitive conditions, operate somewhere at *EE*, and thus maximize its factor productivities. It is also useful to recall that along *EE* the technology is 'locally' subject to constant returns to scale, and to the left and below that locus returns to scale are increasing. To the right and above, returns to scale are diminishing, or in the 'realistic' situation noted above, constant to scale. All the forces described in the preceding section for the case of constant returns to scale are 'locally' valid along the locus *EE* and, as we will see presently, for that reason no equilibrium of a collectively self-financing participatory firm could ever exist anywhere along that locus.

Rather, the equilibrium of the firm with collective ownership and financing will have to be somewhere at the locus *aa* which is located in the increasing-returns zone and which is technically inefficient. It is the locus along which the average and marginal products of labor are equalized (for any level of employment of capital) and along which, as is well known, the average product of labor is at a maximum. The result is obvious, because indeed it is the average product of labor that the community wants to maximize under self-financing (i.e. no payment of rental for capital) so as to maximize every member's income.

The inefficient operation at *aa* is in effect the analogue of the two self-extinction effects noted for the constant-returns technology. The difference here is that the community could never reduce itself to a single member because this would make it extremely inefficient on grounds of considerable losses due to nonrealization of economies of scale.

5 Empirical studies indicate that diminishing returns are rarely present for high levels of capital and labor employment, except where land is utilized intensively as a productive factor.
6 For a detailed discussion of this locus see Vanek, 1970, ch. 2.

The underinvestment effect explained in the preceding section remains unchanged. Again, with collective ownership and savings the equilibrium marginal product of capital must fall well above the rate of time preference R, at a rate which we can again refer to as $A^* = R + D$. Corresponding to $x_K = A^*$, we have another locus in Figure 2. It is at the intersection of aa and $x_K = A^*$, at a^*, that we find the full equilibrium of our participatory self-financed firm, both equilibrium conditions being fulfilled at that point.

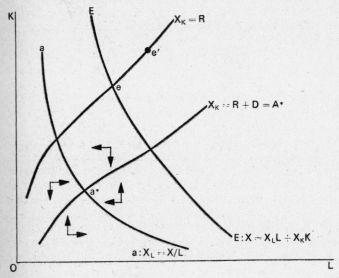

Figure 2

The dynamic forces of adjustment for any point away from equilibrium are indicated by arrows, leading to the conclusion that a^* is a stable position. It will be noted that to the right (left) of aa employment will be declining (rising) so as to increase the income per worker, while below (above) $x_K = A^*$ there will be accumulation (decumulation) of capital in accordance with the members' time preference.

By contrast, under external financing at a capital cost equal to the time preference R, the equilibrium of a participatory firm must be along the locus defined in Figure 2 as $x_K = R$. Under these conditions the income per worker will be maximized at some point on the locus of maximum physical efficiency EE. The equilibrium of a labor-managed externally financed firm thus will be at the intersection of the two loci at e. As is well known, e will also be the equilibrium of a capitalist firm provided that it operates without profit. If it makes positive profits, its equilibrium will be somewhere in the diminishing returns zone of the production function on $x_K = R$, at a point such as e'.

Comparing points e and a^* it thus becomes apparent that in the case studied in this section where the technology is subject to increasing returns to scale for relatively low levels of output – a highly realistic condition in most situations – self-financing by a participatory firm leads to both inefficient production at a low level of output and to underinvestment, as compared to a solution obtained with external financing at a price of capital equal to the rate of time preference. Undercapitalization and a small size are also the most significant drawbacks of traditional workers' cooperatives.

Before concluding this section, we may realistically relax the assumption of a 100 per cent collective internal funding and permit some external funding or individualized redeemable internal funding. The general conclusion is that such an alteration of conditions will weaken the inefficiency explained in this section – largely in proportion to the degree of external funding – but will never eliminate it altogether.

To demonstrate this, it need only be realized that if, for a portion of the capital stock, the cooperative must pay a market price (rate of interest), this will move the locus of maximum labor incomes (no longer the locus of maximum average labor productivity) from aa in Figure 2 to the right, but not as far as EE (the locus attained with full external funding). On the other hand, if the working collective can at all times count on a given proportion of any investment to be financed externally, at the rate R, this will reduce the necessary differential D, and thus bring A^* closer to R and shift the locus $x_K = A^*$ in Figure 2 upwards. Thus the solution point a^* will travel, roughly speaking, toward e on account of both forces (both shifting loci).

The results in real perspective

Looking at Figure 2, the comparison between points a^* and points such as e or e' seems to offer a good deal of the explanation of why in the real world the producer cooperatives – as we have noted in the first section, basically internally and collectively financed participatory firms – have fared so poorly in a capitalist environment. The hostility and prejudice of that environment could explain only a part, and perhaps only a small part, of the difficulties of the cooperatives. The real economic reasons appear as very powerful if we realize how large the orders of magnitude of the underinvestment and underproduction effects corresponding to point a^* actually can be in the real world.

To make this comparison more clear and more tangible let us contemplate a situation of two similar workers, one working in a self-financing production cooperative and the other in a capitalist firm operating (with zero profit) at the minimum average cost point, both firms producing the same product and selling in the same capitalist market. Provided that technologies are unaffected by economic organization and that both workers have the same time preference, but one saves collectively in his cooperative while the other individually through a capital market which finances the capitalist's firm, the situation in equilibrium can be as shown in Table 1 in terms of hypothetical figures.

Table 1

	Cooperative firm	Capitalist firm
product per man	30	50
wage	30	30
interest income from accumulated savings	0	20
recuperable actual accumulation of savings per worker	0	100
irrecuperable accumulation (collective) per worker	100	0
total capital accumulation	10 000	20 000
employment	100	200

In our competitive capitalist firm the typical worker not only earns a considerably higher current aggregate income than in the self-financed production cooperative, but he retains the command over his accumulated savings of one hundred. As we have defined the situation, the worker's only advantage in the cooperative is the moral and psychological one, because he works in a humanly more pleasant environment with a good deal less or no alienation. What we have not considered in our example are the incentive effects of participation on productivity and effort. But these advantages, compared to the considerable drawbacks of a lower productivity and earning power and a lack of command over wealth once accumulated, in many situations were not sufficient counterweights. When in the context of, say, nineteenth-century England or Germany, the factors of a hostile environment, lack of understanding and class resentment are added, no wonder that the production cooperative remained not much more than the utopian dream of a handful of idealistic men.

By contrast to the collectively financed production cooperative illustrated in the first column of Table 1, the economic performance of a participatory firm with external financing would lead to the pattern illustrated in the second column, for an 'ideal' capitalist firm. But in addition, the human and economic advantages of participation, incentives, higher productivity, absence of alienation and a no-conflict atmosphere of work, absent in the capitalist firm, would be added to the redesigned participatory firm.

But of course, to have full external financing (as here defined) and thereby obtain the benefits noted, one can never rely on the conventional private banking system. Conventional banks, whether in Victorian England or the modern United States, would hardly lend much to a producer cooperative, and the cooperatives themselves might shun such funding. It must take an act of political will, or a philanthropic (not profit- and power-oriented) group of men to provide the necessary characteristics of the capital market which would support the smooth and efficient operation of a participatory economy or a participatory sector. Such an economy or sector would then be optimal both humanly and in terms of economic efficiency, superior to all existing forms of productive organization.

References

VANEK, J. (1970), *The General Theory of Labor-Managed Market Economies*, Cornell University Press.

VANEK, J. (1973), 'Some fundamental considerations on financing and the form of ownership under labor management', in H. C. Bos (ed.), *Economic Structure and Development*, North Holland, Amsterdam.

Further Reading

This is a selected and annotated bibliography of books in English on Labour Management and related topics, with emphasis on post-1960 publications. While only more substantial works are included, the selections contain extensive references to other books and articles related to labour management. Also actual case and country studies have been kept to a minimum. The excellent *Bibliography* of the International Institute for Labour Studies contains many such references. In addition there are good select bibliographies in the books by Jan Vanek, and Clarke, Fatchett and Roberts.

I. Adizes, *Industrial Democracy: Yugoslav Style*, Free Press, New York, 1971.
An analysis of the limits of democratic decision-making in firms in the context of a competitive market economy.

H. Arendt, *On Revolution*, Viking Press, 1963; Penguin, 1973.
The author discusses the spontaneous emergence of workers' councils during revolutionary movements, suggesting their political nature as the cause of their failure.

C. Bellas, *Industrial Democracy and the Worker-Owned Firm*, Praeger, 1972.
Supplements the Berman book with a summary analysis and examines some of the problems of the firms from a psychological perspective.

C. Benello and D. Roussopoulos (eds.), *The Case for Participatory Democracy: Some Prospects for a Radical Society*, Grossman Publishers, New York, 1971.
A collection of articles representing a New Left effort toward developing a theory of participatory democracy.

K. Berman, *Worker-Owned Plywood Companies: An Economic Analysis*, Washington State University Press, 1967.
A comprehensive account of worker-owned firms, their relation to the industry and their significance as cooperative ventures.

M. Berthelot, *Works Councils in Germany*, International Labour Office, Geneva, 1924.
An account of the evolution of works councils in Germany after the First World War.

R. Bicanic, *The Turning Point of Economic Development*, Studies in the Social Sciences, vol. 4, Mouton, The Hague, 1972.

R. Bicanic, *Economic Policy in Socialist Yugoslavia*, Soviet and East European Studies Series, Cambridge University Press, 1973.
These collections overlap to some extent and both contain the essay 'Some Aspects of the Policy of Workers' Income in Yugoslavia' as well as the complete bibliography of Bicanic's books and articles.

T. Blair, *The Land to Those Who Work It: Algeria's Experiment in Workers' Management*, Doubleday, 1969.
Less comprehensive than the book by Clegg below. Like Clegg's account it

indicates that any lessons drawn from Algerian workers' councils must be considered in the context of the turbulent situation in Algeria after the National Government came to power.

R. Blauner, *Alienation and Freedom*, University of Chicago Press, 1964.
An analysis of technologically different industries in America and the manifestations of alienation in each.

F. Blum, *Work and Community. The Scott Bader Commonwealth and the Quest for a New Social Order*, Routledge & Kegan Paul, 1968.
A comprehensive account of the Scott Bader Commonwealth.

P. Blumberg, *Industrial Democracy: The Sociology of Participation*, Constable, 1968.
The work of E. Mayo and the most important sociological studies on participation of the preceding two decades are reviewed.

T. Bottomore, *Elites and Society*, C. A. Watts, 1964; Penguin, 1966.
In the relevant parts of this book the author argues powerfully that for political democracy to survive people must have decision-making power in one of the most important spheres of life, work.

J. Bowie, *Sharing Profits with Employees: A Critical Study of Methods in Light of Present Conditions*, Pitman, 1922.
Drawing on his analysis of profit-sharing schemes in Britain during the preceding half-century, the author issued a critique of profit sharing that has still much validity and relevance.

M. Broekmeyer, *Yugoslav Workers' Self-Management*, Reidel, Dordrecht, Holland, 1970.
The papers and discussions of an important and in-depth symposium held in Amsterdam in 1970.

R. Clarke, D. Fatchett and B. Roberts, *Workers' Participation in Management in Britain*, London School of Economics Industrial Relations Series, Heinemann, 1972.
Contains a brief review of various types and ideas of participation and a survey of the extent and types of participation in Britain.

H. A. Clegg, *A New Approach to Industrial Democracy*, Blackwell, 1960.
The author proposes a scheme for industrial democracy based on trade unions fulfilling the role of an opposition and check on management power.

I. Clegg, *Workers' Self-Management in Algeria*, Allen Lane, 1971.
Mainly an informational and political account of the emergence and struggle by workers following Algerian liberation. Little analysis of workers' councils *per se*, but the Algerian experience demonstrates how, in a turbulent situation, workers turn to cooperative organization.

K. Coates (ed.), *Can the Workers Run Industry?*, Sphere Books, 1968.
An examination of British industry, emphasizing the insufficiency of nationalization and the need for new forms of decision-making organization.

K. Coates and A. Topham (eds.), *Industrial Democracy in Great Britain*, MacGibbon & Kee, 1968.
A large collection of readings dealing exclusively with British sources and issues. A trade-union-oriented view of industrial democracy is predominant.

G. D. H. Cole, *Guild Socialism: A Plan for Economic Democracy*, F. A. Stokes, New York, 1920.
A comprehensive and detailed account of a guild socialist society founded on democratic work organizations.

H. Daly (ed.), *Essays Toward a Steady-State Economy*, Freeman, New York, 1973.
A treatment of what the editor refers to as 'an emerging paradigm shift in political economy'.

P. Derrick and F. J. Phipps (eds.), *Co-Ownership Cooperation and Control: An Industrial Objective*, Longman, 1969.
A study of collectives and workers' councils in Israel, the Soviet Union, and Yugoslavia, as well as treatment of the theory, practice, moral and legal aspects of co-ownership.

J. Dirlam and J. Plummer, *An Introduction to the Yugoslav Economy*, Merrill, Columbus, 1973.
Mainly a study of changes in the Yugoslav economy between 1965 and 1971. A final chapter assesses the operation of self-management.

Dubrovnik Papers. First International Sociological Conference on Participation and Self-Management, Zagreb, 1972.
A large collection of mostly sociological papers and studies of participation.

F. Emery and E. Thorsrud, *Form and Content in Industrial Democracy*, Tavistock, 1969.
This study draws on experience from Norway and other European countries in an analysis of the relationship between technology and humanity in the context of viewing the work process as a socio-technical system requiring efficient organization of workers and machines.

A. Flanders, R. Pomeranz and J. Woodward. *Experiment in Industrial Democracy*, Faber and Faber, 1968.
An account of an experiment initiated from the top, involving consultation, profit sharing and large doses of paternalism.

P. Freire, *Pedagogy of the Oppressed*, Herder and Herder, 1970; Penguin, 1972.
The author stresses the importance of education for liberation and the need for cooperation.

R. Garaudy, *The Turning Point of Socialism*, Fontana, 1970.
A once prominent member of the French Communist Party discusses, in this book that led to his expulsion, the need for a more humanitarian socialism.

D. Gorupic and I. Paj, *Workers Self-Management in Yugoslav Undertakings*, Ekonomski Institut, Zagreb, 1970.
A presentation of the organizational structure and mechanisms of workers' participation in Yugoslavia.

A. Gorz, *Strategy for Labor*, Beacon Press, Boston, 1968.
The author argues that strategy for gaining control over work and its nature should be one of 'non-reformist reforms'.

D. Guerin, *Anarchism*, Monthly Review Press, New York, 1970.
A good account of anarchism and contains Noam Chomsky's 'Notes on Anarchism' as an introduction.

B. Horvat, *An Essay on Yugoslav Society*, International Arts & Sciences Press, New York, 1969.
A statement of Yugoslav Marxism and the ideological rationale for self-management.

G. Hunnius, G. Garson and J. Case (eds.), *Workers Control: A Reader on Labour and Social Change*, Random House, 1973.
Divided into four sections the readings cover the nature of work and outdated attitude of unions; role of collective bargaining and failure to cope with many contemporary problems, participation in Sweden, Israel, Germany and Yugoslavia and a range of views on the nature and strategy of workers' control.

International Institute for Labour Studies, *Workers Participation in Management: Selected Bibliography, 1950–1970*, IILS, Geneva, 1971.
Two sections on general and comparative material are followed by a country listing covering forty-eight countries and over 1000 items in English, French, German, Spanish, Italian and Portuguese.

International Labour Office, *Participation of Workers in Decisions within Undertakings*, ILO Labour–Management Relations Series, no. 33, Geneva, 1969.
Papers from conference held in Geneva, 20–29 November 1967.
Covers many special aspects of participation-aims, methods and criticisms, as well as reviewing its adoption and operation in many countries.

International Labour Office, *Workers Management in Yugoslavia*, ILO, Geneva, 1962.
An influential study of the institutional structure and practice of workers' management in Yugoslavia.

International Labour Office, *Report on the International Seminar on Workers' Participation in Decisions within Undertakings*, ILO, Geneva, 1970.
Report on Seminar held in Belgrade, 2–11 December 1969.
Very good summary coverage of participation in twenty-two countries.

G. Ionescu and M. de Madariaga, *Opposition*, C. A. Watts, 1968; Penguin, 1972.
Although somewhat dated, particularly in light of recent constitutional changes, the section on Yugoslavia still gives a good impression of the overall political environment and system.

K. Kanovsky, *The Economy of the Israeli Kibbutz*, Harvard Middle East Monographs no. 13, Harvard University Press, 1966.
The author looks at the history, structure, economic operation and profitability of kibbutzim. Consumption and production are collectivized and it is suggested that the profit motive is followed only to the extent that it is necessary to a self-sustaining economic unit.

J. Klatzman, B. Ilan and Y. Levi (eds.), *The Role of Group Action in the Industrialization of Rural Areas*, Studies in International Economics, Praeger, 1971.
The transition from agriculture to industry as well as specific problems are discussed in the context of cooperative and group action.

J. Knapp, *The Rise of American Cooperative Enterprise, 1620–1920*, Interstate Printers and Publishers, Danville, Illinois, 1969.
A comprehensive historical account of the spontaneous and natural growth of various types of cooperatives and institutions.

J. Kolaja, *Workers' Councils: The Yugoslav Experience*, Tavistock, 1965.
Study of the functioning of workers' councils in two Belgrade factories. Also considered are the roles played by the trade unions, League of Communists and youth organizations in the firms.

L. Kohr, *The Breakdown of Nations*, Routledge & Kegan Paul, 1959.
Drawing on sociocultural and economic arguments, the author proposes the decentralization of political power.

M. Kotler, *Neighborhood Government: The Local Foundation of Political Life*, Bobbs-Merrill, 1969.
This short book puts the case for decentralization and limiting power in cities and giving control to federations based on local community governments.

G. Lakey, *Strategy for a Living Revolution*, Freeman, New York, 1973.
A Quaker view of the non-violent social transformation of the United States. International aspects for developing countries are also explored.

P. Lambert, *Studies in the Social Philosophy of Cooperation*, Cooperative Union, Manchester, 1963.
A presentation and analysis of cooperative principles and experiences. Discusses the issue of producer versus consumer supremacy.

K. Marx and F. Engels, *Writings on the Paris Commune* (H. Draper, ed.), Monthly Review Press, New York, 1971.
The classic authors on one of the great historical examples of an attempt, albeit short-lived, to form an alternative society.

A. H. Maslow, *The Further Reaches of Human Nature*, Penguin, 1973.
In two essays the author draws on the idea of *synergy* and the inadequate theory of human motivation of 'classical economic theory' to stress the need for social conditions in any organization such that the goals of the individual and organization are merged.

D. Milenkovitch, *Plan and Market in Yugoslav Economic Thought*, Yale Russian and East European Studies, Yale University Press, 1971.
A thorough presentation of the economics of socialist development in Yugoslavia within the wider context of the evolution of centralized systems.

J. S. Mill, *Principles of Political Economy, with Some of Their Applications to Social Philosophy*, Penguin, 1970.
Especially relevant for a discussion of cooperation is Chapter 7, section 4, 'On the probable futurity of the laboring classes'.

D. Napagopal, *Experiments in Industrial Democracy*, Asia Publishing House, New York, 1964.
A study of the basic principles underlying experiments in industrial democracy throughout the world in the context of their relevance for India.

J. Nyerere, *Ujamaa. Essays on Socialism*, Oxford University Press, 1968.
A statement of basic humanist principles and goals of development by a leader of African socialism.

C. Pateman, *Participation and Democratic Theory*, Cambridge University Press, 1970.
Discussion of the literature on political theory and industrial democratization. Includes a review of the Yugoslav experience of worker-management. Stresses the need for democratic work-organizations as a base for a truly democratic society and politics.

P.-J. Proudhon, *What is Property?*, Dover, 1970.
This nineteenth-century classic was one of the earlier attempts to develop a theory of property and remains a pillar of anarchism.

E. Rhenman, *Industrial Democracy and Industrial Management: A Critical Essay on the Possible Meanings and Implications of Industrial Democracy*, Technology and Democratic Society Series, Tavistock, 1968.
Examination of the meaning of industrial democracy from the perspective of organization theory.

A. Sturmthal, *Workers' Councils: A Study of Workplace Organization on both sides of the Iron Curtain*, Harvard University Press, 1964.
Case studies of workers' participation in France, Germany, Yugoslavia and Poland.

Jan Vanek, *The Economics of Workers' Management: A Yugoslav Case Study*, Allen & Unwin, 1972.
An effort to explore the behavioural motivation of firms in a society where the profit motive is dominated by others.

Jaroslav Vanek, *The General Theory of Labor-Managed Market Economies*, Cornell University Press, 1970.
To date, the most comprehensive and theoretically rigorous economic analysis of labour management. Microeconomic and macroeconomic aspects, as well as the special dimensions involved when the work collective plays the managerial role, are examined.

Jaroslav Vanek, *The Participatory Economy: An Evolutionary Hypothesis and a Strategy for Development*, Cornell University Press, 1971.
Complements *The General Theory of Labor-Managed Market Economies* by a more general and philosophical discussion. The social and humanistic aspects are stressed and the relevance and potential of labour management for economic growth and development are considered. Labour management is integrated into a theory of history.

V. Vucinich, *Soviet Economic Institutions: The Social Structure of Production Units*, Stanford University Press, 1952.
The chapter on the kolkhoz returns Domar's idealized model of a Soviet collective farm to the harsh reality of Soviet Russia where 'kolkhoz democracy' was devised to make State interference in every aspect of life as inconspicuous as possible.

W. S. Vucinich (ed.), *Contemporary Yugoslavia: Twenty Years of Socialist Experiment*, University of California Press, 1969.
An overall introductory survey of the Yugoslav experience and the particular features of Yugoslavia which have interacted with ideology to yield Yugoslav socialism.

H. Wachtel, *Workers' Management and Workers' Wages in Yugoslavia*, Cornell University Press, 1973.
The early ideas on 'participatory socialism' and the main economic theories of worker management (of Lange, Ward, Domar, Vanek and Horvat) are reviewed. The Yugoslav system of worker management is described and in the most substantial part the determination of wage and inter-industry wage differentials are analysed empirically and theoretically.

B. Ward, *The Socialist Economy: A Study of Organizational Alternatives*, Random House, 1967.
Chapter 8 is a slightly revised version of the author's 1958 paper on the theory of worker management, 'The Firm in Illyria: Market Syndicalism'. The analysis is extended into broader economic issues of Illyria in Chapters 9 and 10.

S. Webb and B. Webb, *Industrial Democracy*, Longman, Green, 1897.
A discussion of the function and characteristics of trade unionism in both the economic and social context and a final chapter considers the interaction of trade unions and democracy.

J. Weinstein, *The Corporate Ideal in the Liberal State, 1900-1918*, Beacon, 1968.
Illustrates the importance of a comprehensive political and economic base, in this case corporate liberalism, in order to influence social order in a certain desired direction.

W. Weisskopf, *Alienation and Economics*, Dutton, 1971.
A treatment of economics as a normative discipline and its contribution to the consequences of the dominant values of industrial society.

Work in America: Report of the Special Task Force to the Secretary of Health, Education and Welfare, Massachusetts Institute of Technology Press, 1973.
This important document draws attention to many of the problems related to work and society. It ranges widely over aspects of work and health, education, job dissatisfaction and redesign as well as problems of specific work and worker categories. Supports the view that a change in the attitude toward work is urgently required.

Author Index

Subject Index

Accumulation,
  capital and land returns, 34–5
  maximization under prescribed wage
    levels, 31
Affluence, 93, 94
Algeria, 'auto-gestation' systems, 91
Amalgamated Engineering Union
  (AEU), 92n
  shop steward representation, 98
America, 18, 23
  chattel-slavery, 145, 149–52, 158
  corporate boards of directors, 86n
  economies of scale, 344
  Junior Republics, 334
  and participation, 324, 328
  and political activity, 332
  prisoner self-government, 334–7
  syndicalism, 66
  worker ownership, 203f
Anarchism, 18, 19, 102
  in syndicalism, 20, 62, 147n
Appropriation, philosophical
  foundations, 21
Association of Jewelry-workers in Gold, 43
L'Atelier, foundation, 43, 44, 45
Austria, 75n
  Federation of Trade Unions, 181
  student participation, 181
  works-councils, 180–1, 183
Authoritarianism, 75n
  capitalist, 79
  in economic enterprises, 330
  industrial, 97
  Marxism, 18

Banks,
  for labour-managed firms, 445, 455
  for working class capital, 40, 41
Beeching, Lord, 102
Belgium,
  Catholic and socialist labour wings,
    176–7
  codetermination, 176–7
  left-wing extremists, 177
  and workers' control, 163–4, 176–7

Bevin, Aneurin, 97
Boards of directors, 94, 104, 161–2
  cooperatives, 206
  identification upwards, 302
  worker representation, 168, 172, 179,
    180, 181, 183–4
Bourgeoisie, 54, 110
Bratislava, Slovnaft workers' council,
  288
British Employers' Confederation, 105
British Industrial Copartnership
  Association, 228
Bulgaria,
  centrally-planned economy, 339, 349
  economic performance, 339, 340, 342,
    343, 348
  factor productivity, 346, 347, 348
Bureau for Programming Scientific
  Research, 137
Burghard de Schorlemer Alst, Baron,
  112
Business Europe, 179

Capital, 23, 33
  co-existence with trade union
    movement, 102–3
  external funding, 33, 34
  in workers' associations, 112
  income from in self-management,
    15–16, 17
  remuneration for, 34, 35
Capital-controlled systems
  (dehumanized), 12–15, 17, 28, 107,
    156–8
  institutionalized theft and tyranny,
    152, 156, 158
  labour rights, 146, 150
  natural rights, 148
Capitalism, 28, 49, 57
  centralized economy, 356
  compared with labour-management,
    353–6, 358, 362
  compared with market socialism, 321
  divisive category, 36, 67, 227
  effort/income relationship, 438, 440

classical theory, 147, 152
personal, 71
'theft', 152, 156

Quadragesimo Anno,
  analysis of capitalism, 115
  work and wages, 115–16
  worker participation, 116, 117, 118,
  120, 121, 122

Reification, 91
Republic in the Workshop, 39, 45
Rerum Novarum, 110–11
  capital–labour coexistence, 114, 115
  private property, 113–14
  work and wages, 114, 116
  worker participation, 114–15
Revolutions, 17, 20, 21
  Marxist concept, 60, 61
Rochdale Pioneers, 17–18, 26
Romania, economic factors, 339, 340,
  342, 343, 347, 348, 349
Rookes v. Barnard judgment, 102
Rowen Onllwyn Ltd, 24, 249, 255–6
  bankruptcy solution, 246–7, 251,
  254–5
  disagreements, 245–6
  diversification, 247–9, 252, 253
  economic history, 242–8
  formation, 239–42
  labour force, 242–4, 248, 252, 253, 255
  production, 244–8
  social and economic lessons, 251–2,
  254
  work organization and conditions,
  248–51, 255
Russia, 21, 115, 218n, 274–5 *see also*
  Soviet Union

Scandinavia,
  voluntary tradition, 172, 183
  worker participation, 172–5
Scott Bader Commonwealth Ltd, 25,
  227
  Board of Directors, 234
  Christian ethos, 229, 230, 233, 237
  foundation, 232–7
  Rowen Onllwyn, 238, 241, 248, 253
  tasks, 233–4
  Trust Company, 232–3, 234
  work organization, 234, 235

Self-government,
  in industry, 20, 81
  of producers, 47, 59, 60, 65
Self-Managed Socialist Economy, 127–8
  decision making, 132, 133–5, 137,
  140–2
  democratic efficiency maximization,
  140–3
  distribution according to need, 70, 139
  distribution according to work, 128,
  132
  economic growth, 132, 135, 136
  economic institutions, 136, 137
  economic systems, 130–6
  economic sub-systems, 131–42
  Executive Board, 143–4
  financial policy, 133–6, 138–9
  investment harmonization, 135–6, 138
  market mechanism, 130–5, 138
  non-productive services, 138–9
  organizational structure, 137–8, 141–4
  Planning Bureau, 136–7
  Prices and Incomes Board, 134–5
  work units, 141, 142–3
Self-management, 11, 19, 21, 69–73,
  91–2, 106, 108, 128
  characteristics, 14, 15, 22, 91, 133
  doctrine, 13, 26, 239
  delegation of authority, 14n, 26, 27
  efficiency conclusions, 29–32, 33–6
  humanistic principle, 24, 26, 34
  Marxian socialism, 47, 57–8, 60
  national ownership, 15
  voting equality, 14, 25, 34
Share ownership, 34
  capital assets, 148, 150
  industrial power, 271
  Inegalitarian Cooperatives, 416–17
  Joint Stock firms, 411–12
  worker stockholding, 170, 171, 173,
  175, 188
Shelter organizations, 35, 36
Shopstewards' movement, 98, 105
  character, 101
  development, 77, 94, 97, 99, 102
  Great Britain, 166, 169, 183, 279
  wage bargaining, 99, 100, 101, 103,
  104
  working aims and role, 100
Skoda Works, 285, 287
Social Democrats, 77–8, 172, 175

West Germany – *Contd.*
  Works Constitution Act, 164
  works-councils, 164, 165
Workers' associations, 19, 39f, 112
Workers' control, 11, 18, 20, 98, 161,
    329
  a 'balance of hostile forces', 91
  concepts, 21, 66–7, 90, 91
  literal interpretation, 91, 271–2
  retreat from idea, 77, 81, 92
  renewed interest in, 92, 93
  self-management, 91, 106
  Trade union–Labour government
    confrontation, 104–6
  unachieved, 289
Workers' management, 11, 14, 15, 77,
    78, 80–1, 92, 352
Workers' participation, 29, 158, 290
  decentralization of economic
    decisions, 58
  European development, 22–3, 161f
  Fabianism, 19–20
  historical development, 16–21, 26–7
  human behaviour, 28
  increasing adherence, 290
  papal pronouncements, 114–19
Workers' self-determination in USSR,
    21
Workers' self-management, 145–58,
    321
  labour management principles, 148–9,
    158
  legal rights, 147–8, 150–2
  moral responsibility, 147,
  natural rights of workforce, 70, 71,
    147, 148, 150–2
  see also Rowen Onllwyn, Yugoslavian
    Constitution
Working man, 69–73
  access to ruling classes, 59–60
  affluence equation, 93
  autocracy, 330
  emancipation through unionism, 66,
    67, 80
  motivation compared with capitalists',
    426–7
  near-full employment, 94, 101

  renovation of traditional loyalties, 93
  subservient fate, 12, 13, 27, 95–6
Working Man's Production Association,
    39–46
  Christian ideal, 42
  credit difficulties, 40
  democratic base, 39, 46
  ideology of 1848, 44–5
  indivisible and inalienable capital,
    40–5 *passim*
Workmen's associations, concept, 17, 19

Yugoslavia, 28, 123, 129, 140, 289, 299
  agriculture, 134
  autonomous provinces, 71n, 138n
  centralized decision-making, 132, 424
  Constitution, 69–73
  Constitutional Court, 135
  decentralized socialist system, 339,
    348, 350, 424–5
  deviant case analysis (industrial
    democracy), 85
  economic affairs, 27, 342–5, 347, 348,
    423–4
  Economic Court, 142n
  enterprise function compared with
    capitalist, 423, 424–6
  income distribution, 71, 425, 426,
    427, 428
  investment decisions, 424, 425, 427
  labour- (worker-) managed economies,
    15, 24, 25, 72, 423–9, 445
  market economy, 135, 320–1, 423,
    426
  means/ends conflict in social
    objective, 423
  monopolies, 136
  Price Board, 135
  profit-maximization, 32, 426–8
  self-management, 69–72, 81, 91, 108,
    133, 183, 286, 337, 342–5
  voting equality, 25
  Western analysis, 424
  working collectives, 425, 426–7

Zigliara, Fr., 113
Zionism, impact of kibbutz, 213